Laying Down the Law

Laying Down the Law

THE AMERICAN LEGAL REVOLUTIONS IN OCCUPIED GERMANY AND JAPAN

R. W. Kostal

Harvard University Press
Cambridge, Massachusetts | London, England
2019

Printed in the United States of America

First printing

Library of Congress Cataloging-in-Publication Data

Names: Kostal, R. W. (Rande W.), author.
Title: Laying down the law : the American legal revolutions in Occupied Germany and Japan / R. W. Kostal.
Description: Cambridge, Massachusetts : Harvard University Press, 2019. | Includes bibliographical references and index.
Identifiers: LCCN 2019010205 | ISBN 9780674052413 (alk. paper)
Subjects: LCSH: Law—American influences—History—20th century. | Law—Germany—History—20th century. | Law—Japan—History—20th century. | Germany—Politics and government—1945–1990. | Germany—History—1945–1955. | Japan—Politics and government—1945–1989. | Japan—History—Allied occupation, 1945–1952. | Reconstruction (1939–1951)—Germany. | Reconstruction (1939–1951)—Japan. | Germany—Civilization—American influences. | Japan—Civilization—American influences.
Classification: LCC K559 .K67 2019 | DDC 347.43009/044—dc23
LC record available at https://lccn.loc.gov/2019010205

For Leslie

Contents

Introduction

LAYING DOWN THE LAW IN OCCUPIED GERMANY AND JAPAN

At the widest setting of its lens, this book is about the destruction and reconstruction of two captive legal systems in the years immediately following the Second World War. In tighter focus, it tells the story of how and why the United States moved to raze the fascist legal orders of occupied Nazi Germany and imperial Japan so to rebuild them as liberal rule-of-law regimes.

These initiatives issued from the conviction among America's wartime leadership that fascism—this "terrifying manifestation of modernity"—had engendered a new and epochal mode of international violence and disorder.[1] In this view, there would be no enduring postwar peace with Germany or Japan until their fascisms, or more precisely, the cultural mainsprings of their fascisms, had been eradicated, the void filled by democratic systems of law and government.[2]

These lines of thought were perceptible in January 1943 at the Casablanca Conference. There, Franklin Roosevelt, Winston Churchill at his side, proclaimed that the principal Allied war aim was to cause the unconditional surrender of the Axis powers. Roosevelt explained that the Allies fought to destroy not only the military might of the Axis states but also the "philosophies in those countries which are based on conquest and the subjugation of other people."[3] In this view, the fascist states were so incorrigibly warlike, their means of war so catastrophically destructive, that it had become necessary to devise strategies for their complete and permanent political disarmament.

In the development of this doctrine, American leaders were fortified by the new and unparalleled capacities of the American nation state.[4] While by the summer of 1945 the human and physical capital of Germany, Japan, and many of its allies had been diminished by bombing and siege, American economic, military, and governmental resources had expanded dramatically.[5] As President Harry Truman explained to the American people in a national radio address in August 1945, "We have emerged from this war the most powerful nation in the world—the most powerful nation, perhaps, in all history."[6]

A salient feature of the American position in 1945 was the widely shared confidence of its leadership class that its power might be used to construct an "American-inspired world order" founded on liberal precepts of personal rights, commerce, and the rule of law.[7] At the end of the Second World War, American leaders had come to possess global reach and aspiration in roughly equal measure.[8] Two years after Roosevelt vowed to destroy the philosophies of the Axis powers, fate had united motive and opportunity. For Truman and his leading policymakers, it now seemed conceivable—even essential—to reimagine postwar military occupations as occasions for transformative reconstruction.[9] In this intoxicating moment of power and possibility, power might be exercised not only to conquer but correct the defective modernity of a rogue state. Under American leadership, Truman declared, even Nazi Germany might be made "into a decent nation."[10]

At Potsdam, American negotiators were content to couch this transformative intent in the deliberately vague language of "democratization." With its British and Soviet allies, the United States agreed that among the central goals of the collective occupation of Nazi Germany was to effect the "reconstruction of German political life on a democratic basis."[11] It was similarly agreed that on securing the unconditional surrender of imperial Japan, the Allied occupation there would "remove all obstacles to the revival and strengthening of democratic tendencies among the Japanese people."[12]

Behind the scenes, however, American postwar planners were formulating far more ambitious and intrusive models of democratic transformation. In contemplation was the design and implementation of top-down "democratic revolution" in American-occupied Germany and Japan.[13] More precisely, American agencies began to plan for the imposition of *liberal*-democratic revolution in postwar Germany and Japan.

This brings us to the overarching thesis of this book: that in prosecuting the military occupations of Germany and Japan among the primary missions of the United States—quintessentially *American* missions—was to replace fascist with liberal legal and political modernity in those vanquished states.[14] As the Second World War unfolded, American leaders had come to understand the conflict as a death struggle between incompatible models of the mass industrial society.[15] As Truman stated in his radio address of August 1945, the American-led victory over Nazi Germany was properly understood as "a victory of one way of life over another . . . a victory of an ideal founded on the rights of the common man, on the dignity of the human being, on the conception of the State as the servant—and not the master—of its people."[16]

For Truman and his planners, therefore, it was an imperative aim of the postwar occupations of Nazi Germany and imperial Japan to remake the legal and political systems of those defeated nations into a particular kind of political and legal modernity, one predicated on individual rights as vindicated by autonomous systems of lawyers and courts.[17] At the base of America's political policy for occupied Germany and Japan, of its democratic aspirations there, was the determination to wield power to remake these nations as liberal rule-of-law states.

The term "democracy" is almost endlessly flexible. Its plasticity explains why nations as dissimilar as the United States and the Soviet Union might agree on the need to democratize postwar Germany and Japan. But here we should make no mistake. The Americans who designed and implemented the American contribution to democratization in the former Axis powers operated from a manifestly liberal definition of the purposes and processes of the democratic community. In this thinking, the *raison d'etre* of democracy—its bony spine—was the promotion and vindication of individual rights by the rule of law.[18] As Secretary of State George Marshall explained in 1947, "I realize that the word *democracy* is given many interpretations. To the American Government and citizen it has a basic meaning. We believe that human beings have certain inalienable rights, that is, rights which may not be given or taken away."[19]

In this statement, Marshall had sought to distinguish American from Soviet intent in the democratization of occupied Germany. For Americans, the term denoted the reconstruction of Germany as a liberal polity in which individual rights were secured by law and, crucially, autonomous legal institutions.[20] In the words of Charles Fahy, the former federal solicitor general, then director of Legal Division in American-occupied Germany, the special distinction of the United States was that it was "a government of law and desire[d] to spread such a concept throughout the world."[21] In the words of another official, the crucial purpose of the occupation was to "teach the Germans the meaning of rights . . . and to help [them] learn that might does not make right, and that the rule of law . . . is the individual's greatest single protection against a capricious and willful expression of governmental power."[22]

American goals in Japan were described in similar fashion. The Supreme Commander in Japan, General Douglas MacArthur, stated in October 1945 that American initiatives in Japan "will unquestionably involve the liberalization of the Constitution."[23] MacArthur's second-in-command remembered that it had been crucial to American philosophy in Japan to induce the construction of a liberal rule-of-law system, one providing "untrammelled recourse to judicial process against any Japanese law or action taken thereunder."[24] In this account, the main tenet of American occupation doctrine in Japan had been to "entrench political freedom based on the rights and dignity of the individual . . . these fundamentals to American life and progress" previously unknown there.[25]

As they devised the occupations of Germany and Japan in 1945, American leaders advocated for a specific matrix of individual legal rights, institutions, and practices. As the American Bar Association summarized in 1958, the touchstone of the rule of law was a written constitution that established "the body of precepts of fundamental individual legal rights" enforced by institutions "vested with power effectively to transmute precepts into fundamental and accepted rights."[26] The twin engines of the system were "courts staffed by judges who are independent of *ad hoc* government pressures" and a "professionally trained bar, free from government direction, without taint of private corruption, devoted solely to the lawful interests of clients within the rules of the legal system of the country."

In the view of American leadership, the compulsory introduction of these liberal modes of law was justified by history—more specifically, by the historical absence in Germany and Japan of successful liberal-democratic political and legal revolutions. As one senior American official rationalized in relation to Japan, because the Japanese people had been unable to mount a "revolution against despotism" in the nineteenth century, the Americans had become obliged to mount the "revolution of 1945."[27] In regard to Germany, the central aim of American policy was not so much to invent as revive, embellish, and consolidate the liberal constitutional state that had been established there, on paper, in 1921.

The transformative goals of the United States were also impelled by the fact that the Allied occupation of Germany after the First World War had been an abject failure. Plainly and disastrously, that occupation, while it temporarily subdued the German military, had signally failed to destroy the mainsprings of German militarism. Now, in the aftermath of a second and still more catastrophic global war, it was clear to American policy-makers that the indispensable prerequisite of permanent German and Japanese pacification was their compulsory political demilitarization.[28] In this way the transformative occupation was innovated as a "national security liberalism."[29] As Under Secretary of State Dean Acheson explained about the occupation of Germany, "You can't have security without a democratic government over there. The two go together."[30]

A second major premise of American occupation policy in 1945 was that during military occupation it was possible to "uproot the spirit as well as the structure of totalitarian government in order to provide for the healthy growth of a democratic system."[31] This optimism stemmed from the supposition, George Kennan observed, that "men everywhere are basically like [Americans]—that they are animated by substantially the same hopes and aspirations."[32] For many American leaders, Allied (read: *American*) victory in the Second World War was at once the direct consequence of the patent superiority and universal allure of the liberal-democratic (read: *American*) model of modernity.[33] In this view, militarism was not the product of race or ethnicity but, again, of contingent historical trajectories. Accordingly, the challenge in American-occupied Germany and Japan was to intervene decisively to redirect these trajectories; that is, to provide swift and decisive liberal revolution from above.

Thus, the Charter of the International Military Tribunal (and other initiatives regarding the defeated enemy's punishment) notwithstanding, American occupation policy toward Germany (and Japan) was always mainly about reconstruction, not retribution. It figured negligibly to American occupation policy that the Third Reich had orchestrated world-historical crimes of genocide and mass murder. (The American-made documents relating to the design and implementation of transformative occupation in Germany almost never contained references to German culpability for genocidal crimes or the implications of such culpability for American-driven legal and political reconstruction.) Similarly in relation to Japan, whatever anger was felt by Americans for the attack on Pearl Harbor or the mistreatment of American prisoners of war, vengeance also played little or no part in shaping policy for the occupation of that nation. If there was a prevailing justification among American planners and decision-makers as to why it was necessary to cause Germany and Japan to become liberal rule-of-law states, it was to secure national security in the longer term, not retribution in the shorter.

The American occupation doctrine of democratization as liberal legal reconstruction, centrally important though it was, did not emerge in a single historical moment or as a single or coherent program. In terms both of planning and execution there were always multiple American occupations of Nazi Germany and imperial Japan and based on a range of (often contradictory) ideas, voices, interests, and aspirations. Liberal legal reconstruction was only one among many core occupation aims and doctrines competing for favor among the disparate American decision-makers in Washington, Berlin, and Tokyo.

By the fall of 1945, for instance, General Lucius Clay, America's chief proconsul in occupied Germany, had been briefed on the need to "denazify," then democratize the German legal and political systems in the U.S. zone. In the actual exercise of his discretion, however, Clay tended to focus scarce administrative resources on (what the general regarded as) more urgent problems of food supply, housing, and economic recovery for the some 14 million Germans in the zone. In contrast, General Douglas MacArthur, the American and Allied Supreme Commander in occupied Japan, even though he had received no explicit orders in this respect, tended to prioritize the swift and radical legal and political reconstruction of Japan. Unlike his counterpart in Germany, MacArthur became and remained deeply invested personally in the liberalization of Japanese law and legal institutions. And far more than Clay, far more than perhaps any other American leader in 1945, MacArthur believed that he and a few thousand Americans could and should cause the Japanese to revolutionize their legal and political modernity.

Thus far I have discussed the grandiose ambition of American power in the military occupations of Germany and Japan. But this book equally is a study of the *limits* of American power in this period, particularly in causing the liberal legal reconstruction of two foreign nation states. That by the fall of 1945 the Truman administration had decided on the need to implement transformative legal and political reconstruction in Germany and Japan says nothing about that policy's coherence, or indeed about the ability of Americans and their agencies to achieve these epic goals. While the United States began this work from a position of unrivalled economic and military power, its capacity to use this power, to harness it to the purpose of transformative occupation, proved much less sure. Clearly it is one thing for a leadership class to embark on epochal transformative tasks, another thing entirely to achieve them.

This raises the second principal thesis of the study: that in its efforts to use power to remake the legal modernities of Germany and Japan, agencies of the United States proved capable of effecting substantial but, at the end of the day, incomplete transformational change. While significant inroads were made in the displacement of the most visible manifestations of authoritarian public law and legal institutions, and in their replacement with liberal legal frameworks, in both occupied nations American agencies proved unable—at crucial junctures *unwilling*—to consolidate the operational substance of legal liberalism and the rule of law.

We will see that failures of organization, intellect, and will all figured importantly in the shortcomings of American reconstructive projects in occupied Germany and Japan. But perhaps the largest impediment was the (slowly acknowledged) fact that the destruction and reconstruction of the German and Japanese systems of law were monumentally complex undertakings, two veritable "Manhattan Projects" of sociolegal engineering. In their first phases, the projects entailed the demolition and displacement of deeply entrenched laws, legal institutions, and professional elites. In their second phases, they entailed the swift and effective design and implementation of new liberal constitutions, courts, and complementary institutions of legal practice and decision-making. In the final phase, the project implied the reconstruction not only of laws but the normative systems and "interpretive communities" that underpinned them.[34] To render them fit to rejoin the family of nations, American legal system-builders would need to cause the leading personnel of two mature legal systems to abandon authoritarianism for liberal habits of legal thought and action. All of this was to be achieved in the space of a few years, in the context of nearly ruined states and societies, and as between agencies with different cultural, linguistic and, in the case of the Americans and Japanese, racial identities.

Although the United States had undertaken previous nation-building projects (as recently as the 1930s in the Philippines) its agencies treated the transformative occupations of Germany and Japan as sui generis, as an entirely new order of intercession. In the planning and execution of these projects, American agencies did not draw on precedent or institutional memory. The operative assumption of their principals was that the techniques and templates of liberal legal reconstruction might be, of necessity had to be, cut from whole cloth.

But during the war years Americans had proved capable of solving the novel intellectual and organizational problems associated with the design and construction of the atomic bomb, they demonstrated less capability in the redesign and construction of foreign systems of law.[35] In important respects, the American atomic bomb project was brilliantly successful for the reasons that liberal legal reconstruction was not. Seen as crucial to victory at war, it was propelled by a combination of steadfast political will and vast physical and human resources. More than this, however, in the making of atom bombs American leadership gave scientific and technical intellectuals wide latitude to theorize, design, and execute the project.[36] In contrast, the liberal legal reconstruction of occupied Germany and Japan, seen less urgently by the Truman administration as a *peace*-winning strategy, constantly wanted for political commitment and adequate resources. And while legal reconstruction engendered a plethora of perplexing theoretical problems, relevantly trained intellectuals and experts were not afforded institutional space to think about and resolve them. I will show that from their inception the American legal reconstruction projects in Germany and Japan painfully lacked for a jurisprudential Robert Oppenheimer and subordinate corps of relevantly trained legal thinkers and technicians.

In consequence, American-directed legal reconstruction in postwar Germany and Japan was grossly undertheorized. While the atomic bomb project was born of an explicit and potent model of atomic matter and behavior, legal reconstruction was born of implicit and imprecise models of foreign laws, institutions, and behaviors. Specifically, American agencies began reconstructive legal projects in Germany and Japan lacking a coherent and well-informed theory of fascist legality or legal order, or of the German or Japanese models thereof. They began work lacking theory about how to identify and remove the fascist elements of the German or Japanese legal orders or how best to introduce liberal ideas and legal structures. In every important respect, Americans started and sustained legal reconstructive projects in occupied Germany and Japan without having theorized the liberal legal revolution from above; that is, without strong backing either from local revolutionary elites or the masses.

A more amply documented obstacle to American-sponsored reconstruction in occupied Germany and Japan was that it unfolded within dynamic and complex diplomatic environments. With regard to the transformative occupation of Germany especially, American priorities and prerogatives were limited by a web of multilateral pacts and undertakings culminating in the Potsdam Agreement and Declaration of August 1945.[37] There the Allies had agreed that with respect to matters affecting Germany as a whole, the former Reich would be governed *directly*—all German-operated government having been extinguished—by a centralized Allied Control Council (ACC) led jointly by the in-theater army commanders of the United States, Great Britain, the Soviet Union, and France.[38] Under Potsdam, the quadpartite ACC was to achieve four general goals: the denazification, decartelization, decentralization, and democratization of Germany.[39] Subject to these collective goals and strictures, the four powers were left to govern their assigned zones of occupation as they saw fit. For the purposes of the denazification and democratization of the German legal system, therefore, American Military Government (AMG) in Germany worked within a bifurcated system of political authority. Although AMG had a free hand in legal matters in the U.S. zone, all reforms to German law affecting Germany as a whole had to be negotiated with three other powers.[40]

For American occupation agencies in postwar Japan, on the other hand, the diplomatic and political structure of military government and administration was less convoluted.[41] The United States dominated the occupation of Japan because politically and militarily it had dominated the instrument—the Supreme Commander for the Allied Powers (SCAP)—that on August 15, 1945, had caused Japan to capitulate.[42] In theory, SCAP was a multilateral organization. In practice, SCAP, this "elaborate Army super-government," was an American operation conducted by American interpretations of Allied policy on postwar Japan.[43]

That policy was summarized in the imprecise provisions of the Potsdam Declaration regarding Japan, the declaration calling on SCAP to "remove all obstacles to the revival and strengthening of democratic tendencies among the Japanese people."[44] From the outset of the occupation, MacArthur took a broad view of these words. In fact, within a few months of his arrival in Japan, the Supreme Commander began to take bold steps toward the construction of a liberal-democratic state.[45]

Just as there were many American occupations, equally German and Japanese officials responded to them in diverse ways. One way was to offer active support to American initiatives, including the liberal reconstruction of legal and political institutions. Another way, conversely, was to engage in active if necessarily stealthy resistance to American legal initiatives. In the course of these pages we will see that in Germany and Japan alike, such resistance arose, grew, and was sustained by factors beyond the natural resentment felt by the conquered toward a foreign conqueror. One was that Japanese and German soon came to realize that in attaining reconstructive ends American occupiers (this standing in stark contrast to the Soviet occupation of its German zone) generally would not rely on violently coercive means.[46] Another was that American occupiers clearly lacked sufficient intellectual or administrative resources to dominate the laws, lawyers, and legal institutions of Germany and Japan. Yet another factor was the heavy dependence of American occupiers on the expertise and labor of the occupied. These factors coalesced to create ample political space for German and Japanese jurists to inhibit, curb, sometimes to repel reconstructive initiatives.

This provides linkage to another thesis of this study: that German and Japanese resistance to liberal legal reconstruction was amplified by the dubious moral authority of the American law reformers. If atoms are indifferent to the hypocrisy of their rulers, subjugated peoples are not. One of the many factors that inhibited Americans in the exportation of liberalism and the rule of law was that their own legal liberalism was flagrantly compromised, not least of all by endemic racism. We will see that German and Japanese officials, those learned in law and legal affairs particularly, were cognizant that in the United States racialized groups suffered from an array of legally entrenched disabilities. As educated men, they knew moreover that as recently as 1942, in the aftermath of Pearl Harbor, America had been the kind of "liberal" nation state that with the blessing of its Supreme Court might consign tens of thousands of its citizens to concentration camps solely on grounds of their race or ancestry.

This hypocrisy reinforced the predisposition of occupied elites to resist foreign innovation or, on the other hand, to conserve extant laws or legal institutions. The German and Japanese jurists who engaged with Americans on matters of law and legal reform mainly did not do so as penitents. Nor in their majorities did they agree easily that extant laws and legal institutions were pathological, archaic, or in some other way inherently inferior to American liberal models. After the surrender, most German jurists were unwilling to accept responsibility for the supposed perversion of law and justice during the Hitler period. After the surrender of Japan, most Japanese jurists did not readily concede that their legal order was mired in outmoded "feudal" norms and practices. Indeed, although they could not always act on these dispositions, Japanese and German jurists were far more apt to reject than accept American criticisms of their laws and legal practices.

In the first phase of the occupation, the American legal occupiers enjoyed one important source of momentum: the German and Japanese elites, including leading lawyers, judges, and state functionaries faced far more pressing concerns than the fate of their systems of law. In the aftermath of catastrophic defeat at war, the populations of both countries were in the grip of acute existential crises. The family members of millions of Germans and Japanese had been killed, displaced, or were unaccounted for.[47] German and Japanese cities and infrastructure were in ruins. Millions had lost their homes and places of work and worship. Hunger was widespread. In these ruined worlds, the physical, social, and psychological bases of modern systems of law had been undercut.

In these hungry years of the occupations, with German and Japanese elites set back on their heels, the American agencies in charge of legal reconstruction were able to make substantial headway first in the displacement and then reconstruction of the key anchors and institutions of German and Japanese public law. In structural terms, meaning, in terms of the frameworks of constitutional law and the judicial branch of government—considerable strides were made by 1948 in the introduction of the rudiments of liberal rule-of-law regimes. This trajectory, however, did not persist in the historically decisive year of 1948 or in the final four years of the occupation.

The final principal thesis of this book concerns the historical consequences of the national security realism that underpinned American transformative aspirations in occupied Germany and Japan. It is notoriously well known that by 1949 the Truman administration had come to recognize the Soviet Union and international communism as the chief sources of menace to American security, domestic and foreign. Less well known are the consequences of this recalibration for the liberal legal reconstruction of Germany and Japan. Historians have tended to credit the United States for its successful role in fostering liberal rule-of-law democracies in occupied Germany and Japan, without awareness of the degree to which American agencies in both places actively intervened in the period 1948 to 1952 to curb, constrain, and even roll back these innovations.[48] We will see that by 1950 American officials in both occupied countries had felt compelled to take deliberate (if covert) steps to prevent German and Japanese lawyers and judges from instituting liberal rule-of-law regimes in those places. By 1950, so it will be argued here, the American Saturn had begun to gobble up its liberal children.

As will be apparent in its endnotes, the present study is indebted to the rich historiography of the American military occupations of post–Second World War Germany and Japan. Its pillars are set in the extensive diplomatic, political, and administrative histories of the American occupations of both countries. The study also has benefited from the rich body of research on the performance of the American military and military leadership in occupied Germany and Japan, and from the works of the historians who have explored the experience of American occupation from the standpoint of the occupied.[49] Important historical studies have also been published on aspects of the postwar denazification of German law and in helping to forge new constitutions for Japan in 1946 to 1947 and for the west German entities in 1948 to 1949.[50]

Here it is necessary to generalize (inevitably, to overgeneralize) the findings of this scholarship in reference to its most pertinent theme:

the historical nature, motivation, and expression of American power in two occupied foreign nations at the end of the Second World War.

The historiography is in broad agreement that the American military regimes in occupied Germany and Japan were constructive, restrained, and pragmatic. From the outset, they were led by exceptionally able professional soldiers, Generals Lucius Clay (in American Germany) and Douglas MacArthur (in Japan). Both officers established and vigilantly enforced a pattern of firm, businesslike, and largely nonviolent conduct toward the occupied populations. Broadly speaking, American Military Government treated the bodies and minds (if not the property) of the occupied populations with appropriate respect. Similarly, American common soldiers were restrained by (mainly) effective discipline. For Clay, MacArthur, and their administrative agencies, the ethos of the occupations was to stabilize, govern, and construct, not to stigmatize, punish, and destroy.

The historians also generally agree that in the immediate postwar period the military and civilian agencies of the United States were woefully ill-equipped to provide efficient, still less transformative, government in two populous countries at opposite ends of the world. The American military occupations of Germany and Japan were incoherently planned, defined, and communicated by the Truman administration and its various subordinate arms. On the ground in Germany and Japan, the functional subdivisions of the occupations were often poorly led and always underresourced. The vitally important legal subdepartments of the occupations were staffed almost exclusively by American lawyers lacking specialized knowledge of German or Japanese law or legal history. Few American legal officers in Germany read or spoke German. Almost no American legal officers in Japan read or spoke Japanese. In American Germany, aptly trained legal specialists were subordinated to ineptly trained superiors. The legal reconstruction of occupied Japan was undertaken almost entirely absent of American experts in Japanese law and society.

The American mission in Germany and Japan was also made exponentially more difficult by the fact that the human and physical capital of both nations had been devastated by war. The abstract purposes of the United States were obviated by the need to avert apocalyptic disaster among the occupied populations. In Germany, the American mission was made still more difficult because it held exclusive sway only in one zone of occupation. In Japan, American power was mediated and deflected less by other Allies than by the persistence of the Japanese state.

In Germany and Japan, historians broadly concur, there was a pronounced tendency for American occupation officers to defer to German (white European) officials while evincing racially tinged chauvinism toward the Japanese. In each occupied country, but especially in Japan, American officers identified and promoted go-betweens, proxies, and agencies, who, at least ostensibly, were willing to carry out American policy initiatives and demands. The inherently fraught relationship between occupier and occupied was further distorted by the pervasive ignorance of American officers of the language, culture, and history of their counterparts in Germany and especially Japan. American policy-makers and program officers evinced a general willingness to adjust plans and actions to circumstances on the ground, including to the needs and desires of the occupied.

More explicitly and deeply than in previous works, the ensuing chapters investigate the American decision in the immediate aftermath of the Second World War to remove and replace the authoritarian modernity of their foes. It is an original study of the attempt by the military and civilian agencies of one self-defined liberal-democratic state to revolutionize simultaneously the legal and political superstructures of two subjugated states, one European, one Asiatic. In this focus this book fundamentally is a work of American history, one which seeks to redefine the historical aspirations of American leadership class for occupied Germany and Japan while assessing its functional capacity of that class to realize them. Its core historical questions pertain to American motives, agencies, perceptions, and reactions. Its main arguments and conclusions describe the character and significance of American historical conduct and are advanced in the context of principally of American historiography.

Although it focuses mainly on American points of view and actions, the study also takes pains to document the perceptions, actions, and reactions of German and Japanese actors and organizations. And while the American-archived English-language sources cannot yield a complete picture of German and Japanese perceptions and activities in relation to legal reconstruction (or any other topic), they can and in these pages do provide an abundance of highly germane and credible evidence on these subjects.

As stated, this study mirrors the historical emphasis of American agencies on German and Japanese "public law"—that is, on the array of constitutional and institutional structures associated with the German and Japanese states and their legal relationship to their citizens. Accordingly the study focuses on constitution drafting, the reconstruction of judiciaries and bar associations, and American interventions with respect to criminal law and procedure, this largely to the exclusion of American interventions relating to "private law."[51] By the same token, the study at hand concerns "transitional justice" only as that term denotes the American-directed structural transitions in Germany and Japan from authoritarian to the rule of law-based constitutionalism.[52] These inclusions and exclusions are justified in terms of the historical record, but also on grounds of both manageability and extant historiography. A great deal of work already has been published on the American role in the Nuremberg and Tokyo war crimes trials.[53] Furthermore, the subdivisions of the American occupations responsible for the prosecution of war crimes was all but completely detached from those engaged in reconstruction. On the other hand, although structural reconstruction dominated the attention of American legal officers in occupied Germany and Japan, all too little work has been completed on their efforts.

In regard to any compelling historical investigation, whatever its points of focus, the devil is in the empirical details. More than any previously published work, therefore, this study focuses on the coalface of American-driven public law reform in occupied Germany and Japan as revealed in the archives of the American legal administrations in both countries. This rich but underexploited bounty of primary source materials, as well as the published and unpublished papers of leading American law reformers, is used to describe the character and contours of American legal activity in Germany and Japan.

While these sources form the basis of a history of American power in the mid-twentieth century at the same time they connect American with world histories of liberalism and the rule of law. For if Americans were innovators of the post-Second World War era, if they were they were part of a world-historical vanguard, it was as the self-appointed architects of a liberal *legal* conception of democracy and the still embryonic practices of "democratization." By their own lights, in mounting transformative occupations of Germany and Japan, American leaders had set out to provide object lessons in a civilized modernity; a modernity of laws and legal institutions devised to shield individual human beings from arbitrary exertions of power. At the core of this book, therefore, is the story of how agencies of three modern states asserted, rejected, refined, and reconfigured the ideas and institutions of the rule of law.

It has been cogently observed that for the historian of American military occupations after the Second World War, it is "almost impossible *not* to compare" the aims and actions of American agencies in Germany and Japan.[54] For the purposes of this study, the astonishing coincidence of American-driven legal reconstruction in two foreign nation states in the same time frame affords that rare occasion to refine historical knowledge of Americans and American agencies by comparing how they designed and directed legal reconstruction in distinct geographic, racial, and cultural fields.[55] It is an opportunity to identify the key factor or factors that caused, or failed to cause, directed legal change in occupied Germany or Japan.

In relation to Americans and their legal reconstructive projects in Germany and Japan, the study therefore poses a set of comparative questions. How did American agencies comprehend the National Socialist and imperial Japanese public systems of law and their relationship to "fascist" political modernity? In what specific ways were these systems found lacking or in need of liberal-minded renovation? To what degree did plans for legal reconstruction in Germany and Japan differ, and to what extent were differences rooted in American racial, cultural, or historical perceptions? What role did American intellectuals and experts play in the legal reconstruction of Germany and Japan? How did American legal officers conceive of and organize their engagement with German and Japanese officials? To what degree did German and Japanese legal officers consent to or resist American initiatives? In the course of the occupations, in what ways were the trajectories of legal destruction and reconstruction the same or different? To what relative extent did American intellectual, moral, and administrative capacities and incapacities figure in legal reconstructive outcomes? Did American agency introduce or reintroduce liberal models of the rule of law in Germany and Japan, and how were these innovations affected by shifting currents in American domestic politics and foreign policy? In the final analysis, to what degree, if any, did American agency foster liberal rule-of-law regimes in occupied Germany and Japan?

In addressing these questions the study employs a mode of comparative methodology in which the historical character of a single subject (the United States, 1944 to 1952) is characterized in its similar aims, policies, and interactions with two different subjects, Germany and Japan.[56] The study aims to identify and document how Americans, in approaching and implementing the radical reconstruction of German and Japanese legal modernities, constructed, and responded to various independent variables. For instance, what bearing did the different diplomatic and political structures of the American occupations have on design and delivery of legal reconstruction in the occupied countries? What bearing did American perceptions of the racial, cultural, and historical character of captive lawyers and legal systems have on their programs of legal intervention and change?

These questions are explored in relation to parallel and multilayered studies. Each of the book's six chapters examines a particular dimension of American efforts to demolish the vestiges of German and Japanese legal authoritarianism and to construct new liberal laws and legal institutions. The chapters unfold with respect to the historical chronology of American-sponsored legal reconstruction in its three main phases: the subjugation and demolition of legal authoritarianism; the introduction of liberal structures of public law and the rule of law; and the later efforts of American agencies to cultivate (and subdue) civil libertarianism among German and Japanese jurists and lay populations. After brief introductions to specific themes, lines of inquiry, and hypotheses, each chapter provides closely documented analytical narratives of six distinct sets of American actions and interactions with the German and Japanese public law systems and their representatives. Similarly, each chapter concludes with brief analytical commentary on American thought and action regarding a specific facet of legal reconstruction and regarding how and why that thought and action might have differed in American-occupied Germany and Japan.

This brings us to a brief preview of the six chapters of *Laying Down the Law.* The prologue to Chapter 1 concerns how, in twenty months after President Roosevelt's call for the destruction of the fascist political modernity, civilian and military agencies of the United States generated policies, plans, and organizational capacities for the realization of this goal. The main body of the chapter traces the genesis of American policy and planning in regard to the democratization and thus the liberalization of German and Japanese systems of law and government. As an integrated whole, the chapter, titled "The 'Destruction of Philosophies'" is therefore about the imaginative process by which American soldiers and civil servants formed collective ideas about German and Japanese legal fascisms and their elimination. The chapter documents how before September 1945 American postwar planning energy was focused on Germany and German fascism, specifically on aims and means for the denazification of Germany's legal and political modernity. It documents both the strengths and weaknesses of American capacity to generate, evaluate, and organize knowledge about the German and Japanese legal systems and their compulsory liberalization during a period of military occupation.

Chapter 2, "Occupying the Legal Other," examines the subjugation of the German and Japanese legal systems by American organizations from first contact to the introduction (some eighteen months later) of new constitutional instruments. It examines the specialized legal subdivisions of the American occupations and how they were organized, staffed, and deployed. The chapter examines how American groups charged with the denazification of German laws and legal institutions quickly became hamstrung by overlapping jurisdiction, weak leadership, and lack of skilled personnel on their side and by mounting

German resistance on the other. In American-occupied Japan, in contrast, MacArthur took swift advantage of American predominance on the ground to organize a small but adroit functional unit (Government Section) devoted exclusively to the swift and radical liberal-democratic reconstruction of Japanese law and government. Among other issues, the chapter will also document, compare, and contrast the role of intellectuals and experts in the reconstruction of the German and Japanese legal systems during the first phase of the occupations.

Chapter 3, "Captive Constitutions," considers why and how in 1946 American political and legal agencies began to initiate and superintend constitutional reform in American-occupied Japan and Germany. The chapter begins by revisiting the story of how under MacArthur's aggressive leadership Americans instigated the comprehensive overhaul of Japan's "Meiji" constitution—how American intervention caused the Japanese to adopt and ratify a constitution reflecting American liberal conviction in constitutionalized rights as enforced by politically independent courts. These events are then contrasted with the less well-known story of how, in the U.S. zone of occupation, American legal agencies prompted groups of German lawyers, legal academics, and politicians to promulgate new liberal rule-of-law constitutions in the regional states of American-occupied Germany.

Chapter 4, "Crafting Liberal Courts," concerns perhaps the most pivotal subproject of liberal legal reconstruction in American-occupied Germany and Japan: the establishment of courts and judiciaries willing and able to defend and enforce liberal constitutional rights and the rule of law. The chapter traces how, in occupied Germany, American legal officers encountered what they saw as an advanced system of courts and adjudication debased by National Socialist imperatives. Their challenge was to rebuild and staff a system of German courts that would vindicate liberal constitutional rights and the rule of law, this in the context of a demonstrably flawed program of denazification. In American-occupied Japan, American officials encountered what they saw as a weak and timorous judiciary, one acutely lacking in prestige and power. Here Americans faced the daunting task of inducing the captive Japanese state to organize and staff a new and potent system of judges and judicial institutions, including a new national Supreme Court equipped with broad powers of judicial review.

The subject of Chapter 5, "Clearing the Spiritual Rubble," is the American-directed reconstruction of the Japanese and German systems of criminal justice. It will examine how, in both occupied nations, American legal agencies viewed criminal law and procedure as critical arenas of directed legal change. American officials agreed that the criminal justice systems of both countries had been suborned—by Nazis in Germany, ultranationalists in Japan—as instruments of tyranny. It was incumbent on American agencies, therefore, to cause German and Japanese officials to establish the components of liberal due process in criminal litigation. One indispensable aspect of these reforms, also canvassed in this chapter, was the American-driven reformation of the legal professions of Japan and American Germany. Significantly, however, these reforms were debated and implemented after the advent of the Cold War, and during a period in which the United States was at odds with itself over the conflicting demands of liberal idealism and national security.

Chapter 6, "Twilight of the Gods," documents the increasingly self-contradictory character of American legal reconstruction in Germany and Japan in the early Cold War. It charts how in 1948 and 1949, with Japan's constitutional and structural reforms nearly complete, American legal agencies implemented a range of programs for the cultivation and consolidation of civil liberties. In 1949, in helping to form and consolidate a new West German state, American agencies supervised drafting (by Germans) of a new liberal-democratic constitution, or "Basic Law." In the same time frame, however, American agencies began to collaborate with German and Japanese conservative elites in the harsh suppression of leftist political and labor activism. The chapter documents how at a number of key junctures the nascent rule-of-law liberalism of American-occupied Germany and Japan was impeded and even undermined.

The final section of the book, "Laying Down the Law: Americans as Legal Revolutionaries," is a thematic essay generalizing the historical data and lines of interpretation presented in the book's six empirical chapters. The essay draws final conclusions about American capacities and incapacities after the Second World War in remaking the legal modernity of two foreign states. It examines and compares patterns of refraction and convergence in American legal reconstruction in Germany and Japan. The essay argues that while the federal governing elite of the United States possessed the military, financial, and psychological resources to attempt the liberal reconstruction of two captive legal systems simultaneously, in a number of crucial respects—administratively, politically, intellectually, morally—it lacked capability to fully realize these goals.

1

The "Destruction of Philosophies"

PLANNING THE LEGAL RECONSTRUCTION OF GERMANY AND JAPAN

THIS CHAPTER CONCERNS the time from the winter of 1943 to the autumn of 1945, during which agencies of the United States laid down plans for directed legal reconstruction in postwar Nazi Germany and imperial Japan. The chapter consists of two parts. The first, a prologue, will identify the ideological, diplomatic, and legal origins of the American policy of transformative occupation. This section also will describe the development of new institutions for planning and implementation of directed legal change in the occupied states.

The second part of the chapter will document the evolving content of American planning for the destruction and subsequent reconstruction of the German and Japanese legal systems. It examines how with considerable urgency in 1944 and 1945 American civilian and military officials strove to assemble actionable knowledge about the character and operation of German and Japanese legal authoritarianisms. The chapter focuses on how American agencies assembled knowledge about the German and Japanese legal systems and the extent to which they used this knowledge to plan for the destruction and reconstruction of those systems.

The central thesis of the chapter is that due to a number of factors, including the dearth of intellectual resources on one side and the novelty, scale, and complexity of the projects on the other, American planning for the capture and reconstruction of German and especially Japanese laws and legal institutions was perfunctory and, even at war's end, incomplete. American policy-makers and planners were more effective, if still not *very* effective, in creating knowledge about the Nazi than the imperial Japanese system of law. In American eyes, laws and legal institutions had been vital instruments of German but not Japanese authoritarianism. For this reason, American agencies (with British counterparts) invested considerable time and resources planning the comprehensive denazification of German laws and legal institutions, while paying scant attention to the renovation of the Japanese legal system. At war's end, however, the poor quality of legal planning for both occupied countries obliged American officials to improvise approaches to the destruction and reconstruction of extant legal systems.

A final preliminary observation about the American planning process is the absence of history. In formulating their approach to planning issues, American agencies focused entirely on present problems, not past performance. Whatever institutional knowledge and experience had been accumulated on nation-building, it was not brought to bear in devising protocols for the democratization of occupied Germany or Japan. These were seen as novel problems calling for novel solutions.

Prologue: The Origins of Transformative Occupation

At the Casablanca Conference in the early winter of 1943, Roosevelt and Churchill agreed that the imperative war aim was to secure the unconditional surrender of the Axis powers as a first step in effecting their complete and permanent demilitarization.[1] Roosevelt hastened to add that this would entail the destruction not only of enemy war machines but also the political "philosophies" and institutions that fueled them.[2]

Roosevelt's remarks reflected the growing conviction of his administration that fascist modernity, this lethal mobilization of racialist militarism and technology, was incompatible with liberal-democratic modes of government and diplomacy.[3] For the president and his circle, the Second World War had become a struggle to the death between the benign modernity of the Western liberal democracies—the Soviet Union being the outlier—and the perverted modernity of the fascist powers. The unresolved question of the war was whether liberals or fascists would become the "masters of modernization," whether liberals or fascists would exert the power to remake the other's political modernity.[4]

Although the president's remarks appear to have been extemporized, in the months following they became the touchstones of American war policy.[5] In a national radio address of April 1944, Secretary of State Cordell Hull affirmed that with its allies the United States had two war aims: the "defeat of our enemies *and* the destruction of the Nazi and Fascist systems"(emphasis added).[6] The war would be pressed until the Allies had secured the unconditional surrender, then permanent pacification, of the Axis powers. This policy, Hull explained, was informed by a bitter lesson of history. After the First World War, because the United States and its allies had not implemented a transformative occupation, Germany had quickly reverted to aggressive nationalism.[7] Hull assured Americans that at the conclusion of the second Great War, the mistake would not be repeated.[8] This time, there would be no "careless tolerance of evil institutions," no "compromise with fascism and Nazism." This time, when the "Nazi state and its Japanese counterpart" were vanquished, pains would be taken to "destroy these systems to their very foundations." The entire system of fascist modernity, "[its] leaders, its institutions, the power which supports it," Hull informed listeners, "[all] must go."

Hull's address was about American aims for war and peace.[9] He made clear that in the political vacuum left by fascism the United States would build "the institutions of a free and democratic way of life." The path to a prosperous world, in this essentially Wilsonian view, was in the proliferation of sovereign states founded on individual rights, democracy, and the rule of law.[10] This then was to be the focus of American policy with regard to the future military occupation of Germany and Japan: to undertake their reconstruction as liberal democracies.

But first things first. The wars in Europe and the Pacific were not only still to be won but won totally. According to emerging American doctrine, the necessary prerequisite of transformative occupation was the unconditional surrender of an enemy state.[11] The doctrine was the logical outgrowth of the unprecedented menace posed by the modern fascist war state and its doctrine of "total war." For policy-makers in the Roosevelt administration, unconditional surrender entailed the complete capitulation of the defeated state as well as complete exercise of power by the "victor nations."[12] Unlike previous instruments of surrender, unconditional surrender would authorize the "imposition of any measures which those nations might deem requisite for future peace and security." American policy-makers sought to justify such impositions in a postwar legal context that did not entail the annexation of vanquished enemy states.[13] With regard to Hitler's Germany, for instance, unconditional surrender was seen to authorize the Allies to undertake the "obliteration of the Nazi state" and its replacement with one more conducive to Allied security.[14]

For most of the duration of the war in Europe, however, American (and British) planners and policy-makers continued to wrestle with a pressing question: was it in fact permissible under international law for nations victorious in war to effect the destruction and permanent reconstruction of the domestic laws and institutions of defeated and occupied nations?

As early as the winter of 1943, postwar planning agencies in the United States and Britain had put the question to some leading experts in international law. The initial answers were not the ones wanted.[15] In November 1943, the War Department was advised unequivocally that in consequence of international agreements (i.e., the Hague Conventions), the occupying power "may not make permanent changes in the constitutional or fundamental laws."[16] In May 1944, Philip Jessup, the preeminent American scholar of international law, informed the War Department that as legal grounds for the "total submission of the enemy state," unconditional surrender had no basis in international law.[17]

By the spring of 1944, the D-Day landings imminent, the Roosevelt administration was determined to secure a more congenial opinion on the legality of transformative occupation. By the time Germany's unconditional surrender was secured in May 1945, the War Department had obtained new legal advice based on the premise that Allied war efforts and aims with respect to Germany were "unprecedented" in that they had been prosecuted in "an attempt to change her warlike character, and form of government, etc., without destroying her existence as a nation."[18] The lethal menace of the fascist war state, combined with the declared Allied war aim to cause its "total and complete defeat and unconditional surrender," authorized the transformative military occupation *ex post bellum*.[19] According to this emerging doctrine, the victors in war against a fascist aggressor was legally entitled to make "major organic changes" to the legal and political system of the aggressive state.[20] When by force of arms it caused the unconditional surrenders of the Axis powers, the Allies would "free themselves of any limitations of international law in their further treatment of Germany."[21] In this view, the Allies would exercise "absolute power and sovereignty" to alter such laws and institutions there as they saw fit.

Legal ambiguities notwithstanding, after D-Day American and British agencies continued to plan, jointly and severally, for the "obliteration" and replacement of the Nazi-era laws and political formations.[22] At the Yalta and Potsdam Conferences, moreover, the Allies formally agreed that the unconditional surrender of an Axis state was to signify that its "sovereign power" had been "assumed and exercised by right of conquest."[23] Bold strategic thinking about the war was to be complemented by equally bold planning for the transformational peace. By the time the Allied occupations of Germany and Japan began in earnest in the fall of 1945, the operational premise of the United States was that unconditional surrender authorized the compulsory democratization of the enemy's domestic laws and institutions.

Constructing the Reconstructors: Planning Mechanisms

Until the early winter of 1944, the American brief on the transformative occupation of Germany and Japan consisted mainly of the high-minded pronouncements of leading statesmen. But as the Allied invasion of western Europe was imminent, urgently worded orders came down—from the White House to the executive reaches of the departments of War and State, then down to their civilian and military planning groups—stating that the unconditional surrenders first of Nazi Germany and then of imperial Japan would occasion the root and branch destruction of two fascist systems of law and government.

But clearly it is one thing, an easy thing, for statesmen to make bold declarations about the wholesale demolition and replacement of the laws and governmental institutions of a foreign state. It is another thing, fantastically difficult, for agencies of state to design and implement undertakings so novel and complex. Even in the closing months of the war in Europe and later in the Pacific, there was a yawning chasm between American aspirations for postwar Germany and Japan and the capacity to realize them.

In 1944 and 1945, no American official or agency possessed a sensible answer to the question of how actually to occupy two foreign bodies politic, remove their authoritarian entrails, and reconstitute them as viable systems of law and government. More to the point, in the last eighteen months of the Second World War, no American official or agency had developed a coherent mechanism even for research and thought about that question.

The historiography of American action in occupied Germany and Japan is largely indiscriminate about preoccupation planning, overrating both its sophistication and tangible impact on events on the ground.[24] American designs were especially shallow and unfinished in regard to the postwar reconstruction of the German (and even more emphatically) Japanese legal systems. When the Germans capitulated in May 1945, American military and civilian agencies had made some crude plans for the denazification of the German legal system and no realized plans for its liberal reconstruction. On the Japanese surrender in August, planning in the legal field was limited to some tentative ideas about the emperor's constitutional status.

A number of factors caused these failures, starting with the reality that for the Roosevelt and Truman administrations legal reconstruction was only one of many national and diplomatic commitments associated with the postwar democratization of Nazi Germany and imperial Japan. In addition, the main centers of postwar planning—the departments of War, State, and (until FDR's death in April 1945) Treasury—were inadequately coordinated, staffed, and resourced.[25] Making matters worse, the leaders of these departments engaged in protracted and divisive struggles over content and control of postwar planning throughout the war.[26] While military conflict continued on two fronts, it was convenient for the White House not to resolve interdepartmental disputes over the peace.

Effective planning for the legal reconstruction of Germany and Japan was also obstructed by the fact that the policy had embedded in it new and exceptionally difficult sociolegal issues and challenges. To make headway, the people working on the planning required expertise in German and Japanese history, culture, law, and government. They would also need expertise, or the capacity to create it, in the transition of the societies and their laws and politics from one archetype to another.

In the event, however, American planning for the legal reconstruction of Germany and Japan was undertaken by officials with, at best, imperfect expertise on German law and its nazification, and by officials with almost no genuine expertise on Japanese culture, law, and legal history. We will see, too, that American planning in this field suffered from the stubborn unwillingness of senior civilian and military officers to defer to the few genuinely learned officials in their midst.

In the eighteen months after January 1944, a hodgepodge of civilian and military agencies undertook research and generated planning advice on the subject of American-directed political and legal change, especially in occupied Germany.[27] In addition to the work by the War Department and its Civil Affairs Division (CAD), scores of papers and operational plans were prepared by multiple planning groups working simultaneously and largely independently within the departments of State, Treasury, and Justice, as well as by the Federal Economic Administration (FEA) and the Office of Strategic Services (OSS). In December 1944, in order to impose some semblance of order on the process, the Roosevelt administration formed the State-War-Navy

Coordinating Committee (SWNCC), de facto an interdepartmental nerve center for postwar planning and policy-making.[28]

But even with the advent of SWNCC, the United States lacked an effective and coherent means to think about the myriad perplexing issues raised by the transformative occupations of Germany and Japan.[29] Another layer of complication was added by the agreement with Great Britain to forge a common policy for the invasion and posttactical military government of German territory captured on the western front after D-Day.

In the American planning for legal democratization in 1944 and 1945, an often discordant medley of semi-autonomous conversations took place within and among several departments of the U.S. government and within the confines of American and American-British military units in Washington and London. Most of the conversations focused on Nazi Germany. They unfolded on the basis of little or no policy briefing from the White House or cabinet and were carried forward mainly by highly conscientious professional men who had no specialized or academic training in politics or public law, still less in German politics or public law.

Disproportionately, the key planners of legal reconstruction were Harvard-trained, Wall Street lawyers, elite American professionals who had volunteered for duty in government service or the U.S. Army after Pearl Harbor. In regard to Germany, these lawyer-planners were assisted by German lawyers, almost all of them émigré Jews who had fled the Third Reich in the 1930s. None of the American and few of the German legal experts, however, had any schooling that might have been helpful in the identification and resolution of the difficult theoretical problems associated with the destruction and reconstruction of captive legal systems. Asking these men to plan for the reconstruction of legal systems was tantamount to asking butchers to plan brain surgeries.

By 1944, of the many chains of command with hands in occupation policy and planning, the most influential ran downward from the White House into the War Department.[30] Near the top of the chain, just below Presidents Roosevelt and Truman, was Secretary of War Henry Stimson. In turn, Stimson delegated most strategic thinking and oversight of postwar planning to Assistant Secretary of War John McCloy.[31] For the development of detailed plans for the military occupations of Germany and Japan, McCloy depended on General John Hilldring, the officer in charge of the War Department's CAD. Hilldring's brief was to "coordinate all planning as well as training" for the postwar military occupations. Hilldring was able to delegate some critical postwar planning tasks to the senior military officers at the War Department's Operations Division (OPD).[32]

By 1944, the War Department and the U.S. Army emerged as the primary sites of American occupation planning, even as the titans of the Roosevelt administration continued to clash over basic postwar policy toward Germany.[33] Many, including FDR himself, expressed uneasiness that soldiers, even *American* ones, might exercise the functions and powers of government.[34] As one senior Roosevelt administration official noted in 1943, to American sensibilities it was "disturbing" that soldiers, if only by "default," might "be trusted with political missions."[35] But, schooled by American misadventures in the posttactical occupation of French North Africa in 1943, the White House was convinced that the army was the only American institution equipped to organize and implement the occupation of enemy territory and civilian populations.[36] In the course of time, then, the liberal reconstruction of the German and Japanese legal systems would be organized, supervised, and administered by the least democratic branch of the American state.

Stimson, an overburdened man in his mid-seventies, was not himself deeply involved in planning the occupations of Germany and Japan. The task of mustering War Department resources in this field fell to his brilliant and enormously capable second-in-command, McCloy, another former Wall Street lawyer.[37] Typical of the highest reaches of Roosevelt's wartime civil service, McCloy came to the War Department, and to the bureaucratic exigencies of a global war, with no previous experience of military affairs. Nor did he have any specialized knowledge of military occupations or of the history, politics, or languages of the Axis powers. What McCloy emphatically *did* bring to his tasks was a sharp and orderly mind, boundless energy, and the ability to identify and delegate to other very able men.

McCloy lived by the conviction that a hard-working and well-educated American—especially one trained as a lawyer—could excel at just about any kind of administrative task.[38] In this view, the American lawyer epitomized the methodical, rational, and pragmatic problem-solver, who, McCloy believed, was ideally suited to operations and management in America's improvised war state.[39] Lawyers knew how to discern the relevant facts of a problem. They knew how to resolve conflict and how to get a thing done. Although McCloy was fully aware of the enormous challenges associated with transformative occupation of enemy states (he thought the pacification of Germany as "terrifying in its complexities and significances"), he never wavered in his determination to see these jobs through.[40]

While in the course of time American lawyers would contribute significantly to the design and execution of legal reconstruction in postwar Germany and Japan, in the eighteen months before Allied victory the key figure was army General John Hilldring. Like McCloy, Hilldring was a person of outstanding intelligence, industry, and dedication. He took control of the new but largely hollow shell of the army's CAD late in 1943 and, by sheer force of will, spurred it to make at least rudimentary plans for the democratization of American-occupied Germany and Japan.[41] It is worth noting that Hilldring did these things not because he thought this mission suitable for the army—in fact, he harbored grave doubts—but because as a soldier he had been ordered to do it.[42]

Like most other senior American military officers of the Second World War, Hilldring was acutely aware that, with regard to the occupation of Germany particularly, the War Department was contemplating an "unprecedented mission" that would involve the short- and longer-term elimination of "totalitarian governmental and economic systems."[43] In Hilldring's private view, the U.S. Army was congenitally unsuited for these "essentially political tasks."[44] In the middle of the most arduous war it had ever waged, the army was being asked not only to win battles but also shoulder the "major role in achieving the political and economic objectives of the war."

There was nothing about this mission that Hilldring liked. Putting aside the unsuitability of the army in achieving it, Hilldring thought that serious planning had started far too late and with too few relevant resources.[45] In his view, the sole reason that the army had been assigned the task late in 1943 was that the key policy- and decision-makers knew that the civilian bureaucracy of the United States had no capacity to design and implement the occupation, still less the transformative occupation, of an enemy nation-state.[46] In delegating the job to an ill-prepared and reluctant military branch, the Washington leadership elite set a precedent for an improvised and often makeshift approach to key postwar policy goals. "I am confident that it is no exaggeration to say that 90 percent of the troubles of Military Government in the smallest towns and units was traceable to Washington," Hilldring later wrote.[47]

It was also traceable to Washington—that is, to the Roosevelt and then Truman cabinets—that by 1944, planning for the postwar occupations was strongly Eurocentric.[48] The prevailing theme was "dispose of Germany first, and Japan will take care of itself later."[49] This was a function of Allied strategic doctrine to defeat Nazi Germany first.[50] By the winter of 1944, the invasion of German-held territory in western Europe, of Germany itself, was on the near horizon. Long before their training had been completed, American civil affair officers were "uprooted from their training centers in the United States" and rushed to staging areas in Britain. These events, Hilldring recalled, were typical of the "wild disorder" of American preparations for the occupation of the German homeland.[51]

There were also cultural reasons that American planning for the reconstruction of Germany, especially for the *legal and political* dimensions of reconstruction, was Eurocentric. These include the strong historical, cultural, and economic kinship felt by the American leadership class toward Germany.[52] America's wartime leaders were predisposed to think the crucial hinge of peace in the postwar world was the successful resolution of the "German question." They thought the critical planning challenge was finding a way to coax Germans to accept liberal-democratic modernity.

For these reasons, American planning for the denazification and liberal reconstruction of the German legal system, as inadequate as it was, was far more extensive and detailed than any such planning for

Japan. To American planners, some of whom were Jews born and trained in Germany, German law and institutions were visible, impressive, and pertinent in ways that Japanese law was not. German laws and legal institutions, even if perverted by the Third Reich, were seen as products of enlightened European rationality. Even if they had been corrupted as instruments of racialized oppression, the premise of American planning was that the German legal system and its personnel were capable of redemption. More to the point, the purification and liberal reconstruction of German law and legal institutions were viewed as essential preconditions of Germany's rehabilitation as a modern political community.

In contrast, we will see that among the handful of American postwar planners who had authentic expertise in Japanese history and society, few, perhaps none, thought of the reconstruction or redemption of its legal system as a priority. To leading American policy-makers, the Japanese legal system of the wartime era was neither visible nor pertinent. There was no sense that the Japanese ultranationalists had perverted a distinguished or celebrated tradition of law and justice. The fixed idea of American policy-makers about the Japanese legal order was that it was a facet of an anachronistically "feudal" system of government. But although the United States began the occupation of Japan without a definite plan for its reconstruction as a liberal rule of law state, within a few months MacArthur began to improvise and institute this transformative change.

Razing the Nazi Legal System: Planning for the Legal Reconstruction of Germany

While American and British planners disagreed about many aspects of the postwar occupation of Germany, they agreed that the capture of German territory should trigger the capture, control, and, crucially, the denazification of German public institutions including its legal system.[53] In this shared view, German law, once a beacon of humane rationality, had been subverted by the Nazis as an instrument of naked political oppression. Soon after Hitler came to power in 1933, something had gone grotesquely wrong in the German manner of law and justice. Were Germany ever to regain its place among civilized nations, that wrong would need urgently to be put right.

These postulations raised a number of novel and hard policy and planning issues. How exactly was one nation state (or an alliance of states) to cause a moment of radical discontinuity in the legal and political institutions of another? By what criteria might its agents discern the legitimate or illegitimate legal idea, actor, process, or institution? By what surgical method might particular laws, legal understandings, and decisions be removed from a body politic? How were American agencies to determine the pace, order and mechanism of directed legal and political change? How were they to ensure the permanence of directed legal change? More specifically in relation to Germany, what was the National Socialist theory of law and legality? How deeply had Nazi ideology and idea-holders penetrated German law and legal institutions? How might the Allies expunge dense and imbricated system of laws, personnel, and legal institutions without creating a chaotic legal vacuum?

In 1943, American officials grappling with these questions faced a serious problem beyond their inherent complexity: the wartime government of the United States lacked coordinated structures for the production, dissemination, and analysis of reliable knowledge about law or government in an enemy state. Indeed, it lacked a coherent plan even for the formation of such structures.

This explains why in the final months of 1943 American research on Nazi law was being undertaken independently by a number of unspecialized planning groups, including at the War Department, within the army, at the OSS, the Federal Economic Administration, and the Justice Department.[54] The work was based on sundry amounts of credible intelligence about Nazi laws and legal processes. It was completed by researchers of varied amounts of expertise in German law and legal history. For the most part, however, an inverse proportionality existed within American planning ranks between those with the most knowledge (German émigré law scholars) and those with the most policy-making power (American civilian and military officials).

Although the War Department, in the form of its Civilian Affairs Division (CAD), ostensibly was in charge of coordinating planning for legal denazification,[55] in fact the leaders at CAD had no effective means to control either the creation or evaluation of information about Germany, legal or otherwise. In September 1943, therefore, General Hilldring was feeling his way in the dark when he informed the Justice Department about the immediate need of CAD for a "detailed study of various aspects of the laws of the Nazi regime."[56] The study was to distinguish "which German laws are inspired by Nazi principles" from those "fundamentally sound in principle and may be freely utilized in connection with the projected military government of Germany."

To underline the urgency of Hilldring's request, on two occasions in the fall of 1943 Assistant Secretary of War John McCloy wrote directly to Attorney General Francis Biddle on the matter. "One of the most important, as well as difficult, of the problems of military government," McCloy stated, "will be that of dealing with the legal systems existing in areas which our armies will occupy."[57] That was why the War Department felt an immediate need for "an index to the German laws which have been adopted under the Nazi regime for the purposes of spreading Nazi principles."[58] It was also urgent that Justice begin to prepare the handbooks that American officers would use in the administration of justice in occupied Germany. "In view of the size and difficulty of this project," McCloy emphasized, "it is of urgent importance that it be started soon." McCloy also requested (fruitlessly, so it turned out) that the attorney general coordinate and consolidate the federal government's array of research initiatives on Nazi law and its prospective destruction and replacement.

In the meantime, the Central European Section of the OSS, staffed by several eminent German émigré jurists, already had completed an intelligence report on the "The Reorganization of the German Administration of Justice in 1942."[59] The report contained an intriguing thesis: that since the German invasion of Poland in 1939, a crisis had arisen in German justice in the Third Reich, stemming from the fact that a number of prominent lawyers and judges, including a number of senior officials in the Justice Ministry, had resisted the escalating incursions and usurpations of Nazi officials in legal matters.

According to this analysis, the resistance persisted even as Hitler, now waging total war in Europe, demanded strict discipline on the home front. For all of the outward signs of its nazification, German justice in the Hitler era had remained in the hands of conservative nationalists who felt greater fealty to the principle of the *rechtsstaat,* the idea of government by formal principles and procedures of law, than to Adolf Hitler or his movement. In this view, a number of senior German jurists continued to impede the Nazi takeover of the German legal system even as the tide of war shifted against the Reich. By the close of 1942, OSS analysts concluded, a "critical situation had arisen in the German administration of justice by reason of the conflict between Nazi principles and practices and older standards."

The OSS report offered a potentially consequential thesis to American planning: that German law and legal professions had not been hopelessly corrupted by National Socialism. The report suggested that it might be sufficient during the occupation for the Allies simply to reset the German legal clock to the settings of the Weimar republic.

But the OSS report was far from the last American word on this subject. In 1943, the new Special War Section of the Justice Department commissioned an expatriate German legal scholar and political scientist to prepare a brief on legal denazification.[60] This brings us to the first of the study's many contacts with the redoubtable Professor Karl Loewenstein, an important future participant in American-driven legal reconstruction in postwar Germany.[61] A Munich-born lawyer and jurisprudent, Loewenstein had been a practicing lawyer and part-time university lecturer in Bavaria when the Nazis came to power in January 1933. Jewish in ancestry, liberal in politics, Loewenstein left Germany the next year, having secured lectureships in law and government at Yale and then Amherst College.

When approached by the Justice Department in 1943, Loewenstein had become a distinguished (and now naturalized American) scholar on fascist political movements in Europe and South America. His report on legal denazification was characteristically incisive and forthright. In contrast to the OSS report, moreover, his report emphasized the culpability of the German legal professions for the perversion of German law and justice.[62]

In Loewenstein's assessment, in the 1930s most German jurists were antidemocratic conservatives who had willingly embraced the

Nazis as means of restoring public order in Germany. When the Nazis persecuted Jewish and liberal jurists, most German jurists had either endorsed these policies or looked the other way. Furthermore, German jurists had been indispensable to both the formation and implementation of the Nazi legal program. By the early 1940s the German legal professions, especially the judiciary, had been "incurably contaminated" by Nazi affiliation or ideology. "Nazism," he explained, "has made deep inroads in the German legal life and has revolutionized practically all its aspects." On this basis Loewenstein contended that when the Nazis were defeated at arms the "task of restoring a decent legal system [in Germany] will present itself as urgent and imperative."

Loewenstein predicted that German jurists would stand together in denying complicity with the Third Reich and its crimes. They would claim that a few "Nazis gangsters" had forced them to make and enforce tyrannous laws. Loewenstein further predicted that after the war German lawyers would promote themselves as the natural leaders of postwar German society. His report was emphatic that such pleadings were to be rejected, that during a period of military occupation the Allies would need to *impose* transformational change from the *outside.* "[The] reconstruction of German law," Loewenstein emphasized, "should under no conditions be left to the discretion of the German authorities, whatever may be their political complexion." Denazification, if it was to succeed, was a task for the "civilian authorities of the Allied governments . . . part and parcel of the planned reconstruction of Germany as whole."

Loewenstein further emphasized that legal denazification was certain to be slow and arduous work. German law could not be decontaminated by a "sweeping blanket clause." The German legal professions could not be cleansed of Nazi influence except by a comprehensive purge. The success of these programs would turn on planning that anticipated and curtailed the ill effects of "expediency, opportunism, and even ignorance." The cost of failure would be grave. If the German legal system was not thoroughly cleansed of Nazi ideas and influences, "no conversion of the German people to constitutional government is feasible."

While in 1943 the work of Karl Loewenstein and the OSS analysts provided some useful starting points to an American planning conversation about legal denazification, there is little evidence that it was treated as such. In the first weeks of 1944, the Justice Department continued to send ambiguous signals about its readiness to complete a comprehensive survey of law under the Third Reich.[63] In subsequent weeks, Hilldring's office tried to arrange for this work to be completed (for $20,000) by professors at the Harvard Law School.[64] Justice tried to complete an inventory of Nazi-era laws, and in January 1944 CAD commissioned a series of joint studies or guides on Nazi laws from the FEA.[65]

In April 1944, CAD circulated a draft guide on the "Elimination of Fundamental Nazi Political Laws" which described legal denazification as a crucial prerequisite of "the reconstruction of democratic Germany."[66] Upon capture of German territory the discriminatory laws of the Third Reich were to be annulled.[67] To avoid creating a dangerous legal void in occupied Germany, Nazi-era laws were to be repealed (or abrogated) selectively, starting with those supporting Nazi dictatorship and persecution on account of race or creed. These were to be the first moves toward the comprehensive denazification of German laws.

The guide attracted criticism. One army civil affairs adviser, the German-literate Harvard law school graduate W. Ward Fearnside, advised against the selective abrogation of Nazi laws.[68] Based on his assessment of "15,082 double column pages" of Nazi-era legislation, Fearnside concluded that Nazi philosophy had become so pervasive in German law that it could only be eradicated by a general repeal of all decrees and laws of the Nazi regime after a "suitable interim period during which new legislation could be prepared and passed by the new German [democratic] government."[69] Blanket repeal was a drastic measure justified by the perversion of an entire system of law. In this view, comprehensive legal denazification was a crucial precondition of the American policy to revolutionize Germany as a liberal-democratic state. "If one wishes to enjoy the position of a crusader," Fearnside commented, "one must *be* a crusader."

Before the CAD came to grips with Fearnside's report, the Teheran Conference of Allied leaders (in late November 1943) accelerated the timetable of planning for legal denazification. At Teheran, Churchill and FDR pledged (to Stalin) to mount a second front invasion of western Europe by May 1944. All going to plan, Allied forces would capture German territory before the end of that year. This left American and now American-British planning groups with six months to craft final plans for the denazification of German law and legal institutions.[70]

With an American-led invasion of western Europe on the near horizon, the War Department moved swiftly to create new civilian, military, and integrated civilian-military groups to plan and implement the civilian affairs dimensions of the invasion of western Europe, including legal denazification. Among Hilldring's first decisions in this regard was to organize an entity called the United States Group Control Council (USGCC), the embryonic American element of prospective Allied military government in postsurrender Germany.[71] The USGCC was set up to assume control of the American occupation effort in Germany upon conclusion of the tactical phase of operations.[72]

Hilldring's decision created an on-paper organization almost devoid of staff.[73] While American, British, and Soviet diplomats continued to negotiate the terms of trilateral control authority over Germany, the directors of the USGCC's twelve functional divisions, including its Legal Division, prepared plans for the denazification and general governance of German territory and people.[74]

The wartime director of USGCC's Legal Division was John B. Marsh, another Wall Street lawyer turned army officer and postwar planner.[75] By the winter of 1944, Marsh's division had been organized into three subdivisions of four officers each: Legal Advice, Judiciary, and Prisons. The division's mission was to seize control of the German legal system in the U.S. zone "with a view to its immediate de-nazification and later long range reform."[76] The division was also slated to work with its British and Soviet counterparts on the planning and implementation of the democratic reconstruction of German law on a national basis.[77]

Like the other directors of USGCC departments in the run-up to D-Day, Marsh's most urgent responsibility was his work as the senior

American legal officer assigned to the German section of the Civil Affairs Section (G-5) of the new joint American-British military command for the invasion of western Europe, the Supreme Headquarters of the Allied Expeditionary Force (SHAEF).[78] Until early in 1946, therefore, Marsh and his subordinates operated in the chains of command both of General Hilldring (in Washington) and General Eisenhower (in England and the western front).

Based in London, the bilateral German Country Unit (GCU) of SHAEF was the nerve center of planning for the short-term occupation of Germany. Its mission was to "crystallize ideas" about the occupation into a program of action.[79] Legal planning was carried out by the equal numbers of American and British army assigned to the GCU's Legal Branch.[80] The branch's first task was to develop a set of edicts for the suspension of German laws closely associated with the Nazi Party and its programs.

Legal Branch was activated in March 1944 and consisted of a small but talented group of American and British lawyers, all of whom had been practicing law as civilians in 1939.[81] The British element of Legal Branch was led successively by two senior barristers, (Brigadiers) Andrew E. J. Clark, KC, and in the spring of 1945, Sir Alfred Brown, KC. The second-in-command was John G. Foster, an accomplished Australian-born and German-literate international commercial lawyer and Oxford don.[82] Working closely with Foster was the English barrister and fellow of All Souls College, Oxford, Richard Wilberforce.

In directing the American contingent at Legal Branch, John Marsh was assisted closely by another former Wall Street lawyer, Hayden N. Smith, and on an assignment basis by the American legal scholar Mitchell Franklin.[83] Also in American army uniform with the branch was Fritz E. Oppenheimer, a German émigré lawyer from Berlin.[84]A very influential figure in legal denazification, his personal story merits a brief digression.

A decorated German veteran of the First World War, by the early 1930s Oppenheimer was a leading international commercial lawyer in Berlin. Facing a mounting wave of anti-Semitic persecution, Oppenheimer immigrated to England in 1936 and was called to the

English bar in 1940. In 1942, Oppenheimer left England to practice law in New York. In June 1943, he enlisted as a private in the U.S. Army. Eight months later, Oppenheimer's high intelligence, training and fluency in both the Anglo-American and German legal worlds earned him an officer's commission and an advisory role with both Eisenhower's staff and SHAEF's Legal Branch.

To support its research on legal denazification, by 1944 SHAEF also had organized the London-based Special Legal Unit, Germany and Austria (SLU), a joint American and British group whose shifting personnel consisted, in its first manifestation, of two German and two Austrian expatriate legal experts in American uniform, all Jewish and refugees from Hitler.[85] While the SLU was assigned a number of rather banal legal information-gathering, manual-writing, and translation jobs,[86] its core mission was one of unusual breadth, difficulty, and significance: to provide a systematic assessment of the impact of Nazism on substantive law and administration of justice in Germany since 1933 and to provide a blueprint for the "repeal or modification of Nazi law."[87] As John Foster stated in March 1945, when it was completed, and when the German army was brought to surrender, this crucial legal research was to "constitute the basis for the elimination [by Allied edict] of discriminatory legislation."[88]

In terms of military chain of command, Fritz Oppenheimer was the ranking officer of the SLU. By midwinter of 1945, however, the unit's intellectual leader and "most important member" was Ernst J. Cohn, the distinguished German expatriate legal scholar.[89] A noncommissioned officer, Cohn coordinated the work of a number of other German émigré jurists.[90] Otto Kahn-Freund, Kurt Lipstein, F. A. Mann, and Max Grunhut were among the other German-Jewish émigré legal academics who accepted assignment work for the SLU, as did Wolfgang Friedmann, seconded from the Political Intelligence Section of the British Foreign Office.[91] The SLU, while lacking quantity, did not lack in quality of personnel.

Legal Branch and its SLU research arm were assigned a wide-ranging set of planning problems associated with legal denazification in the immediate posttactical phase. The branch planned the law-related aspects of the Western Allied invasion of Germany while completing the protocols for control of captured German legal institutions. The branch also was to establish the theoretical and empirical basis of subsequent Allied efforts to normalize German law and legal institutions.

By the early winter of 1944, with new American and bilateral planning organizations in place, work began in earnest on the development of a well-informed and unified approach to legal denazification—that is, on the initial steps to be taken upon conquest of enemy soil.

American and British aims in this regard had been summarized for SHAEF by a subcommittee of the British War Cabinet in early March 1944.[92] In the short term, the SHAEF authorities would act as a kind of legal demolition team. Its main tasks were to suspend "repugnant" laws, abolish Nazi Special Courts, release political prisoners, and purge the German judiciary and legal civil service of "unreliable or politically undesirable judges or magistrates or officials." The long-term objective of the occupation was to "create conditions in which German law can be fundamentally reformed so as to provide a basis for the civilised and democratic way of life in Germany." This goal would in turn depend on the abolition of all racially discriminatory legislation and the establishment in Germany both of "the equality of all citizens before the law" and the "re-establishment of the 'rule of law' and of the authority and impartiality of the courts and judges." These goals would be complemented by the firm establishment of civil and political liberties.

Before the SLU had been established, the British already had commissioned one important study of the legal denazification problem, completed in 1943 by a Foreign Office planning group called the Research Committee for the Revision of German Law.[93] This group was staffed by nine distinguished German émigré jurists led by Ernst Wolff, a former president of the Berlin bar.[94] The Wolff committee's two principal tasks were to survey the impact of Nazi ideology on German statutory and procedural law and formulate an approach to their denazification.

The prologue of the Wolff committee's final report commented on the vexing theoretical issues raised by its assignment, prominently whether the racist or otherwise tyrannical laws of the Third Reich had validity and status as law. "On the one hand," the committee stated, "the 'law' created by National Socialism cannot be retained in its entirety, as it must, to a large extent, be considered incompatible with fundamental principles of humanity and civilization." In this view, Nazi law was an invalid nullity, "law" in quotes. In adopting this position, the committee had been "guided by a recent development in the Law of Nations, namely, the tendency to grant to the individual certain minimum rights under International Law." In superseding these rights the Nazi regime "has even betrayed the idea that the law has its basis in morality." For this reason alone, the committee contended, "It would be possible to argue with some force that all such National Socialist legislation is *ipso facto* null and void."

The Wolff committee was not insensible to the implications of this position. If, on the one hand, Nazi law might be regarded as a nullity, "on the other hand, it would not seem sound policy simply to cancel all Nazi-created law and to revert to the German law as it stood before the Nazis came into power." Such action would erase the foundation of numberless legal decisions and relationships, destabilizing Germany in the postwar period. Furthermore, "A small minority of the legal provisions introduced by the Nazis bear no political stamp and in no way depend on the basic national-socialist outlook." For these reasons the committee's report did not endorse the comprehensive abrogation of Nazi law.

The Wolff committee alternatively advised that on taking the German surrender the Allies introduce an "interim constitution" restoring individual rights and the rule of law in the German territories. This document would provide for the immediate but selective nullification of Nazi-era "statutes, decrees or rules" inimical to these rights. The committee also advised that, where needed, replacement laws might be devised by an advisory committee of non-Nazi German legal experts. The thrust of the committee's recommendations was for the Allies to permit carefully vetted groups of German jurists to denazify and liberalize German law in the immediate postwar period.

The tacit premise of this report was that the Nazis were an army of juristic barbarians who had sacked Germany's legal citadel. In this account legal Nazism was an externality of German law and decision-making, a violent imposition on its integrity. Ernst Wolff, by way of example, agreed that a priority of the Allied occupation authority in Germany should be to "clear the Bench of Nazi elements."[95] This policy was rooted in Wolff's perception that the Weimar-era judiciary had been fundamentally sound both in its political outlook and jurisprudence. When "the Nazis came into power," Wolff explained, "German judges enjoyed full independence from interference by the Executive and were appointed for life." As Wolff saw it, there was no problem with German judges or laws that could not be resolved by eliminating Nazi appointees and influences. The way forward was to go backward, to turn the legal clock back to 1932.

While it made no direct references to the Wolff report, Fritz Oppenheimer's first important SHAEF memo on legal denazification, of April 27, 1944, reflected similar ideas.[96] Oppenheimer's memo focused on the issue of how the Allies, on capture of German national lands, might implement the mandated annulment of German laws. Did annulment (or abrogation) denote a mere temporary suspension or did it mean permanent extirpation?

For Oppenheimer, best answers to these questions hinged on whether Allied authorities had the legal and moral authority to make permanent changes to the domestic institutions of a conquered nation. Then there was the practical issue of whether the Germans would be pacified under laws inflicted on them by foreign occupiers. On this point Oppenheimer suggested that "it may be preferable to leave actual abrogation to the German people so as not to give the impression that a new legal system was imposed upon the Germans by force of arms." He further recommended that on taking German territory the most prudent first step would be to proclaim the suspension of "10 or even fewer significant [Nazi] laws." This or a second proclamation would contain a "general clause" preventing the "application of any other law which is based on Nazi ideology and whose application in individual cases would lead to grave injustice." By D-Day in June 1944, SHAEF had adopted these recommendations as official policy. The only remaining task was to draft the legal denazification edicts.[97]

By June 15, 1944, D-Day plus nine days, SHAEF had finalized a protocol of law-related action on the capture of German soil.[98] Immediately upon the capture of German territory, army group commanders were to issue an edict suspending the operation of a (yet unspecified) list of the "most obnoxious" of Nazi-era laws.[99] German courts in captured areas were to be closed, law-related buildings and records seized. Nazi war criminals were to be arrested while provision was made for the restitution to rightful owners of property seized by the Nazis further to racial or other discriminatory laws.[100]

By the late summer of 1944, the Western Allies now breaking out of Normandy, it was a matter of real urgency for SHAEF's Legal Branch to finalize the list of most pernicious Nazi laws. But just as it moved to do so, the diplomatic context of its work destabilized. In Washington, Roosevelt had endorsed the Morgenthau Plan, a vindictively stern policy toward postwar Germany. Accordingly, the War Department's newly minted "handbooks" on civil affairs policy in occupied Germany were sent back for revision.[101] At the same time, British leaders attempted to relocate civil affairs planning for postwar Germany away from SHAEF and to the incipient tripartite control mechanism.[102]

By the late fall of 1944, as Allied armies neared the Rhine, many of the details and also the very legality of the denazification directives remained at issue, at least among British military lawyers. In October 1944, Colonel H. A. Smith, before 1940 a leading scholar of international law, now senior legal officer at the headquarters of the British 21st Army Group, reviewed SHAEF's draft directives on German law and then weighed in with a scathing memorandum.[103] Addressed to the War Office, Smith's "Legislation for Germany" contended that the SHAEF directives were so ill-considered in principle, so marred by "vagueness and obscurity of language," that their implementation was certain to instigate "a state of legal confusion in which it will be almost impossible in many cases to know what law is actually in force in the occupied territory."[104] Smith further contended that the closure of German courts, even if lawful, was likely only to lead to unrest among German civilians while depriving Nazi victims of "legal remedies for wrongs suffered" during the Third Reich.[105]

Drawing on his expertise in international law, Smith advanced another and even more elemental objection to Allied legal policy for

Germany. "It is also clear," he contended, "that in some respects the enactments seriously transgress the limits which international law sets upon the rights of the occupying power."[106] Smith was convinced that it "is not within the competence of an occupying power to alter the law in an occupied country upon such a matter as marriage." If the British condoned such a move, almost certainly it would be "treated as *ultra vires* by British courts and indeed everywhere outside the occupying territory."

Smith's memorandum alarmed the executive officers at Legal Branch. Its research arm in London, the SLU, was ordered to undertake a general review of the content, legality, and implications of SHAEF's draft directives on German law. Its ensuing report (to John Foster) consisted of a point-by-point rebuttal of all but one of Smith's contentions.[107] Tellingly, however, the report did not dispute the force of Smith's claim that international law forbade an occupying power from making permanent alterations to the domestic law of the occupied territory. But if adopted as policy, the report stated, the Smith finding would "severely limit the action of Military Government . . . to maintain in existence some of the most flagrant examples of National Socialist injustice."

The questions raised by the Smith memorandum were seen as serious enough that SHAEF quickly organized a plenary session (attended by Smith) of British and American military and government lawyers.[108] At the outset of the meeting, Brigadier Clark "emphasized the importance of maintaining the closest cooperation" between the multiplicity of "Departments and Headquarters" engaged in the planning process. He thought that "from time to time differences of opinion between legal experts were inevitable," especially when planning programs "for which no adequate precedents exist." Clark thought that if the lawyers assembled could not reach consensus on the issues, they might be resolved by "high legal authority." But his preference was to thrash the problems out within SHAEF. In the result, Smith was prevailed upon to stay his objections. At the same time it was agreed that SHAEF's "Abrogation of Nazi Law" directive had been drawn too broadly and that "it would be eminently desirable to issue a detailed list of the precise laws rendered inoperative by the clause suspending Nazi laws." Wilberforce and Marsh closed the meeting with the gloomy observation that the compilation of such a list was nothing less than a "monumental undertaking" that "would take very considerable time to bring to completion."

Of course "considerable time" is precisely what SHAEF G-5 did not have. The call for greater "refinement" in the legal denazification directive jeopardized the entire mission.[109] On January 27, 1945, a subcommittee of Legal Branch met to oversee the preparation of a detailed list of German laws and legal decisions that were to be suspended by the "abrogation directive" (Law No. 1).[110] A final list was then approved, henceforth to be regarded as the "basic charter for the denazification of the [*sic*] German legislation."[111] Under Article I of the directive, a list of nine statutes identified as fundamental to the Nazi regime were to be "deprived of effect" within the occupied territory.[112] Article II was to state that "No German law, however and whenever enacted, shall be applied judicially or administratively in any instance, within the occupied territory where such application would cause injustice or inequality."

The central issue now was how to determine how many Nazi-era laws would be affected by the second article, whether only those which were discriminatory (toward Jews and other "enemies of the state") or also laws supporting the Nazi Party and its institutions.[113] Uncertainty on this point persisted even as an officer was assigned to compile an exhaustive inventory, divided into seventeen legal subcategories, of Nazi-era laws that would be abrogated (but not named) by Law No. 1.[114]

By mid-February 1945, the war against Germany having entered its final phase, senior officers at Legal Branch had lost confidence in the feasibility of this project.[115] No inventory that could be finished in time was thought likely to be exhaustive.[116] In any event, the branch's remit was limited to a short list of the most objectionable Nazi laws. As Brigadier Clark put the matter to John Marsh on February 13, comprehensive legal denazification "is inherently work which should be performed by the German administration after it has been brought under control and reconstituted with reliable personnel."[117] For his part, Marsh agreed that the branch should devote remaining time to the "obviously discriminatory legislation, rather than to general revision and long term reform."[118]

Allied forces crossed the Rhine on March 23, 1945. In early April, having received approval from the White House, the Joint Chiefs issued their General Directive (JCS 1067) to General Eisenhower.[119] The document set forth American policy on occupied Germany for the "initial post-defeat period," reaffirming American commitment both to the permanent "elimination of militarism and Nazism in all their forms" and the "eventual reconstruction of German political life on a democratic basis."[120] The directive made a number of references to the need for compulsory legal denazification.[121] It specified that in German territory under American control the "laws purporting to establish the political structure of National Socialism and the basis of the Hitler regime and all laws, decrees, and regulations which establish discriminations on grounds of race, nationality, creed or political opinions" were to be rendered inoperative pending their permanent abrogation by the Control Council.[122] The directive called for Nazi-era Special Courts to be abolished immediately and for ordinary courts to be closed until their "Nazi features and personnel" were eliminated.

On the capture of German soil in March and April 1945, SHAEF tactical commanders proclaimed Law No. 1. The proclamation purported to eliminate "from German law and administration . . . the policies and doctrines of the National Socialist Party, and to restore to the German people the rule of justice and equality before law." The first article of Law No. 1 named nine "fundamental Nazi laws," declaring them "deprived of effect in the occupied territory."[123] The second article contained a "General Suspending Clause" forbidding reopened German courts and tribunals from decisions based on "race, nationality, religious beliefs or opposition to the National Socialist Party or its doctrines." The third article of the proclamation forbade German legal decision-makers from drawing on National Socialist doctrines in the promulgation of decisions.

The final language of Law No. 1 was therefore a victory of sorts for Legal Branch. The pith and substance of its advice had been accepted and deployed.[124] By the same token, Law No. 1 represented the barest start to legal denazification. While the most obvious and obnoxious of Nazi-era German laws had been suspended, Allied lawyers and consultants had yet to develop a detailed plan for the comprehensive denazification of German law.[125] Nor had they finished studies of the presence and impact of National Socialism in the most critical areas of German public and private law, including on criminal, marriage, property, labor, and commercial law.[126] Indeed, the various American and British groups at work on legal denazification still had not agreed on a working definition of the term "Nazi law."[127] How many of the some 9,500 statutes promulgated by the Third Reich would need to be repealed in whole or in part?[128] Moreover, what was the legal status of countless Nazi-era proclamations, decrees, ordinances, notices, and regulations?

Then there was the still unresolved issue of how to rid the German bar, judiciary, and legal bureaucracies of National Socialist operatives. As Ernst Wolff put the matter in July 1944, the "reform of [Nazi] personnel is undoubtedly not less important than the question of the reform of the law."[129] Wolff knew from personal experience that the Hitler regime had taken pains to purge, co-opt, and intimidate the German legal professions, a process that had accelerated during the war years. The prevailing view among Allied planners in 1944 was that Nazi Party members and ways of thought were ubiquitous in the German legal state and that its democratic reconstruction would depend on the thorough denazification of the German legal professions and bureaucracies.

By the end of the war in Europe in May 1945, American planning and policy on the denazification of legal personnel had advanced mainly in terms of goals.[130] In the short term, SHAEF's "Basic Preliminary Plan" called for local military government to "remove and exclude from public office and responsible and important positions in quasi-public and private enterprise all active supporters of Nazism or militarism."[131] German legal officials who had been merely "nominal" members of the Nazi Party were to be permitted to retain positions and professional standing. The most urgent task of SHAEF's Legal Branch was the location and arrest of prominent Nazi legal personnel, especially the judges and prosecutors of Hitler's Special Courts.[132]

It was all too easy to contemplate a general purge of leading Nazi legal officials. The much more difficult task was to create a viable plan for the *reactivation* of a denazified German bench, bar, and legal technocracy. The first impediment in this regard was that by 1945 virtually all German legal officeholders had become members of the Nazi Party. All of them, moreover, were at least indirectly implicated in the oppressions of the Third Reich. But given that American occupiers would need to reactivate many, perhaps a majority of these officials, how to distinguish the pardonable from the unpardonable Nazi?[133]

In the immediate wake of the U.S. Army's tactical occupation of German territory, surviving German courts and tribunals were closed. This and the general havoc of German civilian life after the surrender bought the army's civilian affairs units some time in dealing with the problem of Nazi legal personnel. Having issued its initial proclamations, the army's legal teams were content mainly to kick the legal denazification can down the road.

When the United States began to assemble its posttactical occupation apparatus in Germany in the summer of 1945, few of the key destructive and none of the constructive tasks of legal denazification had been achieved. Most German laws had not been abrogated. Most German legal personnel had not been vetted. More worryingly to American legal officers of the USGCC, little progress had been made in the development of cogent policies and procedures in these areas. As John Marsh acknowledged in June 1945, the time was nigh to commence "affirmative, rather than merely negative or preventive" denazification in the legal field.[134] It was far from clear, however, either to Marsh or any other American legal officer in occupied Germany, how this goal would be realized.

The Other Fascism: Planning the Legal Reconstruction of Imperial Japan

If America's policy for the postwar legal reconstruction of Germany had a score of disputatious fathers, its policy for the postwar reformation of law in imperial Japan was an orphan. We have seen that beginning in the winter of 1943 and then for more than two years groups of American and British officials were more or less continuously engaged in intelligence gathering, deliberating, and planning the denazification of the German legal system. American and British policy-makers believed it pertinent to invest substantial amounts of their scarce human and material resources in research and analysis of Nazi law and legal institutions. Their working hypothesis was that law and legality, having figured importantly in the tyrannies and persecutions of the Third Reich, would figure equally in its reconstruction as a liberal democracy.

In a host of significant ways, however, American planning with respect to postwar Japan stands in sharp contrast. The Allies' "defeat Germany first" policy inhibited all aspects of planning for the postwar occupation of Japan, as did the utter foreignness of Japan to the American policy-making elite.[135] Few American policy-makers had or *believed* they possessed even rudimentary knowledge of Japanese history, politics, or customs. Few knew or thought they knew the genesis or character of the Japanese mode of fascist nationalism. As for Japan's laws and legal system, these subjects barely registered among American planners. Consequently the historian of the American occupation of Japan searches in vain for memoranda on the "de-ultranationalization" of Japanese laws and legal professions. The historian also looks in vain for the reports and position papers of American or Japanese (expatriate) experts, for the equivalent expertise and input on Japanese law and law reform of a Karl Loewenstein, Ernst Cohn, Ernst Wolff, or Fritz Oppenheimer. In the fall of 1945, American agencies began the liberal legal reconstruction of Japan with next to no useful knowledge about Japan's laws and legal system.

In the last days of July 1945, as the Truman administration weighed the use of atomic bombs in Japan, some of the most fundamental American policy questions about the occupation remained unanswered. On the unconditional surrender of Japan, what were to be the principal American aims of its occupation? Would occupied Japan be administered by the United States or by a coalition of Allied states? Would Japan be governed directly or indirectly through the postsurrender vestiges of the Japanese state? Would the emperor be retained as the nation's head of state? To what degree and by what means would the United States and its allies compel the reconfiguration of Japan's authoritarian legal and political institutions?

Another major obstacle to the development of cogent answers to such questions was that American planning unfolded along two mainly distinct paths.[136] Because the U.S. Army was to have principal carriage of the occupation, the War Department and its agencies had primary responsibility over policy and planning. As in the German case, it was Secretary of War Stimson's prerogative to advise the president on the postwar treatment of Japan. But more than in the German case, the State Department (specifically, its Office of Far Eastern Affairs) figured prominently in American preparations, especially for deep background on likely responses of the Japanese leadership elite to a period of occupation.[137]

In the result, however, the State Department proved slow and tentative in the delivery of policy guidance to McCloy and his planners. Although State boasted the single largest concentration of scarce American expertise on Japan, its units were also short of personnel who were fully trained in Japanese language, history, politics, and culture.[138] In the years before the Pacific war there had been no sudden influx to the United States of highly educated Japanese émigrés. Already having raided the American universities for relevant expertise, there was nowhere for the State or War Departments (or the OSS) to turn for usefully educated personnel.[139] The fact is that in the critical planning period, 1943 to 1945, the United States government lacked intellectual resources enough to produce strongly researched and reasoned plans for the reconstruction of Japan.

Stimson depended on McCloy and War Department resources to generate basic planning policy. In turn, McCloy depended on General Hilldring's Civilian Affairs Division (CAD) to generate detailed planning options. Hilldring in his turn depended on a disparate range of sources for primary research and analysis: on the State Department, but also the Operations Policy Division of the Joint Chiefs, the OSS and, in 1945, on the synthetic policy advice of the State-War-Navy Coordinating Committee (SWNCC).[140]

As early as May 1942, State Department planners had begun to assess some of the most salient policy issues facing the Allies on the occupation of a defeated Japan,[141] including the "future of the Imperial House . . . and the question of establishing a responsible government, and possibly the undertaking of social and economic reforms."[142] The single unifying theme of the plethora of policy studies generated by State over the next three years, echoing Roosevelt's public rhetoric, was the "long-range desirability of ridding Japan of the political organism responsible for long-standing aggressive tendencies. It was emphasized that our aim must be to effect a permanent change in Japanese political institutions."[143] But the precise nature of these permanent changes remained unclear. Which political institutions required modification and by whom were these modifications to be made? Would the United States spearhead radical constitutional change in Japan and, if so, on what ideological model?

Much to the exasperation of McCloy and especially General Hilldring, the State Department was slow to deliver straight answers to these central questions.[144] What was urgently needed, Hilldring informed State in April 1945, was a "short policy statement" on the occupation of Japan, endorsed by the president, which would guide CAD planners in drafting specific orders and directives for American occupying forces in Japan.[145]

In some measure, State can be forgiven these delays. Not only was it desperately short of relevant expertise, but, as late as the summer of 1945, its planners worked on the false premises that the military occupation of Japan would not commence before 1946, after a drawn-out and destructive invasion of the Japanese home islands.[146] This engendered a third false premise: the invasion of Japan was thought likely to destroy most of Japan's functional civil and state infrastructure, making it necessary for the United States and its allies to govern the country directly.

The prospect of a full-scale military invasion of Japan was so grim and unpalatable to American leadership that in 1945 it began anxiously to debate how the Japanese might be induced to surrender. For Truman and his closest advisors one possible answer, pending success of the Manhattan Project, was to drop atomic weapons on selected Japanese cities. For the majority of policy-makers not privy to the atomic secret, however, the key Allied policy issue was the fate of the emperor and imperial house in postwar Japan.[147] This question split the American planning community. For War Department planners, it became a nonnegotiable feature of American policy that Japan would be forced to surrender unconditionally and that such surrender meant the removal of the emperor and his dynastic house. The emerging consensus at the State Department, on the other hand, was that the United States was more likely to induce the surrender of Japan, and then govern occupied Japan more effectively, having given the Japanese assurances that the emperor and his house would persist in some dignified position.[148]

When the war with Japan was brought to an abrupt end in August 1945, this debate had not yet been concluded. To its final day, planning groups at State and War continued work based on mixed signals about American occupation policy. On two key theses, however, there was broad consensus. The first was that Japanese militarism was an aberrant deviation from an otherwise evolutionary path toward democratization. The second was that this path would resume once Japan had been purged of ultranationalist elites.[149] On this basis the thrust of State Department planning was to delimit a facilitative, not a transformative, military occupation.

The planning material delivered by State to the War Department (and SWNCC) in 1945 was replete with ends but short on means. State's "Summary of United States Initial Post-Defeat Policy Relating to Japan," delivered in June 1945, recited the orthodoxy that Japan would be occupied in order to "create conditions which will insure that Japan will not again become a menace to the peace and security of the World."[150] Toward this goal, Japan would be subjected to the "stern discipline of occupation," one dedicated to "the abolition of militarism, the strengthening of democratic tendencies and processes, the encouragement of liberal political elements and the . . . emergence of a liberal government with which the United Nations can deal."

The summary further advised that the War Department should prepare the army for a phased occupation, one commencing with the comprehensive disarmament of the Japanese armed forces. This initial phase would then give way to another indefinite period of "close surveillance." The occupation would be wound up when Japan, now pacified, was "properly discharging its responsibilities in the family of peaceful nations." The memo then described, with similar imprecision, how the occupation would be implemented by a "predominately American" military government, one that was to be "effective, just, but stern." In this spirit the emperor's constitutional powers were to be suspended and the "policy-making agencies of the Japanese government [were] to be utterly discarded." While Americans would wield final decision-making authority in Japan, it was to do so while "placing upon the Japanese officials themselves maximum responsibility for the carrying out of the policies and directives of the Military Government."

Perhaps in the realization that these instructions were unlikely to be useful to Hilldring, State supplied a list of ten special planning tasks for a military government of Japan. These tasks involved the substantial modification of Japanese legal and political institutions and norms. Japanese political parties were to be dissolved. The dissemination of nationalist propaganda, including by radio, newspapers and film, was to be terminated. Political prisoners were to be released and suspected war criminals apprehended. The summary also included some highly abstract comments on the postwar modification of the Japanese legal system. Although Japanese trial courts were to "continue to function with their existing officials," all Japanese laws "obnoxious" to the aims and methods of military government were to be "suspended or repealed."[151] The process of criminal justice in Japan was to be modified so that all accused persons would "have the right to a prompt, fair and public trial."

These prescriptions were taken up and embellished by SWNCC in its final policy document of June 1945, SWNCC 150.[152] SWNCC recommended that the Japanese people "be encouraged to develop a desire for individual liberties and respect for fundamental human rights, particularly freedom of religion, assembly, speech, and the press." It was also recommended that military government foster the development of "democratic political parties, with rights of assembly and public discussion." At the same time, Japanese laws that enforced "discriminations on grounds of race, nationality, creed or political opinion" were to be repealed.

The summary went through a number of redrafts until it was published (as SWNCC 150/4/A) when the occupation of Japan commenced in September, 1945.[153] Although some provisions were altered in the course of the redrafts (for instance, those pertaining to the fate of Japanese territories) the substance of American policy was not.[154] The occupation was to be an American-dominated mission that would govern Japan by recourse to the Japanese state and bureaucracy purged of radical nationalists and militarists. In its initial phase, moreover, the Americans would govern Japan with the assistance of an imperial institution stripped of its constitutional prerogatives.

Allied agreements at the Potsdam Conference of July and August 1945 introduced few new wrinkles to the planning process. According to Article 10 of the Potsdam Declaration, during the period of military occupation, the Japanese government was required to "remove all obstacles to the revival and strengthening of democratic tendencies among the Japanese people. Freedom of speech, of religion, and of thought, as well as respect for the fundamental human rights shall be established."

The Potsdam Declaration was broadly consistent with SWNCC 150. So too was emphasis on the noncoercive aspects of political change. The declaration did not commit the Allies to the compulsory democratization of Japan. In line with the Atlantic Charter's commitment to national self-determination, the declaration pledged that the military occupation of Japan would end when "there has been established in accordance with the freely expressed will of the Japanese people a peacefully inclined and responsible government."[155] The declaration was silent on the fate of the emperor and his dynastic house, leaving the Japanese leadership to hope that they might be retained.[156] In all, the declaration set forth a cautious and moderate program for the postsurrender occupation of Japan, one that did not stipulate a program of transformative legal and political change.[157]

The general outlines of American policy for the occupation of Japan had been settled by the first of August 1945. Operational planning, however, was far from complete. The War Department still had not completed orders for the Supreme Commander in Japan. We have seen why this was the case—none of its planners knew about the atomic bombs and how they might bring the war against Japan to a swift end. On the contrary, their working assumption was that the occupation of Japan would follow in the aftermath of invasion, this no earlier than November 1945.

The principal authors of the initial occupation directive for Japan were staff officers at the War Department's Operations and Planning Division.[158] In their planning work OPD tended to rely strongly on the precedents established in 1944 and 1945 by the War Department in the context of the post D-Day campaign in Europe.[159] The OPD draft described a more or less "orthodox military government in Japan based on a combat invasion."[160] On the assumption that surrender would follow the prolonged and bloody siege of Japan, the draft called for the arrest and trial of the emperor for war crimes and the direct military government of occupied Japan by American and allied forces.[161]

The draft did not garner support from Colonel William Chanler and Colonel Edgar Crossman, two nonprofessional lawyer-soldiers assigned to oversee OPD. Chanler and Crossman were well known to each other. In the 1920s, both had begun elite legal careers as junior associates of Henry Stimson at a prestigious Wall Street firm.[162] Both men, but Crossman especially, had maintained close personal and professional ties with Stimson before and during the war. Both men had been handpicked by Stimson in their wartime commissions, Chanler as deputy director (under General Hilldring) at CAD, Crossman as General MacArthur's personal civil affairs liaison to CAD in Washington.[163] Now in late July 1945, Chanler and Crossman were of one mind that the main provisions of the OPD draft to MacArthur, as Crossman later wrote, were "utterly idiotic" and needed to be drastically altered.[164] This they set out to do, one way or another.

Neither Chanler nor Crossman agreed with OPD that the invasion of Japan would reduce the country to stateless anarchy. Their proposals were based on the contrary assumption that, unlike Germany, Japan would have a "going government when she surrendered." On this premise they thought that to be effective in the pacification and reconstruction of a nation as large and populous as Japan, an American occupying force would need to "use whatever Japanese government machinery [it] found and take full advantage of the prestige of the Emperor." This evaluation was soon confided in Crossman's old friend and former Yale European history lecturer turned Army Air Force intelligence officer DeForest Van Slyck.[165]

When Van Slyck joined the army in 1942, he had no expert knowledge either of Japan or Asia.[166] Nor had he been a specialist in military affairs or American foreign relations. His acumen with regard to the prospective occupation of Japan was based on a reading of the "lessons taught by history with respect to the relations between the conquered and the conqueror" and on the eighteen months he had spent working up intelligence on Japanese civilian and military morale for Army Air Force General "Hap" Arnold.[167]

Like Crossman and Chanler, Van Slyck had read the OPD's draft directive on Japan. Like them, he also believed it incorrect both in its assumptions and prescriptions. With encouragement from Chanler and Crossman, Van Slyck agreed to compose a memorandum (he was regarded as the superior writer of the three), signed by Van Slyck alone, on "realistic" suppositions of a successful American occupation of Japan, "Observations on the Post Hostilities Policy Toward Japan."[168] Van Slyck's memo, and the means by which it came to the attention of Stimson, illustrates the informality, fluidity, and contingency of American policy formation for the occupation of Japan.

Van Slyck's memo advanced the thesis that a credible American postwar policy toward Japan had to be based on sober realism about the limits of American power to introduce change in a conquered nation state. In its most optimistic depiction, the transformational occupation of one state by another, if such a thing was possible, would succeed only on the investment of enormous time and resources. "The conquering nation," Van Slyck wrote, "cannot impose its form of government, ideals, or way of life upon a conquered nation except by permanent military occupation and immigration." But that was the rub. In a democratic nation like the United States, how could its leaders maintain "public support" for so ponderous, expensive, and uncertain an enterprise as transformative occupation? In Van Slyck's view, the likelihood was that soon after Japan's surrender, "war hysteria" in America would quickly evaporate. Soon thereafter an increasingly "restive" American public would exert enormous pressure on politicians to get out of Japan.

For this reason alone it was the height of unrealism, Van Slyck argued, for American planners to presume, as the OPD had done, that Americans had the political will to sustain a program of transformational change in a foreign nation, still less a nation as old, populous, and alien as Japan. Further to the point, given its relative inexperience with colonial administration, and shortage of personnel trained in Japanese law, language, and politics, an American-led military government was "bound to be bungling, undiplomatic, and inefficient."[169] For these reasons it now behooved American policy-makers for Japan to "give full recognition to the fact that we do not have sufficient personnel with the proper vision, training and ability to carry out the task effectively."

In the alternative, Van Slyck contended, the premise of American planning should be to "retain the Emperor and the civil administration." Once purged of its ultranationalist elements, the executive apparatus of the Japanese government might then effectuate the policy of a "Supreme Allied Council" led by an American. The main policy of such a body, Van Slyck maintained, was to "give every encouragement to the Japanese to undertake under their own leadership the development of democratic institutions." This in view of the fact that before the ultranationalist takeover in 1931, the Japanese, an "essentially imitative people," had begun to adopt Western democratic norms of government. On the surrender of Japan, its military discredited, the Japanese people will be "ripe . . . for a genuine democratic movement." The wise policy of the United States was to enable the Japanese to make their own political revolution.

At the end of July 1945, with General Hilldring away at the Potsdam Conference, Chanler and Crossman took advantage of a private dinner at Stimson's home to call the secretary's attention to Van Slyck's memo.[170] Over dinner, the two men complained about the "awful" OPD directive on Japan. Disregarding chain of command, they invited Stimson to read the Van Slyck memo, reminding the secretary that, like him, Van Slyck was a member of Yale's exclusive Skull and Bones fraternity. According to Crossman's recollection, on reading the memo Stimson instantly declared, "That is my policy and I am going to do something about it."

What Stimson did about it was instantly to commit the War Department to the policy that occupied Japan was to be governed indirectly through its own national state. In the short term, and to enhance stability in Japan, the emperor would not be subjected to arrest or prosecution.

Having sent an endorsed copy of the Van Slyck memo to Secretary of State Cordell Hull on August 1, Stimson had the memo endorsed by General Marshall and the Joint Chiefs on August 2.[171] Then, during a presidential briefing on the atomic bombing of Hiroshima on August 8, Stimson persuaded the president to endorse Van Slyck's recommendations. After nearly two years of planning work, the framework of American policy on the occupation of Japan stemmed from a three-page memorandum written a month before the end of the war by a nonspecialist on Japan, one with extraordinary contacts.

It was now official U.S. policy that when the Pacific war ended, the American military, with some Allied input and support, would occupy and govern Japan indirectly through the largely intact Japanese state. Until a final decision was made on the imperial institution, the emperor, stripped of his constitutional powers, was to be maintained as a symbol of state.

Neither Hilldring nor MacArthur was privy to these policy decisions until days before the end of the Pacific war. When the Japanese surrendered on August 14, 1945, neither they nor the forces at their disposal were ready to institute even the most cursory civil administration of Japan.

Until the second week of August, MacArthur's civil affairs staff, headquartered in Manila, continued their work on the assumption that the United States and its Allies would implement an "orthodox" direct military government in Japan no earlier than December 1945.[172] The sudden end of the war in mid-August, one senior officer recalled, caused "utter confusion" among MacArthur's tiny civil affairs staff.[173] In the three weeks before MacArthur was to establish headquarters on Japanese soil (and in the absence of their commanding officer, General William Crist), the unit scrambled to draft the Supreme Commander's first salvo of edicts.

Back in Washington, the War Department worked with similar resolve to finalize MacArthur's initial orders regarding American policy and aims for occupied Japan. Unable to complete the directive until November, the Joint Chiefs cabled a summary to MacArthur just prior to his arrival in Japan on August 30. These orders, the "Joint Chiefs of Staff Basic Directive for Post-Surrender Military Government in Japan Proper" (JCS 1380/15), defined the scope of the Supreme Commander Allied Pacific (SCAP) authority and the policies that were to guide "the occupation and control of Japan in the initial period after surrender."[174] As Supreme Commander, MacArthur was to "have the power to take any steps deemed advisable and proper . . . to effectuate the surrender and the provisions of the Potsdam Declaration." Consistent with Van Slyck's recommendation, MacArthur was not however to "establish direct military government," but to exercise power "through the Emperor of Japan or the Japanese Government."

In its description of MacArthur's mission in Japan, JCS 1380 faithfully reflected, sometimes quoted, the Potsdam Declaration. The main goal of the occupation was to ensure that Japan would not again be a "menace to the peace and security of the world." Further to this goal, MacArthur was ordered to eliminate Japan's heavy armaments while purging its public life of "militarism and ultra-nationalism in all their forms." On securing the disarmament of the Japanese, General MacArthur was to promote "democratic tendencies and processes in governmental, economic and social institutions; and the encouragement and support of liberal political tendencies in Japan." The Supreme Commander also was informed that while the United States desired for the Japanese government to "conform as closely as may be to principles of democratic self-government . . . it is not the responsibility of the occupation forces to impose on Japan any form of government not supported by the freely expressed will of the people."

The official line of the Truman administration at the outset of the occupation was thus to disavow transformational intentions; more specifically, to disavow the imposition of transformational legal or political reconstruction. Just as War and State Department planners had been mainly disinterested in revolutionizing Japanese law and politics, so too was JCS 1380 largely silent on this subject.

JCS 1380 enjoined the Supreme Commander to "abrogate all laws, ordinances, decrees and regulations which would prejudice the objectives set forth in the Potsdam Declaration or which conflict with the instrument of surrender." In particular, MacArthur was to suspend "all laws, orders and regulations which established and maintained restrictions on political and civil liberties and discriminations on the grounds of race, nationality, creed or political opinion." With regard to the administration of justice, the directive also called for the ordinary courts of Japan, purged of ultranationalist judges and prosecutors, to remain open during the occupation.[175] However, while these actions were prerequisite of a thoroughgoing liberal-democratization of Japanese law, 1380 made no explicit reference to a program of American-directed constitutional change. It is all the more remarkable, then, that in just a few months MacArthur had initiated liberal legal and political revolution in Japan.

Planning and the Legal Reconstruction of Germany and Japan

After 1942, the first precept of American war doctrine was "defeat Germany first." After 1943, the first precept of American peace doctrine was "pacify Germany first." These precepts arose from the perception that of all the enemy fascisms Nazism was the most menacing, that Germany had perfected the most dangerous fusion of racialist ideology, technology, and the bureaucratic state. More efficiently and comprehensively than in the other enemy states, the Nazis had suborned the modern state, including its laws and legal institutions, to the purposes of imperial military conquest. On these perceptions, American policy-makers bade the War Department to plan for the comprehensive denazification of German political and legal structures during a period of military occupation.

In contrast, in the last two years of the Second World War American policy-makers were relatively complacent about the Japanese brand of fascism. While some American officials were alarmed by how the Nazis had weaponized German law and institutions, virtually no American officials were concerned about the possible role of law and legality in the rise and consolidation of ultranationalist cliques in Japan. Consequently, as late as the summer of 1945, American agencies had made no definite plans for legal or political reconstruction there.

The disparities in American postwar planning aims and resources were not a function of careful study and deliberation. Nor were they a product of informed comparison and analysis of the German and Japanese modes of fascism (which in fact were real and many).[176] Instead the disparities arose from a combination of institutional inertia, incapacity, and more or less accidental decisions of the War Department officials about planning priorities.

In the 1940s, American foreign policy did not hinge on an intractable "Japan problem." Therefore, the legal and political demilitarization of Japan in the postwar period was not prioritized. In any event, the United States government lacked the prerequisite intellectual resources on any aspect of Japanese history, language, politics, or culture. (It is not obvious in this period that the War Department could have identified even one American scholar working in the field of modern Japanese law or legal history.) Lacking a critical mass of Japan experts (and no complement of Japanese émigré scholars and intellectuals), the War and State Departments had limited capacity to comprehend Japanese authoritarianism. They had limited capacity therefore to plan for its liberal democratization.

American planning for the legal reconstruction of Germany, while far more extensive than for Japan, was embedded in a highly discordant debate about the origins, development, and ultimate elimination of National Socialism.[177] In this regard consensus emerged on one key point: the Nazis had gained and held absolute power in Germany in having neutralized and then nazified its *rechtsstaat,* its formidable system of law and legal institutions. Understanding that the German people had an ingrained respect of law, the Nazis had moved swiftly after 1933 to dominate and manipulate the production and use of legal forms. For American planners, the Nazis were expert if sinister innovators of legal tyranny. The thorough penetration of the German legal system by Nazi personnel and ideology made its comprehensive denazification an imperative of American occupation policy.

These perceptions explain why in 1943 to 1945 American officials, sometimes with British partners, invested substantially in planning for the denazification of German law. It would be easy to exaggerate, however, the progress made with the perplexing theoretical and practical problems presented by this task. When early in 1945 the armed forces of the Western Allies began to capture German soil and citizens, their commanders had been prepared for only one law-related mission: the repeal (or abrogation) by military fiat of a dozen Nazi-era laws. Underresourced, short of qualified personnel and time, American planners had assembled almost no actionable advice on the destruction, still less reconstruction, of the Nazi legal edifice. Planning for legal denazification had not progressed much beyond the identification and elimination of the most visible excrescences of the National Socialist legal system. The planning and tactical phases of legal denazification left most of the most challenging tasks undone.

In the same period, the legal dimensions of Japanese ultranationalism remained almost invisible to American policy-makers and planners. For many Americans set to planning work on the occupation of Japan, their subject was ineffably strange, even unknowable.[178] As one planner observed, "In any planning for the military government of Japan, it must be studiously kept in mind that, of all the Axis nations, Japan, by reason of its complete contrast to the United Nations, presents the most difficult problem from almost every point of view. The Germans, Italians, and satellite European Axis nations will be far easier for us to understand and govern than the Japanese."[179] Insofar as key American policy-makers held any views on Japan, these views tended to be rooted in racialized clichés about the feudal and even mystical character of the Japanese outlook, this "peculiar mixture of childish mythological beliefs and adult realism."[180] Fixated on Germany and the defeat of Nazism, the American leadership elite simply could not and did not assemble a coherent view either of Japanese fascism or its reconstruction.

Historians of wartime planning for the occupation of Japan have generally been impressed, to some extent justly so, by the breadth and depth of this work.[181] In 1944 and 1945, planning groups of career diplomats and Japan specialists at the State Department generated a plethora of reports, memoranda, and position papers on the prospective occupation of Japan.[182] As events unfolded, however, the same historians have tended to overrate the importance of this work both to policy formation and especially to decision-making after the occupation began in September 1945. It is right to think of American efforts in this regard as, in the words of one distinguished historian, an "exercise in 'planned' or 'directed' political change."[183] However, it is wrong to think that planning greatly affected the nature and pace of change on Japanese soil.

For whatever confluence of factors, when the final policy documents were pulled together in Washington in mid-August 1945, they were patently lacking in a cogent vision for the democratization of the Japanese legal and / or political systems, one based on a clear articulation of the causes and cures for Japanese fascist modernity.[184] But if in this regard these plans were even more lacking than those placed in the hands of American leaders of occupied Germany, it is far from clear that it was a consequential problem. As we will discover in the following chapter, apart from some vague handbooks provided to all American occupation officers, very little of the planning material generated by American agencies was actually communicated to officials working on the ground in Germany or Japan.[185] Furthermore, by those officials charged with the task of subjugating the legal systems of occupied Germany and Japan, policy material was either ignored or deemed to have been overridden by "facts on the ground." Paradoxically, while Americans engineered transformational legal and political change in Japan, they did so on the basis of improvisation "in country," not presurrender planning.

2

Occupying the Legal Other

THE SUBJUGATION OF THE GERMAN AND JAPANESE LEGAL SYSTEMS

THIS CHAPTER CONCERNS the period from the conclusion of the wars with Germany and Japan, in May and August 1945 respectively, until the first months of 1946. In this brief window, the American occupations of Germany and Japan—until then existing mainly as projections, proposals, and plans—became palpable as engagement between American civil affairs agencies on one side and vestiges of the German and Japanese states on the other. In these months, the United States strove to transition from destroyer to maker of legal worlds. The subdivisions of its occupation forces assigned to legal reconstruction were called upon to activate designs for the subjugation, then elimination, of the legal fascisms of Germany and Japan.

In neither case was the transition a smooth one. In both occupied countries, American officials moved to actuate their missions with unready tools and in the context of two veritable ghost-countries of shattered cities, citizens, and institutions. In both countries too, but especially in occupied Germany, American legal officers labored to devise effective ideas and means by which to engage and renovate the remnants of the German and Japanese legal "other." In neither case, moreover, was planning informed by a nuanced understanding of the distinctive sociologies, structures, or practices of the German and Japanese varieties of fascist political and legal modernity.

An orthodoxy of American and Allied policy, in 1945 and afterward, was that "The first prerequisite in preparing Germany for democracy is to free Germany from the bondage of Nazism and all other totalitarian systems of government."[1] But in the summer and fall of 1945, the American officers in charge of the Legal Division of the United States Group Control Council (USGCC) were beginning to comprehend how difficult it would be to achieve denazification in the legal field.[2] In its dozen years in power, the Hitler regime had infused German law and legal institutions with National Socialist personnel and ideology. In the Third Reich, the Nazis constructed a modern leviathan of racially motivated, exclusionary, and despotic state practice. As USGCC legal executives began to take up positions in Berlin in July 1945, not one of them had a good idea of how that leviathan might be grappled with, still less cleansed and transformed.

We have seen that the legal arm of the U.S. Army in occupied Germany, the Frankfurt-based United States Forces European Theater (USFET), had barely scratched the surface of the problem. Although ably led by Fritz Oppenheimer, planning and policy materials for legal denazification were incomplete and imprecise. Making matters worse, by the fall of 1945 many of its most experienced staff were being demobilized home to the United States.

In the summer and fall of 1945, the situation at Legal Division in Berlin was hardly better, perhaps worse. When its operations began in August, it was short-staffed, and few recruited personnel, its senior officers included, knew the German language or German law. So while the work of subjugating the physical infrastructure of the German legal system had been made easy (if largely irrelevant) by Allied bombs, the work of subjugating the National Socialist character of the system would prove much more difficult.

The Pacific war having ended abruptly in August 1945, American agencies were even less prepared for the occupation of Japan. When the civil affairs officers of the Supreme Commander for the Allied Powers (SCAP) began to organize functional subdivisions in September, most of its trained staff were in the United States. Indeed, most professional and / or expert personnel, including in legal affairs, were not yet under contract.[3] When these officers did begin to arrive in numbers in the fall of 1945, they were mainly American-born and trained lawyers with no Japanese and little knowledge of its laws or politics. In contrast to American legal groups in Germany, in occupied Japan the dearth of expert knowledge could not be compensated for in the recruitment of Japanese émigré legal scholars. In just about every relevant way, therefore, SCAP's legal and political groups were ill equipped to comprehend, much less to subjugate, and still less to reconstruct the legal system of Japan.

We will see that in terms of executing their transformative mission the executive officers of SCAP, once assembled in Tokyo, enjoyed several advantages over their counterparts in American-occupied Germany. One was that the United States—more particularly the American commander of SCAP, General Douglas MacArthur—wielded nearly complete power over the ostensibly *Allied* occupation of Japan. In deciding when and how to initiate legal or governmental reform, MacArthur had no need to bargain with other powers. Of equal consequence was the contingency of MacArthur's dynamic personality and strong predispositions regarding his mission in Japan. Within two months of setting up SCAP headquarters in Japan, MacArthur, acting well beyond the letter of his orders, already had begun to mount a program of momentous constitutional reform.

By the end of October 1945, it had become abundantly clear to MacArthur that the Japanese would not openly resist their occupation. Military demobilization going smoothly, MacArthur turned his mind to Japan's legal and political transformation. Unlike his counterpart in Germany, Lucius Clay, MacArthur was unconstrained by rigorous civilian supervision, multinational diplomacy, or humility. With ample power and space for its exercise, MacArthur began to contemplate a "thick"—that is to say, comprehensive, intrusive, and sustained—engagement with Japan's remnant state and institutions.

On the other hand, in American-occupied Germany in the first phase of the occupation, General Clay instituted a much more "thin" engagement with the Germans and their institutions. Where MacArthur moved quickly and boldly on legal and political reconstruction, Clay was calculating and cautious. We will see that Clay's caution was the product of multiple factors, including scant resources, racial and cultural deference, diplomatic complexity, and, not incidentally, a natural disinclination toward grandiosity and its projects. Most of all, Clay's policy and decision-making process was a sober response to the colossal challenge that the general and his assets faced in a ruined Germany. As one of his civilian bosses, Assistant Secretary of Defense John McCloy, remarked, "The German job is terrifying in its complexities and significances. God, it appalls me!"[4]

"The German Job": Subjugating the Nazi Legal System

With the German surrender in early May 1945, the American functional elements of Supreme Headquarters Allied Expeditionary Force (SHAEF), its legal affairs unit included, returned to the exclusive command of General Eisenhower's now Frankfurt-based army group, USFET. Having been assembled mainly as a war-fighting, not a peace-keeping force, USFET's purchase on civil affairs in occupied Germany always was to be short-lived. In accordance with the War Department's master plan, after a brief transitional period, American-occupied Germany was to be governed in the longer term by the United States Group Control Council (USGCC), the organization of military and civilian officers trained for this purpose. A majority of USFET's legal officers were slated to transfer to the Legal Division in Berlin when it commenced operations there in August.

"One of the great problems that faced the American authorities in defeated Germany on V-E Day," one senior legal officer later recalled, "was that of restoring the rule of law in a country ruled by Nazi tyranny for twelve years."[5] The American master plan in relation to this problem, however, had at least two significant flaws. First, it failed to anticipate the degree to which the legal affairs elements of SHAEF / USFET would develop a proprietary interest in the work they had done on German legal affairs before the end of the war.[6] Deployed in Europe since before D-Day, having moved with tactical units across the Rhine, and having begun to engage with the Nazi-era legal system, led by German-fluent officers, USFET's legal affairs staff did not yield gracefully to their Johnny-come-lately counterparts in Berlin.

The War Department's second miscalculation was to overestimate its capacity to recruit, train, and assemble a staff of legal officers large and appropriately skilled enough to succeed in a task as daunting and complex as the denazification of German law and legal institutions. Not only did few American lawyers have the right qualifications, even fewer were willing at the end of a long war to sign on to a year or more of hardship duty in bombed-out Germany.

The result of these miscalculations was that the transfer of legal affairs from the USFET to USGCC was anything but a smooth one. In fact, after an initial phase of denazification in which a handful of the most egregious Nazi laws were abrogated by military fiat, the second phase, one demanding a much more active and comprehensive engagement with the Nazi legal system, was a chaotic debacle.

After V-E Day, USFET's legal section, now under the charge of another former Wall Street lawyer, Robert Finley, resumed work on a number of tracks. The first priority was to carry out the law-related provisions of JCS 1067, summarized in SHAEF's "Basic Preliminary Plan."[7] Its key legal mandates were set forth in the plan's fifteenth chapter ("Annex") concerning the administration of justice in occupied Germany. Under the plan, army civil affairs units asserted control over the bureaucracy and operations of the German Reich Ministry of Justice.[8] The functions of the ministry, with their highly centralized hold on German justice, were suspended and all Nazi Special Courts and tribunals closed.[9] Civil affairs teams fanned out to locate and conserve German legal records and libraries. Other teams were sent out to locate and arrest high officials of the Reich Ministry of Justice.

In the summer and fall of 1945, the more pressing issue was the denazification of Germany's system of local courts (Amtsgerichte). A doctrine of the Basic Preliminary Plan was that the recovery of German social and economic life during the occupation would depend on sufficient access to local civil and probate courts, courts staffed by non-Nazi German judges, and applying denazified German law. By D-Day, therefore, it had been decided that while the Amtsgerichte were to be closed upon tactical occupation some would be reopened as an urgent priority and staffed by white-listed (that is, non-Nazi) judges and prosecutors to dispense justice in a manner consistent with Allied occupation policy.[10]

By the early fall of 1945, only a few German courts had been reopened in the U.S. zone. This and other crucial legal denazification projects remained incomplete or unstarted. As was made clear in Finley's final report to John Marsh (director of the USGCC's Legal Division), the hardest work on the denazification of German law and legal institutions had just begun. Even the single job of cleansing the Nazi-era statute books, Finley explained, had been far too big and forbidding for his unit.[11] In fewer than twelve years, the Nazis had passed "not less than 9,573 different laws," a third of which were "either discriminatory in character or otherwise tainted with Nazi ideology." Of the more than 3,000 statutes infused with Nazi ideology, the Allies had abrogated only nine "fundamental" Nazi laws and two "basic racial laws."[12]

While a start had been made, Finley acknowledged that "There remains a vast field of legislation imbued with Nazi doctrines which has still to be modified, revised or replaced by new laws." At least sixteen fields of statutory law (including criminal, family, farm, inheritance, labor, education, and constitutional law) had not yet been denazified. In Finley's opinion, with so few resources at its command, Legal Division's sole practical option on this front was to employ research teams of "German legal specialists."

Back in Washington, McCloy and his staff were working furiously to find and recruit American lawyers and academics suitable for legal work in occupied Germany. In fact, they were up against it in trying in the space of a few months to staff large civilian administrations for American-occupied Germany. There was no obvious place to turn for men (women were not recruited) who had both apposite training and willingness to serve abroad for at least one year. Unlike Britain, so experienced in imperial administration, America had "no large corps of civilian administrators" that for generations had governed a global empire.[13] McCloy, Hilldring, and the other senior officials at the War Department had therefore to rely on the recruitment of individual persons on short-term contracts. In the winter and spring of

1945, however, the acceptance rate of qualified recruits was so miserably low that Stimson himself was obliged to seek Truman's personal intervention.[14]

Stimson was under no illusions about the challenge facing occupation officers in Germany and the need therefore for the USGCC to recruit first-class personnel. In the immediate aftermath of German surrender, Stimson informed the president, the conditions in that country were in "violent flux."[15] The "control and disarmament of Germany is a momentous task," he wrote, one that was to have "a direct bearing on the well-being of Europe." In light of these discomfiting facts, Stimson was emphatic that "We must send over our first team for this toughest job in the history of the country. . . . Our men of outstanding ability in Government and industries, professions and other private activities must realize that while our troops have won a decisive victory at great cost we cannot establish a satisfactory peace unless this tough job is handled successfully."[16] Stimson was equally blunt about what this entailed: "In order to make possible the recruitment of the highly competent personnel required, the president should request the various agencies to give the highest priority to the office's request for assistance."

The recruitment shortfalls continued unabated and were especially large and acutely felt with regard to the USGCC's embryonic Legal Division. As the secretary of war grasped, if the United States was to build a rule-of-law state in Germany, it would need to fill the USGCC's top legal offices with the "best brains of the legal profession."[17] (It underlines the perceived importance of Legal Division and its mission that John Marsh, its current director, was regarded by Stimson as not "quite big enough for the overall responsibility.")[18] But the reality was different. Leading members of the American bar simply were not interested in giving up their offices and practices for what they saw as relatively unimportant positions. The amount of extremely difficult legal tasks in occupied Germany greatly exceeded the number of tasks that came with prestigious titles and emoluments.

In the spring of 1945, yet another Wall Street lawyer turned soldier, Brigadier General Cornelius Wickersham, was put in charge of enlisting this vital legal brainpower. In this regard, Wickersham's instructions (issued to him by Stimson personally) were clear, if somewhat self-contradictory. He was to sign legal professionals quickly and in numbers while at the same time confining his search to "really top-notch men," the "real leaders of the bench and bar."[19] To expedite the search process, Wickersham put together an advisory committee of distinguished lawyers, judges, and legal academics. They did not enjoy immediate success. "There is so much to be done and so little talent to do it with,"[20] Wickersham lamented. After several eminent jurists declined the directorship of Legal Division,[21] McCloy intervened to persuade Charles H. Fahy, since 1942 the solicitor general of the United States, to accept the post.

In Fahy, McCloy had chosen a devout Catholic southerner, born to an Irish-born merchant father and (ethnically Jewish) mother in Rome, Georgia, in 1892. His career was practically the archetypal case of American social and political mobility in the Depression era, accelerated in Fahy's case by the opportunities created by the New Deal.

Called to the bar in the District of Columbia in 1914, Fahy became a decorated naval aviator in 1918 and then a successful lawyer and Democratic Party operative in New Mexico. In 1933, his loyal service to the party was rewarded with a job in one of Washington's New Deal agencies. In 1935, Fahy was appointed general counsel to the National Labor Relations Board (working for Warren Madden). But even as he rapidly ascended the Democratic patronage ladder, finally and fatefully to become the solicitor general of the United States just before Pearl Harbor, the southern Catholic Georgetown graduate remained something of an outlier to the northeastern Protestant elite that dominated the highest reaches of American law, business, and both political parties. For an ambitious man like Fahy, striving for a seat on the Supreme Court, there was an overriding need to prove one's worth, to do what was necessary to earn the next and higher office of state.

Fahy the man was admired for the courtliness of his manner. Fahy the advocate was renowned for the intelligence, diligence, and precise craftsmanship he brought to his trial briefs.[22] But Fahy the tireless New Deal climber had a darker and, for our purposes, more consequential dimension of character. Like so many other New Deal liberals, when war came, Fahy proved vulnerable to the seductive elixir of patriotism and personal ambition.

After the United States declared war on the Axis powers, Fahy, in his dual capacities as solicitor general and director of the War Division at Justice, at once an officer of the court and spear-carrier for the state, advocated doggedly, in at least one infamous case with dubious ethics, for the constitutionality of some of the most draconian federal policies in the history of the United States.[23] In Washington, as later in occupied Berlin, Charles Fahy proved himself that useful kind of man who could be counted on to set aside scruples when his higher-ups wanted something done.

When he was approached by McCloy about leading Legal Division, Fahy had no German language skills or advanced learning in German law, politics, or history.[24] He took the job for lack of better options. After all, in May 1945 Fahy was a Roman Catholic and FDR loyalist whose liege man was now dead, numbering his days as solicitor general and foreclosing his chances for the vacant post of attorney general or his prized seat on the Supreme Court.[25] Having reset his sights on a legal advisory role at the State Department, the directorship of Legal Division was a useful and not entirely undignified consolation prize.[26] A stint in Germany was certain to expand his contacts in the United States' burgeoning foreign affairs community while burnishing his credentials as an international lawyer. With the lemons dealt him by FDR's death, Fahy decided to make some careerist lemonade.

Fahy had been the second or third choice to lead Legal Division, underlining that when it came time to select the executive leaders of Legal Division, a candidate's actual knowledge of German, Germany, and German law was not of primary concern. In fact, in his very modest attainments in this respect Fahy was the rule, not the exception. Unlike in relation to the Manhattan Project, when it came time to hire staff for the legal reconstruction of Germany, the War Department did not—perhaps simply could not—insist that its principal directors have specialized expertise.

That is not to say that Charles Fahy brought no relevant assets or ideals to the German mission. When approached by McCloy, Fahy was a mature and accomplished lawyer-administrator of government organizations. Career considerations aside, he also brought a devoted New Dealer's ostensible allegiance to the precepts of liberal-democracy and the rule of law. As he later affirmed to his chief in Germany, Lucius Clay, the most important attribute brought to the occupation by the United States was that "we are a government of law and desire to spread such a concept throughout the world."[27] To the practical tasks of management and self-advancement in Germany, Fahy also brought a measure, if a dispensable one, of liberal missionary zeal.

Once he had accepted the directorship of Legal Division, Fahy was left to appoint a senior deputy of his own choosing. Fahy picked his close friend and former boss J. Warren Madden, a federal judge. The second deputyship went to Herman Phleger, an eminent corporations and appellate lawyer (and Republican operative) from California. Together this triumvirate of American lawyers—not one of them conversant in the German language or laws—was to be responsible for all aspects of German legal subjugation and reconstruction in the crucial first full year of the occupation.

His senior staff in place, Fahy's most pressing chore in the month before departing for Germany was to hire at least two senior expert advisors in German law. An approach to at least one eminent German jurist (Otto Kirchheimer) had come to nothing.[28] Then Max Rheinstein, an accomplished German-born legal scholar (and Jewish refugee from the Third Reich) at the law school at the University of Chicago, accepted a job. Fahy's second appointment in this regard, a fateful one, was the German expatriate lawyer and law professor Karl Loewenstein.

Uniquely among American legal officials in occupied Germany, Loewenstein was a distinguished scholar of comparative law and politics, a professional intellectual who had both studied and experienced German fascism.[29] Born in 1891 into Munich's assimilated German-Jewish bourgeoisie, Loewenstein received a gilt-edged education at universities in Munich, Heidelberg, Paris, and Berlin.[30] Called to the Bavarian bar in 1918, he received a doctorate in law from Munich University in 1919.

In the 1920s, Loewenstein was a scholar want-to-be who cultivated a law practice in international commercial law in order to make ends meet. By 1931, having completed postgraduate work in comparative government, Lowenstein was a part-time lecturer in law at Munich University. But when the Nazis came to power in January 1933, Loewenstein was quick to realize that there was no future in Germany for a liberal jurist of Jewish blood. In the spring of 1933, Loewenstein immigrated to the United States, spending the next two years as lecturer in politics at Yale. When Yale did not offer further work, in 1936 Loewenstein accepted the chair in political science and jurisprudence at Amherst College. In the late 1930s, Loewenstein became an American citizen, was called to the bar in Massachusetts, and published extensively on fascist movements in Europe and South America.

As a scholar of modern politics, Loewenstein was intensely analytical about his subject matter (the threat posed by fascism to liberal-democratic states, for instance). His scholarly work abjured sentimentality or wishful thinking. Its aim was to penetrate to the hard core of political realities, whatever was found there.

As a man, Loewenstein was austere, intense, and work-obsessed. In his dealings with others Loewenstein was perceived as superior to the point of arrogance. It was an unceasing source of trouble in his time at Legal Division that Loewenstein found it all but impossible to disguise his contempt for persons whom he thought lazy or ignorant, including almost everybody in his group. Preternaturally energetic and industrious, Loewenstein also was meddlesome, tactless, and impatient. That he was also genuinely learned in German law, history, and culture, in the subject matter of Legal Division, rendered him at once its most invaluable and difficult officer.

For all of its cerebral detachment, Loewenstein's life and work also evinced a deeply emotional connection to his homeland. A passionate devotee of German language and culture, for Loewenstein Germany's fatal embrace of Nazism was a source of enormous shame and sorrow.

In his politics, Loewenstein was an ardent liberal-democrat and in his scholarship as well as personal actions he was a ceaseless and militant fighter for the protection and redemption of liberal legal and political ideals.[31] Loewenstein volunteered for duty in American-occupied German because it promised intellectual fascination and significance but also, in his own words, because he counted himself among the "sincere idealists who did not mind considerable personal sacrifice . . . for the sake of assisting in the reconstruction of a democratic Germany."[32] Not unjustifiably, Loewenstein saw himself as ideally equipped by background and education to help in the liberal democratic reconstruction of his homeland.

Rather predictably, then, when the war in Europe ended, Loewenstein, then employed in the Justice Department, did not wait to be invited to join Legal Division as an expert consultant.[33] In a letter of application to Fahy, Loewenstein stated, credibly if not modestly, that he had "probably more knowledge of German legal matters than most American-trained lawyers and twelve years in this country have enabled me to learn the spirit and system of our law."[34] Further to his qualifications, Loewenstein explained how in the previous year he had completed a monograph book on the theory and practice of postwar political reconstruction.[35]

Suitably impressed, Fahy made some discreet inquiries about this promising applicant. A former boss at Justice was candid: Loewenstein was a person of "tremendous energy and capacity to dedicate himself to tasks" but "his desire to be mixed up in most everything going on, requires that he work under fairly close supervision."[36] There was a further caveat: "Like many Germans, and particularly German scholars, he tends to be opinionated in relation to his juniors or his equals." Then the writer offered a final and more dubious assessment: as a German, Loewenstein had displayed "great respect for superior authority." Reference in hand, short of time and alternatives, Fahy hired Loewenstein. It turned out this decision was far more fortuitous for historians than for the first director of Legal Division.

When Fahy arrived in Germany in late July 1945, his division still was a work in progress.[37] With a projected staff of some fifty persons (fewer than a third of whom were legally trained professionals, fewer than a fifth of whom were even slightly conversant with German language or law), Fahy was to operate a de facto department of justice for American-occupied Germany. In addition to its mission with regard to the denazification of German laws and legal personnel, the division was responsible for a long list of other tasks, including the denazification and reform of all German courts, tribunals, and prisons situated within the four sub-zonal states (or *Länder*) of the American zone. It also fell upon Legal Division to provide legal advice both to the executive officers of the USGCC and to its eleven operational subdivisions.

In taking command of the group from Marsh, Fahy's first task was to build operational capacity from the ground up.[38] In terms of its organizational chart, Fahy led an executive staff of six officers, three regular military officers, and three civilians. His senior deputies, Madden and Phleger, superintended three functional subdivisions: Legal Advice, Administration of Justice, and Prisons. (A fourth legal field, War Crimes, was supervised by other AMG agencies.) About half of the division's strength, another mixture of soldiers and civilians, were American-born and trained lawyers. Fewer than ten of these officers (*none* of its executive leadership) were German literate and fluent. At the start of operations, no more than four of Legal Division's personnel could claim expertise in some area of German law.

The formal objectives of the division were set forth in the first instance by JCS 1067 and then, on August 2, 1945, confirmed in the articles of the Potsdam Agreement. In that document the signatories agreed that on a national basis in occupied Germany "All Nazi laws which provided the basis of the Hitler regime or established discriminations on grounds of race, creed, or political opinion shall be abolished." The comprehensive denazification of German life, including its legal culture, was to pave the way for the "eventual reconstruction of German political life on a democratic basis and for eventual peaceful cooperation in international life by Germany." Further to that end, the Allies had pledged to work together to reorganize the German judicial system "in accordance with the principles of democracy, of justice under law, and of equal rights for all citizens without distinction of race, nationality or religion."

The law-related commitments of the Potsdam Agreement were reflected in the USGCC general orders ("Basic Responsibilities") for Legal Division.[39] With regard to the American zone of occupation (and on a national basis with the Allied Control Council), the main mission was to help achieve the "Total elimination of all Nazi ideology, institutions, and methods from the administration of justice and legal system in Germany."[40] The division's second responsibility was to help secure the "Reorganization and denazification of the Reich Ministry of Justice including the Patent Office and other central agencies supervised by the Ministry." Its third major mission was to denazify then reconstruct "along democratic lines" the German system of courts and tribunals in the American zone. The division's brief not only concerned German laws or legal institutions, it also pertained to the German legal personnel. It was to assist in the identification and removal of "all members of the Nazi Party and ardent supporters of Nazism from . . . all leading positions."[41] Taken together, these tasks were to be understood as prerequisites of the overarching objective "that the rule of law shall be re-established in Germany."[42]

As the Finley report documented, when Fahy arrived in Germany in late July, American legal officers in Germany, first with SHAEF, then with USFET, had yet to make even an appreciable dent in any of its central assignments. Only a tiny fraction of the Third Reich's statute book—the most conspicuous nine laws of several thousands—had been suspended. Few of the numberless Hitler-era legal decisions had been reviewed or reversed. The denazification of the German bench, bar, and Ministry of Justice had just been started. Only a handful of German courts had been denazified and reopened. In the summer of 1945, Germany had no viable system of law, nazified or not.

But the problem was worse than that. Not only did Germany have no viable system of law, it no longer had the physical underpinnings of one. As all of Legal Division's officers were moved to observe upon arrival in the country, Germany's principal cities and towns were in ruin.[43] The physical context of modern social, economic, and legal life there had been degraded in every case, destroyed in many cases. Young and middle-aged German men, the men who might be employed by rehabilitated legal institutions, were almost not to be seen. The visible population was reeling from violence, loss, and deprivation. In early August 1945, as Fahy and senior deputies passed through the bombed-out streets of Frankfurt and then Berlin, as they rode past the shocked, demoralized, and hungry people on German streets, they might well have reflected on the logic of their mission. Was it possible, relevant even, to reconstruct the laws and legal system of a society experiencing what the State Department termed an "utter collapse"?

General Lucius Clay was not convinced it was. When he took up the reins of the USGCC in Germany in the summer of 1945, Clay, a career soldier and civil engineer, was nothing if not a realist.[44] He had known before arriving in Germany that the AMG's functional subdivisions were unready and that they would be hard pressed to provide even minimal government in the U.S. zone of occupation.

Unlike Douglas MacArthur, Clay had not yearned to lead an American occupation.[45] Still more unlike MacArthur, he had no pretense of being a nation-building visionary. Nor was he ambitious (as many of his key lieutenants were) to leverage his assignment in Germany to obtain other and better offices of government. While cognizant of longer-term transformative aims, Clay was more cognizant of shorter-term material aims—particularly the need to take sure steps to avert outright humanitarian crises in Germany.

The historians of the American occupation of Germany after the Second World War, both American and German, are basically of one mind that Lucius Clay brought unfailing intelligence, diligence, and pragmatism to the command of AMG in the U.S. zone.[46] But perhaps his greatest asset in the job was the ability to face hard facts. One of the hardest of these was that American planning for the occupation had been botched by Washington bureaucrats who, to Clay's mind, had "lived too cloistered and academic a life."[47] Their innocence of modern warfare and its aftereffects had led to very consequential planning mistakes. The first was to grossly overestimate the viability and therefore administrative value of German institutions in the postconflict period.[48] An outgrowth of this error was the gross underestimation of the number and quality of personnel required for the destructive and reconstructive aims of the occupation. In Clay's frank assessment, when he assumed command of the USGCC, the USGCC having assumed control of the American zone of occupation, the

American occupation lacked administrative mechanisms "for the restoration of German organizations."[49]

Like Clay, Karl Loewenstein also was a steely-eyed realist. When he arrived in Berlin in August 1945, he began to detect an air of unreality, even fantasy, at Legal Division.[50] The plain fact was that in multiple ways the division was woefully unprepared to make an effective start on its mission in Germany. The equally plain fact was that the leaders of Legal Division were determined to carry on, the facts be damned.

By end of August 1945, director Fahy had a great many problems to be unrealistic about. He had too few qualified staff. His Berlin offices were physically remote from legal reconstruction in American-occupied Germany. For months prior to the activation of Legal Division, the American legal group at USFET headquarters in Frankfurt (led by Fritz Oppenheimer) had been making and implementing legal policy "according to their own discretion".[51] Throughout the fall of 1945, to Fahy's increasing exasperation, Oppenheimer's unit continued to pursue its own legal agenda in the U.S. zone, contrary to the chain of command. By the close of the year, Berlin and Frankfurt were locked in an increasingly antagonistic institutional rivalry. As Loewenstein later observed, "Much time and labor was lost in eliminating this friction."[52]

Much of Legal Division's time and labor was also lost in compulsory if largely fruitless participation in the deliberative and legislative functions of the legal section, Directorate-Legal (DLeg), of the four-power Allied Control Council (ACC).[53] Since Yalta and recently affirmed at Potsdam, it was American policy to work closely with its three allies, including the Soviets, to achieve the denazification and democratization of Germany on a national basis.[54] As General Clay informed his divisional chiefs in the wake of the Potsdam Conference, the mandate of the USGCC was that "Germany will be governed as a whole."[55]

It therefore fell to Fahy to find a way by which Americans might work with the other three powers to coordinate legal denazification and democratization.[56] From the outset, this task "presented a comical yet tragic paradox."[57] Like the Allied Control Council (ACC) and all of its functional directorates, DLeg was premised on the fanciful idea that a league of three disparate democracies and one violently oppressive authoritarian dictatorship shared a coherent idea of the democratic legal, political, and social system.[58] How this was to be achieved, the French being implacably opposed to the resurrection of any centralized German institutions and the Soviets being the world's most powerful authoritarian dictatorship, was any mad person's guess.

Not only did the Allies disagree about what was denoted by the "democratization" of German politics and law, but also about the meaning and content of "denazification." At the outset of the occupation, American policy called for the comprehensive purge of all but nominal Nazis from all but menial employments—this a necessary precursor to radical destruction and reconstruction of German political culture.[59] The British and French, conversely, were skeptical both of the practicality and efficacy of sweeping programs of denazification.[60] In the especially violent and chaotic Soviet zone, competing agencies struggled to forge a coherent approach to the problem.[61] In all four zones, whatever their policy start points, occupation administration was overwhelmed by the scale, complexity, and practical implications of denazification. In all four zones, stringency yielded to the exigency and expedience.

The directorate met for the first of its twice-weekly meetings on August 21, 1945. Fahy attended with two civilian deputies and two military officers, one an expert in Soviet and international law. France, Britain, and the Soviet Union were also represented by their most senior legal officials. Elected the first chairman of the directorate, Fahy opened proceedings by stating how "glad he was of this opportunity for the Directorate to work together as lawyers in the great task that lay before them."[62] From the American standpoint, the first series of discussions went smoothly enough.[63] It was quickly agreed that the first item of business should be the denazification of the Nazi-era statute books.

Opening discussion, Fahy thought that the ACC needed to take immediate action on the abrogation of Nazi-era statutes on a national basis. But the body of Nazi statutory law being vast, Fahy recommended a selective approach.[64] The British concurred, adding that the indiscriminate repeal of Nazi laws would cause further havoc in German society and economy while removing all legal "controls on personal liberty, freedom of the press."[65] While desirable in principle, the consensus was that it was too early in the occupation to restore German civil rights. The British therefore proposed that Nazi-era statutes be subject to selective abrogation. Only those laws "the whole and essential object of which was the consolidation of the Nazi regime or [its] discrimination" should be immediately "repealed in toto."

On August 30, DLeg voted to endorse the British model. After a subcommittee or working party completed a draft list, a subcommittee of the plenary completed a draft law on September 13. The ACC enacted the final draft as Law No. 1 a week later. The law "expressly repealed" twenty-six Nazi laws of a "political or discriminatory nature upon which the Nazi regime rested," including all of the Nazi-sponsored emergency legislation passed by the Reichstag in 1933.[66] Law No. 1 also repealed Hitler-era statutes and ordinances pertaining to political symbols, racial purity, citizenship, Gestapo, and anti-Jewish discrimination. Like the SHAEF proclamations suspending Nazi laws, Law No. 1 also contained a clause forbidding a German legal official from applying any Nazi-era law that might "cause injustice or inequality" (undefined terms) by favoring a former Nazi Party member or by "discriminating against any person by reason of his race, nationality, religious beliefs, or opposition" to the Nazi Party.[67] The law made it a criminal offence to contravene this provision.[68]

Law No. 1 was a notable, if readily attainable, achievement for the Legal Directorate. It was a first step in the general denazification of the German legal system.[69] The bulk of the Nazi-era laws remained on the books. Almost none of the tens of thousands of Nazi-era legal professionals had been vetted in any of the four zones. But in the fall of 1945 one point of increasing clarity was that the hardest work toward the denazification of German laws and personnel, if it was to be completed at all, would be completed by the four powers unilaterally in their respective zones of occupation.[70] The Legal Directorate of the ACC, like the other quadpartite agencies, was little more than a sideshow.

As Karl Loewenstein painstakingly detailed in his occupation diary, however, Legal Division was dreadfully ill prepared for its mission. Even when in the fall of 1945 the Division reached full strength, at some fifty staff persons it was absurdly small. Moreover, fewer than half of its number were trained legal professionals. Fewer than a quarter were German-speaking and trained jurists. Given that its mission was to assess and reconstruct a foreign legal system, the division also had a counterintuitive hierarchical structure, with the *least* expert in Germany and German law (Fahy, Madden, Phleger) at the top and regular army officers in the middle. On the bottom, subordinated to unilingual American lawyers, generating the group's actionable knowledge and feeding it upward, were the division's handful of German legal experts, Loewenstein and Rheinstein most notably. In this chain of command, policy decisions were made by those in the least informed position about the object of the mission: the denazification and reconstruction of German law.

From the outset, Legal Division was plagued by low morale, especially among its regular army officers and German experts. As for the officers, the liberal crusaders were greatly outnumbered by tired enlistees who (having been in Europe for two or more years) wanted to go home. Almost to a man the regular military officers had been inadequately trained for their tasks and, in Loewenstein's estimation, "set to work on problems of which they have not the slightest idea and very little professional qualification."[71] Because almost none of them could read German, huge amounts of time and resources were dedicated merely to the translation of legal literature—this for readers who had no specialized learning in their context or meaning. In this and in a host of other ways, Loewenstein perceived, Legal Division exhibited a "deplorable amateurism."[72]

These deficiencies were all prominently displayed in the division's Administration of Justice branch, the subdivision to which Loewenstein had been assigned. The branch was led by two regular army officers, Ernest McLendon and Norman Shepard.[73] For Loewenstein, these officers personified the deficiencies, even absurdity, of Legal Division. The American contribution to the pivotally important denazification of the German justice had been placed in the hands of two American country lawyers with no German and no training in German law. Making matters worse, both men were disinclined to defer to underlings who knew more and better. Lacking knowledge of German legal ideas and institutions, their tendency was to superimpose American legal ideas and models. As Loewenstein colorfully summarized the point, "The basic defect is not only the ignorance of the people here concerning German affairs, but the lofty superciliousness in which they apply the principles of a pioneer country to an old legal civilization."[74] Such men were entrusted with "the most important matters affecting millions of people."[75]

In its first four months of operations, Legal Division began work on a long list of major projects. Some of these, the reorganization of the German judicial system and the denazification of marriage and criminal laws among them, were undertaken in conjunction with the ACC's Legal Directorate. Other projects concerned policy development and implementation of occupation policy only in the U.S. zone. Of these projects, one was of pivotal importance: the reconsideration of the American approach to the policies and procedures governing denazification.

There is a large and impressive body of historical literature on denazification policy development in the U.S. zone.[76] While there are points of contention, the scholarship broadly agrees on a number of points. First, at war's end the United States was committed to a tough and comprehensive policy of German denazification.[77] Second, the Washington-based officials who made this policy had vastly underestimated the infiltration of the Nazi Party and its ideology in German public and private life,[78] just as they had grossly overestimated the capacity of American Military Government to operate an effective denazification program. Third, it is agreed that by the autumn of 1945, General Clay had become convinced, in good faith and for cogent reasons,[79] that the American denazification program was unworkable and that the only viable alternative was to devolve it to Germans.[80] Finally, historians have widely endorsed the conclusion of scholar-participant John Herz that denazification in the U.S. zone was a fiasco.[81] The great majority of Germans in the zone who had been closely linked to the Nazi Party, including a majority of those who had taken part in racially motivated oppression, were little more than ruffled by the denazification process.[82]

Our business here is not to revise this orthodoxy but to embellish it in the documentation of two complementary propositions. The first is that Legal Division, more specifically its director, Charles Fahy, agreed to help legitimate Clay's decision to give Germans principal carriage and control of denazification policy. The second proposition is that the machinations that led to the devolution of denazification policy to Germans were detected and strongly resisted by Fahy's *bête noire* in the division, none other than Karl Lowenstein. That Loewenstein lost this battle, and the way he lost it, exemplified the fatal flaws of Legal Division as an instrument of transformational change.

After August 1945, General Clay became increasingly close to, even dependent on, his chief counsel, Charles Fahy.[83] So when the general decided to commission a Denazification Policy Board to review such policy in the U.S. zone, including the proposal emanating from German anti-Nazis that denazification be turned over to the Germans themselves, Fahy, the eminent lawyer of impeccable credentials, was the ideal choice to lead the policy review. Clay knew that the proposal to give Germans control of denazification would be unwelcome in many quarters in the United States. He knew that Charles Fahy could be relied on absolutely to orchestrate the review process so that it yielded this predetermined conclusion without it being blatantly obvious that the fix had been in from the outset.

As for Karl Loewenstein, he arrived in Germany with strong but well-informed convictions about Nazism and denazification, some of which had been conveyed in his wartime writings. He thought it inarguable that Hitler and the Nazi Party had led a mass movement and that its membership and ideology had deeply penetrated German society and its institutions. For these reasons Loewenstein endorsed the basic premise of American occupation policy that a slow, deliberate, and far-reaching program of German denazification was the necessary precursor of German democratization. However, for Loewenstein there were several reasons beyond the pervasiveness of Nazism to expect that denazification would be very hard to achieve. The first of these was rooted in the likely intransigence of the German people.

Loewenstein predicted in this regard that after their defeat at arms most Germans would not own up either to the ruthless savagery of

Nazism or their complicity with it.[84] He further predicted that German jurists, who had been willing to implement even the most heinous Nazi laws, would lead the way in crafting denials and rationalizations. They would steadfastly deny their individual or collective responsibility for Nazis crimes and do everything in their power to impede denazification. Above all, Loewenstein conjectured, Germans would never impose any punitive form of denazification on other Germans. Germans, anti-Nazis or not, would not punish other Germans for having joined or supported a movement joined and supported by millions of German adults. On this premise, Loewenstein forcefully contended that the denazification of German public institutions, especially those involving law and justice, "should under no conditions be left to the discretion of the German authorities, whatever may be their political complexion."[85] His first contacts with German jurists in the postwar period did nothing to alter these longstanding views.

As one of the few persons at Legal Division who spoke German and knew something of the German legal system, Loewenstein was sent out into the American zone to meet with and gather intelligence on German lawyers and judges. His main task in these trips was to assess the law-related work that USFET had completed in the field and to identify suitable candidates for leading jobs in the denazified legal system. His first stops were at Bremen and Hamburg where (in August and September 1945) he met with leading jurists in the course of a week of interviews.[86]

Never an optimist in this regard, Loewenstein was nonetheless startled by his encounter with these north German lawyers. While many had been members of the Nazi Party, and while some had sent people to their deaths from the bench of Nazi political Special Courts, not even one of the score he interviewed would admit that he had been a Nazi out of conviction. Not one man, moreover, expressed regret about the stigmatization or expulsion of Jews and others from their ranks during the period of National Socialist "coordination."[87]

On the other hand, every one of his interviewees expressed fear and indignation about American (and British) denazification policies.

Fearing the loss of careers and livelihoods, the German jurists were closing ranks around a set of exculpatory claims: that in the context of the German malaise of the early 1930s it had been perfectly excusable to have joined the Nazi Party; that Hitler had promised to act within the law; that no one knew that Hitler and a small knot of "wild Nazis" would hijack German law and politics; that most jurists who joined the Nazi Party after 1933 had done so merely because it was required of them as a condition of holding their offices; that respectable non-Nazi jurists had worked within the system "to prevent worse things" from happening. On these grounds, the German lawyers, even those who had not been Nazi Party members or sympathizers, stood shoulder to shoulder against any "indiscriminate denazification policy."[88]

The more that Loewenstein met and conversed with German legal professionals in the autumn of 1945, the more he was convinced that they were living in a state of collective self-pity and denial. Even obvious and committed Nazis had never been Nazis. The Nazis never led a popular movement. "Not a single one of the anti-Nazi lawyers I talked to," Loewenstein wrote in his diary, "seemed to be aware that the Nazis were a majority of the German people."[89] Among Germans, anxiety about jobs and careers was ever present, but "the problem of German guilt is wholly absent."[90] In November, by this time in the wake of scores of conversations with Germans in many walks of life, Loewenstein could detect "not the slightest trace of a sense of collective guilt among the Germans."[91] As for the trials of major war criminals, these too were having no salutary effect on the collective German demeanor. As educative tools, Loewenstein concluded, the trials of major Nazis were a "complete failure insofar as the German people are concerned." They played into the typical German's conceit that the crimes of Nazis were not the crimes of a nation but of a small band of "gangsters."[92]

In his major memoranda on the denazification question, as in his diary entries, Loewenstein repeatedly indicated that American denazification policy was deeply flawed and, without intelligent revision, doomed to fail. While he was pragmatic enough to accept that any workable program of denazification could not seek to exclude from

German civilian life "at least seven million people, with their families constituting a third or more of the German population," Loewenstein remained steadfast that a selectively harsh approach was both morally and, from the point of view of successful democratization, politically indispensable.[93]

In his first memorandum to Fahy on the subject, he canvassed its moral and political complexities. It was probable, he advised, that a program of indiscriminate removal of jurists based solely on membership in the Nazi Party, even if correct normatively, would prove impractical (leaving too few experienced judges and legal technocrats to operate a revamped system of justice) and impolitic (too many influential Germans, including most anti-Nazis, saw such policy as unjust).[94] A forceful argument was made by German jurists that the blanket enforcement of the denazification policy was likely to damage American prestige and render Germany more difficult to govern and reform.[95]

As he labored to develop a rational and morally defensible policy on legal denazification in the American zone, Loewenstein held fast to three basic precepts. The first was that senior posts within the rehabilitated German legal system were too important to the success of the democratization project to be left to former Nazis of either the "ardent" or "nominal" variety.[96] The second was that the purge of Nazi jurists, if it could not be comprehensive, had to be extensive. His third precept, one that he had advanced since 1943, was that this goal was achievable only by an American-controlled program of identification and expulsion. "It cannot be too strongly emphasized," he informed Fahy, "that [denazification] committees composed of Germans alone would utterly fail."[97] Such committees, even if operated by anti-Nazi lawyers of unimpeachable credentials, would swiftly be undermined by the "solidarity of the legal profession, the pressure of [German] public opinion, the effort to mitigate the rigors of the denazification policy, [and] the understandable desire to let as many fellow-citizens as possible escape from the consequences of party membership and the lost war." For these reasons Loewenstein's advice for Fahy was unequivocal: "Under no circumstances should the denazification of the legal profession be entrusted to the Germans themselves, and not even to recognized anti-Nazis among them."[98]

But just as Loewenstein rendered this advice, Clay, having concluded that the American denazification program was unworkable, already had appointed Fahy to lead his Denazification Policy Board.[99] As the work of the policy board unfolded in November 1945, Fritz Oppenheimer, still the senior legal officer at USFET, was brought in to work with German officials in the development of a plan. Strongly in favor of the swift "Germanification" of denazification,[100] Oppenheimer adopted a Bavarian proposal calling for a system of local denazification tribunals or *spruchkammern* to be staffed by dependably anti-Nazi Germans. The tribunals would attempt to undertake denazification not by category but on an individualized case-by-case basis. In early December, Clay requested that the ministers-presidents of the German Länder meet to draft a "uniform regulation of denazification" based on the Bavarian initiative.[101] By late December, the ministers' draft was in the hands of Fahy's policy board.

Meanwhile, and in the wake of many more meetings with German jurists, Loewenstein's views on denazification were hardening in the opposite direction. On November 30, he reported to Fahy that most German jurists were unrepentant about their work during the Nazi era and that "membership in the party is not considered a stigma."[102] The main source of the Nazi Party's strength was that it had "derived its power from the mass of its supporters," drawing members from all regions and walks of life. Individual autonomy and responsibility had been subsumed within the overarching purposes of the Nazi Party. That was why "the notion of a 'nominal' party member is unintelligible," just as it was unintelligible to excuse nominal or wartime membership because it was motivated by private advantage.[103] If nominal party membership, Loewenstein wrote, "means that a person has abstained from torturing prisoners or that he has not burned people in the stoves at Auschwitz it is hardly serviceable, because it merely draws a line between the activists and the rest."[104] After all, the contributions of "the rest" had been vital to the realization of the Nazi program.

These perceptions informed Loewenstein's most radical recommendation during his tenure with Legal Division. With regard to the high offices of German legal professions, "No former member of the Nazi

Party, whether activist or merely nominal [or as an active supporter without membership] . . . should be tolerated except as [an] ordinary worker." The Nazis, just as the Nuremberg prosecutors alleged, had been a criminal organization, and "guilt by association," Loewenstein had concluded, "is the only way of getting rid of subversive associations."[105] If democratization was to achieve permanent reform in the legal field, there was no scope for compromise on this point. The rapid restoration of former Nazis to important offices in the legal system would "constitute a serious danger to the future of the democratization of Germany as a whole."[106]

But such warnings, Loewenstein himself perceived, were falling on increasingly deaf ears. If men like Fahy had come to Germany with an appropriate degree of fear and loathing of Nazis and Nazism—and here there was room for doubt—by the closing months of 1945 such feelings had been steadily eroded "by the fraternization between the American Military Detachment and the German legal profession."[107] In their various engagements with the American occupiers, German legal officials—well-educated, urbane, white-skinned—were apt to spin tales of how they themselves had not been Nazis, had never supported the Nazis, and fully approved of the purge of the few genuine Nazis who had survived the war.[108] With reason, Loewenstein worried that out of expedience his bosses at Legal Division were lending too much credence to such claims. In this they were being abetted by the two of the most prominent German-Jewish émigrés in the legal field, Fritz Oppenheimer and Max Rheinstein.[109] The elements of a full-scale retreat from a stern and American-controlled policy of denazification were falling into place.

And so it came to pass. When American officials met with the German ministers of justice of the three south German Länder on December 18, 1945, the main topic of discussion was not whether there would be German-operated denazification tribunals, but their composition and procedures.[110] Two days later, Fahy's policy board issued a preliminary report that affirmed the American commitment to purge from public life only those Germans who had "held positions of leadership and authority in Nazi regime." The board recommended that the American denazification program be reconfigured as a "popular" program, one which relied mainly on the assessment of Germans about the culpability, or not, of other Germans for the perversities of the Third Reich.[111]

In early January 1946, Loewenstein was afforded a final opportunity to advise Fahy on this policy.[112] He began by reiterating that any denazification program depending on "rigid formulas" was indefensible on both ethical and practical grounds. He then acknowledged the theoretical advantages to the proposal that "the Germans themselves will undertake the purification of their public, social and economic life." With "resignation" Loewenstein further acknowledged that the German denazification proposal, if amended in certain ways, "might prove serviceable." By the same token, Loewenstein remained unyielding in his conviction that it would be a grave error to cede control of the process to Germans, even to "congenitally anti-Nazi" Germans.[113] As his brief explained, "Even the anti-Nazis in Germany are good Germans and they have to live with their people." In applying the new law, even steadfast anti-Nazis would be inclined to overlook the culpability of many thousands of German men and women who had been enthusiastic Nazi operatives.

Loewenstein implored Fahy to understand that the south German initiative on denazification was a thinly disguised attempt to "protect the German people as a whole" against the judgment of a foreign occupier. Their decisions would be guided by the general "climate of misery" in Germany, not by "abstract principles of justice."[114] In the result, the American denazification program would be reduced to a "superficial gesture."[115]

In the final report, dated January 15, 1946, Fahy's policy board recommended that General Clay adopt the German denazification plan as the basic framework of reform. After further consultation with the Länder ministers of justice, the plan was to be fine-tuned and sent back to Clay for final approval. The policy Board offered one caveat: the new denazification law would require "effective supervision and policing by Military Government."[116] Clay activated the directive on March 5, 1946, informing the minister-presidents that they would be held "strictly accountable for the effective and just enforcement of the law."[117] Loewenstein's objections, if they had not been ignored, had been decisively overruled. The decision had come down to pragmatic judgment about what was workable and possible, not what was right or desirable. As Clay informed the War Department in March 1946, he had turned denazification over to Germans for the uncomplicated reason that AMG was incapable of doing the job.[118] At the end of the day, the ensuing risks had to be taken, even over the strenuous protest of some of its leading experts.[119]

While still in the employ of Legal Division, Loewenstein did not, could not, publish his final assessment of Clay's decision on denazification. Giving control of the program over to the Germans, he wrote in a letter to the *New York Times* later in 1946, was "an unmitigated defeat of Military Government."[120] It signaled to the Germans, to America's partners, that the United States was no longer willing or able to fulfill its national commitment to the transformational occupation of Germany. The lever controlling the pace and content of German democratization, Loewenstein diarized while still in Germany, had now "slipped out of [American] hands."[121] The new program, he presciently predicted, would ensure that "95% of the Nazis will slip through the meshes of the tribunals . . . and be reinstated."

But there was another, more subtle, fallout. If it had been intended that intellectuals and experts were to exert meaningful influence over American occupation policy in Germany, the denazification episode dispelled such notions. Certainly Karl Loewenstein, by any measure the most relevantly educated officer at Legal Division, could no longer harbor illusions about his own influence. He had now been marked out by his superiors as difficult and unrealistic, as someone who could not be relied upon to support pragmatic policy decisions. "This is the way Military Government is conducted," Loewenstein lamented in January 1946, "the experts advise against something and the General does what he pleases."[122] A private meeting with General Clay himself a month later did little to change Loewenstein's mind about the glaring deficiencies of American occupation policy and administration.[123]

The new denazification policy was of a piece with General Clay's (still largely tacit) general policy that German institutions, including legal and political institutions, were to be denazified, reactivated, and restored to German hands on an urgent basis. In line with this stance, Fahy circulated a memo in February 1946 announcing that "the work of Legal Division is reaching the point [only six months after it had begun] where the operational phase is to be succeeded by the supervisory phase of Military Government."[124] This message reflected Clay's policy, but also Fahy's self-serving disposition to claim that Legal Division's nonoperational work in Germany was now largely completed. This was convenient for Fahy to claim because, much to the consternation of General Clay, he recently had been offered the post of legal adviser to the State Department. Fahy accepted the position, leaving Germany in May without completing his contract.

In the aftermath of the denazification debacle, Loewenstein thought that his time with Legal Division might still be redeemed if he were able to stimulate positive action in two key areas: German court supervision and legislative drafting, coordination, and oversight. By the spring of 1946, Loewenstein's hopes in the first area had been dashed. Without much optimism, he turned his focus on the myriad problems associated with legislation on two levels: ACC legislation for Germans and Länder-level legislation by Germans.

Loewenstein had had firsthand experience of the chaotic means by which the ACC (and DLeg, its legal subdivision) had tried to promulgate legislation for Germany as a whole. Since his early days at Legal Division he had been called upon to act as a liaison and consultant to the quadpartite legislative drafting subcommittee of DLeg working on the overhaul of Nazi-era matrimonial and divorce laws. The process had schooled Loewenstein in the challenges, indeed the patent absurdities, of law reform by multicultural and multilinguistic committee.

Even when the delegates of the four powers could agree on the general goals of reform legislation, they legislated without benefit of German input and expertise. As Loewenstein acidly observed in this regard, "Formerly [in Germany] there was a Ministry of Justice with an experienced staff. Now there are some amateur people who write laws for 65 million people."[125] Then there was the added problem that DLeg's drafting committee was obliged to write versions of bills in three different languages only to then waste countless hours trying to comprehend "what the English or the French or Russian term used would make sense in German and what German equivalent would eventually be chosen when the translation was to be undertaken."[126] In the result, too, bills were passed into German law before an authoritative German text was put into circulation.

By the spring of 1946, German lawmakers in the Länder were passing laws willy-nilly and with the tacit assent of Political Division, the AMG supervisory body that had been given charge in this field. German lawmakers were being indulged in this because as Loewenstein saw it, of a pervasive if misguided interpretation of the Allied mandate to "decentralize" Germany.[127] It was also yet another product (within the U.S. zone) of the unintelligent compartmentalization of supervisory authority. As it happened, the promulgation and content of German legislation had been defined exclusively as political activities that were within the province of Political Division. Empire-building bureaucrats within Political Division had largely succeeded in shutting out Legal Division and other AMG units from information and input in this area.

Loewenstein had written memoranda to Fahy warning against this trend as early as November 1945.[128] These memoranda had been ignored. In subsequent months he continued to press for the creation of a centralized AMG mechanism by which proposed legislation might be reviewed and amended by officers within Legal Division.[129] In April 1946, even as AMG accelerated the re-Germanification of public functions in the U.S. zone, little had been done to stem the tide of legal fragmentation.[130] At the end of May, Loewenstein implored Madden to take steps to redress the "the dispersal of authority and responsibility and the lack of coordination between the three Länder and therefore to preserve "a minimum of legal unity in the Zone."[131] Facing enormous socioeconomic problems, the newly revived German legislative entities were now increasing the pace of legislative action. As Loewenstein diarized in late June, 1946, "The coordination of German legislation with the Länderrat and the Control Council will become the most important function of the Legal Division. I painted a dark picture of the entire situation, but not as dark as it actually is."

Madden left Germany in early June, before any action was taken on the legislation issue. Loewenstein admired the intelligence and commitment of Madden's successor, Alvin Rockwell, Legal Division's third American-lawyer director inside of a year. Rockwell's appointment was reason to hope that Legal Division might finally provide effective legislative oversight. But it was not to be, not during Loewenstein's tenure. As of August 7, just days before Lowenstein's departure, "nothing had been done on the examination of legislation." Loewenstein left Germany utterly disillusioned. In his opinion, Legal Division, that "very poor organization," had squandered its opportunity to manage the content and pace of legal change in American-occupied Germany.[132]

MacArthur's "August Revolution": Subjugating the Japanese Legal System, 1945–1946

When General Douglas MacArthur, the Supreme Commander for the Allied Powers (SCAP), landed on a Japanese airfield near Yokohoma on August 28, 1945, he had ready access to an impressive war machine but not a similarly impressive machine of postwar administration.[133] Even as the general established his headquarters in Tokyo, the functional subdivisions of SCAP administration were incompletely organized and staffed. More than a thousand Japan-bound civil affairs officers, their training incomplete, were still scattered across the Pacific. Another thousand men were in California, still waiting to ship out to Japan.[134] Many more hundreds of civilian experts had yet to be recruited to SCAP's ranks.

We have seen that American goals in the occupation of Japan were set forth in a number of vague policy and diplomatic documents, the most ostensibly important being the Potsdam Declaration, issued jointly before the end of the war in the Pacific by the United States, Britain, and China. The declaration underlined the collective determination of the Allied states to fight Japan until it had surrendered on such terms that its "irresponsible militarism," and those responsible for it, might be permanently expunged from the Japanese body politic during a period of military occupation.[135] But with regard to the reformation of Japan's domestic political and legal institutions during this period, the declaration was mainly silent. The Allies pledged only that the occupying authority would act to "remove all obstacles to the revival and strengthening of democratic tendencies."[136]

In the immediate aftermath of the surrender, the Truman administration moved quickly behind the scenes to settle two important but lingering issues of occupation policy.[137] The first was that the United States, having been the preponderate force in the defeat of Japan, also would be the preponderate force in its postwar administration.[138] While the Americans made bows to the multilateral administration of occupied Japan, these were not deep bows.[139] From its beginning to end, the occupation of Japan was an American-dominated show.[140] The second principle was that in Japan "the Supreme Commander will exercise his authority through Japanese governmental machinery and agencies, including the emperor, to the extent that this satisfactorily furthers United States objectives."[141] During the occupation period, in sum, Americans would lead the government of occupied Japan through the residue of the Japanese state, one thoroughly purged of ultranationalists and war criminals.

A more detailed description of American policy in occupied Japan was set forth in the "Initial Post-Surrender Policy for Japan," a document drafted by SWNCC and endorsed by Truman before MacArthur landed in Japan.[142] According to this document, the primary objective of the occupation was to ensure that "Japan will not again become a menace to the United States or to the peace and security of the world."[143] The secondary objective was to cause "eventual establishment of a peaceful and responsible government" in Japan. This not being an urgent goal, the document did not provide guidance on how this was to be achieved. It made clear only that the Supreme Commander of Allied Powers (SCAP) in Japan, in addition to the "strengthening of democratic tendencies," would vacate Japanese laws restricting freedoms "of speech, of religion, and of thought, as well as respect for the fundamental human rights." At the same time, SCAP was to encourage the Japanese "to develop a desire for individual liberties and respect for fundamental human rights" and to "form democratic and representative organizations."

The Initial Post-Surrender Policy also set forth the American position that the enhancement of individual rights and democracy in Japan dictated the "wholesale reform of the Japanese judicial and policing systems."[144] What the policy did not do, however, was provide direction to the Supreme Commander with regard to reform of the Japanese constitution. As for more searching reform of Japan's manner of government, and to the construction of a liberal rule-of-law state, the document, echoing the Potsdam Declaration, stated that it was "not the responsibility of the Allied Powers to impose upon Japan any form of government not supported by the freely expressed will of the people."

As its title suggested, the Initial Policy was the first, not the last, word on America policy in occupied Japan. The second came eight weeks later in the form of MacArthur's classified orders from the Joint Chiefs of Staff. The "Basic Directive for Post-Surrender Military Government in Japan Proper" (JCS 1380/15) was basically a more detailed restatement of the policy commitments set forth in the Initial Policy, but with one signal difference.[145] In the context of the very permissive civilian oversight, the broad language of 1380 created space for MacArthur to exercise an extraordinarily broad discretion in the interpretation and implementation of its provisions.[146]

On the one hand, then, the directive merely restated the American government's principal commitment to the demilitarization of Japan and also its unwillingness to impose democratization on Japan.[147] On the other hand, the directive also authorized MacArthur "to take any steps deemed advisable and proper by you to effectuate the surrender and the provisions of the Potsdam Declaration." On this score the directive explicitly contemplated that the Supreme Commander's actions "will in large measure be determined by developing circumstances" in Japan. It was therefore open to MacArthur to decide as events unfolded what appropriate measures were required to achieve basic policy goals. "Occupation administration," as two scholars summarized, "was military administration."[148] The upshot was plain: MacArthur would be at liberty to improvise the content, pace, and intensity of the American program of occupation in Japan.[149]

These prerogatives help us to comprehend what happened next: that within six months of the commencement of the occupation of Japan,

American officers of SCAP in Tokyo had drafted a model liberal-democratic constitution for Japan. Moreover, before the close of 1946, SCAP had caused the Japanese to adopt an only slightly amended version of the model as its basic law. At the same time SCAP was deeply engaged with the Japanese politico-legal elite on the rapid construction of the complementary laws and institutions of a liberal rule-of-law state. This remarkable turn of events, it must be emphasized, was not the inevitable result of either Washington's Initial Policy or its successor policy documents. It was the contingent result of the convergence of an extraordinarily ambitious man and an unusually propitious moment for the exercise of his power.

From the hefty stock of primary documents, published biographical works[150] and studies of his tenure as Supreme Commander of the occupation of Japan, a remarkably consistent picture emerges of Douglas MacArthur's personality and character.[151] It is uniformly accepted that MacArthur was a man of unusually great attributes and failings. On the positive side of the ledger, MacArthur was unquestionably an unusually intelligent, articulate, diligent, and, at close quarters, powerfully charismatic personality. Among American leaders of his time he was perhaps the most accomplished speaker and writer, especially for the grand occasion. But equally there is no disagreement that MacArthur was an epically egomaniacal, arrogant, and vainglorious man, incapable of acknowledging fallibility. In his combination of energy, willfulness, and American-style romanticism, MacArthur came to Japan well disposed to instigate transformative occupation.

In August 1945, Harry Truman did not count himself among MacArthur's legion of admirers. Truman had serious misgivings about MacArthur's vanity and pomposity, feelings that only intensified in his time as president. By the same token, as the Pacific war came to a close Truman did not seriously consider any other person for the position of Supreme Commander in occupied Japan.[152] As for the general himself, at war's end he readily, perhaps eagerly, accepted the post (when he might have returned to the United States a national war hero). From MacArthur's point of view, a number of factors (not least his sense of duty as a professional soldier) weighed in favor of accepting command of SCAP.

It was enormously flattering to MacArthur's ego, first of all, to be asked first to take the surrender of a great foe, then to lead American forces in the demobilization of its armed forces. But finally and decisively, the office of Supreme Commander offered MacArthur that rare opportunity for a master of war to be metamorphosed into a herald of peace. The command flattered the general's ego just as it squared with the high-mindedness so prominent in his personality and public utterances. It also was consistent with what by the end of the Pacific war had become a declared weariness and dread of modern war and the menace it posed for humanity.[153]

In this regard we do not have to believe (as was later alleged by one of the general's circle) that on the plane to Japan MacArthur already had begun to make a blueprint for its democratization.[154] But clearly the Supreme Command of occupied Japan was a job that strongly appealed to MacArthur's grandiosity, sense of destiny, and perhaps political ambition. As his aide later wrote, MacArthur viewed the proconsulship of Japan as a fated "rendezvous with history."[155] The general hinted as much in his first dispatch to Truman from Tokyo, telling the president that he was "deeply grateful" for the Japan command as it would enable him to "capitalize [upon] this situation along the magnificently constructive lines you have conceived for the peace of the world."[156]

On arrival in Japan, however, MacArthur did not yet know to what ends and by what means he might "capitalize" on his nation's nearly absolute power over the fate of some 70,000,000 Japanese. For this practical reason alone, for the first two months of the occupation MacArthur exerted authority cautiously.[157] In this time the general, reasonably enough, was preoccupied with the quick and orderly demobilization of the Japanese armed forces. But it did not take long for MacArthur's natural boldness and self-assertiveness, to say nothing of his personal ambition, to come to the fore.[158] As soon as it became clear that the Japanese were "utterly defeated" and would not resist the occupation,[159] MacArthur quickly began to turn his mind to how he might transform a comprehensively defeated nation into "the world's great laboratory for an experiment in the liberation of a people from totalitarian military rule and for the liberalization of government from within."[160]

The most remarkable and, for MacArthur scholars, most puzzling aspect of his tenure as Supreme Commander is the tenacity and seeming sincerity of his commitment to the introduction to Japan of a fully realized liberal-democratic modernity. Until the fall of 1945 MacArthur had been widely perceived in the United States as a career military man of a typically conservative-Republican cast of mind.[161] When liberal-minded New Dealers began to join the ranks of SCAP in 1945, many did so with serious apprehensions about MacArthur's character and motives.[162] Almost to a man (and one woman), however, by the end of their tenure with SCAP's functional subdivisions, Government Section (GS) only most conspicuously, the New Dealers were won over by the steadfastness of MacArthur's leadership in the liberal-democratic reconstruction of Japan.[163]

If in his years as Supreme Commander in Japan Douglas MacArthur was a dyed-in-the-wool soldier-authoritarian, his progressive persona deceived a large number of ardent liberals. In the estimation of Roger Nash Baldwin, president of the American Civil Liberties Union in the 1940s, "MacArthur's reputation as a conservative and aloof autocrat [was] wrong."[164] Baldwin publically attested that he had "met no man in public life with a keener understanding of the principles and practices of liberal democracy, and a deeper faith in them."

Meanwhile, even as his staff officers struggled to assemble a credible administrative apparatus in Japan, MacArthur did not lack confidence in his preparation and capacities as an agent of transformational change in an Asian country. On the basis of his extensive prewar experience of civilian and military administration in the Philippines, the general regarded himself as an expert in the "Asiatic Mind"[165] and the "lessons of the Orient."[166] In other words and more generally, MacArthur thought himself an expert on the Asiatic races.

In his invocation of tropes such as "Asiatic Mind"[167] and "lessons of the Orient" MacArthur betrayed a racially stereotyped vision of the Japanese and other peoples of the Far East. On this basis, some historians have excoriated MacArthur and the American occupation as a whole for having implemented a racist occupation of Japan.[168] On an undifferentiated definition of "racism," there is substance to these claims. There can be little doubt that like all paternalisms, American paternalism in Japan was tinged by racism. However, in the context of MacArthur's (and American) policy regarding the legal and political reconstruction of Japan, the term "racist" in fact has limited explanatory value.

On close inspection of that part of the public and private records of the American occupation of Japan relating to law and the rule of law, most American attitudes and actions toward the Japanese were more chauvinistic than racist. The record conveys that American officials regarded the Japanese as culturally and historically but not *racially* inferior. In regard to legal reconstruction, policy and decision-making were based on the assumption that Japanese legal evolution had been inhibited by backward (feudal) leadership and cultural norms, not by imperatives of race.[169] Indeed, at the core of MacArthur's legal revolution of 1946 and 1947 was the thesis that, prior to the occupation, the Japanese people had been cheated by history of their natural endowment as human beings of natural rights and liberties. According to SCAP's official propaganda, the reason why Japan required an American-driven liberal revolution in 1946 was because it had failed to experience one in 1868.[170] In MacArthur's opinion, the Japanese people were ready for their democratic moment, even if their conservative leadership was not.[171]

In this regard it is noteworthy the degree to which the viciously racist tenor of American wartime propaganda about the Japanese people figured *so little* in the occupation work (or even private correspondence) of MacArthur or the executive officers put in charge of directing legal change in postwar Japan.[172] In fact, their documented outlook on Japan and the Japanese during the occupation period is remarkable in the absence of personal enmity toward a recent foe of rare martial ferocity.[173] In his dealings with the emperor, Japanese officials, and the people of Japan en masse, MacArthur never seemed moved by anger or vindictive malice. Except for one notorious case involving a rival Japanese army general, neither did he indulge in score-settling.[174] There is strong evidence that MacArthur's liberal demeanor as Supreme Commander was very favorably received by the Japanese people, especially in the first phase of the occupation.[175]

This trait was evinced especially in MacArthur's strategic stance toward Emperor Hirohito. Absent contrary instructions by Washington, MacArthur was content to suborn the emperor and his prestige as a tool of American reform policy.[176] Consequently, SCAP did not go out of its way to gather intelligence implicating Hirohito in war-making or war crimes.[177]

MacArthur's personal ideas and attitudes toward the Japanese people and their emperor mattered decisively in occupied Japan because in the first phase of the occupation they were not much tempered or even influenced from outside. The scores of Japan studies and policy papers prepared at the departments of State and War, even when they were known to MacArthur and his officers, had no appreciable bearing on policy-making or implementation. In the field of Japanese law and government particularly, the nuts and bolts of SCAP's program were improvised by American officers in Japan.

The first move of these officers was made on October 1 in the form of a high-level conference between officials of SCAP Legal Section and the Japanese Ministry of Justice.[178] The conference minutes strongly suggest that presurrender research and planning in this field, if it existed, had not reached SCAP's delegates.[179] The American officers in attendance knew pitifully little about the structure or operation of the Japanese legal system. They did not know, for instance, the organizational scheme of the Ministry of Justice or how it operated in relation to the executive and legislative branches of the Japanese government. They were obliged to request basic information (in English, please) also about the structure and operation of the Japanese courts, including whether political crimes were still being prosecuted in them. (Ministry officials stated that they were not.) Nor did the American officers possess (but now requisitioned) a complete set of Japanese laws and ordinances. There was another urgent request: SCAP officers required a list of Japanese jurists—judges, bureaucrats, law scholars, and lawyers in practice—who spoke English.

A few weeks later, with none of this work yet complete but now certain that the Japanese military would fully disarm,[180] MacArthur resolved on two courses of action: to ramp up the pace and reach of his legal and political reform agenda and to shake up SCAP's capacity to orchestrate such reforms.[181] If inroads were to be made in Japanese legal and political reform, the governmental reform section of SCAP, blatantly dysfunctional in the first two months of the occupation, needed to be better organized and led.[182] These changes were complete by mid-December 1945.

MacArthur achieved this end in three steps. Having fully established his general headquarters (GHQ) in Tokyo on October 1, 1945, the general set up a new set of functional subdepartments or sections, these mirroring the key departments of Japanese national government.[183] The idea was to centralize and streamline decision-making regarding civilian affairs.[184] In early October 1945, MacArthur established Government Section (GS), a special staff section of his headquarters to oversee the political and legal democratization of the Japanese state.[185] By mid-December, eager to get on with this crucial reform work, MacArthur installed forty-six-year-old Brigadier General Courtney Whitney as the commanding officer of the fifty-odd person staff of the section, easily the most significant of SCAP's functional subdivisions in the first two years of the occupation.[186] Given Whitney's close relationship with the Supreme Commander, this appointment unmistakably marked the paramount importance of GS in MacArthur's vision for the American occupation of Japan.

Courtney Whitney was that rarest of organizational birds, the sycophant of substance. A night-school law graduate from Maryland, an Army Air Corps officer and then entrepreneurial lawyer in Manila (where he first met MacArthur), Whitney returned to the United States with a family and a considerable fortune the year before Pearl Harbor. After his reenlistment as a lieutenant-colonel, in 1943, Whitney was sent to MacArthur's army headquarters in Australia.[187] Under MacArthur's command, Whitney directed an intelligence operation in support of the Filipino guerillas. In this context the two men became close personally, if in the asymmetrical manner typical of MacArthur's pattern of friendship. In return for reverential respect and unflagging loyalty, MacArthur invested confidence and trust.[188] Whitney's reverence for MacArthur was so complete that the officers of GS regarded him as the general's "alter ego."[189] Although MacArthur himself was aloof from the section, when Whitney spoke it was understood that he spoke for the Supreme Commander.

Whitney had been handpicked by MacArthur to organize and galvanize Government Section, SCAP's main instrument of legal and political reform in occupied Japan. His task was to cause the Japanese political class to construct and embrace a new liberal-democratic framework of law and government. The section was mandated to advise the Supreme Commander on the "internal structure of civil government of Japan," but further to eliminate from Japanese law and government of all "feudal and totalitarian practices which tended to prevent government by the people." GS also was charged with the task of organizing and implementing the purge of ultranationalists from all positions of public influence in Japan. Taken together these were the first great tasks in the demolition of the Japanese genus of fascist authoritarianism, a prelude to what Whitney later called the American "crusade" for liberal-democracy in Japan.[190]

If MacArthur was the architect of Japanese legal and political reconstruction during the occupation, then as of December 1945 Whitney was his resourceful general contractor. One of his first jobs in this regard was to staff the senior echelon of GS. MacArthur's orders on this point were plain: Whitney was to recruit officers "imbued with the crusading spirit."[191] It was also a fortuitous effect of these developments that it meant the rise of Colonel Charles L. Kades to a position of prominence within SCAP. While MacArthur provided general impetus and supervision to the work of GS, and while Whitney was his senior project manager, Charles Kades quickly became the driving force within the section in the critical year of 1946, "a tutor in practical liberalism to his boss."[192]

Like Whitney, before the Second World War Kades had been a modestly successful lawyer. Born to Alsatian Jewish immigrants in 1906, Kades studied government at Cornell and then law at Harvard. Nothing about his career at Harvard law in the late 1920s marked him out as a future driver of a new constitutional order in Japan twenty years later.

Kades had been a solid B-student at Harvard law, having shown no particular interest even in American constitutional law.[193] In his young adulthood Kades became a public finance lawyer and loyal New Deal Democrat. These twin assets ultimately led to a job as legal counsel to Harold Ickes at the Public Works Administration. In 1937, Kades landed a better job with Internal Revenue and then was quickly promoted to a still more important job working under Henry Morgenthau in Treasury on military procurement and lend-lease contracts. By the time he accepted an officer's commission in the army in 1942, Kades had become an accomplished and enthusiastic New Deal lawyer-technocrat.[194] As he shipped out to fight (as an artillery officer) in Europe in 1944, there was nothing about Kades's professional profile that portended a pivotal role in the legal reconstruction of Japan.

In many ways Charles Kades exemplified the best traits of the well-educated American lawyer of the era. He possessed a sharp and highly adroit intelligence. He was perceptive and world-wise. He possessed a sound grasp of the ideas underpinning American law and democracy. He was undogmatic in his thinking, pragmatic in his approach to problems. Kades also was a highly conscientious man who worked relentlessly on tasks assigned him. Those who knew him later were of one mind that Kades was an outstandingly effective officer, an unusually potent combination of acuity, tact, extreme competence, and affability.[195] He inspired confidence, even affection, in his superiors and subordinates alike. For a host of reasons, then, Kades was an excellent leader and, as events unfolded, the ideal "point man" at GS.

From 1942 until the spring of 1944, Kades distinguished himself as a staff officer with General Hilldring at Civilian Affairs.[196] In this period he had no involvement whatsoever with postwar planning for Japan. After the D-Day landings, Kades was dispatched to help coordinate civilian affairs for the U.S. Army group operating in southern France.[197] Soon after Kades returned to the United States in the spring of 1945, Hilldring, responding to an urgent request for personnel from MacArthur, promoted Kades to full colonel and, with ten days of preparation, sent him to Japan to work in SCAP's governmental affairs section. Kades's pre-mission briefing papers consisted of a file of directives to MacArthur from the Joint Chiefs.[198] As Kades himself later repeatedly stated, he had arrived in Japan (one plane behind MacArthur) knowing nothing about Japanese language, history, politics, or law.[199] Kades admitted that he had been assigned a critically important position with SCAP with no training at all.

In his lack of specialized knowledge or preparation for legal and political reform work in Japan, Kades was not in the least unusual. In fact, back in the United States, SCAP's "bodysnatcher" recruiters had been explicitly instructed by MacArthur *not* to recruit from the ranks of American academic or diplomatic specialists in Japan or Asia.[200] In MacArthur's view, those who knew a great deal about Japanese history were likely to be too respectful of it.

This policy had made the recruiters' hard job even harder. In the result, in the first phase of the occupation, SCAP (just as the USGCC had done) had to get on with its work with too few civilian staff and far too few having Japanese-specific expertise. Making matters worse, even SCAP's supposedly trained personnel had received rudimentary instruction in their assigned fields,[201] only a tiny percentage (none of the most senior executive staff) being conversant in Japanese.[202] For those so inclined, moreover, there was no simple way to become more expert on Japanese issues while in Japan, as SCAP operated without a library of books and materials on Japan. Among the few officers who had come to the country with specialized expertise, a common complaint was that they were able to exert little influence on SCAP policy or procedures.[203] In the specific context of legal and political reconstruction, relevantly trained experts and intellectuals were almost entirely shut out of the process.

And so it came to be that, in the first two years of the occupation, momentous liberal democratic reforms were introduced to Japan's legal and political system by Americans with scant knowledge of Japanese history or culture. As naïve agencies of change in Japan, they were highly optimistic, if not always effective, socio-legal engineers.

In assembling the leaders of a GS team to work on Japanese legal and political reconstruction, Whitney selected men like Charles Kades—men who, like himself, had received no systematic training for the work they had been ordered to undertake. They were men (all but one were men) who during the 1920s or 1930s had been privileged enough to receive a university and in many cases professional legal education.[204] They also broadly shared another characteristic:

apart from MacArthur and Whitney, virtually all of the leading figures at GS—Kades only most prominently—were fervent New Deal Democrats.[205] They approached the reform agenda in Japan strongly committed (from the point of view of MacArthur's security people, suspiciously so) to the New Deal's emphasis on democracy and civil libertarianism in politics and to state interventionism and regulation in economics. With regard to basic human rights, GS's New Dealers were proponents of liberal universalism. In their view, the Japanese, in their innate capacity to enjoy liberty, were more alike than different from Americans. In their own unsystematic way, the leaders of GS became apostles of an emerging theory of universal human rights.[206]

In the course of the first year of the occupation, Whitney and Kades, using the Potsdam Declaration, the policy directives of the Joint Chiefs, and MacArthur's orders as starting points, cobbled together what Whitney would later refer to as MacArthur's "philosophy" of the occupation of Japan.[207] That philosophy set forth the basic precepts for the administration of Japan and the historical and ethical assumptions underscoring them. As a democratizing occupier, first of all, it behooved SCAP to avoid the unilateral imposition of reform. To demonstrate its good faith in this respect and to effect permanent improvements to the Japanese democracy, SCAP's declared policy was to "encourage the Japanese themselves, on their own initiative, to take the necessary steps forward under the broad outline of Allied policy."[208] Every major reform to Japanese law or politics would be preceded by an exhaustive process of consultation, advice-giving, and encouragement.[209] SCAP's goal was to avoid any intervention that would taint a reform measure or "vitiate its character as a Japanese instrument," still more to avoid having to impose liberal-democratic reform by diktat. The American slogan in this regard, as Kades summarized in 1948, was to build a "catalytic rather than catastrophic" relationship with the Japanese state.[210]

SCAP's philosophy of occupation was also informed by a reading of both the unique history and shared humanity of the Japanese people. In this view, the Japanese nation had become a militaristic rogue state in the twentieth century due to historical (not racial) exigencies. Like Germany but unlike Britain, France, and the United

States, Japan's ruling classes had modernized the Japanese state and economy while suppressing the development of liberal-democratic legal and political institutions.[211] In the 1920s and 1930s, facing strong challenges from liberal and leftist political alignments, reactionary ruling cliques had contrived to retain and increase their power by imposing a "modern totalitarian police state,"[212] one dedicated to sociopolitical stasis at home and aggressive territorial expansion abroad.

The salient contention of this account, the key to understanding why SCAP saw Japan as ripe for a "great offensive for democracy," was the idea that Japan's authoritarian past had been the product of powerful but contingent historical forces. In its early engagement with the Japanese, the official line of SCAP was one of liberal-universalism, based in a gospel of individual rights reinforced by law. This line, we have already noted, came in flat contradiction to the wartime propaganda of the United States that the Japanese were a primitive sub-race stuck in a time warp, replacing it with a conception of the Japanese as an aggregate of natural rights–bearing individuals who until September 1945 had been the hapless victims of artificial restraints.[213] Their oppressors subdued by war and purged in peace, the Japanese were poised to cast off their chains in constructing, under American auspices, new "national institutions on a democratic base."

In keeping with this vision, and further to the Initial Policy, in October 1945 MacArthur moved unilaterally to issue a series of directives (known as SCAPINs, short for SCAP index[214]) to the Japanese government.[215] These directives marked the beginning of what one Tokyo University law professor later termed the American-initiated "August Revolution" in Japan.[216] The Japanese government was to take immediate steps to abolish the remaining vestiges of the wartime police state, including the centralized police forces and all law imposing restrictions on freedom of speech and assembly. Political prisoners were to be released from Japan's jails, including all Communists.[217] When the government balked, claiming that such an action would lead to serious disorder at a time of widespread social and economic distress, MacArthur moved swiftly to issue a Civil Liberties Directive (SCAPIN 93), abrogating a long list of Japanese laws restricting freedom of thought, religion, assembly, and speech.[218] The directive also ordered the removal of the Japanese minister in charge of internal security and a number of senior police officials just as it abolished the Japanese secret police forces. Before the close of 1945, MacArthur issued SCAPINs giving women the vote, expanding access to trade unions, and disestablishing Shinto.[219]

If SCAP's line was that the Japanese people as a whole were natural liberals who were certain to welcome the new American-induced rule-of-law state, the line was more ambivalent about the Japanese political elites.[220] In truth, while Japan's crushing defeat at arms dealt a crippling blow to the prestige of ultranationalism and militarism in Japan, tradition-bound forms of conservatism persisted.[221] The scholarship in this area strongly suggests that for the Japanese—including those who before the 1930s had been liberals, democrats, and socialists—a strong allegiance continued to be felt to the peculiarly Japanese political notion of the *kokutai,* the idea of the "immutable and indestructible" historical and cultural communion of the Japanese people and the imperial dynasty.[222] As MacArthur began to issue aggressively liberal directives, as he began to piece together a program for the liberal-democratic reconstruction of Japan, strong factions within the Japanese Diet and largely intact imperial bureaucracy resisted initiatives thought likely to threaten the *kokutai.*[223]

The American decision to govern occupied Japan indirectly through the remnants of the Japanese state afforded Japanese politicians (and especially bureaucrats) abundant psychological and organizational space in which to resist American-directed change.[224] While Japan's military defeat was total, and while it is clear that many sectors of Japanese society, in John Dower's resonant phrase, "embraced" defeat, it is equally clear that elements within Japan's political and bureaucratic elite—the Japanese "deep state"—emerged from the war determined to impede, obstruct, and inhibit American-sponsored legal and political initiatives and reforms.[225]

Indeed, before the end of the second full month of the occupation, senior GS officials already had begun to detect what was generalized as "an attitude of growing intransigence on the part of the Japanese" regarding SCAP reform initiatives.[226] In November 1945, for instance, it had become apparent that the Japanese government was deliberately stalling on the implementation of instructions to lift a long list of statutory restrictions on civil liberties. One intelligence officer had come to the conclusion that since the surrender "the apparent Japanese adherence to the ways of democracy is insincere."[227] As one GS officer observed on this point, "It has recently become quite evident that the Japanese government is either unwilling or unable so to conduct its own reorganization. Consequently the Japanese are being specifically directed to submit all proposed changes in the organization and structure of their government to this HQ for prior approval."[228] In a similar vein, George Atcheson, the State Department's senior officer in Japan, had come to believe that "Japanese ruling groups are delaying the attainment of Allied objectives . . . The conservatives, unless checked, will prevent democratic forms to insure continuation of their authoritarian control."[229] Atcheson further noted, "The present outwardly cooperative attitude of Japan's ruling groups stems from a desire to preserve the emperor institution and its semi-feudalism rather from any real changes in their traditional reactionary outlook." None of SCAP's legal or political reforms were likely to be achieved except through vigilant oversight and prodding.

Charles Kades weighed in on the same theme in December: "Every officer without exception," he informed his chief, "has noted a growing tendency on the part of the Japanese government to delay compliance with official requests. . . . Instructions are misconstrued, technical discrepancies are made use of, subterfuges are indulged in, flimsy excuses are offered, direct evasion or non-compliance is practiced."[230] In a host of subtle ways, therefore, the Japanese old guard was closing ranks against pressure to make significant changes to the nature and structure of their politics.[231]

This show of recalcitrance ultimately backfired. It served mainly to spur MacArthur to take a much more aggressively interventionist hand with the Japanese.[232] Although MacArthur remained reluctant to govern Japan by recourse to fiat, by the close of 1945 he had called on his GS to take back the initiative from the Japanese, especially with regard to the broader strokes of legal and constitutional reform.

On December 24, his tenth day in the job, Whitney assembled the GS staff and told them that they were about to embark on a historic enterprise and that he wanted an open, deliberative section in order to achieve goals.[233] This speech—a speech that obviously enjoyed the imprimatur of MacArthur—instantaneously galvanized morale in the section.[234] According to Kades's recollection, from this point in time the leading officers of GS felt that they "were in a way carrying a crusade. Everybody's heart was in what he was doing."[235]

MacArthur's directives on civil liberties had caused one Japanese government to resign and put its successor very much in defensive mode. But it too would soon learn that MacArthur was prepared to use power—hard or soft—to impose American policy unilaterally. The show of resolve at the end of 1945 was a prelude to SCAP initiatives on the reform of the Japanese constitution, reforms that the Japanese political elite itself "would not have dreamed of initiating."[236]

Occupying the Legal Other: The Subjugation of the German and Japanese Legal Systems, 1945–1946

In October 1945, Assistant Secretary of War John McCloy sent a handwritten note, remarkable in its candor, to Herman Phleger, the Californian corporate lawyer turned civilian executive of AMG-Legal Division in Berlin.[237] McCloy began by apologizing that he had not seen Phleger when in Berlin, the reason being that he had been "on my way through to Japan," the *other* of the United States' two monumental projects of transformational occupation. Overwhelmed by the sheer enormity of his government's new global commitments, wearied by five years at the nerve center of the American war effort, McCloy confided in Phleger that he had become especially distressed ("appalled" was the word chosen) by the "terrifying" gravity and complexity of the United States mission in occupied Germany. How to orchestrate the destruction and renovation of Germany's stubbornly entrenched militarism? "There is so much to be done," McCloy observed, "and so little talent to do it with."

McCloy knew only too well that America's new operational groups in Germany and Japan were unready to achieve their missions, that they were in fact woefully short of people who (like Phleger) were willing to "try to cope" with the challenges presented in those ruined countries. McCloy implored Phleger to consider staying on with Legal Division beyond his six months contract. In the end, however, neither Phleger nor his own boss, Charles Fahy, were still in Germany in the spring of 1946.

Indeed, it is hard to imagine a document more illuminating of the patterns set down in the critical first half year of the occupations of Germany and Japan, the first half year of American attempts to subjugate and reform the legal systems of those defeated nations. More than passing strange it was that McCloy, himself untrained in the legal and political structures of the former Axis powers, was obliged to delegate to persons even less prepared to plan and direct legal reconstruction in Germany.[238]

By October 1945, McCloy had intuited that while the United States had nearly unlimited capacity to win global wars it had much less capacity to win global peace. This was most conspicuously true with regard to the destruction and reconstruction of occupied legal and political systems and their grundnorms. In the weeks—even months—after the Potsdam Conference settled the broad outlines of their mission, the organizational mechanisms by which the United States was to engage with the legal systems of Germany and Japan, invented from whole cloth in the previous eighteen months, were in no fashion ready for effective operations. In the fall of 1945, the legal subdivisions of AMG and SCAP were in reality little more than hastily assembled associations of professional and conscripted soldiers, political placemen, and "expert" consultants. What bound them was mainly shared bewilderment in being stationed in one of two ruined foreign ghost-countries, assigned to tasks they neither fully understood nor knew how to accomplish.

In Berlin, Charles Fahy and Karl Loewenstein embodied the incoherence and malaise of the American legal mission in Germany. The paradox here is that Fahy, an utter novice in German affairs, ill equipped for his assignment in Berlin, only there because it was the best (if roundabout) path to more desired office, was the institutional superior to a man like Loewenstein. It is a paradox that an untutored

Democratic Party apparatchik such as Fahy, more or less uncommitted to particular policy outcomes in Germany, held complete decision-making authority in relation to Karl Loewenstein, who in every imaginable way (save for temperament) was a man better qualified to formulate policy. In his intimate personal and academic knowledge of German law and history, in his intimate knowledge also of the rise of National Socialism and its catastrophic consequences, Loewenstein had no intellectual peer at Legal Division. He had come to Germany, moreover, for no reason of personal advantage but because he genuinely wanted to rid German law of the Nazi taint, to place its law and society on the path of liberal modernity. From the outset, however, the die of Legal Division was cast: Fahy and his peers would keep power and influence to themselves, using that power in the service of what they thought politic, not what intellectuals and experts thought right to do.

A striking fact about Legal Division in the first phase of the occupation of Germany was its willingness to accede to the signal, emanating from General Clay's office, that it was inconvenient to adopt a pessimistic stance on denazification. It was inconvenient, in other words, to act on the view, however compelling it might be, that the Nazis jurists had been complicit in a lawless persecution state and, after the demise of that state, remained (according to the most credible intelligence) in a "mentally sick" state of collective denial and rationalization.[239] Sensing what was wanted, perhaps needed, by his superiors at AMG, Fahy forged policy on legal denazification that squared with what was necessary and possible, not what was plausible or desirable, to believe about German jurists. From the outset, the officials who designed and implemented legal reconstruction in American-occupied Germany were moved mainly by their sense of having limited power.

In Japan, conversely, MacArthur did not feel similarly inhibited. In his memoir of MacArthur's command there, Whitney plausibly observed, "No proconsul, no conqueror, no generalissimo ever had more power over his subjects than MacArthur had over the people of Japan."[240] Nor was the Supreme Commander burdened by Lucius Clay's basic humility or (what one historian alternatively styled as) his weakly developed "will for domination."[241]

Just as Clay began to stage-manage a subtle disengagement from destructive and reconstructive undertakings in Germany, MacArthur began to lay the groundwork for "thick" engagement between his meager civil affairs assets and the Japanese state. Unhindered by Washington, by American allies, or know-it-all Japan experts, by the end of the fall of 1945 MacArthur already had begun to organize the basis of a SCAP-directed structural upheaval of Japanese constitutional law and government.

3

Captive Constitutions

REMAKING CONSTITUTIONAL LAW IN OCCUPIED GERMANY AND JAPAN

On having secured the unconditional surrender of the Third Reich and imperial Japan, the doctrine of the United States and its allies was that they had captured the sovereignty and thus the constitutional autonomy of both states. From the moment the relevant instruments of surrender were endorsed, the national and subnational constitutions of Germany and Japan were regarded as subordinated to Allied postwar policy aims.

Charles Fahy, after his brief tenure as director of Legal Division in American-occupied Germany, having reinvented himself as an authority on public international law, published a scholarly article in which he argued that one of the key incidents of the unconditional surrender of Nazi Germany was that it had created a "legal vacuum" in that country, one filled by the shared and zonal military governments of the Allied powers.[1] The absolute capitulation of civilian and military authority in Germany had generated the "simple fact" that its sovereign power was "assumed and exercised by right of conquest." In Fahy's opinion, furthermore, all of the functions and privileges of German sovereignty would be reposed in the Allies jointly and severally "pending accomplishment of the purposes of the war and occupation, and until final settlement."[2]

We have seen that the central purpose of the United States in making war on Germany and Japan was threefold: to defeat their fascist militarisms by force of arms; then, during periods of military occupation, extirpate the wellsprings and manifestations of fascism in German and Japanese society; and lastly, in the final phase of military occupation to guide the German and Japanese populace in the establishment or, in Germany's case, reestablishment of democratic systems of law and government. "After some preliminary hesitation," Carl Friedrich wrote in 1950, "democratization was made the major positive objective of military government following the . . . Second World War."[3] The deliberate destruction and then reconstruction of the political system in Germany and Japan, one eminent German émigré law scholar wrote in 1947, is "required for the maintenance and safety of the occupying Powers and the consummation of their victory."[4] In this view, there was no impediment to the revision of the constitutional law of occupied Germany or Japan. As Charles Fahy summarized the point, "It can properly be said from a legal standpoint the United States stood on the proposition that every law of Germany [of Japan, equally] was subject to the authority of the occupying powers to further the purposes of the war and the occupation."[5]

While the Potsdam agreements made reference to the compulsory democratization of the occupied nation-states, they did not stipulate the alteration of their constitutional laws. In the first iterations of their general orders, similarly, neither General Clay in Germany nor MacArthur in Japan was explicitly directed to commence constitutional reform programs. That they did so—early in their terms, largely on their own command initiative, and on the basis of no predetermined constitutional theory or planning—are facts bearing careful study.

For reasons to be explored here, when Clay and MacArthur moved to instigate liberal-democratic constitutional reform in occupied Germany and Japan, they were men in a hurry. Professional soldiers without formal training in law or government, the generals proceeded to assemble and implement far-reaching constitutional programs. They did so, moreover, without systematic learning about the Weimar or Meiji constitutions, or how these constitutional arrangements might have contributed to the rise of fascism in Germany or Japan.

They also moved ahead without coherent ideas about how to cause subjugated elites and populations to embrace and actuate new liberal-democratic constitutional orders. In short, they did not think much beyond the compulsory introduction of democracy and the rule of law as a set of abstractions.

In their constitutional interventions, nor were American commanders much moved or informed by previous American actions. Although some agencies under their sway had considerable institutional experience in the design and imposition of liberal-democratic constitutions, such experience had little or no bearing on American constitutional interventions in occupied Germany or Japan.[6]

Before the American occupations of Germany and Japan were six months and three months old respectively, both Generals Clay and MacArthur had already triggered processes that led to significant and radically discontinuous constitutional change. In American-occupied Germany, General Clay, having an exclusive political authority only in the U.S. zone of occupation, wasted little time in kick-starting constitutional innovation in the zone's three newly created Länder or regional substates. Adopting an approach that would be repeated in the context of west German state construction in 1948 to 1949, Clay gave Germans wide latitude to remake their own state constitutions. Before the close of 1946, the American Länder had ratified new and, on their face, liberal democratic constitutional instruments. In American-occupied Japan, General Douglas MacArthur, having a de facto exclusive authority over the entire Japanese homeland, also decided to initiate wholesale constitutional reform there. Before the close of 1946, Japan had an altogether new and radically liberal-democratic constitutional framework.

Consistent with his personal predisposition to promote a transformational concept of occupation, MacArthur quickly concluded that sweeping reform of Japan's Meiji constitution—whether commenced by the Japanese government or by the Supreme Commander for the Allied Powers (SCAP)—was the indispensable precondition of the successful democratization of Japan. Lucius Clay, on the other hand, eschewing any grandiose vision of his mission in Germany, his hands tied by quadpartite control of the German nation as a whole, pursued constitutional reform for altogether different reasons, by an altogether different process, and on an altogether different scale. In the fall of 1945, saddled with the responsibility of governing a large but destitute population with inadequate resources and without the benefit of a remnant German state, Clay decided that the only means of averting humanitarian disaster in the zone was to urgently revive German economic and political activity. Of course it was also vital that such moves were consistent with American and Allied commitments to the democratization of Germany. There could be no recovery of German political autonomy except in the visible presence of new and demonstrably liberal-democratic constitutional frameworks.

Several important historical questions arise in relation to the constitutional innovations fostered by Americans in Germany and Japan. If Generals Clay and MacArthur were the primary instigators of the new constitutions, who was responsible for their specific architectures? What was the nature and source of the ideas informing the constitutional reform process? To what degree were German and Japanese personnel permitted to participate in and affect the process? To what degree, if any, were the new constitutions understood as antidotes to, or firewalls against, the reemergence of fascism? What factors caused the final formulations of the new constitutions of Japan and of the German Länder? To what degree, if any, were the new constitutional instruments *imposed* on the Germans and Japanese by American authorities? What was the significance of constitutional change for the subsequent reconstruction of the German and Japanese legal systems?

Freedom in a Box: Remaking the Constitution of Japan

The most striking aspect of American action toward the Japanese legal system in the first year of the occupation is that so much of great importance was done so rapidly by officials with so little relevant knowledge. Within six months of their first tentative contacts with Japanese legal officialdom, a small coterie of American officials had already presumed to draft a radically new model constitution for a foreign state and people.

In this regard we might usefully recall the first high level conference between officials of SCAP Legal Section and Japan's Ministry of Justice, held in Tokyo on October 1, 1945.[7] American officers had no option but to make a series of requests for rudimentary information about Japanese jurists, laws, and legal institutions. With painful clarity the meeting exposed the unpreparedness of the American legal operation in Japan.

This was the end result of a sequence of planning failures then exacerbated by the abrupt end of the Pacific war. These were rooted in the fact that the key planners and policy-makers at the War and State departments had themselves lacked interest and expertise in legal subjects.[8] Leading American planners had simply not given much thought to the subject of Japan's constitution and its possible revision.[9] The first iteration of SCAP Legal Section was dreadfully short of officers with even a passing acquaintance of Japanese law or legal institutions, lacking even one expert in the history, structure, or operation of Japan's Meiji constitution of 1889.[10] In the result, SCAP Legal Section commenced its work in the fall of 1945 without advanced knowledge of Japanese constitutional law and, with perhaps one exception, lacking means to create such knowledge.[11]

SCAP's unsure and ill-informed start was also explicable in the ambivalence of American and Allied policy at war's end on the subject of Japanese governmental and constitutional reform. As we have seen, the Potsdam Declaration was ambiguous on this point, calling for the removal of "all obstacles to the revival and strengthening of democratic tendencies among the Japanese people. Freedom of speech, of religion, and of thought, as well as respect for the fundamental human rights shall be established."[12] The declaration did not specify whether Japan's Meiji constitution, in operation since 1889, was itself an obstacle to the democratization of Japan. Nor did it state that constitutional reform in Japan was a necessary prerequisite of "a peacefully inclined and responsible government" there.[13] It was definitive only on the *source* of any significant legal change in Japan, specifying that it was to be made "in accordance with the freely expressed will of the Japanese people." In early August 1945, the war in the Pacific not yet over, in hopes that the Japanese might yet be enticed to surrender, the Allies had vowed not to impose substantial legal or political change on the Japanese from the outside.

MacArthur arrived in Japan without definite orders in regard to the constitution of Japan. In fact, as late as November 1945, the Truman administration continued to stress that "it is not the responsibility of the occupation forces to impose on Japan any form of government not supported by the freely expressed will of the people."[14] These orders reflected the widely held view of American planners that Japan might become a functional liberal democracy without sweeping changes to its constitution, that it might be possible for the Japanese government, once purged of ultranationalists, to align the constitution with fundamental democratic precepts.

From the outset of his command, however, MacArthur read his orders to require some significant adjustments to the constitutional status quo in Japan. Clearly, for instance, the constitutional position of the emperor and his dynasty would be untenable in a democratic Japan.[15] It was equally clear that the legal rights of Japanese citizens were too few and insecure.[16] Toward this end, MacArthur, in his first meeting with the leader of Japan's "surrender cabinet," Prince Naruhiko Higashikuni, identified constitutional change as a SCAP priority for his government.[17] In MacArthur's rapidly evolving view on this subject, "No political reform that did not encompass revision of the constitution would be worth serious consideration."[18]

To underline the seriousness of American intent in respect of liberal reform in Japan, on October 4, 1945, over the strong objection of the Japanese cabinet,[19] MacArthur ordered the release of all remaining political prisoners and the repeal of Japan's draconian security legislation.[20] The restoration of civil rights under the Meiji constitution was a prelude to directed reform of the actual constitutional instrument.

During the fall of 1945 and winter of 1946, four key developments impelled constitutional change in Japan. The first was that Japanese governmental and nongovernmental groups began to work on and propose constitutional reform. The second was that MacArthur became deeply invested personally in the wholesale reform of Japan's constitutional law. The third was that MacArthur created a means—SCAP's Government Section (GS)—by which to achieve that reform.

Finally, in the last weeks of 1945, the Truman administration revised MacArthur's orders in a way that, in the general's mind, authorized swift and bold action on constitutional change.

We have already met the American officials, MacArthur and the executive officers of GS, who in two frenetic weeks of February 1946 fashioned a new liberal democratic constitutional model for Japan. The historical accounts of this group and their work tend to underplay its marked deficiencies as constitution-makers.[21]

None of the American officers who played a major part in the constitutional reconstruction of Japan had expertise in constitutional law, theory, or practice, still less in the constitutional law, theory, or practice in Japan. The principal architect of the project, Douglas MacArthur, was a career soldier who brought nothing to the project but conviction in the merits of American-style constitutionalism and a potentate's resolve to impose change on a conquered people and state. Similarly, the chief superintendent of the project, MacArthur's second-in-command, General Courtney Whitney, also brought no asset to constitutional reconstruction of Japan other than determination to see MacArthur's will be done.[22]

The American officer with direct oversight of constitutional reconstruction in occupied Japan—in effect its foreman—was Colonel Charles Kades. Before enlisting in the U.S. Army in 1942, Kades had worked with a number of New Deal federal agencies as a legal specialist in municipal-bonds and public finance.[23] While a highly intelligent and effective occupation officer, Kades lacked specialized training in constitutional law. Nor did Kades's two top site managers, Commander A. Rodman Hussey and Major Milo E. Rowell,[24] bring genuine erudition or experience to either the assessment of the Meiji constitution or alternative constitutional models.[25] No deliberate planning but rather accidents of war and peace had put this small group of Americans in a position to make and introduce a new constitution for a great, if captive, nation-state.

The process was started in November 1945, when Milo Rowell, before the war a business law attorney in Fresno, California, was ordered to make an assessment of the strengths and weaknesses of the Meiji constitution.[26] Rowell's report of December 6, 1945, the only one of its kind submitted to SCAP-GS, was less technical analysis than summary of the "many abuses of authority" committed by the Japanese militarists in the "actual operation of government" from the 1930s to the end of the Pacific war.[27] The document argued the trite thesis that if democratic tendencies were to flourish in postwar Japan, then "certain of the abuses" would need to be halted. What was required was a constitutional instrument that protected individual rights and was "responsible to the will of the people." Rowell urged that SCAP move quickly to create such an instrument.

Rowell's report offered basic proposals for the reform of the Meiji constitution but not the historical and political justification of such reform. This was supplied (after the fact) by Charles Kades, Whitney's executive officer on constitutional reform.[28] In Kades's account, the Meiji constitution, instead of being born of popular revolution from below, had been the product of conservative revolution from above. In the late nineteenth century, a "small group of feudal lords," men who "knew exactly what they were doing," crafted (from a Prussian model) an authoritarian legal and political framework for Japan. Their constitution established a polity in which "the source of all political power and legal authority was the Emperor and that the administration of government was carried out in his name and by virtue of limited delegations."[29]

In Kades's assessment, the Meiji constitution "was not the all-embracing organic law of the land but merely one of a collection of laws, rescripts and customs which altogether made up the constitution of the Japanese state."[30] In reality, it had operated as the "slimmest kind of skeleton,"[31] a constitutional framework that had led to government by "clique and counter-clique, by family group and military cabal, and through all the hidden channels of intrigue, duress, bribery and seduction."[32] In the 1930s, a "modern industrial totalitarian oligarchy"[33] of militarists, ultranationalists, and monopoly capitalists consolidated what for all intents and purposes was an "extraconstitutional" dictatorship in Japan, one acting "without regard to human rights and with no concern for law."[34]

In this analysis, the cardinal defect of the Meiji constitution was that it had facilitated and then obscured what was essentially a lawless triumvirate of emperor, military, and bureaucracy. In other words, Japan of the wartime era represented an archetypal case of a state "as a government of men rather than laws. All authority stemmed from the top. . . . The agents of that ruler governed with complete despotism."[35] The Japanese people enjoyed individual constitutional rights not absolutely but within the unilaterally defined limits of law.[36] In the Japan of the Meiji constitution, there were no effective means for the citizen to "seek redress or remedy through the channels provided by law—the ballot box or the courts of justice."[37]

The GS analysis of the Meiji constitution concluded with this prognostication. If the Japanese people were to be liberated from authoritarian modernity, SCAP would need to introduce a radically different constitutional framework, one based on a handful of new and nonnegotiable precepts: "sovereignty of the people, the supremacy of law, the absolute guarantee of basic rights and liberties, the independence of the courts, the recognition of the individual."[38]

We have seen that on a number of occasions in the fall of 1945 MacArthur had sent signals to Japanese officialdom, first to the "surrender cabinet" and then to its successor, that he expected the Japanese government to initiate constitutional reform.[39] For a host of reasons, however, among them a deep-seated reluctance to take any action that might jeopardize the prestige of the emperor or his house, the second (Shidehara) postwar cabinet stalled until alarmed that MacArthur would act by fiat.[40] In late October, the cabinet quietly commissioned a group of Japanese law scholars and civil servants to study constitutional reform.[41] Led by the distinguished statesman and legal scholar Joji Matsumoto, the committee's tacit operational premise was that the Meiji constitution did not need to be reinvented but revised.[42] In supervising these essentially conservative revisions, Matsumoto's staunchly held belief was that the democratization of Japan could (and should) be achieved in a manner consistent with the *kokutai,* the elemental bond between the Japanese people and the imperial dynasty.[43]

By the end of January 1946, Matsumoto's group had worked up two models for the democratic revision of the Meiji constitution, both of which retained the emperor as sovereign and neither of which was responsive to American expectations.[44] Although both versions would significantly enhance the democratic accountability of the Japanese state and its officials (including the imperial house), neither proposed to constitutionalize inviolable individual rights. On February 1, 1946, a summary of one of these drafts was published in a prominent Japanese daily newspaper, probably as a result of a strategic leak arranged by GS.[45] The draft was then quickly and roundly condemned by leading Japanese and American officials in the (SCAP-controlled) media. More consequentially, the draft's unmistakable conservativism convinced MacArthur as well as Japanese liberals and socialists that old-guard Japanese officials would never initiate or endorse constitutional reforms that threatened the *kokutai*.[46] If major reforms were to be made by the governing elites of Japan, the Supreme Commander would have to compel them to be made.

The Matsumoto affair was only one factor in MacArthur's decision early in 1946 to move unilaterally on constitutional reform.[47] In late December, he had received new guidance on the subject in the shape of State-War-Navy Coordinating Committee (SWNCC) 228, a policy paper on the "the constitutional reforms which the occupation authorities should insist be carried out in Japan."[48] It briefed MacArthur on American policy as it entered talks in 1946 with the Far Eastern Commission (FEC), the Allied body made up of eleven nations, including the Soviet Union and Britain, set up to oversee the occupation of Japan.[49] In essence, SWNCC 228 set forth primary American goals for these talks. On the liberal side of the ledger, the United States desired that a new constitution guarantee "fundamental civil rights to Japanese subjects." On the democratic side, SWNCC called for a framework in which the government of Japan would be "responsible to an electorate based on a wide representative suffrage." Finally, 228 ruled out "the retention of the Emperor institution in its present form."

SWNCC 228 also reaffirmed that the "ultimate form of government in Japan is to be established by the freely expressed will of the Japanese people." This policy stemmed from the practical judgment that the "effectiveness of governmental reforms in preventing the resurgence of military control in Japan will depend in large measure upon acceptance by the Japanese people of the entire program."[50] For this reason, "Only as a last resort should the Supreme Commander order the Japanese Government to effect" constitutional reform.

From MacArthur's point of view, SWNCC 228, even though it was transmitted to him as "guidance" only, reinforced his inclination to cause wholesale constitutional reform in Japan.[51] At the close of 1945, there was another compelling reason for MacArthur to move swiftly on this front. The window for unilateral action on the constitution was about to close. By the spring of 1946, the FEC would be in position to participate in or obstruct any major reform proposal. This was not a development that MacArthur, jealous of his own prerogatives in Japan, increasingly confident in his role as visionary of its democratic reconstruction, was prepared to tolerate.[52]

Although the precise moment of epiphany is uncertain, at some point between late December 1945 and February 1946, MacArthur decided to pull out all the stops to secure major constitutional reform in Japan before the FEC became fully operational.[53] In late January, MacArthur asked Courtney Whitney for legal advice on the extent of his unilateral authority in constitutional matters. Whitney (having taken counsel on the issue from Charles Kades) informed MacArthur on February 1 that under the Potsdam Agreement, and in the absence of a clear policy directive on constitutional reform by the FEC ("which would, of course, be controlling"), SCAP was at liberty to "effectuate constitutional reform" and to extinguish "feudal and authoritarian tendencies" in Japan while "strengthening democratic tendencies" there.[54] In Whitney's view, these provisions were broad enough to justify MacArthur introducing, even imposing, a new democratic constitution on Japan.

Two days later, MacArthur informed Whitney of his decision that Government Section would, in little more than a week, draft a model constitution for Japan, one "embodying basic principles acceptable to the Allied Powers."[55] When the draft was complete, the Japanese would be invited, in short order, to either emulate or adopt SCAP's design.[56] The next day, February 4, 1946, Whitney briefed the senior officers of the section on how they were to form a convention to draft the model. The Supreme Commander's strategy, Whitney explained, was to use the GS draft to cause the Japanese to "change their ideas on constitutional revision."[57] It was hoped that, with an American-made model document in hand, the Japanese government would move with alacrity to make their own liberal-democratic constitution. On the other hand, if the Japanese still did not take up the bit, the American model would serve as the basis of unilateral action on constitutional reform.[58]

MacArthur himself had mandated some of the features of the new document.[59] The American-made model was to abolish all feudal rights and obligations and feature a bill of individual rights. While retaining the emperor as a dynastic head of state, his strictly limited role was to be "exercised in accordance with the Constitution and responsive to will of the people." Crucially, sovereignty was to be reposed in the people of Japan. The draft was also to include a clause, unprecedented in the constitutional law of modern states, abolishing the war-making powers of the Japanese state.

As chief foreman of Whitney's model constitution project, it fell to Kades to supervise and coordinate the drafting work of eight subcommittees, each reflecting the various "structures and headings" of the Meiji constitution.[60] The task of each subcommittee was to replace or embellish the articles of the current constitution with new articles consistent with the precepts of liberal democracy.[61]

The two dozen GS officials, twenty-three men and one woman, assigned to these drafting tasks came from a wide range of civilian backgrounds, including education, business, and government.[62] Only four had formal legal training. None of the subcommittee members had specialized training in constitutional law. Japanese experts were deliberately excluded from what was a secret American initiative.[63] Only one official, a twenty-two-year-old woman (the only woman who had been assigned substantive drafting tasks), was a fluent reader or speaker of Japanese.[64] A disparate group, the GS constitution drafters had one important characteristic in common: a willingness to earnestly get on with a task that was absurd on its face and for which they, individually and collectively, were absurdly unqualified to do.

The next week Kades and his subcommittees worked with an almost maniacal energy and commitment to fill MacArthur's order. That they succeeded in drafting a credible document in a single week is rightly remembered as the single most impressive and consequential achievement of the American occupation of Japan.

But at least two aspects of these events have been inadequately addressed and explained. The first is the ironic fact that MacArthur's constitutional convention was able to complete its mission in eight days not because of an abundance of relevant talent and training but because of its scarcity. The second is that some sections of the model constitution, the sections of which GS officers later professed to be most proud, were drafted with almost complete indifference to their legal, intellectual, or cultural coherence.

Taking the first point first, the principal reason that GS was able to complete a model constitution for Japan in a week is that individually and collectively the drafters were so ill equipped for the task that they did not recognize its inherent absurdity. Here we might plausibly speculate that if in February 1946, a committee of *experts* in constitutional law had been approached to design and draft the basic law of a foreign nation (whose language and history they did not know) in eight days, such committee would have dismissed the idea as a joke in bad taste. As it was, however, the conceit, naïveté, and uncomplicated ignorance of the GS officers involved actually aided them in the completion of the task.[65] That the drafters knew so little about Japan's language, about its legal and political history, about the Meiji constitution,[66] about the legal theory of bills of rights and judicial review, about the subtleties and complexities of constitutional jurisprudence generally—all these deficits left them with little to argue about.[67] If the orthodox constitutional convention is often slowed, sometimes paralyzed, by the clash of nuanced ideas, that was not a factor here.

Instructive on this point was the makeup and deliberations of the subcommittee on civil rights. Although revision of the Meiji constitution's qualified treatment of individual rights was a key objective of the project, the subcommittee assigned to this drafting work consisted of only three variously educated officials.[68] Prior to their assignment to GS, one of these Madisons of American-occupied Japan had been a sociologist (Dr. Pieter Roest), another a political economist (Dr. Harry Emerson Wildes) and the other, Beata Sirota, was a linguist without advanced education in any field.

The common credential of the committee was the shared if largely untutored view that individual rights might be inviolably secured by their enumeration (at length) in a constitutionalized instrument. Drawing on contemporary examples of such instruments, including the U.S. Constitution, the trio synthesized a hugely ambitious and complex model "bill of rights" for Japan.[69] In the longer-term result, their work formed the basis of the individual rights chapter of the new constitution of Japan.

Required to finish the drafting task in one week, it was fortuitous that GS officers were Americans, all of them operating on an unspoken belief in the moral and functional excellence of the Constitution of the United States. To be sure, there were moments of discord.[70] But even the most contentious issues (for instance, concerning division of powers and the inclusion of "social rights" in the bill of rights) were resolved by the intercessions of Kades or Whitney.[71] At the end of the day—at the end of the week, more accurately—disputes arose among officials who agreed on the grundnorms of modern constitutions. Disagreement was not about basic principle but technique. Lingering disagreement was settled quickly and unilaterally by the chain of command.

In keeping with MacArthur's tight timetable, a complete draft of the model constitution was delivered to MacArthur on February 10, 1946, And in keeping with the intellectual shallowness of the whole enterprise, the Supreme Commander approved the draft, with minor textual adjustments, on February 11.

The GS document was a hybrid of the American, British, and modern European republican constitutions.[72] Its general thrust was to replace the Prussian authoritarianism of the old constitution with popular sovereignty, representative democracy, and "universal" individual human rights.[73] Sovereignty, this "sacred trust," was to be reposed in the people, not the emperor of Japan. In the British manner, the emperor was to be retained, stripped of constitutional powers, as "the symbol of the State and the unity of the people." Also in the British manner, the cabinet and its prime minister were to be responsible to a bicameral legislature (the Diet) elected on a wide adult suffrage of male and—a significant innovation—female voters.[74] The

Diet was designated as "the highest organ of state power . . . and the sole lawmaking authority of the state." In this constitutional regime, local legislatures, also elected on a broad franchise, were to enjoy substantial autonomy from the central government. Further to MacArthur's explicit instructions, finally, the draft called for the abolition of war-making as a sovereign right of the Japanese people.

The true centerpiece of the GS draft, however, was the third chapter, consisting of thirty articles purporting to define the individual rights and duties of the people of Japan, such rights to be safeguarded by a "strong and independent judiciary" presiding over a new system of trial and appellate courts. At the apex of the system, at the apex of the constitutional model as a whole, was to be an American-style Supreme Court possessed of broad powers of judicial review.

The "MacArthur constitution" had been the product of blatantly undemocratic procedures, a hypocrisy not lost on at least one participant. Milton Esman, in 1946 a young American political scientist assigned to Government Section, later recalled that he had been "appalled and disgusted by the whole process."[75] In Esman's opinion, in an effort to establish a *fait accompli,* MacArthur instigated a recklessly fast, anti-intellectual drafting process, one that excluded "Japanese scholars, many of whom were very liberal men who had suffered under the military regime and who wanted a constitution that would not be a mere patching up of the Meiji constitution."[76] Had cynical politics not triumphed over good sense, Esman contended, the new constitution of Japan "would have been informed by some understanding of the dynamics and the styles of Japanese society, so that it would appear a more authentic document—a more authentically Japanese document than the one that emerged."

The MacArthur draft was also deeply anti-intellectual in the sense that it was preceded by so little careful thought about the efficacy or ethics of imposing radical constitutional change in the context of military occupation. Little thought had been given to the implications of introducing liberal-democratic constitutional norms by illiberal and undemocratic means. With a few strokes of a pen—a pen held by foreigners—MacArthur and his Government Section purported to change the way in which an ancient society and culture regarded such terms as "authority" "citizenship" and "rights." With a few strokes the limited rights of the subject, gifts of the emperor, were to be replaced by copious rights of the individual human being, the gifts of nature.[77]

The GS draft was presented by Whitney (accompanied by Kades and two other senior officers) to Japanese cabinet officials on February 13.[78] The Japanese side believed that the meeting would concern the Matsumoto draft. They had no inkling that in the preceding two weeks GS had created a constitutional document of its own. Nor had they been forewarned that MacArthur had come to the conclusion that the Japanese political elite was dug in against liberal-democratic constitutional reform and that it was now time, in effect, for their line to be outflanked. Whitney informed the cabinet members that the Matsumoto draft was unacceptable to SCAP and that its own officers had written a model constitution for Japan. The American-made document, Whitney told the Japanese officials, after it was translated from courtly into colloquial Japanese,[79] was to be adopted by the government of Japan either without amendment or amended in a manner consistent with its liberal-democratic norms.[80]

To underline the seriousness of American intent, Whitney (the sources disagree on the exact language used) intimated a threat.[81] If the Japanese government was eager to protect the emperor from further and still greater indignities, then it would adopt the SCAP constitution as its own. If it declined to do so, Whitney indicated, the Supreme Commander would bypass the Japanese government altogether, taking the GS model directly to the Japanese people or to the Far Eastern Commission. In either event, the Supreme Commander could not guarantee even the symbolic persistence of the emperor, his dynastic house, or the *kokutai*.[82]

The response of the handful of elite Japanese politicians and bureaucrats privy to the GS draft—and the brusque manner of its presentation—was almost uniformly "scathing."[83] They were angered by its brazen disrespect for the emperor and perplexed by its alien and prolix (English) language of popular sovereignty and individual rights.[84] The draft provisions regarding popular sovereignty were an obvious and frontal assault on the *kokutai*. The liberal individualist slant of the document posed an equally direct threat to the "communitarian orientation" of Japanese law.[85]

For these reasons alone it was never likely that the Japanese political establishment would instantly embrace the MacArthur constitution. And it did nothing to reconcile Japanese leaders to the draft that they were afforded little time or leeway in making significant changes to the GS model.[86] But historians of the GS draft have not adequately documented another reason why many Japanese officials rejected this document: in terms of constitutional design and craftsmanship, the American model, most conspicuously its convoluted chapter on "Rights and Duties," was a demonstrably vague specimen of constitutional drafting.[87] Its thirty separate articles, representing fully a third of the GS draft, read rather less like a bill than a haphazard catalogue of rights.[88]

The first paragraph (Article 9) of the chapter, for instance, granted to the people of Japan the "enjoyment without interference of all fundamental human rights." Instead of offering more precise definition, Article 10 stated only that "fundamental rights" were to be held "for all time inviolate." The article then traced the origin of these rights to the "age-old struggle of man to be free." Article 11 was scarcely more precise, stating that the (as yet undefined) "freedoms, rights and opportunities enunciated by this Constitution are maintained by the eternal vigilance of the people to prevent their abuse and to employ them always for the common good." With similar obscurity, Article 12 called for the cessation of the "feudal system" (without defining its attributes as a set of legal relationships) declaring that "All Japanese by virtue of their humanity shall be respected as individuals." The Article concluded with a Jeffersonian flourish: The citizen's "right to life, liberty and the pursuit of happiness within the limits of the general welfare [this is the first suggestion of some limitation on the scope of rights] shall be the supreme consideration of all law and of all governmental action."

Chapter III continued in a similarly high-minded manner for another seventeen articles, some multiple sentences long. Now, on American paper in American English, the Japanese were to have the broadest and deepest set of human rights guarantees of any people in the world. In this way the GS draft reflected an unbounded if innocent confidence in the ability of constitutional language to deliver real-world rights and liberties. It is passing strange given the ambivalent American history in 1946 of civil rights litigation that the document should have harbored such an idea.

In subsequent chapters (especially VI and X), the GS model set forth the elements of a constitutional rule-of-law state, one in which a newly powerful and independent judiciary in Japan would exercise substantial powers of review, guidance, and enforcement. In this regard, Article 90 described the constitution as the "supreme law of the nation." No other "law or ordinance or imperial rescript" was to "have legal force or validity." In the American fashion, Articles 68 through 75 set forth the elements of a new and politically independent judiciary led by a new Supreme Court charged with broad powers of judicial review.[89] As Article 68 stated, "being the bulwark of the people's rights, the whole judicial power is vested in a Supreme Court and in such inferior courts as the Diet from time shall establish." Article 73 bestowed the Supreme Court with the unreviewable power to determine the "constitutionality of any law, order, regulation or official act" affecting the rights set forth in the "Rights and Duties" section of the document.

In their ardent enthusiasm for individual rights–based constitutionalism, the GS drafters had given little thought to the implications of their work for the Japanese lawyers who would be left to translate the document, literally and figuratively, into a viable instrument of law. In one fell swoop, laying on the liberal rights thick and heavy, GS had purported to transform an Asiatic authoritarian constitutional instrument into a Western liberal one. But the MacArthur constitution raised a number of thorny questions. How was such a foreign and complicated English-language document to be rendered as intelligible Japanese? If this problem could be resolved, how was the Japanese bar and judiciary, wholly inexperienced—technically, ideologically—with civil rights litigation or judicial review to operate such a complex constitutional instrument?

These questions remained unanswered as the Shidehara government engaged in the immensely difficult process first of translating, then of amending the GS draft.[90] From the outset of these exchanges, however, Whitney forcefully underlined that SCAP presented the GS as an integrated package of constitutional reform and therefore would not countenance any major change to its structure or content.[91] If the Japanese government was to avert a public confrontation over constitutional change, one that would jeopardize the emperor, the GS "model" would have to be adopted by the Japanese in pith and substance.

Fearing the consequences otherwise, Prime Minister Kijuro Shidehara and his foreign minister, Shigeru Yoshida, agreed to present the draft to the Japanese people as their government's work.[92] Making the best of a bad deal, government officials used the translation process to make the final draft more consonant with Japanese values and sensibilities. The final English and Japanese texts of the document were hammered out in long joint sessions of Japanese cabinet members and GS officials in the last week of February 1946.[93] Before the end of the first week of March, after a number of acrimonious bilateral sessions, the two groups agreed on a Japanese-language version of the GS constitution.[94]

On March 6, 1946, the Shidehara cabinet released a translated summary of the draft constitution. SCAP's official line was that the Japanese were free to evaluate and discuss the draft in their media and in public meetings.[95] Following the general election of April 1946, moreover, the Diet would be free to revise the document in context of the "fullest freedom of debate and action." In this way the Americans burnished the claim that it had kept faith with the Potsdam Declaration and that the new constitution of Japan reflected the "freely expressed will" of its people.

But the official line was challenged in its time, just as it has been challenged by leading historians in our own time. In the spring of 1946, no significant Japanese official believed other than that the new constitutional model was utterly an American concoction. More than this, the same politicians understood with perfect clarity that General MacArthur, the American proconsul in Japan, had staked his and his home nation's prestige on the ratification of all or most of its provisions. The notion that the Diet or any other Japanese institution or person was at liberty to make major changes to the document—that is, to reject any articles relating to the emperor, popular sovereignty, individual rights, or to the renunciation of war—was to endorse what one historian has called the "make-believe aura" that SCAP had created around the process.[96]

In an act of powerful symbolic endorsement, Emperor Hirohito himself presented the draft constitution to the Diet to muted if generally positive public reception.[97] When deliberations on its contents and merits began in the summer and fall of 1946, Japanese politicians did not know that by moving so swiftly and decisively on constitutional reform MacArthur had overreached. They did not know that the Supreme Commander had rebuffed efforts by the FEC to slow down the constitutional reform train.[98] Nor were they aware that the Truman administration worried that the Supreme Commander in Japan was about to trigger a major diplomatic imbroglio.[99] In their occupied state, the only safe assumption was that MacArthur had power and determination enough to impose a constitutional arrangement that would eliminate the imperial institution. Their best option, therefore, was to accept the basic framework of the GS model while rounding off some of its sharpest inward-facing edges. If this was freedom of action, it was "freedom in a box."[100]

MacArthur's constitutional box, it must be acknowledged, even if American-made, won proponents among the Japanese. The broadly favorable reception of the document leavened by SCAP censorship and the implicit imprimatur of the emperor, was a product also of the content of the document itself. The evidence suggests that most Japanese people and groups having an opinion on the matter (the Communists excepted) endorsed the basic thrust of the draft document: the decisive rejection of ultranationalist authoritarianism.[101] Many Japanese welcomed the retention of dynastic monarchy. Japanese liberals liked that it purported to guarantee individual rights. Educated Japanese women warmly endorsed the adult female franchise, even if many Japanese men did not.[102] Others were attracted to the extension of representative democracy and by the proposed constitutional ban on militarism and aggressive war.

The generally positive public reception of the draft helps explain why, putting aside other political realities, the Diet's and then House of Peers' deliberations on the document unfolded on the basis of its inevitable ratification. No serious effort was mounted to disturb draft articles on personal rights or judicial review.[103] For the most part, the main point of contention was the language of articles relating to popular sovereignty and the renunciation of war.[104] The Diet, after the general elections "preponderately conservative" in its basic ideology, viewed its ratification as a painful means by which to sustain the imperial institution.[105]

The draft constitution was debated in plenary sessions of the Diet until midsummer.[106] In late August, the Diet voted overwhelmingly to support the bill containing the new constitution, this as an amendment to the Meiji law. After the House of Peers spent another five weeks deliberating the bill and proposing a few marginal amendments, it too voted to approve the bill. In early October, the bill returned to the Diet and was ratified in its final version on a vote of 342 in favor, 5 opposed. The new constitution of Japan was promulgated on November 3, 1946, and came into force six months later on May 3, 1947.

In final draft, the new constitution was in its essential structure, wording, and ideological thrust much the same document that Whitney had placed in the hands of Japanese cabinet members in 1946. The process of translation and amendment, while not an empty charade, had done little to alter the draft or to redress its serious technical deficiencies, most especially with respect to its long third chapter (still a full thirty articles in length) setting forth the "Rights and Duties of the People." Technical issues aside, at least one prominent Japanese law scholar had no doubt of the aim and import of the document: "The new Constitution takes the dignity of the individual as its fundamental principle and aims at making it the principle of the Japanese way of life."[107] This, the professor believed, was "clearly a revolutionary happening" that had revolutionary implications for Japanese law and society.

Liberalizing the Länder: Remaking German State Constitutions

Like MacArthur in Japan, Lucius Clay initiated liberal-democratic constitutional change in American-occupied Germany early in 1946.

The similarity ends there. Clay's constitutional program was only incidentally the product of legal or political idealism and nothing to do with ego or grandiosity. It stemmed rather from Clay's trademark administrative pragmatism. By the early winter of 1946, Clay knew what previously he had only suspected: American Military Government (AMG) lacked the personnel, organization, and resources required to provide effective government in the U.S. zone. The prolonged direct military government of more than 15 million distressed Germans (and growing numbers of refugees) was simply not sustainable.[108] Given Clay's imperative "to get work [and] agriculture going, to keep the country alive," the only viable policy option was to move swiftly and effectively to revive German politics and public administration in the zone within a new liberal-democratic constitutional framework.[109]

Even if they had been of a mind to do it, moreover, neither Clay personally nor the United States generally enjoyed the political and diplomatic sway in Germany to replicate what MacArthur had done in Japan—that is, to unilaterally cause root and branch constitutional reform on a national basis. As but one member of a quadpartite governing entity in occupied Germany, each member possessing a veto in matters affecting Germany as a whole, Clay's constitutional engineering projects had therefore to be confined to the regional political subdivisions—the "Länder"—of the U.S. zone.[110]

With characteristic resolution, and in line with Allied commitments to German decentralization, Clay decided that by the close of 1946 the American Länder would be renovated as semi-autonomous democratic entities.[111] According to a plan devised by Clay's chief advisor on German politics, James K. Pollock, AMG would hold local elections in the Länder as a prelude to constitutional conventions.[112] Subject to American oversight, Germans would themselves "frame the structure for democratic state governments, each with an elected legislature, a responsible executive, and an independent judiciary."

This plan was strongly reinforced in the winter of 1946 by shifts in American policy in the occupation of Germany, particularly in the decision of the Truman administration to abandon the last vestiges of "Morgenthausim" for accelerated German social and economic recovery.[113] In the U.S. zone, the accent now was to be on increased

German autonomy in political affairs, government, and, crucially, the promulgation of new liberal-democratic constitutions.[114]

This was a remarkable policy shift, one that hinged on the disposition of American leaders to trade principles for administrative expedience. The shift also hinged on their willingness to disregard the awkward fact that, little more than a year earlier, most adult Germans in the U.S. zone had been consensual participants in a systematically lethal regime.

As for General Clay, he endorsed and implemented the rapid Germanization of law and politics in the zone while being aware that denazification was a chaotic mess.[115] If the identification, purge, and punishment of Nazi wrongdoers had been a central aim of America's postwar planning, now Clay had demoted it to a secondary purpose, one to be dealt with mainly by the Germans themselves. Far from stigmatizing the postwar Germans under his authority or limiting their role in the development of new constitutions, it became Clay's steadfast policy to let Germans not obviously compromised by Nazi-era crimes get on with the job free from intrusive interference by American officials.

The leading historians of postwar German law reform in the American zone have almost uniformly praised Clay both for initiating constitutional reform in the American Länder and for his "wise and discreet" decision to permit Germans to do the job with minimum interference.[116] In this view, General Clay had been right to trust the Germans to democratize their constitutional law—this less than two years after German-made war and genocide, and even as the American denazification program was unraveling. He had been right, the argument goes, that German political leaders in the U.S. zone were ready to make a clean break from Germany's authoritarian and militarist past. He had been right to overrule expert advisors, such as Karl Loewenstein, who thought that in 1946 the Germans were too war-shocked, hungry, and demoralized to participate meaningfully in constitutional reform. He had been right to set aside that German news media was too disorganized and censored (and short on newsprint) to educate public opinion. Above all, Clay had been right in his judgment that only Germans could draft and ratify legitimate German constitutions.[117]

Some primary sources, however, provide reasons to doubt this historical interpretation, especially in its tendency to read history backwards. The received wisdom on these events, this subchapter will argue, has largely disregarded that Clay's constitutional initiatives, in regard to process and substance, attracted cogent American and German critics and criticisms.

By mid-December 1945, Clay was already "reducing personnel and withdrawing from certain functional fields . . . as German administrative machinery is set up."[118] It was now his declared intention in this regard that by January 1, the Länder "were to carry out all government functions except those explicitly reserved by US, subject to oversight."[119] We have seen how at the same time, despairing of the ability of AMG to denazify the zone, Clay had commissioned a policy group to advise him on how best to turn denazification over to Germans without delay.[120] German-driven reform of constitutional law was therefore only one facet, if an obviously important one, of a much larger policy of American disengagement from the direct administration of the U.S. zone. As Clay later summarized, when it came down to chewing the hardtack of German economic, legal, and political reconstruction, "I thought the Germans could do it better than we could."[121]

Clay decided to move constitutional reform forward on two parallel tracks. On the first, AMG would oversee the gradual restoration of German democratic institutions at the local level. The first step in this regard was for provisional cabinets in the Länder to write new codes of municipal and county government.[122] These were reviewed, revised, and approved by the end of November 1945. The next step was the organization and supervision of the first postwar elections in the U.S. zone. Elections were held in small towns in January 1946, at the county (*kreis*) level in April, and in the larger towns and cities in May. The elections were at once a series of progressively harder tests of democratic feeling and conduct in the zone and a means of generating elected bodies and officials with political legitimacy enough to draft and ratify credible state constitutions.[123]

The second track concerned the content of the constitutions. On this subject, Clay relied mainly on James Pollock, his chief advisor on

German politics. A professor of comparative government at the University of Michigan, fluent in German and German political history, Pollock had spent much of the previous two war years training American officers for civil affairs work in occupied Germany.[124] Clay and Pollock quickly developed a close working relationship—a relationship, at least one critic (Karl Loewenstein) believed, in which Pollock was an empire-building toady lacking the spine to challenge Clay's *idée fixe* that less than year after the surrender, the Germans were ready to embrace the liberal-democratic reinvention of their nation.[125]

In late December 1945, Clay directed Pollock to consult informally with the ministers-president of the Länder on the question of "holding elections for delegates to Constitutional Conventions" by late spring of 1946.[126] In early January, Pollock reported to Clay that all three ministers thought that spring was too soon, both because German political opinion in the zone had not yet had time to form and because "more time [was] needed for the preparation of Constitutional proposals." The ministers-president believed that October was a more realistic goal. But Pollock, in probability only too aware that the general was firmly committed to the spring timetable, indicated that he was not entirely convinced by the ministers-presidents' caution. Pollock opined that because of "our recent progress in reviving the German administrative machine in our zone," and assuming the county and city elections went well, the earlier date for constitutional reform "is not objectionable." Pollock concluded his report with the politically astute comment that "if in your [Clay's] judgment . . . it is desirable to speed up the restoration of Democratic institutions, then I find it would be sound and justifiable to do so."

This may or may not lend support to Loewenstein's opinion of Pollock that he was an obsequious nonentity.[127] In any event, by the first week of February 1946, Clay had decided to move ahead with German-crafted constitutional reform, wanting finished draft documents in all three Länder by summer. On February 4, the ministers-president were instructed to appoint "preparatory constitutional commissions" made up of political party officials and legal experts.[128] These were to review constitutional issues and prepare or amend draft instruments for the consideration of elected state constitutional assemblies in late June. In the fall of 1946, each of the states would then move to ratify, or not, the final text of documents. In this regard, in May 1946, Clay also created a new ad hoc group within AMG, the Interdivisional Committee on German Governmental Structure (ICGGS), whose task it would be to provide supervision and support to German constitution-making efforts.[129]

It cannot be emphasized too strongly that the mandate of the ICGGS was to support, not to supplant, German-driven constitutional conventions. For Clay had made it abundantly clear that the German delegates were to be given maximum autonomy in the drafting process.[130] The General's operative assumption (the reverse of MacArthur's policy in Japan) was that "democracy could not spring from a dictated constitution." If there was to be genuine democratic reform in Germany, the constitutions underpinning this reform "must represent [German] will and not that of the occupation forces."[131] The primary job of the ICGGS was to provide guidance and education to the Germans, to set forth the broad principles by which the new constitutional documents would ultimately be evaluated by AMG. In a report to the War Department in July 1946, Clay described his policy as follows: "We have told the German authorities of the basic principles which we consider necessary to a democratic constitution and these principles have been furnished to you and to the State Department. As long as these principles are safeguarded in the constitution, we do not propose to comment on the details or on the governmental procedures established in the constitutions."[132]

As early as the spring of 1946, just as Clay's plan was building steam, the constitutional initiative began to attract criticism within the American camp. In fact, both of its two main tracks—early elections and the short timetable to ratified constitutions—met with forceful resistance from leading figures inside and outside of AMG, both Americans and Germans.

When they first got wind of Clay's plans, all three of Clay's hand-picked German ministers-president persisted in making the case that the general wanted to go too far too fast. Clay's proposals seemed oddly detached from the harsh reality that the Germans under his control were a shocked, exposed, and hungry people for whom politics and constitutions were irrelevant.[133] As one American official reported, virtually all leading Germans agreed "that the elections were premature because little political interest could be generated among people whose primary objective in life is the search for food."[134] Further to the point, General Clay was proposing the rapid repoliticization of an electorate which had not voted in real elections since 1933 and for whom democracy was "synonymous with frustration and defeat."[135]

Readers will not be surprised that the most vociferous internal critic of Clay's electoral and constitutional program was Karl Loewenstein, the irascible Legal Division advisor and intellectual without portfolio. By virtue of his expertise in German law and politics, Loewenstein had become a member of the ICGGs, AMG's advisory group on constitutional reform. Aware that momentum was building for rapid, German-led constitutional change in the zone, in his work with this group Loewenstein felt obligated to express reasons for caution.[136]

Some context is in order here. Loewenstein had come to Germany as an expert thinker, not a diplomat or political actor. He believed therefore that his job was to apply knowledge and analytical method to problems with academic detachment. The trademark of Loewenstein's official memoranda was their candor to the point of bluntness. In his public communications, however, even Loewenstein, the opposite of a diplomat or political climber, made some concessions to etiquette. He did not do so in his private diary.

Publically, Loewenstein's main objection to Clay's program was that it was too soon for AMG to delegate critically important processes such as constitution-making (this "momentous occasion for self-assertion and self-expression for any nation") to Germans, this obdurately illiberal, undemocratic, and still deeply disordered political community.[137] In Loewenstein's view, the Germans, including the German legal elite, had emerged from war in a state of dissociative denial.[138] In his private discussions with Germans in the zone and with leading Nazi-era jurists, it had become clear to Loewenstein that the Germans were pathologically unwilling to confront the sources or consequences of their ride with the Nazi devil. It had shocked Loewenstein to hear educated Germans justify the Third Reich in terms of the Versailles Treaty—this in the immediate aftermath of cataclysmic defeat, to say nothing of the systematic mass murder of European Jewry. He was bewildered that this stubbornly amoral and impenitent elite was thought ready to create and consolidate a functional liberal democracy before its "re-education" had even nicely begun.[139]

Then there was the related objection based in the unfolding debacle of denazification. As we have seen, early in 1946 when General Clay had begun to set Germans to work on constitutional reform in the U.S. zone, he was also orchestrating a full-scale retreat from American-operated denazification. Loewenstein thought this policy particularly significant in the realm of German law and legal institutions. From the outset of the occupation, AMG had evinced an alarming willingness to rehabilitate Nazi jurists, even those who had partaken in political and racial cases.[140] When the denazification process was devolved to the Germans, Loewenstein predicted that this "superficial gesture of denazification" would lead to the nearly wholesale rehabilitation of the deeply compromised German legal professions.[141] These were the men who in their roles as lawyers, judges, and ministry officials would then be the frontline "defenders of the new democratic state," responsible for the vindication of the new constitutional rights of those living in the American Länder.[142]

There were other reasons of practical politics why it was not timely for AMG to move quickly on constitutional reform. In January 1946, German political parties in the U.S. zone were either barely back on their feet or just being born. The German people, still grappling with the physical and psychological aftershocks of defeat, had little interest in party politics. It did not help that the mainline parties were led by uncharismatic older men, Weimar-era relics who inspired little popular enthusiasm even among supporters. Neither the center-right nor socialist alignments, moreover, were adherents to American-style political liberalism. In Bavaria particularly, parties were reviving deeply conservative regional-nationalist politics, more monarchistic than democratic.[143] Moreover, in Bavaria as in the rest of the U.S. zone, the "unfortunate experiment of Weimar" continued to mar the appeal and prestige of the liberal-democratic model of politics.[144]

For these reasons, so Loewenstein contended in a widely circulated memo of June 5, Clay's push to establish new constitutional regimes in the Länder was unfolding in what amounted to "an intellectual and political vacuum." Instead of waiting until conditions were more conducive to popular democratic change in the zone, Clay was hoping to wave his "magic wand" and induce it from above.

With no false modesty, Loewenstein had penned his memorandum of June 5 as "an essay on the education of General Clay." The memo was a blunt summary of the manifold reasons why he thought AMG was being dangerously "over-optimistic" about German readiness to frame and operate democratic constitutions. But all warnings notwithstanding, "Clay," Loewenstein lamented, "pats his boys on the back . . . and praises them for the good work they are doing while he fails to see that in Bavaria the same old crowd is in control again."[145] Elections had always been a poor barometer of German commitment to democracy and "Yet they are to be held because General Clay, on the way out, wishes to democratize Germany . . . ramming down the throat of people an alien form of government."[146] Ironically enough, Clay's democracy push was the product of "the one man rule set up of MG."

By June 1946, Loewenstein no longer suffered from the delusion that his memoranda, on any topic, were likely to be influential with the leaders of AMG or indeed of Legal Division. He was thinking and writing about problems ("danger areas," Loewenstein called them) "for the record," more than for the purpose of affecting policy or decision-making.[147] This is how we should read Loewenstein's memorandum on the first drafts of the three regional state constitutions.

The central theme of this piece was that leopards do not change their spots. In Loewenstein's view, Germany's antidemocratic past was manifest in the documents, "if in democratic disguise."[148] Judging by the draft Bavarian constitution he had seen, AMG would have to be on its guard "against the inclusion in the constitutions of government institutions or devices which . . . would lend themselves to non-democratic application in the future."[149] For Loewenstein, the key point was for AMG to ensure that the constitutions guaranteed individual rights and the uniform accountability of all state actors to law. What was wanted were plainly written instruments that contained "no provisions that place the government or state over the citizen." The main requirement was that the new documents be made consistent with liberal principles of "the rule of law, that is the accessibility of judicial or legal procedure for all citizens and with rights equal to those of the state."

In Loewenstein's view, in any genuinely *liberal* constitution, "stress should be laid on the extensive judicialization of state functions as far as it is compatible with the main function of government, namely that of governing." But this raised another caveat: the mainstay of such a constitution was judicial review under an independent judiciary, a process "which nowhere in Europe has proved workable because the sociological structure of the European judiciary is not suited for it." Here Loewenstein reiterated the dangers posed by the heedlessly fast pace of Clay's constitutional reform program. The ultimate success of the liberal-democratic constitutional projects depended on the presence of judiciaries of the kind that had not in history existed in Germany. Success would turn on entirely unjustified belief in the collective commitment of German judges to the priority of individual rights.

Loewenstein offered one final word of caution about the draft constitutions. Given the inexperience of German judges with liberal approaches to constitutional interpretation and judicial review, given also the "German [judicial] propensity for moralizing," it was imperative that the drafters avoid "purely semantic" phrasing.[150] In the German context, such rhetorical flourishes were likely to incite the "constitutional speculation and legal insecurity from which the public life under the Weimar republic suffered."

In the result, Loewenstein was correct that his caveats did not stop or even slow down Clay's constitutional program. If anything, by the late spring of 1946, Clay had become even more unyielding about these reforms, if only because he saw them as the necessary precursor of the next major development in Germany: an American-sponsored push for the tighter economic and political integration of the western zones of occupation.[151]

Before the state constitutional assemblies convened in mid-July, Clay, with the endorsement of his chain of command, restated the general precepts that were to guide their work.[152] First, each constitution would need to entrench the principle of popular sovereignty. Second, all political office–holders were to hold power by virtue of frequent and competitive elections on an adult franchise. Each of the new constitutions was also to guarantee a slate of basic individual rights by judges and courts not subject to political oversight. Further to Potsdam's decentralization principle, jurisdiction over local affairs was to be reposed in elected town, city, or county councils.[153] In the post-occupied Germany, the Länder governments would replace the central state as the "highest levels of government."[154] The constitutions were also to provide for the eventual reintegration of the German states into a national (federal) constitutional system. Finally, all of the new constitutions were to include a general provision that at all levels of state power was to be "exercised through the rule of law."[155]

The constitutional assemblies were elected on June 30, 1946, and began work in mid-July. On a regional basis and as a function of election fortunes, the delegates varied substantially in party and ideological affiliations.[156] In Hesse, the Social Democrats had a slim majority, the Christian Democrats in Württemberg-Baden. In Bavaria, delegates of the conservative-nationalist Christian Social Union greatly outnumbered those of the left and liberal parties. As the drafting unfolded, these differences had telling impacts on content, most especially with regard to the constitutional status of individual rights.

In his general instructions to the ministers-president, Clay renewed his pledge that the assemblies would be left alone to write final drafts of their own design, subject to their conformity with fundamental principles. As one historian summarizes, Clay brought American advisors to heel, ordering them to be "highly tolerant of German ideas" on key issues, including the "structure of government, the question of a second chamber, the electoral system, emergency legislation, and even of the question of Capitalism versus Socialism."[157]

In defusing potential opposition to his constitutional program, Clay was aided by the arrival in July of his handpicked constitutional advisor, the German born and educated Harvard professor Carl Friedrich.[158] An eminent authority on German and comparative constitutional law,

Friedrich had been flown to Berlin to advise with the ICGGS during its assessment of the draft constitutions.

Friedrich brought a number of assets to the projects, not least was credibility with Germans flowing from his native fluency in the German language and its public law.[159] Born in 1901 to a prominent family of academics and capitalists, Friedrich left Germany for the United States in the 1920s, before the rise of National Socialism. An adamant critic of all totalitarianisms, Friedrich remained in the United States, becoming a naturalized American citizen.[160]

Friedrich arrived in American Germany a cautious optimist about the prospects for enduring liberal-democratic constitutional reform there. He thought that the war had shattered German support for fascist political and legal modernity. He further believed that AMG was right to move quickly to fill the vacuum with new, German-made, constitutional arrangements. He felt that the coalition of (non-Nazi) German politicians and academics who dominated the constitutional assemblies were genuinely committed to fostering a decisive moment of discontinuity in the U.S. zone and to making a strong bridge from the authoritarian past to the democratic future.[161] An unabashed elitist in his approach to the drafting process, Friedrich did not share Loewenstein's concern that new liberal-democratic constitutional frameworks were being made by men with scant democratic legitimacy.

It was perhaps not just a happy coincidence that from the outset of his visit, Friedrich lined up squarely behind Clay and his decision to give the Germans a wide berth in writing their own constitutions.[162] In return, Clay could not have been but pleased by Friedrich's initial assessment of the three draft constitutions that, if they were "looked at with reasonable tolerance, they will be found to contain little or nothing objectionable."[163] In effect, the general's principal expert had now signed off on the project.

But to less sanguine eyes the draft documents, and the intended press of their assessment, gave cause for concern. When the assemblies delivered the documents in mid-July, Henry Parkman (formerly a prominent Bostonian and lawyer), one of Clay's senior officials in AMG's Civil Administration Division (CAD), deigned to point out that since the drafts already had been voted on by the assemblies, it raised a worrying "presumption that anything contained in these drafts that we do not object to now is presumably unobjectionable."[164] On this ground, and because he was aware of provisions that would need amendment, Parkman thought it crucial that AMG send a clear signal that it had not yet endorsed the drafts, that it was still prepared to overrule "extremely objectionable provisions," if only by recourse to "informal advice rather than mandatory objective." But Clay did not heed this advice. No communications of the kind were sent. On July 21, Clay ordered the ICGGS to initiate and complete its assessment by August 1. Then, on July 22, Carl Friedrich (and Loewenstein) in attendance, the ICGGS met all day and for six more days.

Theirs was a formidable task, especially under pressure of time. All three draft constitutions contained from more than 100 often internally complex articles (Württemberg-Baden) to more than 185 articles (Bavaria). To compound the problem, some individual articles consisted of as many as ten sentences of constitutional language. Still other articles (in the Hesse constitution) purported to constitutionalize some novel social and economic prerogatives, including the socialization of major industries.[165] Then there was the problem that all three draft constitutions contained articles that had been copied verbatim from the Weimar constitution.[166] For all of these reasons, the ICGGS meetings on the draft documents took place under quite extraordinary conditions. They were to be the first and last opportunity for American experts in the U.S. zone to ensure that the Germans had kept faith with AMG and its strictures.

In his diary entries about these meetings, Loewenstein recorded his respect for Carl Friedrich and the "fresh air" he had brought to deliberations.[167] In Loewenstein's estimation, Friedrich was "less conceited and more to the point than [he] had expected and there were no fireworks." Far too much for Loewenstein's liking, however, Friedrich was willing to passively accept Clay's ludicrously tight timetable for review and revision. It was obvious that the Germans, having so little beneficial experience, could not draft three credible liberal-democratic constitutions within two months.[168] And how was the ICGGS to provide meaningful feedback in only ten days? On these crucial issues, in Loewenstein's opinion, Friedrich was "as much under the spell of Clay as everyone else." In terms of actual capacity to assess and improve the drafts, the meetings had to be regarded as a "bad farce."

Loewenstein was not alone in this line of thought. In a richly detailed final report to Clay on the drafts, CAD advisor Henry Parkman also did not pull his punches, especially regarding individual rights.[169] In Parkman's opinion, all of the draft documents offered only contingent protections of basic rights. Individual rights were to be held to unspecified "exceptions to be declared by legislation."[170] Another telling flaw was that the documents contained provisions subordinating the judicial to the "legislative and executive branches" of government. In other words, the German-drafted documents failed to establish either the inviolability of basic rights or the political independence of the courts, two indispensable features of liberal rule-of-law states. Parkman then pointed to the related defect that the drafts purported to confine powers of judicial review to single constitutional courts, even though "constitutional violations are more frequently connected with the exercise of another right which will be prosecuted in a lower court." These observations led to a blunt conclusion: "The draft constitutions indicate a complete misunderstanding of the position of the judiciary and the protection of the constitutional rights."

In the end, however, Parkman's memo was conciliatory. Although the German drafts had many serious defects, Parkman thought that after a short period of "diplomatic negotiations" between AMG and the constitutional assemblies, "there is every reason to expect that the Germans will correct [the defects] themselves."[171] How and why the Germans would make such corrections, given the obvious ideological and theoretical convictions that had brought them into being, Parkman did not say.

Loewenstein's and Parkman's doubts about the draft constitutions were shared by Robert Murphy, the ranking State Department official in Germany.[172] In July, a State Department staff study concluded that the "drafts contain many questionable and objectionable provisions, are full of obscurities and inadequate in their present form to meet our objectives." Worryingly, none of the drafts had made "adequate provision for establishment of [a] constitutional system of courts truly independent and clearly empowered to decide constitutional issues in accordance with our concept of the reign of law." The report's over-arching conclusion was that the liberal elements of the constitutions were insufficient, in that "Civil rights are badly defined and inadequately guaranteed."[173]

On the basis of this advice, Murphy concluded that Clay's constitutional program was "operating on too rapid a timetable," and that the train needed to be slowed down. While he agreed that it was desirable to afford Germans substantial leeway in making new constitutions, Murphy did not think that they should be permitted to disregard the liberal-democratic requirements laid down by American policy. Consequently, Murphy asked the Secretary of State for permission to "advise General Clay to extend the period of deliberation of [the Länder] constitutional assemblies for as long as may be necessary," certainly beyond the October 5 deadline as set by General Clay.

Murphy's was not the only request of this kind. In early September, the constitutional assemblies both of Württemberg-Baden and Hesse formally requested an extension of time to make further adjustments to the new laws.[174] "The reason for the request," Parkman explained, "is the time required to reconsider certain provisions" of the draft documents. Although American suggestions had been favorably received, including on the protection of individual rights, they had not yet been incorporated.

In October, all three constitutional assemblies having submitted final draft documents, the eminent Heidelberg social scientist Alfred Weber added his name to the growing list of credible persons, American and now German, who thought that Clay's constitutional reform agenda was being moved along too fast.[175] Weber was a German scholar of impeccable liberal (and anti-Nazi) credentials. He was also an extremely well-informed student of German society and politics. In sending his letter to Clay personally, Weber exerted the moral authority of a German intellectual who had not bowed to Hitlerism.

The new draft constitutions, Weber contended, lacked legitimacy because they had not "been subjected to the regulating influences of an effective public opinion" in the Länder. Moreover, massive socio-economic dislocation in the U.S. zone meant that it was all but impossible for ordinary Germans, the future electorate of democratic states, to monitor or engage with constitutional development. As matters now stood, the new constitutional instruments had "no roots in the population," most Germans being almost completely ignorant of their content.

Weber was also alarmed that in some cases (the Hessian text particularly) the drafts borrowed heavily from the Weimar constitution and its reliance on "proportional representation and the system of party lists."[176] In his view, such voting systems tended to entrench political elites and their outdated ideas, just as they had done before the Hitler coup, impeding the emergence of a new, younger, and democratic political community. At the end of his letter, Weber urged Clay not to allow the Germans to repeat "mistakes of earlier times." If the ratification of the new documents were to go ahead, Weber wondered whether Clay would ensure that "the separate sections of the constitutions be voted on individually and that time be allowed for public discussion of each section."

By early October, the draft constitutions now undergoing their final assessment before approval and possible ratification, Clay's constitutional program had attracted an impressive array of detractors among the Germans, members of his own camp, and even his superiors in Washington. But Clay was not a man for turning. His response was monotonously consistent: he would entertain proposals that did not injure German prestige or cause undue delay. Clay summarized this position in a terse communication with the War Department on October 15.[177] In his view, the German drafts, while imperfect, were "the best that can be obtained by suggestion." Clay reminded Washington that the impugned documents were the product of "three months of sincere and conscientious effort" by "representatives freely elected by the people." Moreover, neither Clay nor Friedrich and Pollock, his two most trusted advisors on constitutional issues, agreed that the draft documents were fundamentally flawed. Nor did they agree that AMG should direct their amendment. It was thus Clay's firm conviction that (at this point) American intervention would do more harm than good; among other things, it would undo fragile compromises among German political factions in the assemblies. The use of fiat at this stage of the process, Clay warned, would be nothing short of disastrous, first for the ratification process, then for American administration in the U.S. zone.

By the end of October 1946, Clay was more convinced than before that his constitutional project was an indispensable keystone of the American policy that the "German people should be permitted increasingly to govern themselves," a policy that had now been publically endorsed (during a major address at Stuttgart) by Secretary of State James Byrnes.[178] In fact, so convinced was the general of the unwisdom of the State Department's position that on October 9 he had asked the secretary of war to intervene with Secretary of State Byrne and, failing that, to "go to the President if necessary."[179]

In the end, push did not come to shove. Washington did not order Clay to change the draft documents.[180] The War Department had obliged State to concede that Clay and his advisers were "in a peculiar and advantageous position to determine the best method of handling the situation."[181] On this green light, Clay continued to fast-track the draft constitutions, even over the persistent objection of some German officials.[182] After the ICGGS (less Friedrich) was given one or two days with each of the drafts, their comments were given over to CAD for the preparation of final staff studies.[183] The staff studies consisted of advice to General Clay about what, if any, suggestions would be made about changes to the draft documents.

On October 7, the staff study undertaken by Henry Parkman's CAD concluded that, "No amendments need be required by Military Government in the Hessian Constitution."[184] From the point of view of the protection of basic individual rights, not including property rights, the Hessian draft presented the strongest case for positive endorsement by AMG. The draft described the most elemental human rights as "inviolable." According to Article 26, basic rights were further described as "unalterable and impose a direct obligation upon legislators, judges and administrators." The document also set forth a long and detailed list of the social and economic rights. Along these lines, the draft's controversial Article 41 called for compulsory state ownership and administration of heavy industry and "large banks and insurance undertakings." The Hessian draft, then, very much a constitution of the Left, was strongly steeped in the tenets of democratic socialism.[185] In the final result, on October 7, Clay wrote privately to Otto Witte, the president of the Hessian assembly, to inform him that, with minor alterations, AMG was satisfied that its draft constitution was "consistent with the fundamentals of democracy and safeguard[ed] the rights of individuals," and that it was "approved for presentation to the people" subject to minor adjustments.[186]

Similar letters were sent the same day to the presidents of the constitutional assemblies of Bavaria and Württemberg-Baden, although in these cases the draft constitutions were seen as more problematic. In his communication with the Bavarian president, Clay made final approval of the draft document contingent on some alterations of text, including provisions guaranteeing local election of local officials, a ban on closed sessions of the Bavarian legislature, and a ban on sitting members serving as judges in constitutional cases.[187] If individual rights were to be adequately protected, moreover, more needed to be done to ensure that citizens might trigger impartial "judicial review of laws passed by the Landtag." Clay also made it clear that while AMG would countenance the use of the term "Bavarian National" in a state constitution, it "did not thereby express any approval of separatism for Bavaria." In his communication with the president of the assembly in Württemberg-Baden, Clay called for a provision requiring the election of local government officials as well as new language protecting citizens from abuse of power by administrative tribunals.[188]

During the second and third weeks of October, the drafting committees of the three Länder incorporated required amendments while they considered amendments further to the suggestions that had been made by the CAD. Some of these suggestions were incorporated in the final texts, but some (like the alteration to Article 41 of the Hessian draft) were not. But to focus on the particulars of these last adjustments to text would be to miss a larger point. When Clay gave his formal and public approval to all three Länder constitutions (between October 21 and October 29), in two out of three instances (Bavaria and Württemberg-Baden) he did so with regard to draft documents that were deeply suspect from the standpoint of civil rights and judicial review. Both contained provisions that, in the hands of conservative-minded judges, might be invoked to undermine the liberty of citizens. In other words, both contained the type and kind of provision that Loewenstein and other experts had warned against.

The draft constitution of Bavaria, by way of example, pointedly and defiantly began with twelve articles describing the character and dignity not of the individual Bavarian citizen but of the Bavarian state and of "nationality" within that state.[189] The fundamental rights and freedoms of the individual person were not mentioned until Article 98 and then qualified by what might be urgently required by "public safety, morality, health and welfare." Article 60 established the new Bavarian Constitutional Court as the "supreme court for constitutional questions." Article 68 called for the election by legislators of the president and eight co-judges of that court—judges not to enjoy security of tenure. If this were not worry enough to liberal critics of the document, in the event of a public emergency, Article 81 was to permit the Landtag to suspend freedom of speech, assembly, and association without constitutionally guaranteed limits on the suspension power. In Loewenstein's opinion, this opened "the door to the same encroachments on individual rights as under the Weimar constitution."[190] When looked on as a whole, Loewenstein concluded, the Bavarian draft was "basically authoritarian in spite of its democratic trimmings."

There were similar, if less blatantly statist, provisions present in the final constitutional text of Württemberg-Baden. This document more conventionally began with multiple articles setting forth basic rights. Article 2, for instance, described how all persons "are free and equal before the law." But the same article also indicated that the exercise of basic rights was to be limited by "what does not encroach upon another person's rights or honor *or upon public order*" (emphasis added).[191] Articles 6 to 13 purported to enumerate a number of additional individual constitutional rights. But as one (anonymous) American official noted, these rights, "like those in the Bavarian constitution, are subject to restriction by general law." Such a provision, it was further commented, was entirely inconsistent with AMG policy that the basic rights of German citizens in the Länder should be subject to inviolable safeguards.

The final documents were problematic for at least one other reason: in an effort to be comprehensive all three documents were long and convoluted, their articles verbose or drafted in "lofty, general expressions" likely to confound citizens, lawyers, and judges.[192] Still other articles smacked of the ideological dogma of their authors—for example, the call for the nationalization of industry by socialists in Hesse and frequent invocation of morality by Catholic conservatives in Bavaria.

By the same token, the plain and palpable defects of the new constitutional instruments did not seem to trouble clear majorities of constitutional assembly members or general voters. Between October 24 and 29, the constitutional assemblies of the three Länder voted by wide margins to adopt the draft constitutions.[193] In a series of state elections and referenda in November, voters in each of three German states within the U.S. zone approved the constitutions, again by wide margins of plurality.[194]

By early December 1946, plebiscites in the three German Länder delivered strong majorities in favor of ratification.[195] With these votes, Clay's victory was complete. On December 6, the general's immediate superior in Washington, General O. P. Echols, the new director of the Civil Affairs Division of the War Department (replacing Hilldring), offered his congratulations: "While there are points in the Constitutions which we all agree could be improved, it is felt that a splendid job has been done and that substantial progress has been made by you and your organization towards guiding the German Government in the U.S. zone along democratic lines."[196] That important and positive, if arguably premature, steps had been taken toward the establishment of democratic political patterns in American-occupied Germany could hardly be doubted. However, whether significant and concrete strides had been made with regard to the liberalization of the same German states remained very much an open question.

On paper, the three new constitutions indicated a return to a manner of representative democracy in the American Länder, these the new focal points of government in a decentralized German polity.[197] All three called for the reestablishment of the *rechtsstaat* or the "law-bound state" in the new Länder, whereby, in the words of the new

Hessian constitution, "No one shall be compelled to take, abstain or tolerate any action *unless a law or provision based in a law* so requires or permits" (emphasis added).[198] But more than this, all three constitutions contained provisions that, with various degrees of clarity and resolution, pointed to a liberal *rechtsstaat,* a state bound not to make any law or take any action that might abridge the individual rights of persons.

In every case, however, the authors of the new constitutional instruments refused to describe individual rights in unqualified terms. In the "democratic social free state" of Württemberg-Baden,[199] for instance, the constitution was dedicated to "freedom and in fulfillment of the eternal moral code within the human community."[200] The extensive individual and collective constitutional rights of its citizens was to be "restricted only by law." Rights were inviolable except when they did not encroach on public order[201] or the limits of law.[202] In Württemberg-Baden, the ability to pursue the work of one's choice was understood as both a constitutional right and, less liberally, a "moral duty."[203]

In Hesse, the social-democrats who dominated the constitutional convention posited that man is "free to do or not do" whatever he pleased, so long he did not "infringe on the rights of others" or, more ominously, did not do so "to the detriment of the social order."[204] In several articles personal rights and freedoms were described as "inviolable"[205] or "unalterable"[206] only for another article to posit that the same rights might be restricted "within the scope of existing legislation."[207]

As for the Bavarian constitution, its drafters were noticeably less given over even to liberal pretence. The Bavarian document began with definitions of the state and the investment of state power in its people.[208] Some ninety constitutional articles before individual rights were set forth (in the 98th article of its *second* part of the document), the drafters felt moved to describe the constitutional definition and requirements of Bavarian nationality.[209] Although the constitution included at least two articles designed to equip the state to resist antidemocratic movements and political extremism, it also provided for potentially stringent limits on individual and collective rights and freedoms.[210] It would seem that the drafters did not think they were creating broad constraints on rights when they specified, in Article 98, that such limits "are permitted *only* if public safety, morality, health and welfare urgently require" (emphasis added).

As if to make a respectful bow to the liberal predilections of their American overseers, all of the Länder constitutions posited various and sundry individual and social rights. In every case, however, they also posited the mechanisms by which the executive and or legislative branches of the Länder might also ignore or implement strict limits on the same rights. In the context of a declared public emergency, moreover, personal rights might be suspended altogether. In this regard the new constitutions failed to make a clean break from the similar provisions of the Weimar constitution. There was another echo from Weimar: in every case the new constitutions provided for potentially powerful systems of courts, especially the new state supreme constitutional courts. In every case these bodies would possess explicit legal authority to review the constitutionality of state action and to nullify or correct official illegality. If in the post-occupation the Länder were to become, for the first time in German history, authentically liberal regimes in which individual rights enjoyed robust protection, it would be a consequence mainly of liberal-minded vigilance of German appellate judges.

As we will see in the next chapter, the centrality of judges, court process, and judicial review in the new constitutions of the American Länder greatly increased the importance of the successful denazification and reconstruction of the German judiciary.

Captive Constitutions: Remaking Constitutional Law in Occupied Germany and Japan

In 1946, agencies of the United States brought about significant and, in the case of Japan, momentous constitutional change in the occupied countries. In both cases, in Germany on a sub-zonal, in Japan on a national basis, the American military regimes caused occupied elites to adopt and ratify the constitutional basis of liberal-democratic rule of law regimes. In both occupied countries, these changes were improvised; the captive constitutions of the U.S. zone and Japan were reconstructed as a function of the contingent personalities, predilections, and political circumstances of the commanders-in-chief.

In occupied Japan, for instance, the overwhelmingly important reason that 1946 was a year of dramatic constitutional change was that MacArthur willed it to be so.[211] Enormously attracted to the role of modernizer and law-giver, presented with a clear-cut but brief opportunity to exert power without foreign interference, possessing at least the implicit authorization of Washington, by sheer force of will MacArthur utilized all the resources at his disposal to make a liberal-democratic constitution for Japan and then to cause the Japanese to make that constitution their own.

In the early winter of 1946, MacArthur had become so fervently committed to the rapid manufacture and ratification of a new constitution in Japan that he thought it a sound idea to assemble two dozen ill-equipped Americans to draft—in just over a week—a model constitution for a foreign nation-state. So besotted was MacArthur with his newfound role as the liberal-democratic Moses of Japan that he seemed not to comprehend that his in-house constitutional "convention" was a patent absurdity in which a handful of men and one woman of almost no relevant expertise or skill purported to draft a document of enormous complexity and significance for a foreign people whose history and language they did not know. In his haste to install a new constitution in Japan before the Far Eastern Commission could intervene, MacArthur had made mockery of his "philosophy" of occupation: that SCAP's agencies should be gauged to maximize the legitimacy, practical value, and enduring impact of liberal-democratic reconstruction.

As time proved, moreover, the much celebrated rights liberalism of the SCAP constitution was built on a foundation of sand. At the bottom layer was Japan's ancient and persistent culture and its deeply engrained and almost comprehensively illiberal patterns of social cohesion, interaction, and identity.[212] In their unreflective enthusiasm for constitutionalized rights, SCAP's legal engineers had given little thought to how Japan's newly enfranchised and dignified groups, its women, peasant farmers, and urban working classes, were to comprehend, still less to assert rights claims. Nor had adequate consideration been given to how Japan's lawyers and courts, utterly inexperienced in liberal rights litigation and judicial review, would actuate a prolix and culturally alien bill of rights.[213]

In its demotion of the emperor, in its commitment to popular sovereignty and representative democracy, in its extravagant bill of rights liberalism and severe limitation of war-making powers, the MacArthur model constitution marked a radical break from Japan's Meiji constitution. It marked a radical break, therefore, from the *kokutai*. For that reason alone it was not a break that the Japanese governing elite would have made themselves, in 1946 or any other year. That is why it is right to contend that the model was imposed on the Japanese from without.[214] When in February 1946 the government of Japan was informed that the American model constitution had been endorsed by MacArthur, and that the emperor's fate hinged on its acceptance, the die was cast. From that point forward there was no practical option but to accept the imposition of liberal democracy from above.

Douglas MacArthur dominated the content and process of liberal-democratic constitutional change in Japan. In American-occupied Germany, Lucius Clay decided that he wanted only to dominate the process. The most remarkable aspect of Clay's constitutional initiative in the U.S. zone is that he delegated most of it to Germans, this little more than a year after the fall of the Third Reich. He did so by discounting a number of alarming facts. The first was that the German legal establishment in the U.S. zone was replete with unrepentant Nazis and Nazi accommodationists. The second was that the American-operated denazification program in the zone was a chaotic shambles that, even when turned over to Germans, was unlikely to keep former Nazis from returning to key positions in the German legal professions. New German-made liberal constitutions in place, their proper functioning was to depend on the same lawyers and judges who had abetted the destruction of justice and the rule of law.

In Japan, the Japanese elite accepted the MacArthur constitution believing they had no feasible alternative. In American Germany, Clay accepted the risks associated with an accelerated and German-led program of constitutional reform believing he had no feasible alternative.

Given the looming socioeconomic crisis, given the administrative limitations of AMG, the general needed proficient regional government in the U.S. zone.[215] Clay needed such government fast and for it to operate within a liberal-democratic constitutional framework.

At the end of the day, then, Clay's constitutional program of 1946 was driven by practical not intellectual concerns. That is why it was not preceded by intensive American assessment of German constitutional law or of German readiness (or lack of readiness) to engage with constitutional issues. Practical priorities also explain why the changes were made without sober assessment of whether German lawyers and judges in the zone were ready or willing to support three new liberal-democratic constitutional orders. Just as in the French and (in 1947) the British zone, AMG saw no feasible alternative to constitutional reform processes led by German political parties and legal experts.[216] In the U.S. zone, new and ostensibly liberal-democratic state constitutions were developed for Germans by Germans. Even if for lack of a practical alternative, Americans trusted Germans to democratize their own regional states.

When the new Länder constitutions were ratified in the late fall of 1946, General Clay could rightly claim to have achieved a milestone in the liberal reconstruction of American-occupied Germany. On their faces, all of the constitutional documents purported to go beyond the mere reestablishment of the *rechtsstaat* or law-bound state.[217] In every case there were indications that the Germans had aspired also to the liberal *rechtsstaat,* to a polity in which some individual and group rights could not be violated even by law-based action.[218] In every case, too, the new constitutions set forth the exclusive jurisdiction of a specialized constitutional court to engage in the binding judicial review of the action or legislation of a state.[219]

But as the ink dried on these new constitutional arrangements, no one was in a position to confidently predict how, when greater autonomy was devolved to the Länder, they would operate in practice. It could be predicted with certainty only that if the new constitutions delivered on their various liberal and democratic promises, it would be because communities of German jurists—lawyers, judges, prosecutors, legal academics, and legal bureaucrats—had made it so; in other words, if the German legal professions operated as they had never once operated in German history.

Like the new basic law of Japan, the idea for new constitutions for the American Länder was born in the mind of a soldier-turned-military-governor. In both instances, military governors had pressed ahead mainly in the absence of expertise in Japanese or German or, indeed, any manner of constitutional law. In both instances, consequently, constitutional change was prosecuted by Americans in the absence of explicit theories about why the German and Japanese legal and political communities had succumbed to fascist militarisms and, more pertinently, why American-sponsored constitutional change was likely to foreclose the revival of the same.

In occupied Japan, having seized the initiative on constitutional reform, General MacArthur did not yield more than fractional and largely symbolic control of the process to the Japanese. MacArthur's staff drafted the framework of a liberal-democratic rule-of-law state for Japan and, after its politicians made some marginal amendments, the Japanese electorate, including now all of the country's adult women, were invited to "accept" and ratify that document. Although it is probable that a majority of Japanese voters were amenable to the change, it was understood that this was an offer that could not be refused.

In occupied Germany, in contrast, General Clay almost immediately yielded the initiative on constitutional reform to postwar German elites. Having stipulated only that new constitutions establish representative democracies and constitutionalize basic individual rights, Clay and his consultants kept a respectful distance while Germans fleshed out new basic laws and, in the first instance, in their own language. Just as MacArthur was steadfast in defense of SCAP's right to direct the form and content of constitutional reform, with equal steadfastness Clay shielded German-directed constitutional reform from intrusive meddling.

In one significant way, however, the two American roads to constitutional reform had led to one uncertain place. By the close of 1946, American-occupied Japan and the Länder of American-occupied Germany possessed new if not yet deployed liberal-democratic frameworks of law and government. If there was a comparatively easy step in the liberal reconstruction of previously authoritarian societies, that step had been taken. But if constitutional change was to make a palpable difference to the lives of citizens, then many more steps lay ahead, steps that would turn on the perceptions and actions particularly of the judiciaries of Germany and Japan.

4

Crafting Liberal Courts

RECONSTITUTING THE GERMAN AND JAPANESE JUDICIARIES

BY THE CLOSE OF 1946, the United States had instigated new liberal constitutions in American-occupied Germany and Japan. Senior American legal officers knew, however, that liberal rule-of-law revolutions were not made of paper. If these new basic laws and their gaudy bills of individual rights were to become features of lived experience in postwar Germany and Japan, this would be a consequence, in no small measure, of the sympathetic attitude and action of the German and Japanese judiciaries. As an American legal officer in Japan observed in this respect, liberal democracy "stands or falls with an independent judiciary."[1]

At Potsdam, more than a year before the Americans had compelled constitutional change in Germany and Japan, the Allies agreed that the German judicial system, seen as hopelessly corrupted by National Socialism, was to be "reorganized in accordance with the principles of democracy, of justice under law, and of equal rights for all citizens without distinction of race, nationality or religion."[2] And although the Potsdam Declaration did not provide explicit undertakings with regard to the Japanese courts or judiciary, it was no less obvious, one American official contended, that such reforms would be an inevitable feature of democratization in occupied Japan.[3]

In their broad commitments to personal rights and the rule of law, the new constitutions of Japan and the American Länder had positioned judges and judicial institutions to the pivotal center of state. According to the liberal architecture of these documents, in every case at least one court of law—the Supreme or Constitutional court—was explicitly empowered to engage in potent forms of judicial review, to evaluate, or even to nullify, the laws, decisions, or actions of state officials. In this way the new constitutional frameworks of the liberal rule-of-law state were to be safeguarded by judicial intervention and action.

For American officers responsible for the reconstruction of occupied judiciaries, however, formidable challenges lay in store. Where to find the scores of German and Japanese judges—jurists of technical proficiency and liberal cast of mind—needed to staff the courts of new rule-of-law states? Where to find scores of such men in countries in which the judiciaries were historically antidemocratic and illiberal? How to find so many suitable jurists, moreover, in countries whose judiciaries had fresh blood on their hands?

Centering Justice: Remaking the Japanese Judiciary

That the democratization of Japan would entail the intensive renovation of its system of courts and adjudication was an established assumption of American planning long before the end of the Pacific war.[4] Court and judicial reform was viewed as a key element of the broader American (and, after Potsdam, Allied) policy to advance liberal-democratic reconstruction in postwar Japan. As the Joint Chiefs stated in their orders to MacArthur, "The judicial, legal and police systems shall be reformed . . . and thereafter shall be progressively influenced to protect individual liberties and civil rights."[5]

Japan's system of courts and adjudication, never a focal point of social or political conflict in Japan, had been marginalized to the point of irrelevance by the rise and consolidation of ultranationalism.[6] When the ultranationalist clique escalated domestic repression during the wartime period, the courts of Japan were not an important site of either state-sanctioned terror or resistance.[7] The highly charged social and political conflicts of the era only rarely crystallized as litigation. Under the Meiji constitution, the Japanese courts had no authority to engage in the judicial review of legislation,[8] and limited authority to review administrative action.[9] If a Prussian-style *rechtsstaat* had been enforced by Japanese judges before 1945, it was not still being enforced after the army's invasion of Manchuria in 1931.[10] While during the ultranationalist ascendancy some judges had tried to vindicate the rule of law, most had either not done so or had no occasion to do so.[11] For American legal officers, the most striking fact about the Japanese judiciary before the occupation was its near complete subordination to senior bureaucrats in the Ministry of Justice (MofJ).[12] By their superiors, Japanese judges had been regarded as second-class bureaucrats, as mediocre men who had been passed over for more prestigious posts within government.[13]

In the American view, this was decidedly not the kind or quality of judiciary required in the new liberal-democratic Japan. Consequently, when the Japanese government endorsed a lightly amended version of the MacArthur draft constitution in the fall of 1946—its articles on civil rights and judicial review still intact—reform of the Japanese judiciary immediately became the highest priority of American-supervised law reform there.

The framework of this reform was established during the constitutional drafting process by two Government Section lawyer-officers, Milo Rowell and Rodman Hussey (neither of whom were experts in any field of constitutional law). Their work was based on two assumptions. The first was that in the liberal constitutional state, the "strong and independent judiciary is the bulwark of the people's rights."[14] The second was that under the Meiji constitution Japan demonstrably lacked such a bulwark, if only because Japanese judges had been closely "supervised and disciplined by the ministerial bureaucracy of the executive branch of Government."[15] In reconstituting the judiciary in Japan, American legal officials could not call upon even a lapsed tradition of judicial independence.

In creating their blueprint for change in this field, Rowell and Hussey were supported by proposals in this respect of some liberal jurists in Japan.[16] Within days of the surrender, a group of Tokyo lawyers had petitioned the Japanese government to move expeditiously on the "liberation of courts from the supervision of the Ministry of Justice."[17] With little expectation of a favorable response, the reform-minded lawyers made a direct appeal to the American occupation authorities.

By early December 1945, some Tokyo lawyers (styling themselves the "Bar Association for Judicial Reform") had already secured a meeting with MacArthur to discuss their plan for fundamental reform of the Japanese judiciary.[18] Most of its members were low-status lawyers in private law practice, men on the outside of the imperial bureaucracy.[19] The association had taken initiative in this area in the belief that the feebleness of the Japanese judiciary and its institutions had been one of the important contributory factors to the consolidation of fascism in Japan.[20] At a number of critical junctures in the 1930s, Japan's judges had proved wholly incapable of bringing law to bear against the ultranationalist "terrorist" campaign. For most of a generation the judiciary had stood by while right-wing extremists undermined the last vestiges of civil rights, democracy, and the rule of law in Japan. By the time of the surrender, the Association contended, Japan lacked the "essential complexion and characteristics of a judiciary."

For these reasons, in their meeting with MacArthur on December 7, 1945 (four years to the day after Pearl Harbor) the petitioners asked the Supreme Commander to exert his "forceful influence" in the liberation of Japan's judges from ministerial control.[21] The association also called for future judges to be appointed exclusively from the senior bar and for new procedures by which citizens might use the courts to challenge the legality of specific actions of state.

In the first weeks of the occupation, therefore, some of Japan's practicing lawyers had seized the moment to offer public support to the American judicial reform agenda. It was the opening salvo of the private bar's political war on the MofJ, one of Japan's most stout redoubts of conservative nationalism.[22] So keen were the Tokyo lawyers to win this battle that they did not hesitate to be seen standing shoulder to shoulder with the foreign occupiers. It can be readily imagined that in taking this risk they fully expected that when push came to shove over court and judicial reform, the Americans would intervene decisively on their behalf.

So when, in February 1946, Rowell and Hussey began to compose constitutional provisions relating to the Japanese judiciary and its jurisdiction, they did so knowing that their ideas were likely to be endorsed by at least some Japanese jurists. With this confidence, then, their draft articles described an entirely new system of Japanese courts led by a potent Supreme Court armed with sweeping powers of judicial review. Under this new basic law, the judges of the regular courts, made secure in their tenure and institutional autonomy, would enjoy an exclusive prerogative to decide legal disputes involving individual rights and the constitutional legality of legislation and administrative action.[23]

So audacious were these proposals that they raised alarm even within the American camp.[24] Some of their colleagues in Government Section (GS), Charles Kades most prominently, worried that if fully implemented these proposals would turn the Supreme Court into a judicial oligarchy of scant democratic accountability.[25] In the end, Kades's concerns were allayed and most of the original proposals on judicial review were retained in the final American draft.[26] And while the Japanese government also had serious misgivings about these provisions, it did not spend political capital on their amendment.[27] From the American perspective, the ratified version of the new constitution still contained the basis of an unprecedentedly potent Supreme Court judiciary, one which established an American style supremacy of the Supreme Court in determining the "constitutionality of legislative and administrative acts."[28]

The statute containing the revised constitution of Japan was signed into law by Emperor Hirohito on November 3, 1946. The new constitution was slated to come into force on May 3, 1947. That left the Japanese government and its American overseers with just six months to revolutionize Japan's courts of law.

From the outset of the occupation, GS evinced a "can do" ethic that bordered on delusion. MacArthur, after all, had thought it plausible for a small and crudely trained group of Americans to draft a model constitution for a foreign nation-state in little more than a week. In carrying out this extraordinary order, GS lawyers did not shrink from concocting—for a nation-state with no previous experience of legal liberalism—one of the world's most expansive, verbose, and internally complex bills of rights. In the same vein, it was also not seen as doable in the space of a half year to help forge an entirely new system of courts equipped to fulfill an altogether novel role.

Neither MacArthur nor Courtney Whitney concerned himself with the technical details of legal reform in Japan. The task of putting institutional flesh on the bones of the new constitution, starting with the construction of a new courts and judiciaries, was delegated late in 1946 to the deputy-chief of GS, Charles Kades. In the last weeks of 1946, Kades, in turn, assigned the job to the newly organized Courts and Law subdivision of the section, a group staffed by a half-dozen American lawyers led, improbably enough, by a German born and trained jurist and former judge, Alfred C. Oppler.[29] In the typical fashion, Oppler, like most of his American colleagues, was wholly lacking in specialist training in Japanese or indeed any Asian laws or societies.[30] His inexpertise notwithstanding, Oppler was given what amounted to a blanket authorization to "democratize" Japan's judicial and courts systems.[31]

We have observed that it was one of the defining traits of American-led legal reconstruction projects in the postwar era that they were designed and executed mainly by American lawyers (Rowell, Hussey, Whitney, Kades, et al.) who before and during the Second World War had done little to equip them for the comprehensive reconstruction of a foreign nation's courts and judiciary. But even among all the accidental tourists of American-led and directed legal change, none had taken a more strange and circuitous route to power and influence than Alfred Oppler.

Born to German-speaking ethnic Jews in the Alsace in 1893, a baptized Protestant raised in Berlin, by the late 1920s Oppler had become a lawyer and then, in 1931, an associate justice of Germany's Supreme Administrative Court.[32] When the Nazis came to power in Germany in 1933, Oppler did not resign. Like many other ethnically Jewish opponents of the new regime, he had hoped that Hitler's regime would be short-lived. When this optimism proved misplaced, Oppler still did not resign, trusting that his being a Christian war veteran, married to a German gentile, might still shield him from persecution. In 1937, however, Oppler was first demoted then removed from the German judiciary.[33] No longer permitted to hold legal office, and after the *Kristallnacht* of November 1938 no longer safe, Oppler and his family left Germany for the United States just before the outbreak of war in Europe in the fall of 1939.

In America, Oppler learned English and sustained himself with a series of marginal employments until gaining some contract work with the federal government in Washington. When the Pacific war ended in August 1945, Oppler, still lacking secure employment, applied for a position with the legal department of the Supreme Command in Japan.[34] He was quickly hired on the basis that he was familiar with continental legal systems (like Japan's) and because, desperate for suitable employment, he was willing to leave his family to take a job halfway around the world. (To his recruiters, Oppler's ignorance of Japanese language, history, and politics was an asset.[35]) In this way and for these reasons Alfred Oppler—ethnic Jew, German jurist, naturalized refugee—became the principal site engineer in the reconstruction of the Japanese judiciary.

Oppler arrived in Japan in February 1946, a mature professional jurist who had firsthand experience of authoritarian and democratic regimes. In a number of important ways, Oppler made an ideal "occupationaire." He was intelligent without being intellectual. His lack of specialized training was offset by earnest dedication to duty. His avuncular maturity and unfailing decency and courtesy made him congenial to both American colleagues and Japanese counterparts.

Harsh historical experience had made Oppler a democratic pragmatist in his politics. He came to Japan believing that "a parliamentary democracy with a reasonable separation of powers and a system of checks and balances constituted the least imperfect form of government, in which the rule of law is guaranteed."[36] Although in his memoirs he referred to himself as a pioneer and missionary of democracy, his long and self-contradictory record of actions and omissions in occupied Japan verifies that Oppler was a man who might—or in circumstances might not—advance or uphold the precepts of liberal democracy and the rule of law.

There is another reason why Alfred Oppler might be regarded as the key American figure in the history of American-driven legal reform in occupied Japan. Not only had he been deeply engaged in law reform work, but he later became its most prolific American participant-historian.[37] To date of writing, Oppler's book-length treatment of American-supervised law reform in Japan, *Legal Reform in Occupied Japan,* a hybrid of memoir, reportage, and analysis, remains the single most comprehensive attempt to chronicle and vindicate SCAP efforts in the liberal legal reconstruction of Japan.[38] Just as Oppler was a key player in what he himself properly called the gigantic task of overseeing a series of rapid and radical changes to Japanese law and court structure after November 1946, he was also among its leading explicators, historians, and apologists.

In terms of their work on Japanese judges and courts, the memoirs of Oppler (and to a lesser degree those of his chief deputy, the Japanese-fluent American lawyer, Thomas Blakemore[39]) are united by a theme: that the work of the Courts and Law Division had been fundamentally successful in that it had induced the Japanese to execute the liberal reformation of their own judicial institutions.[40] Courts and Law had been successful, so the narrative went, because Oppler and his aides had self-consciously rejected as self-defeating a dictatorial and / or chauvinist approach to law and legal change in Japan. Eschewing any pat assumptions about the superiority of the Anglo-Saxon legal tradition or its transplantation to a legal system rooted in Asiatic and Continental traditions, Oppler and company (in Oppler's own words) "made tremendous efforts to understand the sociological and psychological aspects of Japan's society, its traditions and taboos" and on that basis to help craft legal changes that were compatible with Japan's unique history and culture.[41]

In this account, SCAP's goal had been to make useful and enduring improvements to the Japanese legal system. In Oppler's judgment, the only way to effect permanent reform in Japan was in persuading Japanese decision-makers to consent to change. In other words, when Oppler spoke of success in the legal democratization of Japan he meant success in stimulating Japanese jurists to liberalize their own law and legal practices. As Blakemore later summarized the point: "Neither Oppler nor I ever regarded ourselves as 'reformers' in the active sense. The role that we tried to follow was that of a truly minimal supervision of changes inevitably forced by the terms of the new Constitution."[42]

In his copious writings on his law reform work in Japan, Oppler never deviated from the thesis that the Japanese government, intact and operational during the entire occupation, had acted on its own volition in all matters of legal change including to its system of courts and adjudication.[43] In this view, the Japanese had been the authors of all new laws and legal institutions; Oppler's interventions were "advisory rather than obligatory."[44] In this spirit, Oppler and company had been the mentors[45] of postwar Japanese lawmakers, sources of "inspiration and advice"[46] as the Japanese themselves developed "genuinely Japanese solutions" to the problems presented by the new liberal-democratic constitution of that country.[47]

In Oppler's interpretation, one later reflected in the official history of GS, there had been cogent reasons why the Japanese legal elite had embraced a collaborative model of law reform in Japan.[48] One of course was that the model was based on respect for Japanese knowledge, competence, and agency. Another reason was that in 1946 and 1947 the Japanese legal elite broadly agreed with the sense and thrust of the American-sponsored legal reform program. In this view, MacArthur's bold intercession with the Japanese constitution had reactivated the legal elite's own long-standing (but suppressed) liberal modernization project.[49] The main reason why Japanese legal agencies had been "gratifyingly cooperative and open to progressive ideas" was that "for the last two decades before the war a strong reform movement had existed which advocated the modernization of the backward elements of the law." On this premise, Oppler described his work as "helping the Japanese implement the principles of *their* new constitution" (emphasis added).[50] This work had borne fruit because his Japanese counterparts understood and accepted that reformatory action was necessary.[51]

There was another reason to permit the Japanese to manage their own legal program: it maximized the chance that reforms would take hold and persist. As Oppler later put the point, he and his colleagues had been "guided by the deep conviction that no revision would survive the occupation unless the Japanese themselves could be persuaded that the new law . . . meant a real improvement."[52] The Japanese held an appropriate pride in their legal system and would not embrace any changes to it that were imposed on them by outsiders. As Blakemore advised the chief of GS, Courtney Whitney, "Externally imposed reforms may arouse hostility which will lead to repeal when the occupation period is over."[53] In the course of time, it became the official position of GS that the critically important legal reforms of 1946 and 1947, including the reconstruction of Japan's judiciary, had succeeded because the Japanese had done the hard work.

While there is no reason to doubt the sincerity of this account, especially of Oppler's personal contributions to it, there is reason to doubt its credibility. Like most of his American counterparts, Oppler, justly proud of what (and how) GS had accomplished in occupied Japan, his later accounts of this work tended to downplay the harder political facts of directed legal change in Japan. In regard to judicial reform, for instance, Oppler either softened or omitted altogether what his contemporary memoranda had often acknowledged: that many of Japan's leading postwar politicians in alliance with reactionaries in Japan's Ministry of Justice, had fervently and adroitly resisted American efforts in this arena.[54] In 1948, moreover, Oppler knew, but later seems to have forgotten, how during the early Cold War he and other American officials had actually abetted this resistance.

As we have noted, in its avowed commitments to the supremacy of law, separation of powers, civil libertarianism, judicial independence, and judicial review, the new constitution of Japan compelled the creation of a new and robust judiciary, one with complete organizational and functional independence.[55] The constitution promised what at least one Japanese journalist saw as an epoch-making change to this landscape.[56] "In the opinion of many persons," another Japanese newspaper opined, "the most outstanding features of the new Japanese constitution are those provisions which relate to the independence of the judiciary and the powers of the courts."[57] The new Supreme Court, armed with an elaborate bill of rights and powers to enforce it, was now to be relocated from the margins to the center of public life in Japan, and all this at a moment of unprecedented political discontinuity and uncertainty.

In its presurrender pattern, however, the Japanese judiciary bore almost no resemblance to the liberal archetype described in the new constitutional instrument. In that Japan, judges had been regarded mainly as career government bureaucrats, a group of low-status officials appointed, supervised, and controlled by the Justice Ministry.[58] In deciding public law cases, moreover, Japanese judges, most of them former prosecutors and legal civil servants, had been strongly disposed to vindicate the prerogatives of the state. "By virtue of their education and sociological background," Oppler later commented, "[judges in Japan] were primarily legal technicians—servants of the state rather than guardians of justice."[59] These traits had only intensified in the 1930s, as the militarists consolidated their dictatorship. As one of Tokyo's Bar Associations had averred in October 1945, the failure of the Japanese judiciary had been so complete that its complete reformation was the only workable option.[60]

When the new constitution was ratified in November 1946, GS had about six months to bring the Japanese systems of courts into line. The challenges were various and daunting. While the seven articles of the constitution dealing with the judiciary described the new powers and responsibilities of the reformed court system in broad strokes, they were unspecific about a number of important details, including the "number of Supreme Court judges, the organization of the inferior courts, the retirement age of all judges and the popular review of the appointment of Supreme Court judges."[61] Japanese officials were to complete the details in new legislation.

In Oppler's typically over-optimistic view, the silence of the constitution on specifics represented an opportunity for the Japanese government to supplement and strengthen the new judiciary.[62] From the point of view of Japanese conservatives in the MofJ, a group deeply skeptical of judicial review, however, this was an opportunity to weaken future judicial power and autonomy. It was too late for Japanese reactionaries to derail the new constitution, but not too late for them to embed mechanisms of control over the judges who would interpret and enforce it.

The Japanese general election of April 1946 resulted in a coalition government between two deeply conservative political parties, neither of which were sympathetic to liberal law reforms.[63] The new minister of justice, Tokutaro Kimura, was likewise an extreme conservative who worked with senior bureaucrats in the MofJ to try to curb or control the reform program.[64] This involved overcoming the alliance that had grown up between Oppler's Courts and Law Division and the not inconsequential number of Japanese legal officials—judges, lawyers, and civil servants—who strongly *supported* the new constitution and its promise of an independent judiciary.[65] The most important member of this liberal faction was a thirty-eight-year-old former judge, Yorihiro Naito.[66] For Oppler, Naito was the benevolent (if false) face of the Justice Ministry, a man who appeared to be "in full sympathy with [SCAP's] democratization efforts."[67]

The most important of Oppler's allies among the Japanese judges was Nagayohsi Hosono, the newly appointed chief justice or president of the unreformed Supreme Court of Japan. Just as the conservatives waged a covert campaign to maintain control over the composition, qualifications, and budget of the new Supreme Court, some liberal-minded Japanese jurists like Hosono worked with GS to defeat this maneuver.[68] That Minister Kimura bore an extreme personal and ideological animosity toward Hosono (he would later move to block Hosono's bid for a seat on the new Supreme Court) only made Oppler's task harder.[69]

At first, Oppler was very impressed by Hosono's reformist zeal, and how they saw "eye to eye with regard to the independence of the judiciary."[70] Oppler had been surprised and encouraged to find so cooperative a person among the senior Japanese judges. In the course of time, however, Hosono's always strong, sometimes overzealous commitment to radical reform became a source of misgiving.[71]

In Hosono's opinion, echoing the premise of GS, the "democratization of the judiciary is the essence of the democratization of Japan."[72] He strongly endorsed robust judicial review and its central role in the liberal-democratic state. Further to this conviction, however, Hosono believed that for judicial review to work in Japan it would be essential that judges and their institutions were fully insulated from political or bureaucratic interference. He also thought that the new court system of Japan, most especially the Supreme Court, needed highly competent judges willing to stand up to the feudalistic influence of the old guard.[73]

The surviving English language documents created by or about Hosono on these issues reflect fervent personal commitment to these principles. They also reflect Hosono's personal ambition to be a justice, perhaps chief justice, of the new Supreme Court. From bitter experience before and during the war period, Hosono had learned the high price to pay for being cast as the archenemy of the conservative-nationalist clique that had controlled the Japanese justice system.[74] Experience also had taught Hosono not to assume, as Oppler did, that the old guard would yield ground willingly and gracefully to American-backed reform. So when it became apparent to him in the late fall of 1946 that the conservative clique in the MofJ was mustering forces to capture the new Supreme Court, Hosono was moved to raise the alarm directly with Oppler and, on at least one occasion, General MacArthur himself.

In the final months of 1946, the most important item on the agenda of law reform was the seemingly banal Court Organization Law (COL), the Japanese legislation that would put flesh on the court-related bones of the new constitution. The COL was to settle such matters as the structure of the reformed court system and, crucially, the size, composition, selection, and governance of the new Supreme Court of Japan. This legislation would determine who might wield the enhanced powers of the Japanese judiciary and who might control, through budgetary and other mechanisms, those who wielded judicial power in the new Japan. For this reason, when the bill was still being drafted in the MofJ, it was the subject of a (mainly covert) struggle within the Japanese government and MofJ and between these entities and their American overseers.

Even Oppler's upbeat memoirs indicate that the promulgation of the COL was not a harmonious process. From the standpoint of Courts and Law, the first drafts of the bill contained a number of troubling features, including a special and extended retirement age for the chief justice (from seventy to seventy-five years) and a provision that would permit the MofJ to retain crucial budgetary powers over courts.[75] More significantly, however, still other aspects of the bill indicated that the ministry officials did not understand "the true meaning of judicial review by courts." Crucially in this regard, the latest draft of their bill set forth a constitutional reference that would limit occasions for judicial review by the Supreme Court.[76] In response, Oppler and Blakemore wanted the COL bill altered so that lower courts might also rule on constitutional questions.

As of November 1946, the Justice Ministry had not relented. In fact, the leaders of one Tokyo Bar Association (No. 1), were so much perturbed by the MofJ's intransigence on the COL that they were granted a meeting with Blakemore. The meeting was an occasion to protest many of the law's draft provisions, but "especially the retention by the Ministry of budgetary powers over courts and those provisions qualifying for judicial appointment various categories of administrative officials and university professors who have had no experience as practicing attorneys."[77] In the same month, Hosono, in his capacity as chief justice, took the unusual step of issuing a statement to the press, declaiming the provisions of the COL that would permit MofJ officials to direct and supervise the courts.[78]

In December, Oppler himself acknowledged that the draft COL still contained "a great number of deficiencies," including key sections governing the jurisdiction, rule-making authority, budget, and composition of the Supreme Court.[79] The clear imputation was that conservative elements within the MofJ were scheming to retain effective control over the high court. With his habitual understatement, Oppler's report to superiors conceded that some antagonism had arisen on these matters between Chief Justice Hosono and leading elements of the Yoshida government, most notably Yoshida's arch-conservative minister of justice and anti-Communist firebrand, Tokutaro Kimura.[80]

For more insight into the cause and extent of this antagonism, we are best to turn to a confidential letter communicated by back channels to Oppler early in January 1947. The author was Justice Toshiharu Chono, associated with the liberal-minded wing of the still unreformed

Supreme Court.[81] His letter warned that in the more than two years of occupation, SCAP's purge of "undemocratic elements" within the elite reaches of the legal system had scarcely begun. Chono further warned that influential members of Japan's justice system, including deeply entrenched ministry officials, prosecutors, and judges had "all their lives, gone in for undemocratic conduct . . . [and that] these people down in their hearts do not desire a democratization of the judicial system. They are acting in concert to prevent a reform of Japanese justice."[82] In Chono's candid opinion, "The present administration of justice in Japan is feudalistic, militaristic, nationalistic, bureaucratic." As for the minister of justice himself, Kimura, he was accused of "obstructing and thwarting the reform of the judicial system." In Chono's view, therefore, it was now urgently necessary for SCAP to intervene as fast as possible to rein in (what Justice Chono later called) Japan's "clique-ruled bureaucracy" at the MofJ.[83] "The few months that remain before the enforcement of the new constitution, Chono concluded, "are indeed of the greatest importance to the administration of justice."[84]

Given the silence of Oppler's memoir and surviving SCAP documentary record on Judge Chono's letter, or on Chief Judge Hosono's similarly revelatory communications, a plausible inference is that they had been disregarded. In the winter of 1947, Oppler and Blakemore continued to hold regular consultations with the very MofJ officials who had been the subject of Hosono's denunciations. Emboldened by support in the Yoshida government, more pertinently from Kimura, the officials were slow to move, sensing cracks in American resolve.

At this point, the Japanese guessed wrong. Oppler's group continued to find fault with the MofJ bill.[85] Allowed to stand, it believed, the bill would "prove a body-blow" to the legal accountability of state agencies in Japan.[86] In all, Oppler thought that the draft law was entirely out of keeping with the spirit of the new constitution. With time for its amendment running down, Oppler, eschewing his role as passive mentor, informed his counterparts in the MofJ that it was "absolutely essential" that they move swiftly to amend the bill in accordance with Government Section's expectations.[87]

To expedite the revision process, Oppler organized a special conference of senior American and MofJ officials. He pointedly insisted on the attendance of Japanese officials authorized "to give the point of view of the minister of justice." Oppler expressed hope that the meeting would resolve all outstanding issues concerning the courts bill. He also let it be known that if the conference did not result in a bill that complied with the constitution, he [Oppler] would invoke the Supreme Commander's authority to order them made.

While there is no record of the minutes of the March meeting, in the first days of April the Japanese delivered a revised COL bill that satisfied Courts and Law. The revised bill was passed into Japanese law on April 16, 1947, just over two weeks before the new constitution was to become operative. On paper, the COL denoted a major shift in the structure, mission, and control of Japan's justice system. It established a new hierarchy of trial and appellate courts with exclusive jurisdiction over legal disputes in Japan. It also signified the political and institutional liberation of judges and courts from the authority of the MofJ.

Crucially, moreover, the COL also settled most details concerning the composition and operation of the new Supreme Court of Japan. It established that the new highest court would be composed of a chief justice and fourteen associate justices, only ten of whom had to be lawyers.[88] Without doubt, this was a significant defeat for the conservatives, who had wanted to confine appointments to sitting judges.[89] Henceforth, the chief justice of the Supreme Court was to be appointed by the emperor on the binding advice of the cabinet.

Because of the "extreme importance of the choice of suitable personalities for the high position of a justice of the Supreme Court," SCAP insisted that the cabinet strike an advisory committee to assist in the selection of the chief justice and his associate justices.[90] That committee was to be comprised of "outstanding figures from public life rather than political appointees." The chief justice and associate justices were to enjoy security of tenure, subject only to public impeachment or recall by vote of the national electorate. The COL reinforced the power of the Supreme Court both to engage in judicial review of government legislation and make the rules governing litigation before the courts. Not unimportantly, the law also protected the Court's budget from politically motivated interference.[91] In the end, the MofJ capitulated but unmistakably not because its leaders had become enthusiasts of legal liberalism. Their distemper would be more telling in due course.

For the time being, however, the Supreme Court of Japan now had an American-style political character, having the legal and institutional power to enforce the rule of law in Japan. The Court was now empowered, on the basis of cogent pleadings, to regulate or even nullify the unconstitutional actions of legislators, executive officials, and the other agents of state. The COL, as Oppler himself reported to higher-ups, was "designed to increase tremendously the prerogatives and prestige of the Supreme Court as the apex of the judicial branch of government."[92] What Oppler did not say was that the COL had, in effect, been designed and installed by Americans to achieve this end.

But Oppler was fully aware that the ratification of the constitution, even the passage of an accommodating COL, did not guarantee that it would precipitate concrete changes in how the courts actually operated. "Whether and to what extent the objectives behind these provisions will materialize," Oppler conceded in a report to Whitney, "depends mainly on the willingness and ability of those persons who will be in charge of judicial administration, that is to say, of the Supreme Court themselves." Oppler was equally emphatic on this point at a press conference held in April 1947. "The highest tribunal," he reminded Japanese reporters, "may invalidate any law, ordinance, or official act and order contrary to the principles of the Constitution. . . . Much depends upon the spirit in which the judges will perform this function. For that reason the selection of able and independent personalities to the highest bench is of paramount importance and demands the full attention of the people."[93] These remarks proved prescient.

The next pivotal battleground, therefore, was the selection of the first Supreme Court bench of the new era.[94] Even before the final draft of the COL was passed by the Diet, the clash over appointments to the Court already had begun in earnest. In this regard, for instance, through Oppler the Tokyo Bar Association (No. 1) sent a petition to

GS, contending that the democratization of the judiciary absolutely required the appointment of "learned and experienced men of superiority among the lawyers" to positions on the appellate benches, including to the Supreme Court.[95] After all, more than any other group of Japanese jurists, the Tokyo lawyers contended, the private bar had "fought for . . . the rights, liberty and welfare of the people." If liberal reforms were to come to fruition, it would be due largely to the private bar's interventions on behalf of individual clients.

But whatever Oppler and his superiors at GS thought about the appointments issue, Japanese conservatives in the new cabinet and at the MofJ were not ready to concede the field to the private bar or any other rival group. As Oppler himself knew well, the old-guard bureaucrats at the ministry had not been "much affected by the purge" and most were "basically opposed to reforms which might result in weakening of the controls of the Ministry over the judiciary."[96] While structural change was now an inalterable fact, the senior bureaucrats might still curb reform by packing the new court with men who, in Oppler's own words, "would be expected to carry out the objectives of the new Constitution in a lukewarm way and in compliance with ministerial wishes."

Oppler was fully apprised of this threat if only because Chief Justice Hosono and his circle provided him with a steady stream of credible intelligence to this effect. On April 11, 1947, for instance, one member of the circle, Justice Kotaro Tanaka, alleged that the Yoshida cabinet, ahead of the general election scheduled for April 25, had begun to provide assurances to conservative justices of the war era that they would have appointments to the new Supreme Court. In a letter sent directly to Kades, Tanaka warned that the "bureaucrats of the Justice MofJ and the judges and lawyers who belong to the group of present Minister of Justice Kimura . . . are trying to monopolize the important positions of the court under the new constitution."[97] Tanaka further warned that "Japan's democratization is almost hopeless if she does not succeed in the reform of the judiciary."

Meanwhile, on April 16, the Yoshida cabinet, following up on proposals made months before, struck a new consultative committee of experts to create a list of names of potential appointees to the new

Supreme Court.[98] After he rejected the government's politician-heavy initial list of committee members, Oppler endorsed a subsequent list of eleven committee members that included four judges, three private lawyers, two legal academics, and two members of the Diet. The committee was chaired by Chief Justice Hosono.[99] From the outset, the committee's meetings were so acrimonious, sometimes openly confrontational—this is to say, so strikingly un-Japanese—that there can be no doubting the high stakes involved.

When the consultative committee finally convened, Hosono tried to use his authority as chair to draw out and corner his many determined enemies.[100] On opening the first session he announced that for future reference he wanted the committee to establish certain procedural rules for future Supreme Court appointment committees. He wanted minutes to be taken. Before the rules were firmly laid down, he wanted to invite experts to address the committee on how appointments were made to the highest courts in Anglo-Saxon jurisdictions.

Minutes were taken, and they clearly indicate that the other members of the committee were having none of Hosono or his proposals.[101] They greeted the chief justice with open contempt, rejecting out of hand the idea that they should be subjected to "lectures on American and English laws." While Hosono wanted to discuss theory, the other members of the committee wanted to get down to brass tacks. They pressed the chief justice to provide lists of potential appointees, the less talk the better. When Hosono persisted with the idea that the committee should agree on ideal qualifications for the new Supreme Court he was denounced as negligent and shameful. Not one other committee member endorsed Hosono's approach. They had not come prepared to let Hosono tilt the table in favor of his own candidates.

The first meeting ended in turmoil; nothing decided except to reconvene the next day. At the beginning of this equally contentious second meeting, Hosono asserted, "The preparation of the new Supreme Court should be substantially undertaken by the former Supreme Court and should not be performed . . . by the bureaucrats in the present Justice Ministry." He seized the occasion to denounce the wartime MofJ and judiciary for its unwillingness to confront

General Tojo and the militarists when they encroached on the legal system. When the committee members moved again to establish short lists of candidates, Hosono again tried to slow down the process. It was not until a third meeting, on April 25, that the committee finally voted on the lists.

In the aftermath, Hosono then took the extraordinary step of writing directly to MacArthur about how the reactionaries on the committee had "desecrated their appointed task" in a concerted effort to dominate appointments to the Supreme Court.[102] The committee had capitulated to "corrupt influences" in nominating men for the highest judicial appointment, often members of the committee itself, who were demonstrably unfit to fulfill the mission set for judges under the new constitution.[103]

There is no evidence that MacArthur took any direct action on the matter. It is known that in a report to Whitney on April 30, Oppler acknowledged that the bureaucracy in the MofJ, along with its friends in the Yoshida cabinet, was working covertly to pack the new Supreme Court with other conservatives. If the new Court was to fulfill its intended role under the constitution, Oppler thought, it was important that they did not prevail. If court reform was to take hold in Japan, the first chief justice of the new Supreme Court would need to "establish and maintain a judiciary completely independent of the Ministerial bureaucracy."[104] This candidate also would need to be "deeply convinced of the necessity of a fundamental transformation of Japan into a democratic society." In Oppler's view, the best man on the scene was none other than Hosono, a man known to be of impeccable liberal convictions who had led a "well-nigh singlehanded fight against the endeavor of the Justice Ministry to keep its power and influence over the judiciary."

But Oppler also acknowledged that it was unlikely that Hosono, however much he was respected by GS, would now be selected even as an associate justice of the new Supreme Court. In fact, Oppler's confidential sources revealed that Hosono had been very roughly handled, even smeared, by a conservative alliance on the cabinet's consultative committee, so much so that his name did not appear on either of the final lists of possible associate justices or chief justices.[105] The final lists, Oppler conceded, had been manipulated to favor conservative judges. In fact, a judge called Kamamori, an old-guard conservative and second-rate jurist who had worked in Japanese-occupied Asia during the war, was now in line to get the appointment as first chief justice of democratic Japan.

Perhaps understandably, Oppler's report did not explicitly state, but unmistakably implied, that the hands-off policy of his Court and Law section had been an abject failure, that the judicial appointment process had now been hijacked by the old guard. This was so patently clear that, on April 24, MacArthur stepped in to order the cabinet not to make appointments to the Supreme Court until after the general election. This meant that the new constitution would come into effect on May 3, before appointments had been made to the new Supreme Court.

Courts and Law dealt with this embarrassment by cobbling together an interim Supreme Court (led by Hosono) from the former court, thus to avoid a complete vacuum of constitutional adjudication until the elections were held and a new government formed. The infighting between Hosono's faction on the old Court and Kimura's conservative clique at the MofJ continued unabated, even when in May the socialist Tetsu Katayama formed a new coalition government, replacing Kimura with a new minister of justice, Yoshio Suzuki. One of Suzuki's first actions was to form a new eleven-person advisory panel staffed exclusively with judges, lawyers, and legal academics, but no MofJ bureaucrats, to work up a list of nominees to the Supreme Court.[106]

Doubting the willingness of Suzuki to rein in the Justice clique, in the spring and summer of 1947, the Hosono faction continued to press its case for a shake-up. In July, Justice Chono took the unprecedented step of publishing an open letter in the Japanese newspapers condemning the MofJ for maneuvering covertly to "maintain the superiority of executive power" over the new Supreme Court and appointments thereto.[107] The letter warned the public that, in the absence of public pressure, the new cabinet's judicial appointment committee might pass over men of "unyielding independent spirit."

According to Oppler, however, there was no reason for concern. By late July, the reconstituted cabinet advisory committee on appointments to the Supreme Court had compiled an "excellent choice of the best legal brains of Japan."[108] Few of the 139 candidates on the master list were either ministerial bureaucrats (four) or procurators (eight). Oppler informed Whitney that the minister of justice himself had been pleased to offer that "no outstanding figure of legal practice and science was omitted." Although objections could be raised against "one or the other persons included on the list," none were, by Oppler's forgiving lights, so objectionable to justify an official veto on the part of SCAP. Oppler was thus inclined to give the cabinet the go-ahead to select a short list of thirty jurists. It remained Oppler's belief that GS should not deviate from its attitude of neutrality as the cabinet's consultative committee neared its final recommendations on Supreme Court appointments.[109]

Oppler's cheerful optimism about the appointments process is more than passing strange, however, given that Chief Justice Hosono, a man that Oppler had recently backed as candidate for chief justice of the new Court, most definitely did not share this viewpoint. According to a letter sent by the chief justice to Prime Minister Katayama, liberal members of the legal professions, most prominently the judges (like Hosono himself) who had stood up to the militarists, had been largely excluded from the short list.[110] On the other hand, Hosono named seven judges, all of whom had made the long list, who had "prostrated themselves to pander to Tojo" during the war years. The cliques that had dominated the MofJ and high-court benches for so long, instead of having been broken up, had become more powerful than before.

In the last week of July, cabinet and Justice Ministry committees had prepared a new draft of the COL.[111] By the end of July, they had also compiled a short list of thirty potential appointees to the new Supreme Court. Final decisions on the composition of the first Supreme Court under the new constitution were imminent. These decisions, the *Nippon Times* pronounced, were to have a far-reaching influence on the nation's history.[112] And because of the new and potent powers of the new Court, it was "not enough that the first democratic

SC should be composed of competent and upright judges; it is essential as well that they possess a prophetic and creative confidence in the future destiny of the nation."

But even at the eleventh hour, alarm bells were being rung. Of the short list of thirty names, no fewer than six had themselves been members of the cabinet's advisory committee. (In fact, only one extremely elderly member of that committee failed to make the original short list.) This fact did not sit well with at least eight members of the Tokyo Bar Association, men who felt moved enough to register their dissent in a letter to MacArthur.[113] The signatories registered their emphatic opposition to what appeared to them to be a repetition of the cronyism that had continued to plague Japan's judiciary even during Yoshida's postwar government. "For the sake of Japan's democracy and for the sake of the prestige of the SC," the Tokyo lawyers declared, "they [the short-listed advisory committee members] must be excluded."

By this point, however, neither the new government nor SCAP was very interested in reasons to tolerate further delay in the appointment of the new Supreme Court. Announced on August 2, formally installed two days later, the new Court was to be headed by Chief Justice Tadahiko Mibuchi, a sixty-eight-year-old former judge and cartel lawyer who when he himself was a judge, according to the *Nippon Times,* had "taken care to avoid forming cliques."[114] This record, and his reputation as a "fair and non-factious character," had earned "the almost unanimous support of the bar, the Kimura faction and the Hosono faction of the [old] Supreme Court." It did not seem to matter to the advisory committee or, in the end, to GS, that Mibuchi was a civil law and trusts lawyer with no expertise in constitutional law. Furthermore, since his retirement from the bench in 1925 until 1940, far from having established a liberal pedigree, Mibuchi had acted as chief counselor for the large Mitsui conglomerate, a position that made him vulnerable to the American purge directive.[115]

Mibuchi had not been the first choice of either American officials or the advisory committee. At least two persons who had been approached to let their names stand for the position of chief justice turned down the overture.[116] There were reasons not to accept an appointment, meager pay (compared to private practice), a crushing workload, and poor working conditions being prominent among them.[117] With an enormous backlog of cases, with altogether unprecedented cases in the offing, the lot of a Supreme Court justice in the new Japan was not going to be an easy one.

Although Mibuchi was a compromise candidate for chief justice, it was a compromise that tilted strongly toward the conservative right. And so it was, too, with the selection of associate justices. If they did not succeed in getting appointments for all of their allies, the conservatives at the MofJ did succeed in blocking Hosono and two other leading liberal jurists.[118] Conversely, six candidates associated with conservative factions had been given associate appointments to the new Court.[119] Two of the new justices—Hachiro Fujita and Saburo Iwamatsu—had undertaken official legal duties in military-occupied China.[120]

By the end of the summer of 1947, after an elaborate ceremony in the presence of the emperor, Japan had instituted a new Supreme Court, one that, as American officials boasted, "differed completely from the old Supreme in structure, composition and functions."[121] As a consequence of nearly two years of intense negotiation and open and covert conflict, the position and prestige of the Japanese courts, but especially the Supreme Court, on paper, had been strengthened tremendously.

By the same token, Government Section was aware that changes on paper, whether to the trial or appellate courts, or to the Supreme Court, were not the stuff of authentic change in patterns of litigation and judicial decision-making. Indeed, evidence was already mounting that since the beginning of the occupation the kind and quality of justice in occupied Japan, especially in criminal cases, had worsened. In 1946 and 1947, the rise of organized crime combined with the impoverishment of the country's judges and prosecutors caused an epidemic of corruption in the criminal courts.[122] By December 1947, Legal Section was receiving reports of irregularities in criminal litigation, those involving organized crime figures in particular, from all over Japan.[123]

In the highly publicized Ozu case, for instance, a notorious Tokyo gangster and black-market operator, facing a long list of serious charges, was inexplicably released on bail.[124] The decision, taken in September 1947, was widely condemned in the Japanese press. When the Japanese Supreme Court was slow to exercise its supervisory function, Government Section summoned three justices of the Court (absent Chief Justice Mibuchi, then ill) to a conference at SCAP headquarters.

What ensued was not one of Legal Section's moments of friendly and respectful collaboration, but a demeaning dressing-down of insubordinate "natives" by the conqueror foreigner.[125] In an unusual move, one meant to underline Government Section's serious displeasure and dominant authority, Kades attended the meeting and did most of the talking.

He opened the meeting by reminding the justices "that the judiciary, under the new Constitution, was an independent body with an important responsibility for safe-guarding the Constitution and the laws of the land."[126] Since constitutional reform, Kades added, the judges of Japan were now answerable only to "their conscience and bound only by the Constitution and the laws." This meant that "no man is more important than the law, whether Ozu or a judge." It was an unacceptable state of affairs, therefore, that it was being "openly said in Tokyo that Ozu is more powerful than the courts or procurators." The obvious miscarriage of justice in the Ozu case threatened to undermine the rule of law in Japan before it had been properly established. In GS's view, something had to be done.

In this regard, Kades left the justices with a choice: the Supreme Court could take responsibility for the investigation and possible impeachment or defer to SCAP.[127] For the purposes of its independence and prestige, Kades thought it more advisable that the Supreme Court take on the tasks. According to the American account, all three justices agreed that this was the best course.

The matter was not left there. Five days later, on September 17, 1947, Chief Justice Mibuchi himself met Kades at SCAP-HQ.[128] Mibuchi reported that his Court had decided to open an investigation of the Ozu case. In the interim, the original procurator in the case had been "transferred" and Ozu's bail revoked.[129] The chief justice assured Kades that "to maintain the independence of the judiciary system," his Court was "trying to do everything possible ignoring the outside political pressure."[130] Kades expressed satisfaction that the chief justice and his Court had taken bold measures to establish that "all people will be equal under the law."

In the course of 1948, however, the crisis of public (and SCAP) confidence in Japan's courts only worsened, the corruption of judges and procurators becoming even more widespread and brazen.[131] Despite the interventions of the Supreme Court, the Ozu case had still not been resolved in the spring of 1948, Ozu having used all legal and, it was suspected, extralegal means to postpone a reckoning.[132] By this time, too, the Supreme Court itself was riven by dissension and recrimination.[133] To exacerbate an already dire legal and political climate, in the fall of 1948, the Showa Denko scandal hit the newspapers, leading to the resignation of the government.[134] The case nakedly exposed the fact that corruption (orchestrated in this case by a large corporation) had penetrated the highest reaches of the Japanese state, including its trial and appellate courts.

By the close of 1948, an even more intense political and ideological conflict was brewing. Although the Supreme Court had begun to use its powers of judicial review powers, in this regard it had gotten off to a very rocky start.[135] Public confidence (and, behind the scenes, SCAP's confidence) in the ability of the new judiciary to foster and defend liberal legal modernity in Japan was not high. Certainly there was plenty of room to doubt that the court system would, or even could, safeguard the constitutional rights of the Japanese in the context of a state and SCAP-sponsored crackdown on Japan's leftist activists.

In Nazis We Trust: Reconstituting the German Judiciary, 1945 to 1947

We have seen that due to the overlapping jurisdictions of the Allied Control Authority and American Military Government (AMG) in the U.S. zone, court and judicial reform in Germany, like all legal reform, was pursued on two trajectories. Under the Potsdam Agreement, German legal reform on a country-wide basis fell to the quadpartite Legal Directorate (DLeg) of the Allied Control Council (ACC).

Potsdam provided that the German national system of courts and adjudication was to remain closed until it had been "reorganized in accordance with the principles of democracy, of justice under law, and of equal rights for all citizens without distinction of race, nationality or religion."

In October 1945, the ACC issued a general proclamation setting forth certain fundamental principles for the reorganization of the German judicial system.[136] This document affirmed the collective resolve of the four powers to establish in Germany a "new democratic judicial system based on the achievements of democracy, civilization and justice." The reformed system was to be based on the twin tenets of equality before the law and due process of law. In the new German courts, judges were to dispense justice without regard to race, nationality, or religion. In the criminal field the aspiration was for speedy and public trials before judges and courts independent from executive control and obedient only to the law.[137] With regard to personnel, the Allies agreed that German courts were to be purged of "all former members of the Nazi Party who have been more than nominal participants in its activities and all those who directly followed the punitive practices of the Hitler regime must be dismissed from appointments as judges and prosecutors."[138] The purge was viewed as an essential prerequisite of any meaningful democratization of Germany.

The second path to court and judicial reform in Germany were programs developed by Allied powers unilaterally within their exclusive zones of occupation.[139] In the U.S. zone, planning in this field had begun in the War Department in the winter of 1944, focused mainly on the denazification of German court personnel. This work culminated in April 1945, the Joint Chiefs of Staff directing American commanders controlling captured German territory to exclude from judicial office, "All members of the Nazi party who have been more than nominal participants in its activities" as well as "all active supporters of Nazism or militarism."[140] Commanders were also directed to proclaim the immediate abolition of Nazi-era Special Courts and tribunals.[141] The German court system in occupied areas were to be closed and remain closed until completely cleansed of all Nazi features and personnel. Only then might some local courts be reopened under American supervision and control.[142]

The pace and content of court and judicial reform in the U.S. zone were strongly affected by General Clay's decision late in 1945 to move expeditiously to devolve some legal and political functions to German control.[143] We have seen that it became Clay's firm resolve that, by the close of 1946, each of the American Länder was to have functioning legislatures elected on a broad franchise and operated according to German-drafted and ratified liberal-democratic constitutions.[144] The general's policy was for German "ordinary" courts,[145] criminal and civil, to be reopened as soon as enough courtrooms and (denazified) judges and prosecutors could be found.[146]

From the outset of the occupation, however, best-informed insiders (Karl Loewenstein was but one) knew that there would be no authentic reconstitution of the German judiciary until it was comprehensively denazified. Insiders also knew that such denazification was certain to be a long and arduous task.

These perceptions were rooted in some general and, in the American camp, mostly uncontradicted readings of German judicial history before and during the Third Reich. The premise here was that as a body the German judiciary was instinctively and intensely antidemocratic, statist, and nationalistic, traits that had been unsubtly displayed during the Weimar republic. In a series of notorious political cases in that era, German judges had used judicial power to at once protect the far right and undermine the democratic order.[147] During the Third Reich, even more damningly, most German judges had remained in their offices.[148] Nazi and non-Nazis jurists had accommodated themselves and justice to blatantly racist and often lawless government.[149] In the war years especially, German judges were seen as having become complicit in state-sponsored campaigns of terror and judicial murder.[150] As Loewenstein opined to Fahy in September 1945, in the Nazi era the German courts had helped sustain a regime "which programmatically . . . trampled underfoot the rule of law and justice under law."[151] This was the timber from which Americans were now to build a new and liberal-democratic judicial branch.

This historical record, and the misgivings inspired by it, was invested with far more importance by German experts like Loewenstein than political decision-makers like the commander of AMG, Lucius Clay. Ignoring or overruling cautions and caveats, the general brought the same, perhaps more, urgency to court and judicial reactivation as he did to constitutional reform. One reason for Clay's resolve was the escalating crisis in 1946 of public order in the U.S. zone.[152] The miasmic social, economic, and moral climate in south Germany—in its bombed-out, overcrowded, and hungry cities especially—had spawned a veritable plague of interpersonal and commercial crime, one that had quickly overwhelmed the capacity of American military courts to cope. There were still other sources of extreme legal distress in the zone. The death or disappearance during the war of tens of thousands of south Germans, soldiers and civilians alike, had created an enormous backlog of pressing probate, divorce, and commercial cases. For these pressing reasons and more, Clay was urged to reactivate local criminal, civil, and even appellate courts.[153]

But the urgent need for the reactivation of German courts in the U.S. zone could not change the fact that in 1946 very few German judges had passed through a denazification process. Even more troublingly, as we have seen, best available intelligence indicated that most German judges of the Nazi-era, far from being ready to assume roles in a liberal-democratic constitutional framework, adhered to the mindset and rationalizations of the Third Reich.

In the early fall of 1945, during a trip to interview jurists in Bremen, Loewenstein encountered what he later characterized as the stock postwar narrative of the Nazi-era judges.[154] The story began with what could not be denied: that in response to Hitler and the Nazi program, most judges had not resigned, not even when Jews and dissenters were mercilessly persecuted. Instead, most judges had remained in their courts, joined the Nazi Party, and had applied hideous laws, even if (as they reported) always with reluctance and distaste. As the stock exculpation went, German judges had stayed on the bench, not from ideological or selfish motives, but because they had "hoped to temper the blow of the Nazi system." The Nazi-era judges had done their utmost to defend the last remnants of the *rechtsstaat.*

Strikingly absent from these exculpations were references, remorseful or otherwise, to the elimination of German Jews, first from the legal profession then from German society as a whole.[155] While aware of this and "other crude illegalities of the regime," Loewenstein's judicial interviewees were more apt to dwell on their own grievances and anxieties, especially their fear that the Allies might banish from the legal professions all who joined the Nazi Party before 1937. One senior judge, a man who had been temporarily reinstated by AMG-Bremen, opined that "hardly more than one dozen" of his region's 400 professional jurists (in 1945) could *justly* be purged as former Nazis. Warming to his subject, the man argued for the reinstatement of a judge who in the course of his judicial duties during the war had "signed no fewer than 42 death sentences."

In Loewenstein's view, one expressed to his superiors at Legal Division, the exculpations and denials of German judges were symptomatic of a more widespread malaise. The Germans as a whole, he believed, had emerged from the Third Reich in a state of collective disassociation from Hitler, Nazism, and its crimes. Indeed, they tended to see *themselves* as victims. As the scholar Marianne Weber (Max Weber's widow) commented during a meeting with Loewenstein, the Germans had not and would not repent for the crimes of the Third Reich because they "could not see beyond their own suffering."[156]

These dispiriting contacts with German judges reinforced Loewenstein's determination to oppose the proposal, floated at Legal Division in the fall of 1945, that AMG should move quickly to reopen German local and regional courts across the U.S. zone. Loewenstein's advice was that there were compelling reasons to postpone these actions, at least until the Legal Directorate (DLeg) of the ACC had completed its work on the denazification and rehabilitation of the German judiciary on a national basis.

When DLeg began to deliberate in August 1945, among the top items on its agenda was the construction of a program, pursuant to Potsdam, designed to achieve "justice under law" in occupied Germany.[157] A fundamental feature of this program was the reconstruction of the German courts and judiciary. In mid-September, all four national representatives submitted draft proclamations on the reorganization of the judicial system in Germany. After discussion, the delegates agreed to adopt the Soviet proposal to restore the Weimar-era structure of German local and regional courts. The delegates also agreed, in the absence of specific definitions, that "The system of German courts is to be reorganized on the basis of the principles of democracy, legality and equality in law of all citizens."[158]

In September, both the American and British delegations submitted memoranda purporting to educate the Germans on how judicial reorganization fit within a broader conception of the proper function of lawyers, judges, and courts in a constitutional state. For their part, the British strongly contended, Fahy in agreement, that any nationwide law for the reorganization of the German courts should be preceded by a law that would "tell the German legal profession and people the broad principles" on which such reform would be founded.[159]

Although the British and American statements of these principles were not identical, both were based implicitly on an ideologically liberal reading of the law-related provisions of the Potsdam Agreement.[160] Their common precept was that the democratic legal system required that all persons should have inviolable legal rights as against the state, these to be vindicated by judges and courts independent of political authority. And when the state deigned to act against the merely contingent rights of persons, moreover, it might do so only by recourse to preestablished law and due process of law.

In describing the traits of the liberal-democratic legal system, the British and American memoranda referred to the critical importance of selection and admission criteria based entirely on individual merit, without regard to racial origins, wealth, or social status. The memorandum also laid down that the transition from authoritarianism denoted the "reduction of the power of the state" and the "restoration to accused persons of due legal process," here defined as the presumption of innocence, the right not to be convicted by *ex post facto* law, to retain independent counsel, and rights of appeal.

From the American standpoint, these formulations were not just ideals but calls to action. In the fourth general meeting of DLeg, Fahy contended that the reconception and then reconfiguration of the German legal system along liberal lines was "the most important aspect of the work of the Legal Directorate as it was one of the few cases where the Control Council could take positive as opposed to negative action."[161] But here, lest the deliberations veered toward a candid showing of cards, high-minded talk gave way to diplomatic reality. All parties knew that the French would veto any proposal that tended to reconstitute Germany's central state institutions. They also knew that the Soviets were not going to stand by, even during the honeymoon period of quadpartite government, as the American-British alliance in effect wrote a liberal prescription for the reconstruction of the German legal system. The solution, then, was for the delegations to agree to a statement of fundamental principles so vague and ill-defined that all could agree, that is, to something and nothing at the same time.

Accordingly, in the fourth and fifth plenary meetings of DLeg, the Americans and British tabled a proposal for two new laws on German court reorganization, one which spelled out the "fundamental unchanging principles, and a law dealing with details [about German courts] which might be subject to changes."[162] These principles were so vaguely drawn that even the Soviet delegate agreed to endorse them. The Soviet delegate also agreed that the proclamation should protect the independence of judges from executive control. The final document, approved unanimously, reflected only minor changes to the original British draft of what, on October 20, 1945, was passed by the ACC as Proclamation No. 3, "Fundamental Principles of Judicial Reform." By this proclamation, the four powers laid down the structural basis of the new democratic judicial system in Germany.

The five articles of the proclamation purported to guarantee that the reformed German court system would treat all persons as equals before the law. It guaranteed that no person would be subject to a state-based sanction except by due process of law. The proclamation guaranteed access to judicial office without discrimination based on race, social origins, or religion and the independence of the courts from executive control. The Nazi Special Courts of the Third Reich were formally and comprehensively abolished. Ten days later the Control Council passed Law No. 4, which restored the basic structure of the German system as of 1877 and the jurisdiction of those courts as it stood prior to the Nazis coming to power in 1933. The law set out the exceptions to this jurisdiction, these mainly involving offences and actions against the Allied Military Government and command and its members.

The fourth article also set forth some general rules regarding the denazification of the German judiciary. In keeping with the Potsdam Agreement, it banned from reappointment to the bench all members of the Nazi Party "who have been more than nominal participants in its activities." Significantly, and on Soviet urging, the four powers agreed that the ban would also extend to Nazi-era judges "who directly followed the punitive practices of the Hitler regime."[163]

With the passage of Proclamation No. 3 and Law No. 4, Charles Fahy was in a position to claim another (ostensible) success. The main legislative pillars of the Third Reich had been removed. Its system of political Special Courts had been abolished. Under his chairmanship, the four powers had agreed on a statement of general principles that would guide future law reform. They also had agreed on a set of compulsory criteria for the denazification of the German judiciary that, by the Americans at least, were more honored in the breach.

But before the ink was dry on these proclamations, observers in Legal Division (Karl Loewenstein only most critically) were already aware that American policy on denazification, especially regarding the judiciary, was being constructed on two irreconcilable propositions. First, German local and regional appellate courts were to be reopened on an urgent basis in all of the American Länder. Second, Germans should take the lead on the identification and appointment of non-Nazi or denazified judges. Toward these goals, by October 1945 AMG had appointed a German minister of justice in each regional state. It was then to be the responsibility of the ministers to reopen local and regional courts that, crucially, were staffed by judges and prosecutors who were not disqualified under the Control Council's appointment criteria.

The reappointment process did not begin in the zone until the winter of 1946.[164] But when the Courts and Law department of Legal Division began to actually scrutinize these appointments, Nazi worms began to emerge from the apple. Due to haste, gullibility, and shortages of untainted candidates, local detachments of AMG had reinstated judges before they could be adequately screened. As one American officer noted in the fall of 1945, "We are failing to arrest many who should, by this time, have been arrested, and, what disturbs them even more, we are accepting and endorsing for public offices many known Nazis."[165] In fact, the appointment of former Nazis in reopened courts had become so pervasive that, in the opinion of one senior officer, some AMG administrators had been "'softened up' by the Germans and are losing sight of what a Nazi was and of the aim of the Allies to completely eliminate Nazism."[166]

Once set in motion early in 1946, the process of devolving control over judicial appointments to German officials quickly gained momentum. In fact, by the spring of 1946, most judicial appointments were being made by German Ministers of Justice in the Länder.[167] In theory, AMG's Legal Division was vetting these appointments, ensuring that no appointments contravened denazification criteria. In reality, it was apparent to open-eyed Americans that these criteria were being sidestepped by the Germans. Former Nazis, some with deeply disquieting records, were regaining places in German courts all over the zone. Much more disconcertingly to critics of these developments, Loewenstein among them, was that some of the former Nazis judges had not shed authoritarian habits of thought.

A case heard in December 1945 by a tribunal of three ("allegedly politically reliable") reappointed judges illustrates the point.[168] In that case, a deserter from the German army, a man who had left his ranks late in the war on grounds of conscientious objection, entreated the court to vacate the court-martial's conviction and capital sentence. The Bremen court, while commuting the death sentence, upheld the soldier's conviction on the merits of German military law.[169]

For Loewenstein, as for a number of north German newspapers, the Bremen deserter case exemplified a number of very disturbing trends.[170] Of the more than forty judges and prosecutors who had been appointed to legal offices during the occupation, only two had *not* been members of the Nazi Party. On inspection of their actual judgment in the deserter case, it was obvious to Loewenstein that the tribunal had reverted to the same rigid and amoral judicial positivism (that desertion must be interpreted without regard to social or moral context) that he believed characterized justice during the Third Reich. These "allegedly democratic judges," Loewenstein observed, had demonstrated beyond doubt that their judicial outlook still was "entangled in the traditional concepts of German militarism."

When he commented on the Bremen case in his diary in late December 1945, Loewenstein had been at work for Legal Division's Justice Ministry branch for five months. In that time he had watched as the Americans began to release their grip on denazification and German politics. Now he watched, with increasing dread, as German officials in the Länder began to reinstate to important legal offices the same men who only a year before had dispensed Nazi justice—the same men who had sent scores of men and women to the guillotine for political crimes, the same men who one after another had categorically denied the slightest culpability for the state-sanctioned abominations of the Third Reich.

For these reasons, Loewenstein felt moved to make a series of communications to the director of Legal Division, Charles Fahy, warning that the decision rendered in the Bremen deserter case was the thin edge of a wedge. Not only were Nazis being restored to the postwar bench in the zone but so too were their authoritarian habits of thought. In the Bremen case, Loewenstein saw the first portents that, just as they had done in the 1920s, the German judges would use their power to sabotage the liberal reconstruction of German law.[171] "This time," he wrote, "it starts early and there is no excuse that there was not a purge of the bench."

As the number of similar cases grew, Loewenstein's memoranda emphasized that "the decisions of the German courts have to be reviewed in order to prevent relapse into the anti-democratic habits as occurred after 1918."[172] At the end of January, with denazification soon to be turned over to German tribunals, Loewenstein confronted Fahy with what he saw as the hard facts of the matter: "I told [him] that denazification had slipped out of our hands and we had better admit failure. Under the new plan, 95% of the Nazis will slip through."[173] It was imperative, therefore, that "machinery be developed which would permit checking by Military Government on the activities of the courts . . . there will be an urgent need to find out what they are doing."

By winter of 1946, General Clay having resolved to accelerate the Germanification of law and government in the zone, Loewenstein's warnings on the judiciary, like those on constitutional reform, fell on deaf ears. No action was taken on his recommendations, even as evidence continued to mount, this time in the context of the so-called denunciation cases, that German judges continued to adhere to Nazi-era legal norms.

The denunciation cases involved the prosecution of persons, mainly German nationals, who during the Nazi period (most commonly during the war years) had instigated the prosecution of other Germans for alleged transgressions against the Reich's racial or security laws.[174] As one American officer commented in March 1946, "Many Germans have suffered death, torture, humiliation and loss of liberty due to acts of these informers and nearly all decent Germans lived in constant fear lest their neighbors report an imprudent remark critical of the Nazi regime."[175] Such cases began to come before the reopened German courts in the winter of 1946, after the passage in December 1945 of ACC Law No. 10, establishing a uniform legal basis in occupied Germany for the criminal prosecution "of war criminals and other similar offenders."

Loewenstein was a fervent proponent of the idea that the Germans who had denounced other Germans to the Nazi authorities had committed wicked and legally culpable acts, notwithstanding their legality under the law of the Third Reich. He welcomed the opportunity, in January 1946, to draft legislation for the Länder establishing jurisdiction for the criminal prosecution of Germans who, during the Nazi period, had "intentionally and maliciously" denounced other Germans to the police. In February, Loewenstein submitted a draft law and explanatory memorandum under the title "Law for the Redress of National-Socialist Injustice."[176] Its innovation was to provide German courts with jurisdiction to prosecute, convict, and punish denunciation cases on the basis of retroactive criminal law. The draft included a caveat: "Under no circumstances should the German courts be authorized to deal generally with such cases *prior to the enactment of appropriate legislation.*" If such prosecutions were to have legal and moral legitimacy, Loewenstein contended, they had to be based on German statutes that explicitly granted authority to convict for acts that had been legal under Nazi law.

True to the pattern, Loewenstein's advice was rejected, this time both by his peers and superiors. The key catching point was the draft law's aggressive stance on retroactivity: "One of the bogeys of these born American lawyers," Loewenstein lamented, "is the ex post facto law, as if one could clean up the German mess without that ex post facto. They did it in Law No. 10 and are doing it all the time in Nuremberg. . . . a very good defense of intellectual inertia."[177] For Loewenstein, the moral character of these cases was paramount: "A person who denounced another person knowing that he would be arrested or killed or maimed for life in a concentration camp should be subject to retribution even if it is retroactive."[178]

But once again the balance of opinion in Legal Division was otherwise. Loewenstein's superiors thought it both unjust and impolitic for AMG to equip German courts to convict for retroactive crimes.[179] By April 1946, his denunciation proposals had been set aside. In this and in virtually every other important point of contact between the American legal occupiers and the German legal occupied, General Clay and his agencies rejected what Loewenstein referred to as the "militant" approach to legal reform in the U.S. zone.

Meanwhile, AMG continued to stand back while the Ministers of Justice in the Länder appointed former Nazis to the judiciary. While Loewenstein conceded that most of these jurists had not been "affected by Nazi ideology," he advised Fahy that "Democratic conviction as it is understood in Anglo-Saxon countries cannot be assumed to be deep-rooted in this group."[180] By virtue of their training, these judges were likely to take a "strictly positivist" approach to cases. This posed a threat because "at the present time a very considerable volume of German law remains outside denazification." When it came to decide cases, the reappointees were likely to enforce written law even when such law was inconsistent with liberal-democratic norms.

In April 1946, with five months remaining to run on his contract, Loewenstein began to think of his remaining work with Legal Division as triage. In thinking about what legal reform project might still be salvaged, Loewenstein locked in on the supervision and control of

German courts. While it was too late to prevent the former Nazis from regaining positions on the bench, maybe it was not too late to design and realize a program of vigilance and reeducation. If he could convince his bosses on this point, Loewenstein reflected, his work in the zone would not have been in vain.[181]

By the spring of 1946, there were compelling reasons to fear a further loss of control in this sphere. General Clay had moved so quickly on local and state elections in the zone that judicial appointments would soon be made by German officials with a patina of democratic legitimacy. It would be harder than before, politically, to overrule their decisions. And with denazification now in the hands of German-operated tribunals, it was likely that many more former Nazis, some of whom had held important offices in the Nazi justice system, would be "cleansed" and returned to their former judicial offices. "In a "relatively short time," Loewenstein predicted, "many of the judges and prosecutors who were in office during the Hitler regime will be in office again after having been vindicated by the [German tribunals]." By this reckoning there was no way for AMG to advance and protect liberal-democratic constitutional development in the American zone (or future west German entity) without tight and rigorous supervision of Nazi-era returnees to the bench. "In Germany," Loewenstein later wrote, "with her scarcity of democratically-minded judges and the novelty of democratic legal systems, such . . . supervisory methods appear as the minimum requirements to guarantee that no violation of the spirit of the laws would occur."[182] If Americans would not regulate who became a judge in south Germany, it needed to regulate how south German judges did their jobs.

To this end, Loewenstein proposed that Legal Division set up a system of "continuous inspections on circuit."[183] Imagined as a series of spot checks, the inspections would be undertaken by "persons fully conversant with German language and German law . . . with the fullest possible grasp of the existing German legislation." Naturally enough, most of the inspectorate would be German-born and trained, persons (who had not been Nazis) possessing an educated capacity to monitor judicial and prosecutorial conduct.[184] In the first phase of the program, the inspectorate's most important duty was to identify and observe trial cases having political implications. The court inspectorate would be a tangible reminder to the postwar judiciary that it was on probation; it would have to demonstrate fealty both to the letter and the spirit of the new liberal-democratic constitutions.

In May 1946, before final decisions were taken on court supervision in the zone, Fahy left Germany for a new job in the State Department. His responsibilities fell to his deputy, Judge Warren Madden. On reviewing Loewenstein's memoranda on supervision, Madden found them wanting. He thought that any systematic supervision and control of judges—even former Nazi judges—was an anathema to judicial independence, a precept that Americans had sworn to install and defend.[185] In Madden's opinion, no German judicial candidate worth his salt would accept potentially intrusive oversight by an outside agency. As a practical matter, it was not clear that Legal Division had time or money enough to train a staff of German court inspectors. In rejecting Loewenstein's proposals, Madden thought the only practicable way forward was to delegate court supervision to the Ministers of Justice of the Länder. However, in light of Loewenstein's intransigence on the point, Madden invited other Legal Division staff, men known to be more sanguine about German trustworthiness, to devise an alternative plan.[186]

When that plan reached Loewenstein for comment in late May 1946, yet again he found himself fighting a rear-guard action against what he thought was a profoundly misguided policy.[187] Although he now conceded that direct American control of German courts was unfeasible, Loewenstein did not retract his central point.[188] "The importance of the democratization of the German judicial system can hardly be overrated when projected against the background of incipient democracy in Germany as a whole. The generation of judges and prosecutors now in office is basically and intrinsically not democratically-minded." For this reason alone, it would "take years before a new set of judges, trained in the new spirit of democracy . . . has attained office."[189] In the meantime, it was crucial that AMG institute and maintain a rigorous program of German court supervision.

Privately, Loewenstein despaired that Legal Division's supervision initiative "had been watered down to such an extent that it became almost meaningless."[190] He had come to believe, even more emphatically than before, that his immediate superiors at the division, McLendon and Shepard, were incapable of informed and sound decisions in this field.[191] However, in his "on the record" memorandum to Madden on the subject, Loewenstein was conciliatory.[192] If a German-operated system of internal controls was unavoidable, so be it. In that case it was imperative that German Ministers of Justice were insulated from political interference. Effective mechanisms also had to be created so that German citizens might have redress for abuses of judicial and / or prosecutorial power.

The risk of authoritarian restoration in the German courts was compounded further by growing socioeconomic distress and dislocation in the zone. Crime and criminal prosecution were reaching epic levels.[193] Functional German courts were in short supply. As more and more former Nazi judges took up positions in the postwar courts, it seemed even more critical than before for AMG to deploy at least some rudimentary system of court supervision.

But no such system was implemented. Once the decision had been made to reopen German trial and regional appellate courts in the zone on an urgent basis, once it had been decided to permit German officials in the Länder to appoint whomever they wished to sit as judges in those courts, there was no plausible means to reverse the trend, especially not in the context of creeping socioeconomic crisis. By January 1947, the case workload of the German courts had increased at least threefold over wartime figures.[194] On the other hand, the number of available judges had decreased by about two-thirds, a substantial number of them being "very old, badly nourished, badly clothed and housed and therefore frequently ill." In fact, the conditions of work and rates of pay in the postwar courts were so miserable that only former Nazis, men without other options, were willing (in numbers) to take up judicial posts.

For all of these reasons Madden and then his successor, Alvin J. Rockwell, saw no practical alternative but to countenance the *re*nazification of the judiciary in the U.S. zone.[195] "The only hope," one Legal Division official reported, "is to . . . restore to their former positions many of the capable judges and prosecutors that have been removed. . . . By the very nature of things this will ultimately have to be done."[196] By September 1947, 330 German local courts, 37 county courts and 5 appellate courts were back in operation in the U.S. zone, but with only 40 percent of wartime personnel.[197] The great majority of the judges and prosecutors in these courts had been at least nominal members of the Nazi Party. Many had held senior legal offices during the Third Reich. The denazification dam had burst.

By the close of 1946, the Soviets were well aware that the Americans and their Western partners had reneged on their agreement to purge all but nominal former members of the Nazi Party from the German legal systems in their zones. By this time, too, relations between the Soviet Union and the other three powers had chilled to the point that the Soviets took the deliberate decision to exploit the situation for propaganda value.

A prime opportunity presented itself in January 1947, when the Legal Directorate (DLeg), along with the other functional subdivisions of the Control Council, prepared a joint progress report to the Council of Foreign Ministers on the denazification of German legal personnel in the respective zones. In the first meeting of DLeg in the new year, the Soviet delegate, Karasev, signaled that the Soviet Union no longer was willing to condone their retreat from denazification.[198] He requested that all four powers proffer complete "statistical information regarding the number of judges, prosecutors and barristers employed before the reform of the German judicial system began, the number of removals and the number of Nazis who were still in the offices of judges, prosecutors and barristers." Karasev insisted that the reports provide an "objective report showing the true situation" of what was going on in terms of the reinstatement of former Nazis. The Soviet Union also wanted to nail down a strict definition of grounds (under Control Council Law No. 4) for exclusion from the postwar German legal professions. In his opinion, "Any person who participated in the punitive policy of the Hitler regime, whether he was a member of the Nazi Party or not, could not be employed as a Judge, Prosecutor or Barrister."[199]

A supplementary report by the Soviets (of late January 1947) contained what the British delegate termed a "severe attack upon the failure to carry out Control Council legislation in the western zones and also . . . upon the failure to reform the judiciary in the western zones."[200] Among other assertions, the report claimed that "in the American zone 40 percent of the judges are Nazis who presumably ought to have been expelled under Law No. 4." The estimate was based on a reading of Law No. 4—that it required the permanent purge of German judges who enforced harsh Nazi laws.

After two contentious meetings on the joint report, the other three powers rejected the Soviet interpretation of their obligations under Law No. 4. But the final joint report nonetheless contained some rather embarrassing admissions for the Western powers. With regard to the American zone, Legal Division admitted that 35 percent of the newly appointed judges and prosecutors and 50 percent of reinstated private lawyers in the zone had been at least nominal members of the Nazi party. The figures did not reveal how many had participated in the implementation of the most notorious of Hitler's laws and decrees.

But Legal Division's report was not entirely forthright, neglecting to mention that Nazi-era jurists, including many who had prosecuted or judged cases in the political Special Courts of the Third Reich, were streaming back in swelling numbers.[201] Local and regional courts were being reopened all over the U.S. zone, staffed by lawyers and judges who had been scrubbed clean of Nazi taint by lenient (German-operated) denazification tribunals.[202] The cleansing process was making it easy for the Ministers of Justice in the Länder to do what they were strongly predisposed to do: reappoint judges without regard for their Nazi-era careers or records of conduct.

The widespread reinstatement of Nazi-era jurists coincided with Clay's policy to restore German control over administrative functions in the zone. The trend also coincided with the new general orders of the Joint Chiefs of Staff, JCS 1779.[203] These orders redefined Clay's mandate as "fundamentally that of helping to lay the economic and educational bases of a sound German democracy."[204] Toward this end, the General was to "continue to promote . . . the assumption of direct responsibility by German governmental agencies." In so doing, Clay's functional subdivisions were to help construct democratic legal and political institutions, while giving German officials wide latitude to determine the "ultimate constitutional form of German political life."

With regard to "Courts and Judicial Procedures," JCS 1779 required AMG to "exercise such supervision . . . as is necessary to prevent the revival of National Socialist doctrines." On the other hand, Clay's Legal Division was to "foster the independence of the German judiciary by allowing freedom in their interpretation and application of law and by limiting control measures . . . to the minimum consistent with the accomplishment of the aims of the occupation."[205] The German courts were to be given jurisdiction over all kinds of cases "not involving the interests of Military Government." The "basic objective of the occupation," it was reiterated, "is the establishment of the rule of law in Germany."

In relation to the German courts in the U.S. zone, these orders simply confirmed the status quo on the ground. By the summer of 1947, AMG already had relinquished control over law-related appointments, including of judges. By the same token, in making personnel decisions about judges and other legal offices, German agencies in the Länder were flouting AMG denazification directives.[206] The top officials at Legal Division no longer even pretended to screen appointments before they were made, not even to the appellate courts. As one Legal Division officer reported to the director in July 1947, "A great number of nominal members of the Nazi party have been appointed during the last few months to positions of judges and prosecutors and the percentage of nominal Nazis in the German courts is continuously increasing."[207]

It did not take long for the presence of former Nazis to be felt. Once the majority of German criminal courts had reopened, by January 1948, the number of controversial decisions in Nazi crime cases—that is, cases involving denunciation or crimes against humanity, defined by AMG as crimes "committed during the Hitler-era by National-Socialists for political, racial or religious reasons"—began to mount, as did the adverse publicity in the German and American press.[208]

In February 1947, by way of example, a court in Mannheim acquitted (on charges of murder) a former SS officer and two policemen who had summarily executed three German civilians found in a house that had raised a white flag of surrender.[209] The police were acquitted outright on the basis that they had carried out an order, while the SS man was convicted *in absentia* of manslaughter and sentenced to two years. Later, two former Nazi henchmen received light sentences after a panel of three German judges (two of whom had been Nazi Party members) found them guilty of beating a Jewish businessman to death in 1938.[210] In yet another case, this in Bavaria, a former Nazi judge relied on a discredited coroner's report to exonerate a former Nazi assassin for the prewar murder of a Jewish man.[211] Then, in Berlin, a panel of German judges handed down "clearly false exculpatory sentences on Nazi criminals," in one case exonerating an accused for having been "overcome by a fanatical faith in the original Nazi ideology."[212]

As Alvin Rockwell, the new director of Legal Division, stated in a report written in the spring of 1948, all of these cases involved Germans who acted against other Germans with the "purpose of maintaining Nazi tyranny . . . or in order to promote the realization of Nazi ideas or tendencies."[213] The trials had been conducted by biased judges who contrived to find pretexts to either acquit the accused on the basis of the supposed legality of their acts during the Third Reich or hand down absurdly lenient sentences. Rockwell noted that these results had been severely criticized in the German press, some leading to public protests. "It seems beyond cavil," one of Rockwell's officers commented, "that the participation of biased judges and prosecutors in trials of Nazi crimes cases is in derogation of the reestablishment of the 'rule of law'" and could not therefore be tolerated by American authorities.[214]

In Rockwell's view, if such miscarriages of justice persisted, there was "danger that the confidence of the German people in their judiciary will be greatly damaged." On this basis he sent a directive to local detachments of AMG in the U.S. zone that no person who had been a member of the Nazi party "will participate as judge or prosecutor in the trial of crimes committed for the purpose of maintaining the Nazi tyranny." Rockwell's directive was to go one step further, also banning former Nazis from appointment "to hold certain key positions in the German administration of justice."

When in the late spring of 1948 John Raymond took over for Rockwell as Legal Division's fourth director, he endorsed the "imperative that the trial of Nazi crimes in German courts be conducted with a high standard of fairness and impartiality."[215] He also wanted to defend the line that his predecessors had drawn against the reappointment of former Nazis jurists to key judicial and governmental positions in the zone.

The auguries were not favorable. In the summer of 1948 Raymond received reports that, openly and not, the Ministers of Justice (most blatantly the Bavarian minister) in the Länder continued to disregard renewed American directives in these fields.[216] Men who had held high legal offices during the Third Reich were taking up key positions in supposedly denazified legal systems. One Legal Division officer opined, "The German administration of justice will not be kept materially free from Nazi militaristic ideologies repugnant to democratic concepts and ideals unless substantial immediate control over the justice agencies is retained and exercised by Military Government."[217]

In the summer of 1948, in the context now of the Berlin airlift and incipient Cold War, it was far from obvious that American officials like John Raymond had either the political or administrative capacity to do more than finger-wag at recalcitrant German charges. American admonitions and intercessions on denazification were looking more like perfunctory gestures. One of Raymond's chief lieutenants reported in July 1948 that all evidence from the American Länder indicated a "dangerous and ominous" situation in which the Ministers of Justice flaunted American orders prohibiting the appointment of former Nazis to key legal offices.[218] It had already come to pass that 60 to 70 percent of judges and prosecutors in the U.S. zone were former Nazis.[219] Across the board, the "percentage of politically incriminated judges and prosecutors is increasing alarmingly."[220] In Bavaria, according to one Legal Division report, the minister of justice had been emboldened to "organize the Supreme Court [there] in such a manner that 4 out of 8 judges of this court" were former Nazis. Left to stand, the report concluded, the appointments would deliver a "serious blow" to the democratic reconstruction of German justice in the zone, a "complete breakdown" of American efforts in the legal field.

The same report indicated that AMG could not safely assume that former Nazi judges or prosecutors had shed authoritarian for liberal-democratic outlooks on justice. In fact, according to best evidence from Bavaria, "court decisions and actions of prosecutors . . . reflect a growing sympathy for Nazis and Nazi militaristic ideologies."[221] This was an alarming trend, if only because no fewer than 353 criminal cases involving Nazi war crimes were soon to come to trial there. And although the director of AMG-Bavaria had "informed the Minister President that former members of the Nazi party are disqualified from sitting as judges in criminal cases involving Nazi crimes and atrocities," no American could be confident that this directive would (or could) be respected. In regard to the denazification of the courts, the German genie now was fully and irredeemably out of the bottle.

Americans Remake the German and Japanese Judiciaries

In causing its occupied Germans and Japanese to draft and ratify constitutions in 1946 to 1947 the American occupiers had accomplished something like a start but nothing like an end to liberal-democratic reconstruction there. The indispensable next step, in both places, was to stimulate the formation of technically competent and ideologically sympathetic judiciaries that might breathe liberal life into the constitutional paper. "The adoption of constitutions in the Länder of the U.S. zone," one AMG official commented in June 1947, "has laid the foundations for the re-organization of the German judicial system in accordance with the principles of democracy, justice under law, and of equal rights for all citizens."[222] The official had correctly observed that constitutional reform had laid down foundations for a revamped judiciary, one with expanded jurisdiction and responsibility. But most assuredly it had not made those principles into substantive facts of German or Japanese legal life.

We have seen that senior American legal officers in Germany and Japan were apt to be credulous on the subject of judicial reform. But none were such fools as to think that even the best-drawn and most inspirational constitutional phrases guaranteed change on the ground, still less in two countries where constitutional law had been either irrelevant or undercut as factors of civil society or political conduct. Indeed, most American officers were aware about their own national experience that, as one observed, "Constitutionally guaranteed rights and judicial review do not always protect civil liberties against loosely-worded legislative definitions of political crime, especially in time of crisis when the need for such protections is most urgent."[223] While there were perhaps many reasons why constitutional rights were or were not actualized, a key variable in every case was the willingness of a nation's judges and courts to animate and defend them. As a SCAP press release put the point early in 1947, judicial review was a fine thing in theory, but "Much depends upon the spirit in which the judges will perform this function."[224] That is why it was seen as of paramount importance that the Americans insist on the appointment of German and Japanese judicial personnel likely to bring such spirit to their judicial duties.

There are three fundamental reasons why American legal agencies there failed abjectly to achieve this last goal in occupied south Germany and Japan. The first is that, from the outset, Americans worked from the premise that the postwar German and Japanese judiciaries would need to be staffed by experienced legal professionals. Impliedly, they became obliged to appoint judges who had been willing to operate the courts of two authoritarian and ruthlessly repressive regimes. The second reason is that in both occupied areas the judicial ranks of American-occupied Germany and Japan had been very ineffectually purged of men who either had caused serious miscarriages of justice or were hostile to liberal and democratic legal and political ideas. The third reason was that in American Germany and Japan the Americans were lax in fending off attempts by conservative bureaucrats to capture the judicial reform process and restore presurrender legal elites to their former influence and offices.

In American-occupied Germany, the liberal-democratic reconstruction of the Länder judiciaries, from beginning to end, was tied to the heavy stone of denazification or, more accurately, the unfolding debacle of denazification. By 1947—and on this point Karl Loewenstein's forewarnings had proved prophetic—German-operated denazification, emphatically in relation to the Nazi-era legal professions, had devolved into a process of "mass rehabilitation."[225] The incoming intelligence was abundant and unambiguous that German denazification tribunals routinely exonerated (as mere followers) judges and jurists who had been cold-blooded and well-rewarded instruments of the Nazi murder state.[226]

For the American legal officers charged with the task of overseeing the installation of denazified judges sympathetic to liberal-democratic norms, the situation in south Germany in the spring of 1948 was grim. "The German judiciary in our zone," Hans Weigert, the senior divisional expert on the administration of justice reported in May, "consists in its majority former party members; the average percentage at present is likely to exceed 70%."[227] In some of the Länder the fraction may have reached 80 and even 90 percent, a not inconsequential fraction having been members of the SS.[228]

In the American zone, then, little more than three years after the defeat of the Third Reich, Hitler's judges were back or were making their way back to their former offices in the German legal establishment—all this under the noses of their American overseers. While careers had been interrupted and former Nazi judges returned to sit for long sessions in half-ruined courts on short rations, for most this was the only reckoning faced.[229]

Looking back on the renovation of the courts of Japan, Alfred Oppler, SCAP's point man on judicial reform, drew attention to the "strong individualism" of the new constitution and what it had meant for the postwar judiciary there.[230] Oppler knew that if the liberal theory of the constitution was to become a lived reality in the country, two things would need happen. Individual citizens in Japan would need to "fight for their rights." Just as crucially, Japanese judges, bolstered by their functional independence and enhanced powers, would need to vindicate those rights. Although Oppler himself proved reluctant to confront this truth, it was not at all clear that either he or his brother officers at Government Section had helped construct a judicial branch in Japan that was either willing or able to fulfill this responsibility.

One obstacle was an unpromising start point: that the Japanese judiciary of the presurrender period had been so poorly trained and little respected.[231] Steeped in a continental judicial tradition, subjected to the rigid administrative discipline of the Ministry of Justice, judges in Japan had been groomed not to be assertive, not to be creative, and not to challenge the actions or prerogatives of political leadership. In the 1930s, the judiciary of Japan had been timorous, even servile, in the face of ultranationalist insults to the rule of law. Not only had it not resisted encroachments against the Meiji constitution, there had been no cultural or institutional basis for such resistance. In contrast to the German judiciary, Japan's judges were not seen as having had enough power or prestige to have experienced a tragic fall from grace. Thus, for American legal engineers in Japan, the job was less a matter of reclamation than of fabrication in the first place.

In virtually every relevant respect, the Japanese judiciary of the presurrender era presented unpromising timber for the construction of a robustly liberal-democratic judicial branch, its judges ready to stand between the individual citizen and despotic politicians, prosecutors, and bureaucrats. Apart from the unpreparedness of the judges themselves, another obstacle loomed large. Government Section permitted Japan's Ministry of Justice, a stronghold of statist conservatism, to preside over the liberal reformation of Japan's judiciary.

In their majority, senior bureaucrats at the MofJ were unreconciled both to the strong individualism of the new constitution and to the theory that judges should be independent of their supervision and control. Fortified by the electoral resurgence of conservative political alignments in the Diet, fearing that liberality in the courts would play into the hands of Communist agitators, the bureaucrats responded to Government Section's initiatives in this field with a thinly veiled combination of misdirection, prevarication, and delay. At no point, however, not even when evidence mounted that the leaders of MofJ were impeding the liberal reconstruction of the judiciary, did Government Section use its undoubted power to purge the ministry (or, in 1948, its successor agency) of its reactionary element. At no point, moreover, did Oppler deign even to recommend such a move.

At every turn, in fact, Oppler's Courts and Law group seemed either to discount or underestimate adverse forces. Instead of making common cause with the liberal and socialist elements of the Japanese bar, instead of offering steadfast support to liberal reformist judges like Hosono and Chono, Oppler continued to invest in the misplaced belief that his collaborative approach to the bureaucrats in the MofJ would yield positive and lasting results.[232] For the most part, it did not.

To the still greater disadvantage of judicial reform, Oppler's group, just as SCAP as a whole, also tended in 1947 and 1948 to underestimate the corrosive effects on its reform agenda of Japan's growing social and economic crisis. At the dawn of 1947, Japan's criminal gangs were arguably the country's best-capitalized and most effective organizations, making enormous profits in vice and black-marketeering. Reports began to pour into Government Section that in alarmingly large numbers the judges of the new Japan, especially those presiding over the criminal law trials of gangsters, were being corrupted, a trend exacerbated by the judiciary's poverty and limited prestige. By the end of 1948, indications were that even the new flagship Supreme Court of Japan, staffed mainly by the mediocrities and time-servers favored by the conservative elite, had itself begun to founder in the same polluted seas. Before it had heard its first big constitutional case, the Supreme Court docket was crowded with its own cases of perfidy and impeachment.

In American-occupied Germany and Japan, in December 1948, the judicial renovation projects of both occupations—that is to say the liberal-democratic reconstruction projects in both countries—were in jeopardy. In the south German Länder, the Nazi-era opportunists and fellow-travelers, and not a few keen National Socialist killers, were resuming seats in the courts and in the justice ministries en masse. Their renewed presence was being felt in the willingness of many of these jurists, even as they were bitterly condemned in the German press, to exonerate other former Nazis for Hitler-period political and racial crimes. Those within American ranks who had predicted these outcomes, who reported on them, were shoved aside. General Clay's fixed determination to restore German economy and self-government outstripped of every other concern, including renazification. In the result, if the Germans ultimately were to realize a judicial system based on democracy, civilization, and justice, they were to realize it with the judges and legal bureaucracy of the Third Reich.

In Japan, the problem was not so much the return of a potent and influential judicial elite, but the failure to foster a potent and liberal-spirited judicial elite in the first instance. Unlike AMG-Legal Division, Oppler's Courts and Law group did not generate internal dissension about the shortcomings and then outright failures of the judicial renovation program. As the evidence increased that the critical judicial reform project was going desperately wrong, derailed by conservative machinations and endemic corruption, Oppler and Government Section remained invested, in 1948 and for decades to come, in the mythology that they had introduced—and the occupied had enthusiastically embraced—the liberal reconstruction of the Japanese judiciary.

5

Clearing the Spiritual Rubble

REFORMING CRIMINAL JUSTICE IN OCCUPIED GERMANY AND JAPAN

FOR AMERICAN LEGAL officers in occupied Germany and Japan, criminal justice was a fundamental arena of directed law reform. In no other field of substantive or procedural law was the key norm of American legal policy—the physical integrity and liberty of the individual person vis-à-vis the state—so obviously implicated. "Nothing affects more the very lives of men and women," one American official proclaimed in 1947, "than the methods by which criminal justice is administered in a country."[1] Unlike other areas of individual contact with law, criminal prosecution jeopardized the life, personal liberty, and honor but also the property and employment of individual persons. On these grounds no other reforms were of more concern and none were the product of more meticulous scrutiny.[2]

In American-occupied Japan and Germany, the "democratization" of criminal justice was propelled in 1946 by two parallel developments. The first was the impending introduction of new constitutional instruments which, among other things, set forth extensive individual and due process rights for those prosecuted for criminal wrongdoing. It now behooved the occupation authorities to ensure that the substantive and procedural criminal law of Japan and south German Länder, including the criminal defense bar in those places, was aligned with these developments. As one SCAP legal officer observed in this regard, "The extent to which these general [constitutional] guarantees will actually operate in insuring civil liberties will of course depend to some extent on provisions in the Criminal Code."[3]

The second important factor was that, by the winter of 1946, American occupation authorities in Japan and south Germany had become alarmed by explosive rates of crime and social disorder, and by the political implications of such disorder. In both places, American military courts were groaning under the weight of untried criminal cases. The absence of effective criminal justice was affording too much space for organized criminals and their political analogues, the radical Left. For American leaders in occupied Germany and Japan, therefore, it became an increasingly urgent necessity to stimulate the construction of effective, yet liberal, systems of criminal justice.

In broader perspective, criminal justice reform was a key prerequisite of a larger aim: to establish and consolidate liberal rule-of-law regimes in the occupied nations. The directed reconstruction of criminal law and procedure, along with the segment of the bar dedicated to criminal defense, was thus seen as having a major structural and symbolic importance. At the beating heart of the liberal state was criminal justice that respected the accused and constrained the accuser. As a SCAP press release summarized, the new constitution of Japan "is designed to build up a government by law so that the scope of interference by the State in the private sphere of the individual is legally defined and limited."[4] For that reason, the construction in Japan of a liberal-minded system of criminal law and procedure was among Government Section's central priorities.

In regard to Nazi Germany, the American line was that by the end of the Second World War criminal justice had "assumed the character of non-contradictory administrative proceedings."[5] In the twelve years of the Third Reich the Nazis had systematically destroyed the foundations of German criminal law and procedure in the *rechtsstaat*. On this premise, leading Allied experts on the reconstruction of German criminal law bore in mind the bigger picture, that "the elimination of certain Nazi changes in field of criminal law [were to] depend for their effectiveness on the restoration of the Rule of Law in Germany."[6]

The core thesis of this chapter is that in the period of 1946 to 1947, American officials in Japan and Germany adopted distinctive approaches to criminal justice reform in those places. In Japan, and largely in the absence of input from specialists in Japanese law, the American reform program in this field was based on the perception that criminal justice in presurrender Japan, its European pedigree notwithstanding, exemplified premodern and profoundly illiberal patterns of Asiatic feudalism. On this basis, General MacArthur called for the abolition of systems, criminal justice most prominently, which "through secret inquisition and abuse have held the people in constant fear—substituting therefore a system of justice designed to afford the people protection against despotic, arbitrary and unjust methods."[7]

In contrast, American officials in Germany, led by German émigré legal experts, worked from the different premise that before the rise to power of the National Socialists, the German codes of criminal law and procedure had been broadly consistent with the norms of liberal due process. In this view the challenge facing the United States and its allies in this field was to redeem an essentially modern and rationally defensible system of criminal justice, one that had been defiled by Nazi ideology, practices, and personnel.

Accordingly, as SCAP's lawyers prepared to oversee highly intrusive legal change in Japan's manner of criminal prosecution and trial, AMG lawyers prepared more straightforwardly to cleanse a basically sound system of Nazi taint.

Kokutai and Punishment: Humanizing Criminal Justice in Japan

As Government Section's work on Japan's judiciary unfolded in 1946 and 1947, another urgent priority was the modernization and humanization of its system of criminal justice.[8] According to the section's official line, since the Meiji period the Japanese had adopted the outward structures but not the rights liberalism of west European criminal justice. In American eyes, the technical definition of criminal action, especially its actual prosecution and punishment, had remained pervasively authoritarian and often cruel.

When in 1946 it was decided that Japan would ratify a new liberal-democratic constitution by the close of 1947, modernization meant bringing criminal law and procedure into alignment with the redefinition of Japanese persons as rights-bearing individuals.[9] As a SCAP press release reminded, "Life, personal liberty and honor, property and employment are at stake when crime is prosecuted and tried. Therefore, the new Constitution has established elaborate safeguards for the protection of the individual in the field of criminal justice."[10] Marking an abrupt departure from Japanese legal tradition, the new constitution rendered "all of the people" (by definition, including the emperor and members of his imperial house[11]) as equal under the law.[12] The social status of an accused in relation to hierarchy and community, potent legal factors in Japanese law before 1945, was to have no bearing on legal rights or obligations.[13]

More significantly for the reconfiguration of Japanese criminal justice, no fewer than ten articles of the constitution set forth an entirely novel set of due process rights and entitlements.[14] In Japan, just as in the United States, no person was to be "deprived of life or liberty" or "any other criminal penalty . . . except according to procedure established by law."[15] Nor was a person to be arrested "except upon warrant issued by a competent judicial officer" or detained except after being informed of the charge and having had "the immediate privilege of counsel."[16] The new constitution also purported to guarantee that persons accused of criminal offenses would receive speedy and public trials. At trial, the accused might be defended by a lawyer of his choosing who was to have broad leeway in calling and questioning witnesses.[17] According to these strictures, an accused could not lawfully be tortured or by any other means be compelled to incriminate himself.[18]

In drafting these articles, Government Section (GS) had meant to cause a clean break from Japan's statist norms of criminal law rights and powers. These were to be supplanted by a slate of individual rights, by what General MacArthur himself once called these "simple yet transcendental principles which modern civilization demands." Just as a liberal theory informed American notions of the just constitution, so it informed the American view that Japan's extant system of criminal justice—this exotic hybrid of Confucian status-based social ethics and continental (chiefly French and German) legal codes—was an incoherent anachronism.[19]

The American assessment of criminal justice in Japan was unified by a single theme: Japanese laws in this field had good (European) bones but weak (Asiatic) flesh. In other words, the thrust of GS criticism was that the formal rationality and liberality of Japanese criminal justice had been undermined by the operational irrationality of Japan's criminal justice agencies—that is, its police, prosecutors, and judges.[20] In its actual operation, Japanese criminal justice was fueled by illiberal ideas of social hierarchy and order. It was a system in which physical and psychological pressure, including torture, were customary practices.[21] It was a system in which the criminal trial had become debased as the ritualized assignment of guilt.[22]

This assessment focused on Japan's public prosecutors (or procurators) as the dominant agencies of presurrender criminal justice. As the professional civil servant–employees of the Ministry of Justice (MofJ), with offices attached to the courts,[23] procurators had enjoyed status equal to that of trial judges and much superior to defense lawyers.[24] In their investigative and discretionary powers, the procurators wielded more power than judges and far more power than the defense.[25] They controlled criminal investigations, interrogations, and charging. With the police, procurators enjoyed all but unlimited access to the accused. In this system, almost every criminal investigation and interrogation produced an admissible confession.[26] Most criminal proceedings began and ended when the procurator presented the investigatory record, usually including a signed confession. In the typical criminal case, the main task of trial judges was to validate confession, find guilt, and fix punishment.

In the tiny percentage of cases in which the accused contested guilt, trials were held according to the French and German pattern, the judges taking a proactive role in the examination of witnesses and, there being no jury system, making all findings of law and fact. Upon a guilty verdict and sentencing, convicted persons had limited (and seldom exercised) rights of appeal.

In the GS analysis, the authoritarian character of criminal justice in Japan was seen to have intensified in the 1920s, in the form especially of the Peace Preservation Law of 1925,[27] and in the rapid expansion of police and prosecutorial powers in the wartime period, 1933 to 1945.[28] In this period, criminal justice in Japan, never scrupulous of due process rights, was reduced to a more or less unalloyed means of domestic repression, particularly in regard to the Communist Left.[29] As one GS lawyer summarized, "In the past, the Home Ministry, through the Police, exercised a tyrannical power over the private lives of the people. It was through this power that the Ministry was able to subdue political opposition and lead the nation into a disastrous career of brigandage."[30] Thus, when Americans took up criminal justice reform in the second half of 1946, they did so on the premise that the "psychology and methods of the police state had been . . . thoroughly integrated in the Japanese system and official attitude."[31]

When Government Section undertook to stimulate root and branch reform in occupied Japan, it justified the initiative in two ways. One justification was that, in its concrete operation, criminal justice in Japan was almost the mirror opposite of a liberal, rational, and therefore enlightened system of crime and punishment. In light of liberal constitutional development in Japan, it was essential that crime and punishment, the centerpiece of justice in the liberal rule-of-law state, were brought into proper alignment.

The second justification, offered mainly after the fact, was that criminal justice reform during the occupation had been consensual; it had been the product principally of Japanese initiative and actions. In this account, no reform legislation, including the crucial amendments to criminal procedure, had been "categorically required or dictated."[32] It had been gratifying to GS, so the story was told, that officials at Japan's Ministry of Justice "on the whole demonstrated themselves as gratifyingly cooperative and open to progressive ideas." It had been possible, therefore, for American officials to have assumed an "advisory rather than obligatory" stance toward the key reform programs.[33]

As if these contentions were not convincing enough, the GS account offered yet another reason why the Japanese had, of their own volition, taken the lead on criminal justice reform. When it had become time to flesh out proposals, "No attempt had been made by the Occupation to impose the introduction of legal concepts and institutions patterned on Anglo-Saxon law upon basically different Japanese law."[34] As Thomas Blakemore, one of GS's lead hands on the criminal justice brief, summarized the policy: "SCAP's relationship toward reform is simply that of a stimulant, or at times when necessary a spur, to the development of genuinely Japanese solutions. Only when all efforts to incite self-reform have failed, and only when the subject-matter is of vital importance to the objectives of the occupation should SCAP draft and initiate legislation."[35]

On a frank assessment of available primary source materials, however, even those made by Americans for American purposes, Government Section's official account looks suspect. The records indicate that from the outset of the reform drive in 1946, Japanese officials, uneasy with what they saw as alien and externally imposed constitutional reform, deeply concerned by the implications of liberal reform in the criminal justice field, did not embrace but in fact strongly resisted these initiatives.[36] Notwithstanding GS claims to the contrary,[37] in intensity and effectiveness, this resistance increased as Japanese conservatives reformed their ranks in both the Diet and MofJ.[38]

When it came time in the early summer of 1947 for work to begin on the renovation of Japanese criminal justice, the *modus operandi* between American and Japanese officials was firmly established. The process began when officials at GS signaled to the government of Japan that it needed to legislate sweeping reform of criminal law and procedure within one year, bringing both bodies of law in line with new constitutional norms.[39] Having set forth this general objective, the GS stood back while the government superintended the necessary research, deliberative, and drafting work. Once draft bills had been completed, they were to be sent for assessment by Alfred Oppler's Courts and Law subdivision of GS.

When Courts and Law completed its initial assessment of a bill, a delegation of its criminal justice specialists, typically headed by Oppler, met with officials at Japan's MofJ in order to "receive full information of the Japanese view."[40] Any unresolved issues were recorded in "problem sheets" to be discussed in subsequent bilateral conferences.[41] These conferences, so Oppler later insisted, were conducted on the basis of absolute freedom of discussion between American and

Japanese officials. There was one proviso: the deliberative process ended when and only when Oppler was satisfied that the proposed legislation was consonant with the letter and spirit of the constitution.

In essence, then, the drafting process in the criminal justice field was delegated to the Japanese but controlled by the Americans. It was controlled by Americans, moreover, who (predictably) had no specialist education in the criminal justice of Japan. As we have seen, Oppler, the chief of the Courts and Law group, had been trained as an administrative law lawyer and judge in Germany. Nonetheless, he brought at least one genuine asset to the criminal justice project: advanced training in continental codes of law and procedure.[42] Although Oppler's immediate subordinate, Thomas Blakemore, began work on the project with no expertise in the criminal justice, he brought another invaluable asset to the table: fluency in the language and laws of Japan, rare among American legal officers.

The two other American officers assigned to the criminal justice file, Howard Meyers and Richard B. Appleton, were less well equipped for the criminal justice program. Meyers was a Harvard-educated lawyer who had worked in counterintelligence during the Pacific war.[43] Appleton was an American lawyer who came to GS from the Civil Affairs Division of American occupation forces in Korea. Before they began to oversee the overhaul of the criminal justice system in Japan, neither man had been expert in the criminal law of the United States. While Oppler came to admire the "penetrating" and "far above average" legal minds of both men, it is far from clear that the same view was shared by their Japanese counterparts.[44]

In the winter of 1947, the government of Japan, now led by the emerging leader of Japan's democratic Right, Yoshida Shigeru, had formed a special Legislative Investigation Committee (LIC) on reform of the criminal code.[45] The committee consisted of twenty-six Japanese jurists, including several senior judges and legal academics. Controversially, however, the LIC also included a number of senior prosecutors and no fewer than nine delegates from the arch-conservative MofJ. When the composition of the committee was announced, the Tokyo Bar Association led the call for more political and ideological diversity.[46] According to the chairman of the Federation of Japanese

Bar Associations, the collective mindset of the LIC was "strongly influenced by prewar thinking . . . dominated by the Emperor system."[47] The committee was criticized for its predisposition in criminal justice to promote the power of the government over the individual's human rights.

By spring, the LIC had produced a draft criminal code, and a series of bilateral conferences on the code were held over three weeks in mid-May 1947. Howard Meyers led the American delegation.

The American and Japanese contingents quickly agreed that some provisions in the former criminal code (for instance, those that reflected outdated notions of social status or provided for extreme sentences for status-based offenses) were to be excised as inconsistent with the liberal precepts of the new constitution.[48] Both groups also agreed that in light of Japan's "tradition of violence and of the exercise of force" in politics, punishments for these kinds of crimes should be increased.

It had been more difficult to reach consensus on a number of other issues, especially regarding the decriminalization, pursuant to new constitutional rights, of a range of speech acts that in the years before the surrender would have attracted charges of criminal libel.[49] There was also discord within the Japanese legal community, and between the Japanese and the Americans, regarding the decriminalization of female adultery and other issues relating to criminal liability and the family.[50]

In the result, every point of contention but one was resolved without prolonged acrimony. By far the most contentious point of reform were Articles 73 to 76 of the old code, which described crimes of *lèse-majesté*—that is, crimes against the person or reputation of the emperor or his family. With regard to these crimes and punishments, the point of intersection of criminal law and the *kokutai,* the conservative politicians and MofJ were intransigent. This was the hill they were prepared to die on.

Although Courtney Whitney, the chief of Government Section, only rarely intervened in the section's law reform projects, he made an exception regarding the criminal code. Having reviewed the first Japanese draft, Whitney wanted a number of amendments, but most emphatically to those articles of the code that purported to preserve crimes of *lèse-majesté*.[51] Whitney, backed by MacArthur, was particularly adamant on this point because, even as the reform process was unfolding, Japanese authorities continued to prosecute *lèse-majesté* criminal charges in the so-called placard case.[52] This case was soon to become the symbolic focal point of an intense clash between SCAP and Japan's resurgent coalition of conservative politicians and bureaucrats.

In the decade before the Japanese surrender, prosecution (or the threat of prosecution) for *lèse-majesté* had become a potent weapon of political repression.[53] All public criticisms of the emperor, his household, or of the imperial system as a whole could and did attract vigorous prosecution and for a capital crime. The crime was based on the flatly inegalitarian premise that the supremely elevated status of the emperor and his household justified extraordinary protections of their persons and dignity. Direct interference with either interest was considered a grave affront not just against the body of a venerated person but against the spiritual bond between the imperial house and the Japanese people, the *kokutai*.

In SCAP's view, its civil liberties directives and the impending constitution of Japan ought to mark a decisive end both to the ideological and legal basis of *lèse-majesté*. Thus, on May 19, 1946, when a self-described Communist office worker named Matsushima was charged in Tokyo for having carried a placard insulting the emperor during a public protest against hunger, the stage was set for conflict between SCAP and Japanese conservatives.[54] At stake (apart from the liberty of the accused) was the credibility of SCAP's liberal reform program.

With the support of leftist and liberal lawyers, journalists, and activists, Matsushima's case quickly became a *cause célèbre* of the occupation period, minutely covered in the Japanese press. For the Left, the case was about the persistence in the postwar period of fascism and its emperor-worshipping superstitions. For conservatives, Matsushima's insult underlined the continued importance of the *lèse-majesté* offense.

The first trial of the placard case began in Tokyo on August 2, 1946, before a courtroom packed with spectators, reporters, and news cameramen.[55] Matsushima's defense was led by Tatsuji Fuse, the now elderly leader of Japan's radical bar, who had come out of retirement for this case.[56] Fuse's appearance for the defense (along with a team of no fewer than fifteen other defense lawyers) was evidence of the enormous symbolic significance of the case for the Japanese Left.

Fuse opened Matsushima's defense before a panel of three judges by setting forth a series of queries concerning the legal validity of the *lèse-majesté* provisions of the criminal code.[57] Specifically, the defense asked how, in the face of the Potsdam Declaration and SCAP directives, their client could be lawfully prosecuted for exercising his speech rights.[58] After Fuse submitted his questions, five more defense lawyers took turns challenging the legal validity of criminal charges that had been based on the discredited notion, recanted by the emperor himself, that he and his household were sacred. The defense asked that all charges be withdrawn. When Matsushima himself addressed the court, he was unrepentant. Embodying the changed times and mores in Japan, he brazenly denounced the emperor system "as a mummy with rotten flesh." Said mummy, Matsushima added, "should be put in the grave."

The senior procurator Mitsusada Yoshikawa then made a case for the accused's legally valid arraignment and prosecution for crimes of *lèse-majesté*.[59] He argued that the relevant articles of the criminal code were less about the rights of one individual than the "rights of the State [*sic*] existence and that of the nation's unified body, symbolized by the Emperor himself."[60] In this submission, *lèse-majesté* protected the integrity and prestige not of a person but of the national polity, the *kokutai*. Yoshikawa further submitted that freedom of speech, while an important value, as it was here, "should not be in contradiction to the 'public welfare.'" In view of the novelty and complexity of the case, the presiding judges adjourned the matter so that counsel could prepare further written and oral argument on the legal issues.

As the Matsushima case was prosecuted to a verdict, it was a matter of no small alarm to the leaders of GS that in 1946 and 1947 the Japanese authorities were willing to bring, justify, and sustain *lèse-majesté* prosecutions.[61] This stance provoked a stern response. In a memorandum reviewing the section's options on the issue, Oppler observed that "the humanization of the Emperor as announced by himself and as implied by the draft constitution should find its legal expression in a revision of the [*lèse-majesté*] articles." The time had come for the Japanese political class to accept that "the Emperor has become a public figure of political life exposed to criticism." While it was arguable that as the symbol of the state the emperor might properly enjoy some enhanced protection from criminal libel, the articles in the extant criminal code of Japan were too widely drawn and too punitive in effect. This view was endorsed by Kades, and, in a September 1946 meeting with the executive committee of the LIC, Oppler informed the Japanese that SCAP opposed the retention of *lèse-majesté* in the revised code.[62]

To underline the gravity of SCAP's concerns, Oppler ordered that an inventory be taken of all persons who had been charged or convicted of *lèse-majesté* offenses since the surrender. All persons serving sentences for such offenses were to be released immediately. Oppler also demanded a full explanation from the MofJ as to why some official had sanctioned the prosecution in the Matsushima's case in the face of SCAP's explicit opposition.

Later in September, having owned up to approving the prosecution of Matsushima, the MofJ remained defiant.[63] In the ministry's view, neither Potsdam nor SCAP directives had foreclosed prosecution of persons for having made plainly defamatory public statements about the emperor. In the placard case specifically, ministry officials insisted, "The defendant went far beyond the limits of fair and reasonable criticism." The ministry's position (clearly disingenuous) was that in the placard prosecution it was purely incidental that the emperor, not some ordinary citizen, had been the victim of the defamatory remarks. In that case, the emperor was only being afford the protections enjoyed by all other Japanese persons.

GS did not find these arguments in the least compelling. Oppler's September 23 memorandum on "Lese majesty" set forth the section's rebuttal.[64] The prosecution of Matsushima underscored that the slowness of Japanese officials to accept the revolutionary intent of American policy and its goal to radically alter the traditional tenets of Japanese criminal law, the sacredness and inviolability of the emperor among them. The new constitution had normalized the emperor as but another figure of political life. Although the emperor remained a symbol of the state and unity of the people, in Oppler's view, "This cannot be construed as meaning any limitation upon the fundamental human rights of the people." Matsushima's placard doubtlessly had been vulgar and tactless, but it "did not go beyond the limits usually recognized in democratic countries to political criticism of the head of state."

The placard prosecution directly contradicted SCAP's declared policy that under Japan's new constitution, fully ratified or not, individual rights invalidated illiberal laws of all kinds, including those relating to the emperor. But the hopeful confidence that this policy would be respected by Japan's governing elite was no longer tenable.[65] At the end of September 1946, Oppler was obliged to state the obvious: "The trial in the placard case gives evidence that the Japanese authorities have not yet grasped the true meaning of this change or refuse to draw the necessary conclusions from it."

It did not take much longer to realize that on *lèse-majesté* SCAP was dealing rather more with refusal than incomprehension. On September 26, the Japanese LIC provided yet another plan for the revision of the criminal code, one that "would continue the crime of Lese-majeste, although with certain changes and perhaps under a new name."[66] Before GS had formulated a response, the placard case returned to trial on October 2, 1946.[67]

Neither the procurator nor the accused, Matsushima, was prepared to relent. In answer to questions from the bench, Matsushima explained that he had been moved to paint a sign critical of the emperor because of his belief, unchanged since the "Food Day" demonstration, that the "food crisis confronting this country could not be solved without establishing a complete democratic structure."[68] In their summing up for the defense, Matsushima's lawyers argued that SCAP's civil liberties directive, combined with impending constitutional change, nullified the legal basis of charges against their client. In his turn, the procurator reasserted both the legal validity of the *lèse-majesté* offenses and their applicability on the facts of the case.

Before the court provided its verdict in the placard case, there were further public and private maneuverings regarding the *lèse-majesté* issue. The MofJ announced a general amnesty of all persons (there were two) in Japan who had been convicted and sentenced on *lèse-majesté* charges.

Matushima would not go to jail even if convicted. Then a procurator in Tokyo dismissed *lèse-majesté* charges against five members of the Communist Party.[69] Behind the scenes, Oppler met with the chief of the Criminal Affairs Section of the MofJ and informed him that SCAP wanted the judges to provide a verdict in the case before November 1. If that was not possible, SCAP would leave it for the MofJ to decide whether to "drop the prosecution or to have the defendant benefit from the general amnesty."[70]

On November 2, the Tokyo court rendered a guilty verdict in the placard case. The court found that the words on Matsushima's sign were "vulgar, mean, insulting and sensational," and had been calculated to injure the reputation of the emperor. The contention of the defense that the placard was merely satirical political criticism, not criminal defamation, was dismissed. The panel of judges ruled that "all the rights of freedom guaranteed to the people must not be abused and [must] always be useful for the public welfare." Then, in a surprising twist, the court also ruled that the Potsdam Declaration and the directives of SCAP had in fact altered the law of *lèse-majesté* in Japan. The accused was guilty of a criminal offense but not for *lèse-majesté;* these charges had been abolished *de facto.* The court found Matsushima guilty of having committed criminal libel against the reputation of the emperor as a private citizen.[71] With regard to sentence, there were conflicting factors. On one hand, because the emperor was a "symbol of the unity of the people and the state," the offense in this case was an egregious one. On the other, since the defamation had been uttered by a man out of sincere if misguided political conviction, the correct sentence was a comparatively short jail term of eight months.

In his memorandum on the judgment, Oppler thought the court's reasoning "not at all convincing." While it was a positive development that it had ruled that the *lèse-majesté* provisions of the old criminal code had "become obsolete and that defamation of the emperor must be punished under the general provisions concerning libel and insult," the decision of the court to waive the requirement of a personal complaint was "highly objectionable from a legal point of view."[72]

In the meantime, MacArthur himself released a public statement that the "continuation of specific *lese-majeste* provisions would be contrary to the letter and spirit of the new Constitution."[73] A week later, Kades and Oppler met with senior officials at the MofJ to inform them that SCAP was frustrated by the seeming unwillingness of the government to abolish *lèse-majesté*. Kades indicated to the Japanese that it was the expectation of SCAP that this would be done and that, henceforth, the emperor and imperial household would enjoy the same protections, no more and no less, than as provided by the general provisions of the law. In the face of further remonstrations from the Japanese officials, Kades concluded the meeting by stating that he considered the meeting the "final discussion of the matter at that level." If the minister of justice still labored under any doubts as to SCAP's policy, Kades stated that "he should let us know so that a meeting between General Whitney and the Minister could be arranged."

The Japanese were so unyielding on this point that the meeting was requested and took place. Whitney stated unequivocally that the "Japanese Government was under an obligation to abolish the lese-majeste provisions" of the old criminal code.[74] He conveyed the Supreme Commander's great displeasure that the provisions had not been repealed in spite of repeated warnings. When the minister of justice demurred, stating that it was too late in the current Diet's term to repeal *lèse-majesté,* Whitney stressed that the demand was to be treated as "an official directive from the Supreme Commander, which can be carried out through an Imperial Ordinance." The minister was then told to provide an update on his progress before the end of business the next day. In regard to *lèse-majesté,* the Americans had finally laid down the law.[75]

But even when confronted with Whitney's dictat, the government still did not immediately capitulate—not, that is, until its leaders had made the point clearly that the governing class of Japan remained steadfast in its devotion to traditional political values, to the *kokutai.*

In this spirit, on December 27, 1946, Prime Minister Yoshida sent a letter to MacArthur in reference to the *lèse-majesté* directive.[76] Once again, even at great risk of infuriating the Supreme Commander, Yoshida reiterated the "several reasons" that necessitated the retention of *lèse-majesté* offenses in the criminal code. The prime minister contended that in the new constitutional framework, the imperial house persisted as a symbol of the state. The "traditional faith" remained that "the Emperor is ethically the center of national veneration." On that basis, any indignity directed toward the emperor or his household was rightly regarded as "subversive of the State, and deserving of . . . a severer punishment than any act of violence against the person of an ordinary individual." The letter also reminded the Supreme Commander that other constitutional monarchies had retained *lèse-majesté* offenses in their criminal law.

MacArthur was remarkably mild in his first response to Yoshida's defiance. Instead of issuing a SCAPIN forcing the government's hand, he invited GS to study the issue further, particularly Yoshida's claims about *lèse-majesté* in Western constitutional monarchies. On December 31, Oppler filed a research memorandum claiming that *lèse-majesté* was moribund in all of the countries cited by Yoshida.[77] On February 19, 1947, Oppler met with the minister of justice, reiterating GS's demand that *lèse-majesté* was to be immediately expunged from the criminal code by imperial ordinance. In a remarkable demonstration of defiance, however, the minister informed Oppler that the prime minister would accede to this demand only on receipt of a "formal directive" from the Supreme Commander.

Yoshida received the directive on February 25, complete with an explanatory letter from MacArthur. The Supreme Commander stated that the emperor was "entitled to no more or less legal protection than that accorded to all other citizens." To suggest otherwise, MacArthur wrote, is to "violate the fundamental concept, clearly and unequivocally expressed . . . that all men are equal before the law."[78] In reference to the *kokutai,* MacArthur added, "The former concept of a peculiar Japanese national ethic distinctly different from universally recognized ethical principles was repudiated by the Emperor himself in his Rescript of January 1st 1946, eschewing the myths and legends from which the concept was created." As an outgrowth of these myths and legends, it was time that *lèse-majesté* was expunged from Japanese law.

Two months later, Yoshida's conservatives were obliged to yield to Katayama's socialists. Not accidentally, Yoshida left office without having abolished *lèse-majesté.* At the end of April 1947, Oppler was in the humiliating position of having to remind a third minister of justice that "the Supreme Commander is extremely concerned with the question of the revision of the Penal Code" and that he "insists that the Lese-majeste provisions must disappear completely."[79] But in July, not only had these instructions not been carried out, to Oppler's "astonishment" the placard case still was being litigated in the appellate courts. Adding insult to this injury, the procurators, with the support of the minister of justice, contended both that *lèse-majesté* remained a crime in Japan and on the facts established at trial Matsushima was guilty of that crime.[80]

Soon thereafter, the Japanese appeals court ruled on the case, finding that the equality article of the constitution "does not demand that every individual 'should be uniformly protected regardless of their social position.'"[81] In the court's view, because the constitution defined the emperor as the symbol of the state, he was to enjoy special protections from defamation. And because the crimes of *lèse-majesté* had not been abolished when Matsushima was charged, he had been convicted under valid law. However, the appellate court decided that Matsushima was entitled to an acquittal based on an amnesty passed by the Diet subsequent to his conviction.

In the late fall of 1947, as the socialists inched forward with a bill to revise the criminal code, Yoshida Shigeru, now in opposition, continued to maneuver so that his Liberal Party would not be implicated in the abolition of *lèse-majesté.*[82] Using back channels, he informed GS that the Liberal Party planned to propose a last-minute amendment to the government's bill, one that would retain at least a diluted version of the offenses. In no uncertain terms, Kades condemned this bit of political theater as an affront to the explicit policy of the Supreme Commander and as "untenable, ill-advised, and wholly outrageous." Yoshida's move was yet another calculated show of defiance, one meant to underscore the depth of his party's willingness to defend the *kokutai.* When the next general election was held, Yoshida would be able to state, with perfect sincerity, that he and the Liberals had done everything in their power to impede the abolition of *lèse-majesté*.

On October 14, 1947, the Katayama's government passed the bill amending the criminal code.[83] The *lèse-majesté* offenses of the old code had been eliminated. In the new law, SCAP's press release stated, the emperor was "now one of the people" enjoying "no more and no less than the protection accorded the ordinary citizen."[84] "The abolition of *lèse-majesté*, SCAP further pronounced, "will certainly be a cornerstone on the Japan's way to a free society."

The new code notwithstanding, the status of Matsushima's conviction in the placard case remained unclear until May 1948.[85] At that time, the Supreme Court of Japan ruled that because of the general amnesty for *lèse-majesté* convictions, the Matsushima appeal was moot. The amnesty eliminated any necessity to decide the legal issues raised by the charge and conviction.[86] Accordingly, the Supreme Court declined to render a retroactive judgment on these issues. After more than two years of litigation and political wrangling, the *lèse-majesté* imbroglio finally was over. However, the fight over the content and operation of the criminal justice reforms of 1947 was far from over.

At the close of 1947, although the clash over *lèse-majesté* had left bruises, Government Section was content with piecemeal reform of Japan's criminal code. After all, the French code (on which the Japanese law had been based) provided basic protections for the rights and dignity of the accused. On the other hand, the senior law reformers at the section—Kades, Oppler, and now Thomas Blakemore—were resolved not to settle for anything less than the comprehensive "modernization and humanization" of Japanese criminal procedure.[87] While Japan's criminal procedure also had been based on a modern European model, the 1922 German Imperial Code of Criminal Procedure, in this instance the code's pedigree presented a serious problem. The German and then Japanese codes, both in their written content and practical functioning, did not respect the liberal due process commitments of "the Anglo-Saxon system."[88]

In the presurrender system of criminal procedure in Japan, we noted, police and procurators wielded wide and largely unsupervised powers in the arrest, detention, and interrogation of criminal suspects. The police, procurators, and courts operated in a manner that amounted to the presumption of the accused's guilt.[89] Most criminal charges led to prolonged pretrial detention and unsupervised interrogation (by police and prosecutors), often involving physical force or intimidation. Almost invariably, detention concluded with a sworn confession. In the criminal courts of Japan, the main role of judges was to find guilt based on confession and sentence. In this way the judges acted primarily as "the representative and protector of the majesty and force of the state."[90] The main role of defense lawyers in this system was to minimize the penal impact of conviction.

Criminal justice in Japan had been authoritarian before the embellishments of the wartime era. During the war years, however, a harsh system was made far harsher by the formal and informal expansion of police and prosecutorial power.[91] The prevailing American view was that, by 1945, Japanese criminal process had become little more than a means by which the imperial state deterred or punished dissent.[92]

The goal of American-supervised reform in this field, therefore, was to assist the Japanese government in making comprehensive reform to criminal procedure so to provide "elaborate safeguards for the protection of the individual" in every stage of his contact with the criminal justice apparatus, from arrest to trial and possible punishment.[93] As for the Japanese politicians and bureaucrats who were to draft the new code, their goal was quite different. Realizing that the new constitution and its liberal ideological slant were *faits accompli,* they sought to conserve as much of the extant system of criminal process as circumstances would allow.

In the winter of 1946, little more than a year before the new constitution was to be ratified, GS officers devised a plan by which the Japanese government would overhaul criminal procedure in two stages. In the first stage it would draft and enact a temporary procedural code that would, as one of the American lawyers put the point, "reform immediately the worst abuses which could not wait the drafting of an entirely new Code."[94] In the second phase, to be completed by the summer of 1948, the Japanese government would devise and pass into law a completely revised new code, one that reflected liberal constitutional norms and due process requirements.

In May 1946, in a departure from GS policy that the Japanese were to initiate all reform proposals, an American lawyer at the Public Safety Section of the counterintelligence division of SCAP circulated an "extremely painstaking" revision of the code of criminal procedure. The Maniscalco Code (named for the Texas lawyer who produced it) was a synthesis of a number of American state codes of criminal procedure, all based on adversarial due process and jury trials.[95] If adopted by the Japanese, the Maniscalco Code would signal a decisive shift in Japanese law from a continental to an Anglo-American model of criminal procedure.

Revealingly, the Maniscalco Code was killed by GS before being sent to the Japanese government. The section's reasoning was that reform of criminal procedure was primarily a Japanese problem that ought to be driven by the Japanese themselves in a manner consistent with their domestic legal traditions.[96] "A general shift to Anglo-American practices," Blakemore commented, "would require a major transformation of legal thought." In supervising reform in this field, Oppler concurred, SCAP was ill advised to cause the "abolition of basically sound institutions."[97] In any event, it was thought fruitless to impose a foreign model of procedure if only because the "Japanese courts, procurators, and lawyers, accustomed to a completely different system, would not be able to apply it adequately."[98]

In the spring and summer of 1946, the Legislative Revision Committee (LRC) of the new Yoshida government, made up of Ministry of Justice bureaucrats and legal academics, were invited to create first drafts of interim and then permanent codes of criminal procedure. It submitted draft codes for review by Courts and Law in September. For Oppler and associates the drafts were a rude shock. Key provisions—for instance, those governing police and prosecutorial powers to arrest, detain, and interrogate—blatantly did not conform to the plain language or underlying norms of the constitution.[99] Police and procurators were to continue to wield wide discretionary power over the persons and liberties of suspects.

When the Americans requested amendments to the draft bills, they faced stalling tactics.[100] It was now obvious that the Japanese government had dug in against the liberalization of criminal procedure. Oppler responded to the impasse by arranging a series of bilateral conferences between GS officers and the LRC. In the first round of meetings, Blakemore noted, substantial differences of opinion had arisen on a number of issues, especially relating to the legal powers of police, procurators, and judges to cause the warrantless arrest and detention of persons.[101] On the American side, these powers were seen as dangerous and unnecessary and as contrary to the spirit, if not the letter, of the new Constitution.[102] It seemed that the Japanese wanted to override the fact that the constitution had been designed "to state and safeguard civil liberties."

In the result, Oppler refused to endorse any move to "grant to procurators powers which are without parallel in other democratic countries."[103] In a rare open departure from the pretense that law reform was a collaboration between equal partners, Oppler "made it completely clear [to his counterparts in the Japanese government] that the proposed provisions, insofar as they deal with arrest and detention, cannot be approved by SCAP."

By the close of 1946, GS had drawn some lines in the sand. It would permit the Japanese to reform their own code of criminal procedure. GS would also tolerate the persistence of some vestiges of the presurrender system. But a clear signal had been sent that GS would withhold approval from procedure that was patently inconsistent with the new constitution. GS would not for instance sign off on provisions that preserved the power of prosecutors (or other nonjudicial officials) to issue warrants of arrest, that did not strictly limit periods of pretrial detention, that did not include a presumptive right to bail, that did not provide accused persons with generous access to defense counsel, and, finally, that did not, in the course of a criminal trial, provide the accused and his counsel ample opportunity to impeach the state's evidence and legal case.

In the course of deliberations with the Americans, Japanese officials with the LRC resisted on all these points. They continued to do so until it was made plain by GS, in the first weeks of 1947, that it was prepared to act unilaterally on interim reform. Only then was the temporary measures bill amended and sent to the Diet.

When the bill became law in April 1947, just a few weeks before the new constitution took effect, both procurators and police in Japan had in fact lost legal powers to issue warrants of arrest or detention.[104] Procurators had lost legal powers to control judges and trial proceedings. The law also severely limited the pretrial inquisition of accused persons. With regard to criminal trial itself, the accused and their counsel were also to enjoy new and extensive rights to "examine all witnesses who have given testimony against them." Overstating the case, SCAP's propaganda machine[105] trumpeted that the people of Japan were "no longer at the mercy of law" when facing criminal investigation or trial.[106] In devising a new constitution and now provisional laws of criminal procedure, so the narrative went, the Japanese government had moved to "protect the people from arbitrary acts on the part of the police, the public procurator and the judiciary."

All such self-congratulatory talk aside, the senior American lawyers at the Courts and Law division knew that much of the hardest work on criminal procedure had yet to be done. As Oppler reminded a group of senior Japanese procurators in February 1948, the interim Code of Criminal Procedure was a stopgap measure containing "only the most elementary implementation of the new Constitution and its principles of fundamental human rights."[107] For Oppler the challenge now was to complete the comprehensive and permanent revision of criminal procedure and, in so doing, "do away with the vicious features of the police state of the past."

During the winter of 1948, now against the backdrop of a full-blown socioeconomic crisis and crime wave, the socialist Katayama government organized a new special legislative committee, this one staffed by senior judges and procurators, legal academics and both private and MofJ lawyers, to design and draft a permanent Code of Criminal Procedure. The committee began work with Oppler's personal assurance that neither he nor any other SCAP official would interfere with its draft bill so long as it "properly implements the principles of the Constitution and is not contrary to the objectives of occupation."[108]

In Oppler's account, these assurances engendered a climate of cooperation and goodwill as between American and Japanese. A product of "arduous" but constructive labor, the bill was drafted and amended without rancor.[109] This, at least, was the official American view of what had transpired.

The new bill contained a draft code consisting of more than 500 articles and described the complete arc of procedural rights and state obligations in the criminal prosecution of an accused person. When in receipt of the first complete English language draft of the code, Oppler broke it down into five subject areas and assigned a Courts and Law lawyer to evaluate each one.[110] Their job was to create "problem sheets" for any issues raised by particular provisions of the draft law. Before they committed an issue to a problem sheet, the lawyers were cautioned not to find fault with a provision solely on grounds that it was inconsistent with the American or Anglo-Saxon approach to the same procedural point.[111] Once again, so far as they respected the broad strokes of the constitution, the Japanese were to be given purchase to write their own law.

The general conference on the new Japanese code of criminal procedure convened on April 13, 1948. With the goal of submitting a finished bill to the Diet before the end of its current session, the conference met almost daily for the next three weeks. Oppler and three other GS lawyers represented SCAP in the deliberations. Most of the entire Japanese drafting committee, some thirty jurists in all, were in attendance most days. Oppler chaired the sessions, which consisted of discussion, one by one, of the eighty-eight problem sheets.

According to Oppler's recollection, at the outset of these sessions he had taken pains to explain to the Japanese that it was not American policy to impose its own version of a code of criminal procedure.[112] Oppler and the other American lawyers were there to offer information and advice on points of law and to moderate the debate, to be held principally in the Japanese language (Blakemore translating for the other Americans). As chair, Oppler had been determined to foster free discussion among the Japanese and between the Japanese and Americans. In his own estimation, he succeeded. As the meetings unfolded, Oppler recalled, "We were able to overcome . . . the initial stiffness of our discussion partners, after they realized that we not only wanted to give them a hearing, but were genuinely eager to learn from them."[113] In this account, the American and Japanese lawyers soon "felt and acted like international colleagues in law." Most issues were resolved by consensus, some by show-of-hands vote.

The American-made minutes of these meetings depict sessions that were technical and businesslike to the point of tedium.[114] If there was strong disagreement about the permanent shape and content of criminal procedure in Japan, it is not in evidence. Indeed, the final version of the bill had been so entirely satisfactory to both sides that on conclusion of the conference on May 5, 1948, the Japanese in attendance "tossed bouquets to one another and to SCAP for the successful completion of discussions regarding the revision of the Code."[115]

In his later account of these proceedings, however, Oppler hinted at a rather less harmonious process.[116] The criminal defense and civil liberties lawyers present for the meetings had frequently been at odds with the judges (but especially with the procurators) over a number of substantive points of procedure and their implementation. These lawyers had advocated for procedural rules that maximized the rights of accused persons at every stage of criminal process. Conversely, the procurators and ministry officials at the table strongly contended for rules that vindicated the interests of state and community. As one procurator was recorded to have stated during deliberations, "It is equally important to protect the public against criminals as it is to protect the rights of an accused."[117]

The final bill reflected, on its face, some substantial victories for liberal reform.[118] The new code, like the interim one, was based on the principle that the accused and his counsel should be in a position of rough equality with the procurator. It also reinforced the institutional separation of police and prosecutorial actors. It was now to be more difficult for agents of state to cause accused persons to be arrested without warrant or make self-incriminating statements before being charged or tried. The code consolidated the rights of accused persons to consult defense counsel and know the nature of charges and the legal basis of detention. It also prohibited police and prosecutors from their former practice of appending the entire file of police and procurators' records to the judge's trial book. Furthermore, for the first time in Japanese history persons under detention might apply for bail as a matter of right.

The new draft code also called for substantial changes in the criminal trial. Henceforth, trials would be held before a judge (in felony cases, before a panel of three judges) equipped, as in the continental tradition, with extensive authority to interrogate witnesses. In a key innovation, accused persons and their counsel also were to have extensive rights of examination and cross-examination. Under new rules the credibility of witnesses might now be directly impeached.[119] Judges were not to convict solely on the basis of an accused's uncorroborated confession. Upon a guilty verdict, convicted persons were to have more and broader rights of appeal.

After further consideration and slight amendment by Diet committees, the new Code of Criminal Procedure became law on July 10, 1948. It was to come into effect on January 1 the next year. The stated purpose of the law was to "realize criminal laws and ordinances fairly and speedily" and to do so in the interest of "public welfare and security of fundamental human rights of individuals."[120]

According to the American line on the new code, there was "no doubt that its passage was a momentous step in the direction of human freedom and the rule of law in Japan."[121] For the first time in the history of Japan, the Supreme Court's press release stated, criminal trials were to be regulated by "rigid rules of evidence and the strengthening of the principle of direct examination." In a host of ways, including new and robust rights of appeal, the criminal law of Japan was to safeguard "the fundamental human rights of the accused person."[122] On its face, all of the main parties to the reform process agreed, the code represented a decisive shift in Japanese criminal justice.

The key question now, as General MacArthur himself put it, was not the letter of law, but whether the legal professionals of Japan—judges, procurators, and private defense attorneys—had the resolve to actually "*practice* the simple yet transcendental principles which modern civilization demands" (emphasis added).

In American eyes, great latitude had been afforded the Japanese experts and lawmakers in rendering change as they saw right and proper, even when SCAP might have wanted reforms to go farther. But even as GS made concessions to Japanese autonomy and preference, it was abundantly clear that many constituencies within the Japanese state—legal bureaucrats, conservative politicians, and criminal prosecutors most prominently—were not reconciled to the new law and its liberal innovations. By the time it was activated, some members of these groups, encouraged by conservatives in the office of the attorney general, were preparing to do whatever might be done to sabotage the liberal reform program.

In December 1947, in his press release on the new criminal code, Howard Meyers trenchantly observed that law reform projects were a fine thing but that "on the whole, the unsatisfactory administration of criminal justice in Japan of the past was not to be blamed on the law, but the methods employed in enforcing it."[123] The upshot of this remark (and of similar comments by Alfred Oppler) was plain: GS could exert influence over the content of new law codes but not the spirit in which they were read and actuated.[124]

What Meyers and Oppler knew—but were not stating publically—is that by the time the new criminal justice codes came fully into effect in 1949, a coalition of conservative Japanese politicians and bureaucrats, together with the majority of police and prosecutors, were disposed to ignore or undermine them. Japanese conservatives were fearful of liberal law reform, in particular of its ill effects on public order. By the summer of 1947, with Japan in the grip of a full-blown socioeconomic crisis, these concerns became magnified. Anxiety was rising that American-sponsored reform of criminal justice would hamper efforts to contain Japan's militant Left. Fortunately for the Japanese Right, unfortunately for liberal law reform, these concerns were shared by a growing number of American officials in Japan and Washington.

Japan's new Code of Criminal Procedure came into effect on January 1, 1949. On paper, this was a major event in the legal history of Japan. In terms of the actual operation of the new system, however, Yoshida and his Liberal Party won the general election on January 3. The most influential and, on issues of law and order, staunchly conservative politician of the postwar era had come to power just in time to exert potent influence on criminal justice reform.

As previously noted, Yoshida was passionately devoted to the shibboleths of postwar Japanese conservatism, beginning with his allegiance to a constitutional monarchy and the *kokutai.* The twin aims of Yoshida's government were to revive Japan's corporate business sector while crushing the hard left–dominated labor movement and its radical leadership.[125] In so doing Yoshida was determined to restore stability and discipline in Japan's cities and factories. His program called for a stern "law and order" brand of criminal justice, one valuing public order and collective security over individual rights and due process.

The Yoshida government was the second to have the prerogative to appoint a new attorney general (AG), the office having been established in December 1947.[126] One of the AG's key responsibilities was to oversee Japan's new system of criminal investigation and prosecution and to ensure that police and procurators exercised their powers in ways consistent with the constitution. It did not take long for Japanese politicians to realize that the AG, the senior law officer of the national state, wielded vast discretionary power over which persons or groups would feel the force of criminal law. The AG's office was also certain to make an indelible impact on the interpretation and application of the new law of criminal justice.

Little wonder then that, in October 1948, the first appointment to the office of AG was fiercely contested. The president of one of the Tokyo Bar Associations was adamant that the first appointee should be a person "not affiliated with any political parties."[127] A former justice of the old Supreme Court (Noritaka Nemoto) lobbied SCAP to appoint former Chief Justice Nagayoshi Hosono.[128] Nemoto hoped that Hosono would ensure that the AG's office would be "politically neutralized in light of the existing corruption." Hosono was also endorsed by yet another former Supreme Court Justice, who told Oppler that it was vital to the neutral operation of the criminal justice system that politicians be prevented from appointing a "Fascist" to the AG's office.[129]

These and other similar entreaties about the appointment of legal officers were rebuffed by GS.[130] The time had passed when SCAP would intercede to select a cabinet member for an elected Japanese government.[131] Thus, when Yoshida was returned to power in late October 1948, he was left alone to appoint an AG of his choosing. His conservative and thus steadfastly anti-Communist disposition in this matter was about to be reinforced by the rightward shift (the so-called reverse course[132]) in the Truman administration's policy stance toward the occupation of Japan and the corresponding decline in power, prestige, and personnel of the liberal reform faction within SCAP.[133] In this climate, Yoshida was unembarrassed to appoint Shunkichi Ueda, a rabidly anti-Communist political operative and bureaucrat, as Japan's AG.[134]

This appointment was an unmistakable sign—to SCAP, members of the legal professions, and the Japanese people—that the government was to be more committed to the "order" part of "law and order." Shortly after taking office, Ueda informed Japan's law enforcement officials that his policy was to mobilize the criminal justice system in support of social and economic recovery and in resolute opposition to left-wing militancy. "Our country now stands at a truly critical moment," Ueda told a conference of Japan's senior procurators in June 1949, "and her rise or fall will be decided by our determination and conduct in the next few months."[135] In a speech to lawyers, Ueda emphasized his government's *economic* policy initiatives, how it was imperative (for instance) to "suppress inflation and promote foreign trade to regain the stability and independence of our national economy at all costs." In this regard, Ueda warned that in the short term socioeconomic conditions in Japan were likely to become even more "straitened and austere, and the impending personal retrenchment . . . must bring acute sufferings and friction to the national life in all its phases." Ueda thought it probable, therefore, that for a period of time strikes and other forms of civil unrest would become still more prevalent.

Ueda's speech underscored the connectedness of the government's economic and law enforcement programs. "The more the social stability is threatened," Ueda explained, "the stronger becomes the necessity of vigilance over peace and security, and your responsibility will become greater in proportion." What was the principal responsibility of the procurators in this historical moment? Was it to protect the new and extensive due process rights of persons accused of crimes? Was it to perfect the rule of law under the new constitution? "It is my earnest wish," Ueda explained by way of answer, "that you [procurators] will exercise your correct judgment in the interest of the country's future prosperity and give full play to your sacred function for the achievement *of our economic recovery*" [emphasis added].

In case of doubt as to his meaning, Ueda enlarged the point: "In particular, I want you to take resolute measures, as stern as the law permits, against any lawless and malignant activities of undemocratic elements who aim at the destruction of democratic government under the cloak of democracy, and nip evils in the bud." Stressing the point, Ueda added, "In exhorting you to manage the affairs of prosecution from the standpoint of economic reconstruction and the establishment of democracy I do not mean that you discharge your duties with any political end in view." Nor did he mean to imply, so there was no misunderstanding on this point, that procurators were to "serve the interests particularly of industrialists or conservative forces."

The upshot of Ueda's statement was plain: repeal of the American-sponsored new Code of Criminal Procedure being out of the question, law enforcement officials were encouraged by the highest law officer of state to subordinate constitutional rights and due process to political and economic goals. In Japan in 1948, liberal due process in criminal matters remaining alien to most police and prosecutors, Ueda's remarks might have been heard as implicit repudiation of the reform program.

In fact, as the general reform of Japan's constitution and system of criminal justice neared completion at the end of 1947, reconstructive work had hardly begun on the institutions and norms of lawyers in private practice.[136] To that point, the most striking feature of the private bar in Japan was its social, political, and legal insignificance.[137] "The lawyers in Japan," Alfred Oppler observed in 1947, "are far from enjoying the prestige of their brethren in western countries and also from exercising any important political influence. Here the legal profession is a predominately technical and business character."[138]

Barely fifty years old at midcentury, Japan's legal profession was small by Anglo-American standards, fractious, and dominated by a department of state, the Ministry of Justice. At the time of the surrender, no more than a few thousand men (and a tiny handful of women) were engaged in the private practice of law in Japan.[139] The bar lacked both for numbers and for centralized institutions. It also lacked for a numerous segment of the bar devoted to criminal defense and other forms of civil libertarian practice. In the 1920s and 1930s, only a few score of intrepid liberal and leftist attorneys advocated for the defense in criminal cases,[140] including in a number of sensational anti-Communist "political" trials.[141] In a profession occupied mainly with domestic and commercial work, lawyers specializing in criminal defense or civil rights litigation were both uncommon and, even against the measure of lawyering in other continental legal regimes, uncommonly passive.[142]

In Japan it was unlikely for trial advocates, still less criminal trial advocates, to emerge as leaders of the bar. In part this was a function of custom. The low status of criminal law advocacy was due to the fact that the presurrender system of criminal justice had afforded so little scope to defend an accused person from criminal prosecution.

We have seen that defense counsel had little pretrial access to the accused or potential defense witnesses. When cases came to court, opportunities were limited to impeach the state's evidence or raise points of law. On the other hand, the almost unlimited access to accused persons of police and prosecutors (and routine recourse to torture) almost invariably yielded decisive confessions. In this system of justice, one strongly imbued with a Confucian ethic of conciliation, the principal goal was to vindicate communal rather than individual interests.[143] The customary role of the defense attorney was to "humbly point out extenuating circumstances, beg leniency and promise no future violations."[144]

As early as January 1946, a law professor of Tokyo's Imperial University, Kenzo Takayangi, publically argued for the reinvention of

Japan's bar as free and fearless advocates for the individual rights of persons accused of criminal offenses.[145] "The democratic and liberal Japan if ever it comes," the professor prophesized, "will be . . . the golden age of the advocate." With Takayangi, Japan's liberal and leftist trial lawyers had earnestly hoped in 1945 that the abject defeat of authoritarianism in Japan, combined with the advent of liberal constitutionalism, portended a golden age of vigorous liberal advocacy.

A few weeks after the start of the occupation, a coalition of socialist, Communist, and liberal lawyers formed the Liberal Lawyers' League and began to lobby SCAP for law reform while acting for labor unionists and other activists. Indeed, it became a cause of concern at GS in 1946 that civil liberties work in Japan soon became "restricted to a handful of extreme leftist lawyers."[146]

At the close of 1946, the MofJ decided, in light of imminent constitutional change, that it should thoroughly revise the Lawyers' Law governing the legal profession. A committee made up of the leading local bar associations, MofJ bureaucrats, some judges, and legal academics was struck for the purpose of making a draft law.[147] The advertised motivation for this reform was to "protect human rights, maintenance of social justice, and clarification of the mission of lawyers."[148] Improvement was also sought in the standards of bar admission and professional discipline. The basic thrust of the draft bill was to abolish the supervisory role of the MofJ over the bar, locating these powers in the hands of autonomous local and national bar associations.[149] While the lawyers at GS thought that the MofJ's draft law reflected "reasonably sound and progressive" ideas, political infighting within the Yoshida governing coalition, plus controversy about the bar admission of previously purged procurators and judges, delayed progress of the bill.[150]

The bill was *not* delayed, on the other hand, by the attempted intercession of Japan's tiny but assertive contingent of women lawyers (eleven in total). In the advent of this American occupation, an occupation ostensibly rooted in liberal principles of equality, the women lawyers of Japan had not waited long to press their case.[151] As early as March 1946, one contingent of five women lawyers met with GS officials, Oppler included, to advance their views on the need for SCAP to appoint a new cohort of politically independent Japanese judges and prosecutors.[152] But no sooner had they established credentials as "natural fighters for legal equality and for the cause of democracy," the women lawyers and their aspirations were shunted to the margins of American attention. In the documents relating to reform of the Lawyers' Law, women are nowhere evident. Japan's women lawyers had been assigned a segregated bar association, one (men on both sides agreed) appropriately devoted to "family law and those legal aspects which affect the status of the female sex."[153]

Not until the winter of 1948, the new constitution now ratified and criminal justice reform imminent, was the general Lawyers' Law back on the Diet's agenda. The first articles of the draft law identified the "Mission and Duties of the Lawyer" being to "defend the fundamental human rights and realize social justice."[154] While this mission statement generated little debate, the question of the eligibility of former procurators and judges for calls to the practicing bar was highly contentious.[155] After months of additional deliberation, lobbying, and delay, a new Lawyers' Law bill was submitted to the Diet on May 9, 1949. The bill, complete with its idealistic preamble, passed in June 1949. Oppler later called the passage of this bill the "last important reform within the jurisdiction of my division."[156]

When it came into effect on September 1, 1949, the new Lawyers' Law established a national regulatory organization (the Federation of Japanese Bar Associations) that was to be independent from state supervision and control.[157] Only the Supreme Court of Japan, itself independent from state control, was to have authority to make rules governing the bar.[158] To practice law in Japan every lawyer was now required to achieve bar admission and maintain good standing in at least one local bar association (associated with the jurisdiction of a Japanese district court) and the national body. Based on norms established and enforced by the national federation, lawyers in Japan now exerted self-governing powers over bar admission, ethics, and discipline. Once again, on paper at least, the Lawyers' Law was a major step toward the creation of a bar that was, at least in theory, free to practice law in a way that might vindicate the legal rights of its clients, even when those clients faced the disfavor of the state or its officials.

In SCAP's propaganda, the Lawyers' Law was described as a kind of Emancipation Proclamation for lawyers. As a consequence of their own striving, so the story was told, Japanese lawyers finally had achieved "freedom from government domination."[159] In refusing to capitulate to former and would-be masters of state, the bar had elevated itself "to an independent status unique in Japan's history." But with such privilege, MacArthur himself emphasized in a message to the bar, came grave responsibilities.[160] The first article of the statute committed the bar to the "purposeful calling" of "defending and advancing those fundamental rights and liberties now held by the Japanese people under the Constitution." Whether Japan would or would not realize such rights and liberties, MacArthur stated, in substantial measure would turn on the bar's commitment to these "sacred precepts."

This reform cycle all but complete (on paper, at least) before the end of 1949, Japan now possessed the institutional ingredients of a liberal rule-of-law state. It had a liberal constitution and politically independent institutions of the judiciary and bar. It now possessed new codes of criminal law and procedure, laws reshaped to conform to liberal precepts of individual rights and due process. In all, Government Section had overseen perhaps the most dramatic structural revolutions of a legal system the world had ever seen. All the more remarkable then that the revolution came under purposeful and effective attack before its ink was dry.

Picking through the Spiritual Rubble: Reconstructing Nazi Criminal Justice

Most American knowledge about German criminal law and procedure and its denazification was created in 1944 to 1946 by the German émigré lawyers working for the London-based Special Legal Unit Germany / Austria (SLU) formerly attached to the Supreme Headquarters of the Allied Expeditionary Force (SHAEF). The SLU's first order of business had been to answer a series of questions on the nature and operation of German criminal justice from the Weimar republic through the war years of the Third Reich. What was the juristic nature and content of pre-Nazi criminal law and procedure? To what extent and on what principles had the National Socialists altered the definition, prosecution, and punishment of crime in Germany? On the assumption that these alterations had been extensive and authoritarian, how might they be eliminated? Had criminal law during the Weimar republic been sufficiently democratic that the Allies might wish to restore status quo circa 1932? If not, what would be entailed by the democratization of German criminal justice?

In the spring of 1945, the central thesis of SLU experts on these points was that the pre-Hitler criminal justice, while skewed by a "certain amount of bureaucratic authoritarianism," had been a "child of the liberal age" and therefore might be salvaged as the basis of a postwar German justice system.[161] The German penal code, for example, was admired for its "scholarly and scientific drafting."[162] Its Prussian heritage notwithstanding, the code had upheld the "rights of the defendant, stressed the publicity of hearings, and, above all, upheld a very liberal system of appeals."[163] Theoretically speaking, therefore, when the Nazis came to power German criminal law reflected modern liberal rationality. It was precisely because of its liberalism, because it had imposed genuine constraints on the state, that the Nazis had moved so decisively to circumvent and amend it.

Just as the SLU experts broadly admired the German system of criminal justice, equally they deplored the perversion of that system at the hands of the Nazis.[164] According to the Nazi ideology of the Third Reich, the imperative of authentically German law, criminal law or otherwise, was to support and develop the *volkgemeinschaft,* or pure racial community.[165] To Nationalist Socialist ideologues, legal ideas based on liberal rights or egalitarianism, based on "anything beyond race were bloodless abstractions, the vestiges of the Jewish conspiracy to undermine the German racial community."[166] The Nazis began to remove such abstractions with the suspension in March 1933 of the Weimar constitution and its due process guarantees.[167]

The Nazis then embarked on the more complex task of aligning all aspects of German criminal justice with the party's racial and political program.[168] In the first phase, in the form of the infamous Nuremberg Laws, the Nazis criminalized aspects of the social interaction of "Aryan" and non-Aryan persons. In the second phase, the Nazis created a new system of Special Courts to prosecute racial and political crime. In both the special and regular courts judges were directed to apply new, expanded, and ideologically motivated criteria of criminal culpability.[169] Thereafter, persons accused of crimes in Germany might be convicted on the basis of *ex post facto* law, or when, according to the unfettered discretion of judges, they were deemed to have acted against the *gesundes Volkssempfinden* or "sound feeling of the people."[170] Here the positivistic, law-bound approach to criminal guilt was supplanted by discretionary interpretation and application of the nebulous concept of "Nazi morality."[171] The Nazis had taken a rational theory of criminal culpability only to corrupt and debase it with an externally imposed cluster of emotions, prejudices, and mysticisms.

The advent of war in Europe, and by 1941 total war on two fronts, stimulated the Nazis to make still more—and more ruthless—innovations in German criminal law. We have noted that in 1942, American analysts had detected that "a critical situation had arisen in the German administration of justice by reason of the conflict between Nazi principles and practices and older standards."[172] With vast armies in foreign fields, with its cities under attack, with millions of alien laborers within its borders, with the Red Army pressing on the eastern front, Hitler and his circle now wanted Germany's prosecutors and judges to focus exclusively on the punishment of dissent and disorder.[173] By 1942, an American intelligence report summarized, these efforts had rendered German criminal justice as "a one-sided affair in which the police, the state attorney and the judge alike had the duty to hunt down and convict the criminal."

According to Allied legal analysts, however, the most important story was not how the Nazis had altered the principal definitions, frameworks, and procedures of criminal justice. While Nazi inroads had been significant, they had not changed the basic character of the system. For these analysts, the most significant development of

Nazi-era criminal justice was the degree to which arrests, detentions, and punishments were being inflicted entirely outside the purview of formal law or procedure.[174] By the end of the war, German and non-Germans alike lived in jeopardy of unwarranted arrest, indefinite detention, torture, and summary execution.[175] "Under such a rule without law," SLU analysts observed in February 1945, "the changes in individual legal provisions assume only secondary importance." One German jurist observed in 1946 that the once great edifice of Reich justice had been reduced to "spiritual rubble."[176] The thrust of American policy was to sift the rubble for the materials needed for the restoration of a liberal and law-based system of criminal justice.

With respect to the denazification and democratic reconstruction of German law and legal systems—criminal and otherwise—SHAEF-Legal Branch had operated under a limited mandate. Its job had been to devise and execute a plan exclusively for the initial phase of western Allied occupation of German soil—that is, the period between the first conquest of German soil by SHAEF military formations and the occupation and governance of Germany by the Allies as a whole. SHAEF's single responsibility was to plan and implement what was described as a "surgical operation," one by which legal officers were to exert control over German legal structures, personnel, and records.[177] In this initial phase, too, military proclamations drafted by SHAEF-Legal suspended Nazi-era racial and security laws and those upholding the power and wealth of the Nazi party.[178]

Thus, in March 1945, as Allied tactical units began to take and occupy German soil, SHAEF-HQ issued Military Proclamation No. 1, "The Abrogation of Nazi Law," which suspended a list of nine Nazi-era laws deemed fundamental to the power and policies of the Nazi party.[179] While the German criminal code was not on this list, the proclamation explicitly abrogated the Nuremberg Laws along with its inventory of racial crimes and punishments.

We have seen that in August 1945 Allied military proclamations were superseded by the Potsdam Agreement and new Allied undertakings to abolish all Nazi-era laws forming "the basis of the Hitler regime or established discriminations on grounds of race, creed, or political opinion."[180] On September 20, 1945, the newly constituted Allied Control Council (ACC), the quadpartite organ of central government in occupied Germany, approved its own Law No. 1. The nine Nazi-era statutes previously abrogated by military proclamation and an additional seventeen discriminatory laws were permanently repealed.[181]

These initiatives did little more than scratch the surface of criminal justice during the Third Reich. Of repealed Nazi laws, only one, a statute passed in April 1934 to amend selected provisions of criminal law and procedure, was directly relevant to criminal offenses, prosecution, and punishment. Not only were Nazi-era codes of criminal law and procedure largely untouched, but the denazification of criminal justice personnel barely had begun.

In the American zone, the balance of the legal denazification mission, its most difficult facets, were assigned to the Legal Divisions first of the United States Group Control Council (USGCC), then its successor, Office of Military Government, United States (AMG) based in Berlin. We have seen how, in grappling with this novel and enormously complex assignment, Legal Division (its executive leadership and professional staff) was woefully lacking in adequate training, knowledge, and resources. In no area were these deficiencies more nakedly apparent than with regard to the reform of south German criminal law and procedure. None of the roughly three dozen legal professionals who worked at Legal Division from 1945 to 1947, including the German (and Austrian) émigrés, had specialist training in any aspect of German criminal justice during Weimar or the Third Reich. The American contribution to legal denazification in the criminal justice field was carried out by American novices and German generalists.

It must therefore have come as no small relief to Legal Division's first director, Charles Fahy, when, on October 2, 1945, it was confirmed by the ACC that the denazification of German criminal justice was to be undertaken not on a zonal but on a national basis. Accordingly, the Legal Directorate (DLeg) of the council appointed a working party called the Committee on Revising the German Criminal Code to devise an action plan in the criminal law field. Staffed by jurists from each of the four occupying powers, the mandate of the working party was twofold. First, it would undertake a definitive and up-to-date survey of Nazi-era criminal justice law. Second, with this information in hand, the committee was to draft revised German codes of criminal law and procedure for enactment by the ACC. The four powers would then implement the revised codes at the zonal level.

It was typical of the American legal mission in Germany that its first delegate in this key area of legal denazification was one Ernest Schopler, a German émigré who had been a small-town lawyer in northern Bavaria. Although all indications are that Schopler was a hardworking and earnest man, having (in Karl Loewenstein's estimation) an excellent legal mind, he had taken this assignment without expert or academic knowledge of Weimar or Nazi-era criminal law.[182] Nor did he possess a scholar's training in the theoretical or comparative aspects of criminal law systems. For Loewenstein, at least, it was difficult to see what contribution Schopler could make to deliberations about the nature of democratic criminal law or procedure, or about the democratization of German criminal justice by the Allied powers.

Fortunately for Legal Division, by the fall of 1946, Schopler had been replaced on the working party by Max Rheinstein, a German born and trained jurist of impressive scholarly attainment.[183] It was now for Rheinstein to negotiate the formidable obstacles in the way of progress. By rule, first of all, before becoming an official part of record or discussion, every German legal text and every document created by the working party about such text had to be translated "with identical meaning" into the Control Council's three official languages. In all plenary sessions, moreover, the eight lawyer-delegates (two from each of the four powers) found themselves surrounded by interpreters and translators.[184]

Formidable as they were, these impediments were slight compared to achieving consensus among four disparate partners—one of which was itself an authoritarian state with an illiberal system of criminal justice—on the many unresolved conceptual and political issues. What was the archetypal "nazification" of some aspect of German criminal law or procedure? What was the main goal of denazification in the criminal justice field? Would it suffice simply to eliminate every Nazi-era law, restoring the Weimar system of criminal justice? Should the committee revive and adopt one of many pre-Nazi German-made schemes for the renovation of criminal justice? If the revision of German criminal justice was to be forward-looking, was it even conceivable that all four powers might agree on its precepts?

In the fall of 1945, the working party wrestled with these questions—if not productively, in the absence of overt conflict.[185] It did so on two implicit points of order. The first was that their work should focus on the destructive dimension of their task: the elimination of Nazi ideology from all facets of the German system of criminal justice. The second was to take pains to avoid any direct reference to the elephant (or one might more aptly say, *bear*) in the room—the unbridgeable chasm between the Western and Soviet delegations on the purpose, form, and content of criminal law and justice.[186]

In rigid adherence to this protocol, work started with the business of preparing the Allied Control Council (ACC) to abrogate those sections of the German code that bore the obvious taint of Nazi racial or political norms.[187] A draft enactment was completed by December 1945 and approved by the directorate in January 1946.[188] On January 30, the ACC enacted the draft as Law No. 11, "Repealing Certain Provisions of Criminal Legislation," a law which purported to abolish the "most flagrant Nazi innovations" in the criminal code, including provisions relating to the criteria of criminal guilt, treason, and political libel.[189] No. 11 also repealed seventeen Nazi-era legal instruments (these external to the criminal code) that, in the view of the council, had unduly increased either the scope of criminal culpability or the harshness of its punishment.

In taking this action, the ACC rejected a proposal of the British delegation to "undertake the denazification of German law as a whole," by effect to restore German law, including its criminal law, to its position on the last day, effectively, of the Weimar republic.[190] DLeg spurned this option, but not only because it would cause a staggering amount of uncertainty about the legal status of countless persons and transactions. The proposal was also rejected because the four powers came to agree that in some fields of German law Nazi lawmakers had achieved "technical and substantial improvements."[191] On this premise, the ACC defined Nazi law as laws promulgated during the Third Reich that in their character or purpose reflected National Socialist ideology. The ACC's Legal Directorate was thus charged to undertake legal denazification by an individuated procedure by which specialized working parties, the criminal law group being one of many, focused on single fields of law.[192]

By the winter of 1946, some of DLeg's best brains were now working on the further denazification and potential revision of the German criminal code and "the numerous enactments of an essentially penal character."[193] The ostensible goal now was to produce draft codes that would enable the Control Council to complete the denazification, democratization, and general modernization of German criminal law on a uniform basis throughout postwar Germany.[194]

In what Karl Loewenstein, who had sometimes attended DLeg meetings in 1945 and 1946, called the "most significant project of legal reform" of the early occupation period, the working party on criminal law toiled on the project through most of the spring and summer of 1946. In twenty-five meetings, having reached nearly all the decisions unanimously, the group submitted a full draft of the revised German criminal code in early December 1946.[195]

By this point in the occupation, however, there was no question that the Allied Control Council might agree simply to *impose* the new code on the Germans without thorough consultation. The reconstitution of German-operated government in the zones, while it was far from complete, had advanced too far. Accordingly, in October 1946 the council directed that copies of the draft code be circulated among various Ministries of Justice in the German Länder. But before discussing how the code was received by them, it is apt to bring the American zone, and the work of Legal Division within that zone, back into focus.

In the summer of 1945, the American zone contained some 15 million German people, a large percentage of whom were living in deeply degraded circumstances in south Germany's ruined cities.[196] Tens of thousands of non-Germans, most of them displaced persons, many traumatized by brutal mistreatment, were at large in the zone. From the outset of the occupation, the zone's occupied population was afflicted by housing shortages and hunger, situations made worse by the accelerating influx of tens of thousands of impoverished ethnic German refugees. Just as in occupied Japan, but worse because of the growing social incoherence of the population, these straitened circumstances spawned an epidemic of incidental and organized crime, overwhelming the capacity of American military courts to cope.[197] For American leadership in Germany, the only plausible response to this crisis was to reactivate more German criminal justice.

This response squared with Clay's decision to devolve German governmental and legal functions to denazified German officials at the earliest possible moment, beginning with the subdivision of the zone into zonal substates or Länder. In October 1945, American Military Government established a Länderrat or General Council consisting of American-appointed German executive officials. By the close of 1945, each of the Länder had organized Ministries of Justice led by American-approved German jurists.

It was in this context that AMG implemented its "Basic Plan for the Administration of Justice" in the U.S. zone. Taking its cues from the Potsdam Agreement, the plan set forth a framework for reopening trial and appellate courts in the American Länder. Implemented by the newly appointed German Ministers of Justice, the plan called for, among other things, the reactivation of local and district criminal courts staffed by denazified German prosecutors and judges applying denazified criminal law and procedure. The operative assumption of the basic plan—its very dubious assumption—was that these preconditions would be satisfied soon after the occupation.

In August 1945, as action was taken to reopen some German criminal courts in their zones, both the British and American military governments supplanted the Nazi-era Code of Criminal Procedure with a "streamlined version of the Code existing before Hitler."[198] In the fall of 1945, the Ministers of Justice in the American Länder undertook similar work on the German criminal code. Then, in December, the ministers settled on a new code, one expunged of Nazi racial and political content. The new codes, as one American legal officer commented in 1945, were mere stopgap measures; they did not "constitute a definitive reform" of German criminal justice.[199] In adopting them, the goal was to restore "safeguards which were available under the German Code of Criminal Procedure in the pre-Nazi version."[200] In the U.S. zone, all persons prosecuted for criminal offenses in German courts would enjoy the same procedural rights as during the Weimar republic.

The reactivation of German criminal justice attracted criticism in the American camp. Objections were raised by AMG officials and American journalists about the large number of former Nazi Party members (allegedly nominal members) who had secured appointments as criminal prosecutors and judges by the close of 1946. Alarm also was raised when former Nazi prosecutors and judges were lenient with Germans accused of racial or political crimes during the Third Reich.[201] For some American legal officers, Loewesntein being one, the real threat relating to German criminal justice was not the denazification of criminal law or procedure but the potential *renazification* of criminal law decision-making.[202]

By the late fall of 1946, DLeg had completed the final draft of the revised German criminal code. In an effort to drum up support for the code among German officials, it was circulated among the Ministers of Justice in the German Länder and to other appropriate authorities, including Allied specialists in German law.

The Special Legal Unit, in 1946, still staffed by eminent German émigré jurists (such as Ernst Cohn) produced a particularly thorough and widely circulated evaluation of the DLeg code.[203] The SLU pointed out that the draft was something more, and more discerning, than merely the negative exercise of removing "the implements of Nazi ideology." In fact, it was clear DLeg lawyers had purposefully decided to retain some Nazi-era innovations, those that redressed any "obvious defect of the traditional [criminal] law."[204]

In producing their new revised code, moreover, DLeg's draftsmen had not thought only in terms of the legal rights of persons accused of crimes. They also had been mindful to maintain enough penal bite in the new law that the German authorities might cope with the "political, economic and social upheaval after the collapse of the Nazi regime." The code had been drafted as a compromise between liberal due process and deterrence.

By way of illustration, the draft code replaced Nazi-inspired criteria of criminal guilt with more precise and, from the point of view of criminal prosecution, more onerous legal criteria. By the same token, the code permitted the preventative detention of habitual criminals and retained the death penalty for crimes such as politically motivated murder and kidnapping that might threaten new democratic orders in postwar Germany. On similar reasoning, the code gave German judges authority to mete out long prison sentences for crimes—forgery, embezzlement, fraud—that might threaten economic recovery in postwar Germany.

None of the purported advantages of the DLeg criminal code guaranteed its quick acceptance either by the ACC or, more pertinently, by Germans in the Länder. In the U.S. zone particularly, in the last months of 1946, Germans were being given substantial discretion in the reconstruction of regional laws and legal institutions. From this point forward, neither the Länder nor the Länderrat (their general council) were willing to simply rubber-stamp any law—still less legislation as elemental as a code of criminal law—that had been drafted by foreigners. In October 1946, accordingly, the Ministries of Justice in the U.S. zone were granted more time to consult with German legal experts about the DLeg code.[205]

The consultative process continued into December 1946, when on American bidding some eighty high-ranking German legal officials from all four zones, along with a number of German judges and legal academics, were brought to the Hessian capital of Wiesbaden (in the U.S. zone) for the Second Inter-zonal Conference of Chiefs of Judicial Administrations.[206] As heavy equipment cleared bomb debris outside the hotel, one American observer (a German émigré) was struck by the irony that inside the hotel German jurists were clearing the symbolic debris "left upon the German legal system by the destruction of Hitler's edifice."[207]

Little more than eighteen months after surrender, German jurists were being given broad scope to shape important German laws. In his welcoming address, Franklin Potter, the director of AMG's Legal

Division in Hesse, informed the mainly German assembly that he had not come to the Wiesbaden as a decision-maker but merely as a guest. Potter expressed the personal gratification he felt in the fact that in so short a time the deliberations were lawyer to lawyer, not enemy to enemy.

On this principle, the American officers stood back as German lawyers discussed the possible features of a new general criminal code (and a draft code tabled by the Bavarian delegation) in relation to two contentious issues: the nature and content of legal denazification in the criminal law field and its probable impact on the German crisis of crime and public order.

The first question for debate concerned the meaning of "denazification" in the criminal law field. Did it entail ridding criminal law and procedure of *all* Nazi-era amendments or only those that bore the mark of its racial or political ideology? After an indecisive discussion of this question, attention turned to the specific provisions of the DLeg code, especially to those relating to protective custody, treason, murder, and abortion.[208] In every case (but particularly with regard to narrow redefinitions of murder and protective custody) the delegates worried about the impact of more liberal laws on "rampant" petty and organized criminality. In the end, the delegates refused to endorse any changes, even to provisions introduced during the Third Reich, which might hamper "the struggle against the professional criminal."[209] More significantly, it was also agreed that this body of German delegates, given that it had not been elected by German voters, lacked the political legitimacy needed for the acceptance of permanent change. "The basic reform of the Criminal Code," it was acknowledged, "must be reserved to a future German parliament democratically elected and acting on behalf of the whole of Germany."[210]

If at the beginning of 1946 it looked possible politically for the Allied Control Council to reform the German criminal code, by the end of the year it did not.

The quadpartite control mechanism in Germany was coming unglued. In the western zones, German political and administrative elites had regrouped enough that they would not now acquiesce while foreign occupiers made major changes to a major German law.

In the U.S. zone, emphatically, the window of unilateral policy and decision-making by AMG in matters of law reform had closed. American governance in the zone already was too much based, even dependent, on the active and consensual participation of German politicians and civil servants. By the dawn of 1947, moreover, the increasingly estranged and fractious state of quadpartite government, exacerbated by the unwillingness of the French to countenance any revival of national institutions in Germany, rendered it entirely unlikely that the Control Council would mount any further law reform on a national basis.

In 1947, seemingly oblivious to the mounting diplomatic tension between the Americans and Soviets (and as between the French and all three powers) on the Control Council, DLeg's criminal law group earnestly continued its work. In August, now in possession of feedback from the Länder and in the wake of further plenary sessions within the directorate, the working party produced a voluminous draft German criminal code.[211] In September, the directorate invited the working party to "prepare this law in final form as soon as possible."[212] At the close of October, quadpartite government now coming apart at the seams, DLeg continued to maintain the pretense that its criminal law program might still reach fruition.[213] But now it was clear that the ACC would not attempt to make any more legislation for occupied Germany as a whole. The best that could be hoped for in the field of criminal justice was the abrogation of further Nazi-era statutes with a bearing on crime and punishment.

As for the subject of the denazification of German criminal procedure, it had been shelved altogether. Apart from the general legal denazification diktat of the Allied Control Council (Law No. 1), there had been no specific, certainly no systematic reform initiative regarding procedure. In the U.S. zone, Legal Division was content in this field for the Ministers of Justice in the Länder to restore the system of criminal procedure in place during the Weimar republic. There was no sense at Legal Division that its lawyers could do the job better. But while the Americans demurred on the subject of criminal procedure, initiatives were taken with regard to the related subject of German lawyers and their role in criminal justice.

It was a premise of the Anglo-American conception of criminal justice that it depended on the presence of a criminal defense bar that was free to vindicate the procedural rights of accused persons without meddling or control by state authorities.[214] The authentically liberal legal system afforded lawyers—alone and in their governing bodies—the political space or independence required for the unhindered vindication of their clients' legal rights. In this view, too, the archetypal independent legal practice was that of a criminal defense attorney, whose vital job it was to vindicate personal legal rights and thereby to police the *state* as it caused the arrest, indictment, detention, trial, and punishment of private citizens.[215]

As lawyers at Legal Division-Berlin worked on plans for the denazification and reform of German criminal justice, these points of theory and their applicability to the German case were points of debate. "Foremost among the custodians of democratic liberties in the legal sphere," Loewenstein commented, "are the practicing lawyers."[216] As a widely circulated report of the Special Legal Unit observed in 1945, "It is one of the main tasks of the Bar to defend the liberty of the citizen."[217] In this view, if the Allies were to succeed in establishing a liberal system of law in occupied Germany, it would be imperative for the Allies to take steps early in the occupation "to liberate the German Bar from the curtailments . . . imposed on it by the Nazis." The very first measure in this regard would be to restore the "full independence of the Bar Council as it existed in pre-Nazi times."[218]

Although in Germany the independence of the bar from state authority had been less complete than in Britain or the United States, the German émigré analysts working at Legal Division in 1945 agreed that during the Weimar republic the German private bar (slightly more than 19,000 lawyers in 1932[219]) had performed reasonably well as guardians *de facto* of the *rechtsstaat*.[220] As Loewenstein knew from personal experience, some lawyers in this period, men strongly committed to civil libertarian ideals, had been willing to take on tough and unpopular political cases, even in the face of threats and popular backlash.[221]

When the Nazis took power in 1933, they instituted the systematic subjugation and centralization of the German bar associations.[222] The German defense bar, in Nazi eyes too Jewish and liberal, was seen as an especially important target for "coordination" with Nazi racial and political policies.[223] In the span of a few years, Jews, liberals, and socialists, including decorated war veterans, were purged from legal training and practice. When the Nazis promulgated a new national "Lawyer's Code" in 1936, it became a condition of licensed law practice that racially eligible lawyers join a Nazi-controlled Legal Association and swear a loyalty oath to Adolf Hitler. Whatever legal or institutional autonomy from the state formerly enjoyed by German private lawyers and their bar associations had now been eliminated.

With regard to criminal trial process, in the late 1930s the Nazis took steps to limit the procedural rights of accused persons and the capacity of lawyers to defend the accused or appeal their convictions.[224] After war started in 1939, but especially when the war started to go badly in 1942, the Nazis escalated pressure on judges, prosecutors, and defense lawyers to limit due process in criminal cases.[225] In 1944, in an effort to deter dissent and indiscipline on the home front, the Nazi Ministry of Justice ordered German judges to increase the rate of conviction and the harshness of punishments.[226] By 1945, the role of criminal defense advocates in German courts had been reduced to making petitions for mercy.[227]

Although most members of the private bars in Germany had either joined or otherwise accommodated themselves to the Nazi party, the consensus at Legal Division was that the private bar was not as broadly complicit in Nazi criminality as other legal professionals.[228] (The intelligence indicated for instance that the most eminent German lawyers in private practice had not taken leadership roles in Nazi-dominated programs and bar associations.[229]) Most American legal officers, Loewenstein included, viewed the postwar German bar as more readily salvageable than Nazi-era judges or legal bureaucrats.[230] "On the whole," Loewenstein later observed, "the practicing lawyers had stood the moral test of the Nazi period much better than the Court personnel."[231] For this reason, Legal Division condoned the readmission to private law practice of all Nazi-era German lawyers who had not been members of the SS, prosecutors in the political courts, or implicated in miscarriages of justice. This policy was informed by the fact that by the spring of 1946, the Americans needed

German lawyers to be at work in the reopened German court system in the zone.[232]

Before the end of the war, American planning had contemplated two integrated initiatives regarding private lawyers in the U.S. zone: the denazification first of the "Lawyer's Code" and then of the bar associations established by it.[233] By the spring of 1946, neither of these goals had been achieved. At the local level in the zone, moreover, the denazification of German lawyers had taken place in what Loewenstein saw as a chaotic manner, one "devoid of general principles."[234] Some merely nominal Nazi lawyers had been purged, while devoted Nazi operatives, some with blood on their hands, had been rehabilitated. So long as most German courts in the zone remained closed, the threat created by this incongruity was more theoretical than real. But in the latter half of 1946, with scores of courts reopening across the zone, the denazification of the German bar took on great importance.

Legal Division had begun to take action on this front in November 1945, when Loewenstein, himself a purged member of the Munich and Bavarian bar associations, was invited to draft a new Lawyers Code for consideration by the Legal Directorate of the Control Council. His first effort had a modest goal. "My plan is simple," Loewenstein recorded in his diary, "to abolish the [statute of 1936], restore the conditions existing before, but preserve of the law of 1936 what is valuable."[235] His draft called for the abolition of all racial and political criteria for the practice of law. However, the uniform standards regarding qualification for the bar and in the organization of local bar associations were to be retained. In a bow to the liberal tone of American-sponsored law reform, Loewenstein's draft required members of the bar to report the actions of other lawyers that might "cause injustice or inequality by discrimination."[236] In this way the draft underscored the importance of onus placed on German lawyers to regulate themselves as jurists in a liberal society.

Loewenstein had been modest in his goals for the Lawyers Code because, in November 1945, he still thought it plausible to entertain radical goals in the denazification of the German bar. In his view, what the decline and fall of the Weimar-era bar demonstrated was that laws and legal structures were not nearly as important as the ethical and political character of the lawyers leading them. The most liberal Lawyers Code was bound to fail if reactionaries were permitted to interpret and apply its strictures. At the same time that Loewenstein was drafting a revised code, he was also advising his boss, Charles Fahy, that "Those professions [like the profession of law] which are vital for the social and moral life of the German people should be subjected to the most rigid standard of denazification."[237] In this view, all German lawyers who had either joined the Nazi Party (none had been compelled to do so) or who (as non-Party members) had implemented its program should be permanently disqualified from legal practice.

In the result, DLeg never got far with the development of a quadpartite policy for either the denazification or reorganization and regulation of the German bar on a national basis. Whatever was done in these areas was done on a zonal basis. In the U.S. zone, after a period of seemingly uncontentious consultation with the Länderrat in 1946, a slightly amended version of Loewenstein's Lawyers Code was adopted on November 6, 1946.

In theory, this marked a victory for liberal law reform in the zone. The formal vestiges of Nazi ideology had been expunged from the governing articles and ethics of the bar. The bar associations of south Germany now possessed greater degrees of self-governance and institutional independence than at any time in their histories.

In terms of practicality, however, there were reasons to doubt that the new Lawyers Code represented an authentic step toward the liberal-democratization of the legal system as a whole. Contrary to Loewenstein's prescription, bar reform had occurred in the absence of thorough and accurate denazification before there had been a proper reckoning with those lawyers who had "trampled underfoot the rule of law and justice under law."[238]

In the U.S. zone in 1946 to 1947, former Nazis, many of whom had been intimately involved in its legal projects and practices, were being readmitted to the practice of law in large numbers.[239] In stark contrast, only a negligible few of the lawyers—Jews and political dissenters—who had been purged from the private bar during the Reich were still alive and otherwise willing to return to their practices. In substantial measure, therefore, the fate of so many vital interests, of the thousands accused of serious crimes, of the denazified codes of criminal law and procedure, of the rights and due process guarantees of the new south German constitutions, now hinged on the same German lawyers who had defiled justice during the Third Reich.

Clearing the Spiritual Rubble: Reforming Criminal Justice in Occupied Germany and Japan

In the installation of new constitutions in Japan and south Germany, the American occupations signaled commitments not only to the rule of law but to strongly liberal modes of the rule of law. A principal aim of American-driven constitutional (then judicial reform) initiatives was to consolidate the rights and prerogatives of individual German and Japanese persons as against their states. In no area was this aim more signally important than in the fields of criminal law and procedure, these formal mechanisms of state-sanctioned coercion.

The major premise of American policy in this field was that German and Japanese criminal law and process, once recognizable as subsystems of law, had been corrupted during fascist periods as subsystems of lawless coercion and intimidation. The minimum task of the respective American occupations, therefore, was to purge German and Japanese criminal justice of fascist concepts, personnel, and practices. Whether the American occupiers would attempt more far-reaching reforms depended on hastily generated answers to three questions: To what degree did the pre-fascist Japanese and German systems of criminal law and procedure satisfy the minimum requirements of liberal legal modernity? To what degree might pre-fascist systems be salvaged as the basis of permanent postsurrender systems of criminal justice? Should American intervention in this field aim to restore or reconstruct all or some parts of Japanese and German criminal law and procedure?

In broaching these questions, American legal officials in Japan and Germany betrayed a distinctly eurocentric bias. Pre-fascist criminal law and procedure were deemed salvageable to the extent that they reflected continental legal modernity of the late nineteenth and early twentieth centuries. Continental legal modernity in the criminal law field, America's German émigré experts explained, was itself embedded in liberal ideas about the dignity and integrity of individual persons. On this test, the core of Japanese criminal justice was seen as in need of humanization and modernization. The core of German criminal justice, on the other hand, was not.

In the estimation of American legal officials in Japan, the German-born and trained jurist Alfred Oppler leading the way, the main strength of Japanese criminal justice was that it was patterned on Continental law.[240] But its main weakness was that these patterns had become deeply inlaid with Japan's notoriously backward social mores and norms. In terms of methods of enforcement especially, Japanese criminal justice actually bore little resemblance to its European antecedents. The Japanese system of crime and punishment had conspicuously failed, before and during the fascist period, to "protect the people from arbitrary acts on the part of police, the procurator and the judiciary."[241] In 1946, it seemed clear, the system was radically at odds with the new constitution and the political and social revolution that had inspired it.[242]

On the basis of this analysis American legal officials did not rest until they had caused their Japanese counterparts to make major changes to Japanese criminal justice law, especially the procedural law governing criminal arrest, detention, confession, and trial. The Americans also insisted on the expurgation from Japan's penal code of all extraordinary criminal culpability and punishment for offenses against the emperor or imperial house.

We have seen that an entirely different tack was taken by American officials in occupied Germany. Under the influence of its teams of German émigré legal experts, the American occupation quickly came to embrace the thesis that German criminal law and procedure, if far from satisfactory before the Nazis came to power, was grounded in liberal legal modernity.[243] The German codes of criminal law and procedure, even if dating back to the 1870s, were depicted as exemplars of late-nineteenth-century enlightened rationality; internally coherent and scrupulously drafted to protect the dignity of the individual person. In this view, the problem with German criminal justice in 1946 was not its underlying philosophy or structure, these being fundamentally sound. The problem was that, after 1933, the citadel of

German criminal law and procedure had been besieged and sacked by the Nazi barbarians. By 1945, a system that had once upheld the dignity of men and women had been crudely adapted to terrorize them.[244]

But if the Nazis had disfigured the surface of German criminal law and procedure, the underlying substructure of liberal modernity had remained intact. In this view, adopted by the Americans in relation to their own Länder and the Control Council, there was nothing wrong with German criminal justice that could not be repaired by its comprehensive denazification. Subject to reforms that the Germans themselves were better placed to make, the basic theme of American criminal law policy in Germany in 1946 and 1947 was *restoration* by denazification.

The broad strokes of this process were taken by the Americans, unilaterally in the short term, collectively with the Allies in the longer. Among the first actions of American military formations upon taking German territory in 1945 was to issue proclamations closing German criminal courts and abrogating its most "obnoxious" criminal laws. We have seen further that among the first official legislative actions of the Allied Control Council was to cause the permanent expurgation of Nazi-era legislation in the criminal law field. This part of the denazification process, the uncomplicated part, was successful, so far as it went. The parts of substantive criminal law and procedure that had been most visibly affected by Nazi ideology were cleansed of taint.

Readers will readily detect the central flaw of this approach: that it was based on the naïve premise that the American occupation authorities would identify and purge the German lawyers, prosecutors, and judges who had played significant roles in the systemic injustice of German criminal process during the Third Reich. As early as the fall of 1945, some Americans in Germany, Karl Loewenstein most loudly, already had registered concerns that this would not happen. By 1947, former Nazi jurists of all stripes, including many who had participated in the criminal prosecution and punishment of racial and political crimes, were being hired in increasing numbers to operate a reviving German justice system. By 1948, the denazified systems of criminal law and procedure in the American Länder had been returned to the care of many of the same lawyers and judges who had corrupted those systems only a few years earlier.

Japanese jurists, in their efforts to wrest control of the postwar criminal system, faced a tougher challenge. Where Germans had been shown deference in relation to criminal justice, the Japanese were imposed upon. The difference in treatment stemmed from the fact that in regard to criminal law and procedure, in regard to Japan's legal system as a whole, leading officials at SCAP's Government Section looked upon Japan as a "less advanced and oriental civilization."[245] While the liberal modernity of German criminal law and procedure had been degraded by the Nazis, the Japanese criminal law, in these American eyes, had never achieved liberal modernity in the first place. Convinced that criminal justice in Japan always had been "despotic, arbitrary and unjust," MacArthur mandated that there should be radical discontinuity in this field; all vestiges of illiberal custom, including linkages to the *kokutai,* were be rooted out in both the letter and execution of the law.

SCAP implemented this policy mainly by recourse to legal officers who, before the surrender, had known no Japanese law or sociolegal history and neither read nor spoke Japanese. And unlike its counterpart in Germany, American reform policy in the field was formulated and implemented without internal support by Japanese born and trained experts.

This is not to suggest that Americans were able to simply impose reform to criminal justice from the outside. Indeed, in 1946 and with increasing force in 1947, the Japanese legal-bureaucratic elite, buoyed by the electoral success of Shigeru Yoshida's coalition of conservative political factions, orchestrated an effective campaign of passive resistance to American-driven law reform.

In broad terms, Japanese resistance in the criminal justice field stemmed from the discontent of conservative elites with the American-imposed constitutional settlement, particularly in its extravagant and alien liberalism. Their estrangement was especially palpable in the context of American-driven criminal justice reform, and the threat it posed to the prestige of the imperial house (by repeal of *lèse-majesté*), to the reconciliatory model of criminal justice (hinging on the confession of the accused), and to law and order generally. Japanese conservatives, reconciled to a demilitarized and democratized Japan, were unreconciled to destruction of the *kokutai*. They were unreconciled also to the decidedly un-Japanese softening of criminal justice and its implications for the fight against communism.

In Japan, in the short term, SCAP's legal officers got their way in the criminal justice field. They caused the Ministry of Justice to accept a long list of unwelcome liberal reforms to imperial-era criminal law and procedure. In getting their way, however, the Americans failed to forge effective links with the Japanese jurists—the liberal and leftist (to say nothing of women) lawyers—most dedicated to liberal legal modernity in the criminal law context. On the other hand, by permitting the bureaucrats to dominate the Japanese side of the reform equation, SCAP legitimated a conservative monopoly of law reform work. By the close of 1948, fortified both by the Yoshida government and conservative elements within the American occupation establishment, Ministry of Justice bureaucrats began to orchestrate a campaign to blunt the effects of liberal reform while enlisting criminal justice in a move to suppress the Japanese Left.

In Germany, apart from the abrogation of the most visible and objectionable of Nazi legislative innovations, neither the Americans nor the Allied Control Council had made significant inroads in the reformation of German criminal justice. By 1947, Weimar-era criminal law and practices were being revived in the U.S. zone. In south Germany, AMG permitted the rapid rehabilitation of all but the most manifestly compromised members of the Nazi-era legal establishment. Just as in Japan, the liberal and leftist elements of the German bar, that is, those who had survived twelve years of Nazi persecution, were kept to the margins of the reform process.[246] An objective observer would have been hard pressed in 1948, the socioeconomic and crime crisis in the zone gaining momentum, to comprehend how and by whom a liberal legal system of criminal justice was likely to emerge. In 1949, American and German legal authorities now finding common cause in the fight against Communism in the zone, the same observer would surely be perplexed by how the civil liberties of accused persons, of all south Germans, might be so eagerly given and taken away.

6

Twilight of the Gods

THE RISE AND FALL OF CIVIL LIBERTIES IN OCCUPIED GERMANY AND JAPAN

IN THE PERIOD from 1948 to 1951, liberal legal reconstruction in American-occupied Germany and Japan unspooled in a tangle of contradictory policies and programs, some conducive, others corrosive of liberty. In the main, however, American-instigated civil rights and freedoms, instead of being consolidated as facts of postwar German and Japanese social and political life, were weakened, in some respects destroyed, by a combination of American intervention from without and German and Japanese elite intervention from within.

This illiberal turn was rooted in four elemental truths about American military occupations after the Second World War. The first is that they were conceived not in liberty but as instruments of national security. American leaders instituted and sustained liberal legal revolution in occupied Germany and Japan insofar as such measures facilitated the pacification of former enemies. Liberal-democratization was a contingent, not fixed aim of the occupations.

The second truth is that all foreign military occupations, American and otherwise, are despotisms. In a host of ways, recourse to retributive violence excepted, the American occupations of Germany and Japan were archetypally harsh.[1] From start to finish, Clay and MacArthur led authoritarian regimes which, among other repressive practices, occasioned the indefinite detention of tens of thousands of military and civilian personnel. Both regimes appropriated without compensation enormous quantities of commercial property and scarce private and public building stock. They moved to control food supplies, political, and economic behavior and personal mobility. The occupation authorities censored media, monitored private mail and effected thousands of warrantless searches and seizures.[2] Germans and Japanese accused of crimes were subjected to summary military justice without rights of appeal. Of obvious relevance to this study, moreover, in both occupied countries American officials unilaterally imposed or mandated major changes to captive legal and political institutions.

The third truth is that in the postwar American homeland, too, liberal modernity was a bitterly contested terrain.[3] The turbulence of American policy in occupied Germany and Japan after 1947 mirrored the turbulence of American domestic politics in the same period. When the wartime armistice of political Right and Left dissolved in the fall of 1945, American political alignments rejoined the fight over the role of the federal state in the social and economic life of the nation.[4] The American Right remained unreconciled to the New Deal and its proponents on the moderate and radical Left. At the close of 1946, conservative Republicans, many having run on rabidly anti-Communist platforms, made large gains in midterm congressional elections. Pressure soon began to mount to constrain legal and political liberalism in the United States and in American-occupied Germany and Japan.

The fourth truth was that the Soviet Union, in quitting quadpartite control of Germany in March 1947, shattered any pretense that the four powers might yet agree on the nature and content of democratization in the former Axis powers.[5] This first salvo of an ensuing Cold War caused the Truman administration to reassess its strategic goals in the occupation of Germany and Japan.[6] Increasingly, American national security interests were seen as lining up with German and Japanese economic and political recovery, and the rehabilitation of elites was viewed as vital to such recovery. The emerging policy was for the United States to devise and implement new policy initiatives that might tend to enlist the Japanese and western German populations in stemming the tide of Soviet Communism.

These developments intensified the contradictions of American ideas and actions in occupied Germany and Japan. On the one hand, military government in both countries continued and sometimes accelerated programs promoting the liberalization of law and legal institutions. In both occupied countries, experts were brought in, courses of action were devised, and money was spent to promote and protect the personal rights and civil liberties of German and Japanese citizens. In Germany, beginning in 1948, the United States spearheaded a drive to consolidate the western German zones as a state entity under a new liberal-democratic constitution or "Basic Law."

On the other hand, just as civil libertarian conceptions and patterns of law and the rule of law were being built up by American military government, so they were also being broken down. In both occupied countries after 1947, and in the name of anti-Communism, elements within the American administrations began to form common cause with resurgent conservative elites to orchestrate repressive crackdowns on the leaders, activities, and ideas of the German and Japanese Left. By 1950, we will see, this crackdown had become so aggressive, so flagrantly contrary to liberal conceptions of legal rights and civil liberties, that it threatened the legitimacy and integrity of the nascent German and Japanese rule-of-law states.

"The German Problem" Revisited: Cultivating Liberty in West Germany, 1948 to 1952

For the Truman administration, the withdrawal of the Soviets from the Allied Control Council (ACC) in March and the ensuing Berlin crisis of spring 1948 accentuated the importance of winning German hearts and minds. In the face of increasing economic malaise and Soviet belligerence in Germany, it seemed critically important now to devise and implement policies likely to court favor with the tens of millions of Germans living in the western zones of the occupation.[7] One prong of American policy was to promote rapid reintegration and growth in the west German economies.[8] Another, far more speculative initiative was to cause Germans to reject authoritarianism and to embrace liberalism. As the American Civil Liberties Union (ACLU) generalized the project in 1948, the aim here was to "build up a positive response in German political opinion to the moral values inherent in the respect for the dignity and responsibility of the individual . . . and to point out the danger of neglecting to provide adequate safeguards against the encroachment of basic civil liberties."[9]

The thrust of American policy was to use the twin engines of economic recovery and liberal reorientation to pull the western Germans securely into a Western political and ideological orbit.[10] If history was a guide, however, so long as the German material world remained poor and disordered, the German mental world would remain susceptible to authoritarian appeals and panaceas, now of the Communist Left. In 1948, one American official commented, the liberal-democratic reorientation of western Germany was "especially urgent because of the threat to democratic institutions from totalitarian forms of government and politics which have attempted to exploit and exaggerate the frustrations and political despair of the German people and to discredit democratic principles and methods."[11]

Thus, in 1948, American Military Government (AMG) in Germany shifted its policy focus from the structural or outward frame of German authoritarianism[12] to the inner frame of the German *weltanschauung*.[13] The urgent goal in Germany, a State Department bulletin declared in the spring of 1948, was to "uproot the spirit as well as the structure of totalitarian government in order to provide for the healthy growth of a democratic system."[14] A recently revised American policy and operations handbook made a similar point: "It is universally agreed that the seeds of democracy can never take permanent root in Germany through a mere change of political and governmental forms, but rather, fundamental changes must be effected in the German mind and outlook."[15] In this diplomatic moment, the American aim was to cause an abrupt break in a cultural pattern in which Germans eschewed freedom and equality for authoritarianism and hierarchy.[16] The "political and moral reorientation of the German people," one American policy document declared, "will foster the reestablishment of universally valid principles of justice."[17]

An important first step was to moderate the American dictatorship over German institutions and citizens in the U.S. zone. In this regard, the War Department advised Lucius Clay that "a basic objective of the occupation is the reestablishment of the rule of law in Germany."[18] The General was to "require all agencies under [his] control to refrain from arbitrary and oppressive measures."[19] The vital second step was for American agencies in the zone to facilitate German citizens and voluntary associations in the promotion and protection of their new constitutional rights and liberties. This campaign was to be bolstered by new American programs for the cultivation of a civil libertarian ethos among Germans.

In 1947, National Socialist law and institutions having been eradicated, American doctrine was that the Germans—so long as they respected liberal-democratic norms—were to be permitted to design and implement their own legal and political reforms.[20] Government by American fiat was now to be a last resort. In the words of the new operational handbook, "With the Germans so largely 'on their own' the methods of democratization become altered and at the same time the task becomes more difficult. Education, persuasion, diplomacy, and example must more and more take the place of commands."[21] General Clay himself emphasized the same point: "In the final analysis, [Military Government] can only suggest, advise, and ensure that democratic legislation is enacted, but any lasting benefit in this field must come from the reorientation of the German people themselves."[22]

To advance and expedite these goals, scores of civilian experts, many of them prewar German émigrés, were recruited to advise Germans (and the American functional units overseeing them) on how best to foster liberal-democratic norms.[23] Some were to work with German mass media and cultural institutions to "build a positive response in German public opinion to the moral values inherent in the respect for the dignity and responsibility of the individual."[24] For the first time in the history of the American occupation, nongovernmental entities, most prominently the ACLU, were invited by General Clay personally to observe and advise the American occupation on how to promote and consolidate the civil liberties of Germans.[25]

On the reorientation front, German ground had been taken only with great difficulty. In 1948, in fact, this only two-and-a-half years after the surrender, the German economist Alfred Weber thought that the Western Allies had "accomplished nothing in implanting democracy" in Germany.[26] Senior American officials agreed that if the democratization project was ended in 1948, "nothing much would have been accomplished yet."[27]

There were compelling reasons why not. As American experts were frequently moved to observe, the impediments to the swift liberal reorientation of German minds were numerous and formidable. It was more than slightly optimistic, first of all, to expect the German people to embrace the ideological program of a foreign military occupier. On this point, Roger Baldwin, president of the ACLU, offered this sobering reminder: "The remarkable fact about the [American] occupations is that we should expect an autocratic military machine to act as the agent for democracy. Never before has a military establishment been charged with such a duty, and it would be Quixotic to look for democratic results."[28]

It was inescapable, too, that American military occupiers in Germany were now to liberalize a people who, only a couple of years earlier, had lent prodigious loyalty and support to a totalitarian dictatorship. National Socialism, as Karl Loewenstein and most other American experts understood, had been a mass movement among a people who closely associated liberalism and democracy with political disorder and economic collapse.

Nor did it augur well for liberal reorientation that the mass of Germans in the U.S. and western zones remained ill fed, ill housed, and psychologically damaged by defeat and personal loss. Due to the strictures and impositions of military government, adult Germans were obliged to live reduced and subordinated lives. In this distressed and infantilized state, one American expert commented, Germans tended to "trust neither the government nor themselves and have no faith in their future. In this atmosphere, the German people have thought and acted in terms of survival. Their civil rights seem to be a luxury they cannot afford."[29]

Another obstacle to liberal reorientation was that, in German eyes, American prestige and moral credibility were deeply compromised by the chaotic muddle of the American denazification program.[30] In this view, widely held in the U.S. zone by 1947, the Americans (and the German quislings who took their places) had concocted a system that seemed to punish those who had been nominal Nazis while it exonerated the fervent Nazis.[31] And if moral credibility is indispensable to the proselytizer, it also weighed in some German minds that the United States itself had a checkered record on liberal rights and the rule of law. As educated Germans knew, and as a Truman-appointed commission had amply documented in 1946, the homeland of the liberal crusaders was riven by stark racial, social, and political inequalities of its own, many reinforced by law.[32] Americans, some Germans were bold enough to suggest, preached liberal-egalitarianism in Germany while they practiced authoritarian segregation at home.

In explaining why Germans were unlikely converts to liberalism, American experts, predictably enough, tended to focus on German, not American political culture. In this regard, the memoranda of the Cornell-trained historian Harold W. Landin, since 1947 the chief of AMG's Democratization Branch, received wide distribution inside the American occupation establishment.[33]

According to Landin's assessment, even in the wake of a second catastrophic military and societal defeat in a generation, the German people continued to evince the same habitual "enslavement to authority and tradition, to power and caste, to state and officialdom."[34] As a result of generations of grooming by Germany's staunchly illiberal and antidemocratic political and bureaucratic elites, Germans failed to acquire the love of individual freedom that might have caused them to prefer the liberal disorder of the Weimar republic to the dictatorial order of the Third Reich. "Basically," one of Landin's colleagues offered, "the German people have no understanding of what democracy means in practice, either as rights or obligations."[35] By virtue of their "tradition and training, Germans are unduly submissive to authority, power, and position."

Survey data from the late 1940s tend to confirm that American efforts to foster civil libertarianism among Germans were apt to meet with apathy at best,[36] strong resistance from a population "seething with victimhood and grievance" at worst.[37] These data indicated that more than half (55 percent) of Germans surveyed continued to think that National Socialism was a sound political program that had been "mishandled" by its leaders.[38] In the postwar era, less than half of all Germans followed political developments in the zone. Six in ten adults desired economic prosperity more than personal freedom.[39] Similar numbers regarded Germans who worked for the American authorities as traitors. Later data showed that clear majorities rejected the proposition that Germans as a people were morally responsible for either war in Europe or the extermination of millions of Jews.[40] The data also indicated that defeat had only hardened intolerance of Jews and other "outsiders." Indeed, the evidence was that the Jew, displaced person, or ethnic German refugee was generally seen as "something less than an honorable German citizen" and bore stigma in the western zones.[41]

AMERICAN REORIENTATION OF THE GERMAN LEGAL PROFESSIONS

In the American zone, reorientation was informed but seemingly not much hindered by gloomy revelations of German collective political identity and character. While the architects of German reorientation could afford to indulge themselves in grand—but in the larger picture, quite useless—abstractions, leaders of AMG's functional units had to get on with the work of making, staffing, and delivering actual programs. In 1947, for instance, Legal Division (LD) had begun to shift emphasis from structural to ideological assignments.[42] While they completed the denazification of the German judicial and criminal justice systems, work also began on the philosophical outlook of the German lawyers and bureaucrats who would operate the reformed system over the long haul. The elemental truth here was that only liberal-minded lawyers could realize the promise of a liberal-minded system of law.

Mortimer Kollender, in 1947 to 1948 a senior operative at Legal Division, was certain that going forward the denazification of German legal minds was at least as important as the denazification of German legal structures. "It is not enough," Kollender contended in a memo on reorientation, "to eliminate the laws and practices which, under the Hitler regime, led to the prostitution of justice in Germany." According to Kollender's information, "The sickness of the German judicial system went deeper. It affected both the legal system and legal thinking, as such, by destroying faith in the dignity and possibilities of all men. It thus depraved the thinking of many of those Germans who are today representing the legal system. . . . Only a restoration of the moral values upon which law and justice rest in a democratic society can eventually restore a democratic legal system which will be accepted by the German people."[43] The aim of Legal Division's reorientation project, Kollender summarized, was no less than to bring into existence "a professional corps dedicated to the establishment and maintenance of the rule of law," a body of lawyers who not only outwardly but spiritually embraced their roles as guardians of a liberal-democratic constitution.[44]

In the same vein, another Legal Division expert, William McCurdy, stated that "One of the great needs in Germany is reorientation work among the legal profession."[45] Even among Germany's deeply conservative elites, the legal professions stood out in having "exhibited strong reactionary and anti-democratic tendencies during the Nazi regime and even earlier." That was why it behooved AMG to make a "concentrated effort to indoctrinate the Bench, the Bar, law students and the public with the fundamentals of the democratic legal system as contrasted with the Nazi and Communist totalitarian legal systems." German jurists required urgent training in all elements of liberal legality, including "constitutional guarantees, due process of law, the basic rights of the individual and the rule of law."[46] The chief goal of reorientation was to induce German jurists to abandon authoritarian habits of thought, to think of individual rights and freedoms, not the prerogatives of the state, as the *summum bonum* of law-related practices.

Legal reorientation had become still more urgent in sober realization at Legal Division that American efforts to prevent former Nazis from regaining positions in postwar German legal institutions had largely failed. As Hans Weigert, a senior LD official wrote in 1947, "The percentage of judges and prosecutors reinstated in the administration of justice in spite of the fact that they once had been members of the Nazi party, is steadily growing."[47] As we have seen, by 1948 the denazification process was more about the rehabilitation than punishment of Nazi-era jurists.

Here American realism about the failures of denazification gave way to bureaucratically mandated unrealism about reorientation. In 1947, Legal Division became formally committed to the fantasy that a tiny group of American lawyers might somehow persuade scores of German lawyers to embrace legal and political liberalism.

The fantasy had three operational elements. One was for American experts (mainly émigré Germans) to deliver a series of lectures and short courses of university study on the nature and operation of liberal-democratic legal regimes. Another involved sending a few hundred German law students, lawyers, and judges to training programs in the United States. The third element was the liberal reorientation of German legal education in the U.S. zone.

Of these three, the legal education initiative was thought to have the most potential as a catalyst of change. As Karl Loewenstein put the point in 1946, "It need hardly be emphasized that the proper training of law students, particularly of those having been for a long time exclusively under the Nazi influence or in the militaristic atmosphere of the German army, is of paramount importance for the reconstruction of German legal life . . . Legal education at the law school level is the key-stone of a democratically built Hall of Justice in Germany."[48]

In theory, the great advantage of the legal education program was that it would address comparatively large numbers of comparatively young and, it was rather hopefully presumed, pliable legal minds.[49] The inherent flaw of the program, however, was that it was based on the dubious premise that the supposedly pliant minds of law trainees might be infused with liberal values in the context of law schools staffed mainly by conservative nationalists and former Nazis.[50] There was nothing about the historical culture or postwar mindset of the German professoriate, legal or otherwise, that could inspire genuine confidence in their willingness to inculcate liberal legal values and techniques.[51]

By 1947, in fact, the evidence was mounting about the German schools of law in the U.S. zone—about the law school at Munich University, especially—that many former Nazis, some who had either published pro-Nazi tracts or had been closely linked to Nazi legal programs, had resumed their tenure as faculty.[52] Indeed, reports suggested that across the zone senior law school officials were contriving to hold positions open for former Nazi jurists who had not yet passed through the (increasingly lenient) denazification tribunals.[53] By 1948, upwards of a third of German law professors in the western zones had been Nazis party members. While perhaps few of these had been or remained ideological Nazis, there was no reason to believe that they were sympathetic to liberal-democratic legal reform.[54] Nor, in numbers, were their students.

Like their professors, German law students and referendars (graduate trainees for the bench or bar) in the late 1940s were poor grist for the American reorientation mill. Most were from wealthy backgrounds and were political conservatives even if they had not been ideological Nazis. Many were battle-hardened war veterans diminished by war and humiliated by the occupation. Harsh experience had made them unusually cynical, especially about politics, and extremely wary of being "indoctrinated by propagandists."[55] As one American legal officer generalized, on the whole university students in the zone were "actually just a bunch of terribly disillusioned, hungry, young people, with no direction whatsoever."[56] Most wanted nothing more than to get on with their private and professional lives without having to confront the past.[57]

According to Mort Kollender, the American official in charge of legal education in the zone, its most glaring deficiency was that few German law students had received sound education in history and politics.[58] In the German schools of law, moreover, technical proficiency was emphasized above the normative nature or impact of law in society. "A dangerous gap in their education," Kollender opined, "stems from the fact that only insufficient attempts are made to broaden the background of the students and awaken in them an understanding of the vital ideological and social issues involved."[59] German law school graduates had been prepared as mere "technicians of law, [as men] who have no appreciation of the moral and social significance of the legal problems which they are to deal." These deficiencies had been worsened by the nazification of German law and legal education after 1933. What young German jurists knew about the politics of law was a National Socialist politics of law. In every vital respect, then, in 1947 Germany's future legal elite was ill prepared—and was being poorly prepared—to take on key legal roles in the new German liberal rule-of-law state.

As of November 1947, American agencies had made no real progress in the liberal reform of German legal education in the zone. In the result, AMG settled for what must be regarded a series of token, if expensive,[60] gestures.[61] In the period 1949 to 1952, the west German law schools were obliged to play host to a succession of guest lecturers and visiting professors, mainly from the United States.[62] A series of training conferences were held for referendars. Money was provided to law schools and bar associations for the purchase of foreign law books. A few score of German jurists and law students were sent to the United States on exchange.[63] However, no thoroughgoing reconfiguration of the faculties or curricula of law schools of the Federal Republic of Germany (FRG), or in the training of referendars, was ever really attempted by the American authorities. Nor had one been possible.

CIVIL RIGHTS IN AMERICAN-OCCUPIED GERMANY

By the time of the Berlin crisis in June 1948, American efforts in the field of civil rights and freedoms had been mainly concerned with laws and legal structures. In this regard certain promises had been made. As a consequence of American-sponsored constitutional change in the U.S. Länder, Germans were to imminently enjoy long lists of individual and due process rights all bolstered by politically independent bar associations and judiciaries. Those Germans prosecuted for criminal offences were set to benefit from thoroughly denazified if largely unreformed Codes of criminal law and procedure.

It remained an open question, of course, whether this on-paper liberal reform would translate into meaningful changes in behavior among German state actors and institutions. Most pertinently for our purposes, an open question was whether politically active Germans, especially those active on the far Left, were to enjoy tangible gains in liberties of thought, access to information, political speech, and assembly. Another open question was whether politically active Germans would enjoy liberal legal protections when they challenged American or German political and ideological preferences and policies. In such circumstances what individual and due process rights might dissenters assert and vindicate?

With regard to *law*-based legal rights in relation to AMG, the simple answer was that Germans had few formal rights to assert. As a consequence of unconditional surrender, German citizens were subject to the martial law of the occupiers. "To sum up," Henry Parkman, a senior American official with the Civil Affairs Division (CAD) stated in the summer of 1947, "the German constitutions are not legally binding upon us as members of the Occupying Forces. . . . We are here by right of conquest and in the last analysis our position depends upon force."[64] Insofar as German nationals enjoyed civil rights and liberties in the U.S. zone, they did so at the pleasure of the American military authorities. "Above the [German] law and constitutions ourselves," Parkman explained, "we are nevertheless trying to teach the Germans the meaning of rights which we are not bound to recognize."

Although the military dictatorship of AMG in the U.S. zone was relatively mild, it remained a dictatorship, one that by 1947 plainly had not delivered meaningfully on the promise of German civil rights and freedoms.[65] Dangerously, in the context of mounting cold war, both AMG and the nascent German administrations had become (this according to AMG's own intelligence) "discredited in the eyes of the German public by the degree to which basic rights, guaranteed by the constitutions, were being infringed by the occupation authorities and troops; arbitrary searches and seizures, interference with freedom of the press, of assembly, and of association continued."[66] For American policy-makers and administrators, the time was nigh to make good on their civil libertarian promises.

We have seen that this process began in the spring of 1947 when the Truman administration issued a new policy directive (JCS 1779) to General Clay to recalibrate AMG in Germany so to bring it in line with fundamental human rights and freedoms.[67] The directive called for AMG to provide an object lesson to Germans in how to use power in a manner consistent with a liberal-democratic ideology and constitution.[68] To better achieve this goal, Clay began to engage the assistance of American experts on civil liberties.[69]

THE ACLU COMES TO GERMANY

An important initiative in this regard occurred in the spring of 1948 when the army, in a move endorsed by General Clay, formally invited Roger Baldwin, president of the ACLU, to visit Germany to assess the state of German civil rights and liberties there.[70] This invitation, urged by Baldwin himself, was offered in the wake of (from the points of view of the army, MacArthur, and Baldwin himself) a very productive visit to occupied Japan the previous year.

As an unyielding advocate of liberal causes, a stone in the shoe of the American conservative establishment, Baldwin was an unnatural friend of the War Department and its agencies. But his undoubted expertise in the now vital civil liberties field, combined with his impeccable credentials as an anti-Communist, had made him a plausible choice to consult on civil liberties in occupied Japan.[71] When that gamble was seen both by MacArthur and the War Department to have paid off handsomely, Baldwin and the ACLU seemed a risk amply worth taking in Germany. After all, by the beginning of 1948 AMG had already devolved substantial liberal and democratic rights back to Germans in the U.S. zone. As Clay himself boasted in a letter to Baldwin, AMG "has led the way in restoring civil liberties to the German people. . . . We have led the way in abolishing pre-censorship and in encouraging free speech. We have granted the right of habeas corpus to *Germans* charged with violating Military Government law, and have devoted our main effort in the educational field to stressing the importance of the individual and necessity of guarding his liberties."[72] By the summer of 1948, furthermore, AMG became a largely civilian-operated administration whose leading officials were generally liberal in political outlook.[73]

On arrival in Berlin, Baldwin met with Clay, whom he soon praised as "approachable, keen, calm, simple, wholly lacking in vanity or pride of position."[74] Baldwin was immediately convinced of the sincerity of Clay's decision to secure the civil rights of western Germans. "The direction at the top," Baldwin reported to the ACLU board, "is certainly liberal, even a bit New-Dealish. General Clay is an amazing administrator, quiet, effective, democratic, meeting everyone who wants to see him, with a grasp of both factual detail and overall policy rare in public life."[75] His ACLU associate, Arthur Hays, was similarly impressed with Clay and his senior civil affairs officers, men seen as "civil libertarians of the highest and most idealistic order."[76]

Baldwin and Hays quickly found that their German sources were highly critical of AMG, delivering many "frank kicks" to its liberal pretenses.[77] The consensus view among Germans was that, public relations gestures to the contrary, AMG continued to exert authoritarian control over all aspects of social and political life in the U.S. zone.[78] Private communications were monitored. The German press operated under a repressive licensing system. AMG's monopoly on newsprint suppressed left-wing news and opinion. German-language radio and cinema were censored. International travel and communications were strictly controlled. Public assembly was arbitrarily restricted. Military courts continued to convict Germans on the basis of vague criminal laws and procedures. Germans were subjected to demeaning ("Hans Crow") discrimination in housing and public services.[79] Germans were also routinely subjected to warrantless arrests, searches, and seizures.[80] While in theory AMG had devolved meaningful governmental and social power back to Germans, in reality it remained domineering and repressive.

One or another of these complaints was registered by almost all the Germans who met with the ACLU men. In fact, Baldwin, summarizing his notes, detected nearly "universal resentment at the occupation and universal fear of the Russians. The Germans are either bored with all the talk of democratizing them or they ridicule the varied vague concepts promoted. . . . They sense at once the contradiction between the autocratic methods of occupation and the precepts of democracy. Under such conditions they do not feel that they can take effective responsibility; hence the apathy in public affairs, and the criticism of the 'collaborators.'"[81]

In his official memoranda to Clay and the ACLU on civil liberties in Germany, Baldwin did not pull punches. While acknowledging Clay's good faith, in his opinion the general had not succeeded in this crucial field of American-directed reform.[82] Baldwin wrote, "There is an evident lack at the top of any coherent concept of what democracy requires in institutions or spirit. The approach is diffused and unplanned. It is little wonder that the response of the Germans is so apathetic." Baldwin also reported his surprise and dismay that AMG had done nothing while scores of former Nazis had resumed positions of influence in the U.S. zone.[83]

In his final reports to Clay and the ACLU board, Baldwin, while recognizing the enormity of AMG's task in Germany, expressed the opinion that not nearly enough had been done to promote civil rights or a civil libertarian culture in the U.S. zone.[84] As a consequence, German civil rights and freedoms, despite pronouncements to the contrary, continued to be suppressed by illiberal policies and actions, including the active constraint of the most promising source of democratic activity in the zone, the trade unions.

To redress these ills, Baldwin recommended, *inter alia,* that AMG lead efforts to promulgate a new occupation statute, one that provided Germans with an explicit bill of rights *vis-à-vis* military government and judicial means for their vindication. It was further recommended that AMG establish new mechanisms for civil rights oversight within AMG and German regional government. Baldwin's report called for the end of interference with strikes and the prescribed participation of trade unions in private business corporations and government. Baldwin also called on AMG to end all forms of censorship and for German rights to foreign travel and communications to be restored. Finally, Baldwin recommended that immediate steps be taken to encourage leading German liberals to establish local and zonal civil liberties unions on the American model.

In his response, Clay was encouraging but noncommittal. In a letter to Arthur Hays, he expressed his "sincere hope" that the visits of the ACLU executives "will result in the beginning of an organized movement among the German population for civil liberties protection."[85] Although he could not promise the same crusade for civil liberties that MacArthur had sponsored in Japan, Clay stated that he considered it "one of our primary tasks of reorientation to instill in the minds of the German governments and German people a respect and sincere desire for personal liberties and personal freedom." In previous meetings with Baldwin, the general already had agreed in principle to create a Civil Liberties Bureau within AMG.[86] He also pledged to continue to consult with experts, including those of the ACLU, on the further embellishment of civil liberties programs in the U.S. zone and with regard to the unified western zones.

By the spring of 1949, with the transfer of AMG authority from the U.S. Army to the State Department in the form of the United States High Commissioner for Germany (HICOG) nearly complete, actual changes made in the civil liberties were mainly of the symbolic or promissory kind (such as finally establishing a Civil Liberties Bureau).[87]

Then there was the persistent problem of arbitrary arrest and search in the American Länder, particularly those instigated by German police. Studies commissioned by AMG in 1948 revealed, for example, that 45,000 house searches and 270,000 arrests had been made without warrant by Bavarian police alone in 1948. Few of these were justified by Bavarian state law.[88] And while the warrantless search of a domicile was expressly forbidden under all of the Länder constitutions (except in situations presenting imminent danger to persons), over 90 percent of house searches had been without warrant.[89] AMG's own survey data revealed that 75 percent of the Germans polled believed that "the police have a right to search a private dwelling without a warrant, merely on suspicion."[90] AMG data indicated that, in Bavaria especially, the authoritarian (and now unconstitutional) search and seizure practices of the police continued unabated.[91] HICOG did not move to put an end to these abuses until the spring of 1949.[92]

GERMAN CIVIL LIBERTIES UNIONS

It was always the conviction of Baldwin that if the Germans were to make any permanent headway in redressing wrongful arrest, search, or any other glaring offence against their constitutional civil rights and freedoms, they needed to organize American-style local and national civil liberties unions of private citizens.

The basic story of how, over two years starting in the spring of 1949, Germans (with American encouragement and financial support) organized the first unions (*bunds*) for civil rights (*burgerrechcte*) in the U.S. zone has been told elsewhere.[93] For our purposes there are a number of salient points.

The first is that the German civil liberties unions' project was, from beginning to end, an American project funded by American money. Although Americans worked assiduously to entice Germans to lead and develop the new unions, these efforts had not taken root in German civil society.[94] Even after civil liberties unions were organized in most major West German cities, they met with the apparent indifference of German elites and working classes.[95] Many of the unions were riven by disagreement about the nature of civil rights and the means of their effective promotion.[96] The unions tended to die soon after American funding for them ran out.

The taint of an occupier's touch was one reason.[97] The historical indifference of Germans to liberal ideas of civil liberties was another.[98] The preoccupation of Germans with material issues was another contributing factor. It did not help that the major political parties of West Germany looked on civil liberties unions with suspicion. Nor did the American constitutional litigation model for the promotion of civil liberties, one that became plausible with the advent in 1949 of the new West German constitution, resonate strongly with Germans.

TOWARD A NEW BASIC LAW

In Germany, as in Japan, American-engineered transformative occupation enjoyed more success when it was less about hearts and minds than grand-scale structural change. The final American program of this kind, forging a new West German state entity complete with its own constitutional instrument (the Basic Law), played out in the twelve months following the failed London Conference of Allied foreign ministers in June 1948.[99] In that period, the United States, with the passive support of Britain and France, steered and superintended while western German politicians and consultants hammered out the structural framework of a liberal-democratic rule-of-law state, one which, on paper, would recognize and respect a long list of inviolable individual rights and freedoms.[100] The American goal was to expedite the transformation of the western German states into an entity tightly integrated with the liberal-democratic and capitalist west.

For the United States, an essential element of this policy was to fuse western German states and peoples together in a new and improved liberal constitutional state. In explaining the widening diplomatic rift (in the spring of 1947) between the Western Allies and the Soviet Union, Secretary of State George Marshall stated that, "The protection of the individual in the modern state rests upon the constitutional guarantees of his basic rights and liberties. I assume my colleagues will agree that adequate guaranties of these basic rights of the individual should be contained in every German constitution."[101]

Although German nationals—politicians and expert consultants—drafted the new constitutional instrument with little direct interference by the occupiers, this was mainly an American initiative. The Truman administration, not the Germans (who did not want to legitimize partition of the former German state), catalyzed the project and, Britain and France in tow, mandated most of its elemental features, including federalism, an extensive bill of individual rights, judicial review, and representative democracy.[102]

For the western Germans, its foreign origins was reason enough to be leery of the plan.[103] As matters stood, the new West German state and its constitution would be drafted while west Germans remained subjugated and financially dependent.[104] The document would also tend to validate the permanent division of the German homeland. Making matters worse, the Germans were being asked to set down the constitutional basis of a new state before the Allies had, in a new occupation statute, established the formal limits on the sovereignty of that state.[105]

At a meeting in Frankfurt on July 1, 1948, the three Western Allied military governors met with the German ministers-president of the western Länder (plus two mayors) to communicate the "Frankfurt documents," a statement of intent and list of instructions.[106] The

Allies intended to move swiftly to unify the three west German zones as a single state entity. The assemblies of the west German Länder were directed to elect a temporary entity (the Parliamentary Council), a subcommittee of which would draft the details of a new constitution, one that created a liberal-democratic west German federal state.

After the Frankfurt meeting, German party leaders agreed, if grudgingly, to participate in the first phase of the constitution drafting process,[107] if on the pretense that the document under consideration was not a permanent national constitution but the *Grundgesetz* or Basic Law of a temporarily partitioned German state.[108]

The complex diplomacy and negotiations as between the Allies and German political factions that led to the finalization and ratification of the Basic Law of the FRG have been described in detail elsewhere.[109] Here it will be enough to recount the evolution of the Basic Law as the framework of a west German liberal rule-of-law state.

In the summer of 1948, leading German constitutional experts, with the aid of American consultant Carl Friedrich, created a first draft of the Basic Law, one which respected the American guidelines set forth at Frankfurt.[110] The 1948 draft included an extensive Western-style bill of individual rights and, consistent with Allied requirements, a "formidable scheme of constitutional review" to be undertaken by a new federal constitutional court.[111]

While negotiations over some final provisions were divisive (with regard, for instance, to federalism, division of powers, and taxation) a clear majority of delegates supported the inclusion of extensive personal rights and freedoms enforced by judicial review.[112] More ambivalence was expressed about what, if anything, the Basic Law should provide in terms of the justiciability of personal rights in the federal courts.[113] Should individual citizens have a constitutional right to challenge the legal validity of a law or legal decision? Which federal courts would have jurisdiction to review and potentially to invalidate the laws or decisions of the state?

In coming to grips with these questions, it is useful to recall that in 1949, not one nation in the world, not even the United States, could provide an unproblematic model of constitutional rights litigation and judicial review.[114] Not only did the drafters lack for instructive examples, but their decision-making was complicated by Germany's unusually tragic legal history.[115] The Weimar experiment with constitutional liberalism had been undermined, in part, by Germany's illiberal and antidemocratic judiciary. Still, the widely held view of the delegates to the Parliamentary Council was that judicial review was an indispensable safeguard of individual rights and democratic political practices.[116]

The general disrepute of the German judiciary in 1949, that so many German judges had either actively supported or passively tolerated the legal program of National Socialism, threatened to undermine the constitutionalization of individual rights and judicial review.[117] There were a host of compelling reasons, then, why even the most liberal members of the Parliamentary Council hesitated to endorse constitutional provisions that would give German judges—any judges—the final say about legislation.

THE BASIC LAW AS LIBERAL AND ILLIBERAL CONSTITUTION

The final version of the Basic Law, ratified by the Parliamentary Council on May 23, 1949, was a grand display of ostensible liberality. Pointedly, the articles concerning the basic rights of the individual ("*Die Würde des Menschen*") were set forth at the beginning of the document and in bold and unequivocal language.[118] The first article of the first chapter declared that "The dignity of man is inviolable."[119] The first duty of the new West German state, it continued, was to "respect and protect [human dignity]." The third article, in effect the preamble to a series of articles describing basic personal rights (to life, liberty, speech, assembly, religion), pronounced that these "inviolable and inalienable human rights" are the basis of "every community, of peace and of justice in the world." Such basic rights, the document further proclaimed, "bind the legislature, the executive and the judiciary as directly enforceable law."

Here the Basic Law purported to lay down fixed constitutional limits on the legal authority of West German state actors, legislatures, and courts.[120] For the first time in the history of German public law,

Carl Friedrich observed, the individual person had been "put above the state."[121] For the first time, the German *rechtsstaat* or rule-of-law state, according to a founding constitutional instrument, was embedded in liberal precepts, in the priority and sanctity of the individual person. Not only was the decision-making power of West Germany's state actors always to be constrained by law but also by the law's transcendent commitment to the rights of the individual person.

To complement and enforce these liberal precepts, the Basic Law also established a potent federal judiciary, whose judges would enjoy security of tenure and institutional independence from the executive, legislative, and administrative arms of government.[122] For the first time in German history the judicial branch was to be a coequal of the executive and legislative branches of the state. In this regard, Article 93 created a new Federal Constitutional Court (FCC), one empowered to engage in two general types of judicial review: (1) with regard to challenges to the constitutional validity of federal legislation, and (2), with regard to the consideration of constitutional issues as they might arise in general, including in cases involving individual rights.[123] In the estimation of one of its architects, Carl Friedrich, the FCC was "the central institution in the experiment with constitutionalism initiated by the Basic Law—it is 'the final step in building a state based upon the rule of law (rechtsstaat).'"[124]

However, because of the Parliamentary Council's disagreement on this point,[125] the Basic Law did not stipulate the procedural mechanism by which persons might establish the justiciability of an alleged infringement of constitutional rights.[126] In the end result, the federal legislature (the *Bundestag*) of the FRG was left to determine the precise jurisdiction, powers, and procedures of the constitutional court.[127] This was done in March 1951.[128]

These elements of the Basic Law notwithstanding, it is a mistake to imagine that the new constitution was drafted by Germans moved mainly by liberal inspiration. In fact, most of the delegates who drafted the constitution, the Adenauer conservatives on the center Right and the Schumacher socialists on the center Left, while they made obligatory bows to liberalism, had other and more vital political goals. In general, the drafters were preoccupied far more with the democratic and structural than the liberal and procedural dimensions of the new constitutional order. Their main concern was not the quality of German liberalism but federalism. The drafting priority, therefore, was to design and install a system of shared powers flexible enough to reconcile West German regional with national social and economic interests and programs. They also wanted to devise a national democratic system flexible enough to accommodate the economic liberalism of the Right and the planned economy and social welfare aims of the Left. Finally, they wanted a constitution that would permit the federal state to defend itself against political extremism of the far Right and Left.

The Basic Law was constructed by a Parliamentary Council divided along party and ideological lines but united, almost to a person, by the conviction that German democracy must not be permitted to fall prey to the machinations of a new Hitler or Stalin. The councilors completed their work in the context of a dangerous past and present. They weighed and drafted constitutional Articles while cognizant of the forces, historical and current, aligned against a new German democratic experiment. They drafted for a people who, only a handful of years earlier, had firmly rejected liberalism and democracy. They also drafted in a moment of crippling social, psychological, and economic dislocation, and with an aggressive totalitarian regime on their eastern boundary.

For all of those reasons, but especially the menace posed by Soviet power, agitation, and intrigue, the Basic Law was inspired by the theory of "militant democracy" more than personal rights liberalism.[129] The final draft of the Basic Law was strongly influenced by the premise that any new West German liberal-democracy would be vulnerable to destabilization, even destruction, by the overt and covert actions of the Soviets and their surrogates. No accident, then, that the Basic Rights section of the Basic Law concluded with an Article (18) which contemplated the forfeiture of basic rights.[130] No wonder, therefore, that another Article (21) contemplated the illegality of totalitarian political parties. It was also no coincidence that these articles purported to limit personal and collective political rights in West Germany.[131]

Further to the theory of militant democracy, Article 21 of the Basic Law concerned political parties and how they might be freely formed and operated. Article 21(1) required that political parties be organized on democratic principles. Article 21(2) went further, declaring that political parties that "seek to abolish the free and democratic basic order . . . shall be unconstitutional." Taken together (in Carl Friedrich's opinion) these articles had been included in order to ensure that the West German state might "nip in the bud any totalitarian movements that try to address themselves to the electorate with an appeal to the change of the system."[132] But although Friedrich was a strong proponent of the doctrine of militant democracy, he harbored concerns that these provisions of the Basic Law were vaguely drawn and might someday be abused to suppress legitimate political activity.[133]

When the Basic Law came into effect in May 1949, the United States had chalked up another major victory in the abstract reconstruction of the west German zones. But its leaders could not credibly claim that these embellishments were certain, or even very likely, to have measureable impact on the worldview or lived experience of Germans. After all, the new West German constitution had been designed, drafted, and ratified without popular participation. The new Basic Law (Article 131) also left the door open to the reemployment by the Länder of Germany's deeply conservative and morally compromised civil service elite.[134] There is little evidence, moreover, that the high-minded liberalism of its first seventeen articles had penetrated the hearts and minds either of German political elites or ordinary German men and women.

Certainly this was Roger Baldwin's dour conclusion in the early autumn of 1950. In the course of a two-month fact-finding mission to the FRG in the early autumn of 1950 (this time sponsored by the State Department), Baldwin had encountered West Germany as "completely split up into small pieces," a dislocated physical and cultural space lacking in cohesive civil agency, private or public.[135] The void left by the Third Reich was being filled, not by vigorous young leaders, voluntary associations and pressure groups, but by Germany's timeworn men and institutions—the staid political parties and placemen, the Catholic Church, bureaucrats, and business corporations. In the ostensibly new republic, Germany's conservative elites were quietly reforming their ranks. The old gang was back, Baldwin lamented, and "Order, not liberty, is their chief concern."

In the face of liberal revolution in theory, conservative revival in fact, Baldwin observed, the West German populace remained passive and detached, evincing immovable "apathy in all public affairs." Although he thought the Americans had made structural inroads with liberal reform,[136] there was no mistaking that Germany's authoritarian dispositions were "again strong under various guises, with so few Germans taking any interest in politics."[137] Membership in political parties had not reached even 5 percent, the parties themselves "dictatorial in their leadership, the Socialists like the others." If the West Germans now had access to liberty, they remained steadfast in refusing to exercise it. In Baldwin's view, the "whole concept of protecting civil liberties by citizen action is a novelty in a country where officials are supposed to govern and citizens obey." Senior American civil affairs officers concurred with Baldwin's grim assessment, admitting that "all the preaching of democracy for five years has not changed German habits of discipline, obedience and government from the top down. All my audiences confirm it."

In Baldwin's opinion, the West Germans in 1950 were worse off than in 1948 in that "the sense of change" detectable then was lacking two years later.[138] Ironically, the transition from a military-dominated occupation under General Clay to the largely civilianized administration of the first High Commissioner, John McCloy, seemed somehow to have disrupted the momentum of liberal-democratic reorientation in West Germany. "Instead of change, drama and excitement," Baldwin dolefully reported, "there's now a let's-wait-and-see-what's-coming attitude, while the Germans fall back on secure old patterns and the Occupation just keeps its machine going."

We might be tempted to devalue Baldwin's observations as those of a non-German speaking, nonspecialist outsider, except that nearly identical reports, this time the formal reports to the American authorities from one of their own expert consultants, were rendered in 1950 by persons like Wilhelm Sollman, a man of unassailable knowledge, experience, and fluency in German affairs. Sollman was a German born and educated socialist politician and lawyer, an émigré refugee from Hitler, who had returned to Germany as an expert consultant on civil liberties several times in the late 1940s. During his final visit, from spring through the summer of 1950, Sollman was a guest professor of politics at the University of Cologne, helped found a new chapter of the German Civil Liberties *Bund* and interviewed, among others, leading American officials and a number of prominent German politicians and eminences—Konrad Adenauer and Kurt Schumacher included—on the subject of civil liberties in the new FRG.[139]

Like Roger Baldwin, by the close of his work in West Germany in August 1950 Sollman had become alarmed by the debased state of political and civic culture there. As a result of the various dismemberments of the occupation, the German nation had "practically nothing in common except its language. . . . even in the West the Germans are deeply divided and for the most part with no faith in a national community."[140] For all of its liberal-democratic promise, the new Basic Law of the FRG had been met with "indifference from a majority and hostility from a minority of Germans." Alarmingly, too, Sollman detected "grave doubts in all parts of society and all political parties as to whether democracy is suitable for the Germans. Many antidemocratic groups . . . are much more active in their attacks on the present state than the supporters of the democratic republic are in its defense." Most Germans clung to conservative and nationalists ideals, in Bavaria to a revived nationalism. In a host of ways, then, psychological and ideological resistance to liberal-democratic patterns of thought remained strong.

In Sollman's view, one that was widely shared by analysts of West German affairs in 1950, a resurgent German *beamtenschaften,* the insular and privileged cliques of senior bureaucrats who ran Germany's state and federal governments, once again were tightening their grip on public administration in the FRG.[141] From the point of view of democratization, the threat here was not that the various civil service bureaucracies were brimming with ex-Nazis (although they were), but that whether Nazis or not, notoriously the bureaucratic elite, the *beamten,* were dominated by old-school German lawyers, men steadfastly statist and antidemocratic in outlook.[142] This group, now regaining day-to-day operation of policing and criminal justice in West

Germany, had successfully resisted American attempts in their reform.[143] Not much impressed by liberal-minded structural change, the *beamten* seemed determine to retard or derail efforts to liberalize German society.

As the American German affairs expert Harold Landin reported in 1950, the evidence suggested that at all levels of West German government, elected officials had failed to exploit opportunities to consolidate liberal-democratic reform.[144] In the area of civil liberties particularly, politicians had deferred to the *beamten,* who, in turn had permitted police, prosecutors, and judges to run roughshod over the new constitutional rights of citizens. This trend was reinforced by the predisposition of ordinary Germans to accept the authoritarianism of state officials. "The German people," Landin commented, "are not only intimidated by judges and other high officials, they are also the victims of the arbitrary, ruthless and undemocratic authority of the lower civil service. The most offensive have been the police whose daily violation of basic civil rights has brought discredit upon the new German administration." In Landin's opinion, American intervention had done little to alter this historical pattern. "What is more tragic," his reported emphasized, "is the fact that the great majority of citizens, ignorant of their rights, accept this state of affairs. The few who may know their rights in law do not dare exercise them in the face of the police-state behavior of the government."

Such subservience was not a matter of habit only but a rational response to the predisposition of officials to punish recalcitrance. German citizens who deigned to criticize state officials in the media, for instance, were liable to be prosecuted criminally for insulting their public reputation or honor.[145] Such prosecutions served to remind Germans that the formal liberalization of federal and state laws notwithstanding, the weak were vulnerable to backlash by the powerful.

THE ANTI-COMMUNIST CAMPAIGN, 1949 TO 1952

The litmus test of civil rights and liberties—in West Germany in 1949 to 1952 or anywhere else in any time frame—is whether the power of state actors is limited by law even when such actors feel threatened. In the relevant period, the West German federal and state authorities abjectly failed that test. They did so by orchestrating, with the backing of their American overseers, an increasingly aggressive campaign of state-sponsored repression directed at Communists, the West German Communist Party (KPD), and other and sundry left-wing activists.[146]

Before the Berlin crisis began in June 1948, American leadership generally and Clay emphatically discounted the threats posed by Moscow or the KPD in the West German zone.[147] As late as October 1947, Clay assured the assistant secretary of the army that the "march westward of Communism and world revolution has been stopped in central Germany. Western Germany and western Europe do not desire to live in police states. . . . We do not need to fear for democracy in western Germany."[148] To Clay's mind, in fact, the best strategy for winning the hearts and minds of western Germans was not in the domestic suppression but in the liberation of the German people to engage in economic and political behavior.

But as the estrangement of the United States and the Soviet Union deepened in 1948, with the loss of China to Communism in the fall of 1949, the Truman administration reassessed the prospects of Communism's westward march. Although in western Germany the KPD was a minor political party with little public support. Its Soviet masters, in the words of one historian, were "shunned by an overwhelmingly hostile society with a long pedigree of anti-Communist behavior," in 1949 American and German authorities began to take manifestly illiberal steps to crush it.[149]

In this regard, the Truman administration adopted what became the standard rationale of anti-Communist repression in Germany (and the United States): that as a revolutionary party the KPD was, at least tacitly, a subversive political organization. On this basis the White House felt justified in discarding its previous neutrality in the authorization, supervision, and control of German political parties, including the KPD.[150] In 1949 and afterward, American policy was placed on a new footing, one of active support for democratic parties and active suppression of the KPD.[151] The implicit policy of the United States was to support the nascent West German government agencies as they practiced the doctrine of militant democracy—that is, their taking deliberately illiberal steps to protect the democratic state from antidemocratic threats.[152]

In adopting this militantly anti-Communist posture, the Americans found a devoted German partner in the first chancellor of the FRG, Konrad Adenauer. On the plus side was the chancellor's deep disdain of totalitarianism, both of the Right and the Left. Another asset was Adenauer's unrivalled capacity to enlist West Germans in support of a popular and "Made in Germany" program of anti-Communist repression.[153] From the point of view of the consolidation of liberal-democratic norms of thought and practice in the FRG, however, Adenauer was a dubious partner. While the chancellor's anti-Communism was beyond doubt, his commitment to democracy and civil libertarianism was not. As one American analyst noted, Adenauer evinced no "real sympathy for public government, nor for democracy in practice as we understand it. He is the product of German officialdom with its belief in the authority of the state over the people and in the professional civil servant as the representative of the state."[154] In subduing the Communist threat, Adenauer had few scruples about civil rights and freedoms.

In 1949, HICOG and the new West German state ramped up their attack on the hard Left, curtailing the KPD newspaper and its political activities.[155] By September 1949, furthermore, "All Western German Länder have followed the Bonn lead in ousting Communists from the civil service."[156] But the pivotal moment in this regard, the event that caused American and West German leaders to take further and still more illiberal action against the hard Left, was when North Korean Communist forces invaded South Korea in June 1950. In their eyes the Communist invasion of Korea signaled the willingness of the Soviet Union to use military force to challenge the post–Second World War settlement. In the grip of a "red scare," HICOG stood back while Adenauer further escalated his war on the Communist Left.[157]

While adhering to American-made policy of not banning the KPD outright, German security agencies at the federal and regional levels were deployed to close KPD newspapers and to constrain its propaganda and public meetings.[158] KPD officials were subjected to various forms of harassment and arbitrary arrest. The elimination of former Nazis from German public life abandoned, the elimination of the Communist Left had begun.

The repressive vigor of these moves left German and American authorities open to the plausible claim that they undercut the *raison d'être* of the West German state: to exemplify "the benefits of free life under a truly democratic governmental system." McCloy was especially alive to American vulnerability on this point. In response to the worried inquiry of Roger Baldwin, he offered assurance that it was American policy "to discourage the prosecutions of persons identified with Communist activities (such as the distribution of subversive posters, etc.) unless it can clearly be established that these persons are habitual offenders or have been apprehended in some real disturbance of public order."[159] Just as in the United States, McCloy disingenuously added, Communists were in no jeopardy except when they had broken or threatened to break the law. If the German police sometimes had gone too far, it was because the Communists had waged cold war in West Germany.[160] McCloy advised Baldwin that in respect to police action against the Left in the FRG "the 'clear and present danger' rule is generally regarded as controlling, although its application is, of course, difficult to ascertain in certain situations."[161]

In 1951, Adenauer's government sought legal validation for its claim that both the KPD and a far-Right political faction (the Socialist Reich Party) were illegal political parties under Article 21 of the Basic Law.[162] Within a year, the FCC ruled that the Reich Party was illegal and subject to lawful ban. While Adenauer waited for the FCC's decision on the KPD, his government passed new criminal law legislation (the "Blitz Law") that greatly expanded the federal state's legal authority to charge and prosecute persons for very broadly drawn political crimes such as "endangering the state."[163] In the next five years, thousands of alleged Communists and their associates were convicted under these provisions.[164] In the same period, federal authorities pressed more criminal prosecutions against leading KPD officials on charges of conspiracy and treason.

In theory at least, it was possible for West German Communists, or other persons believing their legal or constitutional rights had been wrongfully abridged, to challenge the legality of such incursions. It was altogether possible, in fact it was now "guaranteed" under state and federal constitutional law, that such persons should have their civil rights vindicated in the West German courts of law. But, in fact, in the period 1949 to 1952, this rarely happened. If West Germans knew or cared about their constitutional rights, they did not often seek to vindicate them in the courts. In the first five years of its jurisdiction, the Basic Law, far from vindicating civil liberties in West Germany, more often and decisively served as the basis of state-sanctioned repression.

Nor were the new West German civil liberties unions, or German radicals themselves, inclined to fight German state authorities in the courts.[165] Civil libertarian litigation was deterred by the absence of libertarian habits of thought both among potential litigants and German lawyers. In some measure, too, it was deterred by the deeply engrained illiberalism of the German judiciary, especially in relation to Communist political activity. In this stance, Germany's judges found support in the almost uniformly anti-Communist consensus among West Germans of all regions and classes. This also explains why few learned observers were surprised when, in the summer of 1956, some five years after the FRG's petition had been submitted, the Federal Constitutional Court ruled that the KPD was unconstitutional and was to be dissolved for having sought to "impair or destroy the free democratic order."[166] This landmark decision prompted further state-backed and now legally sanctioned repression of leftist political activity.

While no friend to Communism, Baldwin came away from his final trip to the FRG in 1950 disappointed in the state of political liberties there. He particularly bemoaned that unelected federal and regional bureaucrats were wielding outsized amounts of influence and power in the new West German democracy. "The wrong men are at the top of government," he observed, "the old bureaucracy and the conservatives. Former Nazis hold too many posts, especially in the courts (some 80% of judges in Bavaria)."[167] In this context, the German habit of "letting officials attend to problems" remained unaltered. In the democratic arena, too, Baldwin saw the same German tendency to defer to the old parties, party leaders, and ideas. He was especially disillusioned in the "rejection of the youth in all movements." Even Germany's otherwise promising trades union movement, Baldwin lamented, were "like all other organizations, are run from the top down, the center out."[168]

The coincidence of the Cold War, birth of the FRG, and the rise to national power of Adenauer and his conservative coalition had produced an almost perfect storm of factors militating against a civil libertarian cultural shift in West Germany. "Reorienting the Germans," Baldwin recorded in his notes, "has not worked, despite five years of attempts. It is an unworkable theory."[169] The new German political class, taking advantage of the indifference of the German people and the tacit support of the Allied occupiers, had by the closing weeks of 1950 constructed a quasi-authoritarian state entity in West Germany.

As for Baldwin, against all odds he remained invested in the idea that the civil libertarian promise of the new German constitutional law might still be realized by the creation and activation of a German national agency devoted to this mission.[170] Wilhelm Sollman was less sanguine. His final report of 1950 concluded flatly that "The Bonn Basic Law meets with indifference from a majority and hostility from a minority of Germans." According to Sollman's observations, conservatives and statists of various stripes still far outnumbered ideological liberal-democrats in West Germany. Whether because of history or economic malaise or both, Germans seemed disinterested in the idea of building a genuinely liberal-democratic civil society. If anything, Sollman believed, the "social conscience" of the West Germans, this critical prerequisite of a thriving liberal society, was "less developed than before Hitler."

For Sollman, as for other American consultants on Germany such as Karl Loewenstein, there was no escaping the conclusion that, as of 1950, the American-sponsored structural and ideological reorientation program in Germany had had little or no impact on German political patterns or sensibilities.[171] "The fact that working democracy means citizenship participation on all levels of society," Sollman reported, was still not recognized in the FRG, by either the political leaders or the people. Germans at the local, regional, and federal levels still lacked the perquisite civic virtues and habitual conduct of a liberal-democratic community. There still was "no general consciousness of being a citizen in Germany . . . no sense of the need for personal responsibility and action." Among the political leaders, almost all of whom were in their sixties or seventies, there was, as Sollman saw it, a tendency to "conduct politics with political parties and ideas of 1860 and 1870." The leaders seemed stuck in a political netherworld, "no longer monarchists, but not yet for the republic. They are no longer Nazis, nor yet democrats. They are no longer nationalists, but not yet Europeans." The FRG political elite, only theoretically the democratic representatives of voters, were dangerously disconnected from a people who had not yet even nearly recovered from the aftershocks of defeat, occupation, and now partition *de facto*.

Saturn Devours His Children: Civil Liberties in Cold War Japan, 1948 to 1952

In remaking Germans and Japanese as civil libertarians in the late 1940s, American occupation authorities faced uphill battles. In neither country, not even European Germany, was there a strong historical or cultural predisposition toward liberal individualism. In the postwar era, German and Japanese radicalism and dissent was far more likely to be Marxist than liberal in its ideological allegiances. In both occupied countries, leadership elites and the general populations alike were more likely to endorse the repression than the liberation of the far left. In both places, private and public economic recovery was seen as infinitely more pertinent than whether handfuls of radical troublemakers were being deprived of laundry lists of fundamental rights.

In regard to occupied Japan, the Potsdam Declaration had called for the Allied occupation regime to establish "Freedom of speech, of religion, and of thought, as well as respect for the fundamental human rights."[172] In his capacity as Supreme Commander of that regime, MacArthur moved quickly and decisively to make good on this undertaking.

On October 4, 1945, not quite a month after establishing his headquarters in Japan, MacArthur issued a directive (SCAPIN 93) ordering the Japanese government to take immediate action to "remove restrictions on political, civil and religious liberties and discrimination on grounds of race, nationality, creed or political opinion."[173] The directive required the abrogation of the score of laws and ordinances that had underpinned Japan's wartime police state. It also called for the immediate release of all persons who might remain in detention as a consequence of such laws.

SCAPIN 93 was an important moment in the history of civil liberties in postwar Japan. It signaled that all political activists, even leaders of the Communist Party of Japan (CPJ)—for more than ten years harshly stigmatized and suppressed by the Japanese state—would be free to organize, recruit, and advance their claims. To the eventual distress of American and Japanese conservatives, however, the CPJ made ready and effective use of this new legal space.

Previous chapters have documented the dramatic second phase of the American civil liberties program in Japan—that is, the explicit constitutionalization (in 1946 and 1947) not only of inviolate individual and collective rights but the legal mechanisms of their vindication and enforcement.[174] Those Japanese citizens who felt ill used by agencies of state were to have their day in court, their pleadings heard by judges free from political interference and empowered to redress unconstitutional action or conduct. Thus, when the new constitution of Japan was ratified at the close of 1947, Japan, on paper, became a liberal rule-of-law state.

But of course neither lives nor laws are lived on paper or in a sociopolitical vacuum. The second phase of MacArthur's civil liberties program came to fruition in the context of socioeconomic crisis. The physical reconstruction of Japan's ruined cities, infrastructure, and domestic and trade economies had barely begun. Inflation and unemployment were punishingly high and hunger widespread. In such dire circumstances, Japanese men and women had abundant motivation to utilize newfound civil liberties of speech, association, and assembly.

And utilize them they did. The coincidence of socioeconomic hardship and American-sponsored civil libertarianism led to a flourishing of left-wing activism, including aggressive trade unionism, public demonstration, and radical speech.[175] Indeed, as early as May 1946,

MacArthur had become so alarmed by the tenor and destructive effects of this activism that he issued a statement warning the Japanese against its "growing tendency towards mass violence."[176] "While every possible rational freedom of democratic method has been permitted and will be permitted," MacArthur intoned, unruly expressions of dissent "will not be permitted to continue." The most controversial expression of the Supreme Commander's resolve came at the end of January 1947, when MacArthur declared that in "the present impoverished and emaciated condition of Japan," SCAP would prohibit activists from organizing a general strike.[177]

The general strike decree did not otherwise spell the end of SCAP's civil libertarian initiatives in Japan. In the winter of 1947, with the War Department's blessing MacArthur reached out to Roger Baldwin, president of the ACLU and America's most conspicuous champion of liberal causes. Baldwin was invited and, after consulting with the ACLU board, agreed to spend two months in Japan and Korea to complete an independent assessment of "occupation policies in relation to democracy and civil liberty."[178] While in Japan, Baldwin was to be afforded broad and unfettered access to relevant SCAP and Japanese governmental officials as well as to a range of Japanese political and civic leaders and social activists. His mission was to gauge the state of civil liberties in Japan and to advise MacArthur on how they might be further promoted and protected.

In bringing Baldwin to Japan, MacArthur's motives were a comingling of idealism and political calculation. To a man, the New Deal liberals of SCAP's Government Section never doubted the sincerity of the General's commitment to the introduction of American-style civil libertarianism in Japan. MacArthur calculated, correctly as it turned out, that he could also win Baldwin over to this view. He also calculated that Baldwin might provide some genuine insight on how to manage hard-Left activism in Japan in a manner consistent with SCAP's civil libertarian commitments.

There had been another reason for MacArthur and the War Department to encourage Baldwin to make a fact-finding and advice-dispensing tour of occupied Japan.[179] Baldwin, it was well known, was a staunch anti-Communist[180] and under his leadership the ACLU had become disassociated from the radical Left.[181] In arranging for Baldwin to come to Japan, then affording him what Baldwin himself called "complete freedom" in seeing and interviewing politically engaged Japanese and Koreans, MacArthur calculated that the ACLU president was unlikely to embarrass him about steps taken to constrain the radical Left in Japan.[182]

As for Baldwin, he had arrived in Tokyo doubting that an American army general, still less one known to be an out-and-out reactionary, might be a champion of human rights and liberties.[183] However, MacArthur had not been wrong in predicting that he might change Baldwin's mind on that point. Baldwin recalled their first meeting (Sunday dinner at the MacArthur residence) where the general informed his astonished guest that not only were civil liberties important to the American political program in Japan, they "were the essence of the democracy he was trying to implant."[184] Baldwin came away from two hours of conversation convinced that the general was in fact "a real statesman of democracy and liberal-minded philosopher of human relations wholly unrelated to the military spirit." Baldwin did not later find cause to deviate from that view.

So what conclusions did Baldwin draw from two months of meetings with American officials and an array of Japanese lawyers, trade unionists, and politicians? In relation to the Americans, Baldwin concluded that, like MacArthur, they were genuinely dedicated to the liberal-democratic transformation of Japan. In relation to the Japanese, Baldwin encountered people which he thought "child-like enough to be teachable," and almost "pathetically eager to learn" about liberal-democratic precepts and practices.[185] In particular, government officials in Japan had proved unable or unwilling to thwart the authoritarian abuses either of the police or of Communist agitators in the trade unions.[186]

On the other hand, Baldwin also offered some pointed criticisms of SCAP policies on civil liberties. The comprehensive censorship of Japanese private mail and media, for example, he considered "capricious and arbitrary."[187] Baldwin thought that SCAP's purge of alleged ultranationalists and militarists had been indiscriminate in its targets and arbitrary in its procedures.[188] Baldwin also reckoned that Japan's reorganized police and prosecutorial agencies were overriding the new procedural rights and protections of persons accused of criminal offenses. On these grounds, in 1947 Baldwin, now supported by Alfred Oppler and Government Section, urged MacArthur to establish American-style[189] local and national Civil Liberties Unions in Japan.[190]

On his return to the United States in the summer of 1947, Baldwin provided the American reading public with an enthusiastic, even saccharine, portrait of MacArthur and his program.[191] Playing down the authoritarian aspects of American military government in Japan, in a series of publications and ACLU internal reports, Baldwin chose to burnish MacArthur's reputation as a "crusader for democracy."[192] In these writings, the SCAP regime was drawn as a "near-miracle in human relations."[193] They repeatedly stressed that "MacArthur's reputation as a conservative and aloof autocrat is wrong." In fact, Baldwin claimed that he had met "no man in public life with a keener understanding of the principles and practices of liberal democracy, and a deeper faith in them." In two short years, Baldwin contended, MacArthur and his men had transformed a "military autocracy into a democracy."

The centerpiece of the MacArthur revolution in Japan, in Baldwin's view, was Japan's new constitution, now "among the most democratic in the world." Under American guidance, the Japanese people, once systematically oppressed, now lived in a country that "guarantees civil and political rights to all." In the newly liberated Japan, "Freedom of religion, speech, thought, assembly and association have been secured for the Japanese people." There could be no doubt as to the author of this epic achievement: "The key to the great drama is General MacArthur."

Ironically enough, however, just as Baldwin published this tribute in February 1948, the Truman administration—as it positioned itself for reelection in November—was crafting a decisive and, from the standpoint of civil liberties, decidedly illiberal realignment in its policy toward SCAP and the occupation of Japan. As a consequence, the period of expansive civil libertarianism in occupied Japan was fleeting, the casualty of a rightward policy shift. In terms of political rights and freedoms, what some Americans had given, other Americans (in league with Japanese politicians and bureaucrats) began to take away.

In 1947 and 1948, the Truman administration implemented a major change in American policy toward the occupation of Japan.[194] The change was precipitated by a number of factors, starting with pressure it felt from the Republican-controlled and vehemently anti-Communist Congress. Apprehension was building in the United States about Communist influence at home and Soviet belligerence in Europe and east Asia. In the context also of the mounting financial cost of its occupations, Truman had become politically vulnerable to the claim that MacArthur was blundering Japan into the hands of Soviet-backed Communists.[195] In response to attack from its Right, and its own frustration with the slow pace of economic recovery in Japan, the Truman administration began to reset American priorities there.[196] Henceforth, the primary policy focus of the United States in Japan started to be moved away from democratization and toward Communist containment and other considerations relating to national security.

This policy shift, often given the overgeneralized label of "the reverse course," was rooted in the perception, fostered and embellished by Truman's most influential diplomatic and economic advisers, that MacArthur, both his personality and policies, had led Japan to a point of dangerous economic and political instability.[197] Too long left to his own devices, the Supreme Commander had promoted a radical program of legal and political reform in Japan while neglecting economic reconstruction and growth. In this view, at the close of 1947, Japan had too much political freedom, too little economic dynamism. From 1948 until the end of the occupation, MacArthur and his liberal vision of the democratization program in Japan came under relentless and effective political pressure from conservative interest groups and political alignments in Washington.

In the view of Truman's advisers, the problem's most alarming manifestation was the deplorable state of relations between capital and labor in Japan.[198] The policy of making collective bargaining widely available to Japanese workers—a right that was fully constitutionalized at the close of 1947—was seen as having promoted a veritable tidal wave of militant unionization.[199] In the face of declining wages and conditions of work, by 1948 these unions had called scores of strikes, some of them broadly supported by alliances of university students, women, and even farmers. Even more disconcertingly, increasing numbers of Japan's key private and public sector unions were either controlled or strongly influenced by Communists.[200]

The arrival in Tokyo in March 1948 of George Kennan, the State Department's emissary (and principal architect of America's early Cold War diplomacy), signaled the end of MacArthur's largely unsupervised authority in Japan.[201] From that point forward the key shots on occupation policy in Japan were called by the White House.

In the course of the next two years, Washington introduced a new prescription for occupied Japan.[202] While it was impolitic to replace the Supreme Commander, MacArthur was put on an increasingly tight leash, especially with regard to management of the Japanese economy. American banker-economists were sent to Japan to take control over its mainsprings. This entailed a harsh regimen of anti-inflationary and fiscal policies. Wage freezes and massive cuts to public services were accompanied by more and regressive taxes. Overriding MacArthur's objections, previous American commitments (rooted in the Potsdam Declaration) to the destruction of Japan's corporate conglomerates and to the purge of rightists were relaxed, then shelved.[203]

In the short term, Truman's advisers knew, these measures were certain to exacerbate socioeconomic distress in Japan and lead to even higher levels of social unrest and labor militancy. It would be necessary, therefore, for SCAP, working closely with Japan's (conservative) government and bureaucracy, to promote social discipline and public security over liberal values.[204] It would be necessary, in other words, for MacArthur and his Government Section to redefine, from the far Right to the far Left, the principal threat to democracy in Japan. While neither MacArthur nor GS concurred with this change, they had no recourse but to curb, eventually to undercut, the freshly minted civil and constitutional rights of left-wing activists in Japan.

The turbulent spring and summer of 1948 were a crucial turning point in postwar Japan, marking the end of the occupation's civil liberties moment. With increasing frequency and harshness, local Japanese police, sometimes with the direct intervention of U.S. Army units, began to suppress public protests and strike-related demonstrations and rallies.[205] Then, in July, and in the face of established legal rights and in plain contradiction of Article 28 of the new constitution, MacArthur ordered the Japanese government to terminate the legal right of Japan's 2 million public-sector employees to strike and bargain collectively.[206] The Supreme Commander then signaled to the Japanese government to arrest anyone who dared to organize protests or strikes against this law.

In January 1949, the crackdown on the Left gained momentum on the election by a decisive majority in the Diet of the Democratic Liberal Party (DLP), led by Shigeru Yoshida.[207] Staunchly pro-business, rabidly anti-Communist (and anti-Korean), unmoved by the civil libertarianism of the new constitution, Yoshida came to power prepared, even eager, to employ all assets of state to subdue a restive Korean minority and, more emphatically, to crush what he regarded as a Soviet plot to "bring about a revolution by force" in Japan.[208] With the increasingly robust support of SCAP and the Truman administration, in the summer of 1949 Yoshida began to prosecute a major offensive against alleged Communists and their fellow travelers.[209] Yoshida's main goal, as he stated in a letter to MacArthur, was to eliminate Communism domestically while stemming the "tide of Communism now sweeping over the Asiatic continent."

From the standpoint of lives and liberties in Japan, this goal was not attained cheaply. Over the next three years the anti-Communist drive caused tens of thousands of arrests, prosecutions, and prison sentences. For tens of thousands more, the crackdown cost jobs and professional careers. Symbolically, the offensive substantially damaged the integrity of Japan's new constitution and the judiciary sworn to uphold it.

Both the official record of the American occupation of Japan and the published memoirs of key American officials are replete with boasts about the liberal reconstruction of that country.[210] We have seen, for example, how Alfred Oppler wrote extensively of his role in helping institute legal and institutional "safeguards of the fundamental human rights of the individual."[211] For whatever reason—whether shame, embarrassment, or selective forgetfulness—the American memoirists, Oppler especially, were far more reticent about their role in the degradation of the same rights. The sober fact is that by the close of 1948, the primary mission of Oppler's GS unit was no longer to help construct or protect civil rights in Japan so much as to constrain their supposed abuse. Although Oppler's memoir pays scant attention to this fact, from 1948 until the end of the occupation in 1952, the main task of the unit was to work with the Japanese state in taking overt and covert countermeasures against the perceived political and economic subversions of the Japanese Left.[212]

The overt part of this job was the provision of information and advice to the Japanese government and judiciary on the legislative and judicial techniques of law-based countersubversion. (Oppler and his men also pitched in with propaganda, offering a series of public lectures on the "irreconcilability of Communism with fundamental human rights."[213]) The larger but *covert* part of the job involved a series of off-the-record briefings of the chief justice of Japan (and, sometimes, the Supreme Court) on the exigencies of countersubversion. In these secret meetings that flatly contradicted constitutional commitments to judicial independence and the rule of law, Oppler and other American officials communicated SCAP's expectations, sometimes demands, regarding the correct judicial response to the legal issues raised by the countersubversion program.

It ought not to be supposed, however, that all, or even any, senior GS legal officers were enthusiastic about their role in countersubversion. Some, Charles Kades most prominently, were so uneasy with the change of policy course that they resigned commissions and returned to the United States (Kades doing so in April 1949).[214]

Most senior American legal officers stayed the course (Oppler perhaps for lack of attractive options). As for Kades, he was replaced as second-in-command of GS by the career soldier Major Jack Napier.[215] Napier's closest counterpart on the Japanese side was Yoshida's ardently anti-Communist attorney general, Ueda Shunkichi, first officer of the newly reconfigured Office of the Attorney General.[216] Napier and Shunkichi agreed that what was urgently needed in Japan were new and effective means—legal or otherwise—by which to quell leftist activism. A first step in this regard was to permit the government to rebuild and activate Japan's internal security assets, including the formation of an antisubversive Special Investigations Bureau (SIB) within the Office of the Attorney General.[217]

The next step was to forge and maintain "continuous and close contact" between GS and the attorney general's office on the "problem of communism."[218] In order to make his contact productive, Napier and his GS officers began to educate themselves, then their Japanese counterparts, in the contemporary American techniques of countersubversion. This included the preparation of briefing documents for Japanese government lawyers on such items as the Smith Act, the federal laws governing the transmission and importation of political literature and state laws, particularly the recent laws of New York State, regarding the legal regulation and control of Communists and Communist propaganda.[219] When Japanese lawyers drafted new antisubversive legislation, they were to be "furnished with models of American laws and court decisions on subversive activities." The same materials, moreover, were also to be given to the Supreme Court of Japan.

Further to its mandate to review all bills to the Japanese Diet from the legal and constitutional point of view, from 1947 through 1951 GS lawyers approved and assisted in the formulation of legislation that, *de facto,* stripped alleged Communists and their fellow travelers of basic civil rights.[220]

It did not take long for these initiatives to generate vehement complaint and criticism. Some were aired at a remarkable meeting convened at SCAP headquarters on September 9, 1949.[221] On the agenda was a recent decision of Yoshida's attorney general to invoke an imperial ordinance, backed by the SCAP purge directive,[222] disbanding a number of "subversive" organizations.[223] The ordinance, designed as a means of ridding government of ultranationalists, had been used to justify the dissolution of two Korean cooperative organizations and the confiscation of their property. The meeting was attended by delegates of the League of Koreans, the Korean Youth Alliance, the CPJ, and the Free Lawyers Association. The officials wanted SCAP to explain the constitutional basis for the dissolution of nonviolent social and political organizations.

One delegate contended that the move against the Koreans was based on nothing more than the unilateral judgment of the attorney general and as such was very dangerous.[224] Shigeo Katiyama, the Communist delegate, offered that the new law "might be applied to any organization which might have something to do with politics." If the decision was left to stand, there could be no limit to the government's authority to suppress voluntary associations. Katiyama then told the SCAP officers that in 1945 he himself had been "released from imperial prison by SCAP order." He thought that the government's dissolution policy was "reminiscent of the Home Ministry just before the outbreak of the Sino-Japanese incident." It looked to him like the "past practices of the militaristic regime." Then as now, oppression had begun by "fanning national prejudice against Koreans and other peoples of the east." In general, the government's high-handed and authoritarian practice was seen as contrary to the constitutional rights of Japanese citizens to associate freely and to petition their government. The delegates wanted to know what SCAP would do to correct and stop these abuses.

In the absence of their higher-ups (who had begged off) the Americans present at the meeting stated that they were not in a position to make an answer. They would make no comment on the legal problems raised by the delegates until senior officers were consulted. The organizations they represented were invited to submit a formal brief on the legal points raised by their complaints.

It does not appear that, not wanting to waste their time, any of the complainants took up this offer. The writing on the wall all too clearly indicated that neither the government nor SCAP was going to let legal niceties stand in the way of what they saw as a necessary crackdown on radicals and agitators.

The complainants were not wrong in this surmise. The documents are clear that from 1949 until the end of the occupation, SCAP's policy, like that of American Military Government in Germany, was one of "militant democracy," the doctrine that the liberal democratic regime was justified in the suppression of antidemocratic agitation by illiberal and undemocratic means. In this period, the prevailing doctrine among American decision-makers was that Communist agitators and agitations could not, except at unacceptable risk to Japan's nascent democracy, be afforded the benefit of their constitutional rights and the rule of law.

On this reasoning, even the "inviolable" principle of the political independence of judge and courts might justly be violated. As Alfred Oppler dourly noted in his published memoir, "Few principles are without exceptions, and I felt compelled, for different reasons, in two instances to intervene in judicial affairs."[225]

One of those instances was occasioned when the Tokyo High Court acquitted two wartime officials of bribery and breach of the ordinances governing the purge of ultranationalists.[226] Oppler and other GS officers arranged a number of secret meetings with justices of the Supreme Court. At those meetings, on the basis that purge ordinances fell within the exclusive jurisdiction of SCAP, GS dictated the outcome of this litigation.[227] Oppler recounts how he had taken up such cases with the newly appointed chief justice of the Supreme Court, Tanaka Kotaro. The meeting, Oppler writes, "was a command performance, and constituted an obvious interference with a pending judicial procedure."[228]

A number of important episodes of American intervention in Japan's new system of justice are not recounted in Oppler's published writing. In November 1949, for instance, in response to the high-profile criminal trials of alleged Communist railway saboteurs, Whitney had again dispatched Oppler to meet with the chief justice.[229] Oppler informed the chief justice that SCAP was strongly critical of the failures of the trial judges to prevent their courtrooms from becoming platforms for "Communistic propaganda." The chief justice was instructed to take all measures necessary to forestall any further threats to the dignity of the courts.[230]

Then there were the interventions associated with the infamous "red purge." In the summer of 1949, with the tacit endorsement of SCAP, the Yoshida government began to use SCAP's purge ordinance to fire suspected Communists and Communist sympathizers from jobs in the public and, later, private sectors.[231] A program devised by SCAP to punish and deter ultranationalists was now redeployed by Japanese to punish and deter the hard Left. The red purge unfolded in overlapping stages.[232] It began in July 1949 when GS (represented by Jack Napier) formally approved Yoshida's plan for the "release of subversives" from positions with the Japanese public service or public service enterprises.[233] In the result, some 10,790 persons were dismissed from jobs either because they were members of the CPJ or, as per the "implementing statement," because they were viewed as "sympathetic and cooperate [*sic*] with said party, and all the subversive elements who are believed to accept Communism."[234] The first phase of the red purge was now complete.

Commencing in 1950, the second phase of the purge, now publically approved by MacArthur himself, involved the purge of all Communists remaining in public office.[235] In June 1950 alone, on MacArthur's direct orders, some two dozen Communist leaders were both dismissed from their jobs and banned from future participation in public affairs. A few weeks later alleged Communists were purged from Japan's newspapers. In July, the official newspaper of the CPJ, the *Akahata,* was shut down. The purge also claimed some 1,100 educators and another 10,000 in private industry.[236]

Unlike the purge of Japanese militarists, the red purge was not clearly rooted in a Potsdam-inspired SCAP directive. On the contrary, fearing the opprobrium of its erstwhile allies, especially the Soviet Union, SCAP never authorized the purge by formal written directive to the Japanese government.

By the summer of 1950, the red purge was in full flight, claiming thousands of jobs and careers, now also in the private sector of the economy. Japanese employers operating in critical industries had been given broad leeway to summarily discharge any person identified either as a subversive or merely a troublemaker.[237] At this time, Valery Burati, a senior official at SCAP's Labor Division, became disturbed by the long reach and arbitrariness of the private sector purge.[238] In the Japanese labor scene, he informed a contact in the State Department that "grave doubts exist everywhere about the legality of discharging a man because he is a Communist."[239] An expert in the new labor laws of postwar Japan, Burati contended that an employee who was not otherwise derelict in his duties could not "be discharged on the basis of his 'creed' [which] without a shadow of a doubt means 'political opinion' as well as 'religion.'"

Evidently, this view was shared by Burati's chief at Labor Division. In August 1950, the division formally requested that Japan's attorney general provide a formal opinion on the status of the red purge as a matter of Japanese domestic law.[240] In his reply, tellingly, the AG did not pretend to have found a legal basis for the purge other than in two letters of direction from MacArthur to Yoshida. In other words, Burati explained, the AG's reply was not a legal opinion at all. Instead it was an acknowledgment that if the red purge had legal validity, it stemmed from SCAP's fiat. Although plainly correct, the attorney general's statement was so embarrassing to GS's chiefs that (according to Burati) "they killed any possible publication of [it] and filed it away."

According to Valery Burati's credible (but, for him, unverifiable) information, the most senior executive officials of SCAP were well aware that, in its intent and methods, the red purge was illegal. It was illegal, ironically enough, under the constitution that many of the same officials had helped draft a few years earlier.[241] Now Americans were taking pains to short-circuit the system, the liberal rule-of-law system they themselves had designed, promoted, and installed.

In August 1950, Burati confided to his State Department contacts that he had heard a credible rumor to the effect that General Whitney "had directed [Chief Justice] Tanaka to send down word to the courts that they would not entertain any petitions from any of the Communists."[242] Not incidentally, none of the particulars concerning these instructions "was reduced to writing." But in unequivocal terms "Tanaka was told that the courts could not question management's designation of Communist. Anyone so designated was to be considered per se as a Communist and the courts were not to touch his case."

Although the veracity of this claim was later steadfastly denied by Oppler, it was accurate.[243] Whitney *had* in fact ordered Tanaka to endeavor to keep red purge cases out of the Japanese courts but failing that to ensure that any reaching the courts, whatever their merits under Japanese law, were dismissed for lack of jurisdiction.

What Burati strongly suspected but could not prove was that the red purge was an off-the-books operation, the expedient of officials—American and Japanese—not keen to justify it publically. After all, the red purge was precisely the kind of abuse of power that was not supposed to happen in a rule-of-law society like reconstructed Japan, one purporting to guarantee basic freedoms of thought, speech, and association. The red purge was the sort of blatantly unconstitutional program that once detected was certain to be swiftly disarmed and redressed by Japan's politically autonomous courts of law.

Or not. At the end of June 1950, senior officials at GS were informed that having been purged from their employment and political offices, leaders of the CPJ had met with lawyers and filed a suit in the Tokyo District Court seeking injunctive relief against the government's purge order.[244] Significantly, the presiding judge (Kono) who heard the application, instead of dismissing it summarily for want of jurisdiction, asked the CPJ's lawyers to submit a legal brief on the legal issues.

But before this could happen Jack Napier, GS's second-in-command, interceded. In a show of power, Napier "summoned" two Tokyo District Court judges (and two officials of the Supreme Court's Secretariat) to SCAP headquarters.[245] At the ensuing meeting, with Oppler present, he informed the judges that because the new purge was further to a SCAP directive, "the Japanese court had no jurisdiction over the [red purge] cases." Napier then "expressed regret that the Japanese court was used as a sounding board for cheap Communist propaganda."

The judges did not meekly defer to Napier. In their view, the purge raised justiciable issues under Japanese law. When they continued to press this point, Napier cut them short, refusing to listen to their arguments. Oppler then told the judges that their only recourse was to immediately withdraw permission for the submission of a legal brief. When the Japanese jurists continued to defend their contrary position, Napier, now incensed, told them that he had "said all he needed to say and that it was no use to continue the discussion." Just before he withdrew from the conference, Napier acidly remarked that he hoped that the judges felt "big and happy to become martyrs for the

Communist cause." In the end, however, the judges had to face political facts. Before they left the room, Oppler recorded, the two judges promised to comply with the directive. A short time later the Supreme Court reported to GS that the CPJ's case had been dismissed.

Given the increasing number and diversity of red purgees, given the stakes involved, given that the purge was being orchestrated by Japanese state authorities and now private business, given also that on its face it seemed to be carried out in plain contradiction of a long list of constitutional rights, the idea of challenging the purge in court did not go away. In late July 1950, GS became aware that certain Tokyo news agencies, then about to purge lists of leftist employees, had sought counsel from GS on how to respond to the "court actions to be anticipated from those who will be discharged."[246]

On July 28, a number of Japanese officials, representing both the Yoshida government and the Supreme Court, contacted Oppler wanting "instructions with regard to anticipated court actions of Communist employees and workers . . . who will be discharged."[247] The justices of the Supreme Court "wanted to know whether the discharge of employees was made in the implementation of an Occupation order" or an order of the Japanese government. If the latter, they wanted to know whether the "courts were free to consider this a matter of domestic concern on which the courts were allowed to decide." The justices had a final message: "Unless the Supreme Court had [written] instructions to the contrary, the courts would be bound on the Constitution." They would instruct subordinate courts to hear purge cases unless ordered not to do so.

GS now faced a pivotal decision. If it ruled that the red purge did not stem from a SCAP directive, it would touch off a wave of potentially embarrassing civil rights litigation under the reformed constitution and labor laws of Japan. If the contrary ruling was made, some discomfiting litigation would end, but at the cost of the credibility and legitimacy of the rule of law in postwar Japan.

Oppler had been briefed on the answer. He informed the Court that the "Supreme Commander indeed considered the discharge of Communist employees . . . in compliance with the spirit" of his previous purge directives.[248] Internally, however, Oppler expressed the opinion, the obvious one, that if it had been carried out under the domestic law of Japan, the purge and efforts to foreclose its justiciability would be clearly unconstitutional.

Oppler's answer was not SCAP's last word on the subject. In mid-August 1950, Oppler was apprised that on August 7 (Major Napier himself had confirmed to the writer) Tanaka saw General Whitney to discuss the red purge of the press, media, and key industries.[249] In the course of that meeting Whitney communicated to the chief justice SCAP's position that it would not issue a directive on the resolution of the red purge litigation. On this point, "There is nothing in writing and General Whitney indicated that there would not be." Whitney desired the chief justice to know that, even in the absence of "SCAPIN on the subject," the Supreme Commander's position was that "all Communists and fellow-travelers are subversive; there would be no reinstatements of dismissals either directly or on legal technicalities: that the courts are not to be used as sounding boards for subversive or Communist propaganda." The chief justice was instructed to inform his judges that all purge cases brought before their courts were to be summarily terminated. To assist in this regard Whitney had supplied the chief justice with a model decision "for the use of the court in dismissing these cases."

During the same meeting, Whitney broached the subject of the purge in relation to the constitution of Japan and its proper interpretation. The general indicated to the chief justice that "the courts must be realistic in these serious times" and it was therefore imperative that they decide purge cases "not from a narrow technical point of view, but from a wider political standpoint . . . from the standpoint of public welfare as expressed in the Constitution." Whitney wanted Japan's judges to take "judicial notice" that the purge of subversives from key sectors of Japanese society enjoyed the personal endorsement of the Supreme Commander.

Before the meeting ended, Whitney also helpfully offered the chief justice a number of "informal suggestions" about the legal grounds upon which purge litigation was to be rebuffed. The Japanese judges might first of all simply refuse to hear such cases on the basis of no jurisdiction. Alternatively, they might take the cases but render an immediate adverse decision on grounds that it was the "inherent right of any Japanese employer in critical industries involving National welfare and in times of stress to remove subversive elements, or even persons who *might* become subversive (emphasis added)." Whitney then invited the chief justice to "inform judges under each jurisdiction the situation in such cases." In any case in which it could be positively proved that a dismissed person was a "Communist or fellow-traveler," Whitney stated, he "wants the court to dismiss the application of claimants because such dismissal was proper according to GHQ opinion."

The chief justice carried out Whitney's instructions.[250] Although even Whitney recognized that in the absence of a SCAP directive the Supreme Court could not force the judges to rule in any particular way, matters had already overtaken such nice points of law. Immediately after Whitney's meeting with Tanaka, red purge cases, some of which had got past a first hearing,[251] were routinely dismissed.[252] It would appear that Japan's bar saw these widely publicized decisions as decisive of the matter. It is a fair conjecture that by this point lawyers knew that, behind the scenes, SCAP had barred the courtroom doors. The red purge was thus the great constitutional legal battle that never was.

The Twilight of the Gods: Freedom and Unfreedom in Occupied Germany and Japan, 1947 to 1951

In American Germany and Japan, liberal legal modernity was constructed and then undercut in the classic American pattern. In both occupied countries, it was built from the blueprints of rights-based liberalism and the judicially enforced rule of law. Then, just as in the United States itself, it was undercut to repel the menace of Communism and Communist subversion.[253]

"For about two weeks," so Alfred Oppler wrote to a former SCAP Legal Section colleague in 1951, "there was pretty much of a 'twilight of the Gods' atmosphere here [in Tokyo]."[254] Oppler's letter bore witness to the rapid devolution of American power in Japan and, wistfully, to the diminishing scope for godlike revelation about the liberal-democratic polity. In this or other writings Oppler might have but did not offer ironic commentary on the truth that the American gods of occupied Japan had in the previous two years revealed themselves all too human, all too disposed to ungodlike paroxysms of fear, prejudice, and hypocrisy.

We recall that only four years earlier, Secretary of State George Marshall had explained the then-recent American break with the Soviet Union in terms of irreconcilable differences over the meaning of democracy. For Americans, Marshall contended, democracy held a basic meaning, one grounded in the principle that "human beings have certain inalienable rights, that is, rights which may not be given or taken away. They include the right of every individual to develop his mind and his soul in ways of his own choice, free of fear or coercion provided only he does not interfere with the like right of others."[255] The aim of American democracy and of American-style democratic reconstruction in Germany and Japan, Marshall reaffirmed, was to create a system of government under law calculated to shield men from the arbitrary incursions of state, church, and other private persons. Behind a legal bulwark of constitutional rights, independent courts and privately retained lawyers, the individual person might live "without fear of being denied the right to work or deprived of life, liberty, and the pursuit of happiness."

Roger Nash Baldwin, the leading American civil libertarian of his era, could only have endorsed Marshall's depiction of the American mission in Germany, Japan, and the American homeland. It was because of this characterization of the mission that Baldwin accepted invitations in 1947 and 1948, from no less than the War Department, to consult with military government in occupied Japan and Germany about how to improve and consolidate American-sponsored liberal revolutions there. The War Department reached out to Baldwin, it must be noted, not only because of his undoubted *bona fides* and expertise as a civil libertarian but because he was also known to be a stern and uncompromising opponent of Communism and its acolytes.[256] In this respect we might fairly interpret Baldwin's intercessions in the occupied countries as boldly symptomatic of what one contemporary analyst in 1947 viewed as the increasingly "schizophrenic" character of American military government.[257] By the time Baldwin arrived in Japan in the fall of 1947 and American Germany in the spring of 1948, in both places the rights-based rule of law was at the same time being both enhanced and weakened.

In Japan, for example, we have seen how after 1947, GS continued to build and embellish the institutions and laws prerequisite of functioning liberal democracy. Construction proceeded apace on systems of politically independent courts and the bar, and on the liberalization of criminal law and procedure. New programs were being mounted for the dissemination of liberal-democratic values and ideas among Japanese jurists and citizens. In response to Baldwin's recommendations, civil liberties unions began to be established late in 1947.[258] Civil liberties bureaus were established within Japanese government and civil liberties associations in Japanese cities.[259]

For all this frenetic civil libertarian activity, the authentic master narrative of the period 1948 to 1951 in Japan—the narrative *not* told in Oppler's lengthy memoir—was how the fear and loathing of Communists, shared equally by increasingly powerful elements in Washington, SCAP, and the Japanese government, had fueled the systematic, illiberal, and largely illegal crackdown on the democratic and Communist Left. The dominant story in the last years of the occupation was how the liberal legal reconstruction of Japan was undermined and degraded just as its structures and institutions became completed and operational.

In this regressive phase of the occupation Alfred Oppler is the telling figure. Like Baldwin, Oppler was an earnest disciple of liberal-democratic modernity. Experience had taught him that the constraint of power by liberal laws and legal institutions was the last best hope of humankind. Oppler thought that the authoritarian character of military occupation, in Japan or any other country, was vindicated only by principled devotion to the liberal-democratic reconstruction of the occupied state.[260] In the context of civil rights, Oppler worked hard and enthusiastically in 1947 to 1949 in helping build a network of civil liberties unions in Japan and on the civil libertarian orientation of the Japanese judiciary and legal profession.

This is the story, a half-true one, that Oppler tells in his memoir. The other half is less flattering to Oppler the liberal prophet and law reformer. Although he later forgot or suppressed this part of his record, by 1950 Oppler had become a key actor and propagandist in the harsh and often unscrupulous suppression of the radical Left in Japan.[261] In this period Oppler embodied the schizoid character of military government in early Cold War Japan, alternatively talking up and tearing down legal liberalism there. His lecture one day was apt to extol the virtues of an independent court system with a powerful Supreme Court.[262] His actions the next day were apt to entail a secret errand to that Court, informing its justices that they were not to entertain the petitions of citizens whose legal rights had been abridged without due process of law. In early Cold War Japan, as he canted on about the glories of the rule of law, Oppler had been present when it was strangled in its crib.

In rationalizing this state of affairs, Oppler relied on an orthodoxy then invoked at the highest reaches of American government at home and military government abroad: "We are living in a confused and divided world," Oppler observed to a group of Japanese government lawyers dedicated (in 1951) to the state-backed suppression of alleged Communists.[263] In that world, liberal modernity was in a death struggle with authoritarian modernity. In such circumstances, the Communists, however small or fractious their cohort, presented no mere civil liberties problem. Communists and their movement, Oppler contended, "threaten the integrity of the state and security of the nation as a whole. . . . They exploit the privileges of democracy for their purposes." This is why when Communists were arrested and detained without warrant, when public rallies against remilitarization were attacked by police or blocked outright,[264] when their newspapers were shut down and their associations banned, such actions did not engender "real civil liberties cases."[265] As the sworn enemies of liberal-democracy, the Communists could not avail of its protections. While publically Oppler urged the Japanese authorities not to "re-establish the old police state under the guise of patriotism and anti-communism," privately Oppler had abetted that outcome.

Much the same set of contradictions was evident in American-occupied Germany and then in the nascent West German entity. We have seen how Americans sponsored liberal-democratic constitutional reform, first in its Länder and then in the form of the West German Basic Law. We have seen how, while tolerating the rehabilitation of Nazi-era jurists, Americans labored on the design and implementation of politically independent courts, bar associations, and law schools in south Germany. We have seen how they had denazified German statute books, including the codes of criminal law and procedure. By the close of 1949, with their British and French allies Americans had laid down the keel of a functional liberal rights-based rule of law in West Germany.

But just as in Japan, after the Berlin crisis in the spring of 1948 the German hard Left came under increasingly harsh assault by the security forces both of American Military Government and reconstituted German authorities. It is true that from its inception American Military Government in Germany always had been authoritarian. What happened after 1948 is that its illiberality became tightly focused, not on former Nazis, but on the radical German Left. Censorship, warrantless arrest and search, and strict control of the movement of people and information prevailed in West Germany to the end of the occupation. The suppression of the KDP by American and German authorities, leading ultimately to its total ban by the West German government in 1956, were popular policies in Germany, and they were barely impeded by new liberal constitutions, rights or legal structures.[266] Ironically enough, the introduction of the Basic Law, instead of facilitating civil liberties in the early 1950s, actually legitimated their suppression.

It need be noted in this regard that the suppression of the West German Left was broadly consistent with long-standing German patterns. Much to the chagrin of Roger Baldwin and other American civil libertarians, the German people as a whole, as a consequence of deeply rooted cultural proclivities and the dire material conditions of postwar German life, had proved strongly resistant to American-style liberal legal structures and ideology.[267] While the suppression of the radical Left was popular in Germany, the introduction of civil liberties unions was not.[268] Western Germans of this era broadly welcomed American (Marshall Plan) financial aid and, when it was directed at Communists, American-initiated assaults on their civil rights. The West Germans also generally granted the desirability or at least inevitability of democratic politics. But what the West Germans did not grant, what they did not welcome en masse, were high-minded attempts to "re-orientate" them as good American-style liberals. They did not accept, even in theory, that Bolsheviks enjoyed the full protection of liberal laws.

That the United States orchestrated the betrayal of liberal legality and the rule of law in occupied Germany and Japan was perhaps the predictable function of a number of preconditions. The first was that for the American leadership elite the transformative dimensions of the occupations were always subordinated to considerations of national security. Programs were designed and monies were spent on the liberal reconstruction of Germany and Japan so long as it was seen as the straightest road to their permanent pacification. Therefore, when in 1948 it became apparent to the Truman administration that the German and Japanese occupied states were less threatening to American interests than Soviet Communism, liberal reconstruction—never popular with German and Japanese elites—started to look more like a security risk than security imperative.

In occupied Germany and Japan, moreover, the most ideologically liberal American occupationaires, those most strongly committed to liberal-democratic reconstruction, were never in dominant positions in either civilian or military government. Even when the likes of Loewenstein, Oppler, and Baldwin exerted considerable influence, we have seen that they were willing in many cases to stand back while the authorities used militant means to crush the hard Left. All of this played out against a backdrop in which, in the United States itself—the original land of the free—conservative elites at the national and local levels were waging a dirty and often illegal war on the civil rights of American leftists.

The exportation of aggressive anti-Communism—this expression of the "paranoid style" of American politics—from the United States to the occupied countries, had grim implications for embryonic liberal legal modernity and the rule of law in the occupied countries.[269] In American Germany, the habitually conservative-nationalist German legal elite had been given an object lesson in the flexibility, even hypocrisy, of American commitments to liberal equality under law. A military government that had never been entirely bound by law had evinced willingness to disregard what had been recently advertised as inalienable individual and collective legal rights. In Japan, a nation in which the roots of liberal legalism were even more precarious, Americans had reneged on their solemn undertaking to sponsor not only the construction of a liberal legal culture but ensure that it became a functional reality. As a result, in the period 1948 to 1951 the world watched the grim spectacle of the American Saturn eating its liberal children.

Conclusion

LAYING DOWN THE LAW: AMERICANS AS LEGAL REVOLUTIONARIES

IN THE LATE SUMMER OF 1945 the men leading the federal government of the United States were riding high. At home they were the chief beneficiaries of the world's most liberal and prosperous modernity. On the world stage they had prevailed in an epic war and now were to embark on the military occupation and permanent pacification of two vanquished nation-states, one European, one Asiatic. In the aftermath of this great national triumph, it seemed to them desirable and feasible that the United States should move to dominate the physical territory but also the politics, laws, and even the hearts and minds of their vanquished foes. It seemed possible now for Americans to revolutionize Germany and Japan as democratic nation-states and peoples.

An *American* governing elite, these men—politicians, civil servants, lawyers, soldiers—brought a distinctly liberal sensibility to these transformative ideas and projects.[1] As soldier turned statesman George Marshall was moved to explain in 1947, while the term "democracy" might admit to many definitions, "To the American government and citizen it has a basic meaning. We believe that human beings have certain inalienable rights, that is, rights which may not be given or taken away."[2] The dominant tenet of the American political creed, the creed to be implanted in American-occupied Germany and Japan, was liberal individualism as buttressed by constitutionalized personal rights and the rule of law. What marked out American political modernity, what defined the American mission in postwar Germany and Japan, Charles Fahy reminded Lucius Clay in 1945, was that Americans had "a government of law and desire to spread such a concept throughout the world."[3]

That Americans were a people dedicated to individual rights, and the rule of law was a source both of power and confidence in its application. American constitutional liberalism, this supposed mirror of God and nature, was seen as the main reason why the United States had flourished in a world otherwise wasted by tyranny and militarism. From the American standpoint in the fall of 1945, the peoples of Germany and Japan had been cheated by history. In those fascist nation-states, the liberal aspirations of their citizenry had either been crushed by reactionary elites (as in Germany) or indefinitely forestalled by them (as in Japan). Such misfortune provided American planners and decision-makers with the central rationale of the American missions in occupied Germany and Japan: to provide from above the liberal revolutions that had not been secured from below.[4]

When American leaders began to implement the compulsory democratization of occupied Germany and Japan, the fulcrum of both programs was a liberal conception of the rule of law. In 1956, just one year after the West German state gained full sovereignty, a special subcommittee of the American Bar Association defined the rule of law as "the body of precepts of fundamental individual legal rights permeating institutions of government which are vested with appropriate powers of enforcement."[5] For Americans of the postwar era, for the purpose of domestic and occupation policy, the rule of law was the means by which an advanced society secured the "essential interests of the individual . . . through limitations on the authority of the state." In its structural character it entailed constitutional supremacy vindicated by judges and courts independent of politics and wielding stout powers of judicial review. The rule-of-law state was one in which the principal calling of lawyers and judges was to vindicate the equal accountability of state actors to the constitution. Most crucially, it was the state whose key institutions promoted and, when necessary, safeguarded the elemental freedoms of the individual person, including, as the federal attorney general summarized in 1946, the "freedoms of religion, speech and press, right of assembly and petition, freedom from unreasonable search and seizure, right of due process [and] prohibition against taking private property without fair compensation."[6]

American plans to reconstruct Germany and Japan as liberal rule-of-law states were made in the unity of war but executed in the divisiveness of peace. In the wake of world war, America's governing class felt justified, even righteous, in compelling conquered elites to construct or reconstruct liberal regimes. But in the actual achievement of this goal, American leaders were hampered by a number of factors, not the least of which was that, at war's end, America's own liberal rule-of-law project was profoundly flawed. At war's end, as in the first months of peace, Americans were themselves deeply divided over the meaning and scope of their own legal liberalism.

These tensions were plainly evident in a speech on civil rights given to the Chicago Bar Association in June 1946 by the attorney general of the United States, Tom Clark.[7] The main theme of Clark's address was America's "troublesome" postwar moment.[8] Its undercurrent was that for many American citizens, the United States had failed to live up to its moral and constitutional promises. It was a country in which elemental civil rights were often curbed or flouted. Clark took pains to defend recent exertions of the Justice Department to enforce federal civil rights law; in particular, the law protecting the equal right to vote. He assured his audience that, going forward, his department would enforce the law "for *all* the people of every race, creed or political faith." Then, in the closing paragraph of Clark's address, there was an abrupt shift of focus and tone. Having decried civil rights abuses in the United States, the attorney general remarked that "One of the greatest dangers . . . to civil liberties . . . is the method of communism and fascism to shackle democracy by indirection." In Clark's view, indeed, the United States was beset by "a national and international conspiracy to divide our people, to discredit our institutions, and to bring disrespect to our government." On this basis he urged the leaders of the bar to "censure" lawyers who degraded the legal profession by defending persons whose aim it was to "destroy our government by force."[9] The speech of the highest legal official in the federal government had closed with a screed against lawyers who might deign to defend the civil rights of political dissenters.

If inadvertently, Clark's address reflected the self-contradictory forces also at work in the American legal programs in occupied Germany and Japan. It reflected the volatile mixture of liberal idealism, hypocrisy, and fear that churned at the core of American-directed legal reconstruction in those captive states.

From a historically informed standpoint, it is unsurprising that the attorney general should have contradicted himself in this way. After all, Tom Clark had risen to the top of a legal system deeply riven by the same contradictory forces. In the span of Clark's career, American federal and local government had engaged in the systematic and often unlawful suppression of pacifists, socialists, trade unionists, and other "radicals."[10] After Pearl Harbor, moreover, Clark himself, while a lawyer at the Department of Justice, had helped smooth the way for the internment of tens of thousands of American citizens of Japanese ancestry.[11]

Clark's address is revealing also in its oblique references to America's law-based system of racial discrimination, one so extensive and effective that in the 1930s it was studied admiringly by Hitler's legal advisors.[12] But here we might do what Clark's speech did not do, stop to dwell on the particulars of one of the thousands of contemporary American stories regarding the stark illiberality of American law in relation to men, women, and, in one notorious instance, children of color.

In an indirect but informative way, the story of George Stinney Jr. implicates James "Jimmy" Byrnes and the system that promoted and sustained him in the office of secretary of state for the United States from July 1945 until January 1947. During his tenure in that office, Byrnes, a South Carolinian lawyer and former judge, contributed importantly to the reformulation (a decisive *softening*) of American government policy in the occupation of Nazi Germany.[13] In the same years, however, there was no similar softening of the white supremacist regime in Byrnes's home state of South Carolina.

In March 1944, a fourteen-year-old South Carolinian black boy named George Stinney Jr. was charged with the double murder of two white girls.[14] The sole evidence that tied the accused to those crimes was a confession wrested during a police interrogation in the absence of Stinney's parents or counsel. The white lawyer assigned to defend Stinney at trial had not previously defended a criminal case. None of the state's witnesses were cross-examined; none were called for the defense. An all-white jury convicted Stinney on both capital charges after ten minutes of deliberation. No appeal having been filed, Stinney was executed by electric chair (the youngest American so to die) in June 1944, just three months after his initial arrest and just ten days after American troops had landed in Normandy.

The Stinney case did not attract national attention in wartime United States. But when a white mob ruthlessly murdered two black couples in rural Georgia in late July 1946, the incident generated countrywide coverage.[15] In part the difference is explained by the scale, brutality, and lawlessness of the killings, and that two of the mob's victims were young women. In larger part, however, the controversy, like the murders themselves, was a product of a particular historical moment. The prevailing theory was that the white mob had lashed out in defense of the prewar racial status quo, against "uppity" Negroes emboldened by the war and war service to assert voting and other civil rights. In coming to grips with the "Moore's Ford" killings, civil rights activists, desperate to consolidate and extend gains that had been made in the war years, furiously lobbied the federal government for more and better intercession on behalf of black people.

In some measure, these efforts bore fruit. In the fall of 1946, the Truman administration ordered an FBI investigation into the Moore's Ford killings.[16] Truman also moved to establish the President's Committee on Civil Rights, appointed to study how law enforcement in America might be "strengthened and improved to safeguard the civil rights of the people."[17] In the next five years, however, American agencies did more to advance the civil rights of Germans and Japanese than of millions of African Americans.

In the late 1940s, the ironies of American life and foreign policy were thick and dark. During its vaunted liberal legal revolutions in occupied Germany and Japan, educated Germans and Japanese knew that the United States was itself a place of incomplete, if not altogether failed, liberal revolution. It was a country in which political dissenters and radicals, real and imagined, were subjected to increasing levels of state-sanctioned repression. It was a country in which the attorney general might warn lawyers against the vigorous representation of men and women prosecuted and harassed on the basis of their perceived beliefs. America was a country in which some states might subject mere boys to judicial murder by electric chair and in which the lawyers and judges of such states might become national leaders.

These unpleasant facts about the state of liberalism and the rule of law in the American homeland ramified strongly in the battle for hearts and minds in occupied Germany and Japan. As Charles Thompson, a black American journalist commented in 1947, more than any previous time since the Civil War, the United States was a self-conflicted nation, one that tolerated egregious injustice at home while in a "death struggle for the moral leadership of the world."[18] In Thompson's opinion, if Americans "cannot convince the world that we are able and willing to protect those rights which democracy guarantees and on the basis of which it proclaims its superiority to other ways of life, we shall lose the fight."

If atoms are indifferent to the rectitude of their masters, people are not. By the nature of their aims as liberal redeemers of the German and Japanese peoples, the American occupation regimes assumed strong moral postures. In no small measure, their efficacy hinged on the moral credibility of the government of the United States as foreign and domestic actor. In this regard, in the eyes of Germans and Japanese both regimes suffered from the handicap of the conventional and, in Japan, conventional and atomic bombings of cities and civilian populations. Compounding the credibility problem, German and Japanese elites knew of American hypocrisy in its treatment of political dissenters and racial minorities. It was not lost on them that, in its posture as liberal revolutionary, the American colossus had feet of clay.

The American officers at the forefront of legal reconstruction in Germany were often made painfully conscious of American vulnerability in this respect. When, for instance, Karl Loewenstein returned from a summer lecture tour in the new West German state in 1949, he reported that Germans were "fully aware of our difficulties in living up to the letter of the American constitution."[19] Another American lecturer recounted that "The treatment of the Negro popped into every discussion whatever the topic." In this view, the prestige of the United States and its occupation were greatly injured by the fact that many Germans thought that "our colored citizens are not better off than the Jews under Hitler."[20] When ACLU president Roger Baldwin returned from West Germany in 1950 he also noted that many educated Germans, some of them assuming control of the new West German state, saw that the white governing classes of America had experienced only limited success in living up to liberal ideals.[21]

In this study, American efforts in the liberal legal reconstruction in Germany and Japan have been likened to two simultaneous "Manhattan Projects" of sociolegal engineering. Although the one program was essentially scientific, the other essentially social-scientific, both were hugely ambitious national undertakings. Both presented theoretical and practical problems of utmost difficulty. In both cases, too, these problems could only be resolved by the intelligent application of vast amounts of human and financial resources over a period of years.

It has been suggested here that the American atom bomb design and construction project was efficacious for many reasons that American liberal rule-of-law projects in Germany and Japan were not. The atom bomb project, being critically important to war-winning, was supported with vast human, financial, and material resources. It also reflected strong unity and coherence of purpose among American political and military decision-makers. Legal reconstruction, critically important to the less urgent business of making peace, was not sustained by similar amounts of human and material resources. Nor was it the product of a similar unity or coherence of purpose.

This telling contrast was particularly apparent in relation to the organization and use of intellectual resources. The political and military leaders who decided that the United States should design and build an atomic weapon did not know, and did not think they could know, how to construct such a device. The leaders understood that success in the atomic bomb project would hinge on the exertions of specialist intellectuals and technicians. They also comprehended that when the relevantly trained and skilled experts were assembled and equipped, it would be necessary for them to stand back while the experts identified and resolved key theoretical and practical problems. In the result, the government and military men did stand back, and the problems did get resolved.

Like the atomic bomb project, the postwar legal reconstruction of two foreign nation-states were tasks of staggering theoretical, sociological, and technical complexity. But entirely unlike the atomic bomb project, political and military decision-makers decided, in an irregular and piecemeal process, they knew when and how it should be done. They thought (General MacArthur, emphatically so) they grasped the nature and content of liberal legal systems and how to introduce them to foreign political and cultural communities. In directing action on legal destruction and reconstruction in the occupied countries, they did not wait to assemble large numbers of relevantly trained and skilled experts. Nor did they stand back while the few trained specialists at their disposal posed, researched, deliberated, and resolved the key theoretical and practical problems associated with the two most ambitious law reform projects in the history of the world. In the result, we have seen, the key problems did not get resolved and, in both cases in different ways, the projects faltered.

In this regard, one of the striking features of liberal rule-of-law construction in American-occupied Germany and Japan, another salient divergence from the Manhattan Project, was that both initiatives were so little theorized. The two world-historical experiments in directed legal and political change were commenced without a general hypothesis about the linkages between national histories, sociologies, and legal systems. If the Manhattan Project was predicated on accepted scientific theory about matter and energy, the reconstruction of Germany and Japan as rule-of-law states was predicated on untested belief in the universal appeal of liberal individualism, on the hopeful expectation that the German and Japanese populations would readily and gratefully embrace liberal revolution from above.

The United States pursued legal reconstruction in Germany and Japan with woefully deficient means of knowing the sociolegal other.

We have documented, for instance, that when legal destruction and reconstruction began in earnest in the American zone of Germany in the summer of 1945, the Legal Division of military government was patently, in Karl Loewenstein's considered judgment, pathetically ill equipped to study or evaluate German legal ideas and institutions, still less to deploy knowledge in the field. Many, perhaps most, American legal officers had been "set to work on problems of which they have not the slightest idea and very little professional qualification."[22] American lawyers with no German and no training in German law or society were being asked to "knock out the Nazi laws" and replace them with liberal ones. In the formation of basic policy in the field, Loewenstein cogently observed, the leaders of Legal Division (not one of whom was conversant in German or German history) proved incapable of putting aside their "preconceived American ideas," of seeing "the German problems in their own light."[23] One of those problems was how to assess and redress the impact of Nazis and Nazism on German law and its liberal reformation.

Legal Division, and before it the relevant departments of the federal government in Washington, lacked both the will and intellectual means to formulate a coherent theory of the nazification and / or denazification of German law. But what most perturbed professional thinker-turned-*occupationaire* Karl Loewenstein was not "the ignorance with which this occupation of Germany had been prepared," but the bureaucratic (read: anti-intellectual) character of American Military Government.[24] The leaders of Legal Division often made key policy decisions in the absence, sometimes in the face, of relevant learning and critical reflection. Awkward truths (and truth-tellers) were routinely ignored while bureaucratic expedience routinely prevailed.

So it had been with the decisions, all within two years of German surrender, to turn legal denazification over to Germans, to permit Germans to appoint former Nazis to powerful positions within the postwar legal system, then for Legal Division not to superintend their legal actions and decisions. From the standpoint of candid evaluation of the German legal situation, from the related standpoint of modeling a viable path to the liberalization of German law and society, American

Military Government, Loewenstein plausibly concluded, was a "failure which stinks to high heaven."

Even in the immediate aftermath of the war, of Nazi tyranny, domestic and foreign, the basic American inclination was to trust and defer to Germans in matters of law and legality. This stemmed from a number of sources, Clay's practical realism about the limits of American administrative power in the U.S. zone being chief among them. It was a function also of the enormous prestige of German legal science, prestige that persisted even among German-Jewish émigré legal officers.[25]

The predisposition to trust German jurists, to take them at their word, was also rooted in racial and cultural affinity.[26] The American occupation of Germany, after all, was an encounter of two white-dominated societies of Christian-European heritage. In this regard, Roy B. Snapp, an American lawyer and Second World War intelligence staff officer (with the Joint Chiefs), recalled that his unit had tended to regard Germans as very like Americans, as "kind of kissin' cousins."[27]

The upshot of this was significant. Although the Germans had a decidedly illiberal cultural history, it was easy for American officers to presume that Germans, once their authoritarian masters were removed, would embrace their natural endowment of liberty and equality. Another of its consequences was that it made it easy for American legal *occupationaires,* most of the middle ranks and all of the leaders, to be more or less indifferent to the Holocaust. It is another remarkable aspect of the voluminous record of American legal activity in Germany that so few documents indicate that American officers were thinking about or even conscious of the culpability of German jurists for this or other heinous crimes.

As Roy Snapp further recalled of his wartime intelligence work, if he and his fellow officers thought of Germans as racial and cultural kinfolk, they had held a quite different view of the Japanese. Snapp's intelligence group had "a pretty good feeling that the Japanese were a different people, whereas the Germans were not."[28] The cultural gap had not been bridged by extensive training in the language, history, or culture of Japan or by the presence of experts. In the end result,

Snapp concluded, the stark racial and cultural differences between Americans and Japanese had gravely impaired American analysis of intelligence data.[29]

The meager comprehension of the Japanese "other" persisted in the peace. In early September 1945, American occupation forces landed in Japan with far greater military than intellectual resources. Planning had been piecemeal and unfinished. So too the recruitment and training of civil affairs officers for Japan. Even as MacArthur began to contemplate a wide and permissive reading of his mandate to strengthen democratic tendencies in Japan, he was unworried that SCAP, its new Government Section most glaringly, was desperately short of officers learned in Japanese law, government, and society.

Such was MacArthur's confidence in himself and his staff that even as he began to contemplate initiating liberal legal revolution in Japan, it was of no account that neither the Supreme Commander nor any senior member of his Government Section could speak or read Japanese, or that few had read even one book on Japanese history or politics. In fact, so little did this trouble the general that he intervened to prevent recruitment from the State Department's coterie of experts on Japanese affairs.

MacArthur's disdain of intellectuals and experts on Japan was perhaps of little moment. In 1945, in all the United States there were not more than a score of genuinely learned specialists of Japanese history and government, still fewer of its laws and legal institutions.[30] When MacArthur decided, more or less unilaterally, to prioritize liberal legal revolution in Japan, the United States as a nation plainly lacked the intellectual firepower needed to generate plausible answers to the elemental questions about how to reconstruct Japan as a liberal democracy. In sharp contrast to the occupation of Germany, furthermore, the United States government could not make up the deficit with expatriate Japanese lawyers and scholars. There were no Japanese-American equivalents of Fritz Oppenheimer, Karl Loewenstein, Max Rheinstein, or Carl Friedrich.

Remarkably enough, undeterred if not spurred on by the dearth of Japan specialists, deficient of learning but not temerity, MacArthur and his Government Section largely improvised the liberal legal reconstruction of Japan's constitution, then its public and (some private) laws and institutions, with the ideas and predilections of a professional soldier without formal training in law or legal theory, American or Japanese.[31]

One fixed point of MacArthur's thinking was that the American occupation, then Japanese democracy in the longer term, would go better in the presence of an imperial dynasty stripped of constitutional powers. Late in 1945 and in 1946, MacArthur rebuffed a Japanese-designed model of constitutional reform that contemplated reduced but not negligible roles for emperor and the *kokutai,* the indivisible unity of people, state, and imperial dynasty. In the end result, MacArthur ordered his Government Section to draft a model constitution that, when ratified, would signify a clean break from Japan's former legal and political modernity, a constitution based on American-style popular sovereignty, individual rights, and judicial review. Here the quintessential liberal revolution from above: a foreign proconsul and his minions deigning to impose liberal-democratic modernity in a country lacking a liberal-minded movement culture.

Insofar as the American liberal revolution in Japan was explicitly theorized, it was theorized retroactively. In forging a new constitutional model for Japan, MacArthur and his senior Government Section officers later alleged that they had worked from the "general principles"[32] (set down at Potsdam and elaborated in MacArthur's orders) to cause "unprecedented orientation of a government and a people."[33] Because the Japanese had failed to mount a proper liberal-democratic revolution against despotism in 1868,[34] MacArthur had instituted "the Revolution of 1945."[35] Through the instrument of the SCAP, the United States had acted unilaterally to liberate the Japanese people from the constitutional tyranny of the "infallible emperor-god" and his cliques.

In the context of the American occupation of Germany, the leading intellectual involved in legal reconstruction, Karl Loewenstein, was a relentless critic of American-sponsored action there, this before the even more unsettling developments of the Cold War era. In the context of the American-driven liberal legal revolution in Japan, at least in its first intensive phase, there were no Government Section equivalents of Loewenstein—that is, of academically trained specialists in Japanese law and society providing well-informed and critically trenchant memoranda on programs and policies. Of the key designers and engineers of the liberal legal reformation in Japan in 1946 and 1947—Charles Kades, Alfred Oppler, Thomas Blakemore—only Blakemore had been conversant with Japanese laws and language at war's end. In their work for Government Section, even civilian officers like Oppler and Blakemore accepted that their job was not to formulate, certainly not to criticize, but to execute the policy decisions of superiors. At the close of 1947, the structural liberalization of Japanese public law now largely complete, Kades and Oppler became the chief apologists of and propagandists for the motives and effects of the American liberal legal revolution in Japan. Although neither of these men had expected or prepared for historical roles in occupied Japan, neither later disavowed these roles, even in the face of the illiberal retrenchments of the "reverse course."

The veterans of Government Section owned and justified their participation in what was, after all, law reform by foreign military dictatorship. They rationalized their work in Japan on several grounds. They claimed credibly to have acted, in Oppler's words, from a start point of "missionary zeal" for the precepts of liberal-democratic modernity.[36] They were adamant that their programs had helped the Japanese people realize the natural endowment of rights and liberties denied them by their quasi-feudal ruling classes.[37] In their view, they had taken pains to persuade and mentor Japanese counterparts in the ideas and techniques of legal liberalism.[38] Leading Government Section officers insisted that they had been scrupulous in respecting the skill, knowledge, and dignity of Japanese officials and also the particularities of Japanese culture and its implications for legal liberalism. Oppler recalled that the conference rooms had been characterized by "complete freedom of speech and argument based on perfect equality."[39] Japanese law had been brought into alignment with the new liberal constitution by a consensual process, not administrative fiat. It had been done this way as a matter of respect for Japanese sensibilities and so to ensure the legitimacy and therefore longevity of liberal legal change.

In the late 1940s, just as it was thirty years later in the 1970s, the lawyer-revolutionaries of Government Section were unironically proud of the motives, substance, and results of the work they had done in Japan and of MacArthur's leadership. They believed that the American occupation had performed a uniquely important and laudable historical role in Japan. In this self-congratulatory account, SCAP had finally broken the centuries-old hold of reactionary elites on Japanese law and politics. Then, under their benevolent auspices, Japanese officials had themselves and on their own accord had moved to cement Japan's liberal-democratic future. In this way, the Americans had prevailed in the fight for moral leadership in the postwar world. "The opinion may be ventured," Oppler wrote in 1948, "that America, the nation primarily responsible for the occupation of Japan, has become the citadel of the democratic forces in their struggle [with] totalitarianism whether of the left or the right."[40]

This was how the American revolutionaries told their own story. It should not be taken for the story the Japanese might tell of their experience. In fact, individually and collectively, many Japanese resisted American initiatives just as they resisted American "mentoring" on legal subjects.

Here was an important point of contrast between American-occupied Germany and American-occupied Japan. Generally speaking, German officials, once they had emerged from denazification, were not averse to the thrust of American law reform initiatives. They were not averse, first of all, because early in the occupation Germans had been given substantial control over the specific content of law reform. They were not averse, secondly, because American-sponsored constitutional, judicial, and criminal law reform programs, while revolutionary in the face of Nazi legal modernity, were not revolutionary in the face of Weimar-era legal modernity. Once denazification of personnel was neutered by Germans in the U.S. zone, American reforms did not represent a mortal threat either to Germany's legal traditions or its legal elites. In this sense, American legal occupiers did Germany's legal elites a favor by causing a more or less clean break between Germany of the pre- and post-Hitler eras in terms of written laws. The American legal revolution, directed only against Nazi jurisprudence, left ample space for the traditional (inveterately conservative) leaders of the German bench, bar, and legal bureaucracy to reconsolidate their hold on the German legal system.

For Japan's postwar legal elite, however, MacArthur's liberal legal revolution represented a wholly different order of threat. In the first place, the MacArthur constitution was promulgated—by foreigners—as an explicit attack not only on Japan's ultranationalist moment but on a venerable and venerated political tradition, the *kokutai*. It was antithetical, not only to a legal tradition but to national identity and the belief systems in which it was anchored.

In the occupation period, Japanese political activists of all stripes acknowledged that MacArthur's Government Section was attempting to instigate a moment of radical discontinuity in Japan's cultural, legal, and political modernity. There was division only with regard to whether this was a welcome development. Japanese liberals and socialists mainly welcomed MacArthur's "August Revolution" as a necessary break from an authoritarian past.[41] According to Toshimi Miyasawa, a University of Tokyo legal academic, "The new Constitution takes the dignity of the individual as its fundamental principle and aims at making it the principle of the Japanese way of life. This is clearly a revolutionary happening. The true 'modernization' of Japan becomes possible for the first time because of this."[42]

But the Japanese conservative elite, especially of the largely intact imperial Justice bureaucracy, were unreconciled to the liberalism of the MacArthur legal revolution. This group bitterly resented attacks on the *kokutai*. It also deeply feared that the sudden liberalization of Japanese political life, in the context of socioeconomic crisis, would lead to a Communist takeover in Japan.

In the context of a lost war and foreign military occupation, however, it was not possible for elite resistance to be overt. SCAP's most prominent structural initiatives, constitutional and judicial reform, for instance, could not be stopped.

On the other hand, in no meaningful sense was Japan's powerful Ministry of Justice ever entirely or even partly occupied by SCAP. In fact, the ministry's senior ranks were left virtually untouched by postwar purge. Government Section officers worked with, but not within, its subdepartments. With an undisturbed hierarchy and patterns of action, remote from Americans physically, culturally, and psychologically, the Ministry of Justice became an almost ideal platform of passive resistance, for playing the long game against the foreign interloper. The strategy of its leadership clique was to regard the American legal revolution as a political typhoon—intense and potentially destructive to be sure, but likely to pass over, leaving the oldest and most definitive contours unchanged. For these reasons, the American policy to govern Japan indirectly through the largely intact agencies of the Japanese state, its willingness to permit Japanese legal bureaucrats to flesh out law reform initiatives, enabled the Japanese to slow down and blunt American reforms.

If they did not know it in 1945, Japanese and German legal actors came to realize in 1946 that the military occupations of the United States were not monolithic in policy terms, nor all-powerful in political terms, nor likely to be enduring in temporal terms. We have seen that for all their military and economic potency, the Americans had set up military occupations in Germany and Japan with distinct political, moral, and intellectual incapacities. As strongly as these factors resonated in favor of resistance, they paled by comparison to the basic administrative incapacities of AMG and SCAP. As best-informed Americans knew, the Americans had not been adequately prepared in 1945 to mount successful occupations of Japan and a large section of Germany, still less to realize transformative projects there.

The most trenchant witness to these truths was General John H. Hilldring, the U.S. Army Civil Affairs officer instrumental to American occupation planning and implementation. In Hilldring's candid assessment, one provided privately in 1950, American occupation efforts in both Germany and Japan had been very badly planned and executed. The principal reason was traceable back to Washington, to 1943 and 1944, when the decision was made—far too late and too lightly—to saddle the U.S. Army with principal responsibility to win the war *and* the peace.[43] In Hilldring's assessment, the army was ill trained and equipped to achieve the political and economic objectives of the war. In the event, American soldiers were given the wrong orders and then inadequate human and physical resources for their proficient execution. To exacerbate the problem, in American-occupied Germany, Lucius Clay had been asked to effect radical political transformation without the instrument of a German state and in concert with allies whose views of democracy and civil rights were incongruent.

A disciplined soldier, Hilldring had kept his doubts and skepticisms to himself. In the summer of 1945, the perspicacious Air Force colonel and former Yale scholar DeForest Van Slyck, a respected colleague of a number of senior War Department officials, did not. We have seen that in a memorandum written before the occupation of Japan had begun, Van Slyck warned, "The conquering nation cannot impose its form of government, ideals or way of life upon a conquered nation except by permanent military occupation and immigration."[44] Military government, whether operated exclusively by the United States or a coalition of nations, was "bound to be bungling, undiplomatic, and inefficient." Van Slyck thought that the United States should face the fact that it lacked "sufficient personnel with the proper vision, training, and ability to carry out the task effectively."

Those who experienced the American occupation in Germany first-hand (Karl Loewenstein and the constitutional expert Carl Friedrich are but two prime examples) were apt to confirm Van Slyck's prediction. In the realization of its most ambitious legal and political goals, it was clear that the United States did not field enough officers who knew German language, history, or society. Everything that was done by Americans in Germany was done without a specialized overseas or colonial service. As Friedrich remarked in this regard, "Not least of the shortcomings resulting from military administration has been manifest in the field of personnel."[45] The occupation's functional agencies had tended to "put square pegs into round holes especially at the top levels." Time and again crucial moments and operations of the legal reconstruction mission were hindered by the lack of enough appropriately trained American minds.

In a myriad of ways, the dearth of suitably qualified experts and thinkers prominent among them, the American administrative instruments of liberal legal reconstruction in Germany and Japan were inadequate to their missions. The legally specialized subdivisions both of AMG and SCAP, from the first to the last phase of their work in the early 1950s, were chronically lacking in coherent plans for mission statements and lawyers and legal academics who knew the laws and language of the occupied.[46] In both countries, key positions were held down by unilingual American lawyers whose training, one former director of AMG-Legal Division observed, had "no relevancy whatsoever to being a member of the bar in the United States."[47] The American rule-of-law builders in Germany and Japan were therefore consigned to work exclusively from the outside of the construction sites.

Candid witnesses of the rule-of-law projects in American-occupied Germany and Japan knew intuitively what the scholarship of democratization and nation-building has now extensively documented: that the construction of liberal-democratic norms of law and government in previously authoritarian states, by interveners foreign or domestic, after war or civil upheaval, is a forbidding task.[48] Such projects are often inhibited by rash assessments of both initial conditions in the subject nation and the capacity of the intervener to introduce productive and lasting change. Attempts at constructing liberal models of the rule of law are hampered by poor planning and from weak or nonexistent theorization of the relationship of laws and legal institutions to their social, economic, and cultural environments. Interveners tend to overestimate their capacity to foment change while underestimating the capacity of entrenched elites to resist it.

The present study has detailed the presence of all of these (and more) impediments to American success in the introduction of liberal models of law and the rule of law in occupied Germany and Japan from 1945 to 1952. In previous chapters it documented America's many legal setbacks and outright failures in both occupied nations and also in American actions during the early Cold War to "reverse course" on the liberal inroads that Americans had made there. What then to make of the common perception that the American occupations of Germany and Japan after the Second World War revolutionized those countries as liberal-democratic nation-states? Where does the truth lie? To what degree in fact did efforts of agencies of the United States cause West Germany and Japan to join the liberal spectrum of legal regimes? To what degree did the United States cause—

or enable Germans or Japanese to cause—the construction of liberal models of the rule of law? To what degree did American efforts and the success of those efforts vary between Germany and Japan, and if they did, why did they?

The overarching answer offered here is that the received wisdom that during the period of military occupation American agencies successfully imposed functional liberal rule-of-law regimes in Germany and Japan, if not flatly wrong, is misleading. What can be more plausibly averred is that American interventions successfully introduced the constitutional and institutional *superstructures* of liberal rule-of-law regimes. In the legal sphere, American achievement was in the manner of forms, not functionalities.

In a four-year period in Germany, in just more than two years in Japan, American agencies caused the stringent subordination of political and military power to law and legal institutions. Americans oversaw the broad constitutionalization of individual rights and prerogatives while securing the formal political independence of the German and Japanese courts, judiciaries, and bar associations. In American-occupied Germany and Japan, criminal law and procedure were brought into line with the strictures of liberal due process. By these means Americans organized and directed the installation—on paper—of court-centered legal liberalisms crowned by Supreme Courts equipped with extensive legal powers of judicial review. In both occupied countries, too, the systems of criminal law and procedure were brought into alignment with liberal substantive and procedural norms.

Although there was a consistency and coherence in America's legal-revolutionary intent in Germany and Japan, there were salient differences in the ways, circumstances, and outcomes of these revolutionary intercessions from above.

In Japan, a number of contingencies combined to magnify the revolutionary intent and reach of the American legal program there. The first was the power to act unilaterally. The second was MacArthur's personal determination to use that power aggressively to cause the swift and radical liberal-democratic reconstruction of the Japanese legal and political systems. The third was the want of cultural deference to

Japanese history and traditions, particularly telling in the context of law. For lack of training and cultural affinity, American officials were disinclined to respect extant Japanese laws, lawyers, and legal institutions. They tended to see a retrograde otherness in Asian legal officials and their ways of law. By the same token, it was uncomplicated psychologically for American officials to dismiss the structure, content, and practices of Japanese legality as the socially regressive anachronisms of a feudal society.

A fourth factor conducive to the revolutionary reinvention of the Japanese legal system was the profound disorientation of the Japanese political and legal establishments in the crucial first eighteen months of the occupation and their incapacity to mount effective resistance to American incursions. The fifth was the persistence in Japan of the national state and bureaucracy in the same period. So long as the governing class was disordered and weak, SCAP was able to co-opt Japan's remnant state as a means of effecting structural change.

For these reasons it had been possible, in the space of a single year, for Americans to usher in an expansive charter of personal rights and (ostensibly) powerful and politically independent judiciary. By the close of 1948, the nation's primary codes of law having been brought into (ostensible) alignment with the provisions of the MacArthur constitution, the nation's lawyers having been reorganized into (ostensibly) self-governing and politically autonomous bar associations, American power had caused Japan to install the essential structural elements of a liberal rule-of-law state.

In American-occupied Germany, different contingencies had combined to inhibit, if not obviate, AMG's revolutionary intent and reach. The first was that in Germany Americans had been unable to apply power unilaterally, except within the confines of its zone of occupation. The second was that the American commander in Germany, Lucius Clay, had not entertained a vision of himself chiefly as a liberal revolutionary. He had not, as MacArthur had, prioritized a set of revolutionary goals in Germany. A third factor was AMG's obligation in its zone to provide direct government to its German population. From the start, AMG's marked incapacities in this regard engendered dependence on German officialdom. Its dependence dovetailed with the American racial and cultural affinity for Germans. From the outset of the occupation, AMG officials had been predisposed to trust Germans and minimize their sins; indeed, so much so that, little more than a year after the surrender, they had already empowered Germans to decide who among them had been "real" Nazis and culpable for misdeeds. The same American officials went quiet when the answer came back that almost none had been.

In the legal field, American officers were similarly predisposed to minimize the differences between American and German cultures of law, predisposed to esteem the white European heritage of the German legal system. If in Japan American legal officers could barely discern, still less admire, the Japanese legal tradition, American legal officers in Germany were apt to defer to German jurists in their claim that the Third Reich was an aberrant and transient interlude of German legal history. Over the objections of some of their leading experts, for reasons mainly of administrative convenience, senior American legal officers adopted the thesis that most German jurists had been unwilling participants in the crimes of the Third Reich.

The rehabilitation of the Nazi-era legal professions did not, however, presage the revival of Nazi legal norms either in the U.S. zone or, after 1949, in the West German *rechtsstaat*.[49] But neither did it instantly herald a new era of American-style constitutional liberalism. In Germany, liberal reconstruction was revolutionary in its displacement of National Socialist legal theory, laws, and practices. In both occupied countries, however, American agencies found it easier to drive structural and legislative than ideological and operational change. Under American auspices, by the close of 1949 occupied Germany and Japan had become liberal rule-of-law regimes in theory but not in practice. This was due, in part, to the moral and intellectual incapacities of the American occupation regimes in the liberal reorientation of German and Japanese hearts and minds. In larger part, it was due to the historical shift within and among American political leaders and voters away from New Deal liberalism and toward conservative (read: anti-statist and anti-Communist) politics.

From the end of the Second World War, there were always multiple American occupations of Germany and Japan, just as there were multiple responses to its initiatives. In both captive states the Americans devised and implemented various and often self-contradictory policy stances and programs, some of liberal-revolutionary and some of counter-revolutionary intent. These stances were welcomed and rejected by the various constituencies among the occupied. In the first eighteen months of both occupation regimes, if in Japan more clearly, those sympathetic to liberal-democratic reform had had the upper hand. But their grip began to slip when, after 1946, the Truman administration, in concert with resurgent conservative elites in both occupied countries, began to identify Soviet-sponsored Communism as the most urgent threat to American national security.

Here it serves to recall that the American doctrine of transformative military occupation, the compulsory democratization of captive enemy states, was rooted in political realism—that is, in unsentimental calculation about the national security interests of the United States. When in 1947 and afterward the Truman administration began to think of the German and Japanese militarism as less dangerous to the United States than Soviet Communism, basic occupation policy was revisited and altered. In the wake of the Berlin crisis of June 1948, making good rule-of-law liberals out of Germans and Japanese was viewed as less vital than enlisting them as allies in the fight against the Communist Left. Without wholly shutting down programs of liberal democratization in American-occupied Germany and Japan, the Truman administration began to ramp up programs of anti-Communist suppression.

This policy shift converged powerfully with the stubborn fact that even after catastrophic defeats at arms, neither Germany nor Japan had large constituencies of liberal-minded citizens, either among the resurgent political, professional, and bureaucratic elites or among the populace as a whole.[50] In West Germany, Konrad Adenauer's coalition of Christian conservative voters and bureaucrats, with the tacit support of AMG, came to broadly agree on three goals, none being the realization of the civil libertarian promise of the Basic Law. A stable majority of West Germans wanted their federal government to achieve physical reconstruction, economic recovery, and political stability.[51] There was broad consensus also on a fourth point, including among the reconstituted German legal establishment: it was acceptable, even encouraged, for the West German authorities to adopt strong measures so to crush the Communist Left. The strongest shared political conviction among West Germans in the late 1940s and early 1950s was not liberal, or even democratic; it was anti-Communism.[52]

This set the stage for a dramatic walking back by Germans, but more emphatically by their American overseers, of the civil libertarian promises of the occupation and Basic Law. For the truth was that most German radicals of the period, that is to say, the men and women most likely to test the limits of civil rights in West Germany, were leftists, many of them Communists, speaking, publishing, organizing, and demonstrating against (what they saw as) the American-led revival of German fascism and monopoly capitalism. Whether this was a cogent or popular challenge to the new state is beside the point. More germane is whether, in this nascent West German liberal rule-of-law state, legal rights to advance such politics would be tolerated and, when not tolerated, whether they would be vindicated by West German lawyers, judges, and courts.

We have seen that in the short term, the constitutional rights of West German political radicals were not respected by the federal state and were not vindicated by lawyers and judges acting as zealous guardians of such rights. German political conservatives, dominant in elected and unelected office, turned the West Germany of the early 1950s into what Karl Loewenstein termed a "demo-authoritarian" regime, a superficial democracy dominated by a restrained but habitually authoritarian governing class.[53] If the Americans and their allies had in fact established a new *rechtsstaat* in the Federal Republic, it was a decidedly illiberal one.

A remarkably similar convergence of illiberal forces emerged in occupied Japan after 1948. There the first phase of the MacArthur revolution had succeeded only too well. In directing the release of political prisoners, in provoking the ratification of a radically liberal constitution, the Supreme Commander had fostered a political climate in which leftist radicals had been emboldened to test the boundaries of new constitutional rights of free thought, speech, and assembly. But political dissent in Japan gained momentum and veered left just as American domestic politics veered toward the anti-Communist Right. In a series of moves, the Truman administration—MacArthur and his liberal reform programs still in situ—tilted American policy in Japan away from legal and political to economic reconstruction. Just as in West Germany, resurgent conservative political and bureaucratic elites, never reconciled to MacArthur's liberal revolutionary programs, began to organize a harsh crackdown on leftist social, labor, and political agitation in Japan.[54] The Communist victory in China in 1949 and the advent of war on the Korean peninsula in 1950 hardened the resolve of American and Japanese authorities to repress the hard Left.

From 1949 to 1952, the ink barely dry on Japan's liberal rule-of-law constitution, the Japanese authorities, with the explicit and tacit assent of SCAP, began to subject real and supposed Communists (and ethnic Koreans) to an escalating campaign of police harassment, arbitrary arrest, detention, and politically motivated criminal prosecution. The authorities closed down Communist newspapers while limiting rights of assembly. In the same period, thousands of Japanese were deprived of jobs and careers in a government-authorized, American-backed, and patently lawless red purge.

In response to these oppressions, some Japanese citizens were moved to do precisely what American propaganda had urged them to do: retain lawyers so to vindicate their vaunted constitutional rights in Japan's new and ostensibly independent courts of law. Fearing that this move might impede the anti-red crackdown, SCAP officials secretly intervened to prevent the new Japanese courts from exercising jurisdiction in these cases. In other words, at a critical juncture in the postwar history of the rule of law in Japan, Americans sabotaged the substance and credibility of the liberal reconstruction project.

In the early 1950s, for all intents and purposes, the rule of law in Japan reverted to the rule of conservative politicians and bureaucrats. This happened because of a number of factors, of both Japanese and American origin.

On the Japanese side of the equation, the main factor was that the emerging ruling blocs in Japanese government—Yoshida's ironically named Liberal Democratic Party and the national bureaucracy—

were hostile to American-style legal and political liberalism. They believed both that liberal individualistic social philosophy was inimical to Japan's communitarian norms and traditions and that, in the context of Japan's postwar socioeconomic malaise, civil libertarian liberalism played into the hands of the nation's mortal enemies: Communism and the Soviet Union. For this bloc, the MacArthur legal revolution had been an exercise in neocolonial power politics, an alien and alienating imposition from the outside. While it had not been possible for Japanese elites to stop the imposition of liberal legal structures, the anti-Communist imperative made it possible for them to blunt their substance and force.

The failure of liberal legal revolution in Japan during the early Cold War was not, however, solely a function of pushback by conservative politicians and bureaucrats. It also stemmed from American incapacity to make significant headway in the liberal reorientation either of Japanese jurists or among the people at large. Revolutionary legal change is manifest in legal behaviors and outcomes when accompanied by congruent changes in belief systems. There is little evidence that, even in the twin wakes of shattering societal defeat and the MacArthur constitution, large numbers of Japanese lawyers, judges, or citizens had begun suddenly to think of themselves as guardians or holders of individual rights. While the American liberal revolution in Japan was predicated on a new centrality of legal rights and rights litigation, neither Japanese laymen nor law men suddenly abandoned centuries-old habits of thought and being.[55] There was no sudden increase of reliance on law as a means of conflict resolution (not even by the leftist victims of unlawful state action).

American failures in this regard were also rooted in first the decision to govern Japan indirectly through a more or less intact national bureaucracy and then in not having taken bold steps to purge and reconstitute that bureaucracy.[56] This policy, if inadvertently, created and sustained a powerful mechanism by which Japanese officials could mediate, blunt, and after 1950, roll back liberal reform initiatives. In preserving the Japanese bureaucratic state, the Americans, in effect, facilitated and legitimated conservative resistance. More specifically, Government Section's intense engagement with Japan's Ministry of

Justice, this command center of fidelity to the *kokutai,* greatly strengthened the capacity of the Japanese to mediate and deflect liberal legal change. In their dealings with Americans, ministry lawyers accepted what could not be refused while rejecting what could not be imposed: the egalitarian outlook underpinning liberal systems of law. The engagement also tended to marginalize Japan's postwar liberals, social democrats, and reform-minded women, who were the natural allies of American-sponsored law reform.[57] In the actual course of events, therefore, Government Section's mode of operation was more apt to foster opposition than support for liberal legal reconstruction.

The architects of the MacArthur legal revolution had imagined for Japan a lawyer and court-centered legal system by which judges would use stout powers of judicial review to protect citizens from the unconstitutional or otherwise unlawful actions of legislators and other state actors. As a bulwark of individual rights, such legal architecture was problematic enough in the United States. In Japan of the late 1940s and early 1950s, even if the Americans had not intervened, the country was signally lacking in the prerequisites of an effective civil libertarian legal culture. It lacked in numbers liberal rights–minded and trained criminal defense and constitutional litigation lawyers.[58] It lacked a prosecutorial service convinced of the priority of liberal rights and due process over contrition and reconciliation.[59] Most of all, Japan lacked a citizenry prepared to forsake customary understandings of the legitimacy and supremacy of family and community.[60] In the early 1950s the American legal revolution in Japan, while attractive to a small, avant-garde constituency among the Japanese, was barely detectable in the social outlook or *mentalité* of the Japanese masses.[61]

When national sovereignty was restored to Japan (1952) and West Germany (1955), fascist legal and political modernities there had been destroyed. Its formal legal and institutional manifestations had been eradicated by American and Allied interventions in the first phase of occupation. The ideological credibility of racialized nationalism, militarism, and dictatorship had been destroyed by violent military defeat.[62] But while bombs caused Germans and Japanese to reject fascism, it did not cause them to embrace liberalism.

In occupied Japan, defeat had left the Japanese political and bureaucratic elites with no choice but to yield to the introduction by foreigners of a radically liberal legal modernity, one promoting individual rights while demoting the *kokutai*. In American-occupied Germany and then West Germany, the force of Allied arms had caused German political and bureaucratic elites to renounce Nazism while reviving and embellishing the liberal constitutional norms of the Weimar republic. By 1950, the prewar legal elites of both occupied countries, having reestablished ranks and power, had begun to operate systems of law designed to secure the legal rights of the individual and to limit the legal power of state actors. But they did not operate them as philosophical liberals.

Taking their signals from anti-Communist political forces in the United States, West German and Japanese officialdoms did not move quickly to consolidate liberal rule-of-law regimes in West Germany and Japan. Having prioritized economic recovery and political stability, political and bureaucratic elites instituted programs of "militant democracy." Legitimized by democratic elections, the reconstituted West German and Japanese states prioritized the systematic and often lawless suppression of leftists and leftist organizations and politics. In the early 1950s, West Germany and Japan were states with the outward attributes but not the operational substance of the rule of law. They were places where the constitution prevailed except with regard to those persons, political dissenters particularly, whose rights it was designed to protect.

In West Germany of the 1950s, constitutional liberalism had no strong proponents but many staunch antagonists. With the support of the United States, successive West German governments prioritized public order and discipline over liberty and dissent. In civil society, civil libertarianism failed to take root. Predictably, too, the German legal establishment, only a few years removed from dedicated service to National Socialism, remained broadly indifferent if not implacably hostile to liberalism, legal and otherwise. While in the late 1950s, the

Federal Constitutional Court proved willing to validate some individual and group rights assertions as against the state,[63] successful civil libertarian litigation was far more exceptional than the repressive practices of the West German police and other state agencies.[64] Not until the late 1960s did large numbers of West Germans, led by the sons and daughters of the wartime generation, partake of "anti-authoritarian revolt."[65] In the ensuing score of years German citizens and jurists took it upon themselves to take the forms and structures implanted after 1945 to construct a new, robust, and distinctly German form of legal liberalism.[66]

In twenty-first-century Japan, the individual rights liberalism entrenched in the MacArthur constitution has remained fundamentally alien to the communitarian social and legal culture of the nation.[67] The combined actions of SCAP in the liberal reconstruction of Japan had done little to cause the Japanese to acquire the central precondition of legal liberalism: reflexive self-consciousness of themselves as rights-holding individuals. In the six decades after the occupation, individual Japanese persons or organizations were seldom moved to retain legal counsel so to assert individual rights claims in courts of law. In the same period, the Japanese bar, on a per capita basis one of the smallest in the developed world, was ill-equipped by disposition and training to cultivate the mindset and technique of civil libertarian litigation.[68] The criminal justice system of Japan, notwithstanding American-driven efforts to foster a new culture of due process liberalism, remains (as it was before the war) a system that convicts and then discharges almost all accused persons on the basis of confessions.[69] MacArthur's August Revolution did little to change the spirit of either Japan's belief systems or its public and private laws.[70]

In the early twenty-first century, Japan's Supreme Court, exercising extreme caution in the field of constitutional rights and judicial review,[71] presided over a rule-of-law state that continued to privilege social status, consensus, and harmony over individual rights claims.[72] The legal meaning and import of most of the thirty articles of the "Rights and Duties" chapter of the constitution of Japan were left untested in the courts. In the seventy years after its ratification in 1947, the Supreme Court deigned to nullify legislation on fewer than ten occasions.[73] Although few question the formal political independence and professionalism of postwar Japanese judges, both the trial and appellate courts have declined to supplant custom with the rights liberalism baked into the formal fabric of the law since the late 1940s. In the presence of extensive potential power of judicial review, Japanese judges developed elaborate institutional and jurisprudential mechanisms to limit that power.[74] If Japan has become a *liberal*-democratic community since the occupation, it is not an outcome of American-style judicial review.

We have seen that for American leadership August of 1945 was a moment of extraordinary vindication, not only for its war-fighting but an entire way of life. The exhilaration was such that Americans began to contemplate that they might not only defeat but remake the modernities of whole nation states, to school them in the government of laws. But in the revelry, the hubris, of victory, American leadership was apt to overestimate the moral and practical force of its world-shaping capabilities. When the occupations wound down, in Germany and Japan just as in the United States, the rights-based rule of law was an unfinished dream, as much conceit as reality.

Abbreviations

ACC	Allied Control Council, Berlin
ACLUP	American Civil Liberties Union Papers, Mudd Manuscript Library, Princeton
ACOP	Alfred C. Oppler Papers, M. E. Grenander Department of Special Collections and Archives, State University of New York, Albany
AJRP	Alvin J. Rockwell Papers, Harry S. Truman Presidential Library, Independence, Missouri
AMG	American Military Government, Germany
CAD	Civil Affairs Division
CC	Control Council, Germany
CHFP	Charles H. Fahy Papers, Franklin Delano Roosevelt Presidential Library, Hyde Park, New York
CJFP	Carl J. Friedrich Papers, Harvard University Archives
CPJ	Communist Party of Japan
DLEG	Legal Directorate, Allied Control Authority,
DMHP	Dale M. Hellegers Papers, Harry S. Truman Presidential Library, Independence, Missouri
FEA	Foreign Economic Administration
FEC	Far Eastern Commission
FO	Foreign Office, United Kingdom
GFKP	George F. Kennan Papers, Mudd Manuscript Library, Princeton
GS	Government Section, Supreme Commander Allied Powers, Japan
HICOG	High Commissioner for Germany
HFPP	Herman F. Phleger Papers, Bancroft Library, University of California, Berkeley

HLSP	Henry L. Stimson Papers, Yale University Library, Manuscripts and Archives
JFTP	James F. Tent Papers, Hoover Institution, Stanford University
JKPP	James K. Pollock Papers, Bentley Historical Library, University of Michigan
KLP	Karl Loewenstein Papers, Amherst College Archives and Special Collections
KPD	Communist Party of Germany
LOD	Loewenstein Occupation Diary, Loewenstein Papers, Amherst College
MRP	Max Rheinstein Papers, University of Chicago Library
NARA	National Archive and Record Administration, College Park, Maryland
NAUK	National Archive of the United Kingdom
OMGUS	Office of Military Government, United States
OSS	Offices of Overseas Services, United States
PCLK	Papers of Charles L. Kades, Douglas MacArthur Memorial Library, Norfolk, Virginia
PRJ	Political Reorientation of Japan, vols. 1 and 2
RG	Record Group, National Archive and Record Administration, College Park, Maryland
RNBP	Roger Nash Baldwin Papers, Mudd Manuscript Library, Princeton
SCAP	Supreme Commander Allied Powers, Japan
SHAEF	Supreme Headquarters Allied Expeditionary Force
SLU	Special Legal Unit, Germany and Austria
USFET	United States Forces, European Theater
VBP	Valery Burati Papers, Walter P. Reuter Library, Wayne State University
WO	War Office, United Kingdom

Notes

Introduction

1. Thomas Bohlander and Michael Vormbaum, *A Modern History of German Criminal Law*, ed. Michael Bohlander, trans. Margaret Hiley (Berlin: Springer Berlin, 2014), 173.
2. For discussion, see Phillip Bobbit, *The Shield of Achilles: War, Peace, and the Course of History* (New York: Knopf, 2002), 45–46; Tony Judt, *Postwar: A History of Europe Since 1945* (New York: Penguin, 2005), 18.
3. Franklin D. Roosevelt, Joint Press Conference with Prime Minister Churchill at Casablanca, January 24, 1943, *American Presidency Project*, http://www.presidency.ucsb.edu/ws/index.php?pid=16408; Marlene J. Mayo, "American Wartime Planning for Occupied Japan," in *Americans as Proconsuls: United States Military Government in Germany and Japan, 1944–1952*, ed. Robert Wolfe (Carbondale: Southern Illinois University Press, 1984), 3–52, 9.
4. As Joyce and Gabriel Kolko observe: "And so the United States entered the postwar era, incomparably the most powerful nation in modern history." Joyce Kolko and Gabriel Kolko, *The Limits of Power: The World and United States Foreign Policy, 1945–1954* (New York: Harper and Row, 1972), 6. See also Michael H. Hunt, *The American Ascendancy: How the United States Gained and Wielded Global Dominance* (Chapel Hill: University of North Carolina Press, 2007), 2.
5. Hunt, *American Ascendancy*, 1–5; Tony Smith, "Making the World Safe for Democracy in the American Century," *Diplomatic History* 23 no. 2 (1999): 173–188, at 174–175.

6. Radio Report to the American People, August 9, 1945, https://www.trumanlibrary.org/publicpapers/?pid=104.
7. Smith, "Making the World Safe for Democracy," 174. Some of the New Dealers in the FDR administration, the influential treasury secretary Henry Morgenthau among them, were extremely confident in the ability of the United States to make and execute "grand plans" for transformational occupation. Elizabeth Borgwardt, *A New Deal for the World: America's Vision for Human Rights* (Cambridge, MA: Belknap, 2005), 208.
8. Michael Ignatieff, "Messianic America: Can We Explain It?" *New York Review of Books* 18 no. 62 (2005): 28–30, 29.
9. On the theory and practice of modern military occupations, see David M. Edelstein, *Occupational Hazards: Success and Failure in Military Occupations* (Ithaca, NY: Cornell University Press, 2008).
10. Radio Report to the American People, August 9, 1945, https://www.trumanlibrary.org/publicpapers/?pid=104.
11. The Berlin (Potsdam) Conference, July 17–August 2, 1945, Protocol, August 1, 1945, Article 2 A. (iv), *The Avalon Project,* http://avalon.law.yale.edu/20th_century/decade17.asp.
12. The Potsdam Declaration, Proclamation Defining Terms for Japanese Surrender, Issued, at Potsdam, July 26, 1945, Article 10. *Birth of the Constitution of Japan,* http://www.ndl.go.jp/constitution/e/etc/c06.html.
13. John D. Montgomery, *The Artificial Revolution in Germany and Japan* (Chicago: University of Chicago Press, 1957), 1.
14. For the "liberal" character of American foreign policy in this era, see Tony Smith, *America's Mission: The United States and the Worldwide Struggle for Democracy in the Twentieth Century* (Princeton, NJ: Princeton University Press, 1994), 1–6; David Ekbladh, *The Great American Mission: Modernization and the Construction of the American World Order* (Princeton, NJ: Princeton University Press, 2010), 2; Robert Latham, *The Liberal Moment: Modernity, Security, and the Making of the Postwar International Order* (New York: Columbia University Press, 1997), 2.
15. For discussion of modernity, see, generally, Mark Elvin, "A Working Definition of 'Modernity'" *Past & Present* 113 (November 1986): 209–213; Anthony Giddens and Christopher Pierson, *Conversations with Anthony Giddens: Making Sense of Modernity* (Oxford: Policy Press, 1998).
16. Radio Report to the American People, August 9, 1945, https://www.trumanlibrary.org/publicpapers/?pid=104.
17. In this era, American leaders began to identify the rule of law as a universal "elixir" for the ills of authoritarian regimes. Brian Z. Tamanaha, *On the Rule of Law: History, Politics, Theory* (Cambridge: Cambridge University Press, 2004), 48–51. For discussion of the central role of law and legality to the American outlook, see Benjamin Allen Coates, *Legalist Empire: International Law and American Foreign Relations in the Early Twentieth Century* (New York:

Oxford University Press, 2016), 2–3; Francis Fukuyama, "Nation-Building and the Failure of Institutional Memory," in *Nation-Building: Beyond Afghanistan and Iraq,* ed. Francis Fukuyama (Baltimore: Johns Hopkins University Press, 2006), 5–8.

18. The rule of law has been called the "central jewel in liberalism's crown." Allan C. Hutchinson and Patrick Monahan in *The Rule of Law: Ideal or Ideology,* ed. Allan C Hutchinson and Patrick Monahan (Toronto: Carswell, 1987), ix. As another scholar has observed, "The rule of law makes possible individual rights, which are at the core of democracy." Thomas Carothers, *Promoting the Rule of Law Abroad: In Search of Knowledge* (Washington, DC: Carnegie Endowment for International Peace, 2006), vii, 3.
19. George Marshall, "Reconstruction of Germany on a Democratic Basis," Department of State, Bulletin no. 16, March 14, 1947, 524. For a discussion of the different meanings attributed to the term by the Allies, see Carl J. Friedrich, "Military Government and Dictatorship," *Annals of the American Academy of Political and Social Science* 267 (1950): 1–7, at 1, 4.
20. For the institutional dimensions of legal reconstruction, see John Bell, "The Importance of Institutions," in *The Method and Culture of Comparative Law: Essays in Honour of Mark Van* Hoecke, ed. Maurice Adams and Dirk Heirbaut (Oxford: Hart, 2014), 207, 209–215.
21. Fahy to Clay, December 3, 1945, Charles H. Fahy Papers (CHFP), FDR Presidential Library, box 59.
22. Henry Parkman, "Talk on German Constitutional Liberties," undated August 1947, NARA RG 260, OMGUS CAD-Director, box 66.
23. General Douglas MacArthur, "Statement of the Japanese Government Concerning Required Reforms," October 11, 1945, in *Supreme Commander for the Allied Powers: Government Section Report: Political Reorientation of Japan (PRJ),* September 1945 to September 1948, vol. II (Grosse Pointe, MI: Scholarly Press, 1968), 741.
24. Brigadier General Courtney Whitney, "The Philosophy of the Occupation," *PRJ,* vol. I, xx.
25. Ibid.
26. "The Rule of Law in the United States," *A Statement by the Committee to Cooperate with the International Commission of Jurists, ABA Section on International and Comparative Law* (The Hague, 1958), 9–13. For American understandings of the concept of the rule of law, see also Robert W. Gordon, "The Role of Lawyers in Producing the Rule of Law: Some Critical Reflections," *Theoretical Inquires in Law* 11, no. 1 (2010): 441–468.
27. That official was Charles Kades, until the spring of 1947 the chief of the Government Section of the American occupation in Japan. Charles L. Kades, "Representative Government in Japan," *PRJ,* vol. I, xxiii–xxxv, xxiv–xxv.
28. For the Roosevelt administration's planning for national security in the postwar era, see Or Rosenboim, *The Emergence of Globalism: Visions of World*

Order in Britain and the United States 1939–1945 (Princeton, NJ: Princeton University Press, 2017); Patrick J. Hearnden, *Architects of Globalism; Building a New World Order during World War II* (Fayetteville: University of Arkansas Press, 2002), 147–173.

29. Smith, "Making the World Safe," 174–175, 183. See also Smith, *America's Mission,* 71; Coates, *Legalist Empire,* 170–175. For the Roosevelt administration's planning for American and global security in the postwar era, see Hearnden, *Architects of Globalism,* 147–173; Rosenboim, *The Emergence of Globalism.*
30. As Acheson further stated: "The primary purpose of the Potsdam Declaration . . . was—is—to destroy the Nazi war-machine beyond all possibility of resurrection, and to make sure that the German people are in a frame of mind never to want to fight again. At the same time . . . we must go ahead to open the way for democratic institutions." See "Our Military-Government Policy in Germany," *Department of State Bulletin,* no. 323, September 2, 1945, 314–315.
31. Harold W. Landin, chief, Democratization Branch, "Democratizing Germany," *Department of State Bulletin,* no. 133, April 1948, 6–8. For discussion of American reorientation policy in occupied Germany, see Alexandra F. Levy, "Promoting Democracy and Denazification: American Policymaking and German Public Opinion," *Diplomacy & Statecraft* 26 (2015): 614–635.
32. Kennan thought that much of American foreign policy was "conditioned on the premise that men everywhere are basically like ourselves—that they are animated by substantially the same hopes and aspirations—that they will react in substantially the same way." Kennan, "What Is Policy?" December 18, 1947, George F. Kennan Papers (GFKP), Princeton, box 298.
33. As one historian put the matter, the cardinal question of the Second World War era was which "universal model of modernity would in the end prevail." Latham, *The Liberal Moment,* 2.
34. Bell, "The Importance of Institutions," 215.
35. For comprehensive review of the literature on the Manhattan Project to the year 2008, see Rebecca Press Schwartz, "The Making of the History of the Atomic Bomb: Henry DeWolf Smyth and the Historiography of the Manhattan Project," Ph.D. dissertation, Princeton University, 2008), 2–20. See also Jeff Hughes, *The Manhattan Project: Big Science and the Atom Bomb* (London: Icon Books, 2002), 1–10.
36. Schwartz, "History of the Atomic Bomb," 10–11.
37. For a summary, see Edward H. Litchfield, "Political Objectives and Legal Bases of Occupation Government," in *Governing Postwar Germany,* ed. Edward H. Litchfield (Ithaca, NY: Cornell University Press, 1953), 3–4.
38. The Berlin (Potsdam) Conference, July 17–August 2, 1945, Protocol, 1 August 1945, Article 2 A. 1, *The Avalon Project,* http://avalon.law.yale.edu/20th_century/decade17.asp, Potsdam Agreement.
39. The American occupation officer Edward Litchfield referred to these goals as "meaningless generalities." Litchfield, "Political Objectives," 5.

40. Ibid., 3–18. In regard to the legal reconstruction of Germany, this book will focus on American action in the U.S. zone, alluding to developments in the British, French, and Soviet zones only as they provide points of similarity and contrast with American law reform activity. For histories of the British, French, Soviet occupations, see respectively Ian D. T. Turner, ed., *Reconstruction in Post-War Germany: British Occupation Policy and the Western Zones, 1945–55* (Oxford: Berg Press, 1989); F. Roy Willis, *The French in Germany 1945–1949* (Palo Alto, CA: Stanford University Press, 1962), 26–27; Norman N. Naimark, *The Russians in Germany: A History of the Soviet Zone of Occupation, 1945–1949* (Cambridge, MA: Harvard University Press, 1995); Filip Slaveski, *The Soviet Occupation of Germany: Hunger, Mass Violence and the Struggle for Peace* (Cambridge: Cambridge University Press, 2013).
41. For a summary of the genesis and organization of SCAP, see Takemae Eiji, *Inside GHQ: The Allied Occupation of Japan and its Legacy* (London: Continuum, 2002), 93–96.
42. "SCAP" described both the office of the Supreme Commander for the Allied Pacific, General Douglas MacArthur, and the military and administrative agencies under his command. Ibid., xxvii–xxviii.
43. Ibid., xxviii.
44. The Potsdam Declaration, Proclamation Defining Terms for Japanese Surrender, Issued, at Potsdam, July 26, 1945, Article 10. *Birth of the Constitution of Japan,* http://www.ndl.go.jp/constitution/e/etc/c06.html.
45. Theodore Cohen, *Remaking Japan: The American Occupation as New Deal* (New York: Free Press, 1987), 11–12.
46. This is not to suggest that the American occupation of its German zone was free of cruelty and abuses. For an account of American and Allied oppressions of Germans during the occupation, see Giles MacDonough, *After the Reich: The Brutal History of the Allied Occupation* (New York: Basic Books, 2007), 227–249.
47. Giles MacDonough estimates that as a result of the Second World War, 1.8 million German civilians died, 3.6 million homes were destroyed. Over 2 million more Germans died as a result of expulsion from the east. MacDonough, *After the Reich,* 45–46, 158–161. The historian Richard Bessel describes how defeat and disillusion among Germans "left behind an ocean of bitterness . . . altogether, the German population was battered physically, economically and psychologically to an extent unprecedented in living memory." Bessel, *Germany 1945: From War to Peace* (New York: Harpers Collins, 2010), 2–3. 7. See also, Victor Sebestyen, *1946: The Making of the Modern World* (London: Macmillan, 2014), 38–40. For the situation in Japan at war's end, see John W. Dower, *Embracing Defeat: Japan in the Wake of World War II* (New York: Norton, 1999), 45–48. Dower estimates that as a result of the war in the Pacific, the Japanese suffered 1.74 million military and another 1.2 million civilian dead; that one-quarter of Japan's national wealth was destroyed,

including 66 cities seriously damaged, leaving 30 percent of the population homeless (65 percent left homeless in Tokyo alone). In addition, in 1945 some 3.5 million Japanese soldiers were either POWs or unaccounted for.

48. The scholar Shunzo Majima is representative of the school of thought that in terms of legal and political democratization the American occupation of Japan was "one of the most successful cases of occupation in the modern history of war and peace." See "Just Military Occupation? A Case Study of the American Occupation of Japan," in *Jus Post Bellum and Transitional Justice,* ed. Larry May and Elizabeth Edenburg (Cambridge, MA: Cambridge University Press, 2013), 27–43, 27.
49. For this approach to the occupation of Japan, see Dower, *Embracing Defeat,* 19–30. For the occupation of Germany, see Wolfgang Benz, *Zwischen Hitler und Adenauer: Studien zur deutschen Nachkriegsgesellschaft* (Frankfurt: Fischer Taschenbuch, 1991). For an excellent summary of the landmark studies of the late occupation published in German, see Sabine Huth, "Einigkeit und Recht und Freiheit: Selected Themes in Contemporary German Post-War History," *Historical Journal* 37, no. 2 (1994), 487–503.
50. Jeffrey S. Gaab, *Justice Delayed: The Restoration of Justice in Bavaria under American Occupation, 1945–1949* (New York: Peter Lang, 1999); Dieter Waibel, *Von der wohlwollenden Despoties zur Herrschaft des Recht* (Tubingen: J. C. B. Mohr [Paul Siebeck], 1996); Andrew Szanajda, *The Restoration of Justice in Postwar Hesse, 1945–1949* (New York: Lexington, 2007).
51. Apart from its general program of denazification, American Military Government in Germany did not attempt to make significant changes to German private law. Rather more change was instigated by American agencies with regard to the private law of Japan, especially with regard to the so-called "household" systems of family and employment relations. In Japan, Americans also instigated major reforms in landholding. See, generally, Ronald Dore, *Land Reform in Japan* (New York: Oxford University Press, 1959). In occupied Germany and Japan, however, the thrust of American-directed legal reform activity addressed the central precepts and institutions of public law.
52. Edenburg, "Introduction," *Jus Post Bellum and Transitional Justice,* 8. See also Zachary D. Kaufman, *United States Law and Policy on Transitional Justice: Principles, Politics and Pragmatics* (New York: Oxford University Press, 2016).
53. For a useful summary of this literature, see Kaufman, *United States Law and Policy.*
54. See Carol Gluck, "The 'Long Postwar': Japan and Germany in Common and in Contrast," in *Legacies and Ambiguities: Postwar Fiction and Culture in West Germany and Japan,* ed. Ernestine Schlant and J. Thomas Rimer (Washington, DC: Woodrow Wilson Center Press, 1991): 63–78, at 63.
55. See George M. Fredrickson, "From Exceptionalism to Variability: Recent Developments in Cross-National Comparative History," *Journal of American History* 82 no. 2 (1995): 587–604.

56. See Theda Skocpol and Margaret Somers, "The Uses of Comparative History in Macrosocial Inquiry," *Comparative Studies in Society and History* 22 no. 2 (1980): 174–197.

1. The "Destruction of Philosophies"

1. John L. Chase, "Unconditional Surrender Reconsidered," *Political Science Quarterly* 70, no. 2 (1955): 258–279, at 259–260. FDR himself invented the term "unconditional surrender," perhaps without Churchill's prior approval.
2. Ibid., 261.
3. See David Ekbladh, *The Great American Mission: Modernization and the Construction of the American World Order* (Princeton: Princeton University Press, 2010), 2, 41, 164–169. For discussions and debates among the Office of Strategic Services about the nature of German fascism, see Frank Schale, "John H. Herz and the Office of Strategic Services," *International Relations* 22, no. 4 (2008): 411–415.
4. Ekbladh, *Great American Mission,* 41. See also Tony Smith, "Making the World Safe for Democracy in the American Century," *Diplomatic History* 23 (1999): 173–188, at 179; Robert Latham, *The Liberal Moment: Modernity, Security, and the Making of the Postwar International Order* (New York: Columbia University Press, 1997), 50–54.
5. See Thomas Fleming, *The New Dealers' War: Franklin D. Roosevelt and the War Within World War II* (New York: Basic Books, 2001), 180.
6. Cordell Hull, "If We Are Divided We Are Ineffective," radio address, April 9, 1944. See documents relating to World War II (1944), http://www.ibiblio.org/pha/policy/1944/1944 _Document_Relating_to_World_War_II.htm.
7. NARA RG 331, SHAEF G-5, box 109. As General Cornelius Wickersham, the War Department's chief of civil affairs, explained in 1944, after World War I the Allied civil affairs mission to Germany had commenced with "no officers, no plans, no training, no personnel." NARA RG 260, USGCC-Planning, box 11.
8. See Elizabeth Borgwardt, *A New Deal for the World: America's Vision for Human Rights* (Cambridge, MA: Belknap Press, 2005), 14–15.
9. See Smith, "Making the World Safe," 180–184.
10. Borgwardt, *A New Deal,* 15–46; Latham, *Liberal Moment,* 12–14; Smith, *America's Mission,* 7–8, 143–144.
11. Dale Hellegers, *We, the Japanese People: World War II and the Origins of the Japanese Constitution,* vol. 1 (Stanford, CA: Stanford University Press, 2001), 2–7.
12. State Department memorandum drafted by senior diplomat Robert Murphy to Secretary of State, "The Allied Control Authority for Germany: An Analysis of Its Organization and Procedures," January 6, 1947, NARA RG 260, OMGUS Legal Division (LD), box 4.

13. The legal basis of the Allied occupations of Germany and Japan are discussed in Adam Roberts, "Transformative Military Occupation: Applying the Laws of War and Human Rights," *American Journal of International Law* 100 (July 2006), 580–622, at 605; Shunzo Majima, "Just Military Occupation? A Case Study of the American Occupation of Japan," in *Jus Post Bellum and Transitional Justice,* ed. Larry May and Elizabeth Edenburg (Cambridge, MA: Cambridge University Press, 2013), 27–43.
14. Murphy to Secretary of State, *supra,* note 12.
15. For opinions doubting Allied legal authority to change domestic laws and political structures during military occupation, see, for example, War Office to Colonel Ryan, European Theatre of Operations United States Army, November 3, 1943, NARA RG 331, SHAEF Legal Branch, box 235; Memorandum for the Judge Advocate General, January 1, 1944, NARA RG 165, War Department CAD-General, box 20.
16. For instance, this quote in Myron Cramer, Judge Advocate General of the Army to General Hilldring, Director of Civil Affairs, December 1, 1943, NARA RG 165, War Department CAD-General, box 10.
17. Professor Phillip C. Jessup, "The Nature and Consequences of Unconditional Surrender under International Law," informal memorandum prepared for Colonel Chandler, May 1944, CJFP, box 65.
18. William Chanler to John McCloy, "Legal Consequences of Unconditional Surrender," February 3, 1945, NARA RG 107, War Department CAD-General, box 39.
19. By the spring of 1945, the War Department had endorsed this view, one developed by Lt. Colonel William Chanler, a former Wall Street lawyer who, in 1945, was the deputy-director of the department's Civil Affairs Division. Chanler's opinion was that "defeated Germany presented an unprecedented case in international law to which the Hague Rules were never intended to apply." See Chanler, "The Consequences of Unconditional Surrender under International Law," February 12, 1944, CJFP, box 65.
20. The legal position of the United States on this point was summarized in 1948 by Charles H. Fahy, the former solicitor-general and, from 1945 to 1946, the director of OMGUS Legal Division: "Whatever ancient or modern theories or precedents may be advanced to describe the situation, the simple fact is that sovereign power in Germany was assumed and exercised by right of conquest accompanied by unconditional surrender of the armed forces and collapse of civil authority." Charles Fahy, "Legal Problems of German Occupation," *Michigan Law Review* 47, no. 1 (1948): 11–22, at 12. In another contemporary account, transformative occupation was legally justified on the basis that the state of war between the Allies and the Axis powers persisted after their unconditional surrender. R. Y. Jennings, "Government in Commission," 23 *British Yearbook of International Law* 112 (1946): 112–140, at 135–140.

21. "Advice to the U.S. Representative in E.A.C. on Legal Consequences of Unconditional Surrender," February 17, 1945, NARA RG 107, War Department CAD, box 39. For the application of these principles to the occupation of Japan, see "The New Constitution of Japan," *The Political Reorientation of Japan,* vol. 1 (Grosse Pointe, MI: Scholarly Press, 1947), 89.
22. See Smith, "Making the World Safe," 197–198.
23. From a "legal standpoint," Charles Fahy argued, "every law of Germany was subject to the authority of the occupying powers to further the purposes of the war or the occupation." Fahy, "Legal Problems of German Occupation," 15.
24. Takemae Eiji, *Inside GHQ: The Allied Occupation of Japan and its Legacy* (London: Continuum, 2002), 201. For instance, the leading work on the organization and activity of the American command in postwar Japan refers to a "detailed master plan for occupation tailored to that country's precise conditions and requirements." See also D. Clayton James, *The Years of MacArthur,* vol. 3 (Boston: Houghton Mifflin, 1970), 10. See also Robert E. Ward, "Presurrender Planning: Treatment of the Emperor and Constitutional Changes," in *Democratizing Japan,* ed. Robert E. Ward and Shakamoto Yoshikazu (Honolulu: University of Hawaii Press, 1987), 1–41.
25. See Charles E. Neu, "The Rise of the National Security Bureaucracy," in *The New American State: Bureaucracies and Policies since World War II,* ed. Louis Galambos (Baltimore: Johns Hopkins University Press, 1987), 85–108; see also Daniel R. Ernst and Victor Jew, eds., *Total War and the Law: The American Home Front in World War II* (Westport, CT: Praeger, 2002), 2–3.
26. American planning for the occupation of Germany was particularly contentious, oscillating between the hard-peace proposals of Henry Morgenthau at Treasury and the softer-peace models advanced by the War and State departments. Kai Bird, *The Chairman: John J. McCloy, The Making of the American Establishment* (New York: Simon & Schuster, 1992), 223–227; see also Borgwardt, *A New Deal,* 206–210.
27. Edward N. Peterson, *The American Occupation of Germany: Retreat from Victory* (Detroit: Wayne State University Press, 1977), 19.
28. Edward H. Litchfield, "Political Objectives and Legal Bases of Occupation Government," in *Governing Postwar Germany,* ed. Edward H. Litchfield (Ithaca, NY: Cornell University Press, 1953), See also Hellegers, *We, the Japanese People,* vol. 1, 194–195.
29. Yoshiro Miwa and J. Mark Ramseyer, "The Good Occupation? Law in the Allied Occupation of Japan," *Washington University Global Studies Law Review* 8, no. 2 (2009): 363–378.
30. See Melvyn P. Leffler, *A Preponderance of Power: National Security, the Truman Administration, and the Cold War* (Stanford, CA: Stanford University Press, 1992), 28–29.
31. See Sean L. Malloy, *Atomic Tragedy: Henry L. Stimson and the Decision to Use the Atomic Bomb against Japan* (Ithaca, NY: Cornell University Press, 2008).

Among other duties, Stimson was busy advising two presidents about the Manhattan Project.

32. Harry L. Coles and Albert K. Weinberg, *Civil Affairs: Soldiers Become Governors* (Washington, DC: Office of the Chief of Military History, Department of the Army Office, 1964), x; Hellegers, *We, the Japanese People,* vol. 1, 162.
33. See Earl F. Ziemke, *The U.S. Army in the Occupation of Germany, 1944–1946* (Washington, DC: Center of Military History, 1975), 16; Kai Bird, *American Establishment,* 229–233.
34. See Coles and Weinberg, *Soldiers Become Governors,* 3–5, 21–23; see also Earl F. Ziemke, "Improvising Stability and Change in Postwar Germany," in *Americans as Proconsuls: United States Military Government in Germany and Japan, 1944–1952,* ed. Robert Wolfe (Carbondale: Southern Illinois University Press, 1984), 52–66, 53; see also Kenneth O. McCreedy, "Planning the Peace: Operation Eclipse and the Occupation of Germany," *Journal of Military History* 65 (2001): 713, 717.
35. Assistant Secretary of the Interior Saul Padover to Secretary Harold Ickes, as quoted in Coles and Weinberg, *Soldiers Become Governors,* 26.
36. Hilldring to Kent Greenfield, August 7, 1950, CJFP, box 1. In the view of the general in charge of planning the occupations, in 1944–1945, "there was no organization in Washington capable of hammering out these policies and decisions except the War Department."
37. Kai Bird, *American Establishment,* 17–18, 113, 229–233; Peter H. Irons, *The New Deal Lawyers* (Princeton, NJ: Princeton University Press, 1982), 15–18.
38. "McCloy felt a good lawyer could do anything." McCloy used the term "lawyer-like" to mean "good." Interview with Davidson Sommers (former McCloy law partner at Cravath and then in McCloy's office in the War Department), ii, 23, DMHP, box 6.
39. See also Karl N. Llewellyn, "The Crafts of Law Re-Valued," *Rocky Mountain Law Review* 15, no. 1 (1942): 1, 3. As Karl Llewellyn wrote in 1942, "The essence of our craftsmanship lies in skills and wisdoms: in practical, effective, persuasive, inventive skills for getting things done, any kind of thing in any field . . . in skills for moving men into desired action."
40. John McCloy to Herman Phleger, October 1945, HFPP, box 1.
41. Ziemke, *Occupation of Germany,* 16.
42. As Hilldring later wrote, "To the very end of the war some of our best and most enlightened commanders carried out their military government missions because they had been told to. To the very end they entertained profound and sincere reservations as to the wisdom of the [*sic*] using the U.S. Army in this role." Hilldring to Kent Greenfield, August 7, 1950, CJFP, box 1.
43. Cole and Weinberg, *Soldiers Become Governors,* x.
44. In Hilldring's view, the American Army was an institution designed not for governmental work but to "win battles" and in "complete detachment from the political life in the republic." Hilldring to Kent Greenfield, August 7,

1950, CJFP, box 1. See also Cole and Weinberg, *Soldiers Become Governors,* x. On the Army's reluctance to take on long-term civil affairs responsibilities in occupied territory, see McCreedy, "Planning the Peace," 715.

45. Hilldring did not mean "a year too late; I mean twenty years too late." Hilldring to Kent Greenfield, August 7, 1950, CJFP, box 1.
46. As Hilldring himself put the point, "I can successfully refute the validity of all the so-called reasons except one. The civilians weren't ready. They were late too—about twenty years." Ibid.
47. Ibid.
48. "Interview of Charles Kades," DMHP, box 6.
49. "Interview of Davidson Sommers," DMHP, box 6.
50. Louis Morton, "Germany First: The Basic Concept of Allied Strategy in World War II," in *Command Decisions,* ed. Kent Roberts Greenfield (London: Methuen, 1960), 11–47, 36.
51. Hilldring to Greenfield, August 7, 1950, CJFP, box 1.
52. As one American official later commented on this point, "I had a pretty good feeling that the Japanese were a different people, whereas the Germans were not. . . . The Germans were kind of kissin' cousins." Interview with Roy B. Snapp, lawyer from the Office of Naval Intelligence with State Department, DMHP, box 6.
53. See, generally, John Gimbel, *The American Occupation of Germany: Politics and the Military, 1945–1949* (Stanford, CA: Stanford University Press, 1968), 101; Rebecca L. Boehling, *A Question of Priorities: Democratic Reforms and Economic Recovery in Postwar Germany* (New York: Berghahn Books, 1996), 17–20; Jeffrey S. Gaab, *Justice Delayed: The Restoration of Justice in Bavaria under American Occupation, 1945–1949* (New York: Lang, 1999), 49–52; Andrew Szanajda, *The Restoration of Justice in Postwar Hesse, 1945–1949* (Lanham, MD: Lexington, 2007), 31–42.
54. See "Research and Planning on German Law and Administration," September 6, 1944, NAUK FO 937 / 20.
55. Ziemke, *Occupation of Germany,* 16, 19.
56. Hilldring to Hugh Cox, September 11, 1943, NARA RG 165, War Department, CAD-General, box 19.
57. McCloy to Biddle, October 16, 1943, NARA RG 165, War Department CAD-General, box 19.
58. Ibid. General Cornelius Wickersham, Hilldring's second-in-command, kept Hilldring carefully briefed on the progress of this work. Wickersham to Hilldring, September 12, 1943, NARA RG 165, CAD-General, box 19.
59. "The Reorganization of the German Administration of Justice in 1942," Office of Strategic Services (hereafter referred to as OSS) Research and Analysis, memo, no. 850, NARA RG 226, E. 1.
60. Loewenstein to W. C. Smith, "De-contamination of German Law after the Fall of the Nazi System," April 30, 1943, KLP, box 29.

61. See, generally, R. W. Kostal, "The Alchemy of Occupation: Karl Loewenstein and the Legal Reconstruction of Nazi Germany, 1945–1946," *Law and History Review* 29, no. 1 (2011): 1–52.
62. It is unclear whether Loewenstein was privy to the OSS report. Having left Germany soon after the Nazis came to power, Loewenstein had no firsthand knowledge of the response of German jurists to its actions and programs.
63. Biddle to McCloy, February 15, 1944, NARA RG 165, CAD-General, box 20.
64. Lieu-Colonel Burnett to Hilldring, December 22, 1943, NARA RG 165, CAD-General, box 20.
65. McCloy to Biddle, February 17, 1944, NARA RG 165, CAD-General, box 20.
66. "Elimination of Fundamental Nazi Political Laws in Germany," Civil Affairs Guide, prepared by the Federal Economic Administration, April 1944. NARA RG 60, Department of Justice, Economic Warfare, box 61.
67. The United States Manual of Military Government and Civil Affairs, FM 27–5, December 22, 1943, as quoted in "Memorandum on Denazification of German Law," April 26, 1944, NARA RG 331, SHAEF Legal Branch, box 235.
68. Fearnside had learned German at Bowdoin College and then during a research stint in Nazi Germany in 1934. "W. Ward Fearnside," obituary, *Boston Globe,* August 20, 2011.
69. William W. Fearnside, "Suggestion that All Nazi Laws Be Repealed," n.d., NARA RG 260, OMGUS LD-Legal Advice Branch (LAB), box 61.
70. NARA RG 260, OMGUS Control-Historical, box 690; see also "History of the Office of Military Government for Germany to May 1945," NARA RG 260, USGCC-Adjutant General (AG), box 1.
71. The USGCC was a political entity operated by soldiers. The idea was to get the business of military government out of the hands of the general staff (civilian and government affairs G-5) and into the hands of a larger and specially trained unit. The USGCC answered directly to the War Department, not the tactical arm of the army. "History of the Office of Military Government for Germany to May 1945," NARA RG 260, USGCC-AG, box 1; see Ziemke, *Occupation of Germany,* 90–91; Jean E. Smith, *Lucius D. Clay: An American Life* (New York: Holt, 1990), 224–225.
72. See "SLUGA: Priority of Work," September 12, 1944, NAUK FO 937/20.
73. "History of the Office of Military Government in Germany to May 1945," NARA RG 260, USGCC-AG, box 1. Marsh's staff increased to a half dozen lawyers by the time of the surrender. "Historical Notes of Colonel John M. Raymond," NARA RG 260, OMGUS LD-Director, box 9.
74. "History of the OMGUS to 1945," NARA RG 260, USGCC-AG, box 1.
75. "John B. Marsh," obituary, *New York Times,* March 23, 1967.

76. "Plans for Legal Section," September 26, 1944, NARA RG 260, OMGUS LD-Administration of Justice Branch (AJB), box 84.
77. These aims were later expressed as Allied policy after the EAC approved them in the form of an Allied "Directive on the Administration of Justice" in December 1944.
78. For background on SHAEF G-5, see, generally, Cole and Weinberg, *Civil Affairs,* 160, 674, 681; Ziemke, *Occupation of Germany,* 79–80.
79. "Historical Statement of the German Country Unit," August 1944, NARA RG 331, SHAEF Control Office, box 307.
80. Ibid.
81. Ibid., 1–9; see also "Integration of Legal Agencies," May 22, 1945, NARA RG 260, USGCC Executive Office, box 10.
82. "Sir John Galway Foster," *Oxford Dictionary of National Biography* (Oxford: Oxford University Press, 2004–2010). Energetic and intelligent, fluent in German and French, Wilberforce (a future British Law Lord), eventually became the ranking officer in the British group. See, generally, Richard Orme Wilberforce, *Reflections on My Life* (London: Roundtuit, 2003).
83. "Hayden N. Smith," obituary, *New York Times,* June 22, 1981.
84. Oppenheimer, a decorated veteran of the German army in the First World War, practiced corporate and international law in Berlin from 1922 until he emigrated to England in 1936. After becoming a barrister in London, he immigrated to the United States in 1940, enlisting in the U.S. Army as a private soldier in 1942. In the final months of the war in Europe, Oppenheimer was a major assigned to Eisenhower's general staff, helping to coordinate the first American efforts in taking control of the Nazi legal system. After the surrender, he was promoted to lieutenant-colonel and assigned to General Clay's staff as a general advisor of German affairs. See, generally, Oppenheimer obituary, *New York Times,* February 6, 1968.
85. Some had been working on German-law related projects for the British Foreign Office since 1941. Cohn to Sir Alfred Brown, March 16, 1945, NAUK FO 937/20. See Ulrike Walton-Jordan, "Safeguards against Tyranny: The Impact of German Emigre Lawyers on British Legal Policy towards Germany, 1942–1946," in *German-Speaking Exiles in Great Britain,* ed. Anthony Grenville (London: Brill, 2000), 6–8.
86. Worth to Jenkins, "British Legal Research Unit," October 1946, NAUK FO 936/106.
87. Letter to Brigadier AEJ Clark, September 1944, NAUK FO 936/106.
88. March 2, 1945, NAUK FO 937/20.
89. According to a Lt. Col. Aynsley to McLendon, "British Legal Research Unit," March 10, 1945, NAUK FO 937/20. For background on Cohn, see Werner Lorenz, "Ernst J. Cohn (1904–1976)," in *Jurists Uprooted: German-Speaking Émigré Lawyers in Twentieth-Century Britain,* ed. Jack Beatson and

Reinhard Zimmermann (Oxford: Oxford University Press, 2004), 326–327, 331.

90. Cohn was assigned the noncommissioned rank of sergeant because by British War Office rule, former enemy nationals (even if, like Cohn, they had become naturalized British citizens) could not be given officer's rank in the British armed forces. Oppenheimer had circumvented this problem by joining the American army.
91. Friedmann was a German émigré law scholar who worked mainly with the British Political Intelligence Department. "In Memoriam: Wolfgang Gaston Friedmann," *American Journal of International Law* 65 (1973): 102–103.
92. "Preparation of Directives in Connection with the Draft German Armistice . . . Reform of Nazi Law, etc.," March 4, 1944, NAUK WO 220 / 191.
93. For background, see Walton-Jordan, "*Safeguards against Tyranny,* 8–9.
94. "Report of the Committee for the Revision of German Law," NARA RG 331, SHAEF-Legal Branch, box 230.
95. Cohn to Foster, July 27, 1944, NAUK FO 1060 / 099.
96. Oppenheimer to Finlay, "Memorandum on the Denazification of the German Legal System," April 26, 1944, NARA RG 331, SHAEF Legal Branch, box 235.
97. This task was delegated to Major Mitchell Franklin, an American army officer who before the war had been a legal academic. Franklin's unsubtle solution was for the edict to order German judges to interpret German law "so as to effect its genuine meaning, purpose, and justification." On the other hand, German law was "not to be interpreted, applied or administered with aim of realizing National Socialist purposes." Another clause would require that "National Socialist legal theory, judicial and administrative decisions, practices and customs, shall be disregarded in the administration of German law." German judges found to have contravened them were to face prosecution and, on a guilty verdict, dismissal from office. Franklin to Marsh, June 18, 1944, NARA RG 331, SHAEF-Legal Branch, box 229.
98. Foster to Marsh, "Planning a Legal Framework to Underlying German Directives," June 15, 1944, NAUK WO 219 / 3618.
99. Foster's summary was based on a memorandum sent to him by Oppenheimer some weeks earlier. See Oppenheimer to Marsh, May 1, 1944, NARA RG 260, OMGUS LD-LAB, box 61.
100. SLUGA, "Report on 'Fundamental Political Nazi Laws,'" July 25, 1944, NARA RG 260, OMGUS Property Division, box 16.
101. For a discussion of the handbooks dispute, see Patrick J. Hearnden, *Architects of Globalism; Building a New World Order during World War II* (Fayetteville: University of Arkansas Press, 2002), 254–255.
102. "Discouraged in their struggle to have London become the seat of combined post-hostilities policy-making, the British were pushing for conversion to tri-

partite planning and the virtual exclusion of SHAEF." Ziemke, *Occupation of Germany,* 98–99.

103. "Professor H. A. Smith," obituary, *The Times,* April 19, 1961.
104. "Legislation for Germany," October 22, 1944, NARA RG 331, SHAEF Legal Branch, box 229.
105. Ibid.
106. Ibid.
107. Lieu. Loewy to Foster, "Legislation for Germany," October 31, 1944, NARA RG 331, SHAEF Legal Branch, box 229. The report alleged that the directives' references to supplementary and subsidiary laws were based on "a well-known and stock phrase of German law and its meaning will be abundantly clear" to German jurists.
108. "Minutes of Meeting in the Office of Brigadier Andrew Clark," November 2, 1944, RG 331, SHAEF Legal Branch, box 229.
109. Lieutenant General Grassett, minutes of meeting at SHAEF, January 3, 1945, NAUK, WO 219 / 3618.
110. "Notes on Meeting," January 27, 1945, NAUK FO 1060 / 1095.
111. Finley to Marsh, "Denazification of German Law," August 12, 1945, NAUK FO 1060 / 1095.
112. The third article of the law forbade "interpretation and application of German law in accordance with National Socialist doctrines" and the use of Nazi-influenced precedents.
113. "Lists of Nazi Laws to Be Abrogated," Cohn to Malfroy, May 15, 1945, NAUK, WO 219 / 3618.
114. "Notes on Meeting," January 27, 1945, NAUK FO 1060 / 1095.
115. "Discriminatory Laws," Marsh to Clark, March 26, 1945, NAUK FO 1060 / 1095.
116. "Discriminatory German Legislation," April 12, 1945, NARA RG 331, SHAEF Legal Branch, box 229. For instance, a schedule relating to Nazi-era legislation regarding the German civil service; see also "Discriminatory German Laws, May 4, 1945, NAUK FO 1060 / 1095 which listed numerous suspended laws under six headings.
117. Clark to Marsh, February 13, 1945, NAUK FO 1060 / 1095.
118. Marsh to Clark, February 20, 1945, NARA RG 331, SHAEF-Legal Branch, box 229.
119. In fact, this was the sixth revision of these orders, JCS 1067 / 6 "Directive to the Commander-in-Chief of the United States Forces of Occupation Regarding the Military Government of Germany," *Documents on Germany, 1944–1985* (Washington, DC: U.S. State Department, 1985), 15–32.
120. That is, the period between the unconditional surrender and the formation of an Allied control authority. "JCS 1067 and the British Draft Directives," NARA RG 260, USGCC-Planning, box 11. Quote from JCS 1067, Part I, 4. C, *supra,* note 119.

121. Interestingly, the American directive did not go so far as the British directive in this regard. The British Directive No. 1 called for the British commander to "lay the foundations for the rule of law in Germany, and for eventual peaceful cooperation in international life by Germany." The American leaders at SHAEF rejected this language, not in principle, but on grounds that "these are clearly long-term objectives" outside the mandate of SHAEF. "Comparison of JCS 1067 and British Draft Directive," NARA RG 260, USGCC-Planning, box 11.
122. JCS 1067, Part I, 6 b., *supra,* note 119.
123. James K. Pollock and James H. Meisel, eds., *Germany under Occupation: Illustrative Materials and Documents* (Ann Arbor, MI: George Wahr, 1947), 55–67.
124. This was admitted to Brigadier Clark by John Marsh in June 1945 in "Discriminatory German Laws," Marsh to Clark, June 3, 1945, NAUK FO 1060 / 1095.
125. Ibid.
126. Oppenheimer to Marsh, 1 May 1944, NARA RG 331 SHAEF Legal Branch, box 229. The huge body of Nazi-era statute law still was being studied page by page; see also reference in Oppenheimer to Marsh, May 17, 1944, NARA RG 331, SHAEF Legal Branch, box 229. Having read Karl Loewenstein's memo on legal denazification written to the Justice Department in 1943, Oppenheimer lamented that more complete studies had not already been commissioned and completed.
127. "Denazification of German Law," Finlay to Marsh, August 12, 1945, KLP, box 45.
128. See Michael Stolleis, "Law and Lawyers Preparing the Holocaust," *Annual Review of Law and Social Sciences* 3, no. 1 (2007): 213, 215.
129. Wolff to Foster, July 27, 1944, NAUK FO 1060 / 1099.
130. See Gaab, *Justice Delayed,* 3–4; see also Szanadja, *Postwar Hesse,* 109–112.
131. "Denazification: Basic Preliminary Plan," Annex XXXIII, April 5, 1945, NARA RG 260, USGCC-Planning, box 33.
132. McLendon to G-5, "Special Report," June 22, 1945, NARA RG 331, SHAEF Legal Branch, box 229. Records that revealed the existence, for instance, of the hitherto secret Department IV section of the Reich Ministry, responsible for the extrajudicial elimination of perceived enemies of the Third Reich.
133. Even the German émigré lawyers at SLUGA had little useful assistance to offer in this regard. Ernst Wolff, for example, rather unhelpfully recommended that only those Nazi-era jurists who "acted in such a way as they cannot be trusted" should be barred from postwar legal offices. Wolff to Foster, July 27, 1944, NAUK FO 1060 / 1099.
134. Marsh to Alfred Brown, "Discriminatory German Laws," June 3, 1945, NAUK, FO 1060 / 1095.

135. See, generally, Robert E. Ward, "Reflections on the Allied Occupation and Planned Political Change in Japan, in *Political Development in Modern Japan,* ed. Robert E. Ward (Princeton, NJ: Princeton University Press, 1968), 477–535; Hellegers, *We, the Japanese People,* vol. 1, 159–246; Marlene J. Mayo, "American Wartime Planning for Occupied Japan: The Role of Experts," in *Americans as Proconsuls: United States Military Government in Germany and Japan, 1944–1952,* ed. Robert Wolfe (Carbondale: Southern Illinois University Press, 1984), 3–51; Rudolf V. A. Janssens, *"What Future for Japan?" U.S. Wartime Planning for the Postwar Era, 1942–1945* (Amsterdam: Rudopi, 1995); Ray A. Moore and Donald L. Robinson, *Partners for Democracy: Crafting a New Japanese State under MacArthur* (Oxford: Oxford University Press, 2002), 23–35.
136. The organizational chart in Janssens, *Wartime Planning,* 77.
137. Moore and Robinson, *Partners for Democracy,* 24.
138. Most of the leading American scholars on Japan were dependent in their work on translations from the Japanese. See Koseki Shoichi, *The Birth of Japan's Postwar Constitution,* ed. and trans. Ray A. Moore (New York: Westview, 1997), 142; Of all the "experts" at State, only three were literate in Japanese and or had visited Japan. See Mayo, "Wartime Planning for Japan," 5; see also Janssens, *Wartime Planning,* 77.
139. See "Interview with Professor E. O. Reischauer," DMHP, box 5.
140. See "Interview with Davidson Sommers," DMHP, box 6. The OPD was staffed mainly by "professional Army with a healthy sprinkling of West Pointers." Its main function was to advise the Joint Chiefs on "planning and policy implications of planning." The professional soldiers at OPD regarded the planners at Hilldring's Civil Affairs Division as "largely a bunch of Christmas help. They were all civilians."
141. Moore and Robinson, *Partners for Democracy,* 23.
142. "Agenda for the Meeting of March 13, 1943," NARA RG 59 in DMHP, box 16.
143. Minutes, "Department of State Committee on Post-War Programs," April 21, 1944, NARA RG 59; "Postwar Programs Committee," DMHP, box 16.
144. Hellegers, *We, the Japanese People,* vol. 1, 198–199.
145. Mayo, "Wartime Planning for Japan," 38; Janssens, *Wartime Planning,* 349.
146. Hellegers, *We, the People,* 81.
147. Moore and Robinson, *Partners for Democracy,* 25–27.
148. Kimura, "Cultures of Modernity in the Making of the United States-Japan Cold War Alliance" (Ph.D. diss., University of Arizona, 2013), 88–91.
149. Mayo, "Wartime Planning for Japan," 32; Hellegers, *We, the Japanese People,* vol. 1, 233–236.
150. "Summary of United States Initial Post-Defeat Policy relating to Japan," National Diet Library of Japan, http://www.ndl.go.jp/constitution/e/shiryo/01/007/007_001r.html.

151. "Nullification of Obnoxious Laws," March 22, 1944, Department of State, Post-War Committee, DMHP, box 16.
152. "U.S. Initial Post-Surrender Policy for Japan," For SWNCC 150 and its iterations, see National Diet Library of Japan, http://www.ndl.go.jp/constitution/e/shiryo/01/022shoshi.html. See also Hellegers, *We, the Japanese People,* vol. 1, 206–209.
153. Janssens, *Wartime Planning,* 351.
154. Ibid.
155. In the third provision of the Atlantic Charter, FDR and Churchill had pledged that in the postwar world they would "respect the right of all peoples to choose the form of government under which they will live." See, generally, Borgwardt, *A New Deal,* 4–7.
156. Moore and Robinson, *Partners in Democracy,* 28.
157. Mayo, "Wartime Planning for Japan," 44, 124.
158. Interview with Davidson Sommers (former McCloy law partner at Cravath and, during the war, employed in McCloy's division of the War Department), DMHP, box 6.
159. Mayo, "Wartime Planning for Japan," 3.
160. Interview with Loomis Patrick, DMHP, box 6.
161. Crossman to White, January 13, 1973, 2, DMHP, box 2; Hellegers, *We, the Japanese People,* vol. 1, 216.
162. Winthrop Stimson Putnam & Roberts. For a description of their long association, see Crossman to White, January 13, 1973, and Edward G. Crossman, unpublished memoir, 155–156, DMHP, box 2.
163. Crossman memoir, DMHP, box 2. Crossman had served as legal aide to Stimson during his time as governor general of the Philippines. In that time he had also come to know MacArthur socially. Crossman served with MacArthur as a CAD officer during the campaign in the Philippines in 1944.
164. Ibid.
165. Hellegers, *We, the Japanese People,* vol. 1, 215–216, 387.
166. For biographical detail on van Slyck, see Hellegers, *We, the Japanese People,* vol. 1, 387.
167. Ibid.
168. DeForest Van Slyck, "Observations on Post Hostilities Policy toward Japan," July 1945, DMHP, box 16. On Van Slyck's analytical and writing skills, see Crossman memoir, DMHP, box 2. For another account of how the Van Slyck memo came to the attention of Stimson, see Leon V. Sigal, *Fighting to a Finish: The Politics of War Termination in the United States and Japan, 1945* (Ithaca, NY: Cornell University Press, 1988), 246–249.
169. This deficiency had been noted many times by State Department officials during the war. See, for instance, "Japan: The Educations System under Military Government," November 6, 1944, DMHP, box 16.

170. Crossman to White, January 13, 1973, DMHP, box 2; see also Crossman memoir, DMHP.
171. Stimson diary, August 2, 1945, HLSP, reel 9; Chanler to Stimson, "Post-Defeat Policy Relating to Japan," August 6, 1945, DMHP, box 1.
172. Interview with Loomis Patrick, 12. See also James, *Years of MacArthur,* vol. II, 782–783.
173. Interview with Milo E. Rowell, DMHP, box 2.
174. "Basic Initial Post Surrender Directive to Supreme Commander for the Allied Powers for the Occupation and Control of Japan," JCS 1380 / 15, November 3, 1945, 134–168, National Diet Library of Japan, http://www.ndl.go.jp/constitution/e/shiryo/01/036/036tx.html.
175. Ibid., paragraphs 4g to 5e.
176. Carol Gluck, "The 'Long Postwar': Japan and Germany in Common and in Contrast," in *Legacies and Ambiguities: Postwar Fiction and Culture in West Germany and Japan,* ed. Ernestine Schlant and J. Thomas. Rimer (Washington, DC: Woodrow Wilson Center Press, 1991) 63–81; Ben-Ami Shillony, *Politics and Culture in Wartime Japan* (Oxford, NY: Clarendon, 1981), 15–16.
177. Boehling, *A Question of Priorities,* 16–21.
178. Carol Gluck, "Entangling Illusions—Japanese and American Views of the Occupation," in *New Frontiers in American-East Asian Relations,* ed. Warren I. Cohen and Dorothy (New York: Columbia University Press, 1983), 181.
179. Colonel Frank Milani to Adjutant General, War Department, "Plan for the Organization and Training in the U.S." November 10, 1943, in DMHP, box 17.
180. "Unconditional Surrender of Japan," Joint Intelligence Staff, March 13, 1945, DMHP, box 16. See also Moore and Robinson, *Partners for Democracy,* 28.
181. See, for examples, Ward, "Presurrender Planning," 36; Mayo, "American Wartime Planning," 3–41; Takemae, *Inside GHQ,* 201.
182. Janssens, *Wartime Planning,* 60–70.
183. Ward, "Planned Political Change, 477.
184. A point emphasized in Joyce Kolko and Gabriel Kolko, *The Limits of Power: The World and United States Foreign Policy, 1945–1954* (New York: Harper and Row, 1972), 6.
185. The State Department's planning papers were either not communicated, unread, or exerted little influence. Interview with Loomis Patrick, DMHP, box 4.

2. Occupying the Legal Other

1. Harold W. Landin, chief, Democratization Branch, "Democratizing Germany," April 1948, Department of State Bulletin, no. 133, 6–8.
2. The USGCC was soon thereafter renamed the Office of Military Government, United States (OMGUS). For the purposes of simplicity, this study adopts the same shorthand for OMGUS adopted by many of its operatives, i.e., American Military Government (AMG).

3. For an account of his recruitment to Government Section in the fall of 1946, see Alfred Oppler, *Legal Reform in Occupied Japan: A Participant Looks Back* (Princeton, NJ: Princeton University Press, 1976), 11–12.
4. John McCloy to Herman Phleger, October, 1945, HFPP, box 1.
5. Alvin J. Rockwell, "Post-War Problems in Occupied Germany: American Democracy versus Russian Democracy," *American Bar Association Journal* 36, no. 5 (1950): 359–362 and 431–434.
6. Karl Loewenstein, *Legal Reconstruction in Germany,* c. 1948, unpublished ms. 10, KLP, box 24.
7. Basic Preliminary Plan, Allied Control and Occupation of Germany, app. A, German Courts (Civil and Military) to Annex XV (Administration of Justice), NARA RG 260, USGCC-Planning, box 30.
8. According to Legal Branch analysis, during the Weimar period the German Ministry of Justice had become "one of the most nationalist and reactionary of all German bureaucracies." See "Reich Ministry of Justice," April 23, 1945, NAUK War Office 219, 1600 / 347.
9. For American perceptions of the Reich Ministry of Justice, see McLendon to Marsh, June 16, 1945, NARA RG 331, SHAEF Legal Branch, box 235. Allied military courts were established in their place. German superior courts and Special Courts were to be closed permanently. The German local courts were to be closed as long as it took to denazify their personnel. "Minutes of Plenary Meeting of SHAEF G-5," June 29, 1945, NARA RG 498, European Theatre of Operations, United States Army, box 15.
10. Cohn to Foster, July 27, 1944, NAUK FO 1060 / 1099. On the subject of the denazification of the German bench, Legal Branch was advised by Ernst Cohn at SLUGA. In Cohn's view, it was absolutely essential to the restoration of impartial justice in Germany to "clear the Bench of Nazi elements." Cohn understood that this action might lead to a shortage of decent candidates for judicial appointment. See also "Directions to Judges and Prosecutors of the Amtsgerichte," September 18, 1944, NAUK WO 219 / 3618.
11. Finley to Marsh, "Denazification of German Law," August 12, 1945, NAUK FO 1060 / 1095.
12. Ibid. The Nazi-era statutes on criminal procedure and "hereditary health and marriage" were also soon "to be deprived of effect."
13. McCloy speech to Academy of Political Science, November 8, 1945, NARA RG 260 OMGUS-Executive Office, box 317.
14. See Stimson to Truman, "Memorandum for the President," June 2, 1945, NARA RG 165, War Department, CAD-General, box 26. Stimson requested that "the President take cognizance of this problem of staffing the U.S. Group Control Council."
15. Ibid.
16. Ibid.
17. Ibid.

18. Wickersham to Clay, May 22, 1945, NARA RG 260, USGCC-Planning, box 24.
19. Ibid.
20. Ibid.
21. A number of senior federal judges had turned down the directorship before Fahy was considered. See Wickersham to Clay, May 17 and 31, 1945, NARA RG 260, USGCC-Planning, box 24.
22. Fahy was so soft-spoken the justices of the Supreme Court dubbed him "whispering Charlie." See Peter H. Irons, *The New Deal Lawyers* (Princeton, NJ: Princeton University Press, 1982), 234–236.
23. In one wartime case, Fahy advocated (successfully) for the constitutionality of the arrest and internment of Americans of Japanese ancestry. See Peter H. Irons, *Justice at War* (New York: Oxford University Press, 1983), 120, 286–290; see also Malick W. Ghachem and Daniel Gordon, "From Emergency Law to Legal Process: Herbert Wechsler and the Second World War," *Suffolk University Law Review* 40, no. 2 (2007): 333, 339–342. On one occasion as wartime solicitor general, in order to vindicate the constitutionality of the Japanese internment law, Fahy appears to have crossed a bright ethical line when he suppressed evidence that tended to discredit the veracity of an army report material to the government's case. See also David G. Savage, "U.S. Official Cites Misconduct in Japanese American Internment Cases," *Los Angeles Times,* May 24, 2011. In 2011, Acting Attorney General Neil Katyal explicitly accused Fahy of professional misconduct in having misled the Supreme Court in the internment cases. See also Joshua E. Kastenberg and Eric Merriam, *In a Time of Total War: The Federal Judiciary and the National Defense, 1940–1954* (New York: Routledge, 2016), 76.
24. Although Fahy's mother was Jewish born, there is no evidence that he went to Germany in the spirit of revenge.
25. Philip Elman, *With All Deliberate Speed: The Life of Philip Elman: An Oral History Memoir,* ed. Norman I. Sibler (Ann Arbor: University of Michigan Press, 2004), 147.
26. Fahy had had some exposure to international law in having provided legal counsel to the Lend-Lease program in 1941–1942 and then at the San Francisco Conference of April 1945. Fahy to Killion, July 5, 1945, CHFP, box 59. Neither Fahy nor the other senior appointees to Legal Division saw German service as a great prize (although the top post came with a then-handsome $10,000 per annum salary). Fahy's deputy director, Herman Phleger, regarded his tenure in Germany as an occasion of national "service and sacrifice."
27. Fahy, "Memorandum for General Clay," December 3, 1945, CHFP, box 59.
28. In the end, Kirchheimer was judged to be too much of a leftist to be trusted with the job.
29. For background and biographical material on Loewenstein, see R. W. Kostal, "The Alchemy of Occupation: Karl Loewenstein and the Legal Reconstruction

of Nazi Germany, 1945–1946," *Law and History Review* 29, no. 1 (2011): 1–52, at 6–7; see also Udi Greenberg, *The Weimar Century: German Émigrés and the Ideological Foundations of the Cold War* (Princeton, NJ: Princeton University Press, 2014), 195–199.

30. See "Faculty Profile," *The Amherst Student,* September 29, 1955, KLP, box 58. After finishing secondary school in 1908, Loewenstein joined a Munich banking firm and traveled widely on business, including to the United States. He became an excellent linguist, having learned to speak—in addition to German—French, English, Spanish, and Italian.
31. For descriptions of Loewenstein's theory of militant democracy, see *supra,* note 30.
32. Karl Loewenstein, "Brass Hats versus Brass Buttons," draft letter to *New York Times,* n.d., KLP, box 45.
33. Loewenstein had been set to work on anti-fascist counterintelligence in South America.
34. Loewenstein to Fahy, June 27, 1945, CHFP, box 59.
35. See Karl Loewenstein, *Political Reconstruction* (New York: MacMillan, 1946). The book defended the right of liberal-democratic nations to impose liberal-democratic political institutions on defeated authoritarian states.
36. Laurence Knapp to Fahy, July 5, 1945, CHFP, box 596.
37. For Fahy's comments on the early days of Legal Division, see "Legal Problems of German Occupation," *Michigan Law Review* 47, no. 1 (1948): 11, 16–17; Charles Fahy, "The Lawyer in Military Government (Germany)," *Proceedings of the Section of International and Comparative Law—American Bar Association* (1946), 29–37.
38. For a description of this process, see Loewenstein, *Legal Reconstruction in Germany,* KLP, box 24.
39. See "Statement of General Divisional Responsibilities," September 28, 1945, NARA RG 260, USGCC-Planning, box 24.
40. "Legal Division: Basic Responsibilities," n.d., NARA RG 260, SHAEF Legal Branch, box 229.
41. Basic Preliminary Plan, Allied Control and Occupation of Germany, app. A, German Courts (Civil and Military) to Annex XV (Administration of Justice), NARA RG 260, USGCC-Planning, box 30.
42. "Legal and Judicial Affairs: I. Objectives," n.d. NARA RG 331, SHAEF Legal Branch, box 229.
43. See, for example, Charles Fahy, "The Lawyer in Military Government in Germany," 29–30.
44. For the best biographical treatment of Clay in the period, see Jean Edward Smith, *Lucius D. Clay: An American Life* (New York: Holt, 1990), 201–247. For further assessment of Clay's administration in Germany, see Rebecca L. Boehling, *A Question of Priorities: Democratic Reforms and Economic Recovery in*

Postwar Germany: Frankfurt, Munich, and Stuttgart under U.S. Occupation, 1945–1949 (New York: Berghahn, 1998), 43–44.

45. According to Clay, at war's end, "Everyone ambitious, including Ike, wanted to go home to make their political and financial fortunes." "Oral History Interview of Lucius D. Clay," July 16, 1974, Truman Presidential Library, https://www.trumanlibrary.org/oralhist/clayl.htm.
46. For the positive assessment of a German historians, see, generally, Wolfgang Benz, *Zwischen Hitler und Adenauer: Studien zur deustchen Nachkreigsgeschicte* (Frankfurt: Fischer Taschenbuch, 1991).
47. Clay to Hilldring, May 7, 1945, in *The Papers of General Lucius Clay,* vol. 1, ed. Jean Edward Smith (Bloomington: Indiana University Press, 1974), 10–11.
48. Harold Zink, *The United States in Germany, 1944–1955* (Princeton, NJ: Van Nostrand, 1957), 89.
49. Clay to Hilldring, May 7, 1945, Smith, *Clay Papers,* vol. 1, 10–11.
50. For several compelling reasons, Loewenstein's assessment is lent considerable credence in these pages. Loewenstein was one of Legal Division's few intellectuals in the field of the agency's principal endeavor. That he had been a practicing German lawyer (and part-time law professor) enhanced already impressive credentials. As a senior expert consultant to Legal Division, he had generous internal access to the agency's key documents, activities, and personnel. He kept meticulous and contemporaneous notes and records, including a detailed diary. Loewenstein also researched and wrote more than forty Legal Division memoranda. Finally, because of his native fluency in German, he had the atypical capacity at Legal Division to speak directly and naturally with other German lawyers and officials.
51. Loewenstein, *Legal Reconstruction in Germany,* box 24.
52. "Interview of Dr. Karl Loewenstein," July 1946, RG 331 SHAEF Legal Branch-Director, box 40; LOD, April 12, 1946.
53. In their memoranda and correspondence, American officials generally referred to the Directorate-Legal as the "Legal Directorate," or by the abbreviation, "DLeg". These usages are adopted here. The Allied Control Authority was "a continuous four-power diplomatic conference subordinate to the Council of Foreign Ministers . . . but with only minor exceptions no central administration has developed under the aegis of the Council." Carl Friedrich, "Organizational Aspects of the German Program for the US Government," January 2, 1947, CJFP, box 1.
54. See, generally, Carolyn Woods Eisenberg, *Drawing the Line: The American Decision to Divide Germany, 1944–1949* (Cambridge: Cambridge University Press, 1996), 7–8; see also Smith, *An American Life,* 214.
55. USGCC, Staff Meetings, August 4, 1945, NARA RG 260, USGCC-Control Office, box 117.
56. Charles Fahy, "The Lawyer in Military Government in Germany," 38–40.

57. Rockwell had served as a legal officer and then director of Legal Division. Rockwell, "Post-War Problems," 359.
58. For discussion of the divergent definitions of democracy among the four powers, see, generally, Carl J. Friedrich, "Military Government and Dictatorship," *Annals of the American Academy of Political and Social Sciences* 267 (1950): 1–7, at 3.
59. For summary and review of American denazification policy in Germany, see Boehling, *A Question of Priorities,* 62–63, 270–276.
60. For British policy and action on denazification, see Raymond Ebsworth, *Restoring Democracy in Germany: The British Contribution* (London: Stevens, 1960), 11–13; Ian D. Turner, "Denazification in the British Zone," in *Reconstruction in Post-War Germany,* 239–270. For French policy and action on denazification, see Willis, *The French in Germany* (Stanford, CA: Stanford University Press, 1962), 157–158, 247–248.
61. For Soviet denazification, see Timothy R. Vogt, *Denazification in Soviet-Occupied Germany: Brandenburg, 1945–1948* (Cambridge, MA: Harvard University Press, 2000), 78–80; Filip Slaveski, *The Soviet Occupation of Germany: Hunger, Mass Violence and the Struggle for Peace* (Cambridge: Cambridge University Press, 2013), 80.
62. ACA, August 21, 1945, NARA RG 260, ACA-DLeg, box 173.
63. According to Herman Phleger, in the first meetings, more about procedure than substance, there were "no major differences as to major policies." Phleger diary, August 31, September 4, 1945, HFPP, box 1.
64. See DLeg / P(45)11, August 31, 1945, NARA RG 260, ACA-DLeg, box 176.
65. Memorandum of Legal Action, DLeg / P(45)14, 1 September 1945, NARA RG 260, ACA-DLeg., box 176.
66. Law No. 1, "Repealing of Nazi Laws," in "Summary of Multipartite Agreements & Disagreements on Germany, 2nd rev. ed., pt. 1., September 15, 1948," 48–49.
67. Ibid., article 2.
68. Ibid., article 3.
69. See, generally, Jeffrey S. Gaab, *Justice Delayed: The Restoration of Justice in Bavaria under American Occupation, 1945–1949* (New York: Lang, 1999), 52–59; Szanajda, *Justice in Postwar Hesse,* 47–51.
70. Clay believed the diplomatic situation was such that it would "necessitate the operation of the zone governments on an almost independent basis for many months although gradually through long and drawn out negotiations we will be able to establish overall German admin machinery." See Clay to McCloy, June 29, 1945, Smith, *Clay Papers,* vol. 1, 37.
71. LOD, September 18, 1945.
72. Ibid.
73. For relevant personnel files, see NARA RG 331, SHAEF Legal Branch-Director, box 33. Before and during the Second World War, McLendon had

been a career U.S. Army officer. Although as a young man he had taken a degree in law, the army employed him as an infantry instructor and commander. Before enlisting in the army in 1942, Shepard had been a small-town attorney in North Carolina. Before their assignment to Legal Division, neither man had received specialized education in German law or history.

74. LOD, January 8, 1946.
75. LOD, August 26, 1945.
76. For the design and implementation of American denazification policy, see, generally, John H. Herz, "The Fiasco of Denazification in Germany," *Political Science Quarterly* 63, no. 4 (1948): 569–594; see also Lutz Niethammer, *Entnazifizierung in Bayern* (Frankfurt: Fischer, 1972), 244–250; Clemens Vollnhals, ed., *Entnazifizierung Politische Säuberung und Rehabilitierung in den vier Besatzungszone* (Munich: Deutscher Taschenbuch Verlag, 1991); John Gimbel, *A German Community Under American Occupation: Marburg, 1945–1952* (Stanford, CA: Stanford University Press, 1961), 101–110; Edward N. Peterson, *The American Occupation of Germany: Retreat to Victory* (Detroit: Wayne State University Press, 1977), 138–166. For recent research on denazification in the U.S. zone, see Frederick Taylor, *Exorcising Hitler: The Occupation and Denazification of Germany* (London: Bloomsbury, 2011), 278–285; Alexandra F. Levy, "Promoting Democracy and Denazification: American Policymaking and German Public Opinion," *Diplomacy & Statecraft* 26 (2015): 614–635.
77. Gimbel, *American Occupation,* 102; Boehling, *Question of Priorities,* 52–62; Harold Marcuse, *Legacies of Dachau: The Uses and Abuses of a Concentration Camp, 1933–2001* (Cambridge: Cambridge University Press, 2008), 89–93.
78. Boehling, *Question of Priorities,* 58.
79. The denazification job was just too large. Clay thought that even 10,000 American officials could not do the job. Clay, conversation with Hilldring, March 1, 1946, Smith, *Clay Papers,* vol. 1, 172.
80. See Clay to Hilldring, July 5, 1945, Smith, *Clay Papers,* vol. 1, 46–47.
81. Herz, "The Fiasco of Denazification in Germany," 59.
82. Marcuse, *Legacies of Dachau,* 88–95.
83. Clay recalled Fahy as a close confidante and "great tower of strength." Smith, *An American Life,* 303.
84. LOD, August 29, 1945.
85. Loewenstein to W. C. Smith, "De-contamination of German Law after the fall of the Nazi System," April 30, 1943, KLP, box 29.
86. See memorandum, Loewenstein to Fahy, September 14, 1945, KLP, box 45.
87. Szanajda, *Restoration of Justice,* 4–5. The *gleichschaltung* or synchronization was the process by which German state and civil institutions were reduced to National Socialist control, goals, and membership requirements; see also Konrad H. Jarausch, *The Unfree Professions: German Lawyers, Teachers and Engineers, 1900–1950* (New York, Oxford University Press, 1990), 117, 199.

88. Memorandum, Loewenstein to Fahy, September 14, 1945, KLP, box 45. Loewenstein was quite surprised that the non-Nazis supported only an extremely selective denazification and exclusion policy. One Bremen jurist thought that of the 400 members of the bar there, "Hardly more than one dozen" should be permanently disbarred from legal office.
89. LOD, September 14, 1945.
90. LOD, August 29, 1945.
91. Loewenstein Memorandum, "Denazification Policy," November 30, 1945, KLP, box 45.
92. Loewenstein, "Report on Political and Social Conditions in South Germany," November 26, 1945, KLP, box 45.
93. Loewenstein, *supra,* note 92.
94. "Exit Interview of Loewenstein," July 10, 1946, KLP, box 45.
95. See Loewenstein to Fahy, September 14, 1945, KLP, box 45.
96. See B. M. Katz, "The Criticism of Arms: The Frankfurt School Goes to War" *Journal of Modern History* 50, no. 3 (1987) 439, 459–465. Loewenstein was not alone among German émigré scholars in advocating for a "militant" program of postwar denazification in the legal field. In planning work for the OSS, Franz Neumann, John Herz, and Otto Kirchheimer also had endorsed tough denazification policies.
97. Loewenstein to Fahy, September 14, 1945, KLP, box 45.
98. Ibid.
99. See Peterson, *Retreat to Victory,* 147. The board consisted of six men, including Fahy and the chiefs of AMG intelligence and economic affairs, along with the senior political advisor to AMG, Robert Murphy. See, generally, Gimbel, *American Occupation,* 101–103.
100. In his support of this policy, Oppenheimer was in direct and sometimes acrimonious conflict with Loewenstein. The two men clashed on the issue during their time with AMG in Germany and afterward. For an account of their policy differences on denazification, see Fritz Oppenheimer, "Denazifying Germany," *New York Times,* January 12, 1947.
101. Ibid. See also Loewenstein, "Minutes of the Meeting at Stuttgart of the Ministers of Justice of the South-German Länder," December 18, 1945, KLP, box 28.
102. Loewenstein to Fahy, November 30, 1945, KLP, box 28.
103. See Loewenstein, "Comment on Denazification," *Social Research* 14, no. 3 (1947): 367. As Loewenstein later wrote, "I admit that it is a fundamental right of man not to be a hero. But the fact that a person of integrity loaned his name, for selfish and opportunistic reasons, to a party which he now professes to have despised" was no basis either of respect or trust.
104. Loewenstein to Fahy, November 30, 1945, KLP, box 28.
105. LOD, January 31, 1946.
106. LOD, November 30, 1945.

107. LOD, August 29, 1945.
108. This Loewenstein called the "glib and persuasive technique of the Germans in absolving themselves." Loewenstein, "Comment on Denazification," 367.
109. In key meetings with German officials in December 1945, Loewenstein alleged, Oppenheimer "was less rigorous than the Germans themselves. He seemed to protect the Germans against their own proposals." LOD, December 18, 1945. "Rheinstein and Oppenheimer," he diarized on January 31, 1946, "are leaning back to get as many 'nominal' Nazis [as possible] back into the fold."
110. See "Summary of Discussion of Denazification Laws," December 18, 1945, NARA RG 260, SHAEF Legal Branch, box 235. For Oppenheimer's similar account of these meetings, see "Denazifying Germany," *New York Times,* January 12, 1947.
111. "Preliminary Report by Working Committee to Denazification Policy Board," December 20, 1945, CHFP, box 59.
112. See Loewenstein to Fahy, January 5, 1946, KLP, box 28.
113. LOD, January 3, 1946.
114. Loewenstein (through Elman) to Fahy, January 5, 1946, KLP, box 28. Having offered these basic objections, Loewenstein proceeded ("with resignation") to provide a section-by-section analysis of the German proposal, suggesting amendments that might render it at least serviceable.
115. LOD, January 3, 1946; see also Loewenstein, "Reconstruction," 450–52; see also Loewenstein, "Comment on 'Denazification," 365–369.
116. "Report of the Denazification Policy Board," January 15, 1946, KLP, box 45.
117. Clay to Minister-Presidents, March 5, 1946, CHFP, box 60.
118. See Clay, *Papers,* 172. The denazification job was so big, Clay thought, that "It's got to be done by the Germans."
119. Clay was aware that in the United States news of the new denazification policy would garner a "tremendous amount of abuse." Ibid.
120. Karl Loewenstein, "Denazification Report," *New York Times,* December 8, 1946.
121. LOD, January 31, 1946.
122. LOD, January 18, 1946.
123. While Loewenstein left this meeting deeply impressed by Clay's knowledge, intelligence, and personal charm, he also concluded that the general was determined at all costs to press forward with the rapid rehabilitation of Germany's institutions and leadership elite. LOD, February 16, 1946.
124. Loewenstein, untitled memo, February 19, 1946, KLP, box 46.
125. LOD, January 12, 1946.
126. Loewenstein, *Legal Reconstruction in Germany,* KLP, box 24.
127. In Loewenstein's view, the decentralization mandate was being conflated with the idea of legal diversification. He contended that the ACC could decentralize the power of the German state in the presence of more or less uniform laws

and argued strenuously for the need of a central legal agency in the "field of law" in occupied Germany. He detected among the Germans the "universal consciousness of the imperative need of retaining the unity of the Reich, of preserving what is considered the most precious spiritual heritage of German history. . . . Some sort of coordinating and unifying agency in the field of law and legislation is urgently and desperately needed lest Germany would break into fragments of small states." Loewenstein to Fahy, "Proposals for the Reconstruction of Law-Making in Germany," November 17, 1945, NARA RG 260, SHAEF Legal Branch, box 230.

128. See Loewenstein, "Proposals for the Reconstruction of the Law-Making Process in Germany," November 17, 1945, KLP, box 46.
129. See, for instance, Loewenstein's memo on "Committee of the Ministers of Justice," December 3, 1945, KLP, box 46.
130. See memorandum, "Control by AMG of legislation," April 19, 1946, KLP, box 46.
131. Memorandum, "Approval of German Land Legislation," May 31, 1946, KLP, box 46.
132. See LOD, August 7, 1946.
133. The acronymic term SCAP (Supreme Commander for the Allied Powers) referred both to the rank and position of the commander and to the organization under his command. See, generally, Dale M. Hellegers, *We, the Japanese People: World War II and the Origins of the Japanese Constitution,* vol. 1 (Stanford, CA: Stanford University Press, 2001), 419–420. By default the task of orchestrating the first phase of the occupation of Japan had fallen to MacArthur and the handful of senior civilian affairs officers working under his direction at SCAP's pre-occupation headquarters in Manila.
134. In the period October 1945 to December 1946, SCAP civil affairs personnel expanded from a few hundred to 1,600. Theodore Cohen, *Remaking Japan: The American Occupation as New Deal* (New York: Free Press, 1987), 80, 101. See Harry Emerson Wildes, *Typhoon in Tokyo: The Occupation and Its Aftermath* (New York: Macmillan, 1954), 8–9.
135. See Potsdam Declaration, provision 6. See *Report of the Government Section of SCAP, PRJ,* vol. 2, Appendix A (Washington, DC, 1949), 413.
136. "The Instrument of Surrender gave the Allies the right to insist that Japanese basic law should be altered to provide a government responsible to the people and to grant and safeguard the rights commonly enjoyed by citizens of democratic states." Potsdam Declaration, provision 10. See also "History of the Non-Military Activities of the Occupation of Japan, 1945–1951," vol. 5, "Civil Liberties—Part One," NARA RG 331, Historical Branch, box 3634.
137. See Hellegers, *We, the Japanese People,* vol. 1, 220–222.
138. See John W. Dower, *Japan in War and Peace: Selected Essays* (New York: New Press, 1993), 163.

139. "The occupation shall have the character of an operation on behalf of the principal Allied powers acting in the interest of the United Nations at war with Japan. . . . participation will be welcomed and encouraged." "United States Initial Post-Surrender Policy for Japan," November 3, 1945, *PRJ,* vol. 2, 423. For American preeminence in the occupation of Japan, see also Robert E. Ward, "The Origins of the Present Japanese Constitution," *American Political Science Review* 50, no. 4 (1956): 980, 980.
140. John Dower, *Embracing Defeat: Japan in the Wake of World War II* (New York: W. W. Norton, 1999), 73.
141. "Initial Post-Surrender Policy," *PRJ,* vol. 2, app. A, part 1, 423–424.
142. See JCS 1380 / 15, "United States Initial Post-Surrender Policy for Japan," November 3, 1945, *PRJ,* vol. 2, app. A, 423–426.
143. Ibid.
144. "History of the Non-Military Activities of the Occupation of Japan, 1945–1951," vol. 5, "Civil Liberties—Part One," NARA RG 331, Historical Branch, box 3634.
145. "United States Initial Post-Surrender Policy for Japan," November 3, 1945, *PRJ,* vol. 2, app. A, 428–441.
146. As two scholars summarized the point: "In practice the diplomatic representative was merely MacArthur's mouthpiece in the Allied Council, not his confrere in the consideration of policy." Harold S. Quigley and Jones E. Turner, *The New Japan: Government and Politics* (Minneapolis: University of Minnesota Press, 1956), 91. See Cohen, *Remaking Japan,* 13. According to one informed observer, MacArthur had been given "the greatest leeway ever accorded an American officer in peacetime;" see also Takemae Eiji, *Inside GHQ: The Allied Occupation of Japan and Its Legacy* (London: Continuum, 2002), 5, 105, 149–150.
147. *PRJ,* vol. 2, 429.
148. Quigley and Turner, *The New Japan,* 91.
149. See D. Clayton James, *The Years of MacArthur: Triumph and Disaster, 1945–1964,* vol. 3 (Boston: Houghton Mifflin, 1985), 14–16; Takemae, *Inside GHQ,* 104–105.
150. See especially James, *Years of MacArthur;* see also William Manchester, *American Caesar: Douglas MacArthur 1880–1964* (Boston: Little, Brown, 1978); see also Arthur Herman, *Douglas MacArthur: American Warrior* (New York: Random House, 2016).
151. See, generally, Michael Schaller, *The American Occupation of Japan: The Origins of the Cold War in Asia* (New York: Oxford University Press, 1985), 23–25; see also Howard B. Schonberger, *Aftermath of War: Americans and the Remaking of Japan, 1945–1952* (Kent, OH: Kent State University, 1989), 40–90; see also Ray A. Moore and Donald L. Robinson, *Partners for Democracy: Crafting the New Japanese State Under MacArthur* (Oxford: Oxford University Press, 2002), 36–49; Dower, *Embracing Defeat,* 40–44, 203–206; Takemae, *Inside GHQ,* 5, 150.

152. See James, *Years of MacArthur,* vol. 2, 776.
153. For this perception of MacArthur, see Roger Baldwin, *Autobiography (1947–1950),* 500, RNBP, box 21. In his speech on taking the Japanese surrender, MacArthur stated that he detested war, "knowing better than most men the futility and debasement of civilization."
154. See Courtney Whitney, *MacArthur: His Rendezvous with History* (New York: Knopf, 1956), 228.
155. As Whitney's MacArthur homage was titled. Ibid.
156. Ibid.
157. See Hellegers, *We, the Japanese People,* vol. 2, 413.
158. See James, *Years of MacArthur,* vol. 3, 193–199, 648. There is no doubting that perceived success in the liberal-democratization of Japan could only have helped a presidential bid.
159. See Atcheson Dispatch to State Department, no. 176, December 31, 1945, DMHP, box 1.
160. Douglas MacArthur, *Reminiscences* (New York: McGraw-Hill, 1964), 282.
161. MacArthur's extremely poor standing with Democrats was a product also of his prominent part in the violent rousting of the "bonus army" in 1932. Schonberger, *Aftermath of War,* 42–43.
162. One former SCAP official characterized MacArthur as a "self-made political thinker . . . an extraordinary flexibility in unorthodox circumstances." See Cohen, *Remaking Japan,* 70–75.
163. No less a liberal than the ACLU's Roger Baldwin steadfastly maintained that MacArthur had a "profound commitment to democratic liberties, an instinct for the equality of peoples, a respect for the sensitivities of the defeated Japanese and a reformer's zeal." Baldwin, *The Nation,* April 20, 1964; see also Baldwin, "Tokyo–Confidential," April 13, RNBP, box 21.
164. Baldwin, "Japan's American Revolution," 100.
165. Carnes Lord, *Proconsuls: Delegated Political-Military Leadership from Rome to America Today* (Cambridge: Cambridge University Press, 2012), 100.
166. As MacArthur put it in his memoir, "But years of overseas duty had schooled me well in the lessons of the Orient and, what was probably more important, had taught the Far East that I was its friend." MacArthur, *Reminiscences,* 270.
167. Lord, *Proconsuls,* 100.
168. See Lord, *Proconsuls,* 102; for the contrary view, see Dower, *Embracing Defeat,* 211–212; Yokiko Koshiro, *Trans-Pacific Racisms and the U.S. Occupations of Japan* (New York: Columbia University Press, 1999).
169. See Charles L. Kades, "Representative Government in Japan," *PRJ,* vol. 1, xxiii.
170. Ibid.
171. "The Japanese were the most advanced of the oriental peoples, and in that capacity they were bound to exercise in the long run the greatest influence over the others." George Kennan, "Memoranda of Conversations with Gen-

eral of the Army Douglas MacArthur," March 1, 1948, 8. In https://history.state.gov/historicaldocuments/frus1948v06/d519. See also Dower, *Embracing Defeat,* 550–551. I take this view notwithstanding MacArthur's infamous statement to Congress in 1952 that the Japanese had the racial and cultural maturity of a twelve-year old.

172. For the definitive study, see John W. Dower, *War without Mercy: Race and Power in the Pacific War* (New York: Pantheon Books, 1993).
173. Lord, *Proconsuls,* 101.
174. The vindictive and mendacious steps that MacArthur took in the trial and execution of the Japanese Army General Tomoyuki Yamashita are amply documented in Allan A. Ryan, *Yamashita's Ghost: War Crimes, MacArthur's Justice, and Command Accountability* (Lawrence: University Press of Kansas, 2012).
175. Having consulted with a number of his Japanese contacts while in Japan, the Japan expert and scholar Kenneth Colegrove became convinced that in 1946 MacArthur was held in "phenomenal esteem" by the Japanese people. See Colegrove, as quoted in Koseki Shoichi, *The Birth of Japan's Postwar Constitution,* ed. and trans. Ray A. Moore (Boulder, CO: Westview, 1997), 154–155.
176. See Takemae, *Inside GHQ,* 234.
177. Ibid., 235–236. Dower, *Embracing Defeat,* 291–292.
178. See "Report on the Conference with Japanese Officials," October 1, 1946, DMHP, box 16.
179. "Kades Interview of Hellegers," October 27, 1973, 8, 22, DMHP, box 3. When Kades began work in Japan in the fall of 1945, the only policy material he had in his possession was JCS 1380.
180. Ibid.
181. See Hellegers, *We, the Japanese People,* vol. 2, 419.
182. As one SCAP official recalled, "We had the feeling of floundering around a lot until Gen. Whitney arrived. There really wasn't any significant action or decisions. There were simply ad hoc operations from day to day without any clear sense of direction . . . as to why we were there." "Interview of H. E. Robison," DMHP, box 5.
183. See Takemae, *Inside GHQ,* 113.
184. See Hellegers, *We, the Japanese People,* vol. 2, 424.
185. Ibid., 487–499. See also Charles L. Kades, "The American Role in Revising Japan's Imperial Constitution," *Political Science Quarterly* 104 (1989): 219; SCAP, General Orders no. 8, "Government Section," October 2, 1945, *PRJ,* vol. 1, 796.
186. See Hellegers, *We, the Japanese People,* vol. 2, 505–506. Impelled in part by a secret policy communiqué, SWNCC 228, which called for further Japanese-driven political reforms.
187. See James, *Years of MacArthur,* vol. 3, 43.
188. As another officer at GS later put it, Whitney was "a man of real substance and personality who permitted himself to be completely submerged in the

personality of MacArthur." "Interview of Osborne Hauge," DMHP, box 3.

189. See "Oral Reminiscences of Colonel Charles L. Kades," interview of D. Clayton James, July 7, 1977, Papers of Charles L. Kades, MacArthur Memorial Library (MML), RG-5, box 1.
190. See Roger Baldwin, "Confidential Notes from an Interview of MacArthur," May 6, 1947. The general referred to the work of SCAP as a "crusade."
191. Baldwin thought this "sense of crusade" among GS officials was genuine. Baldwin, "Letter to the Board," May 10, 1947, RNBP, box 18.
192. "I think Kades, more than any man, really had a major impact on these civil government programs . . . and the manner of their implementation. Kades was an all-out New Dealer." "Interview of Osborne Hauge," DMHP, box 3; Baldwin, *Autobiography,* 450, RNBP, box 21.
193. Kades thought of himself as a liberal New Dealer. See David Danelski, "Interview of Charles Kades," July 7, 1976, DMHP, box 3.
194. "Interview of Osborne Hauge," DMHP, box 3.
195. See, generally, Moore and Robinson, *Partners for Democracy,* 6–7.
196. Hilldring later referred to Kades as "one of the bright boys of my staff during a large part of the war." Hilldring to Baldwin, January 18, 1951, ACLUP, box 1172.
197. See, generally, Takemae, *Inside GHQ,* 256.
198. "Interview of Kades," 5, 26, 36, DMHP, box 3.
199. Ibid., 23.
200. See Oppler, *Legal Reform in Occupied Japan,* 11–12; see also Mire Koikari, *Pedagogy of Democracy: Feminism and the Cold War in the US Occupation of Japan* (Philadelphia: Temple University Press, 2008), 8, 15–20.
201. "Interview of Kades," 26–27, DMHP, box 3.
202. According to one SCAP officer, "This occupation was carried on by so many men not of high reputation at all, most with no previous knowledge of Japan, not ever having been there or studied it, very few of them knowing the language . . . yet, despite all this, the achievements were considerable." "Interview of Dr. Cyrus Peake," 40, DMHP, box 3.
203. As one SCAP officer recalled, "Even had the occupationnaires cared to investigate, research materials were inadequate. . . . Government Section's library contained not a single authoritative modern book, journal, or paper on Japanese affairs. Nor, apparently, did top brass care to know. Three different staff sections rejected proposals that efficient fact-finding services be established." Wildes, *Typhoon,* 12, 20. "We of the academic world," Wildes later commented, "were put into insignificant places." "Interview of Wildes," DMHP, box 7.
204. See Moore and Robinson, *Partners in Democracy,* 98.
205. See Cohen, *Remaking Japan,* 3–4.

206. See Borgwardt, *New Deal for Human Rights,* 55.
207. See Whitney, "The Philosophy of the Occupation," *PRJ,* vol. 1, xvii–xxii.
208. Ibid., xix.
209. Ibid., xxi.
210. See Kades, "Representative Government in Japan," *PRJ,* vol. 1, xxiii–xxxv, xxvii.
211. Ibid., xxiv.
212. Ibid., xxv.
213. See Dower, *War Without Mercy,* 118–124. Kades, "Representative Government," xxv–xxvi.
214. The acronym SCAPIN was an abbreviation of "SCAP Index." James, *Years of MacArthur,* vol. 3, 56; see also Takemae, *Inside GHQ,*114–115.
215. See, generally, Takemae, *Inside GHQ,* 114–115.
216. "It cannot be denied," Toshimi Miyasawa wrote in 1949, "that these reforms carried out in the various circles as a result of the surrender are really of a revolutionary nature." Translation of Toshimi Miyasawa, "Outline Concerning the Reforms in Japan under the Control of the Allied Powers," January 10, 1949, NARA RG 331, SCAP-GS, box 1522.
217. One Communist detainee, Miki Kiyoshi, had died in prison forty-two days *after* the surrender. See Dimitri Vanoverbek, *Juries in the Japanese Legal System: The Continuing Struggle for Citizen Participation and Democracy* (New York: Routledge, 2015), 92–93.
218. The Japanese government also balked at the idea of releasing from prison Communists who had been convicted of acts of violence. Chalmers Johnson, *Conspiracy at Matsukawa* (Berkeley: University of California Press, 1972), 15–16.
219. Ibid.; for complete list of these directives, see Cohen, *Remaking Japan,* 62.
220. See John W. Dower, "Yoshida in the Scales of History," in *Japan in War and Peace: Selected Essays,* ed. John W. Dower (New York: New Press, 1993), 209, 213–218.
221. See Masami Kimura, "Cultures of Modernity in the Making of the United States-Japan Cold War Alliance," Ph.D. diss., University of Arizona, 2013, 8, 12, 20. See also Cohen, *Remaking Japan,* 98–104; Roger Baldwin, "Notes on Japan," conference with Col. Nugent, RNBP, box 18.
222. See *PRJ,* vol. 1, 83. See also John. W. Dower, *Empire and Aftermath: Yoshida Shigeru and the Japanese Experience, 1878–1954* (Cambridge, MA: Harvard, 1979), 326; Dower, "Yoshida in the Scales of History," 213–218.
223. Little more than 1 percent of Japanese bureaucrats were purged during the occupation. See Haruhiro Fukui, "Postwar Politics, 1945–1973," in *The Cambridge History of Japan,* vol. 6, ed. Peter Duus (Cambridge: Cambridge University Press, 2008), 154–214, 180–181. See also Dower, *Empire and Aftermath,* 306, 318; Kimura, "Cultures of Modernity," 23, 212.

224. In the conclusion of one historian, "The entire effect of SCAP's operations allowed the Japanese government a great deal of informal leeway in dealing with their American overseers." Schaller, *American Occupation,* 28.
225. Dower, *Embracing Defeat,* 23. One American study concluded, "The upper reaches of the [Japanese] bureaucracy . . . constituted an exclusive, tight-knit and self-perpetuating oligarchy who owed their allegiance theoretically to the Emperor. . . . Their authority was never challenged." "Brief Program Report on the Political Reorientation of Japan. Pre-War Government of Japan," Government Section Report, 1949, NARA RG 331, SCAP-GS, box 1446.
226. See Kades, memo for the chief, December 8, 1945, DMHP, box 7; Hellegers, *We, the Japanese People,* vol. 2, 493.
227. McCormack to OPD, "Memorandum from G-3 to OPD," November 27, 1945, DMHP, box 4.
228. Commander A. R. Hussey, "Report on Work Done," circa December 1945, DMHP, box 7.
229. See Generals Bissel and Wackerling, memo for the chief, OPD, "Comment on Cable from Atcheson," November 23, 1945, DMHP, box 30.
230. Kades to chief of staff, December 8, 1945, DMHP, box 3.
231. As one SCAP officer later summarized, "Basically, the Old Guard seems more or less united on policy. It is interested in maintaining its power position despite the occupations reforms in the legal power structure. . . . [They] go through the motions of complying with GHQ-sponsored changes in the legal structure, then capture the altered edifice, and proceed leisurely to sabotage the purpose for which GHQ had demanded a restructuring." Robert B. Textor, *Failure in Japan, with Keystones for Positive Policy* (Westport, CT: Greenwood Press, 1972), 17.
232. Hellegers, *We, the Japanese People,* vol. 2, 424.
233. Justin Williams, *Japan's Political Revolution under MacArthur: A Participant's Account* (Athens: University of Georgia Press, 1979), 75.
234. According to two participants, on Whitney's arrival, "There was difference of night and day. All at once the whole Section was electrified." "Interview of Charles Kades," 42, DMHP, box 3. See also "Interview of H. E. Robison," 14, DMHP, box 5.
235. "Interview of Kades," 42.
236. Ibid., 82.
237. See John McCloy to Herman Phleger, n.d., October 1945, HFPP, box 2.
238. In 1945 and afterward Phleger displayed a painful ignorance about Germany and National Socialism, claiming in a speech on Germany given in the United States that "Though the Nazi party at its maximum had less than 9,000 members out of a population of 70 million, it was able to seize power in Germany." This figure is too small by several million. Notes on speech to "Warden and Fellows of the Golden Bear," n.d., HFPP, box 3.
239. LOD, November 26, 1945.

240. Whitney, *Rendezvous with History,* 229.
241. Peterson, *Retreat to Victory,* 349.

3. Captive Constitutions

1. See Charles Fahy, "Legal Problems of German Occupation," *Michigan Law Review* 47, no. 1 (1948): 11.
2. See, for example, F. A. Mann, "The Present Legal Status of Germany," *Transactions of the Grotius Society* 33 (1947): 119, 136. After 1945, a number of legal scholars denied that Germany's or Japan's "sovereignty," properly defined, was acquired by the Allies.
3. Carl J. Friedrich, "Military Government and Dictatorship," *Annals of the American Academy of Political and Social Sciences* 267 (1950): 1–7, 3.
4. Mann, "Legal Status of Germany," 128.
5. Fahy, "German Occupation," 15.
6. Indeed, as recently as the 1930s, American agencies had been deeply involved in constitution-making in the Philippines. See, for example, Leia Casteneda Anastacio, *The Foundations of the Modern Philippine State: Imperial Rule and the American Constitutional Tradition in the Philippine Islands, 1898–1935* (New York: Cambridge University Press, 2017).
7. See "Report on the Conference with Japanese Officials," October 1, 1946, DMHP, box 22. This meeting took place the day before Government Section was reorganized under General Whitney's leadership.
8. When asked by an historian whether in 1945 constitutional reform had been a high priority of postwar planners, retired General Charles H. Bonesteel replied: "To be honest, I don't think I knew a damned thing about the Japanese constitution." See "Interview of Bonesteel," DMHP, box 1. See, generally, Hellegers, *We, the Japanese People:World War II and the Origins of the Japanese Constitution,* vol. 1 (Stanford, CA: Stanford University Press, 2001), 172–173, 238–242.
9. "Interview of Japan Expert Hugh Borton," 16, DMHP, box 1.
10. Hugh Borton, while an accomplished historian of modern Japanese politics and government, had no specialized training in any aspect of Japanese law. Hugh Borton, *American Presurrender Planning for Postwar Japan* (New York: East Asian Institute, Columbia University, 1967). See also V.A. Janssens, *What Future Japan? U.S. Wartime Planning for the Postwar Era, 1942–1945* (Amsterdam: Rudopi, 1995), 261.
11. The political scientist Dr. Kenneth Colegrove of Northwestern University. In the 1930s, Colegrove, a specialist in Japanese government, had published a series of articles on the subject in the *American Political Science Review.* His expertise notwithstanding, Colegrove was not especially influential at GS. See, generally, Takemae Eiji, *Inside GHQ: The Allied Occupation of Japan and its Legacy* (London: Continuum, 2002), 156.

12. Article 10, in *PRJ,* vol. 2, app. A, 413.
13. Ibid., Article 12.
14. See JCS 1380/15, "United States Initial Post-Surrender Policy for Japan," November 3, 1945, *PRJ,* vol. 2, app. A, 423–426.
15. See "Interview of Hugh Borton," 15, DMHP, box 1. See also Marlene J. Mayo, "Wartime Planning for Occupied Japan: The Role of Experts," in *Americans as Proconsuls: United States Military Government in Germany and Japan, 1944–1952,* ed. Robert Wolfe (Carbondale: Southern Illinois University Press, 1984), 20. As the scholar Edward Reischauer later commented, "I think we all assumed there would be some kind of constitutional revision." "Interview of E. O. Reischauer," 3, DMHP, box 5.
16. See Mayo, "Wartime Planning for Occupied Japan," 25–26. See also Hugh Borton, "Abolition of Militarism and Strengthening of Democratic Process," State Department, Postwar Programs Committee, May 9, 1944, DMHP, box 16.
17. Robert E. Ward, "The Origins of the Present Japanese Constitution," *American Political Science Review* 50, no. 4 (1956): 980, 984.
18. "The New Constitution of Japan," *PRJ,* vol. 1, app. A, 90.
19. The Japanese cabinet believed that the release of Communists would lead to violence and disorder in the country. See, generally, Chalmers Johnson, *Conspiracy at Matsukawa* (Berkeley: University of California Press, 1972), 15; Hellegers, *We, the Japanese People,* vol. 2, 445.
20. See "The Judicial and Legal System," *PRJ,* vol. 1, 193.
21. See, for instance, Justin Williams, "Making the Japanese Constitution: A Further Look," *American Political Science Review* 59, no. 3 (1965): 675; Hellegers, *We, the Japanese People,* vol. 2, 487–517; Alfred Oppler, *Legal Reform in Occupied Japan: A Participant Looks Back* (Princeton, NJ: Princeton University Press, 1976).
22. Unlike MacArthur, Whitney was an American-trained lawyer who had practiced law (mainly in the Philippines). However, Whitney had no specialized expertise in the constitutional law of Japan (or any other nation). For background on Whitney, see D. Clayton James, *The Years of MacArthur,* vol. III, (Boston: Houghton Mifflin, 1970), 43–45.
23. Ibid., 52, 223–224.
24. Some material on the Meiji constitution was being generated by the Office of the Political Advisor (POLAD) in Japan. It is not clear, however, how much of this material was in circulation at GS. See, generally, Hellegers, *We, the Japanese People,* vol. 2, 447–448. Ray A. Moore and Donald L. Robinson, *Partners for Democracy: Crafting a New Japanese State under MacArthur* (Oxford: Oxford University Press, 2002), 82–83.
25. For background on Milo Rowell and Alfred Rodman Hussey, see Moore and Robinson, *Partners for Democracy,* 82–83; 96–97.
26. Hellegers, *We, the Japanese People,* vol. 2, 499–501.

27. See "Report of the Preliminary Studies and Recommendations of Japanese Constitution," December 6, 1945, SCAP-GS, National Diet Library, Japan.
28. Ibid., 82.
29. "The New Constitution of Japan," *PRJ,* vol. 1, App. A, 84.
30. "Brief Program Report on the Political Reorientation of Japan—Pre-War Government of Japan," Government Section Report, 1949, NARA RG 331, SCAP-GS, box 1446.
31. Ibid.
32. Ibid., 83. In the words of the SCAP account, the Meiji constitution "was carefully planned by the top and forced upon the people by a relatively small but extremely vigorous group in control of the movement."
33. Ibid., 86.
34. Ibid., 88.
35. Ibid., 92.
36. Oppler, "Legal Comments," September 1948, NARA RG 331, SCAP-GS, box 1498.
37. Ibid.
38. Ibid., 92.
39. Hellegers, *We, the Japanese People,* vol. 2, 463.
40. Ibid., 465.
41. See, generally, Moore and Robinson, *Partners for Democracy,* 73.
42. Matsumoto was notorious for his extreme arrogance and superiority. See, generally, Kosecki Shoichi, *The Birth of Japan's Postwar Constitution.* Edited and translated by Ray A. Moore (Boulder, CO: Westview Press, 1997), 61–62, 103–104. For the Japanese, the "underlying assumption seems to have been that the Meiji constitution was itself capable of development along democratic lines and that only minor tinkering was necessary to achieve this." Ward, "Present Japanese Constitution," 985.
43. See John Dower, *Embracing Defeat: Japan in the Wake of World War II* (New York: W. W. Norton, 1999), 157–158; Shunsuke Tsurumi, *An Intellectual History of Wartime Japan, 1931–1945* (London: KPI, 1986), 23.
44. See John W. Dower, *Empire and Aftermath: Yoshida Shigeru and the Japanese Experience, 1878–1954* (Cambridge, MA: Harvard University Press, 1988), 321; see also Dower, *Embracing Defeat,* 351–353; "The New Constitution of Japan," *PRJ,* vol. 1, 82.
45. Shoichi, *Japan's Postwar Constitution,* 78.
46. Dower, *Empire and Aftermath,* 321.
47. Hellegers, *We, the Japanese People,* vol. 2, 502–503.
48. Ibid., 505; see also Moore and Robinson, *Partners for Democracy,* 84–86.
49. See Takemae, *Inside GHQ,* 99–100.
50. See Hellegers, *We, the Japanese People,* vol. 2, 502–503.
51. See Ward, "Present Japanese Constitution," 990–991; see also Hellegers, *We, the Japanese People,* vol. 2, 246. For the thesis that SWNCC 228 impelled

SCAP to move forcefully on constitutional reform, see Williams, "Making the Japanese Constitution," 665–668.

52. Michael Schaller, *Altered States: The United States and Japan since the Occupation* (New York: Oxford University Press, 1997), 7; see also Ward, "Present Japanese Constitution," 987–990; Shoichi, *Japan's Postwar Constitution,* 68–69.
53. That the emperor had denied his divinity in an Imperial rescript on January 1, 1946, helped clear the way for constitutional reform involving the Imperial institution. As late as mid-January, at least one senior official at SCAP had told an FEC commissioner that SCAP was not considering amendments to the constitution on grounds that "fundamental changes" of that sort fell solely within the province of the FEC. Charles L. Kades, "The American Role in Revising Japan's Imperial Constitution," *Political Science Quarterly* 104, no. 2 (1989): 215, 218–219.
54. Whitney to MacArthur, "Constitutional Reform," February 1, 1946, DMHP, box 7.
55. Kades, "The American Role," 223.
56. See Hellegers, *We, the Japanese People,* vol. 2, 519–520.
57. Beate Sirota Gordon, *The Only Woman in the Room* (London: Kodansha International, 1997), 105.
58. Ibid.
59. See "The New Constitution of Japan," *PRJ,* vol. 1, 102.
60. Kades, "American Role," 225.
61. See SCAP-GS, "Summary Report on Meeting of the Government Section," February 4, 1946, DMHP, box 7.
62. For the most detailed profiles of the draftspersons, see Dower, *Embracing Defeat,* 364–365; see also Hellegers, *We, the Japanese People,* vol. 2, 521–525.
63. See Hellegers, *We, the Japanese People,* vol. 2, 519. Kades later claimed, however, that the GS drafting committees had reviewed and made "good advantage" of outlines of draft constitutions that had been produced by various groups of Japanese liberals and socialists. Kades, "American Role," 227.
64. Hellegers, *We, the Japanese People,* vol. 2, 580–584. For a more critical assessment of Sirota's contribution, see Mire Koikari, *Pedagogy of Democracy: Feminism and the Cold war in the US Occupation of Japan* (Philadelphia: Temple University Press, 2008), 3, 56–59. See also "Summary Report of Meeting of GS," February 4, 1946.
65. For instance, Beate Sirota was twenty-two years old when put in charge of drafting provisions concerning the basic rights of women. Sirota later admitted that she had known no more about this or any other aspect of constitutional law except what she could recall from her high school social studies classes. Gordon, *Only Woman in the Room,* 106.
66. See "The New Constitution of Japan," *PRJ,* vol. 1, 82–88; see also Shoichi, *Japan's Postwar Constitution,* 103; Ward, "Present Japanese Constitution," 1005.

67. The debate was especially intense over the subjects of executive powers, an amendment formula, judicial review, and civil rights. Hellegers, *We, the Japanese People,* vol. 2, 580.
68. Ibid., 580–581.
69. According to SCAP, the articles describing the fundamental rights of the people was rightly regarded as the "Japanese Bill of Rights." See "Brief Program Report on the Political Reorientation of Japan—Constitution," 1949, NARA RG 331, SCAP-GS, box 1446.
70. Ibid., 524; Moore and Robinson, *Partners for Democracy,* 101–103.
71. See Hellegers, *We, the Japanese People,* vol. 2, 522–524. There was disagreement about how to describe specific rights and over the decision to eliminate a charter of "social rights." See "Interview of Rowell," 93–94, 104–105, DMHP, box 5.
72. Ibid., 582; Robinson and Moore, *Partners for Democracy,* 98, 103.
73. See Shoichi, *Japan's Postwar Constitution,* 87.
74. See Hellegers, *We, the Japanese People,* vol. 2, app. J, 673–709.
75. "Interview with Milton Esman," 9, DMHP, box 2.
76. Ibid.
77. According to one Japanese scholar of the Meiji constitution, in Japan rights "were never thought of as something which existed before the constitution. They were regarded as the rights *of the subjects* but never as *human* rights." Miyazawa Toshiyoshi, as quoted in Richard H. Mitchell, *Justice in Japan: The Notorious Teijin Scandal* (Honolulu: University of Hawaii Press, 2002), 13.
78. See Robinson and Moore, *Partners for Democracy,* 108–109; Hellegers, *We, the Japanese People,* vol. 2, 527–528.
79. As one University of Tokyo law professor commented in 1949, the American insistence that the new constitution be written in the colloquial style (not in the courtly Japanese spoken and read by the Imperial elite) was to be considered of deep significance in terms of the popular comprehension and respect for the document. See translation of Miyazawa Toshiyoshi, "Outline Concerning the Reforms in Japan under the Control of the Allied Powers," January 10, 1949, NARA RG 331, SCAP-GS, box 1522. For detailed analysis of these issues, see Kyoko Inoue, *MacArthur's Japanese Constitution: A Linguistic and Cultural Study of Its Making* (Chicago: University of Chicago Press, 1991), 266–268.
80. See Moore, *Partners for Democracy,* 117.
81. See Shoichi, *Japan's Postwar Constitution,* 100–103; Hellegers, *We, the Japanese People,* vol. 2, 528. To Kades this was less a threat than the plain-spoken advice of a lawyer. Kades, "American Role," 230.
82. See Shoichi, *Japan's Postwar Constitution,* 109; "Record of Events," February 13, 1946, DMHP, box 7. See also Dower, *Empire and Aftermath,* 321
83. H. Fukui, "Twenty Years of Revisionism," *Washington Law Review* 43 (1968): 931, 932. See also Dower, *Embracing Defeat,* 377.

84. See Hellegers, *We, the Japanese People,* vol. 2, 529.
85. See John Owen Haley, *The Spirit of Japanese Law* (Athens: University of Georgia Press 2006), 17.
86. Shigeru Yoshida, *The Yoshida Memoirs: The Story of Japan in Crisis* (Boston: Houghton Mifflin, 1962), 133–135; Inoue, *MacArthur's Japanese Constitution,* 34–35; Hellegers, *We, the Japanese People,* vol. 2, 535.
87. For detailed analyses of the document, Robinson and Moore, *Partners for Democracy,* 107.
88. Ibid., 129.
89. This reflected the American idea of "making the courts, or at least a judicial body, the guardian of the constitution, rather than the legislative and / or executive authorities." See Carl Friedrich, "Political Theory of New Democratic Constitutions," in *Constitutions and Constitutional Trends Since World War II,* ed. Arnold John Zurcher (Westport, CT: Greenwood Press, 1955), 20–21.
90. Many English terms—"democracy" being only one prominent example—had no clear equivalent in colloquial Japanese. New Japanese words and combinations of words had to be invented in the process of translation. See William Manchester, interview of Kades for "American Caesar—Cineworld," with Charles Kades, October 21, 1982, PCLK, RG-5, box 1.
91. See Moore, *Partners for Democracy,* 120–121.
92. Ibid., 141, 331–332.
93. See Hellegers, *We, the Japanese People,* vol. 2, 537–538; see also Kades, "American Role," 233–234. Few Japanese constitutional experts attended these sessions; see also Ward, "Present Japanese Constitution," 998–999.
94. See Shoichi, *Japan's Postwar Constitution,* 111–112.
95. See "The New Constitution," *PRJ,* vol. 1, 109.
96. Dower, *Embracing Defeat,* 385.
97. Ibid.
98. The FEC wanted MacArthur to postpone the general election and pause for an extensive process of consultation and amendment. Shoichi, *Japan's Postwar Constitution,* 147–148.
99. See Shoichi, *Japan's Postwar Constitution,* 122–123.
100. Dower, *Embracing Defeat,* 385
101. See John M. Maki, "The Japanese Constitutional Style," *Washington Law Review* 43 (1968): 893, 903–904.
102. See, generally, Koikari, *Pedagogy of Democracy,* 1–31.
103. In fact, there was a broad consensus among Japanese politicians and law scholars that the new constitution should grant the Supreme Court very extensive powers of judicial review. Po Liang Chen and Jordan T. Wada, "Can the Japanese Supreme Court Overcome the Political Question Hurdle?" *Washington International Law Journal* 26 (April, 2017): 349–379, 352–353.
104. See Yoshida, *Memoirs,* 138.

105. See "The New Constitution," *PRJ,* vol. 1, 110.

106. For a general description of the deliberations of the Diet and other Japanese political institutions, see Theodore H. McNelly, "'Induced Revolution:' The Policy and Process of Constitutional Reform in Japan," in *Democratizing Japan: The Allied Occupation,* ed. Robert E. Ward and Sakamoto Yoshikazu (Honolulu: University of Hawaii Press, 1987), 76–105, 87–93.

107. Miyazawa Toshiyoshi, "Outline Concerning the Reforms in Japan," January 10, 1949, NARA RG 331, SCAP-GS, box 1522.

108. Edward H. Litchfield, "Political Objectives and Legal Bases of the Occupation Government," in *Governing Postwar Germany,* ed. Litchfield et al. (Ithaca, NY: Cornell University Press, 1953), 3–18, 22.

109. Jean Edward Smith, *Lucius D. Clay: An American Life* (New York: Holt, 1990), 238.

110. The French were particularly willing to exercise this veto in response to any attempt by the other three powers to revive German national institutions. John Gimbel, *The American Occupation of Germany: Politics and the Military, 1945–1949* (Stanford, CA: Stanford University Press, 1968), 16–17. See also Carolyn Woods Eisenberg, *Drawing the Line: The American Decision to Divide Germany, 1944–1949* (Cambridge: Cambridge University Press, 1996), 167–170.

111. Gimbel, *American Occupation,* 85–90.

112. Pollock was a University of Michigan political scientist, a specialist in German politics and government. *Constitutions of the German Länder,* AMG-Berlin, February 15, 1947, JKPP, box 61. Before the war ended, Pollock had been working as an expert consultant in German affairs at the War Department's School for Military Government in Virginia. Smith, *Lucius D. Clay,* 231.

113. Gimbel, *American Occupation,* 85–90; Rebecca L. Boehling, *A Question of Priorities: Democratic Reforms and Economic Recovery in Postwar Germany* (New York: Berghahn Books, 1996), 161.

114. Erich J. Hahn, "U.S. Policy on a West German Constitution," in *American Policy and the Reconstruction of West Germany, 1945–1955,* ed. Jeffrey M. Diendorf, Axel Frohn, and Hermann-Josef Rupieper (New York, 1993), 21–44, 23.

115. See "Clay Conversation with Hilldring," March 1, 1946, *The Papers of General Lucius Clay,* vol. 1, ed. Jean Edward Smith (Bloomington: Indiana University Press, 1974), 172. For a succinct summary of the American denazification program and its defects, see Boehling, *Question of Priorities,* 59–63.

116. See, for instance, Frank R. Pfetsch, *Verfassungspolitik der Nachkriegszeit: Theorie und Praxis des Bundesdeutschen Konstitutionalismus* (West Berlin: Wissenschaftliche Buchgesellschaft, 1985), 173. According to one historian, Clay felt that he had to trust the Germans and "when he did, it worked." Edward N. Peterson, *The American Occupation of Germany: Retreat from Victory* (Detroit: Wayne State University Press, 1977), 343.

117. Barbara Fait documents that the Americans took a strict hands-off approach to the development of new state constitutions in Germany. Hermann J. Rupieper, review of Barbara Fait, *Demokratische Erneuerung unter dem Sternenbanner: Amerikanische Kontrolle und Verfassunggebung in Bayern 1946* (Düsseldorf: Droste, 1998), *American Historical Review* 106, no. 2 (2001): 671; see also Hahn, "West German Constitution," 23; Michael Stolleis, "Besatzungsherrschaft und Wiederaufbau 1945–1949," in *Hanbuch des Staatsrechts,* vol. 1, 3rd ed., ed. Josef Isensee and Paul Kirchhof (Heidelberg, 2003), 7; Wilfried Mausbach, review of Adolf M. Birke, *Die Bundesrepublick Deutscheland: Verfassung, Parlament und Parteien* (Munchen: Oldenbourg, 1998), H-Net, August 24, 2017.
118. Clay to Russell, December 15, 1945, *Clay Papers,* vol. 1, 139.
119. Clay to Hilldring, March 1, 1946, *Clay Papers,* vol. 1, 172.
120. Ibid.
121. Smith, *Lucius D. Clay,* 243.
122. Litchfield, "Preface," *Constitutions of the German Länder,* AMG-Berlin, February 15, 1947, JKPP, box 61.
123. See *Clay Papers,* vol. 1, 76–77.
124. Smith, *Lucius D. Clay,* 231.
125. This according to multiple comments along these lines in the occupation diary of Karl Loewenstein. For example, LOD, January 13, 1946.
126. See Pollock to Clay, January 3, 1946, JKPP, box 61.
127. On more than one occasion, Loewenstein thought that Pollock had been less than honest with other advisers on constitutional reform. In one case, Pollock apparently was not forthright about information in January 1946 that "all three German Minister Presidents believe[d] that no election for constituent assemblies should be held in the near future." LOD, January 18, 1946.
128. See *Constitutions of the German Länder,* AMG-Berlin, February 15, 1947, 7, JKPP, box 61.
129. The ICGGS was led by senior civil affairs officer Edward Litchfield. The group consisted of AMG's leading experts on German law and politics, four from AMG's Internal Affairs and two each from the Legal and Political Affairs divisions.
130. Loewenstein to Madden, ICGGS, June 3, 1946, NARA RG 260, OMGUS Legal Division, box 91.
131. *Constitutions of the German Länder,* Civil Affairs Division, AMG Publications, 1947, 7.
132. Clay to War Department, "Constitutions for Länder in US Zone," August 23, 1946, in *Clay Papers,* vol. 1, 260.
133. See Pollock to Clay, January 3, 1946, JKPP, box 61.
134. Seymour Bolten to Deputy of Civil Affairs Division (hereafter referred to as CAD), November 26, 1945, JKPP, box 59.

135. Harold O. Lewis, *New Constitutions in Occupied Germany* (Washington, DC: Foundation for Foreign Affairs, 1948), iv; see also Michael Stolleis, "Besatzungsherrschaft und Wiederaufbau 1945–1949," in *Hanbuch des Staatsrechts,* vol. 1, 3rd ed., ed. Josef Isensee and Paul Kirchhof (Heidelberg, 2003), 7.
136. Loewenstein to Litchfield, "German Länder Constitutions," June 4, 1946, KLP, box 28.
137. Ibid.
138. As Loewenstein wrote in one memorandum on the subject, "But this writer feels that the Germans are performing, on a gigantic scale, what in Freudian psycho-analysis is known as the process of 'Vardrangung,' that is, eliminating from the mental awareness unpleasant facts. Because the Germans do not wish to partake of collective guilt, they pretend that such guilt does not exist." Lowenstein, "Report on Political and Social Conditions in South Germany," November 26, 1945, NARA RG 260, OMGUS Legal Division-Administration of Justice Branch (AJB), box 74.
139. Ibid.
140. In August 1945, Loewenstein learned of a case in which a local military detachment of AMG had reinstated a former Nazi Special Court judge who had sentenced forty-two persons to death by execution. LOD, August 30, 1945.
141. LOD, January 7, 1946.
142. LOD, January 31, 1946.
143. For the same interpretation of Bavarian intentions, see Lewis, *New Constitutions in Occupied Germany,* 6; see also Walter M. Hudson, "The U.S. Military Gov't and Democratic Reform and Denazification in Bavaria, 1945–47," Master of Military Art and Science thesis, faculty of the U.S. Army, 2001, 68.
144. Ibid., 66.
145. See LOD, March 1, 1946.
146. LOD, July 1, 1946.
147. See Loewenstein to Madden, ICGGS, June 3, 1946, NARA RG 260, OMGUS Legal Division, box 91.
148. Loewenstein to Litchfield, "German Länder Constitutions," June 5, 1946, KLP, box 45. See also Edmund Spevack, *Allied Control and German Freedom: American Political and Ideological Influences on the Framing of the West German Constitution (Grundgesetz)* (Munster: LIT, 2001), 101–110.
149. See Loewenstein to Litchfield, "Analysis of the Draft Constitution of Bavaria," June 21, 1946, KLP, box 45. The first Bavarian draft reflected an attempt to centralize political authority in the hands of a president. Lewis, *New Constitutions in Occupied Germany,* 7.
150. And yet, according to one scholar, "The failed constitution of Weimar was a model for most of the constitutional conventions." Spevack, *Allied Control,* 83.

151. Smith, *Clay Papers,* vol. 1, 212–213.
152. See "USFET from Eyster signed McNarney," July 11, 1946, NARA RG 260, OMGUS CAD-Executive Office (EO), box 10.
153. On July 9, Clay's immediate superior, General McNarney, held a press conference in Washington to announce these stipulations. See Smith, *Clay papers,* vol. 1, 241.
154. Robert G. Neumann, "New Constitutions in Germany," *American Political Science Review* 42, no. 3 (1948): 448.
155. Smith, *Clay Papers,* vol. 1, 240–241.
156. Litchfield, "Preface to the Constitutions of the German Länder," AMG-Berlin, February 15, 1947, JKPP, box 61.
157. Spevack, *Allied Control,* 92.
158. As will be discussed in chapter 6, in 1948–1949 Friedrich would also figure prominently in the development of a constitution for the new West German state. For more material on Friedrich's ideas, see Udi Greenberg, *The Weimar Century* (Princeton, NJ: Princeton University Press, 2014), 25–75; see also Udi Greenberg, "The Limits of Dictatorship and the Origins of Democracy: The Political Theory of Carl J. Friedrich from Weimar to the Cold War," in *The Weimar Moment: Liberalism, Political Theology, and Law,* ed. Leonard V. Kaplan and Rudy Koshar (Lanham, MD: Lexington, 2012), 443–464.
159. Spevack, *Allied Control,* 168–169.
160. See Udi Greenberg, "The Limits of Dictatorship and the Origins of Democracy: The Political Theory of Carl J. Friedrich from Weimar to the Cold War," in *The Weimar Moment: Liberalism, Political Theology, and Law,* ed. Rudy Koshar (New York: Roman & Littlefield, 2012), 443–464, at 444–455.
161. See Friedrich, "Military Government and Dictatorship," 5.
162. As Parkman informed American delegates to the constitutional assemblies, "It is important that the preparation of constitutions be considered primarily and fundamentally a problem for German government. . . . Every effort should be made to impress on the constitutional assembly the fact that the documents which they draw will be of their own making, that success in democracy in Germany is dependent upon the effectiveness of their assumption of responsibilities." Henry Parkman, memo to file, July 12, 1946, NARA RG 260, OMGUS CAD-EO, box 10.
163. Friedrich's assessment according to Henry Parkman. Parkman to Clay, "Procedure Relative to Länder Constitutional Assemblies," July 18, 1946, NARA RG 260, OMGUS CAD-EO, box 10.
164. Ibid.
165. See Constitution of Württemberg-Baden, Article 41, in *Constitutions of the German Länder,* AMG-Berlin, February 15, 1947, JKPP, box 61.
166. See Spevack, *Allied Control,* 83.
167. See LOD, July 19, 1946.
168. Ibid.

169. See Parkman to Clay, "Analysis of Land Constitutions," July 31 1946, NARA RG 260, OMGUS-Exec Office, box 10.
170. Neumann, "New Constitutions," 454.
171. For instance, one perceived "defect" of the Bavarian draft constitution was that it called for the establishment of a distinct Bavarian state citizenship. Lewis, *New Constitutions in Occupied Germany,* 7. See also Spevack, *Allied Control,* 86, 100.
172. See Murphy to Byrnes, "Länder Constitutions," July 30, 1946, NARA RG 260, OMGUS CAD-EO, box 10.
173. See Lewis, *New Constitutions in Occupied Germany,* 6–7. Spevack, *Allied Control,* 86, 100.
174. See Parkman to Clay, "Extension of Time," September 25, 1946, NARA RG 260, OMGUS CAD-EO, box 10.
175. See Weber to Clay, October 8, 1946, NARA OMGUS CAD-EO, box 10.
176. Spevack, *Allied Control,* 98–99.
177. Clay to Echols, "Constitutions for Länder in the US Zone," October 15, 1946, Smith, *Clay Papers,* vol. 1, 270–272.
178. Clay to AMG Officers, "Relationships between Military and Civil Government (U.S. Zone)," September 30, 1946, in Litchfield, *Governing Postwar Germany,* app. A, 537; see also Lucius D. Clay, *Decision in Germany* (New York: Doubleday, 1950), 78–80. It was of course very important to Clay that in his "Stuttgart Speech" of early September 1946, Secretary of State Byrnes had endorsed a policy of accelerated western German political and economic integration and development. For detailed analysis of this policy shift, see James McAllister, *No Exit: America and the German Problem, 1943–1954* (Ithaca, NY: Cornell University Press, 2002), 78–98.
179. Clay cable to War Department, October 9, 1946, NARA RG 260, OMGUS CAD-EO, box 10.
180. Spevack, *Allied Control,* 93.
181. War Department cable to Clay, October 10, 1946, NARA RG 260, OMGUS CAD-EO, box 10.
182. Spevack, *Allied Control,* 93.
183. Litchfield to Madden, October 9, 1946, NARA RG 260, OMGUS CAD, box 75.
184. Parkman to chief of staff, "Greater Hesse Constitution," October 7, 1946, NARA RG 260, OMGUS CAD-EO, box 10.
185. Spevack, *Allied Control,* 99.
186. In a rare instance of direct intervention, however, AMG ordered the Hessians to revise Article 41 to make it optional—but not mandatory—for the state to takeover privately-held business or industrial concerns. See Parkman to Clay, "Amendments to Hessian Constitution," October 7 and 14, 1946; Clay to Witte, October 7, 1946, NARA RG 260, OMGUS CAD-EO, box 10.

187. See Clay to Michael Horlacher, October 7, 1946, NARA RG 260, OMGUS CAD-EO, box 10.
188. See Clay to Wilhelm Simpfendpoerfer, October 7, 1946, NARA RG 260, OMGUS CAD-EO, box 10.
189. See "The Constitution of the Free State of Bavaria," in *Constitutions of the German Länder,* AMG-Berlin, February 15, 1947, JKPP, box 61.
190. Loewenstein to Litchfield, "Analysis of the Draft of a Bavarian Constitution," June 21, 1945, KLP, box 45.
191. "Baden-Wurttemberg," July 30, 1946, NARA RG 260, OMGUS CAD-EO, box 10.
192. See Neumann, "New Constitutions," 449–450.
193. In Bavaria, the constitution was adopted by a vote of 136–14, in Württemberg-Baden by a vote of 88–1, and in Hesse by a vote of 82–8. Ibid., 8.
194. In Württemberg-Baden, 72 percent of eligible voters went to the polls and nearly 69 percent voted in favor of the new constitution. In Hesse, nearly 73 percent of eligible voters cast a ballot, nearly 67 percent in favor of the constitution (in Hesse, in a separate referendum, nearly 63 percent voted in favor of Article 410, the provision on the expropriation of heavy industry by the Hessian state). Litchfield, "Preface to the Constitutions of the German Länder," NARA RG 260, OMGUS-Berlin, February 15, 1947, box 61. In Bavaria, 76 percent of the eligible voters voted, and nearly 68 percent voted in favor of adopting the new constitution, despite the anger of some of Bavarian voters in the frustration of their separatist ambitions. Spevack, *Allied Control,* 100–102.
195. See Spevack, *Allied Control,* 91.
196. Echols to Clay, December 6, 1946, NARA RG 260, OMGUS CAD-EO, box 10.
197. The composition of the assemblies determined by systems of proportional representation. Neumann, "New Constitutions," 448.
198. See Constitution of Hesse, Article 2. *Constitutions of the German Länder,* AMG-Berlin, February 15, 1947, JKPP, box 61.
199. Ibid., Article 43, Constitution of Württemberg-Baden.
200. Ibid., Article 1.
201. Ibid., Article 2.
202. Ibid., Article 11.
203. Ibid., Article 20.
204. Constitution of Hesse, Article 2.
205. Ibid., Article 5.
206. Ibid., Article 26.
207. Ibid., Article 24.
208. "Constitution of the Free State of Bavaria," Articles 1 and 2, in *Constitutions of the German Länder,* AMG-Berlin, February 15, 1947, JKPP, box 61.
209. Ibid., Articles 6 and 7.

210. Ibid., Article 15 and Article 119. Article 15 banned groups from acting to "suppress civil liberties or to use force against people." Article 119 forbade the incitement of "racial and national hatred."
211. As one historian observes, MacArthur's "single most important attribute was his vast and imposing authority—and the confidence with which he wielded it." Carol Gluck, "Entangling Illusions—Japanese and American Views of the Occupation," in *New Frontiers in American-East Asian Relations* ed. Warren I. Cohen and Dorothy Borg (New York: Columbia University Press, 1983), 196–197.
212. See, generally, Borgwardt, *A New Deal for the World,* 218–220.
213. Before 1947, the courts of Japan had no powers of judicial review of legislation. See Kisaburo Yokota, "Political Questions and Judicial Review: A Comparison," in *The Constitution of Japan: Its First Twenty Years, 1947–1967,* ed. Dan Fenno Henderson (Seattle: University of Washington Press, 1968), 141–166, 141.
214. For one of the first assertions of the imposition thesis, see Harold S. Quigley and John E. Turner, *The New Japan: Government and Politics* (Minneapolis: The University of Minnesota Press, 1956), 173–174; see also Moore and Robinson, *Partners for Democracy,* 111–112.
215. Gimbel, *American Occupation,* 47–49; Peterson, *Retreat to Victory,* 346.
216. Like the Americans, the French occupation administration set out basic liberal democratic goals for German state constitutions in the French zone and then let the Germans hash out details without intensive interference. In turn, the German drafters in the French zone were strongly influenced by state constitutional models developed in the U.S. zone. See F. Roy Willis, *The French in Germany 1945–1949* (Stanford, CA: Stanford University Press, 1962), 199–207. In the British zone, constitutional reform did not begin until 1947. In any event, the British had never seriously entertained the idea that it might cause the sudden and thorough democratization of German law and politics in its zone. The British occupation administration was content to permit German statesmen to adopt state constitution-making precedents already laid down in the U.S. and French zones, while it engaged in deliberations with its Western allies for the establishment of a West German federal state. See Barbara Marshall, "British Democratisation Policy in Germany," in *Reconstruction in Post-War Germany: British Occupation Policy and the Western Zones, 1945–55,* ed. Ian D. T. Turner (Oxford: Berg, 1989), 189–214.
217. Friedrich, "Military Government and Dictatorship," 5–6.
218. Neumann, "New Constitutions in Germany," 461.
219. Ibid., 463. In the result, ordinary German trial and appellate courts were denied the right to assess the constitutionality of legislation. That right was reserved to special constitutional courts. Donald Kommers, *The Constitutional Jurisprudence of the Federal Republic of Germany* (Durham, NC: Duke University Press, 1989), 8.

4. Crafting Liberal Courts

1. Alfred C. Oppler, "Courts and Law in Transition," *Contemporary Japan* XXI (1952), 19–49, 25.
2. The Berlin (Potsdam) Conference, July 17–August 2, 1945, Protocol, August 1, 1945, II. Political Principles, Article 8. Available at the Avalon Project, http://avalon.law.yale.edu/20th_century/decade17.asp.
3. "The Judicial and Legal System: Induced Revolution," *PRJ,* vol. 1, 186–245, 186.
4. David J. Danelski, "The Constitutional and Legislative Phases of the Creation of the Japanese Supreme Court," in *The Occupation of Japan: The Impact of Legal Reform,* ed. Lawrence H. Redford (Norfolk, VA: MacArthur Memorial, 1977), 29; Hugh Borton, "Abolition of Militarism and Strengthening of Democratic Process," State Department, Postwar Programs Committee, May 9, 1944, DMHP, box 16.
5. "Initial Post-Surrender Policy for Japan," August 29, 1945, *PRJ,* vol. 2, app. A, 423–426.
6. See John Owen Haley, *The Spirit of Japanese Law* (Athens: University of Georgia Press, 2006), 90–91; Haley, "Toward a Reappraisal of Occupation Legal Reforms: Administrative Accountability," in *Eibeihō Ronshū [Essays on Anglo-American Law]* (Hideo Tanaka Festschrift), ed. Fujukura (Tokyo: University of Tokyo Press, 1987), 543–567, at 543–545.
7. Ben-Ami Shillony, *Politics and Culture in Wartime Japan,* (Oxford, NY: Clarendon, 1981), 12–16.
8. See Dan Fenno Henderson, "Law and Political Modernization in Japan," in *Political Development in Modern Japan: Studies in the Modernization of Japan,* ed. Robert E. Ward (Princeton, NJ: Princeton University Press, 1968), 387–456, at 415. By the early twentieth-century, Japan, in one scholar's estimation, had achieved something akin to the German *rechtsstaat.*
9. Ichiro Ogawa, "Judicial Review of Administrative Actions in Japan," *Washington Law Review* 43 (1967–1968): 1075–1094, at 1075.
10. See Henderson, "Law and Political Modernization," 421. See also Alfred Oppler, *Legal Reform in Occupied Japan: A Participant Looks Back* (Princeton, NJ: Princeton University Press, 1976), 100.
11. SCAP's lead hand on judicial reform, Alfred Oppler, perceived that, "While the judges had to apply the rigid political laws during the war and did by no means show unusual courage, it is known that they resisted on the whole the attempts of the public procurators to enforce extremely severe penalties." Oppler, "Selection of Judges to the Supreme Court," April 30, 1947, NARA RG 331, SCAP-GS, box 2142.
12. See "The Pre-Surrender Judicial and Legal System," *PRJ,* vol. 1, 191–192; Oppler, *Legal Reform,* 86.

13. Takaati Hattori, "The Legal Profession in Japan: Its Historical Development and Present State," in *Law in Japan: The Legal Order in a Changing Society,* ed. Arthur Taylor von Mehren (Cambridge, MA: Harvard University Press, 1963), 111–152, 116–119, 121–123; D. S. Law, "Why Has Judicial Review Failed in Japan?" *Washington University Law Review* 88, no. 6 (2011): 1425–1466, at 1436.
14. Dale M. Hellegers, *We, the Japanese People: World War II and the Origins of the Japanese Constitution,* vol. 2 (Stanford, CA: Stanford University Press, 2001), app. G, 645–646.
15. "The Pre-Surrender Judicial and Legal System," *PRJ,* vol. 1, 192.
16. "Request of the Bar Association for Judicial Reform," n.d., DMHP, box 3.
17. "Various Reforms Asked by Lawyers' Federation," *Nippon Times,* September 27, 1945.
18. In their meeting with MacArthur, these lawyers, led by the leading prewar lawyer and politician Ichiro Kiyose, signaled their intention to resume the fight for the democratization of Japan, first taken up in the 1920s but interrupted by state-sponsored violence and intimidation in the 1930s. The lawyers had been outraged to discover that, on September 26, 1945, a political prisoner had died in prison, forty-two days after the surrender. Dmitri Vanoverbeke, *Juries in the Japanese Legal System: The Continuing Struggle for Citizen Participation and Democracy* (London: Routledge, 2015), 92–93.
19. Lawrence Repeta, "Reserved Seats on Japan's Supreme Court," *Washington University Law Review* 88, no. 6 (2011): 1713, 1715–1716.
20. "Leading Barristers Call on MacArthur," *Nippon Times,* December 8, 1945. See also Hussey, "Request of the Bar Association for Judicial Reform," December 7, 1945, DMHP, box 3.
21. Hellegers, *We, the Japanese People,* vol. 2, 646. Hussey, "Request of the Bar Association for Judicial Reform," Hussey papers, 58-A, DMHP, box 3.
22. See "A Thorough Reform of the Justice System," *Mainichi Shimbun,* February 2, 1946.
23. Oppler, *Legal Reform,* 100.
24. See Hellegers, *We, the Japanese People,* vol. 2, 647; see also Danelski, "Japanese Supreme Court," 38–39; see also John Owen Haley, "The Japanese Judiciary: Maintaining Integrity, Autonomy, and the Public Trust," in *The Law in Japan: A Turning Point,* ed. David Foote (Seattle: University of Washington Press, 2007), 99–135, 118.
25. As quoted in Haley, "Japanese Judiciary," 118.
26. See Oppler, *Legal Reform,* 67.
27. See Haley, "Japanese Judiciary," 118. In one scholar's opinion, here the Americans placed "a very large bet on the role played by the Supreme Court in Japan's development as a democratic society." Danelski, "Japanese Supreme Court," 48–49.

28. Alfred C. Oppler, "The Reform of Japan's Judicial and Legal System Under Allied Occupation," n.d., NARA RG 331, SCAP-GS, box 1450.
29. Oppler, *Legal Reform,* 68.
30. In his recruitment interview, Oppler recalled that he had "volunteered the confession that, although I had some familiarity with European affairs, I did not have any knowledge of things Japanese." Oppler further recalled that his ignorance of Japan was viewed as an asset, since MacArthur wanted to recruit men without a lot of preconceived and thus conservative views on Japan. Ibid., 12.
31. Ibid., 66.
32. Ibid., 5–8.
33. Oppler's memoirs do not provide the precise date or year that he was ousted from judicial office. He admitted only to having had "experienced several years of the Nazi regime." See Oppler to Hellegers, March 14, 1969, ACOP, box 43.
34. At that point, Oppler was "fed up with German problems" and had actively sought out work with a "different people and civilization." Oppler, *Legal Reform,* 11.
35. Ibid., 12.
36. Ibid., 34.
37. Apart from his book length study of legal reconstruction in Japan, *Legal Reform in Occupied Japan* (1976), Oppler published a number of scholarly articles on the subject of judicial reform in Japan. For example, see Alfred C. Oppler, "The Reform of Japan's Legal and Judicial System under Allied Occupation," *Washington Law Review* 24 (1949): 290–323.
38. The reviewer Chalmers Johnson dismissed Oppler's book as an "essentially defensive, platitudinous reminiscence." Chalmers Johnson, "Review of Alfred C. Oppler, *Legal Reform in Occupied Japan*," *American Journal of Comparative Law* 25 (1977): 189–192, at 190.
39. For background on Blakemore, see John Owen Haley, *Authority without Power: The Japanese Paradox* (New York: Oxford University Press, 1991), 105.
40. Oppler claimed that the American occupation of Japan was the "most enlightened and effective military occupation in history." Oppler to Dale Hellegers, March 14, 1969, ACOP, box 4.
41. Ibid.
42. "Recurring Encounters: Personal Perspectives on Thomas L. Blakemore's Career Contributions to Japanese Law," in *Law and Practice in Postwar Japan: The Postwar Legal Reforms and their Influence: Symposium Honoring the Contributions and Career of Thomas L. Blakemore* (Tokyo: Blakemore Foundation and International House of Japan, 2010), 27–34, 32.
43. *PRJ,* vol. 1, 186–87.
44. Ibid.
45. Oppler, *Legal Reform,* 37.
46. Ibid., 83.
47. Blakemore to Chief, May 31, 1946, NARA RG 331, SCAP-GS, box 2142.

48. See "Induced Revolution," *PRJ,* vol. 2, 187.
49. Ibid.; Oppler, *Legal Reform,* 36.
50. Oppler, *Legal Reform,* 73.
51. Ibid.
52. Oppler, "Reform of Japan's Legal and Judicial System," 303.
53. Blakemore to Chief, May 31, 1946, NARA RG 331, SCAP-GS, box 2142.
54. Oppler, "Reform of Japan's Legal and Judicial System," 306; "Selection of Judges to the Supreme Court," April 30, 1947, NARA RG 331, SCAP-GS, box 2142. The relevant sections of Oppler's book, *Legal Reform in Occupied Japan,* barely hint that court and judicial reform had been a divisive process, one fiercely resisted by conservative factions within the Japanese political, legal, and bureaucratic elite. For this conflict-free account, see Oppler, *Legal Reform,* 72–103.
55. Oppler, *Legal Reform,* 87–88.
56. "A Thorough Reform of the Justice System."
57. Quoted in "Elections and the Judiciary," NARA RG 331, SCAP-GS, box 1496.
58. Oppler, *Legal Reform,* 190; "Reform of Japan's Legal and Judicial System," 306–307; Hugh Borton, "Abolition of Militarism and Strengthening of Democratic Process," State Department, Postwar Programs Committee, May 9, 1944, NARA RG 59, in DMHP, box 16.
59. Oppler, "Address to the Tokyo Bar Associations," 1949, NARA RG 331, SCAP-GS, box 1450.
60. "Request of the Bar Association for Judicial Reform," n.d., Hussey papers 58-A, DMHP, box 3.
61. Oppler, *Legal Reform,* 88.
62. Ibid., 89.
63. Shigeru Yoshida, *The Yoshida Memoirs: The Story of Japan in Crisis* (Boston: Houghton Mifflin, 1962), 70.
64. Kimura later engineered the reassertion of conservative political control over the Supreme Court. See Setsuo Miyazawa, "Administrative Control of Japanese Judges," *Kobe U. L. Rev.* 25 (1991): 45–61, at 58. On November 1, 1948, in private conversation with Oppler, former Supreme Court Justice Chono condemned Kimura as a fascist. Chono also recommended Hosono for the job. Oppler repeated that this was not possible. Oppler, "Activity Reports," November 1, 1948, NARA RG 331, SCAP-GS, box 1522.
65. Oppler, *Legal Reform,* 76.
66. Given his relative youth (38 years) and newness to a largely unpurged bureaucracy of older and experienced men, one wonders just how influential Naito actually was. Naito came in February 1946 as the government made sweeping personnel changes in the ministry. See "Yorihiro Naito (1908–2000)," obituary, in *Japanese Annual Review of International Law* 44 (2001): 5–7.
67. Oppler, *Legal Reform,* 76.

68. Hosono led a small faction of the justices of the unreformed Supreme Court of Japan who strongly supported the liberal-democratic reform of the Japanese judiciary under the new constitution. See Oppler, "Selection of Judges to the Supreme Court," April 30, 1947, NARA RG 331, SCAP-GS, box 2142.
69. See Oppler to Chief, May 9, 1947, DMHP, box 4.
70. "Memorandum for the Chief," March 28, 1946, NARA RG 331, SCAP-GS, box 1500; see also Hellegers, "Interview with Oppler," March 31, 1969, DMHP, box 4. Here, Hellegers describes the close working relationship he had with Hosono.
71. See Oppler, *Legal Reform,* 39–40.
72. Hosono to MacArthur, September 18, 1946, NARA RG 331, SCAP-GS, box 2142.
73. See Haruhiro Fukui, "Postwar Politics, 1945–1973," in *The Cambridge History of Japan,* vol. 6, ed. Peter Duus (Cambridge: Cambridge University Press, 2008), 180–181.
74. Ibid. Hosono claimed that in the war years he had tried to defy Tojo's meddling with the independence of the courts.
75. "Memorandum for the Executive Committee in Charge of SPLIC," September 30, 1946, NARA RG 331, SCAP-GS, box 1505.
76. Ibid. By this procedure, the Supreme Court was to exercise exclusive jurisdiction to decide the constitutionality of a law without there having been "an initial decision by the judge of an inferior court, as well as their right to refrain from an appeal against the decision of such a court." In Blakemore's view, one that prevailed in the final draft, "The issue of constitutionality of legislation cannot be successfully and properly considered apart from facts."
77. "Conversations with members of the Tokyo Bar Association," November 21, 1946, NARA RG 331, SCAP-GS, box 1484.
78. "Freedom Demanded of Judicial Power," *Nippon Times,* November 14, 1946.
79. Oppler to Chief, December 4, 1946, NARA RG 331, SCAP-GS, box 2142.
80. In the early 1950s, Kimura's anti-communism was so rabid and ruthless that he became known as the "Joe McCarthy of Japan." See, generally, Glenn Davis and John G. Roberts, *An Occupation without Troops: Wall Street's Half-Century Domination of Japan* (Tokyo: Yen Press, 1996), chapter eight, note 4.
81. See "Statement of Justice Chono," January 8, 1947, NARA RG 331, SCAP-GS, box 1499. See also Oppler, "Selection of Judges to the Supreme Court," April 30, 1947, NARA RG 331, SCAP-GS, box 2142.
82. "In Confidence: Statement of Justice Chono to Blakemore," January 8, 1947, NARA RG 331, SCAP-GS, box 1484.
83. Translator Tanaka, "Gist of the Letter Addressed to Minister Kimura from Judge Chono," April 8, 1947, NARA RG 331, SCAP-GS, box 1496.
84. Ibid. In a letter addressed to AG Kimura personally, Chono alleged that Kimura had "done many things inimical to the healthy development of the

judiciary system." Instead of bolstering the "Iwata policy" of judicial independence, Kimura had caused reversals in these areas. See also Vanoverbeke, *Juries,* 93.

85. Among the bill's many perceived defects was that it made no provision to protect the authority of the new Supreme Court to control its rules and procedures. It was also vague regarding the structure, jurisdiction, and powers of the subordinate courts. Nor did it make specific provision to protect the security of judicial tenure or the mechanism by which judicial vacancies would be filled. From the point of view of the independence and integrity of the new system, the bill's most glaring fault was that it restricted jurisdiction for appeals against the administrative actions of the state to the Supreme Court, swelling the cost and time involved in such appeals and thereby severely limiting access of citizens to judicial review. See "Court Organization Law," n.d., NARA RG 331, SCAP-GS, box 1505.
86. "Memorandum for the Record," February 13, 1947, NARA RG 331, SCAP-GS, box 1681.
87. "Conference Proceedings," February 28, 1947, NARA RG 331, SCAP-GS, box 1522.
88. *PRJ,* vol. 1, 201; Repeta, "Reserved Seats on Japan's Supreme Court," 1718–1719.
89. The main goal of the conservatives going forward was to retain the customary practice that appointments to the Supreme Court be limited to "inside lawyers" within the bureaucracy. See Repeta, "Reserved Seats," 1717.
90. See Oppler to Chief, "Gist of the Ministry of Justice Laws passed by the last Diet," May 1, 1947, 4, NARA RG 331, SCAP-GS, box 1496.
91. In this way the resolution of the budget issue marked a significant defeat for the conservatives at the Ministry of Justice. See Repeta, "Reserved Seats," 1716.
92. Oppler, "Selection of Judges to the Supreme Court," April 30, 1947, NARA RG SCAP-GS, box 2142.
93. SCAP Press Conference, "The Reform of Criminal Procedure," April 23, 1947, RG 331, SCAP-GS, box 1498.
94. For the most thorough discussion of the Japanese-language sources on the first postwar Supreme Court, see Shin-ichi Nishikawa, "Saikosai no Rutsu wo Saguru (Uncovering the Roots of the Supreme Court)," *Seikei Ronso* 78, no. 1–2 (2009): 1.
95. Tokyo Bar Association (no. 1) to Oppler, "Petition regarding the democratization of the Judicature of Japan," February 2, 1947, NARA RG 331, SCAP-GS, box 1522.
96. Oppler, "Selection of Judges to the Supreme Court," April 30, 1947, NARA RG 331 SCAP-GS, box 2142.
97. Tanaka, "The Government ignores the New Constitution," Letter from the Supreme Court, April 11, 1947, NARA RG 331, SCAP-GS box 1496.

98. Repeta, "Reserved Seats," 1718–1719.
99. "Judicial Appointment Co-ordinating Committee," Minutes, April 19, 1947, NARA RG 331, SCAP-GS, box 2142.
100. Among them were the private lawyers from the Tokyo Bar Association (No. 1), a group that had already denounced Hosono and his own bid to become chief justice of the new Supreme Court. Tokyo Bar Association (No. 1) to Oppler, "Petition Regarding the Democratization of the Judicature of Japan," February 3, 1947, NARA RG 331, SCAP-GS, box 1522.
101. Ibid.
102. Hosono to MacArthur, April 28, 1947, NARA RG 331, SCAP-GS, box 1499.
103. Members of the Tokyo Bar Association, "Letter of Opinion Regarding the Appointment of Judges of the Supreme Court," August 1, 1947, NARA RG 331, SCAP-GS, box 1498.
104. Oppler, "Selection of Judges to the Supreme Court," April 30, 1947, NARA SCAP-GS, box 2142.
105. Ibid.
106. See Danelski, "Japanese Supreme Court," 52.
107. "Regarding the Recent Court Problems," published in the *Yomiuri Shimbun,* July 11, 1947, RG 331, SCAP-GS, box 1499.
108. Oppler to Chief, "List of Candidates," July 23, 1947, RG 331, SCAP-GS box 1500.
109. Connors to Chief, "Irregularities in the Election of Judges," July 19, 1947, NARA RG 331, SCAP-GS, box 1500.
110. See Hosono to Katayama, July 28, 1947, NARA RG 331, SCAP-GS, box 1498.
111. See Danelski, "Japanese Supreme Court," 52.
112. "Supreme Court Judges," *Nippon Times,* July 27, 1947.
113. "Letter of Opinion Regarding the Appointment of Judges of the Supreme Court," August 1, 1947, NARA RG 331, SCAP-GS box 1498; McCormick to Chief, "Appointment of Judges," August 1, 1947. NARA RG 331, SCAP-GS box 1498.
114. "Tadahiko Mibuchi, Chief Justice of the Supreme Court," *Nippon Times,* August 30, 1947.
115. Ibid.
116. Untitled, *Maimishi Shimbun,* July 30, 1947, in "Press Analysis," August 2, 1947, NARA RG 331, SCAP-GS, box 1445.
117. According to Blakemore, "The appointment to the Court will constitute a financial loss for almost every member of the Court." See Blakemore, "Memo for the Record," August 6, 1947, NARA SCAP-GS, box 1500.
118. Justices Chono and Matsuo Nemoto. See Danielski, "Japanese Supreme Court," 51.
119. Ibid.

120. See "Biographies of Members of Japan's New Supreme Court," NARA RG 331, SCAP-GS, box 1500.
121. Oppler, "Legal and Judicial System," 308.
122. The poor pay and morale of judges was a matter of particular concern to SCAP. "Social and Economic Conditions of Judges," Press Conference, October 8, 1948, NARA RG 331, SCAP-GS, box 1498.
123. See, for example, "The Ozugumi Market Case," December 16, 1947; "The Kikunami Case," December 17, 1947; "The Sekine Case," December 18, 1947, NARA RG 331, SCAP-GS, box 1500.
124. Bail was granted with the consent of the procurator and endorsement of the three presiding judges. Oppler was almost alone in his conclusion that in the Ozu case the Tokyo judges had not been corrupt, merely incompetent. They simply had failed to "grasp the political, ethical and social significance of the individual case they had to decide." Oppler, "Poor Administration of Justice by the Courts," NARA RG 331, SCAP-GS, box 1500; Meyers, "Memo for the Record: Case of Ozu," November 17, 1947, NARA RG 331, SCAP-GS, box 1500.
125. See Oppler, *Legal Reform,* 225.
126. Ibid.
127. Ibid.
128. "Minutes: Conference in Government Section," November 17, 1947, NARA RG 331, SCAP-GS, box 1500.
129. See SCAP-HQ, "History of the Non-Military Activities of the Occupation of Japan—Volume V—Civil Liberties—Part 1," NARA RG 331, SCAP-Historical, box 3634.
130. Ibid.
131. See "Suspension of Bail in the Maki and Sasaki Cases," November 8 and 15, 1948, NARA RG 331, SCAP-GS, box 1500.
132. Ozu finally was convicted and sentenced for black-marketeering and extortion in 1948. See Oppler, "Slow Administration of Justice in the Ozu case," June 5, 1948, NARA RG 331, SCAP-GS, box 1500. See also SCAP-HQ, "History of the Non-Military Activities of the Occupation of Japan—Volume V—Civil Liberties—Part 1," NARA RG 331, SCAP-Historical, box 3634.
133. In one especially damaging incident in February 1948, Justice Riichi Shono publicly accused another jurist (Dr. Eiichi Makino) of taking a bribe in order to cause the purge of a political rival. This led to a divisive conflict within the Supreme Court over whether Justice Shono should be impeached. Shono ultimately resigned from the Court after being sued for libel. See Colonel Jack Napier, "Supreme Court: Shono vs. Makino," NARA RG 331, SCAP-GS, box 2187. See also Oppler, "Minutes of Conference," March 2, 1948, NARA RG 331, SCAP-GS, box 1522.
134. The scandal led to the indicted of sixty-four persons, including a number of cabinet ministers. It also led to the fall of the Asida (Liberal) government.

See, generally, Yoneyuki Sugita, *Pitfall or Panacea: The Irony of U.S. Power in Occupied Japan, 1945–1952* (New York: Routledge, 2003), 55.

135. In at least one case, the Supreme Court reversed, on constitutional grounds, the decision of two lower courts in throwing out a conviction in a criminal case that had been based on a confession elicited after a prolonged period of detention. Oppler warmly endorsed the Court's decision in that case. See "SCAP Chief Lauds Supreme Court," *Nippon Times,* July 31, 1948.
136. "Fundamental Principles of [German] Judicial Reform," Allied Control Council, *Official Gazette of the Control Council for Germany,* No. 1, October 29, 1945, 6; "Reorganization of the German Judicial System," Allied Control Council, *Official Gazette of the Control Council for Germany,* No. 2, November 30, 1945, 26.
137. "Reorganization of the German Judicial System," Article IV.
138. Ibid.
139. See Edith Raim, *Nazi Crimes against Jews and German Post-War Justice: The West German Judicial System During Allied Occupation (1945–1949)* (Berlin: Oldenbourg, 2015), 30–44.
140. "Directive to the Commander-in-Chief of the United States Forces of Occupation Regarding the Military Government of Germany (JCS 1067)," *Documents on Germany, 1944–1985* (Washington, DC: U.S. State Department, 1985), 15–32.
141. Ibid., s. 11 (a).
142. The details were set forth in the "Basic Plan for the Administration of Justice–U.S. Zone." See Karl Loewenstein, "Justice," in *Governing Postwar Germany,* ed. Edward H. Litchfield (Ithaca, NY: Cornell University Press, 1953), 236–262, 237.
143. Ibid., 238.
144. Gimbel, *American Occupation of Germany,* 47–51; Rebecca L. Boehling, *A Question of Priorities: Democratic Reforms and Economic Recovery in Postwar Germany: Frankfurt, Munich, and Stuttgart under U.S. Occupation, 1945–1949* (New York: Berghahn, 1998), 210–214.
145. "Ordinary" courts meaning the local (Amtsgerichte) and state (Landgerichte) courts. See Stolleis, *The Law Under the Swastika: Studies on Legal History in Nazi Germany* (Chicago: University of Chicago Press, 1998), 172.
146. See Raim, *Nazi Crimes against Jews,* 30–33; 68–70.
147. For a discussion of the extreme conservative nationalism of some Bavarian judges during the Weimar republic, see Douglas G. Morris, *Justice Imperiled: The Anti-Nazi Lawyer Max Hirschberg in Weimar Germany* (Ann Arbor: University of Michigan Press, 2005), 1–2, 128–129.
148. For a concise summary, see Thomas Vormbaum and Michael Bohlander, eds., *A Modern History of German Criminal Law* (New York: Springer Verlag, 2014), 200–201.

149. Kenneth F. Ledford, "Judging Judges in the Third Reich," in *The Law in Nazi Germany: Ideology, Opportunism, and the Perversion of Justice,* eds. Alan E. Steinweis and Robert D. Rachlin (New York: Berghahn, 2013), 167–168.
150. For scholarly commentary on this point, see Nikolaus Wachsmann, "'Soldiers on the Home Front': Jurists and Legal Terror during the Second World War," in *Nazism, War and Genocide: Essays in Honour of Jeremy Noakes,* ed. Neil Gregor (Exeter: Exeter University Press, 2008), 75–92, 75–78.
151. Loewenstein to Fahy, September 14, 1945, NARA RG 260, LD-Advice, box 52.
152. As one American civil affairs officer in Hesse had observed in November 1946: "Distress of mind and political and economic tension in the population is reaching a breaking point . . . the government will have to adopt a more rigid attitude in order to prevent the situation from getting out of hand. In order to meet the increase in criminality it is considered necessary to relieve the administration of criminal justice as much as possible from arrears of work." Backer to Potter, "Special Report on Personnel Crisis in the Administration of Justice," November 18, 1946, NARA RG 260, LD-AJB, box 74. See, generally, Thomas Kehoe, "Control, Disempowerment, Fear, and Fantasy: Violent Criminality During the Early American Occupation of Germany, March–July 1945," *Australian Journal of Politics and History* 62 (2016): 561–575, at 561–563.
153. Henry H. Urman to Fahy, "Reopening of the Oberlandesgerichte," September 7, 1945, NARA RG 260, LD-AJB, box 88; Woolf Committee, "Supplemental Report," September 24, 1945, NAUK FO 1060 / 1099.
154. Loewenstein to Fahy, September 14, 1945, NARA RG 260, LD-Advice, box 52.
155. The elimination of the Jews from the professions had been preceded by the annulment of the legal rights of some 800,000 persons stigmatized as Jews or partial Jews. See, generally, Claudia Koonz, *The Nazi Conscience* (Cambridge, MA, Harvard University Press, 2005), 169–172.
156. Ibid. See also Howard Becker, "An Interview of Marianne Weber," *American Journal of Economics and Sociology,* 10 (1951): 401–405.
157. "Legal Action under the Potsdam Decisions," Memorandum by British Member, August 31, 1945, NARA RG 260, ACC-DLeg / P(45)17, box 173; "Legal Action under the Potsdam Decisions," Memorandum by United States Member, September 10, 1945, NARA RG 260, ACC-DLeg / P(45)17, box 173.
158. "Legal Action under the Potsdam Decisions," Memorandum by British Member, August 31, 1945, NARA RG 260, ACC-DLeg / P(45)17, box 173.
159. Fifth Meeting of DLeg, September 19–20, 1945, NARA RG 260, ACC-DLeg / 18(45) 5, box 173.
160. "Legal Action under the Potsdam Decisions," Memorandum by British Member, August 31, 1945, NARA RG 260, ACC-DLeg / P(45) 13.

161. Fourth Meeting of DLeg, September 15, 1945, NARA RG 260, ACC-DLeg/P(45)17, box 173.
162. Ibid.
163. Ibid.
164. To that point the relatively small number of German local and regional courts in operation were staffed by judges appointed on a temporary basis by local detachments of AMG. The decision to reopen (or not) German courts was left to local detachments of American Military Government, then, starting in 1946, to the Ministers of Justice in the Länder. See, generally, Loewenstein, *Legal Reconstruction in Germany,* 44–45, KLP, box 24.
165. Rosenbaum, "Denazification, September 9, 1945, JKPP, box 61.
166. Clarence C. Neslen to Director, September 5, 1945, NARA RG 260, LD-AJB, box 88.
167. Brigadier-General R.B. Lovett to Commanding Generals, Eastern and Western Districts, "Administration of Justice," October 4, 1945, RG 260, OMGUS Legal Division-Administration of Justice Branch (AJB), box 88. According to Loewenstein, by mid-1946, "practically the entire administration of justice in the technical sense was turned over to the Germans and Military Government maintained a marginal supervision." Karl Loewenstein, *Legal Reconstruction in Germany,* c. 1948, unpublished ms., 41, KLP, box 24.
168. LOD, December 28, 1945, KLP, box 46; Loewenstein to Fahy, "Press Report on a Scandalous Trial," December 27, 1945, KLP, box 28.
169. Loewenstein to Fahy, "Press Report on a Scandalous Trial," December 27, 1945, KLP, box 28. The deserter was then discharged on time served (two years) in prison. The tribunal reduced the soldier's sentence to two years based on his war record with the Afrika Corps.
170. Karl Loewenstein, "Reconstruction of the Administration of Justice in American-Occupied Germany," *Harvard Law Review* 61 (1948), 419–467, at 434.
171. LOD, December 28, 1945, KLP, box 46.
172. LOD, January 28, 1946, KLP, box 46.
173. LOD, January 31, 1946, KLP, box 46.
174. See Andrew Szanajda, *Indirect Perpetrators: The Prosecution of Informers in Germany, 1945–1965* (Toronto: Lexington, 2012), 1–5. See also Raim, *Nazi Crimes against Jews and German Post-War Justice,* 115–142.
175. Walter H. Menke to Shepard, "Draft Law on the Redress of National-Socialist Injustice," March 21, 1946, NARA RG 260, OMGUS LD-AJB, box 74.
176. See Loewenstein to Madden, "Draft Law on the Redress of National-Socialist Injustice," February 19, 1946, NARA RG 260, OMGUS LD-AJB, box 74.
177. LOD, March 13, 1946, KLP, box 46.
178. LOD, April 10, 1946, KLP, box 46.
179. LOD, April 5, 1946, KLP, box 46; see also Shepard to Madden, Memorandum, April 5, 1946, NARA RG 260, OMGUS Legal Division-AJB, box 74.

180. Loewenstein to Fahy, "Plan for the Supervision and Administration of the German Courts," March 25, 1946, NARA RG 260, OMGUS LD-AJB, box 74.
181. LOD, April 20, 1946, KLP, box 46.
182. Loewenstein, *Legal Reconstruction in Germany,* 44, KLP, box 24.
183. Loewenstein to McLendon, "Plan for the Supervision of German Courts," April 29, 1946, and May 28, 1946, KLP, box 28.
184. LOD, March 18, 1946, KLP, box 46.
185. LOD, April 20, 1946, KLP, box 46.
186. Madden's pick was the German émigré lawyer, Max Rheinstein. Loewenstein was contemptuous of what he viewed as Rheinstein's strange, even neurotic desire to exonerate former Nazi jurists. As Loewenstein bitterly diarized on April 25, 1946, "Rheinstein is a true fifth columnist and doesn't wish to touch the pure and nice Germans. . . . They will be alright after what they have suffered, look at their wantonly destroyed cities, etc. He does not remember that after 1919 the courts undermined deliberately the young republic, to the delight of the entire bourgeoisie. . . . I try and hold him back so at least the internal controls which the Germans themselves wish to institute will get into our final draft."
187. The draft plan called for the use as supervisors of "former referendars (graduates of law who had not yet qualified for the German bar) who left Germany after Hitler." In Loewenstein's opinion, referendars had far too little experience and prestige "to be capable of exercising the function of control" over judges. Loewenstein to McLendon, April 29, 1946, KLP, box 28.
188. Loewenstein now thought that the best approach was by indirect American supervision of the Läend Ministers of Justice and their direct supervision of "judicial trends." Loewenstein to Madden, "Plan for the Supervision of the German Courts," May 28, 1946, KLP, box 51.
189. Ibid.
190. LOD, May 27, 1946, KLP, box 46.
191. In his private diary, Loewenstein was caustically critical of McLendon and Shepard both in their lack of dedication and relevant expertise. After having working for Shepard for many months, Loewenstein concluded that he was too "stupid" for such a challenging job. As for McLendon, he was "a charming Southern gentleman" in an office far beyond his intellectual depth and training. "Here we have an administration of justice branch run by an army colonel who goes after antiques, a country lawyer who knows no German law and nothing of Germany." LOD, July 2, 1946, KLP, box 46.
192. Loewenstein to Madden, "Plan for the Supervision of the German Courts," May 28, 1946, KLP, box 28.
193. For Clay's own comments on the crime problem in 1948, see *The Papers of General Lucius Clay,* vol. 1, ed. Jean Edward Smith (Bloomington: Indiana University Press, 1974), 566–567.

194. Urman to Rockwell, "German Courts," January 9, 1947, NARA RG 260, OMGUS Legal Division-Advice, box 61.
195. Before the war, Rockwell, like Fahy and Madden before him, had worked at the National Labor Relations Board. Like his predecessors, he came to Legal Division without specialized knowledge of Germany or German law. See "Biographical Sketch," AJRP, box 1; Rockwell, obituary, *New York Times,* May 20, 1999.
196. Robert L. Guthrie to Major Kraus, "Removal of Nazis," January 17, 1947, NARA RG 260, OMGUS Legal Division-AJB, box 76.
197. Jeffrey S. Gaab, *Justice Delayed: The Restoration of Justice in Bavaria under American Occupation, 1945–1949* (New York: Lang, 1999), 62.
198. NARA RG 260, ACC-DLeg, January 24, 1947 (DLEG / M(47)3), 5.
199. NARA RG 260, ACC-DLeg, January 31, 1947 (DLEG / P(47)1), 7.
200. "Extraordinary Meeting of DLeg on Joint Report," ACC-DLeg, January 25, 1947, Allied Control Authority Papers, Hoover Institution, Stanford.
201. "Minutes of the Conference at the Bavarian Ministry of Justice," July 25, 1947, NARA RG 260, OMGUS Legal Division-Weigert correspondence, box 132.
202. See Boehling, *Question of Priorities,* 239. By this time, the main effect of the tribunals was to remove the stigma of Nazism from former Nazi party members and officials. For a thorough review of how this operated in the case of Nazi jurists in Hesse, see Szanajda, *Justice in Postwar Hesse,* 128–136, 139; Gaab, *Justice Delayed,* 64–65.
203. "Directive to the Commander in Chief of the US Forces of Occupation (JCS 1779), in Velma H. Cassidy, *Germany 1947–1949: The Story in Documents* (Honolulu: University Press of the Pacific, 2005), 33–41.
204. Ibid., part IV, 34.
205. Ibid., part IV, sub. 11.
206. By 1948, AMG officials in the Länder reported the "growing tendency to obstructionism and procrastination in carrying out MG directives." See Edward Litchfield, director of CAD, "Democratization of Germany," February 4, 1948, NARA RG 260, OMGUS CAD-Bavaria, box 6.
207. G. H. Garde to Land Directors of OMGUS, "German Courts," July 22, 1947, OMGUS Legal Division-Weigert Correspondence, box 132.
208. For a review of the denunciation subcategory of these cases, see, generally, Szanajda, *Indirect Perpetrators,* 29–49.
209. Weigert to Mr. Haven Parker and Mr. Alvin Rockwell, "Field Trip to Bremen," September 19, 1947, NARA RG 260, OMGUS Legal Division-Weigert Correspondence, box 132.
210. The accused were on trial for killings that had taken place (on order of Nazi officials) on the infamous *Kristallnacht.* On their original trial in 1938, the men had been acquitted. Convicted of murder in the postwar trial, the accused received sentences of six and eight years, respectively. *Der Tagesspiegel,*

May 30, 1947, in NARA RG 260, OMGUS Legal Division-Director, box 25. The tribunal explained its lenient sentence on grounds that the "higher ups" who had ordered the killing had not been identified or charged. In relation to the three judges who had presided over the re-trial in 1947, one German newspaper commented: ". . . in sitting on the bench, they have shown not only that they were former adherents of Nazism but that they are accomplices of the murderers even today . . . protecting their former associates." See "Germans Protest Lenient Sentences," *New York Times,* May 12, 1947. See also Loewenstein, "Comment on 'Denazification," *Social Research* 14, No. 3 (Fall 1947): 365–369, 368.

211. Weigert to Parker, Rockwell, August 25, 1947, NARA RG 260, OMGUS Legal Division-AJB, box 74. This decision was so troubling (even to some German press) that the Bavarian minister of justice, not waiting for Legal Division to intervene, nullified the verdict ordered a new trial of the case.
212. Ibid.
213. Rockwell to the chief of staff, "Denazification of German Administration of Justice," n.d., NARA RG 260, OMGUS Legal Division-Weigert Correspondence, box 132.
214. Major Kraus to Raymond, "Trial of Criminal Offences by Nazis," July 28, 1948, NARA RG 260, OMGUS Legal Division-AJB, box 84. Growing numbers of Nazi war crimes cases were being prosecuted in the Bavarian ordinary courts because of the discontinuance of the war crimes trials at Dachau and at Nuremberg. Sedillo, "Annual Report," NARA RG 260, OMGUS Legal Division-AJB, box 68.
215. Raymond, before the war a Boston-based corporate lawyer, had led the Legal Advice branch of Legal Division since 1945. Like his three predecessor directors, what Raymond knew of Germany and German law he learned on the job at Legal Division. Raymond to chief of staff, "Trial of Criminal Offences by Nazis," June 10, 1948, NARA RG 260, OMGUS Legal Division-Director, box 26; Kraus to Raymond, "Trial of Criminal Offences by Nazis," 28, July 1948, NARA RG 260, OMGUS Legal Division-AJB, box 84.
216. For example, in June 1948, Legal Division learned that the minister of justice in Bavaria had appointed Dr. Andreas Holzbauer to the post of chief prosecutor. Holzbauer had been cleared by a Munich denazification board even though he had served as a Nazi party monitor, or "Blockleiter," in his Munich neighborhood. It was also established that, on a number of occasions, Holzbauer had received promotions and perquisites from the Nazi party. Sedillo to Legal Division, "Promotion of Holzbauer," NARA RG 260, OMGUS Legal Division-AJB, box 84.
217. Richard J. Jackson to director of OMGUS-Bavaria, July 13, 1948, OMGUS Legal Division-AJB, box 84.
218. Mortimer Kollender to Raymond, "Appointment of Former Nazis as Judges of the Supreme Court of Bavaria," OMGUS Legal Division-AJB, box 84.

219. Ibid.
220. Ibid.
221. Ibid.
222. Garde to OMGUS Directors of Land Government, "Administration of Justice," June 13, 1947, NARA RG 260, OMGUS Legal Division-AJB, box 76.
223. "An Evaluation of Japanese Progress in the Field of Civil Liberties Since the Surrender", Intelligence Research Report no. OCL-4120, January 15, 1947, 35, NARA RG 331, SCAP-GS, box 152.
224. "The Reform of Criminal Procedure," SCAP press conference, April 23, 1947, NARA RG 331, SCAP-GS, box 1498.
225. Sabine Huth, "Einigkeit und Recht und Freiheit: Selected Themes in Contemporary German Post-War History," *Historical Journal* 37 (1994): 487–503, at 491–492.
226. For documents relating to the lax or lenient prosecution of Nazi-era war crimes in the south German courts, see "Denazification Scandal still Expanding," report from *Die Neue Zeitung,* January 31, 1950, NARA RG 260, OMGUS Legal Division-AJB, box 83.
227. Weigert to Raymond, May 19, 1948, NARA RG 260, OMGUS Legal Division-AJB, box 74.
228. As one scholar has noted, "By May, 1947, OMGUS estimated that, by the end of 1947, the number of judges and prosecutors who had been NP members might be as high as 90%." Gaab, *Justice Delayed,* 73. See also Szanajda, *Restoration,* 160–161.
229. One historian has observed in this regard that in postwar Germany, "The judiciary was more successful than any other elite in ensuring that its participation in the regimes monstrous crimes was publicly forgotten." Jena S. Steinbacher, "Review of Wachsmann, 'Soldiers on the Home Front,'" *European History Quarterly* 37, no. 2, (2007): 357–358.
230. Oppler, *Legal Reform,* 87–88.
231. Ibid., 86–87.
232. Ibid., 76. Oppler later recalled that he thought Hosono and the other Japanese liberals "went too far in their proposals."

5. Clearing the Spiritual Rubble

1. SCAP Press Conference, "The Reform of Criminal Procedure," April 23, 1947, NARA RG 331, SCAP-GS, box 1498.
2. Ibid.
3. "An Evaluation of Japanese Progress in the Civil Liberties since the Surrender," Intelligence Research Report OCL-4120, Division of Research for Far East, State Department, January 15, 1947, 28, NARA RG 331, SCAP-GS, box 1522.

4. "The Reform of Criminal Procedure," Joint Press Conference Government Section and Civil Information, April 23, 1947, NARA RG 331, SCAP-GS, box 1498.
5. "Nazi Changes in Criminal Procedure," July 10, 1945, OSS, R&A No. 3081, NARA RG 226, E. 2.
6. Special Legal Unit Germany / Austria, "Nazi Changes in the Field of Criminal Law," February 23, 1945, NARA RG 260, USGCC-Control, box 170.
7. MacArthur, "Statement to the Japanese Government Concerning Required Reforms," *PRJ,* vol. 2, app. F, 741.
8. Richard B. Appleton, "Reforms in the Japanese Criminal Procedure," *Washington Law Review* 24 (1949): 401–430, at 401.
9. Under Article 13, all people in Japan were to be "treated as individuals."
10. "The Reform of Criminal Procedure," Joint Press Conference GS and Civil Information, April 23, 1947, NARA RG 331, SCAP-GS, box 1498; Oppler, address to meeting called by the Attorney General's office, July 17, 1948, NARA RG 331, SCAP-GS, box 1522.
11. "SCAP Statement on Lese Majeste," *PRJ,* vol. 2, app. F, 759. MacArthur later stated of the new constitution that "no individual in Japan—not even the Emperor—shall be clothed in legal protection denied the common man."
12. Article 14, *The Constitution of Japan, PRJ,* vol. 2, app. C.
13. John Owen Haley, *Spirit of Japanese Law* (Athens: University of Georgia Press 2006), 3–7.
14. For contemporary American account of the details, see "The Reform of Criminal Procedure," Joint Press Conference GS and Civil Information, April 23, 1947, NARA RG 331, SCAP-GS, box 1498.
15. Article 31, *The Constitution of Japan, PRJ,* vol. 2, app. C.
16. Article 33, ibid.
17. Article 37, ibid.
18. Torture being a common feature of presurrender criminal justice in Japan. See Richard H. Mitchell, *Janus-Faced Justice: Political Criminals in Imperial Japan* (Honolulu: University of Hawaii Press, 1992), 172–175. Howard Meyers, "Revisions of the Criminal Code of Japan During Occupation," *Washington Law Review* 25 (1950): 104–134, at 106.
19. Dan Fenno Henderson, "Law and Political Modernization in Japan" in *Political Development in Modern Japan: Studies in the Modernization of Japan,* ed. Robert E. Ward (Princeton, NJ: Princeton University Press, 1968), 387–388; Mitchell, *Janus-Faced Justice,* 4–7
20. Oppler, "The Judicial and Legal System," *PRJ,* vol. 1, 190; see also Meyers, "Revisions of the Criminal Code," 104–105.
21. Mitchell, *Janus-Faced Justice,* 175; see also Richard H. Mitchell, *Justice in Japan: The Notorious Teijin Scandal* (Honolulu: University of Hawaii Press, 2002), 8;

see also Carl F. Goodman, *The Rule of Law in Japan: A Comparative Analysis* (The Hague: Kluwer Law International, 2003), 382–385.

22. Goodman, *Rule of Law,* 383–387.
23. "Brief Program Report on the Political Reorientation of Japan"—"Judiciary," Government Section Report, 1949, NARA RG 331, SCAP-GS, box 1446.
24. In fact, in Japanese courtrooms, the procurator's station stood at the same height as that of the judges and higher than of defense lawyers. See "Lower the Procurator's Bench," from the *Tokyo Minpo,* July 12, 1948, NARA RG 331, SCAP-GS, box 1502. See, generally, Takaati Hattori, "The Legal Profession in Japan: Its Historical Development and Present State," in *Law in Japan: The Legal Order in a Changing Society,* ed. Arthur Taylor von Mehren (Cambridge, MA: Harvard University Press, 1963), 111, 124–126.
25. On this point Alfred Oppler later commented, "In the administration of criminal law the judges were under the continuous observation and control of the public procurators who, though attached to The Courts, reported to and followed the directives of the Ministry of Justice." Oppler, "Address to the Tokyo Bar Associations," 1949, NARA RG 331, SCAP-GS, box 1450.
26. Alfred Oppler, *Legal Reform in Occupied Japan: A Participant Looks Back* (Princeton: Princeton University Press, 1976), 136, 143.
27. The *Peace Preservation* legislation had been promulgated to aid the state in its crackdown on the Japanese Left. See, generally, Richard H. Mitchell, "Japan's Peace Preservation Law of 1925: Its Origins and Significance," *Monumenta Nipponica* 28, no. 3 (1973): 317, 318–321; see also Appleton, "Japanese Criminal Procedure," 403.
28. The legislation that expanded police and prosecutorial powers (abrogated by SCAP directive in 1945) is listed in "The Judicial and Legal System," *PRJ,* vol. 1, 193–194.
29. In a few instances in the 1920s, politically motivated prosecutions had ended with acquittals. Appleton, "Japanese Criminal Procedure," 401; see also Meyers, "Revisions of the Criminal Code," 106–107; see also Mitchell, *Teijin Incident,* 48, 177–78.
30. Howard Meyers, "Rights of Citizens Protected by Law," *Nippon Times,* July 22, 1947.
31. "The Judicial and Legal System," *PRJ,* vol. 1, 186–245, 189.
32. Oppler, as quoted in "Brief Program Report on the Political Reorientation of Japan"—"Conclusion," Government Section Report, 1949, NARA RG 331, SCAP-GS, box 1446.
33. Ibid.
34. Ibid.
35. Blakemore to the Chief, May 31, 1946, NARA RG 331, SCAP-GS, box 1484.
36. John W. Dower, *Empire and Aftermath: Yoshida Shigeru and the Japanese Experience, 1878–1954* (Cambridge, MA: Harvard University Press, 1979), 313.

37. "The underpinnings of that bureaucracy," Charles Kades claimed in 1947, "have begun to be knocked down." Kades, "Conference, Government Section, 14 October 1947," DMHP, box 7.
38. Ibid., 313.
39. Alfred C. Oppler, "The Reform of Japan's Judicial and Legal System under Allied Occupation," *Washington Law Review* 24 (1949): 290, 319.
40. Ibid., 303–304.
41. Ibid. In the case of draft Code of Criminal Procedure, more than sixty "problem sheets" were discussed in a series of bilateral conferences that went on for the better part of three weeks. In the result, the Japanese drafting committee would produce a final draft for debate and passage by the Diet.
42. Oppler, *Legal Reform,* 66.
43. Ibid., 69.
44. Ibid., 69–70.
45. See, generally, John W. Dower, "Yoshida in the Scales of History," in *Japan in War and Peace: Selected Essays,* ed. John W. Dower (New York: New Press, 1993): 207. See also John W. Dower, *Empire and Aftermath,* 306–310; see also Richard B. Finn, *Winners in Peace: MacArthur, Yoshida, and Postwar Japan* (Berkeley: University of California Press, 1992), 210–227.
46. Mitchell, *Janus-Faced Justice,* 71–72.
47. Ibid.
48. For an excellent summary of suspended sentences, concurrency of crimes, sentences, and repeat offenders, see Meyers to the Chief, "Revision of the Criminal Code of Japan," June 12, 1947, NARA RG 331, SCAP-GS, box 1477.
49. Ibid., 118–121.
50. Ibid., 121–125.
51. The general thought that the articles on criminal libel were so broadly drafted as to have a chilling effect on political speech. Blakemore, File Note, "Revision of the Criminal Code," June 14, 1947, NARA RG 331, SCAP-GS, box 1477.
52. "SCAP Statement on Lese Majeste," *PRJ,* vol. 2, app. F, 759. MacArthur thought that the doctrine of *lèse-majesté* was a "direct negation" of the equal dignity of all citizens, this "one of the basic principles of democratic government."
53. Such prosecution was sometimes based in the criminal code, sometimes on the *Peace Preservation Law. Akahata* newspaper summary, August 5, 1946 in NARA RG 331, SCAP-GS, box 1530.
54. The characters on the placard read: "The Emperor is well-fed while the people starve and die."
55. *Akahata* newspaper report, August 5, 1946 in NARA RG 331, SCAP-GS, box 1530.
56. Ibid. Fuse came out of retirement fore the case. For biographical background on Tatsuji Fuse (1880–1952) and other Japanese radical lawyers, see Mitchell,

Janus-Faced Justice, 175; *Justice in Japan,* 32–33; 71–73; Haley, *Spirit of Japanese Law,* 53.

57. See "Protocol of the First Public Trial," NARA RG 331, SCAP-GS, box 1530.
58. Ibid.
59. For further written elaboration of the procurator's legal argument, see "Statement of Procurator Yoshikawa," NARA RG 331, SCAP-GS, box 1530. "[Lèse-majesté]," the procurator wrote, "is not a law to restrict freedom of speech, but rather a law specifically to protect the honor of the Emperor and the Imperial family as in the case of any individual in regard to the abuse of the right of freedom of speech."
60. Ibid.
61. The Japanese LIC executive set forth a full defense of the *lèse-majesté* provisions at a meeting with Oppler and Blakemore on September 11. Oppler, "Memo for the Executive Committee," September 9, 1946, NARA RG 331, SCAP-GS, box 1500. Blakemore, "Revision of Japanese Criminal Law," September 12, 1946, NARA RG 331, SCAP-GS, box 1500.
62. Oppler, "Memo for the Executive Committee," September 11, 1946, NARA RG 331, SCAP-GS, box 1500.
63. Oppler to the Chief, "Lese Majesty," September 23, 1946, NARA RG 331, SCAP-GS, box 1500.
64. Ibid.
65. Ibid.
66. Memo to Executive Committee, "Revision of Lese-Majeste Provisions," September 26, 1946, NARA RG 331, box 2142.
67. "Third Hearing in the Placard Case," Asahi Shimbun, October 2, 1946, NARA RG 331, box 1530.
68. "Placard Incident Trial," *Asaahi Shimbun,* October 4, 1946, NARA RG 331, SCAP-GS, box 1530.
69. "SCAP Statement on Lese Majeste," *PRJ,* vol. 2, app. F, 759. A move that was publically endorsed by MacArthur personally.
70. Oppler to the Chief, "Lese-Majeste and Other Political Offenses," October 22, 1946, NARA RG 331, SCAP-GS, box 1500.
71. Ibid. The problem in invoking the criminal libel article of the code (230.1) was that it required the victim personally to initiate process by filing a complaint. In the case at bar, predictably, the emperor had not done so. The Court resolved this issue in ruling that the crime depended on the intention of the accused, not the identity of the complainant. Procurators could perfect the charge by lodging the complaint in the emperor's name.
72. Oppler to the Chief, "Lese-Majeste," December 3, 1946, NARA RG 331, SCAP-GS, box 1500.
73. As discussed in Oppler, Memo for the Record, "Abrogation of Lese-Majeste Articles," December 20, 1946, NARA RG 331, SCAP-GS, box 1500.
74. Ibid.

75. Ibid. For another account of this meeting, see Oppler, *Legal Reform,* 164–167. As Oppler recalled: "My impression was that the conservative cabinet did not want such an irreverent action to be taken by the Diet, or any other Japanese government agency without being forced by the higher power of SCAP." But presumably at the behest of MacArthur, Whitney pressed the Japanese government for an immediate report on "action taken."
76. Yoshida to MacArthur, December 27, 1946, *PRJ,* vol. 2, app. C, 679.
77. Oppler, Memo for the Chief, "Legal Protection," December 31, 1946, NARA RG 331, SCAP-GS, box 1500.
78. Yoshida to MacArthur, December 27, 1946, *PRJ,* vol. 2, app. C, 679.
79. Oppler, Memo to the Chief, "Instructions to Minister of Justice," April 29, 1947, NARA RG 331, SCAP-GS, box 1500.
80. Oppler, Memo to the Chief, "Report on Lese-Majeste Case," July 8, 1947, NARA RG 331, SCAP-GS, box 1500.
81. Oppler, Memo to the Chief, July 17, 1947, NARA RG 331, NARA RG 331, SCAP-GS, box 1530.
82. Minutes of Conference in GS, October 6, 1947, NARA RG 331, NARA RG 331, SCAP-GS, box 1530.
83. Press conference, "The Reform of the Penal Code," December 5, 1947, NARA RG 331, SCAP-GS, box 1500.
84. SCAP-HQ, "History of the Non-Military Activities of the Occupation of Japan—Volume V—Civil Liberties—Part 1," NARA RG 331, SCAP-Historical, box 3634.
85. "Judicial and Legal Affairs," May 1948, NARA RG 331, SCAP-GS, box 1500.
86. See "History of the Non-military Activities of the Occupation of Japan," Vol. V, "Civil Liberties—Part 1," 107, NARA RG 331, SCAP-GS, box 3634.
87. Appleton, "Japanese Criminal Procedure," 401.
88. Ibid., 402.
89. Blakemore to the Chief, "Arrest and Detention," October 4, 1946, DMHP, box 1.
90. "Democracy and the Criminal Process," SCAP press conference, January 12, 1948, NARA RG 331, SCAP-GS, box 1529.
91. Elise K. Tipton, *The Japanese Police State: The Tokko in Interwar Japan* (Honolulu: University of Hawaii Press, 1990), 62–64, 55, 69.
92. Ibid.
93. Ibid.; see also Oppler, "The Judicial and Legal System," *PRJ,* vol. 1, 227.
94. Appleton, "Japanese Criminal Procedure," 405–406.
95. Anthony J. Maniscalco, a Texan lawyer since 1927, was a former Texas assistant attorney general; see also Dimitri Vanoverbeke, *Juries in the Japanese Legal System: The Continuing Struggle for Citizen Participation and Democracy* (London: Routledge, 2015), 96–97.

96. Blakemore to the Chief, "Proposed Revision of Criminal Procedure," May 31, 1946, NARA RG 331, SCAP-GS, box 1500.
97. Oppler to the Chief, "Additional Comment," May 31, 1946, NARA RG 331, SCAP-GS, box 1500.
98. Ibid.
99. Blakemore to Executive Committee LIC, September 30, 1946, DMHP, box 1.
100. Blakemore for the Record, "Conference with Supreme Court Justices," October 16, 1946, NARA RG 331, SCAP-GS, box 1484.
101. Blakemore to the Chief, "Arrest and Detention," October 4, 1946, DMHP, box 1.
102. This was thought true especially of the Article governing warrantless arrest. SCAP wanted to restrict this privilege to sitting judges. Oppler to the Chief, "Arrest and Detention in the Code of Criminal Procedure," October 4, 1946, DMHP, box 1.
103. Blakemore to the Chief, "Further Conferences with Supreme Court Justices," October 16, 1946, NARA RG 331, SCAP-GS, box 1484.
104. Exceptions: in capital cases and when the accused was arrested in course of criminal action. Oppler to the Chief, "Gist of the Ministry of Justice Laws," May 1, 1947, 16–17, NARA RG 331, SCAP-GS, box 1496.
105. GS also compelled the MofJ to organize a series of public meetings and broadcasts at which Japanese officials, including senior procurators, would explain the gist of the new law to the Japanese people in their own language. Meyers to the Chief, "Publicity Program," May 2, 1947, NARA RG 331, SCAP-GS, box 2142.
106. "People No Longer at Mercy of Law," *Nippon Times,* April 24, 1947.
107. Oppler, "Untitled Speech to Japanese Procurators," February 9, 1948, NARA RG 331, SCAP-GS, box 1498.
108. Ibid.
109. Oppler, "The Judicial and Legal System," *PRJ,* vol. 1, 198.
110. Oppler, "Revision of the Code," March 5, 1948, NARA RG 331, SCAP-GS, box 1500.
111. Oppler, *Legal Reform,* 147.
112. Ibid., 79–82.
113. Ibid., 81.
114. "Conference on the Code of Criminal Procedure," Record of Proceedings, May 5, 1948, NARA RG 331, SCAP-GS, box 1530.
115. Ibid.
116. Oppler, *Legal Reform,* 80–82.
117. "Conference on the Code of Criminal Procedure," Record of Proceedings, April 21, 1948, NARA RG 331, SCAP-GS, box 1530.
118. These details in Appleton, "Japanese Criminal Procedure," 401–422.
119. Ibid., 422.

120. *Code of Criminal Procedure,* Law No. 131, in *PRJ,* vol. 2, app. H, 1159.
121. Appleton, "Japanese Criminal Procedure," 429.
122. "Recent Developments in the Field of Criminal Justice in Japan," Supreme Court of Japan (August 1950), NARA RG 331, SCAP-GS, box 1482.
123. Press conference, "Reform of the Penal Code," December 5, 1947, NARA RG 331, SCAP-GS, box 1500.
124. Oppler, *Legal Reform,* 73–75; see also Oppler, "Judicial and Legal System," *PRJ,* vol. 1, 187.
125. Ibid.
126. One of the main tasks of the new office was to replace the MofJ as the main source of administrative oversight with respect to Japan's new system of criminal justice. Oppler, *Legal Reform,* 106.
127. Nagano to SCAP, October 15, 1948, NARA RG 331, SCAP-GS-Legis, box 2821.
128. Oppler, "Activity Report," October 8, 1948, NARA RG 331, SCAP-GS, box 1522.
129. The endorsement came from "former Judge of the Supreme Court Chono." In conversing with Oppler, Chono denounced the former minister of justice, Tokutaro Kimura, as a "Fascist" unfit for high legal office in postwar Japan. Oppler, "Activity Report," November 1, 1948, NARA RG 331, SCAP-GS, box 1522.
130. A similar fight arose over the appointment to the post of legal advisor to the Attorney General. The Left politicians wanted Keneko, a nonpolitical scholar. The Yoshida cabinet wanted one of their own, and got its way. Oppler, "Activity Report, April 15 and May 25, 1948, NARA RG 331, SCAP-GS, box 1522.
131. Ibid.
132. The "reverse course" is defined and discussed at length in chapter 6.
133. Takemae Eiji, *Inside GHQ: The Allied Occupation of Japan and Its Legacy* (London: Continuum, 2002), 473–480.
134. Ibid., 220, 478–79. One historian describes Ueda as having been an "Emperor system ideologue" whose principal mission it was to protect the *kokutai* while crushing the communist threat in postwar Japan. Oppler, *Legal Reform,* 106.
135. "Attorney General's Address to the Chief Public Procurators," June 16, 1949, NARA RG 331, SCAP-GS, box 1498.
136. In a message read before an assembly of some 350 lawyers from across Japan, General MacArthur himself warmly endorsed the willingness of Japan's bar to "shoulder the new responsibilities under the recently approved Constitution." "Bar Associations Hear MacArthur's Message," *Nippon Times,* November 12, 1946.
137. That is to say, significant number of lawyers did not begin to appear on behalf of accused in the criminal courts until after 1910. See, generally, Richard W. Rabinowitz, "Historical Development of the Japanese Bar,"

Harvard Law Review 70 (1956): 61–81, at 61, 65; Hattori, "Legal Profession in Japan," 128–131.

138. Oppler to the Chief, "Exclusion from the Bar," January 16, 1947, NARA RG 331, SCAP-GS, box 1479. See also Blakemore, Memo for the Record, "Lawyers Law," July 30, 1949, NARA RG 331, SCAP-GS, box 1525.
139. In March 1946, there were eleven women lawyers in Japan. Since the surrender, however, they actively pressed claims for greater respect and equality within the bar. See Oppler, "Meeting with Japanese Women Lawyers," March 15, 1946, NARA RG 331, SCAP-GS, box 1500; see, generally, Hattori, "Legal Profession in Japan," 128–129.
140. Mitchell, *Janus-Faced Justice,* 71–73.
141. Ibid., 13–15.
142. Oppler, "Address to the Tokyo Bar Associations," 1949, NARA RG 331, SCAP-GS, box 1450; see also Oppler, "With the Tokyo Bar associations," c. 1949, NARA RG 331, NARA RG 331, SCAP-GS, box 1450; Mitchell, *Janus-Faced Justice,* 71. As Oppler later remarked on this point: "Our contacts with the leaders of the bar associations made us see the potentiality of an eventual development of Japan's bar to a protagonist of civil rights." See also Oppler, *Legal Reform,* 108; "Jottings on Criminal Trial," *Nippon Times,* January 6 and 9, 1946.
143. Oppler, "Address to the Tokyo Bar Associations," 1949, NARA RG 331, SCAP-GS, box 1450.
144. See Mitchell, *Janus-Faced Justice,* 71; see also Oppler, *Legal Reform,* 108.
145. In one noteworthy (in their timing, content, and bold tone) series of articles published in the Japanese and English versions of the *Nippon Times,* Takayangi, a specialist in Anglo-American law, provided a thumbnail history and seemingly his personal endorsement not only of the Anglo-American model of adversarial trial but also the crucial role therein of defense counsel. According to the "Anglo-American philosophy" of the criminal trial, he informed readers, the key question was "not whether the accused be guilty, but whether he can be shown to be guilty" by the prosecution. "Jottings on Criminal Trial," *Nippon Times,* January 6 and 9, 1946. Takayangi contended that even General Tojo, this "despicable and flagrant criminal," was entitled to "able and well-prepared defense counsel."
146. Blakemore, Memo for the Record, "Conversations with Members of Number One Tokyo Bar Association," November 21, 1946, NARA RG 331, SCAP-GS, box 1479; see also "Liberal Lawyers' Group," NARA RG 331, SCAP-GS, box 1524.
147. Blakemore, "Draft Revision of Lawyers' Law," January 17, 1947, NARA SCAP-GS, box 1484.
148. "Lawyers' Law Is Set to Undergo Revision," *Nippon Times,* November 12, 1946.

149. Blakemore, "Draft Revision of Lawyers' Law," January 17, 1947, NARA SCAP-GS, box 1484.
150. Oppler, "Exclusion from the Bar," January 16, 1947, NARA RG 331, SCAP-GS, box 1500.
151. For background on women and the American occupation, see John W. Dower, *Embracing Defeat: Japan in the Wake of World War II* (New York: W.W. Norton, 1999), 81–83, 241–243. See also Jeanne M. Gleich-Anthony, "Democratizing Women: American Women and the U.S. Occupation of Japan, 1945–1951," (Ph.D. dissertation, Ohio University, 2007), 10.
152. Oppler, "Meeting with Japanese Women Lawyers," March 15, 1946, ACOP, box 3.
153. Oppler, "The Future of Japan's Bar," *Nippon Times,* October 25, 1951.
154. "Law of Lawyers," June 7, 1948, NARA RG 331, SCAP-GS, box 1523.
155. The postwar private bar was not eager to invite further competition for scarce legal business. Blakemore, Memo for the Record, "Lawyers Law," July 30, 1949, NARA RG 331, SCAP-GS, box 1525.
156. Oppler, *Legal Reform,* 108.
157. Inouye, "Historical Record of Japan Bar Association," March 20, 1959, ACOP, box 3.
158. Ibid.
159. Press Release, "Lawyers Freed from Government Domination," July 10, 1949, NARA RG 331, SCAP-GS, box 1498.
160. Ibid.
161. Special Legal Unit Germany / Austria (SLUGA), "Memorandum on the Revision of German Criminal Law," November 4, 1946, 1–2, NAUK FO 1060 / 860. The prevailing view among the German émigré analysts at the OSS was that the Nazi party was dedicated to the destruction of the German *rechtsstaat,* and that consequently many leading German jurists might later be enlisted to its restoration. See Frank Schale, "The Government Advisor John H. Herz and the Office of Strategic Services," *International Relations,* 22, no. 4 (2008): 411, 415.
162. H. A. S. to SHAEF-Legal, "Draft Crimes Ordinance," July 1944, RG 331, SHAEF Legal Branch, box 229.
163. SLUGA, "Memorandum on the Revision of German Criminal Law," November 4, 1946, 1–2, NAUK FO 1060 / 860.
164. SLUGA, "Nazi Changes in the Field of Criminal Law," February 23, 1945, NARA RG 260, OMGUS-Control, box 170.
165. William W. Fearnside, *National Socialist Ideology in German Criminal Law, 1933–1945* (Ph.D. Thesis, University of California, 1949: 26, 26–27.
166. Timothy Snyder, "Hitler's World," *New York Review of Books* 64, no. 14 (2015): 6, 8.
167. Richard J. Evans, *The Third Reich at War* (New York: Penguin, 2009), 79.

168. Michael Stolleis, "Law and Lawyers Preparing the Holocaust," *Annual Review of Social Science* 3 (2007): 213–231, at 213, 225–226.
169. This including liability for novel criminal wrongs "by analogy" to established crimes. See *The Statutory Criminal Law of Germany,* ed. Eldon R. James (Washington, DC: Library of Congress, 1947), 3–5. See also Fearnside, *National Socialist Ideology,* 114–117.
170. Thus abrogating the rule expressed in the maxim *nulla poena nullum crimen sine lege.* SLUGA, "Memorandum on the Revision of German Criminal Law," November 4, 1946, 3–5, NAUK FO 1060 / 860. See also Fearnside, *National Socialist Ideology,* 14. The Reorganization of the German Administration of Justice in 1942," OSS, R&A No. 850, NARA RG 226, E. 1; Thomas Vormbaum and Michael Bohlander, eds. *A Modern History of German Criminal Law* (Berlin: Springer, 2014), 175; Edith Raim, *Nazi Crimes against Jews and German Post-War Justice; The West German Judicial System During Allied Occupation (1945–1949)* (Berlin: De Gruyter Oldenbourg, 2015), 1–10.
171. "In criminal law, instead of looking to the boundary of expressly forbidden wrong as prescribed by statute, the judge would look to the line between moral right and wrong." Fearnside, *National Socialist Ideology,* 33, 35. See also Vormbaum and Bohlander, *German Criminal Law,* 175; Carolyn Benson and Julian Fink, "Introduction: New Perspectives on Nazi Law," *Discussion: A Symposium on Nazi Law, Jurisprudence* 3, no. 2 (2012): 341, 342.
172. "The Reorganization of the German Administration of Justice in 1942," OSS, R&A No. 850, NARA RG 226, E. 1.
173. In 1942, appalled by the stubborn persistence of legal norms in criminal justice, Hitler was moved publically to excoriate Germany's judges for excessive leniency. Evans, *Third Reich at War,* 513–517.
174. Franz Neumann to Walter Rothschild, "SHAEF Outline of German Criminal Law," August 2, 1944, NAUK WO 219.
175. As one SLUGA report stated, in the Third Reich "the criminal courts no longer were the sole agencies of the state authorized to impose punishment. The police have been granted powers to arrest, detain and execute people without any judicial warrant. . . . In their actions, the police are not bound by criminal laws." SLUGA, "Memorandum on the Revision of German Criminal Law," November 4, 1946, 3–5, NAUK FO 1060 / 860. For scholarly commentary, see *Nikolaus Wachsmann,* "'Soldiers on the Home Front:' Jurists and Legal Terror During the Second World War," in *Nazism, War and Genocide: Essays in Honour of Jeremy Noakes,* ed. Neil Gregor (Exeter: University of Exeter Press, 2008), 75–78.
176. Eberhard Schmidt, professor of criminal law, Leipzig, as quoted in Petra Godecke, "Criminal Law After National Socialism: The Renaissance of Natural Law and the Beginnings of Penal Reform in Nazi Germany," in *Crime and Criminal Justice in Modern Germany,* ed. Richard Wetzel (New York: Berghahn, 2014): 270, 272.

177. T.T. Marye to E. L. McLendon, "Comment on Memo of CC (British Element) German Laws (Criminal)," April 26, 1945, NARA RG 260, USGCC-LD-Legal Advice Branch (LAB), box 62.
178. H. A. S. to SHAEF-Legal, "Draft Crimes Ordinance," July 1944, RG 331, SHAEF Legal Branch, box 229.
179. Military Government, Germany, Law No. 1, "On the Abrogation of Nazi Law," in *Documents on Germany Under Occupation, 1945–1954,* ed. Beate Ruhm von Oppen (London: Oxford, 1955), 9–11. The third article of the law forbade "interpretation and application of German law in accordance with National Socialist doctrines" and the use of Nazi-influenced precedents.
180. Ibid., Article 4. "All Nazi laws which provided the basis of the Hitler regime or established discriminations on grounds of race, creed, or political opinion shall be abolished. No such discriminations, whether legal, administrative or otherwise, shall be tolerated."
181. Law No. 1, "Repealing Nazi Laws" in *Germany Under Occupation: Illustrative Materials and Documents,* ed. James K. Pollock et al. (Ann Arbor, MI: George Wahr, 1949), 55–56. See also Christoph Krehl, "Reforms of the German Criminal Code—Stock Taking and Perspectives—also from a Constitutional Point of View," *German Law Journal* 4, no. 5 (2003): 420, 422.
182. Loewenstein thought that Schopler lacked the "slightest theoretical knowledge" about criminal law. LOD, February 27, 1946.
183. Holding a doctorate in law from the University of Munich, in 1946 Rheinstein was a professor of law (a specialist in comparative law) at the University of Chicago. See "Biographical Note" in MRP, https://www.lib.uchicago.edu/e/scrc/findingaids/view.php?eadid=ICU.SPCL.RHEINSTEIN#idp14100781.
184. "Memorandum Concerning Procedure," DLeg/P(46) 155, NARA RG 260, ACA-DLeg, box 183. Later in 1946, the then members of the committee informally agreed to conduct all their discussions in German. See Joachim von Elbe, *Witness to History: A Refugee from the Third Reich Remembers* (Madison, WI: German-American Cultural Society Inc., 1988), 315–316.
185. Ibid., 306. According to one participant, relations between the representatives of the three Western Allies and the Soviet delegation were tense.
186. Ibid., 309.
187. Ibid., 306–307.
188. Madden to Fahy, "Law No. 11," February 2, 1946, NARA RG 260, OMGUS LD-LAB, box 62.
189. Karl Loewenstein, "Law and Legislative Process in Occupied Germany: I," *Yale Law Journal* 57, no. 5 (1948): 724, 752. Fahy to Deputy Military Governor (Clay), "Draft Law Repealing Certain Provisions of the German Criminal Law," January 23, 1946, NARA RG 260, OMGUS LD-Director, box 23. See also "German Law Reform," Memorandum by the British

Representative," November 30, 1945, DLeg/P(45)47, NARA RG 260, ACA-DLeg, box 176.

190. "German Law Reform," Memorandum by the British Representative," November 30, 1945, DLeg/P(45)47, NARA RG 260, ACA-DLeg, box 176.; Loewenstein, "Law and Legislative Process," 737.

191. SLUGA, "Memorandum on the Revision of German Criminal Law," November 4, 1946, 1–2, NAUK FO 1060/860.

192. Loewenstein, "Law and Legislative Process," 737–738.

193. Ibid., 752.

194. Rockwell to Läender Military Governments, "Reform of German Law—Criminal Procedure," August 20, 1946, NARA RG 260, OMGUS LD-LAB, box 62. As the Special Legal Unit commented: "The pre-Nazi state of German Criminal Law was far from satisfactory . . . the bulk of legal provisions were still the same as promulgated in the Code of 1871. Many legal concepts had long been regarded as out of date. Between 1909 and 1930 numerous Draft Codes and counterproposals seemed to herald a progressive reform of German Criminal Law." SLUGA, "Memorandum on the Revision of German Criminal Law," November 4, 1946, 1–2, NAUK FO 1060/860.

195. Loewenstein, "Law and Legislative Process," 752.

196. Jeffrey S. Gaab, *Justice Delayed: The Restoration of Justice in Bavaria under American Occupation, 1945–1949* (New York: Lang, 1999), 40–41.

197. Szanajda, *Restoration of Justice,* 59–63.

198. LOD, August 16, 1945.

199. Baker to Land MG Directors, "Enactment of German Codes," February 5, 1946, NARA RG 260, OMGUS LD-LAB, box 88.

200. Schopler to Fahy, "Habeas Corpus and the German Criminal Law," May 3, 1946, NARA RG 260, OMGUS LD-LAB, box 88.

201. Andrew Szanajda, *Indirect Perpetrators: The Prosecution of Informers in Germany, 1945–1965* (Toronto: Lexington, 2012), 1–5.

202. See Loewenstein to Madden, "Draft Law on the Redress of National-Socialist Injustice," February 19, 1946, NARA RG 260, OMGUS LD-AJB, box 74.

203. "Memorandum on the Revision of German Criminal Law," November 4, 1946, NAUK FO 1060/80.

204. Ibid.

205. The ministers complained that inadequate time had been afforded for a "sufficiently careful examination of such an important draft law." Kane to Rockwell, October 24, 1946, NARA RG 260, OMGUS LD-LAB, box 62.

206. "Record of the Second Interzonal Conference of Judicial Administrations, December 1946," n.d., NARA RG 260, OMGUS Legal Division-Admin, box 75.

207. Von Elbe to Kramer, "Report on the Meeting of German Jurists," December 16, 1946, NARA RG 260, OMGUS LD-LAB, box 64.

208. Ibid.

209. Ibid. For instance, there was persistent resistance to the proposal of abolishing a Nazi-era provision permitting the state to assert protective custody with regard to habitual criminals.
210. Ibid.
211. Minutes of the 111th Meeting, August 5 and 7, 1947, DLEG / P(47) 51, NARA RG 260, ACA-DLeg, box 178.
212. Criminal Law Committee, "Report of the Chairman," September 26, 1947, DLEG / P(46)133 / 2, NARA RG 260, ACA-DLeg, box 191.
213. For a general account of the deteriorating diplomatic situation between the Soviets and the Western Allies, see Carolyn Eisenberg, *Drawing the Line: The American Decision to Divide Germany, 1944–1949* (Cambridge: Cambridge University Press, 1996), 290–301.
214. For a historical overview of the American theory of the independent bar, see Robert W. Gordon, "The Independence of Lawyers," *Boston University Law Review* 68, no. 1 (1988): 1–83, at 1, 10.
215. As one American legal historian later summarized the point, "The lawyer's prime obligation is to put his best advice and advocacy fearlessly and vigorously at the service of his client's interests. In this respect, they stated a fundamental civil liberty." James W. Hurst, *The Growth of American Law: The Law-Makers* (Boston: Little, Brown, 1950), 330.
216. See Karl Loewenstein, *Legal Reconstruction in Germany,* 47, 57, KLP, box 24.
217. SLUGA, "First Supplementary Report, Revision of Nazi Law, April 11, 1945, NAUK, FO 1060 / 1099.
218. Loewenstein thought that the reconstruction of the German bar was second in importance only to the judiciary. Loewenstein, *Legal Reconstruction,* 57.
219. Udo Reifner, "The Bar in the Third Reich: Anti-Semitism and the Decline of Liberal Advocacy," *McGill Law Journal* 32, no. 1 (1986): 96–124, at 96, 104.
220. See, generally, Konrad H. Jarausch, *The Unfree Professions: German Lawyers, Teachers and Engineers, 1900–1950* (New York: Oxford University Press, 1990), 9–13; 23; 63, 199. As one German émigré jurist commented, "The German legal profession has not at any previous time . . . enjoyed anything like the amount of autonomy and freedom from State supervision which has been so marked a characteristic of the development of the English Bar." E. J. Cohn, "The German Attorney: Experiences with a Unified Profession (II)," *International and Comparative Law Quarterly* 10, no. 1 (1961): 103–122, at 103.
221. See, for instance, the Weimar-era career of Loewenstein's contemporary, the Munich-based lawyer-advocate Max Hirschberg. See, generally, Douglas G. Morris, *Justice Imperiled: The Anti-Nazi Lawyer Max Hirschberg in Weimar Germany* (Ann Arbor: University of Michigan Press, 2005).
222. The "*Reich-Rechtsanwaltsordnung*" was legislated by the Nazis on February 21, 1933. See "Laws Relating to Lawyers, Notaries and Patent Attorneys," NARA RG 260, OMGUS LD-LAB, box 61. See also Gaab, *Justice Delayed,* 29–31.

223. For a general overview of the "coordination" of the German bar by the Nazis, see Kenneth F. Ledford, "German Lawyers and the State in the Weimar Republic," *Law and History Review* 13, no. 2 (1995): 317; see also Reifner, "Bar in the Third Reich," 100.
224. Reifner, "Bar in the Third Reich," 111.
225. Cohn, "The German Attorney (II)," 589–590.
226. Wachsmann, "Soldiers on the Home Front," 76.
227. Gaab, *Justice Delayed,* 35; Reifner, "Bar in the Third Reich," 111.
228. American data indicated that by May 1945, 752 of Bavaria's 924 legal professionals had joined the Nazi party. Gaab, *Justice Delayed,* 68.
229. As one German expert at SLUGA wrote on this point, "It is clear that only outspoken members of the Nazi Party were chosen as benchers. So that in our submission it will be necessary to dismiss all of them without exception." SLUGA, Wolff to Foster, July 27, 1944, NAUK FO 1060/1099.
230. Loewenstein to Fahy, "Basic Problems of the Denazification of the Legal Profession," September 14, 1945, NARA RG 260, OMGUS LD-LAB, box 66.
231. Loewenstein, *Legal Reconstruction in Germany,* 59–60.
232. There was a demonstrable shortage of experienced advocates throughout the U.S. zone. Szanajda, *Justice in Postwar Hesse,* 134–135; Gaab, *Justice Delayed,* 61.
233. "Laws Relating to Lawyers, Notaries and Patent Attornies," May 4, 1945, NARA RG 260, OMGUS LD-LAB, box 61. See also Szanajda, *Justice in Postwar Hesse,* 74–76.
234. In Loewenstein's observation, local detachments of AMG were screening German lawyers in an entirely "haphazard" fashion. But once a denazified lawyer had returned to the practice of law, he became "practically irremovable." *Legal Reconstruction in Germany,* 58.
235. LOD, December 5, 1945.
236. Loewenstein, *Legal Reconstruction in Germany,* 47.
237. Loewenstein to Director, "Denazification Policy," November 30, 1945, NARA RG 260, OMGUS LD-LAB, box 66.
238. Loewenstein to Fahy, "Basic Problems of the Denazification of the Legal Profession," September 14, 1945, NARA RG 260, OMGUS LD-LAB, box 66.
239. For a contemporary report, see Loewenstein, letter to the *New York Times,* December 8, 1946, KLP, box 27. According to one German émigré lawyer, the German bar was "never cleansed even of the most virulent elements which brought disgrace to it during the period 1933–1945." See also Cohn, "The German Attorney (II)," 104; Dietrich Reuschemeyer, *Lawyers and Their Society: A Comparative Study of the Legal Profession in Germany and in the United States* (Cambridge, MA: Harvard University Press, 1973), 182.
240. SCAP press conference, "The Reform of the Penal Code," December 5, 1947, NARA RG 331, SCAP-GS, box 1498.

241. SCAP press conference, "The Reform of the Penal Code," April 23, 1947, NARA RG 331, SCAP-GS, box 1498.
242. SCAP press conference, "The Reform of the Penal Code," December 5, 1947, NARA RG 331, SCAP-GS, box 1498.
243. According to SLUGA analysts, since 1871 a number of attempts by German law reform groups to eliminate the worst anachronisms and anomalies of the original code had failed. SLUGA, "Memorandum on the Revision of German Criminal Law," November 4, 1946, 1–2, NAUK FO 1060/860.
244. Ibid.
245. Alfred C. Oppler, "The Reform of Japan's Legal and Judicial System Under Allied Occupation," *Washington Law Review* 24 (1949): 290, 291.
246. Some one-quarter of the Weimar-era criminal defence bar were Jews. Few of these men were willing (or alive to) take up their roles in postwar Germany. One of the most politically progressive wings of the German bar was thus unavailable to contribute to the liberal reconstruction of German criminal justice. See Reifner "Bar in the Third Reich," 104–106.

6. Twilight of the Gods

1. For an authoritative account of the harsh aspects of the American and Allied occupations of Germany after the Second World War, see Giles MacDonough, *After the Reich* (New York: Basic Books, 2007).
2. For a compelling account of American censorship in occupied Japan, see John W. Dower, *Embracing Defeat: Japan in the Wake of World War II* (New York: W.W. Norton, 1999), 405–440.
3. See, generally, Melvyn P. Leffler, *A Preponderance of Power: National Security, the Truman Administration, and the Cold War* (Palo Alto, CA: Stanford University Press, 1992), 116–130.
4. When the Second World War came to a close in August 1945, so did the informal wartime armistice between these bitterly opposed parties and factions. In the fall of 1946, American conservatives, unreconciled to New Deal statism, sensing Truman's inability to hold together FDR's Democratic voting coalition, scored major victories in the midterm congressional elections. Even when Truman won election in 1948, the Democrats led the federal government with one eye to their right flank. See, generally, Jonathan Bell, *The Liberal State on Trial: The Cold War and American Politics in the Truman Years* (New York: Columbia University Press, 2004), 1–45.
5. According to Carl Friedrich, the American constitutional consultant to Germany, the break between the Soviet Union and the United States became inevitable in 1947 when the United States set forth a firm demand that postwar Germany democratization be defined in liberal-capitalist terms. See Charles J. Friedrich, "Rebuilding the German Constitution, I," *American Political Science Review* 43, no. 3 (1949): 461, 467.

6. Campbell Craig and Fredrik Logevall, *America's Cold War: The Politics of Insecurity* (Cambridge, MA: Harvard University Press, 2009), 62, 68–77; 87–96.
7. According to one historian, "In typical liberal fashion, the Truman administration believed that political radicalism—and Communism was considered one of its quintessential manifestations—prospered in conditions of economic recovery and distress. The rapid recovery of postwar Europe was therefore deemed necessary for both political and economic reasons." Mario del Pero, "Incompatible Universalisms: The United States, the Soviet Union, and the Beginning of the Cold War," in *The Routledge Handbook of the Cold War,* ed. Artemy M. Kalinovsky and Craig Daigle (London: Routledge, 2014): 3, 6.
8. Josef Rupieper, *Die Wurzeln der westdeutschen Nachkriegsdemokratie: der amerikanische Beitrag, 1945–1952* (Opladen: Wesdeutscher Verlag, 1993), 43. See also David B. Posner, "Review of *Die Wurzeln der westdeutschen Nachkriegsdemokratie: der amerikanische Beitrag, 1945–1952,*" *German Studies Review* 20, no. 1 (1997): 183.
9. ACLU pamphlet, "Democratization and Civil Liberties in Germany," 1948, AACLUP, Princeton, box 1170.
10. As one historian has summarized, "However, although the Germans needed the West, the West also needed the Germans as the cornerstone of the policy of anti-communism, economic stabilization, and political democratization in west Europe." Edmund Spevack, *Allied Control and German Freedom. American Political and Ideological Influences on the Framing of the West German Constitution (Grundgesetz)* (Munster: LIT, 2001), 66.
11. "The Cultural Exchange program of the CAD," revised as of October 30, 1948, NARA RG 260, OMGUS Bavaria-CAD, box 8.
12. Harold W. Landin, chief, Democratization Branch, "Democratizing Germany," April 1948, Department of State Bulletin no. 133, 6–8.
13. For introductory overview to reeducation policy and planning, see, generally, James F. Tent, *Mission on the Rhine: Re-Education and Denazification in American-Occupied Germany* (Chicago: University of Chicago Press, 1982), 29–39. See also Udi Greenberg, *The Weimar Century: German Émigrés and the Ideological Foundations of the Cold War* (Princeton, NJ: Princeton University Press, 2014), 64–65.
14. Landin, "Democratizing Germany," 6–8.
15. "Techniques of Democratic Action: A Handbook for Reorientation," 2, NARA RG 260, OMGUS Bavaria-CAD, box 6.
16. As quoted in Rupieper, *Die Wurzeln,* 90.
17. "Long-Range Policy Statement for German Re-education," n.d., JFTP, box 2. See also Tent, *Mission on the Rhine,* 29–36; Masako Shibata, *Japan and Germany Under the US Occupation: A Comparative Analysis of Post-War Education Reform* (Lanham, MD: Lexington Books, 2005), 107–112.

18. JCS 1779, "Directive to the Commander in Chief of the U.S. Forces of Occupation," in U.S. Department of State, Office of Public Affairs, *Germany: 1947–1949: The Story in Documents,* ed. Velma Hastings Cassidy (Honolulu: University Press of the Pacific, 1950), 33.
19. Ibid., section 11d.
20. Ibid., section 5c. The policy of the United States was that it would not "impose its own historically developed forms of democracy and social organization on Germany."
21. "Techniques of Democratic Action: A Handbook for Reorientation," 2, NARA RG 260, OMGUS Bavaria-CAD, box 6.
22. Clay to Hays, November 12, 1948, ACLU Papers, box 10.
23. The number of visiting experts in the legal field increased from 3 to 10 in the fall of 1948. "Visiting Legal Experts to Germany," September 28, 1948, NARA RG 260, OMGUS LD-Weigert Correspondence files. The key German émigrés are profiled in Greenberg, *Weimar Century,* 17–25.
24. "The Cultural Exchange Program of the CAD," revised as of October 30, 1948, NARA OMGUS Bavaria-CAD, box 8.
25. Hermann-Josef Rupieper, "'Der Bund fur Burgerrechte:' Transnational Relations and the Problem of Democratization in Germany, 1949–1954," in *International Politics and German History: The Past Informs the Present,* ed. David Wetzel and Theodore S. Hamerow (Westport, CT: Praeger, 1997), 88–90.
26. Baldwin, interview of Alfred Weber, Baldwin interview notes, October 1948, RNBP, box 17. See also Rupieper, *Die Wurzeln,* 95–6.
27. See Baldwin, interview of A. K. Kramer and other OMGUS officials, October 8, 1948, RNBP, box 17. "Both men agreed that accomplishments to date are so superficial that if we left everything would be lost in six months."
28. Baldwin, "Test for American Democracy," written for *Corps Diplomatique,* Paris, 1948, RNBP, box 22.
29. Atina Grossmann, "Grams, Calories and Food: Languages of Victimization, Entitlement, and Human Rights in Occupied Germany, 1945–1949," *Central European History* 44, no. 1 (2011): 118, 139. Landin, "Civil Rights in Western Germany Today: A Report," 1950, ACLUP, box 1169.
30. ACLU pamphlet, "Democratization and Civil Liberties in Germany," 1948, ACLUP, box 1169.
31. As one ACLU executive put the point, "One fundamental principle of the ACLU is that men should not be deprived of liberty . . . because of their associations or views (past or present) but only because of acts. . . . Guilt by association is a Continental European and not an American doctrine." Hays, "Memo on Civil Liberties in Germany," September 13, 1948, ACLUP, box 1166; see also Simon to Baldwin, March 15, 1950, ACLUP, box 1170.
32. For analysis of Truman's 1946 Presidential Committee on Civil Rights and its findings, see, generally, Michael R. Gardner, *Harry Truman and Civil Rights:*

Moral Courage and Political Risks (Carbondale: Southern Illinois University Press, 2002), 50–60.

33. Born in 1903, Landin graduated with a Ph.D. in European history from Cornell in 1928. After stints at Smith College and Ohio State, he joined the American Council for Learned Societies in 1942 and 1942 and then OMGUS as a civil affairs officer in 1945. Edward Litchfield, chief of AMG's Civil Affairs Division, viewed Landin as an undisciplined maverick who did "not fit within any regularized administrative system." Landin returned to West Germany in 1950, this time as a State Department consultant on civil liberties projects. Landin's writings were widely distributed within AMG and in State Department bulletins. See, for instance, Landin, "Democratizing Germany," 6–8. See also Dayton to Baldwin, February 2, 1950, ACLUP, box 1171.
34. Landin, "Civil Rights in West Germany Today: A Report," September 12, 1949, in JKPP, box 64.
35. "Democratization and Decentralization of the Bavarian Government," April 22, 1947, NARA RG 260, OMGUS Bavaria-CAD, box 112.
36. See Anna J. Merritt and Richard L. Merritt, *Public Opinion in Occupied Germany: The OMGUS Surveys, 1945–1949* (Urbana: University of Illinois Press, 1970), 294–298; see also Richard Merton, September 23, 1948, RNBP, box 17.
37. Jay H. Geller, *Jews in the Post-Holocaust, 1945–1953* (Cambridge: Cambridge University Press, 2005), 124–127.
38. Merrit and Merritt, *Public Opinion,* 294–298.
39. "The Cultural Exchange Program of the CAD," revised as of October 30, 1948, NARA RG 260, OMGUS Bavaria-CAD, box 8.
40. See Merritt and Merritt, *Public Opinion,* 33–35. See also Baldwin, interview of Dr. Robert Kempner, Baldwin interview notes, October 1948, RNBP, box 17. According to Dr. Robert Kempner, a Weimar-era civil libertarian and, after the war, Nuremberg prosecutor, "Too many [Germans] accept the defense thesis that only the top leaders were to blame, or that these men did not know what was going on or their subordinates did it."
41. Baldwin, "The Promotion of Civil Liberties in Germany," n.d., ACLUP, box 1169; see also Baldwin, interview of Fritz Steinkuhle, Baldwin interview notes, October 1948, RNBP, box 17.
42. McCurdy to Chief of Staff, "Reorganization of the Administration of Justice Branch, LD, to Provide for Proper Handling of Reorientation Program," n.d., NARA RG 260, OMGUS LD-Administration of Justice Branch (AJBr), box 4.
43. Mortimer Kollender, "Legal Division Reorientation Program," December 21, 1948, NARA RG 260, OMGUS LD-AJBr, box 6.
44. Ibid.
45. McCurdy to Chief of Staff, "Reorganization of the Administration of Justice Branch, LD, to Provide for Proper Handling of Reorientation Program,"

n.d., NARA RG 260, OMGUS LD-AJBr, box 4. McCurdy was a Harvard law professor who had taken leave to work on legal reorientation in American-occupied Germany in 1949.

46. Ibid.
47. Weigert to Rockwell, "Military Government Participation in Training of Referendars and Law Students," May 14, 1947, NARA RG 260, OMGUS LD-Weigert Correspondence file, box 132. Hans Weigert (1896–1967) was a German-born and trained lawyer and scholar of international relations. In 1938, he emigrated from Germany to the United States, taking up a number of academic posts before joining American Military Government as an expert-consultant to Legal Division in 1947. For biographical detail, see "Hans W. Weigert," obituary, *New York Times,* October 27, 1983.
48. Loewenstein to Fahy, "Report on the Law School of Munich," April 23, 1946, KLP, box 50.
49. Weigert to Rockwell, "Military Government Participation in Training of Referendars and Law Students," May 14, 1947, NARA RG 260, OMGUS LD-Weigert Correspondence file, box 132.
50. See, generally, Tent, *Mission on the Rhine,* 85–86. See also Konrad H. Jarausch, *The Unfree Professions: German Lawyers, Teachers and Engineers, 1900–1950* (New York, Oxford University Press, 1990), 9–13, 23, 63, 199.
51. "The Problem of Re-education in Germany," Office of Intelligence Research, Report no. 4237, June 5, 1947, Department of State, JFTP, box 5.
52. See, generally, Jeffrey S. Gaab, *Justice Delayed: The Restoration of Justice in Bavaria under American Occupation, 1945–1949* (New York: Lang, 1999), 74; Tent, *Mission on the Rhine,* 84–86. Se also Loewenstein to Fahy," Report on the Law School of Munich," April 23, 1946, KLP, box 50.
53. American intelligence reported that the German university hiring boards, "were almost uniformly inclined to protect their colleagues;" "The Problem of Re-education in Germany," Office of Intelligence Research, Report no. 4237, June 5, 1947, Department of State, JFTP, box 5. For scholarly support of this view, see, generally, Steven P. Remy, *The Heidelberg Myth: The Nazification and Denazification of a German University* (Cambridge, MA: Harvard University Press, 2002), 175, 223.
54. One student at a Munich law school, 1948–53, recalled that he and his fellow students were uninterested in any politics. They had just wanted to get on with their education as lawyers, whether under former Nazi professors or not. See James Tent, "Interview of Professor Heinrich Scholler," February 8, 1980, JFTP, box 5.
55. In Sollman's opinion, the wartime period had left German students with "little political interest and conviction. . . . Deeper attachment to democracy has not yet developed. Most students live politically and religiously in a kind of vacuum."

56. George Florsheim (chief interrogator, OMGUS-Bavaria) to Commanding Officer, Information Control, "The Munich University Student Body," May 9, 1946, JFTP, box 5.
57. See "Meeting at Heidelberg University," 1947, NARA RG 260, LD-AJBr, box 89. This was also the view of Walter Jellinek, dean of the law school at Heidelberg. See James Tent, "Interview of Professor Heinrich Scholler," February 8, 1980, in JFTP, box 5.
58. Kollender to Weigert, "Reorientation Project for Trainees (Referendars)," November 12, 1948, NARA RG 260, OMGUS LD-Weigert Correspondence file, box 132.
59. Mortimer Kollender, "Legal Division Reorientation Program," December 21, 1948, NARA RG 260, OMGUS Legal Division-AJBr, box 6.
60. In 1949 alone, the United States spent $184,000 on referendar training, grants, scholarships, chairs, library acquisition and foreign travel.
61. One scholar has called American reorientation efforts at Munich University a "basic failure." Gaab, *Justice Delayed,* 115. For a similar conclusion, see Remy, *Heidelberg Myth.*
62. "The Cultural Exchange Program of Legal Division," n.d., NARA RG 260, OMGUS LD-Weigert Correspondence file, box 132.
63. Weigert to Kollender, "1950 Reorientation Projects," April 18, 1949, NARA RG 260, OMGUS LD-Weigert Correspondence file, box 132. See also Gaab, *Justice Delayed,* 112–113.
64. Henry Parkman, "Talk on German Constitutional Liberties," August 1947, NARA RG 260, OMGUS CAD-Director, box 66.
65. As one AMG report claimed, while the new state constitutions were "basically democratic in their provisions, those provisions have no tradition to support them and their practical implications are understood neither by the people or government. It is especially unfortunate that the courts have no tradition of constitutional protection of individuals, or the public, against the State, nor of contributing independently to the growth of the democratic state." See "Democratization and Decentralization of the Bavarian Government," April 22, 1947, NARA RG 260, OMGUS Bavaria-CAD, box 112.
66. Ibid. See also "Three German Constitutions Compared with the Constitution of the United States," n.d., NARA RG 260, OMGUS Bavaria-CAD, box 112.
67. JCS 1779, "Directive to the Commander in Chief of the U.S. Forces of Occupation," *Germany 1947–1949: The Story in Documents,* 33.
68. As one American expert stated on this point, "And yet our basic objective is to help the Germans learn that might does not make right, and that the rule of law . . . is the individual's greatest single protection against a capricious and willful expression of governmental power." Henry Parkman, "Talk on German Constitutional Liberties," August 1947, NARA RG 260, OMGUS CAD-Director, box 66.

69. Such as the Harvard constitutional law scholar, Carl Friedrich. Clay to Friedrich, June 29, 1948, CJFP, box 5. See also Clay to Draper, April 28, 1948, *The Papers of General Lucius Clay,* vol. 2, ed. Jean Edward Smith (Bloomington: Indiana University Press, 1974), 642.
70. Jean Edward Smith, *Lucius D. Clay: An American Life* (New York: Holt, 1990), 332. For details of Nash's visit to Germany, see also Rupieper, "Der Bund," 90–91; Lora Wildenthal, "Human Rights Activism in Occupied and Early West Germany: The Case of the German League for Human Rights," *Journal of Modern History* 80, no. 3 (2008): 515–556, at 536.
71. For Roger Baldwin's anti-Communist convictions, see, generally, Robert C. Cotterell, *Roger Nash Baldwin and the American Civil Liberties Union* (New York: Columbia University Press, 2000); Judy Kutulas, *The American Civil Liberties Union and the Making of Modern Liberalism, 1930–1960* (Chapel Hill: University of North Carolina Press, 2006).
72. Clay to Baldwin, August 28, 1948, ACLU Papers, box 1166.
73. See Baldwin, "Memo to the State and Army Department on Occupation Policies in Germany," January 1949, RNBP, box 17.
74. Baldwin, "Notes on Interview of General Clay," October 8, 1948, RNBP, box 17.
75. Baldwin, "Letter to ACLU Members," October 10, 1948, RNBP, box 17.
76. Hayes, "Memo on Civil Liberties in Germany," September 13, 1948, ACLUP, box 1166
77. Baldwin, "Letter to ACLU," October 10, 1948, RNBP, box 17.
78. Baldwin, "Facts Concerning Civil Liberties in Germany, n.d., RNBP, box 17.
79. As quoted in Rupieper, "Der Bund," 92.
80. A number of Baldwin's interviewees stated that the Criminal Investigations Division of AMG was regarded by Germans as an "American Gestapo." See Baldwin, interview of Colonel Montgomery, Berlin, Baldwin interview notes, October 1948, RNBP, box 17.
81. Baldwin, "Report on Civil Liberties in Germany," November 1948, NARA RG 260, OMGUS CAD, box 201.
82. Baldwin, "Facts Concerning Civil Liberties in Germany," n.d., RNBP, box 17.
83. In a private meeting with Clay, Baldwin expressed disquiet that scores of ex-Nazi jurists and senior civil servants had been permitted to return to important public offices. When he informed Clay (inaccurately) that in Japan purged ultranationalists had not been permitted to resume important offices, the general replied that "it would be impracticable to do in Germany what was done in Japan, namely to bar forever from office or private responsible posts, the top leaders and responsible Nazis because there were so many of them. Clay thought that the Germans had be trusted to do their own

house-cleaning." Baldwin, "Notes on Interview of General Clay," October 8, 1948, RNBP, box 17.

84. Baldwin, October 3, 1948, ACLU Papers, box 1166. For complete list of suggested reforms, see Baldwin, "Memorandum for General Clay," October 1948, RNBP, box 4. Baldwin worried that his list of needed reforms was so long it would be "too formidable even for a liberal general to swallow." Baldwin, "Report on Civil Liberties in Germany," November 1948, RG 260, OMGUS CAD, box 201. See also Baldwin to Litchfield, November 5, 1948, RG 260, OMGUS CAD, box 201.
85. Clay to Hays, November 12, 1948, ACLUP, box 1169.
86. Baldwin, "Notes on Interview of General Clay," October 8, 1948, RNBP, box 17.
87. Henry Draper pledged to Baldwin that the German civil liberties union project would get funded. Draper to Baldwin, January 28, 1949, RNBP, box 17.
88. Most of these searches, insofar as the police bothered to justify them legally, were justified on the so-called "hot pursuit" or "imminent danger" exception. See "Translation of '*Neue Zeitung*'" clipping, January 13, 1947, NARA RG 260, OMGUS CAD, box 201. But according to some German media, "the exception has become a rule." See also Landis, "Democratizing Germany," 6–8.
89. An AMG study of more than 10,600 German police searches found that 10,550 took place without warrants. About half of Germans surveyed thought policing was, in terms of security, as good as it had been under the Nazis. Garde, ADJ, to all zonal MG, "Searches and Seizures by German Police," January 21, 1949, NARA RG 260, OMGUS Legal Division-AJBr, box 82. See also "Translation of '*Neue Zeitung*'" clipping, January 13, 1947, NARA RG 260, OMGUS CAD, box 201.
90. General Appraisals, April 25, 1949, NARA RG 260, OMGUS CAD, box 201.
91. Clem, "Notes for Briefing, Civil Liberties Campaign," May 13, 1949, NARA RG 260, OMGUS CAD-Bavaria, box 5.
92. Justice ministers of the Länder were ordered to stop warrantless searches except in cases of imminent danger. "Inviolability of the Home," April 13, 1949, NARA RG 260, OMGUS CAD-Bavaria, box 5.
93. Rupieper, "Der Bund," 87–102; Wildenthal, "Human Rights Activism," 536.
94. Baldwin to Dayton, November 14, 1950, RNBP, box 17. As Baldwin reported in November 1950, "There is no structure or organization with any roots sufficient to promise continuation through its own development. . . . That such movement as exists is fumbling around with matters of comparatively little consequence or direction." Baldwin thought that American "aid and stimulation" would continue to be "essential to developing the movement."

95. By 1952, there were some forty local civil liberties chapters in West Germany, and sixty-three by 1952, with a membership of approximately 3,500 members. Rupieper, "Der Bund," 95–97. In the opinion of at least one American field officer, the civil liberties union effort "takes on the appearance of a Military Government stooge organization." Field Officers Seminar, "German Indifference to Civil Liberties," March 15, 1949, NARA RG 260, CAD-Bavaria, box 8.
96. Wildenthal, "Human Rights Activism," 533, 516–522.
97. Baldwin to Bowies, September 25, 1950. RNBP, box 17; Landin to Litchfield, "Civil Rights Program," May 12, 1949, NARA RG 260, OMGUS CAD, box 201.
98. Harold W. Landin, "The 'Bund fuer Buergerrechte' in Germany (Civil Liberties Union)," ACLUP, box 1169.
99. See, generally, John Gimbel, *The American Occupation of Germany: Politics and the Military,* 1945–1949 (Stanford, CA: Stanford University Press, 1968), 200–231; Edmund Spevack "American Pressures on the German Constitutional Tradition: Basic Rights in the West German Constitution of 1949," *International Journal of Politics, Culture, and Society* 10, no. 3 (1997): 411; Udi Greenberg, "The Limits of Dictatorship and the Origins of Democracy: The Political Theory of Carl J. Friedrich from Weimar to the Cold War," in *The Weimar Moment: Liberalism, Political Theology, and Law,* ed. Leonard V. Kaplan and Rudy Koshar (Lanham, MD: Lexington Books, 2012), 443–464. For German language sources on the Basic Law, see Martin Borowski, "The Beginnings of Germany's Federal Constitutional Court," *Ratio Juris* 16, no. 2 (2003): 155, 158–162.
100. Lucius D. Clay, *Decision in Germany* (London: W. Heinemann, 1950), 420–425.
101. George Marshall, "Reconstruction of Germany on a Democratic Basis," Department of State, Bulletin no. 16, March 14, 1947, 524.
102. Spevack, *Allied Control,* 15; Erich J. Hahn, "U.S. Policy on a West German Constitution," in *American Policy and the Reconstruction of West Germany, 1945–1955,* ed. Jeffrey M. Diendorf, Axel Frohn, and Hermann-Josef Rupieper (New York: Cambridge University Press, 1993), 21–44, at 27.
103. Carl J. Friedrich and Herbert J. Spiro, "The Constitution of the Federal Republic," in Edward H. Litchfield, *Governing Postwar Germany* (Ithaca, NY: Cornell University Press, 1953), 117–151, 118.
104. For German reaction to the Allied constitutional initiative, see Roger Wells, "The German Problem in 1948," *Western Political Quarterly* 2 (1949): 208, 215; Gimbel, *American Occupation of Germany,* 212. Friedrich, "German Constitution, I," 472; Carl J. Friedrich, "Rebuilding the German Constitution, II," *American Political Science Review* 43, no. 4 (1949): 704, 704.
105. The nature and parameters of the Allied Occupation Statute of April 1949 are discussed in Friedrich and Spiro, "Constitution of the German Federal

Republic," 119–120. See also H. W. Koch, *A Constitutional History of Germany in the Nineteenth and Twentieth Centuries* (London: Longman, 1984), 266–267; Friedrich, "Rebuilding the German Constitution, I," 469.

106. Gimbel, *American Occupation of Germany,* 209–210.
107. While Americans initiated the process, German officials, if reluctantly at first, took over and settled almost all the details according to the advice of German experts. See Borowski, "Germany's Federal Constitutional Court," 157–159; see also Heinrich A. Winkler, *Germany: The Long Road West,* vol. 2: 1933–1990 (New York: Oxford University Press, 2000), 122.
108. Gimbel, *American Occupation of Germany,* 213; see also Hahn, "U.S. Policy on a West German Constitution," 32; see also Friedrich, "Rebuilding the German Constitution, I," 470.
109. Friedrich, "Rebuilding the German Constitution, I," 479–81; see, generally, Hahn, "U.S. Policy on a West German Constitution;" see also Spevack, *Allied Control,* 340–436.
110. For a detailed analysis of Friedrich's legal and political outlook, see Greenberg, "The Limits of Dictatorship," 443–464. See, generally, Friedrich, "Rebuilding the German Constitution"; Spevack, *Allied Control,* 350–353.
111. Spevack, "American Pressures," 411, 420; Borowski, "Germany's Federal Constitutional Court," 159–161.
112. In one of the most contentious clashes, General Clay and the German Social Democrats locked horns over whether the new federal government should have jurisdiction to centrally plan the West German economy. See Marjorie Lamberti, "General Lucius Clay, German Politicians and the Great Crisis During the Making of West Germany's Constitution," *German Politics and Society* 27, no. 4 (2009): 24, 36–37; Spevack, *Allied Control,* 517.
113. Neither the early nor final drafts set forth a detailed framework for the powers and procedures of the FCC in undertaking judicial review. See Florian Meinel, "The Constitutional Miracle on the Rhine: Towards a History of West German Constitutionalism and the Federal Constitutional Court," *International Journal of Constitutional Law* 14, no. 1 (2016): 277–293, at 278. See also Dieter Grimm, "The Role of Fundamental Rights After Sixty-Five Years of Constitutional Jurisprudence in Germany," *International Journal of Constitutional Law* 13, no. 1 (2015): 9, 12–13.
114. For a discussion of the illiberal rulings of the United States Supreme Court on cases involving Communist activists, see Larry Ceplair, *Anti-Communism in Twentieth-Century America: A Critical History* (Santa Barbara, CA: Praegar, 2011), 106–109. Christoph Mollers, "Scope and Legitimacy of Judicial Review in German Constitutional Law—The Court versus Political Process," in *Debates in German Public Law,* ed. Hermann Punder and Christian Waldhoff (Oxford: Hart, 2014), 3–26, 3–4.

115. Michaela Hailbronner, "Rethinking the Rise of the German Constitutional Court: From Anti-Nazism to Value Formalism," *International Journal of Constitutional Law* 12, no. 3 (2014): 626, 631.
116. See also Donald Kommers, *The Constitutional Jurisprudence of the Federal Republic of Germany* (Durham, NC: Duke University Press, 1989), 8.
117. Hailbronner, "Rethinking the Rise," 639; see also Karl Loewenstein, "Justice," in Litchfield, *Governing Postwar Germany,* 255.
118. Friedrich, "Rebuilding the German Constitution, II," 708–709.
119. *The Basic Law for the Federal Republic of Germany,* Deutscher Bundestag, online, https://www.btg-bestellservice.de/pdf/80201000.pdf.
120. Spevack, "American Pressures," 412; see also Friedrich, "Rebuilding the German Constitution, II," 708.
121. Friedrich, "Rebuilding the German Constitution, II."
122. *Basic Law,* Deutscher Bundestag, online, Articles 18, 20, 97. See Loewenstein, "Justice," 255–258.
123. See, generally, Loewenstein, "Justice," 255–258; Arthur T. von Mehren, "Constitutionalism in Germany—The First Decision of the New Constitutional Court," *American Journal of Comparative Law* 1 (1952): 70, 76.
124. Von Mehren, "Constitutionalism in Germany," 78.
125. Friedrich, "Rebuilding the German Constitution, II," 708.
126. In 1949, the Parliamentary Council had decided not to include in the Basic Law a provision that explicitly guaranteed the legal right of an individual to sue the state on the basis of a rights violation. See Borowski, "Germany's Federal Constitutional Court," 168–169.
127. Ibid., 171.
128. Von Mehren, "Constitutionalism in Germany," 78–79. See also Edward McWhinney, "The German Federal Constitutional Court and the Communist Party Decision," *Indiana Law Journal* 32, no. 3 (1956): 295–312, at 296.
129. For a general summary of the German turn on the theory, see Kommers and Miller, *Constitutional Jurisprudence,* 222. For the theory that democratic political communities needed to be armed to defend themselves against antidemocratic political agitation or subversion, see, generally, Karl Loewenstein, "Militant Democracy and Fundamental Rights, I," *The American Political Science Review* 31, no. 3 (1937): 417. Ironically (given his later criticisms of Adenauer's abuses of the theory in the 1950s), Karl Loewenstein was a leading theorist of militant democracy.
130. As one scholar summarizes the point: "The constitutional scholars who began drafting western Germany's constitution in the summer of 1948 and the politicians who gathered in Bonn at the Parliamentary Council to complete it the following year both agreed that the new republic should be pre-emptively empowered to crush its enemies." Greenberg, *Weimar Century,* 204.
131. Ibid.

132. Friedrich, "Rebuilding the German Constitution, II," 709; for background, see Greenberg, "Limits of Dictatorship," 449–450.
133. Greenberg, *Weimar Century,* 201–202.
134. Meinel, "The Constitutional Miracle on the Rhine," 284.
135. Baldwin, "Report to the ACLU on Mission to Germany," October 30, 1950, RNBP, box 17.
136. Baldwin, "Conference with Leaders of LIGA," September 23, 1950, RNBP, box 17.
137. Baldwin, "Report to the ACLU on Mission to Germany," October 30, 1950, RNBP, box 17.
138. Ibid.
139. During this visit, Sollman spoke with the leaders of all the major political parties and with many of the politicians and experts who participated in drafting the basic law. Sollman also met with many of the leaders of the Länder governments and with leading journalists and scholars. He also interviewed American officials working at the Land level. William Sollman, "Report to the Political Affairs Division of HICOG," October 1950, JKPP, box 64.
140. Ibid.
141. Ibid.
142. Baldwin, "Interview of Mr. Egidi, Vogel, Frazer," September 15, 1950, RNBP, box 17.
143. Bennet M. Rich, "Civil Liberties in Germany," *Political Science Quarterly* 65, no. 1 (1950): 68, 84.
144. Landin, "Civil Rights in Western Germany Today: A Report," 1950, ACLUP, box 1169.
145. Not until the insult law had been invoked multiple times in 1949–1950 did the American authorities apply pressure on the Germans to change it. As Landin commented: "During the last year more than thirty cases have been tried in German courts in the US zone alone involving merely the criticism of public servants. In only one case was the defendant acquitted . . . So long as the average citizen is intimidated by the officials of the gov't it is idle to expect citizens to cry out against abuse and tyranny." Landin, "Civil Rights in Western Germany Today: A Report," 1950, ACLUP, box 1169. For further discussion of the invocation of the insult law in this period, see Josef Muller, State Minister of Justice, April 29, 1949, NARA RG 260, OMGUS CAD-Bavaria, box 5; see also Muller, "Civil Liberties in Germany (Brief Historical Background)," NARA RG 260, OMGUS CAD-Bavaria, box 2; see also Landin, "Civil Rights in West Germany Today: A Report," 1950, ACLUP, box 1169.
146. The KDP was as the western iteration of the East German Communist Party, the SED. The KDP was in fact an instrument of the SED and the Soviets. Patrick Major, *The Death of the KPD: Communism and Anti-Communism in West Germany, 1945–1956* (Oxford: Clarendon Press, 1997), 7, 14.

147. Rebecca L. Boehling, *A Question of Priorities: Democratic Reforms and Economic Recovery in Postwar Germany: Frankfurt, Munich, and Stuttgart under U.S. Occupation, 1945–1949* (New York: Berghahn, 1998), 217–218.
148. Clay to Assistant Secretary of the Army, October 27, 1947, in *Papers of General Lucius Clay,* ed. Smith, 448.
149. The weight of intelligence was that the KPD was too weak to subvert the new Bonn state. Major, *Death of the KPD,* 3, 245. For a summary of AMG's anticommunist program, see "Outline for Program against Communism," October 29, 1947, NARA RG 260, OMGUS CAD-Director, box 72.
150. Boehling, *Question of Priorities,* 234.
151. Support was shown in the form of covert financing and disproportionate newsprint and media time. Simon, "OMGUS Policy Regarding Communism," October 28, 1947, NARA RG 260, CAD-Director, box 72.
152. In this regard, Carlo Schmid, a leader of the SPD in West Germany, spoke of the "courage of intolerance." As quoted in Quinn Slobodian, *Globalists: The End of Empire and the Birth of Neoliberalism* (Cambridge, MA: Harvard University Press, 2018), 14. See also Greenberg, *Weimar Century,* 201–202.
153. In this era, the West German population was very receptive to official repression of the Communists, and the doctrine was (as one historian puts it), more "'Made in Germany' than a McCarthyite import." See Major, *Death of the KDP,* 15.
154. As quoted in Rupieper, *Die Wurzeln,* 43.
155. Major, *Death of the KPD,* 246; see also Boehling, *Question of Priorities,* 222–223.
156. Ibid., 278.
157. Ibid., 253.
158. Ibid., 253–256. See also *Weekly Political Review,* no. 10, September 29, 1950, NARA RG 260, OMGUS Legal Division-AJB, box 67.
159. McCloy to Baldwin, November 14, 1950, RNBP, box 6.
160. Baldwin notes, "Mr. John McCloy," October 4, 1950, RNBP, box 6.
161. McCloy to Baldwin, November 14, 1950, RNBP, box 6.
162. See Paul Franz, "Unconstitutional and Outlawed Political Parties: A German-American Comparison" *Boston College International and Comparative Law Review* 5, no. 1 (1982): 51; Major, *Death of the KPD,* 276–277; McWhinney, "Communist Party Decision," 299.
163. Including efforts to bring the state under "foreign domination." Franz, "Unconstitutional and Outlawed Political Parties." See also Orlan Lee and T. A. Robertson, *Moral Order and the Criminal Law: Reform Efforts in the United States and Western Germany* (The Hague: Nijhoff, 1973), 170.
164. See, generally, Vormbaum and Bohlander, *Modern History of German Criminal Law,* 222; Alexander von Brünneck, *Politische Justiz gegen Kommunisten in der Bundesrepublik, 1949–1968,* (Frankfurt: Suhrkamp, Verlag, 1978).

165. For discussion of the Bund and anti-Communism, see Wildenthal, "Human Rights Activism," 533–537.
166. See Kommers and Miller, *Constitutional Jurisprudence,* 227–229. The FCC had delayed its decision in the case hoping that the problem of the KPD would be resolved politically; see also Franz, "Outlawed Political Parties," 56–63.
167. Baldwin, "Notes on Trip to Bavaria," October 1950, RNBP, box 17.
168. Letter to the ACLU, October 30, 1950, RNBP, box 17.
169. Baldwin, "Germany Trip," November 17, 1950, RNBP, box 17.
170. Ibid.
171. Loewenstein, "The Political Balance Sheet of the Occupation," address before Political Science Association, December 28, 1949, KLP, box 21.
172. The Potsdam Declaration, Proclamation Defining Terms for Japanese Surrender Issued, at Potsdam, July 26, 1945, Article 10. *Birth of the Constitution of Japan,* available at http://www.ndl.go.jp/constitution/e/etc/c06.html.
173. SCAPIN 93 purged some 4,000 people from positions in the Home Ministry and secret police. By December 1946, the directive also had led to the release of some 3,000 political prisoners, abolished wartime Japan's Thought Control Law, and ended police surveillance of more than 2,000 persons. See SCAP-HQ, "Non-Military Activities in Japan and Korea—Establishment of Civil Liberties," Summation(s) no. 1–3, NARA SCAP-HQ, box 847.
174. Article 17 of the 1947 constitution was explicit on this point: "Every person may sue for redress as provided by law from the State or a public entity, in case he has suffered damage through illegal act of any public official." "The Constitution of Japan," *PRJ,* vol. 2, app. C, 672.
175. Howard Schonberger, "American Labor's Cold War in Occupied Japan," *Diplomatic History* 3, no. 3 (1979): 249–272, at 253–255; see also Dower, *Embracing Defeat,* 255.
176. MacArthur, "Warning Against Mob Disorder and Violence," May 20, 1946, *PRJ,* vol. 2, app. F, 750. For the institutional background of this statement, see Theodore Cohen and Herbert Passin, *Remaking Japan: The American Occupation as New Deal* (New York: Free Press, 1987), 286.
177. "Statement Calling Off General Strike," January 31, 1947, *PRJ,* vol. 2, app. F, 762.
178. Baldwin accepted this invitation on the theory that after the Second World War it was right that the ACLU should become "interested in United States' policies in occupied countries." He claimed to have traveled to Japan as a "private citizen and free of military control or censorship." Baldwin, *Autobiography (1947–1950),* 435, RNBP, box 21. See also Kutulas, *American Civil Liberties Union,* 136.
179. On the politically calculating side of the equation, however, in the winter of 1947 MacArthur had not ruled out a run for president the next year. Some positive publicity in the United States of the general's achievements in the democratization of Japan only stood to improve his standing in the eyes of

American voters. D. Clayton James, *Years of MacArthur,* vol. 3 (Boston: Houghton Mifflin, 1970), 201–205.

180. Kutulas, *American Civil Liberties Union,* 128–148. See also Laura Weinrib, *The Taming of Free Speech: America's Civil Liberties Compromise* (Cambridge, MA: Harvard University Press, 2016).
181. Kutulas, *American Civil Liberties Union,* 138.
182. Baldwin, "Tokyo—Confidential," April 13, 1947, RNBP, box 18.
183. Baldwin, *Autobiography (1947–1950*), 448, RNBP, box 21.
184. According to Baldwin's recollection, "The General was better than his reputation, a gracious, kindly, out-going man, with wit and quick understanding and utter frankness. . . . I may have been overcome by charm, but this is one of the greatest guys I ever met." Baldwin, "Why Communism Fails in Japan," RNBP, box 22.
185. Baldwin, *Autobiography (1947–1950),* 446, RNBP, box 21.
186. Baldwin supported MacArthur's decision in 1947 to stop the left from organizing a General Strike. Baldwin, "Why Communism Fails in Japan," RNBP, box 22; see also Baldwin, *Autobiography (1947–1950),* 457–458.
187. Baldwin, *Autobiography (1947–1950),* 457–458.
188. Baldwin, *Autobiography (1947–1950),* 461; see also Baldwin, "Civil Liberties in Japan, June 1947, RNBP, box 18.
189. Baldwin actually started three different associations while in Japan—the JCLU, the United Nations, and one for Japanese-Americans. The JCLU was based directly on the American model. See "By-Laws of the Civil Liberties Union," NARA RG 331, SCAP-GS, box 1527. See also "Civil Liberties Union Here Growing into Big Movement," *Japan Times,* June 25, 1948.
190. Oppler, *Legal Reform,* 178–182. Blakemore, "Civil Liberties Union Meeting," June 5, 1947, RG 331, SCAP-GS, box 1500. The JCLU began operation in November 1947. For background, see also "Donations to . . . Japanese Civil Liberties Society," July 14, 1947, RG 331, LD, box 1527.
191. See Roger N. Baldwin, "Japan's American Revolution," *Current History* 14, no. 78 (1948): 100.
192. MacArthur twice promised Baldwin that he would intervene to curtail censorship, but then did not. Baldwin, *Autobiography (1947–1950),* 468, 490–491, 495, RNBP, box 21; see also Baldwin, "Notes on Japan, Conference with Col. Nugent," RNBP, box 17.
193. Baldwin, "Japan's American Revolution," 100.
194. See, generally, Takemae, *Inside GHQ,* 457–515. See also Sayuri Guthrie-Shimuzu, "Japan, the United States and the Cold War, 1945–1960," in *The Cambridge History of the Cold War,* ed. Melvyn P. Leffler and Odd Arne Westad, vol. 1 (Cambridge: Cambridge University Press, 2010), 244–265, 250–252.
195. As one historian generalized, MacArthur's "early policies of democratization and demilitarization were halted around 1948 and replaced with the priorities of economic recovery and rearmament in the context of the cold war."

Carol Gluck, "Entangling Illusions—Japanese and American Views of the Occupation," in *New Frontiers in American-East Asian Relations,* ed. Warren I. Cohen and Dorothy Borg (New York: Columbia University Press, 1983), 200.

196. James, *Years of MacArthur,* vol. 3, 221–222.
197. Ibid., for a more detailed description of Kennan's intervention in Japan.
198. Takemae, *Inside GHQ,* 457–459.
199. "The right of workers to organize and bargain collectively is guaranteed." Article 28, "The Constitution of Japan," *PRJ,* vol. 2, app. C, 672.
200. See, generally, Cohen and Passin, *Remaking Japan,* 416–417; Ray A. Moore and Donald L. Robinson, *Partners for Democracy: Crafting the New Japanese State Under McArthur* (New York: Oxford University Press, 2002), 319.
201. James, *Years of MacArthur,* vol. 3, 226.
202. Schonberger, "American Labor's Cold War in Occupied Japan," 263; Takemae, *Inside GHQ,* 467–68, 475.
203. Hans H. Baerwald, *Purge of Japanese Leaders Under the Occupation* (Westport, CT: Greenwood, 1977), 99–103; see also Sayuri Guthrie-Shimuzu, "Japan, the United States and the Cold War, 1945–1950," in *Cambridge History of the Cold War,* ed. Melvyn P. Leffler (Cambridge: Cambridge University Press, 2010): 244, 250.
204. Takemae, *Inside GHQ,* 457.
205. Ibid., 462–465.
206. Cohen and Passin, *Remaking Japan,* 392, 389–392. The directive affected some 700,000 government employees, including teachers and communications workers. Michael Schaller, *Origins of Cold War in Asia* (Oxford: Oxford University Press, 1985), 135. See also Takemae, *Inside GHQ,* 462; Cohen, *Remaking Japan,* 384–393; Schonberger, "American Labor's Cold War," 260–261; Baerwald, *Purge of Japanese Leaders,* 99–103.
207. Yoshida's second cabinet, organized in November 1948, is generally regarded as the crucial turning point in the resurgence of Japanese conservativism in postwar Japan. The election marked the beginning of aggressive anti-Communist crackdown in the country. From this point forward Yoshida, supported by American right-wing groups, was able to exert more counterweight against Government Section's liberal-democratic reform program. Gluck, "Entangling," 183–186.
208. Shigeru Yoshida, *The Yoshida Memoirs: The Story of Japan in Crisis* (Boston: Houghton Mifflin, 1962), 180.
209. Takemae, *Inside GHQ,* 470–471.
210. See, for instance, Courtney Whitney, *MacArthur: His Rendezvous with History* (New York: Knopf, 1956); see also Oppler, *Legal Reform;* Justin Williams, *Japan's Political Revolution Under MacArthur: A Participant's Account* (Athens: University of Georgia Press, 1979).
211. Oppler, *Legal Reform,* 86.

212. Colonel Napier, "Counter-Measures Against the Subversive Potential in Japan," n.d., NARA RG 331, SCAP-GS, box 1524.
213. "Legal Section's Activities Connected with the Problem of Communism," 1951, Annex B, NARA RG 331, SCAP-GS, box 1447.
214. In 1948, Kades had been denounced as a Communist fellow-traveler (by an anonymous source) to SCAP's counterintelligence (G-2) division. The political tide in the United States had turned to the point where even MacArthur could not, or did not, shield him. Although Kades was eventually cleared of all "derogatory allegations," this incident prompted Kades to return to the U.S. See R. S. Bratton, Memorandum for the Record: Kades, September 23, 1948, File, CLKP, box 5.
215. Kades left Japan in February 1949 and did not return. Napier had been the chief administrator of the purge of ultranationalists. See Takemae, *Inside GHQ,* 479–482.
216. In 1948, the Diet passed legislation dissolving the Ministry of Justice and reassigning its post-constitutional reform responsibilities to the Office of the Attorney General.
217. Cecil H. Uyehara, *The Subversive Activities Prevention Law of Japan: Its Creation, 1951–52* (Leiden, Boston: Brill, 2009), 4.
218. "Legal Section's Activities Connected with the Problem of Communism," 1951, Annex C, NARA RG 331, SCAP-LS, box 1447.
219. For background on the suppression of civil liberties in the United States in the early Cold War era, see, generally, Michal R. Belknap, *Cold War Political Justice: The Smith Act, the Communist party, and American Civil Liberties* (Westport, CT: Greenwood, 1977); see also Stanley I. Kutler, *The American Inquisition: Justice and Injustice in the Cold War* (New York: Hill and Wang, 1982).
220. "Legal Section's Activities Connected with the Problem of Communism," 1951, Annex C, NARA RG 331, SCAP-GS, box 1447. In the relevant archive of this activity, this historian could find no record that Government Section officers had made and recorded objections or even reservations about the legality or constitutional validity even of the most draconian of antisubversive measures.
221. Untitled meeting, transcript, September 9, 1949, NARA RG331, SCAP-GS, box 1528.
222. Uyehara, *The Subversive Activities,* 3; Takemae, *Inside GHQ,* 479.
223. Ibid.
224. This was recorded by Roger Baldwin. Baldwin also expressed concern to SCAP that the dissolution law would lead to the suppression of legitimate activities. Baldwin to Sullivan, September 27, 1949, ACLUP, box 1169.
225. Oppler, *Legal Reform,* 227–228.
226. Ibid., 228.
227. See Oppler, Memo for the Record, "Decisions of Japanese Courts on Violations of the Purge Ordinance," March 27, 1949, NARA RG 331, SCAP-GS,

box 1500. Whitney dispatched one of his new deputies, Frank Rizzo, to meet with Acting Chief Justice Taukazaki of Japan's Supreme Court. Rizzo communicated GS's "grave concern and severe criticism" of the recent purge decision. Rizzo stated that while GS was reluctant to interfere with judicial independence in Japan, it had no other recourse in this instance. He reminded the acting chief justice that the Japanese law affecting the purge was based on a SCAP directive and therefore was not subject to creative interpretation. If the injunctions were not reversed as soon as possible, Rizzo emphasized, they would threaten to undermine both the purge program and SCAP's basic authority. For this reason it was time once again that the Supreme Court provided "general instructions to the inferior courts including for the proper interpretation" of the relevant purge ordinances.

228. Oppler, *Legal Reform,* 228–229.

229. Oppler, "Mitaka and Komatsu Cases," November 21, 1949, NARA RG 331, SCAP-LD, box 1500. See, generally, Chalmers Johnson, *Conspiracy at Matsukawa* (Berkeley: University of California Press, 1972).

230. In early February 1949, left with no choice, the chief justice issued a direction to his courts that since the "machinery and procedures" of the purge had been established by the Supreme Commander, "the Japanese courts are without jurisdiction over any removal or exclusion proceedings." "Jurisdiction of the Japanese Courts over Purge Cases," n.d., NARA RG 331, SCAP-LD, box 1500.

231. Takemae, *Inside GHQ,* 480; Brice Fauconnier, "The 'Red Purges' and the Democratisation of Japan, 1949–1952" in *Japan's Postwar,* ed. Michael Lucken, Anne Bayard-Sakai, and Emmanuel Lozerand (London: Routledge, 2013), 233–234.

232. Dower, *Embracing Defeat,* 433–438.

233. "Release of Communists and Fellow Travelers from Government Service Begun on SCAP Suggestions (July 21, 1949)," n.d., NARA RG 331, SCAP-GS, box 1524.

234. Ibid.

235. As MacArthur wrote in an open letter to Yoshida, "Acting in common accord, they [the communists] have hurled defiance at constituted authority, show contempt for the processes of law and order." Press release, MacArthur to Yoshida, June 6, 1950, NARA RG 331, SCAP-GS, box 1522. See also Takemae, *Inside GHQ,* 482.

236. See Fauconnier, "Red Purges." Although the final upward tally of red purgees cannot be known with accuracy, the number could not be fewer than 10,000. See John W. Dower and Tetsuo Hirata, "Japan's Red Purge: Lessons from a Saga of Suppression of Free Speech and Thought," *Japan Focus,* online, July 10, 2007, https://apjjf.org/-John-W.-Dower/2462/article.html.

237. At least 1,100 persons were dismissed from their jobs on grounds merely that they were "known troublemakers." See "Release of Communists and Fellow Travelers from Government Service Begun on SCAP Suggestions," July 21, 1950, NARA RG 331, SCAP-GS, box 1524.
238. In 1950, Burati, who began work in SCAP's Labor Division in 1948, had worked to promote the development of independent and affiliated non-Communist trade unions in Japan. See, generally, John Price, "Valery Burati and the Formation of Sohyo During the U.S. Occupation of Japan," *Pacific Affairs* 64, no. 2 (1991): 208.
239. Burati to Sullivan, August 14, 1950, VBP, box 3.
240. Ibid.
241. First reported in Takemae, *Inside GHQ,* 483.
242. Burati to Sullivan, August 22, 1950, VBP, box 3.
243. Oppler to Takemae, September 23, 1981, ACOP, box 5.
244. Aka to Napier, "Conference with Judges of Tokyo District Court," June 29, 1950, NARA RG 331, SCAP-GS, box 2059.
245. Ibid. See also Oppler, "Daily Activity Report," "Communist Purge Case," June 26 to July 1, 1950, NARA RG 331, SCAP-GS, box 1500.
246. Oppler, "Daily Activity Report," "Other Activities," July 24 to 29, 1950, NARA RG 331, SCAP-GS, box 1500.
247. Oppler, Memo for the Record, "Discharge of Communist Employees by Newspapers," July 29, 1950, NARA RG 331, SCAP-GS, box 1524.
248. Ibid.
249. McCormick to Oppler, "Dismissals of Subversives," August 21, 1950, NARA RG 331, SCAP-GS, box 1524.
250. Ibid. At the chief justice's request, "the Judicial Assembly met and came to the conclusion to send officials of the Secretariat to each high court to inform judges under each jurisdiction."
251. Ibid. Such as the case of a dismissed electrical worker who had asked that a requirement that he register as a Communist be declared unconstitutional. A preliminary finding in favor of the applicant was quickly reversed by the same judge.
252. In September 1950, for example, the application of twelve purged journalists that their discharges had been in "violation of the Constitution and other relevant laws" (such as the Labor Standards and Labor Union Law) was rejected. See *Japan Times,* September 10, 1950.
253. For discussions of anti-Communist repression in the United States in the immediate postwar era, see Ceplair, *Anti-Communism,* 75–95; see also Alex Goodall, *Loyalty and Liberty: American Countersubversion from World War I to the McCarthy Era* (Chicago: University of Illinois Press, 2013; Robert Justin Goldstein, ed., *Little "Red Scares:" Anti-communism and Political Repression in the United States* (Farnham, UK: Routledge, 2014).
254. Oppler to Kurt Steiner, January 22, 1951, ACOP, box 5.

255. George Marshall, "Reconstruction of Germany on a Democratic Basis," Department of State, Bulletin no. 16, March 14, 1947, 524.
256. Kukulus, *American Civil Liberties Union,* 3–4.
257. Arnold Wolfers, "United States Policy Toward Germany," February 21, 1947, Yale Institute of International Studies, NARA RG 260, OMGUS-General Records, box 232.
258. By September 1948, the JCLU boasted more than 2,000 members and offices in six cities. See "Extracts from Japanese Newspapers," the "Civil Liberties Bureau," *Tokyo Minpo,* September 12, 1948, in NARA RG 331, SCAP-GS, box 1482. However, always short of funds, the JCLU actually had "limited authority actually to conduct investigations of civil liberties abuses." Oppler, *Legal Reform,* 179; see also "Civil Liberties Activities," press conference of Legal Section, September 10, 1948, NARA RG 331, SCAP-GS, box 1498.
259. Established by statute in May 1949, the bureaus were to operate as civil liberties watchdogs within local Japanese communities. The initiative was a failure. As Tom Blakemore summarized, "My civil liberties branch is almost completely impotent, and the title 'branch' is a good administrative joke. Only a portion of my time, and a rather small one at that, is given to civil liberties work." Blakemore to Baldwin, February 1, 1949, ACLUP, box 1169. See, generally, Ian Neary, "The Civil Liberties Commissioners System and the Protection of Human Rights in Japan," *Japan Forum,* 9, no. 2 (1997): 217.
260. Oppler, *Legal Reform,* 178.
261. Many years later, a Japanese historian of the occupation asked Alfred Oppler in writing whether he had ever heard that "that General Whitney ordered Chief Justice Tanaka . . . not to touch the red purge case?" Whether because of a memory lapse or deception, however, Oppler denied that he had heard of such a thing, and dismissed the rumor as "very improbable." Oppler to Takemae, September 23, 1981, ACOP, box 5.
262. Oppler, "Address at Kyobashi—Meeting on Civil Liberties Sponsored by Tokyo Legal Affairs Bureau of the AG's Office," March 17, 1951, ACOP, box 3.
263. Oppler, "Address to Tokyo Legal Affairs Bureau of the Attorney General's Office," March 17, 1951, NARA RG 331, SCAP-GS, box 1522.
264. Dower, *Embracing Defeat,* 554.
265. Oppler, "Address to Conference of Civil Liberties Commissioners and Mayors in the AG's Office," December 18, 1951, Speeches, Notes, ACOP, box 3.
266. Major, *Death of the KDP,* 277.
267. Rich, "Civil Liberties in Germany," 85.
268. Wildenthal, "Human Rights Activism," 538–540.
269. As historian Richard Hofstadter famously argued about American politics, this trend exemplified in the Cold War era, the American political elite has been prone to exaggerate threats and response to threats. Richard Hofstadter, *The Paranoid Style in American Politics and Other Essays* (Cambridge, MA: Harvard University Press, 1965), 3–40, at 3.

Conclusion

1. David Ekbladh, *The Great American Mission: Modernization and the Construction of the American World Order* (Princeton, NJ: Princeton University Press, 2010), 79.
2. George Marshall, "Reconstruction of Germany on a Democratic Basis," Department of State, Bulletin no. 16, March 14, 1947, 524.
3. Fahy to Clay, December 3, 1945, CHFP, box 59.
4. For an early version of this thesis, see John D. Montgomery, *The Artificial Revolution in Germany and Japan* (Chicago: University of Chicago Press, 1957), 11.
5. American Bar Association, "The Rule of Law in the United States: A Statement by the Committee to Cooperate with the International Commission of Jurists" (The Hague: International Commission of Jurists, 1958), 10.
6. Address of Attorney General Tom C. Clark to Chicago Bar Association, June 21, 1946, 1–15. https://www.justice.gov/sites/default/files/ag/legacy/2011/09/12/06-21-1946.pdf.
7. See Vincent R. Johnson, "Justice Tom C. Clark's Legacy in the Field of Legal Ethics," *Journal of the Legal Profession* 29 (2005): 33–70, at 33–34.
8. Ibid., 1.
9. Ibid.
10. See, generally, David J. Goldberg, *Discontented America: The United States in the 1920s of The American Moment* (Baltimore: Johns Hopkins University Press, 1999).
11. Clark had acted as Justice's legal liaison with the U.S. Army groups overseeing internment. Peter H. Irons, *Justice at War* (New York: Oxford University Press, 1983), 46, 119.
12. See, generally, James Q. Whitman, *Hitler's American Model: The United States and the Making of the Nazi Race Law* (Princeton, NJ: Princeton University Press, 2017).
13. John Gimbel, *American Occupation of Germany: Politics and the Military, 1945–1949* (Stanford, Calif.: Stanford University Press, 1968), 2–4.
14. "George Stinney's Conviction Tossed Out . . . 70 Years After Execution," *New York Times*, December 17, 2014.
15. For details of the lynchings at Moore's Ford Bridge, see Laura Wexler, *Fire in the Canebreak: The Last Mass Lynching in America* (New York: Scribner, 2015). See also Terrence McCoy, "The Ghosts and Terror of America's 'Last Mass Lynching,'" *Washington Post*, February 18, 2015; "A Last Hope for Truth in a Mass Lynching," *New York Times*, October 7, 2018.
16. The FBI investigation led to no arrests. No one was ever indicted for the murders. "The Ghosts and Terror of America's 'Last Mass Lynching,'" *Washington Post*, February 18, 2015.

17. As quoted in Charles H. Thompson, editorial comment, "The Report of the President's Committee on Civil Rights," *Journal of Negro Education* 17, no. 1 (1948): 1–9, 1.
18. Thompson, "Report of the President's Committee on Civil Rights," 8.
19. According to Loewenstein, the credibility of American speakers to German audiences hinged on their willingness "not to gloss over the defects of American democracy and the American way of life." "Report of Loewenstein," visiting expert, August-September 1948, NARA RG 260, CAD-Bavaria, box 111.
20. William Sollman, visiting expert, "Report No. 1 to CAD Democratization Branch," 1949, WFSP, box 18.
21. "Of course I was chased everywhere by German criticism of civil liberties in the U.S. on the general assumption that 'you are as bad as we are'; but I could point out the essential difference between Germany and the U.S., that here at least a host of strong national force constantly fight to maintain civil rights." ACLU press release, November 28, 1950, RNBP, box 17.
22. LOD, August 22, 1945.
23. LOD, September 10, 1945.
24. LOD, December 14, 1945.
25. For prestige of the German law, see, generally, David M. Rabban, "American Responses to German Legal Scholarship: From the Civil War to World War I," *Comparative Legal History* 1, no. 1 (2013): 13–43.
26. For the ready identification of Americans with Germans, see Stephen G. Fritz, *Endkampf: Soldiers, Civilians, and the Death of the Third Reich* (Lexington: University Press of Kentucky, 2004), 54–55.
27. Snapp was the first secretary of the Atomic Energy Commission between 1947 and 1955. See Hellegers, "Interview of Roy B. Snapp," November 17, 1977, DMHP, box 6.
28. Ibid.
29. Ibid. Explaining why with regard to the Pacific war, American military intelligence became almost wholly dependent on code breaking.
30. Edwin O. Reischauer, one of America's most renowned scholars of Japanese politics and society, later recounted how thinly spread America's Japan specialists were during and after the war. Reischauer himself moved from the War Department to the State Department in November 1945, but too far away and too late to have had a large impact on the formation of policy on the ground in MacArthur's Japan. See Hellegers, "Interview of Reischauer," December 2, 1973, DMHP, box 5.
31. For instance, the Americans took steps to cause the Japanese to remove the legal disabilities of women in the private law governing the family and inheritance. See, generally, Alfred C. Oppler, *Legal Reform in Occupied Japan: A Participant Looks Back* (Princeton, NJ: Princeton University Press, 1976), 111–129.
32. Whitney, "The Philosophy of the Occupation," *PRJ*, vol. 1, xix.

33. Ibid., xxi.
34. Kades, "Representative Government in Japan," *PRJ,* vol. 1, xxiv.
35. Ibid., xxv.
36. Oppler, *Legal Reform,* 4.
37. Kurt Steiner, "Foreword," in Oppler, *Legal Reform,* vii–xvi.
38. Ibid., x.
39. Oppler, "Historical Notes on Law and Justice Division," n.d., NARA RG 331, SCAP-GS, box 1455.
40. Ibid.
41. See, for instance, Karube Tadashi, *Maruyama Masao and the Fate of Liberalism in Twentieth Century Japan* (Tokyo: International House of Japan, 2008), 90–92, 102.
42. Translation of Toshimi Miyasawa, "Outline Concerning the Reforms in Japan Under the Control of the Allied Powers," January 10, 1949, NARA RG 331, SCAP-GS, box 1522.
43. Hilldring to Kent Roberts Greenfield, chief historian, Department of the Army, August 7, 1950, CJFP, box 1.
44. DeForest Van Slyck, "Observations on Post Hostilities Policy Toward Japan," July 1945, DMHP, box 6.
45. Friedrich, "Organizational Aspects of the German Program for the US Government," January 2, 1947, CJFP, box 1.
46. John Raymond, "Historical Notes of Colonel John M. Raymond," March 23, 1949, NARA RG 260, LD-Director, box 9.
47. Ibid.
48. Hiram E. Chodosh, *Global Justice Reform: A Comparative Methodology* (New York: New York University Press, 2005), 61, 87–102.
49. See, generally, Michael Stolleis, "Germany's Legal Status, Reconstruction, Two States," in *Public Law in Germany: A Historical Introduction from the 16th to the 21st Century,* ed. Michael Stolleis and Dunlap Thomas (Oxford: Oxford University Press, 2017), 119–126.
50. See, generally, Leonard Krieger, *The German Idea of Freedom: History of Political Tradition* (Boston: Beacon, 1957), 468.
51. For an examination of how Germans experienced defeat, occupation, and the early Federal Republic, see, generally, Konrad H. Jarausch, *Broken Lives: How Ordinary Germans Experienced the Twentieth Century* (Princeton, NJ: Princeton University Press, 2018), 237–278.
52. Axel Schildt, "Sind die Westdeutschen amerikanisiert worden?" *Aus Politik und Zeitgeschicte* 26, no. 5 (2000): 50.
53. Loewenstein, "The Political Balance Sheet of the Occupation," address before Political Science Association, December 28, 1949, KLP, box 21.
54. Carol Gluck, "Entangling Illusions—Japanese and American Views of the Occupation," in *New Frontiers in American-East Asian Relations,* ed. Warren I.

Cohen and Dorothy Borg (New York: Columbia University Press, 1983), 174.

55. See, generally, Seigo Hirowatari, "Post-War Japan and the Law: Mapping Discourses of Legalization and Modernization," *Social Science Japan Journal* 3, no. 2 (2000): 155–169.
56. See, generally, Dower, *Embracing Defeat,* 560–561; Takemae, *Inside GHQ,* 538.
57. Dower, *Embracing Defeat,* 233–244.
58. Hakaru Abe, "Education of the Legal Profession of Japan," in *Law in Japan: The Legal Order in a Changing Society,* ed. Arthur Taylor von Mehren (Cambridge, MA: Harvard University Press, 1963), 161; see also Takaati Hattori, "The Legal Profession in Japan: Its Historical Development and Present State," in von Mehren, ed., *Law in Japan,* 111.
59. Atsushi Nagashima, "The Accused and Society: The Administration of Justice in Japan," in von Mehren, ed., *Law in Japan,* 297.
60. See, generally, Arthur Taylor von Mehren, "The Legal Order in Japan's Society: Some Observations," *Harvard Law Review* 76, no. 6 (1963): 1170–1205; John O. Haley, "Comment: Law and Culture in China and Japan," *Michigan Journal of International Law* 27, no. 3 (2006): 895, 897.
61. Andrew E. Barshay, "Imagining Democracy in Postwar Japan: Reflections on Maruyama Masao and Modernism," *Journal of Japanese Studies* 18, no. 2 (1992): 365–406.
62. Edward N. Peterson, *American Occupation of Germany: Retreat to Victory* (Detroit: Wayne State University Press, 1977), 339–341.
63. See, generally, D. Grimm, "The Role of Fundamental Rights after 65 Years of Constitutional Jurisprudence in Germany," *Con-International Journal of Constitutional Law* 13, no. 1 (2015): 9–29; Justin Collings, *Democracy's Guardians: A History of the German Federal Constitutional Court, 1951–2001* (Oxford: Oxford University Press, 2015); Meinel, "The Constitutional Miracle on the Rhine," 277–293.
64. See, generally, Michaela Hailbronner, "Rethinking the Rise of the German Constitutional Court: From Anti-Nazism to Value Formalism," *International Journal of Constitutional Law* 12, no. 3 (2014): 626–649, at 631.
65. See, generally, Timothy Scott Brown, "1968 in West Germany: the Anti-Authoritarian Revolt," *The Sixties: A Journal of History, Politics, and Culture* 7, no. 2 (2014): 99.
66. See, generally, Edward J. Eberle, *Dignity and Liberty: Constitutional Visions in Germany and the United States* (Westport, CT: Praeger, 2002), 19–21; Grimm, "The Role of Fundamental Rights," 9–29: Grimm, "The role of fundamental rights," 19; Meinel, "The Constitutional Miracle on the Rhine," 278.
67. As one distinguished scholar in the field has summarized: "The defining pattern for Japanese law, during the course of the twentieth century, has been its communitarian orientation." Haley, *Spirit of Japanese Law,* 211. See also Haley, "Comment: Law and Culture in China and Japan," 896. For a discus-

sion of the "powerful inertial forces rooted in the history of law in Japan," see, generally, Mark Levin, "Continuities of Consciousness: Professor John Haley's Writings on Twelve Hundred Years of Japanese Legal History," *Washington University Global Studies Law Review* 8, no. 2 (2009): 317–332.

68. Tomio Kinoshita, "The Nature and Consequences of Lawyers' Market Regulation in Japan," *Contemporary Economic Policy* 18, no. 2 (2000): 181–193.
69. Kazuko Ito, "Wrongful Convictions and Recent Criminal Justice Reform in Japan," *University of Cincinnati Law Review* 80, no. 4 (2012): 1245–1275.
70. Haley, *Spirit of Japanese Law,* 16.
71. John O. Haley, "The Role of Courts in 'Making Law' in Japan: The Communitarian Conservatism of Japanese Judges," *Pacific Rim Law and Policy Journal* 22, no. 3 (2013): 491–503, at 499.
72. See, generally, Masahito Tadano, "The Role of the Judicial Branch in the Protection of Fundamental Rights in Japan," in *Contemporary Issues in Human Rights Law: Europe and Asia,* ed. Yumiko Nakanishi (Singapore: Springer, 2018), 73–89, 74–75.
73. David S. Law, "Why Has Judicial Review Failed in Japan?" *Washington University Law Review* 88, no. 6 (2011): 1426–1466, at 1426; see also Carl F. Goodman, *The Rule of Law in Japan: A Comparative Analysis,* 2nd rev. ed. (Austin, TX: Wolters Kluwer, 2008), 90–99.
74. David Beatty, "Protecting Constitutional Rights in Japan and Canada," *American Journal of Comparative Law* 41, no. 4 (1993): 535, 538. See also Haley, "Comment: Law and Culture in China and Japan," 895–896; Po L. Chen and Jordan T. Wada, "Can the Japanese Supreme Court Overcome the Political Question Hurdle?" *Washington International Law Journal* 26, no. 2 (2017): 349–379.

Acknowledgments

In the many years it took to write this history book I have incurred large institutional and personal debts.

I am extremely grateful, first of all, to Deans Iain Scott and Erika Chamberlain of the Faculty of Law, Western University. By their grace I was afforded space in which to cache extensive source materials and think about, write, and rewrite a legal history book. Iain remained supportive as years passed, still no finished product. Iain, then Erika, accepted assurances that—within the span of their lifetimes—an ambitious book project would come to fruition. Thank you, both of you, for trusting me to get on with it.

A generous grant from Western University's Academic Development Fund defrayed the substantial cost of archival research in the United States, United Kingdom, and Germany. The book would not have been started, still less completed, without this vital financial support. Thank you, Western.

The Faculty of Law at Western underwrote the cost of numerous summer research assistants, including Fred Gjoka and Grant Bodnaryk (who put together excellent first bibliographies and research briefs), Melissa Loucks (German translation), Lawrence Gridin (a searchable database), Jacob Damstra, Stephen Hopkins, Andrew Locatelli (research support at large), and Stuart Borenovich (editing citations). I am very grateful to all these then-students of law for their help in the design and execution of a big project.

In regard to work at archival institutions, I need to acknowledge the patient and skillful interventions of Pauline Schmidt and Eric Van Slander of the National Archive at College Park, Maryland. Pauline helped me navigate the tangled thickets of American civilian and military occupation agencies in post–Second World War Germany. Eric was indispensable in helping me track down the most pertinent of many thousands of record boxes relating to the American occupation of Japan. Eric was, and is, not only a superb archivist but a good friend to me and my work.

Also deserving of special thanks are the excellent professional librarians who oversee the Karl Loewenstein Papers at the Special Collections library of Amherst College. At the Truman Presidential Library, my investigations profited both from skilled staff and from the painstaking previous research of historian Dale M. Hellegers, whose exhaustive source materials now form part of the TPL's permanent collection. The archivists at the MacArthur Memorial Library in Norfolk, Virginia, provided similarly excellent support to my work in that fine institution.

At Western Law, librarian Elizabeth Bruton was always dogged in pursuit of obscure references and materials. Thank you, Elizabeth, for your expertise and unfailing good cheer.

Tigger Jourard did an exceptionally good (and swift) job of proofreading the first complete draft of the manuscript. Hilary Neary brought an equally sharp eye to a second draft. The final draft was far better for their careful and discerning scrutiny. In the final stages of the project, I rang up substantial debts to the courteous and skillful interventions of Westchester Publishing Services, namely, to production editor Angela Piliouras and copyeditor Lunaea Weatherstone. I thank them both very much indeed.

Among administrative staff at Western Law, Vera van Diepen contributed word processing and other support. JiYoun "Rachel" Kim helped prepare manuscript files according to the guidelines of Harvard University Press.

Among scholarly colleagues afield, Marlene Mayo at Maryland and Dieter Waibel at Tubingen provided experienced advice in the early development of this work. I am especially grateful to Dieter for his hospitality during a memorable visit to Swabia and for having generously shared research materials with me.

Among colleagues at Western, I am grateful to Eric Hahn and Eli Nathans for foundational conversations about modern German history. I am also deeply indebted to the eminent Western historical sociologist Samuel Clark. In the course of innumerable meet-ups, Sam coached me on comparative history and generally bucked up my resolve to keep going. Sam is nothing short of an ideal scholarly mentor and friend.

Craig Simpson, lifelong teacher and friend, offered endless support and encouragement.

I am grateful to Michael Aronson, distinguished social sciences editor (retired) at Harvard University Press for endorsing my book prospectus before the Syndics. Sorry, Michael, that I could not finish the job before you moved on. I am extremely grateful, too, to Thomas LeBien, for having taken over the project from Michael and for shepherding me and it through the publication process. Thank you, Thomas for affording me the benefit of your experienced judgment and consummate professionalism.

I am sad to acknowledge my deep appreciation posthumously to Blaine Baker and Tim Edgar, accomplished academics and dear friends. Blaine helped start and then sustain me in my academic career. Tim Edgar endures as a model of dedication and brilliance in the scholar's calling. It is a great sorrow to me that Blaine and Tim did not live to be given this book.

Leslie Kostal, my beloved life partner, lent her prodigious skills in proofreading, word processing, and, most of all, as morale officer. The dedication page of this book is hers alone.

Best efforts notwithstanding, this book surely contains some mistakes of fact, interpretation, or technique. I alone am responsible for them.

Index